Communications in Computer and Information Science 1899

Rationale
The CCIS series is devoted to the publication of proceedings of computer science conferences. Its aim is to efficiently disseminate original research results in informatics in printed and electronic form. While the focus is on publication of peer-reviewed full papers presenting mature work, inclusion of reviewed short papers reporting on work in progress is welcome, too. Besides globally relevant meetings with internationally representative program committees guaranteeing a strict peer-reviewing and paper selection process, conferences run by societies or of high regional or national relevance are also considered for publication.

Topics
The topical scope of CCIS spans the entire spectrum of informatics ranging from foundational topics in the theory of computing to information and communications science and technology and a broad variety of interdisciplinary application fields.

Information for Volume Editors and Authors
Publication in CCIS is free of charge. No royalties are paid, however, we offer registered conference participants temporary free access to the online version of the conference proceedings on SpringerLink (http://link.springer.com) by means of an http referrer from the conference website and/or a number of complimentary printed copies, as specified in the official acceptance email of the event.

CCIS proceedings can be published in time for distribution at conferences or as post-proceedings, and delivered in the form of printed books and/or electronically as USBs and/or e-content licenses for accessing proceedings at SpringerLink. Furthermore, CCIS proceedings are included in the CCIS electronic book series hosted in the SpringerLink digital library at http://link.springer.com/bookseries/7899. Conferences publishing in CCIS are allowed to use Online Conference Service (OCS) for managing the whole proceedings lifecycle (from submission and reviewing to preparing for publication) free of charge.

Publication process
The language of publication is exclusively English. Authors publishing in CCIS have to sign the Springer CCIS copyright transfer form, however, they are free to use their material published in CCIS for substantially changed, more elaborate subsequent publications elsewhere. For the preparation of the camera-ready papers/files, authors have to strictly adhere to the Springer CCIS Authors' Instructions and are strongly encouraged to use the CCIS LaTeX style files or templates.

Abstracting/Indexing
CCIS is abstracted/indexed in DBLP, Google Scholar, EI-Compendex, Mathematical Reviews, SCImago, Scopus. CCIS volumes are also submitted for the inclusion in ISI Proceedings.

How to start
To start the evaluation of your proposal for inclusion in the CCIS series, please send an e-mail to ccis@springer.com.

Jianhou Gan · Yi Pan · Juxiang Zhou · Dong Liu ·
Xianhua Song · Zeguang Lu
Editors

Computer Science and Educational Informatization

5th International Conference, CSEI 2023
Kunming, China, August 11–13, 2023
Revised Selected Papers, Part I

Editors
Jianhou Gan
Yunnan Normal University
Kunming, China

Yi Pan
Georgia State University
Atlanta, GA, USA

Juxiang Zhou
Yunnan Normal University
Kunming, China

Dong Liu
Henan Normal University
Xinxiang, China

Xianhua Song
Harbin University of Science and Technology
Harbin, China

Zeguang Lu
National Academy of Guo Ding Institute
of Data Science
Beijing, China

ISSN 1865-0929 ISSN 1865-0937 (electronic)
Communications in Computer and Information Science
ISBN 978-981-99-9498-4 ISBN 978-981-99-9499-1 (eBook)
https://doi.org/10.1007/978-981-99-9499-1

This Springer imprint is published by the registered company Springer Nature Singapore Pte Ltd.
The registered company address is: 152 Beach Road, #21-01/04 Gateway East, Singapore 189721, Singapore

Paper in this product is recyclable.

Preface

As the program chairs of the Fifth International Conference on Computer Science and Educational Informatization (CSEI 2023), it is our great pleasure to welcome you to the conference proceedings. The conference was held in Kunming, China, August 11–13, 2023, hosted by Yunnan Normal University, Key Laboratory of Educational Informatization for Nationalities (YNNU), Ministry of Education, China, Yunnan Key Laboratory of Smart Education, Key Laboratory of Artificial Intelligence and Personalized Learning in Education of Henan Province (Henan Normal University), Harbin University of Science and Technology and National Academy of Guo Ding Institute of Data Science. The goal of this conference was to provide a forum for computer scientists, engineers, and educators.

This conference attracted 297 paper submissions. After the hard work of the Program Committee, 76 papers were accepted to appear in the conference proceedings, with an acceptance rate of 25.59%. There were at least 3 reviewers for each article, and each reviewer reviewed no more than 5 articles. The major topic of this conference was Computer Science and Education Informatization. The accepted papers cover a wide range of areas related to Educational information science and technology, Educational informatization and big data for education, Innovative application for the deeper integration of education practice and information technology, and University engineering education and education informatization.

We would like to thank all the Program Committee members for their hard work in completing the review tasks. Their collective efforts made it possible to attain quality reviews for all the submissions within a few weeks. Their diverse expertise in each individual research area helped us to create an exciting program for the conference. Their comments and advice helped the authors to improve the quality of their papers and gain deeper insights.

Great thanks should also go to the authors and participants for their tremendous support in making the conference a success.

Besides the technical program, this year CSEI offered different experiences to the participants. We hope you enjoyed the conference.

July 2023

Jianhou Gan
Yi Pan
Juxiang Zhou
Dong Liu

Organization

General Chairs

Jianhou Gan	Yunnan Normal University, China
Yi Pan	Georgia State University, USA

Program Chairs

Juxiang Zhou	Yunnan Normal University, China
Dong Liu	Henan Normal University, China

Program Co-chairs

Zeguang Lu	National Academy of Guo Ding Institute of Data Science, China
Lan Huang	Jilin University, China

Organization Co-chairs

Bin Wen	Yunnan Normal University, China
Jia Hao	Yunnan Normal University, China
Chao Yang	Yunnan Normal University, China
Junna Zhang	Henan Normal University, China

Organization Chair

Lingyun Yuan	Yunnan Normal University, China

Publication Chair

Xianhua Song	Harbin University of Science and Technology, China

Registration/Financial Chair

Zhongchan Sun	National Academy of Guo Ding Institute of Data Science, China

Chairman

Hongzhi Wang	Harbin Institute of Technology, China

Vice-presidents

Jianhou Gan	Yunnan Normal University, China
Liu Dong	Henan Normal University, China
Guanglu Sun	Harbin University of Science and Technology, China

Secretary General

Zeguang Lu	National Academy of Guo Ding Institute of Data Science, China

Executive Members

Xiaoju Dong	Shanghai Jiao Tong University, China
Qilong Han	Harbin Engineering University, China
Lan Huang	Jilin University, China
Ying Jiang	Kunming University of Science and Technology, China
Junna Zhang	Henan Normal University, China
Juxiang Zhou	Yunnan Normal University, China

Program Committee Members

Jinliang An	Henan Institute of Science and Technology, China
Hongtao Bai	Jilin University, China
Chunguang Bi	Jilin Agricultural University, China
Xiaochun Cao	Sun Yat-sen University, China

Contents – Part I

Educational Information Science and Technology

Contents – Part II

Educational Informatization and Big Data for Education

Educational Information Science and Technology

An OS Kernel Based on RISC-V Architecture

Guojun Liu(✉), Jili Huang, and Xiaoyan Liu

Faculty of Computing, Harbin Institute of Technology, Harbin, China
hitliu@hit.edu.cn

Abstract. Few operating system are currently available for teaching purposes, and they are largely based on the x86 architecture, which makes it inevitable to learn about the complex features of x86 and its bloated historical baggage during the learning process. To further promote the teaching and learning of the operating system, we have designed an operating system kernel based on rCore for the RISC-V architecture. The kernel is written in the Rust language, compared with rCore, it supports multiprocessing and multithreading, signal, FAT32 file system, can be booted and run on QEMU, and supports running practical applications such as BusyBox and LUA. Meanwhile, the code is standardised and well documented. The kernel can be used for educational purposes and as an objective contribution to the development of the RISC-V open-source community.

Keywords: OS Kernel · RISC-V · Rust · FAT32 · rCore

1 Introduction

The Instruction Set Architecture (ISA) is an abstract model of a computer that defines the basic mode of how a processor parses and executes instructions. Typically, an instruction set architecture defines a set of supported data types, registers, memory management, basic features and IO models. ISA can be classified according to the complexity of the instruction set as follows: Complex Instruction Set Computer (CISC), represented by the x86 architecture, and Reduced Instruction Set Computer (RISC), represented by the ARM architecture [5].

Although both x86 and ARM are commercially successful, they are closed source and not open enough, and high licensing fees need to be paid to Intel or ARM Holdings plc to use these instruction set architectures. In contrast, Krste Asanovi et al. make the argument that instruction set architectures should be open and use RISC-V as a typical example of an open-source instruction set architecture [3].

RISC-V is an open-source instruction set architecture based on RISC, a project started by the University of California, Berkeley in 2010. Although it was not the first open-source instruction set, RISC-V can be used from embedded devices to large virtualised devices due to its cross-platform nature, and its open-source nature has contributed to an active community. As a result,

J. Gan et al. (Eds.): CSEI 2023, CCIS 1899, pp. 3–16, 2024.
https://doi.org/10.1007/978-981-99-9499-1_1

once RISC-V appeared, many chip designers design SoC based on it [7,10,11]. Compared with ARM, RISC-V has richer instructions and stronger scalability. Compared to Intel's architecture, RISC-V has less historical baggage and does not need to worry about backward compatibility [5], so it can be said to be "lightweight".

In terms of operating system, the RISC-V architecture is more often used to design embedded operating systems [2,4]. At the level of general-purpose OS, apart from the Linux kernel with RISC-V architecture that is officially transplanted from Linux, there are mainly two well-known foreign RISC-V OS projects: one is the xv6-riscv project developed at MIT written in C language, and xv6 is an example OS used in the school's 6.828 OS course. The other is StephenMarz's BlogOS, which came out of a series of teaching blogs he wrote in 2019 that focused on completing a simple RISC-V operating system kernel using the Rust language. The project has had a huge response abroad and spawned a number of RISC-V operating systems implemented by Rust language.

There are few researchers on this aspect in China. Basically only rCore [14] and zCore are used as teaching operating systems, which both developed as Tsinghua University and written in Rust. In particular, rCore's rich and detailed documentation and complete experimental tutorials have attracted many enthusiasts to study and improve it, and its open-source spirit has further promoted the development of the community.

Due to the above, we have written a RISC-V operating system kernel based on rCore. Compared with rCore, our design and implementation differ in several ways. Firstly, we add modules such as thread and signal, which are very important concepts in the OS course. Secondly, we support FAT32 file system and can run practical applications such as BusyBox and LUA. Beginners can learn about how the environment of a real application is set up and how the program is executed. In the end, we have implemented an OS kernel with complete basic functions and detailed documentation, which is also convenient to expand and suitable for teaching. We currently name the operating system SOS temporarily.

In the next section, we will describe the overall design of the kernel, and in the subsequent sections, we will discuss the design and implementation of each module, including process management, signal handling, memory management, and the file system. Due to space limitations, we will only describe the new features added relative to rCore.

2 Overall Design

The SOS is designed with a macro kernel, as shown in Fig. 1, which we have roughly divided into the following modules: process/thread management module, signal handling module, exception handling module, memory management module, virtual file system layer, and FAT32 file system module. RISC-V privileged architecture provides four privilege levels [13]. Our OS kernel is in S-mode, running in the SEE environment built by RustSBI, and interacting with the underlying hardware through the SBI interface. In addition, the OS kernel acts as a layer of execution environment, providing ABI interfaces (system calls) upwards to provide services to upper layer applications.

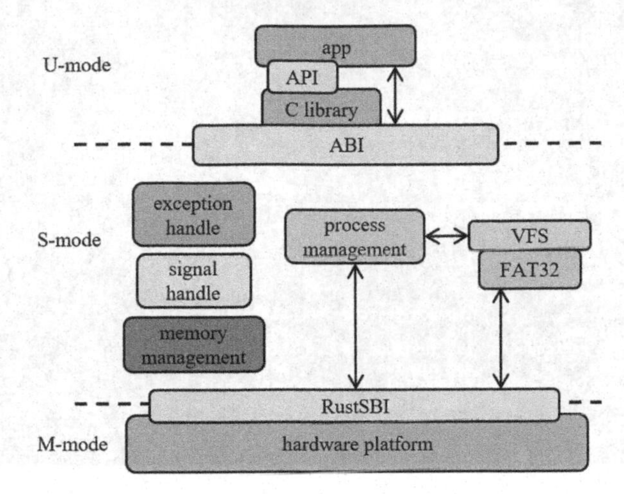

Fig. 1. Overall design of SOS.

The system startup and interactive interface are shown in the Fig. 2 and Fig. 3.

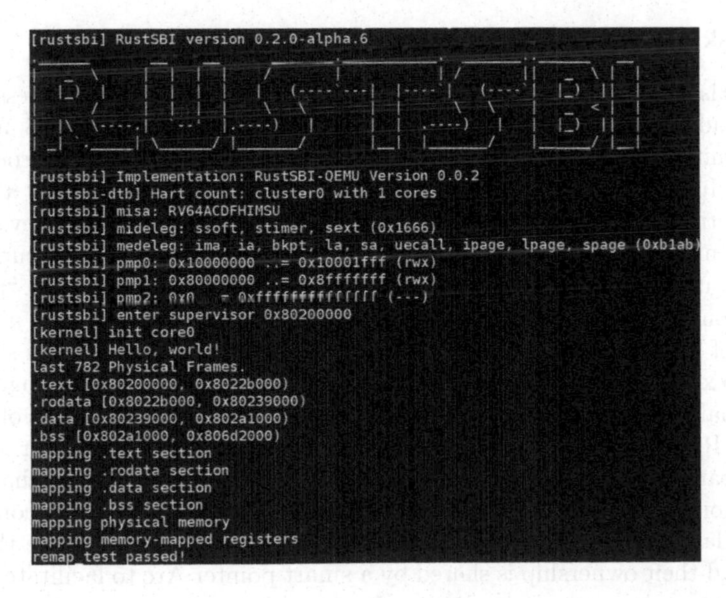

Fig. 2. Startup interface.

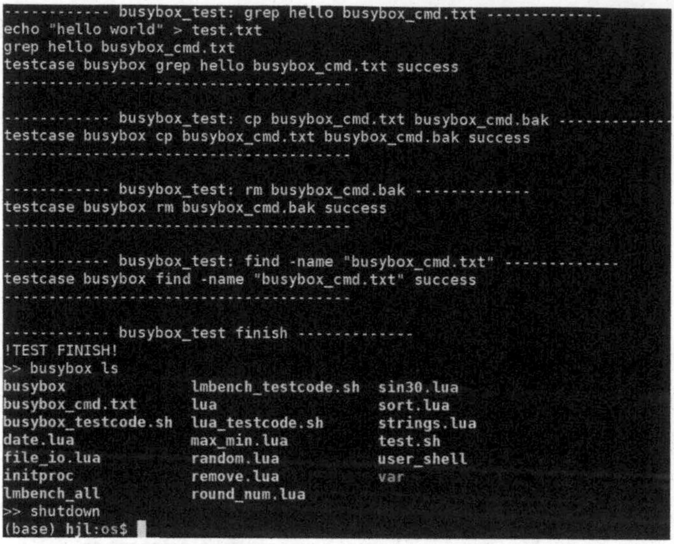

```
----------- busybox_test: grep hello busybox_cmd.txt ------------
echo "hello world" > test.txt
grep hello busybox_cmd.txt
testcase busybox grep hello busybox_cmd.txt success
--------------------------------------

----------- busybox_test: cp busybox_cmd.txt busybox_cmd.bak ------------
testcase busybox cp busybox_cmd.txt busybox_cmd.bak success
--------------------------------------

----------- busybox_test: rm busybox_cmd.bak ------------
testcase busybox rm busybox_cmd.bak success
--------------------------------------

----------- busybox_test: find -name "busybox_cmd.txt" ------------
testcase busybox find -name "busybox_cmd.txt" success
--------------------------------------

----------- busybox_test finish ------------
!TEST FINISH!
>> busybox ls
busybox             lmbench_testcode.sh  sin30.lua
busybox_cmd.txt     lua                  sort.lua
busybox_testcode.sh lua_testcode.sh      strings.lua
date.lua            max_min.lua          test.sh
file_io.lua         random.lua           user_shell
initproc            remove.lua           var
lmbench_all         round_num.lua
>> shutdown
(base) hjl:os$
```

Fig. 3. Interactive interface.

3 Process Management

3.1 Task Control Block

A process is an instance of a running program. SOS supports multiprocessing and multithreading, but does not distinguish between these concepts. SOS abstracts the two uniformly, i.e. a task control block (TCB) represents both a process and a thread. In our system, a thread is just a "lightweight process", and a process is a collection of lightweight processes, i.e. a group of threads. However, some resources may be shared between different processes/threads, thus supporting the user's concept of "process" and "thread". In this paper, the term "process" is used consistently to denote a normal or lightweight process, i.e. a specific member of a thread group. By abstracting this uniformly, our process structure is more flexible and convenient in terms of resource sharing, scheduling, etc.

The main structure of the TCB is shown in Fig. 4. Due to the limits of borrow checks in Rust language, SOS employs a design pattern called interior mutability to separate the immutable and mutable parts, so that we can change the relevant content under the condition of external immutability, while controlling the granularity of locks. The various resources of the process also use the same design, and their ownership is shared by a smart pointer Arc to facilitate sharing of resources.

```
1 pub struct TaskControlBlock {
2     // immutable
3     tid: PidHandle,
4     pub pid: usize,
5     pub ppid: usize,
6     ...
7     // mutable
8     inner: Mutex<TaskControlBlockInner>,
9 }
10 pub struct TaskControlBlockInner {
11     pub memory_set: Arc<MemorySet>,
12     pub fs_info: Arc<FSInfo>,
13     pub fd_table: Arc<FileTable>,
14     pub signal_info: Arc<SignalInfo>,
15     pub signal_actions: Arc<SignalActions>,
16     ...
17 }
```

Fig. 4. Structure of TCB.

For the RISC-V architecture, the *fork()* system call is not supported and is replaced by *clone()* [9]. Compared to *fork()*, *clone()* is more flexible and provides more precise control over whether resources are shared or not: its argument "flags" specifies the resources to be shared and some other settings, the main flags are shown in Table 1.

Table 1. The main flag mask.

Flag mask	Description
CLONE_VM	Share virtual memory address space
CLONE_FS	Share filesystem information
CLONE_FILES	Share file descriptor table
CLONE_SIGHAND	Share table of signal handlers
CLONE_THREAD	The child is placed in the same thread group as the calling process

When *execve()* is called to execute a new program, the initial stack is set up as shown in Fig. 5. SOS puts the environment parameters, program parameters, ELF auxiliary vectors [8], envp, argv, argc from high address to low address in that order.

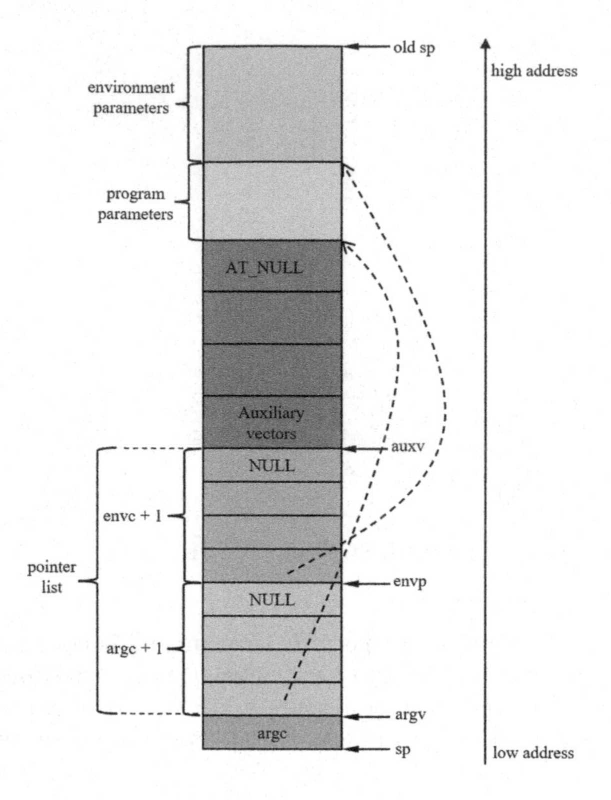

Fig. 5. Initial stack.

3.2 Hash Tables

To manage these processes, SOS uses hash tables to categorise them, and processes that meet the same criteria are hung on the appropriate chain. Currently, there are three hash tables in SOS:

1. In the hash table of type PIDTYPE_TID, TCBs with the same thread ID (TID) will be hung on the same chain, and since the TID must be different between threads, there will be only one node on that chain.
2. In the hash table of type PIDTYPE_TGID, TCBs with the same process ID (PID) are hung on the same chain and the nodes on that chain become a thread group.
3. In the hash table of type PIDTYPE_PPID, TCBs with the same parent process ID (PPID) are hung on the same chain, and only one TCB of the same thread group member will exist in that chain. We can find all the child processes iterate through the hash table with the type PIDTYPE_TGID.

3.3 Process States

Our processes support four states, as follows:

1. Ready: Processes are in the ready queue, waiting to gain access to the CPU to run.
2. Running: The process has been granted CPU access and is running.
3. Zombie: process execution is terminated, waiting for the *wait4()* system call to recycle resources.
4. Stopped: the process is in a suspended state due to a signal.

The process state transitions are illustrated in Fig. 6.

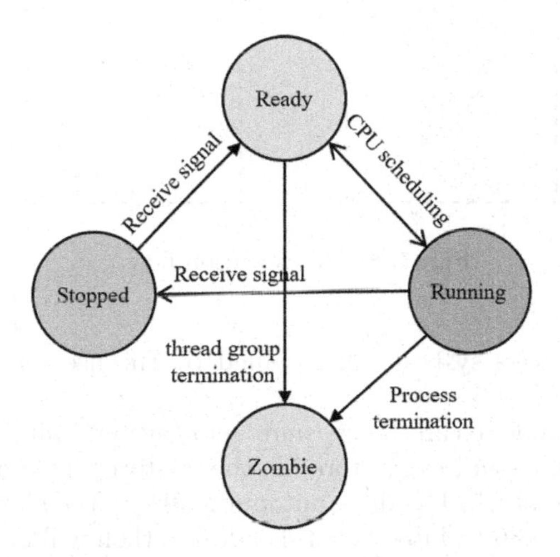

Fig. 6. The process state transition diagram.

4 Signal Management

Signals are short messages that can be sent to a thread group or a group of thread groups (process groups) to trigger specific behaviors. They are a limited form of inter-process communication (IPC). And the kernel can also use signals to notify the process of an event that has occurred.

When the user registers a signal handler function using the *rt_sigaction()* system call, once the corresponding signal hangs, the kernel will create a signal stack frame on the user-mode stack to store the relevant information and then jump to the user mode to execute the corresponding handler function; after the handler function is executed, the *rt_sigreturn()* system call will be called to jump to the kernel mode to restore the previously saved task context and to restore the user mode stack. This allows the process to thus resume its own execution when this system call finishes. The execution flow of the signal handling function is shown in Fig. 7. The *rt_sigreturn()* system call has no specific parameter structure, it depends on the corresponding architecture and is not called directly

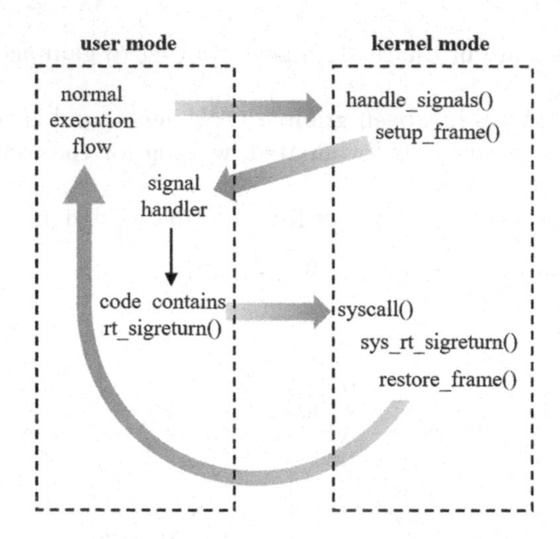

Fig. 7. Signal execution flow.

by the user. When this system call is called by the user, glibc will return -1 directly.

The part of the code to call the *rt_ sigreturn()* system call is provided by vdso or the C library and its address is stored in the "restorer" field of the k_sigaction structure, the filling of which is done automatically by the C library and hidden for the user. For the x86 architecture, this address then will be stored at the top of the stack when the kernel creates the signal stack frame to save the context, so that when the handler function finishes executing, an assembly instruction "ret" will automatically jump to this address to execute the *rt_ sigreturn()* system call. In contrast, for the RISC-V architecture, the address is stored in the "ra" register, so that the system call can also be called after the handler returns.

In SOS, the signal stack frame is created using the *setup_frame()* function, which stores the old trap context, the current set of masked signals from the high address to the low address. In order to check that the top of the stack points to the signal stack frame upon return, we store a check code at the top of stack for verification. The contents of the signal stack frame are shown in Fig. 8.

5 Memory Management

5.1 Buddy System Allocator

SOS allocates some part of memory permanently to the kernel to store kernel code and static data structures, the remainder is called dynamic memory and this is managed using the buddy system allocator. In the buddy system, we use 23 linked lists to connect blocks of memory of the same size, each of which is a power of two. When small memory is needed and there are no free memory blocks on the corresponding lists, allocator will cut the large memory blocks:

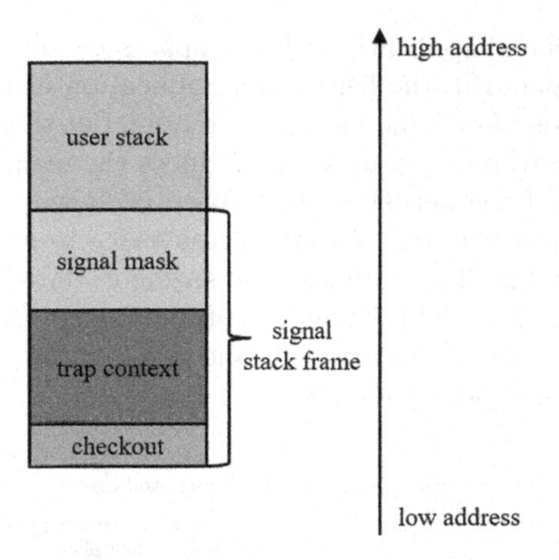

Fig. 8. Signal stack frame.

the needed memory blocks will return to the user, and the remainder of the memory blocks will hang on the corresponding lists. Similarly, when memory is reclaimed, adjacent memory blocks are merged into a large memory block.

In our system, two forms of memory are used: one is allocated in page-based, the other is dynamically allocated in order to support the Rust heap data structures, which are allocated at variable sizes, possibly smaller than a page, or several pages at a time. The Rust language provides a simple and standardised interface GlobalAlloc in alloc crate, as show in Fig. 9. By implementing this interface, the kernel can easily support dynamic memory allocation, and we can use data structures such as containers and smart pointers, thus greatly improving our development efficiency. SOS have implemented this interface on the buddy system allocator and the allocation size of this interface is in powers of two, so as not to cause significant memory fragmentation regardless of the form of memory used.

```
1 pub unsafe fn alloc(&self, layout: Layout) -> *mut u8
2 pub unsafe fn dealloc(&self, ptr: *mut u8, layout: Layout)
```

Fig. 9. GlobalAlloc interface.

5.2 Memory Address Space

SOS uses the 39-bit virtual address spaces (Sv39), where only the lower 39 bits are valid under a 64-bit virtual address, and the other high bits must be the same as the 39th bit, so only the minimum 256GB and maximum 256GB of the virtual address are valid.

In SOS, the kernel and application address spaces are separated into two independent parts. Compared to the kernel and application using the same address space, this way spends more time in trap switching, but there is only one kernel address space for the whole system, which reduces the memory usage overhead.

The distribution of the kernel address space is shown in Fig. 10. We add a Trampoline structure at the top of the address space to smooth the transition between process switches. The kernel's code segment, data segment, etc. utilize identical mapping to map virtual pages to physical page frames. This way, the physical addresses of page tables are also valid virtual addresses. The rest of the logical segments are mapped randomly.

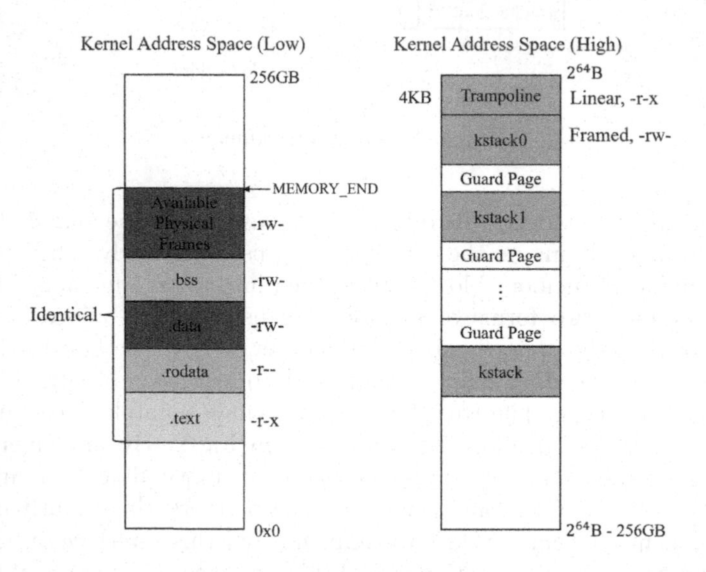

Fig. 10. Kernel address space.

The distribution of the application address space is shown in Fig. 11. The Trampoline structure is also put in the highest address, after which the Trap context of the process is stored. In the lower 256 GB of the application address space, the dynamic linker, user stack, memory map area, heap and user program related logical segments are stored from the high address to the low address in that order.

SOS allocates a user stack and a Trap context to each thread, and a guard page is added between each user stack to detect stack overflows. Some threads are created by specifying the user stack address via the "stack" parameter of the *clone()* system call, where the kernel will not automatically allocate stack and will not manage the associated user resources. The memory map area then grows towards the lower address. Pointer "brk" points to the highest address in the data area (i.e. the heap) and when the *brk()* system call is called, the value of brk is changed, thus allocating heap space, while the heap grows towards the higher address.

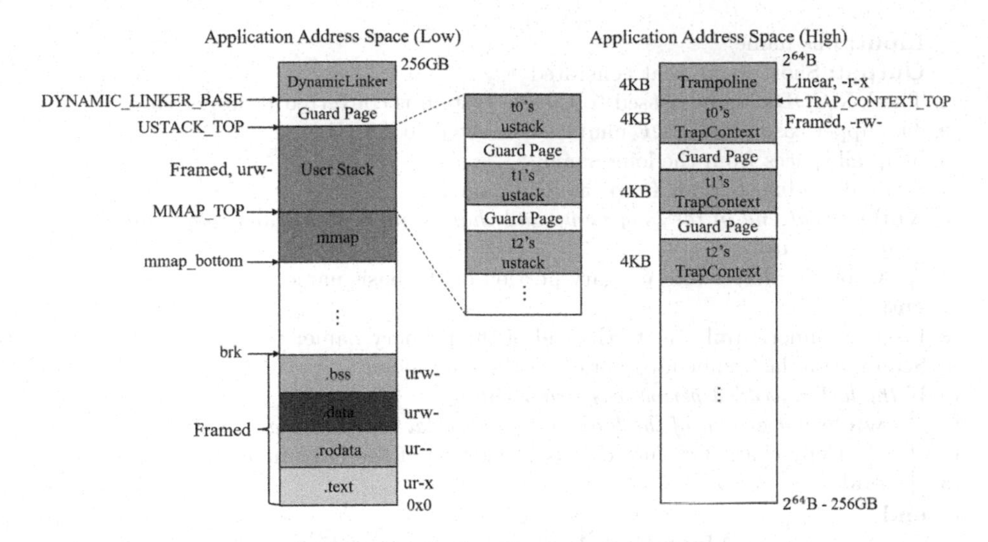

Fig. 11. Application address space.

6 File System

6.1 FAT32 File System

The FAT32 file system divides the data region into clusters for allocation. Whether or not each cluster is used is recorded in the FAT region, and the value of the entry corresponding to each cluster number describes the status of the cluster allocation as well as specifies the cluster number of the next cluster for the file. As a result, the FAT data structure defines a singly linked list of the "extents" (clusters) of a file.

Each file on the FAT32 file system corresponds to a short directory entry, which stores information about the file. However, the length of a file name stored in a short directory entry is limited, so long file names are split out and stored in multiple long directory entries, followed by a short directory entry, forming a collection of directory entries corresponding to the file.

The names contained in the set of all short directory entries are termed the "short name space". The names contained in the set of all long directory entries are termed the "long name space". Together, they form a single unified name space in which no duplicate names can exist [1]. Due to the restriction of the name space, there is no API for specifying the short file name, so the user can only specify the long file name, which is automatically generated using an algorithm to ensure that the file name is unique. As shown in Algorithm 1, the generated short file names conform to the short file name format and do not conflict with the name space.

Input: File name
Output: Short name that generated
1 The UNICODE name passed to the file system is converted to upper case;
2 The upper case UNICODE name is converted to ASCII;
3 Strip all spaces from the long name;
4 Strip all leading periods from the long name;
5 **while** *not at end of the long name and char is not a period and total chars copied* < 8 **do**
6 | Copy characters into primary portion of the basis name
7 **end**
8 Insert a numeric-tail "~n" to the end of the primary name;
9 Scan for the last embedded period in the long name;
10 **if** *the last embedded period was found* **then**
11 | **while** *not at end of the long name and total chars copied* < 3 **do**
12 | | Copy characters into extension portion of the basis name
13 | **end**
14 **end**

Algorithm 1: Short-name generation

6.2 Common File Model

Currently SOS only supports the single file system FAT32. To facilitate extensions to form multiple file systems, we add a virtual file system layer to handle all system calls related to the file system. Its robustness is demonstrated by its ability to provide a common interface to a variety of file systems.

SOS uses a common file model that contains three object types and each object type requires to implement the corresponding interface [6,12]. Once a file system is implemented and the corresponding interface is implemented, we can obtain a file object and thus accesses that file system. The generic file model consists of the following three types of objects:

1. Superblock object: stores information about the installed file system.
2. Index node object (inode): stores general information about a specific file. Each index node object has an index node number that uniquely identifies a file in the file system.
3. File object: stores information about the opened file.

The relationship of the three objects are shown in Fig. 12. Each file system corresponds to a superblock object, and each file in that file system is abstracted into an index node object, of which there is only one in the whole system. We can open the same file multiple times, which creates multiple file objects, but they correspond to the same index node object.

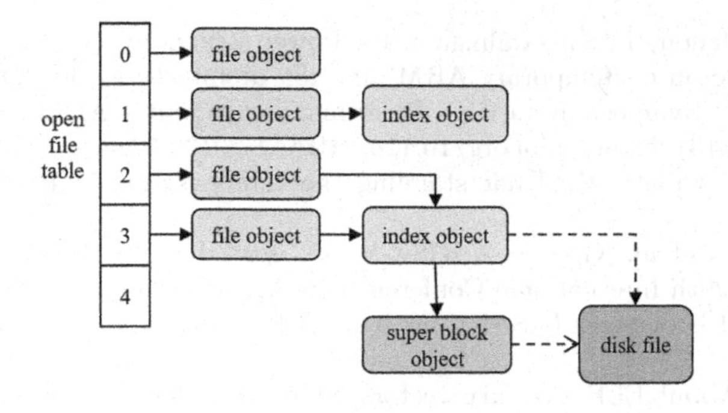

Fig. 12. Common file model.

7 Conclusion

This paper implements a RISC-V operating system kernel written in Rust based on rCore, which has a clear structure and is convenient for horizontal expansion. At the same time, the code conforms to the specification, the comments and documentation are comprehensive and detailed. It also supports real file system and can run real applications such as BusyBox and LUA, which can be used for teaching purposes.

However, this project still has many shortcomings, in the future, we will implement features such as page fault and dynamic linking, as well as presenting the underlying details of the system in a clearer and more explicit way to assist beginners in understanding some complex operating system concepts.

Acknowledgements. This work is supported by the National Natural Science Foundation of China (61976071), and the Natural Science Foundation of Heilongjiang Province of China (LH2020F012).

References

1. Microsoft Extensible Firmware Initiative FAT32 File System Specification. https://download.microsoft.com/download/1/6/1/161ba512-40e2-4cc9-843a-923143f3456c/fatgen103.doc (2000)
2. Akçay, L., Tükel, M., Örs, S.B.: Implementation of an OpenRISC based SoC and Linux Kernel installation on FPGA. In: 2016 24th Signal Processing and Communication Application Conference (SIU), pp. 1969–1972 (2016). https://doi.org/10.1109/SIU.2016.7496153
3. Asanović, K., Patterson, D.A.: Instruction sets should be free: the case for RISC-V. EECS Department, University of California, Berkeley, Tech. Rep. UCB/EECS-2014-146 (2014)
4. Bakiri, M., Titri, S., Izeboudjen, N., Abid, F., Louiz, F., Lazib, D.: Embedded system with Linux Kernel based on OpenRISC 1200–V3. In: 2012 6th International Conference on Sciences of Electronics, Technologies of Information and Telecommunications (SETIT), pp. 177–182 (2012). https://doi.org/10.1109/SETIT.2012.6481909

5. Blem, E., Menon, J., Sankaralingam, K.: Power struggles: revisiting the RISC vs. CISC debate on contemporary ARM and x86 architectures. In: 2013 IEEE 19th International Symposium on High Performance Computer Architecture (HPCA), pp. 1–12 (2013). https://doi.org/10.1109/HPCA.2013.6522302
6. Bovet, D.P., Cesati, M.: Understanding the Linux Kernel. O'Reilly Media, Inc. (2005)
7. Flamand, E., et al.: GAP-8: A RISC-V SoC for AI at the Edge of the IoT. In: 2018 IEEE 29th International Conference on Application-specific Systems, Architectures and Processors (ASAP), pp. 1–4 (2018). https://doi.org/10.1109/ASAP.2018.8445101
8. Garg, M.: About ELF auxiliary vectors. http://articles.manugarg.com/aboutelfauxiliaryvectors.html (2006)
9. Juszkiewicz, M.: Linux kernel system calls for all architectures. https://marcin.juszkiewicz.com.pl/download/tables/syscalls.html (2022)
10. Keller, B., et al.: A RISC-V processor SoC with integrated power management at submicrosecond timescales in 28 nm FD-SOI. IEEE J. Solid-State Circuits **52**(7), 1863–1875 (2017). https://doi.org/10.1109/JSSC.2017.2690859
11. Lee, Y., et al.: An agile approach to building RISC-V microprocessors. IEEE Micro **36**(2), 8–20 (2016). https://doi.org/10.1109/MM.2016.11
12. Love, R.: Linux Kernel Development, 3rd edn. (2010)
13. Waterman, E.A., Asanović, K., Hauser, J.: The RISC-V Instruction set manual, Volume II: Privileged Architecture, Document Version 20211203 (2021)
14. Yu, C., Yifan, W.: rCore-Tutorial-Book. http://rcore-os.cn/rCore-Tutorial-Book-v3 (2022)

Research on the Cultivation of Media Literacy Among Adolescents from the Perspective of Smart Education

Zhijun Yang[1,2,3], Zijia Ren[3(✉)], and Guimei Fan[3]

[1] Educational Instruments and Facilities Service Center, Educational Department of Yunnan Province, Kunming, China
[2] Key Laboratory of Education Informatization for Nationalities of Ministry of Education, Yunnan Normal University, Kunming, China
[3] School of Vocational and Continuing Education, Yunnan University, Kunming, China
645841720@qq.com

Abstract. With the rapid development of the Internet era, social media is widely used in the daily life and learning of adolescents and plays an important role in cultivating their media literacy. Based on the problems and dilemmas faced by adolescents in the use of social media, combined with the research hotspots of smart education, this article proposes the inspiration that smart education brings to the cultivation of adolescents' media literacy, hoping to promote the further development of research on the cultivation of adolescents' media literacy.

Keywords: Smart Education · Media Literacy · Education Informatization · Social Media

1 Introduction

In recent years, due to the rapid development and massive popularity of the Internet and new media, online social media have been widely used in the daily life of the majority of adolescents and have increasingly penetrated into the learning activities of adolescents, becoming an important way for them to learn. In the rich network information environment, the rational use of various media for learning has become an important ability for adolescents in the information age, and the cultivation of media literacy has received increasing attention. China's education informationization has entered the era of smart education, which requires adolescents to have the ability to learn smartly in a smart environment, and the cultivation of smart learning ability is inseparable from the cultivation of media literacy. This paper addresses the problems and dilemmas faced by adolescents in the process of using online social media; combines the hot content of current research on smart education; proposes insights into the cultivation of adolescents' media literacy from the perspective of smart education in terms of environment construction, technology development, and learning and teaching modes; and provides ideas for research on the cultivation of adolescents' media literacy from the perspective of smart education.

J. Gan et al. (Eds.): CSEI 2023, CCIS 1899, pp. 17–25, 2024.
https://doi.org/10.1007/978-981-99-9499-1_2

2 Media Literacy Cultivation and Smart Education

2.1 Media Literacy Cultivation Relies on Social Media

Media is a medium for disseminating information, and traditional media is the main source of information acquisition in people's daily lives in the past. Media literacy refers to people's ability to acquire, collect, discriminate, screen, understand and use information and other information processing in the network environment, as well as their awareness and ability of self-management and self-protection in the use of information [1]. Media literacy education is education that guides individuals to correctly understand and effectively use media, enhance media competence, and cultivate qualified media citizens [2]. With the rapid development of science and technology, various new media relying on the Internet have emerged. Social media is a platform for users to share, communicate and interact with each other relying on Internet technology, which is favoured by the majority of users and widely used in daily life. Common social media in China include WeChat, QQ, Microblog, Tiktok, The Little Red Book, Post Bar, etc., on which people can subscribe and browse hot news, chat with relatives and friends in different places, make new online friends, publish opinions, discuss and communicate with others, share experience and strategies, etc., which plays an important role in improving media literacy. In the process of using various social media, people's media literacy is also improving.

2.2 Social Media is Gradually Being Applied in the Field of Education

Initially, social media was used to meet people's needs for social communication and entertainment in daily life. In the past, teenagers used social media to chat, make friends, relax and engage in other recreational activities after learning. However, with the continuous development of the Internet and the impact of the COVID-19 epidemic in recent years, online education and online courses have rapidly impacted and occupied a large amount of traditional offline teaching and learning. Social media is no longer just an entertainment tool for adolescents but has begun to be widely used in the learning process of teenagers. For example, various functions of WeChat and QQ are used to conduct online classes, hand in homework, hold class meetings, attend lectures and other learning activities, becoming an essential learning tool. The integration of life, learning and entertainment and intelligence has become the trend of adolescents' Internet application in the age of social media [3]. The use of social media is developing into the field of education and has become an important tool and channel for online education. The rational use of social media will be of great help to the education of teenagers.

2.3 The Necessity of Cultivating Media Literacy Among Adolescents

Adolescents are in a special stage and critical period of physical and psychological development, especially in secondary school. They are curious but not yet determined, their values are in the process of formation, and their ability to judge right and wrong is still gradually developing, so they are very vulnerable to the interference and influence of the external environment and peers and often need to bear the negative influence of the dissemination of Internet information, which will seriously affect the physical and mental health of adolescents. This negative information will seriously affect the physical and mental health development of adolescents. Therefore, it is necessary to pay attention to the psychological development of adolescents, improve their information literacy and media literacy, and help them establish correct ideological values [4]. Cultivating adolescents' media literacy can also improve adolescents' information literacy and collaboration and innovation skills and facilitate the establishment of correct values. Currently, most studies on media literacy cultivation focus on teachers and college students in higher education, but there is a lack of studies on media literacy cultivation in adolescents in secondary education.

2.4 Smart Education and Media Literacy Cultivation Complement Each Other

From the development history of education informatization, after experiencing the digitalization of education mainly by computer education in the 1970s and 1980s and the networking of education mainly by Internet education from the 1990s to the beginning of the 21st century, it entered the stage of education intelligence mainly by emerging technologies such as artificial intelligence and big data since 2010. In 2017, the Chinese State Council issued the "New Generation of Artificial Intelligence Development Plan" [5], pointing out the use of intelligent technology to accelerate the promotion of talent training mode, teaching method reform, the construction of a new education system containing intelligent learning, and interactive learning. Yang Xianmin pointed out that smart education is an educational information ecosystem that is connected, intelligent, perceptive, and ubiquitous based on a new generation of information technology [6]. Education informatization provides the environment and technical support for the cultivation of students' media literacy, and smart education cannot be achieved without the Internet and various information technology environments, as well as without various media channels. The realization of smart education requires students to have certain media literacy, and the improvement of media literacy can also promote smart learning.

3 The Current Situation and Problems of Social Media Use Among Adolescents

As we all know, the Internet has two sides. While it brings people fast and convenient information and colorful resources, it also brings many difficult problems. In the process of using social media, adolescents tend to be addicted to the virtual world and neglect reality, and their social skills are reduced; they are not aware of their own safety precautions and are prone to cyber security accidents; they have difficulty in screening and filtering the vast amount of information in the Internet and are not capable of distinguishing right from wrong; their search and browsing records on the Internet tend to form information cocoons and cause self-isolation, which is not conducive to the cultivation of the spirit of collaboration and innovation.

3.1 Indulge in the Virtual Online World and Ignore Reality

Adolescents are curious, receptive and interested in new things, but lack of self-control makes them easily addicted to the virtual network world and ignore reality. With the rapid development of virtual reality, augmented reality and wearable devices, the topic of the "meta-universe" has increased dramatically in recent years, and the connection between the virtual world and the real world will become a future trend. However, this also brings many problems. Adolescents are deeply involved in the Internet and cannot extricate themselves from it, and there are a large number of Internet-addicted young boys and young girls with poor self-control, low social interaction ability and reluctance to communicate with real human beings, and a large amount of Internet information brings a sense of loneliness and fear of missing out to adolescents.

3.2 Frequent Network Security Incidents and Susceptibility to Fraud

Secondary school adolescents are naiver, self-protection and risk prevention awareness is insufficient, and it is easy to walk into the trap of telecommunications network fraud. From various news reports, it is easy to see that in recent years, the adolescent group is vulnerable to network fraud, such as gullible network part-time job brush single rebate, but in fact was cheated of funds; the desire for money into the psychological trap of false investment and network loans; anti-fraud awareness and vigilance is not enough, falling into the impersonation of e-commerce customer service, public prosecution and law and teachers and students, family and friends acquaintances and other fraudulent schemes, in addition to the use of foreign numbers, specific numbers, screen sharing, "phishing" links, fake APP and other fraudulent means cannot be prevented. Once cheated, personal information is leaked and used illegally, and family funds are stolen, causing great physical and psychological damage to adolescents.

3.3 Massive Information is Complex and Difficult to Filter

Adolescents in secondary school are in the process of forming their values of right and wrong, and their ability to distinguish truth from falsehood has yet to be improved. They have difficulty in screening and selecting correct and valuable information from the vast amount of Internet information and are prone to believe and spread rumours. In the traditional media era, information is often released and disseminated to the public only after multiple checks and audits by the person in charge, while in today's new media era, everyone can be the publisher of information, and information is disseminated very quickly and through many channels, so some unconfirmed information is easily spread on a large scale after release. Because the information can be released anonymously, some people take a chance to engage in bad behaviour on the Internet [7]. Adolescents lack the ability to verify information and are prone to listen to rumours and some inaccurate information, and at the same time, they may become disseminators of such information, unable to judge the authenticity and value of the information.

3.4 Preferences Can Easily Become Information Cocoons and Self-imposed Closures

Due to the rapid development of big data, cloud computing, artificial intelligence, learning analysis and other information technology, major social media can infer the topic areas of interest to users based on their usage time, browsing records, search preferences and other information and constantly recommend similar or identical information to users by "guessing what you like". In the long run, users can only see what they want to see and ignore other information, forming the "information cocoon" phenomenon. This phenomenon will create an information gap among adolescents, and individual cognitive differences will become bigger, and the way and channel to obtain information will become single and narrow, which will easily cause information monopoly [8] and not use adolescents to expand their knowledge and broaden their horizons.

4 Enlightenment from the Cultivation of Media Literacy Among Adolescents from the Perspective of Smart Education

In the past decade, research on smart education has developed rapidly and become a hot spot for education research. In this paper, we used the advanced search function of CNKI to search for literature with the topic or keyword "smart education" and retrieved 8403 articles from January 1, 2012, to December 31, 2022. In addition to 2728 articles

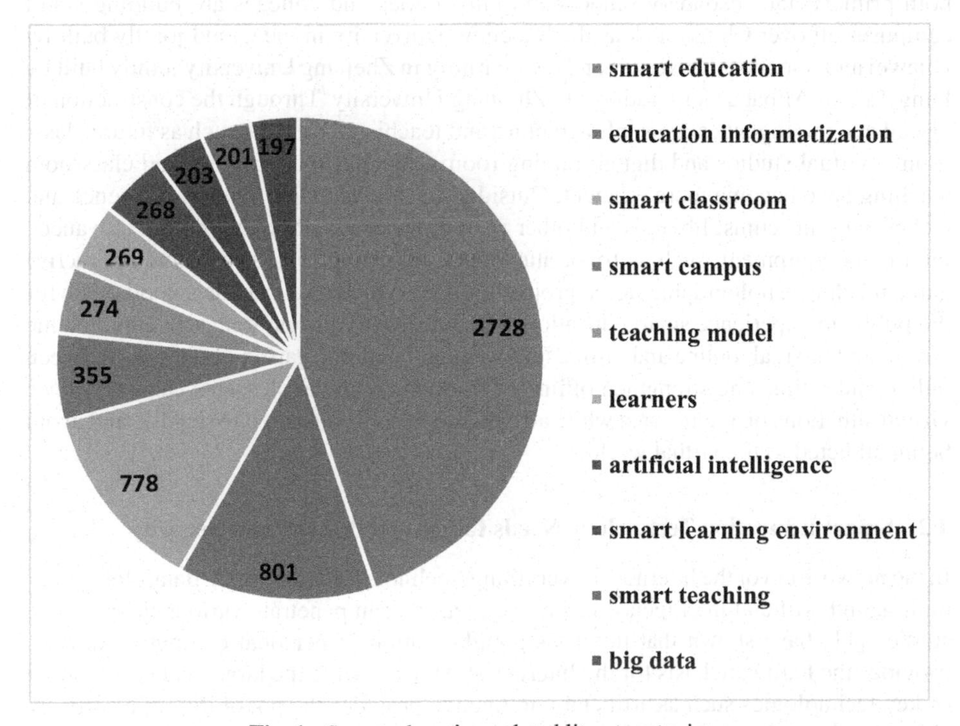

Fig. 1. Smart education-related literature topics

on "smart education," the top 9 topics were "education informatization" (801 articles), "smart classroom" (778 articles), "smart campus" (355 articles), "teaching model" (274 articles), "learners" (269 articles), "artificial intelligence" (268 articles), "smart learning environment" (203 articles), "smart teaching" (201 articles), and "big data" (197 articles), as shown in Fig. 1. The current research hotspots on smart education focus on the construction of smart environments such as smart classrooms, smart campuses, and smart learning environments, the development of smart technologies such as artificial intelligence and big data, and the exploration of smart learning and teaching models focusing on learner learning and teacher teaching. This paper addresses the current situation and problems of adolescents' use of social media, combines the characteristics of smart education in environment construction, technology development, and exploration of learning and teaching models, and proposes the inspiration of smart education for the cultivation of adolescents' media literacy.

4.1 Smart Education Environment Construction Needs to Be Closely Related to the Real World

The smart learning ecosystem is a learning system developed by the integration of the digital learning ecosystem with the smart education concept [9], and the regional education informatization system is turning into a vertically integrated and horizontally integrated smart ecosystem [10], so it can be seen that the construction of the smart environment is developing in the direction of building a universal smart education ecology. Currently, both primary and secondary schools and universities and colleges are building smart campuses all over China, such as the Soochow University in the Cloud jointly built by Huawei and Soochow University and the Learning in Zhejiang University jointly built by Ding Talk of Alibaba Corporation and Zhejiang University. Through the construction of digital and intelligent campus infrastructure and teaching platforms such as future classrooms, virtual studios and digital training rooms, campus management and classroom teaching have become more efficient. Outside of schools, major museums, science and technology museums, libraries and other public places also have even more advanced intelligent equipment, such as robot attendants, human–machine real-time interactive game machines, holographic stereo projection, etc., which also provide a good scene for the public to experience smart education. The future smart ecosystem will combine the virtual and the real, online and offline intermingle, break the gap and boundary between online and offline and strengthen offline interaction so that adolescents can experience virtual situations on the Internet while also being closely connected to real life and avoid being addicted to the virtual world.

4.2 Smart Education Technology Needs to Ensure Privacy and Security

In the network era of the Internet of Everything, technologies such as big data, cloud computing, and artificial intelligence in smart education can penetrate various fields. Some studies [11] have shown that the mass popularization of personal computing devices provides the hardware basis for the Internet of Things, while the large-scale application of key technologies such as artificial intelligence provides the possibility of a software algorithm level for smart education. The technologies in smart education can provide safety prevention for adolescents' socialization, automatically identify and block bad information, spam messages and illegal links to guarantee a clean and green network environment for adolescents, and push anti-fraud tips and network safety microcourses in a timely manner to help adolescents develop critical thinking and discernment skills. It can also intervene safely in adolescents' social networks and build a social media intervention mechanism for adolescents with the help of intelligent technology to track the information records of adolescents' social media activities in their daily study and life and immediately alert students once they identify behaviours that may enter dangerous pages to help them raise their awareness of risk prevention. It can also provide safety remedies for adolescents' social media, identify safety hazards through various technologies, assist adolescents in preserving remaining safety information, freeze fund accounts with one click, and assist in reporting to the police to minimize losses and injuries.

4.3 Smart Education Needs Personalized Recommended Learning Resources

Using seamless perception technology, smart education can comprehensively perceive learners' information in learning scenarios, such as learning environment, learning equipment, and user information, and deeply analyse and mine the data generated by learners in the learning process to identify learners' learning abilities, cognitive styles, and learning preferences and match them with appropriate learning tasks to guide and help [12]. Smart services entering the smart era will shift to active intelligence with everything connected, comprehensive perception, reliable transmission, and intelligent processing [13]. Under a rich intelligent environment, students' learning resources will become more intelligent and personalized. In the face of complicated online information, personalized recommendation can improve the efficiency of information screening for adolescents. Before learning, students' learning situation should be analysed and diagnosed, their ability level and knowledge weaknesses should be determined, and learning resources that meet their physical and mental development characteristics should be recommended according to the theory of the nearest development zone. During the learning process, learning analysis is used to determine students' learning styles and adjust the recommendation of learning resources and personalized content based on their learning time and practice results. After the learning process, the next learning content is recommended through the analysis of students' learning effects to achieve a virtuous cycle.

4.4 Smart Education Needs to Focus on Collaborative Learning and Teaching Model Innovation

Some studies [14] note that smart education integrates a variety of information technologies to promote the optimization of learning scenarios and the transformation of learning and teaching modes and that smart education is moving toward the trend of building an educational ecology. There are also studies [15] that note that smart education is an innovative educational form and educational model implemented in an educational environment with active intelligence as well as a new educational system for cultivating innovative talent in the smart era. Especially in recent years, influenced by the epidemic, online education has developed rapidly, online live streaming for teachers and online classes for students has become the norm, and major smart education platforms have actively played the role of teacher preparation, student prereview, teacher-student classroom interaction, and learning analysis.

Develop Interdisciplinary Integrated Courses and Innovate Learning Methods and Teaching Models through Interdisciplinary Integration. Some studies suggest [16] that media literacy development should attempt to breakdown disciplinary boundaries and focus on disciplinary diversity rather than homogeneity. At the secondary school level, single-subject courses have a long history of development, and the media literacy cultivation that adolescents can receive through a single course is limited and does not take advantage of knowledge transfer and practical application, while interdisciplinary courses can integrate knowledge from various subjects, allowing students to integrate, broaden their knowledge and horizons, and improve their ability to integrate information and knowledge, which is conducive to the improvement of media literacy.

Carry Out Campus-Themed Activities and Develop Adolescents' Teamwork and Communication Skills through Campus-Themed Activities. Outside of the classroom, schools can use various new media means and tools based on their own characteristics to organize campus-themed activities in the form of workshops, interest groups, clubs, etc. Students can work together to complete tasks through online collaboration offline, and students and teachers can ask for advice and guidance on problems through online and offline means to improve practical interaction, communication and collaboration skills.

Encourage After-School Science and Technology Practice, through Science and Technology Practice to Let Adolescents Actually Hands-On, However, Additionally, to Improve the Ability to Innovate. In the context of "double reduction" policy, schools and major public education bases have reached a coeducation mechanism to carry out students' science and innovation practices through adolescents' science education bases such as children's palaces, science and technology museums and other museums. In these places, adolescents can independently explore and learn extracurricular knowledge; to a large extent, they can play an independent and active role in learning, stimulate interest in learning and develop creative thinking skills, and they can be connected with social life, using the knowledge they have learned and various media work to think and solve practical problems in life by themselves.

5 Conclusion

Smart education is developing in China, and media literacy is an important quality for adolescents in the information age. Media literacy cultivation and smart education complement each other, and smart education can provide new ideas for adolescents' media literacy cultivation in terms of environment construction, technology development, and learning and teaching models. At the same time, we should also recognize that the environment, technology, learning and teaching models are only tools and means of education that are used to support better development of education, and we should not focus on technology to neglect the essence of education. Only by adhering to the original intention of student-oriented education, starting from the learners themselves, promoting the cultivation of adolescents' media literacy from the perspective of smart education, and constantly verifying theories in practice over a long period of time, can we truly exert the practical power of educational informatization and improve the media literacy of adolescents in a smart education environment.

Acknowledgements. Thanks for the support from the "Yunnan Province Talent Support Program" for industrial innovation talents (formerly Yunnan Province "Ten Thousand People Plan" for industrial technology leaders).

Thanks for the support from the Wu Zhonghai Expert Workstation Project in Yunnan Province (Project No. 202305AF150045).

References

1. Zhang, X., Ding, Y.: Online media literacy education and youth moral construction. China Radio TV Acad. J. 20–23 (2020)
2. Chen, L.: Improving media literacy. Southeast Commun. 33–34 (2017)
3. Ji, W.: Characteristics of teenagers' internet use trends and growth influence in the social media era–an analysis based on a survey of teenagers' Internet use from 2006 to 2020. News Writ. 43–50 (2020)
4. Liu, Y.: Enhancing online media literacy and taking care of adolescent psychological health–review of "online information communication and adolescent psychological development". Media 98 (2021)
5. Notice of the State Council on the issuance of the development plan of a new generation of artificial intelligence. Bulletin of the State Council of the People's Republic of China, pp. 7–21 (2017)
6. Yang, X.: The connotation and characteristics of intelligent education in the information age. China Educ. Technol. 29–34 (2014)
7. Deng, W.: An analysis of strategies to cultivate and enhance college students' media literacy in the age of social media. J. News Res. 128–131 (2022)
8. Shen, N.: The information cocoons and information equality in algorithm era. J. Xi'an Jiaotong Univ. (Soc. Sci.) 139–144 (2020)
9. Gu, X., Du, H., Peng, H., et al.: The theoretical framework, development and future prospect of smart education. J. East China Norm. Univ. (Educ. Sci.) 20–32 (2021)
10. Wang, Y., Wang, Y., Wang, H., et al.: Construction of regional education smart ecosystem: model, framework and strategies—based on the practical research of Zhejiang education big data project. China Educ. Technol. 114–120 (2022)
11. Yu, S., Liu, E.: Transformation and change of smart education. E-educ. Res. 16–23+62 (2022)
12. Zhu, Z., He, B.: Smart education: the new realm of education informatization. E-educ. Res. 7–15 (2012)
13. Yu, S., Chen, F., Li, S.: Private network construction of 5G-based smart campus. Open Educ. Res. 51–59 (2020)
14. Yang, J.F., Shi, G., Zhuang, R., et al.: 5G+smart education: educational reform based on intelligent technology. China Educ. Technol. 1–7 (2021)
15. Tang, W., Qin, C., Xiang, Y., et al.: Research on the theory and practice of smart education and personalized learning. China Educ. Technol. 124–137 (2021)
16. Li, H.: The development status and new trends of media literacy research at home and abroad–a knowledge map analysis based on CiteSpace (2010–2021). Southeast Commun. 95–99 (2022)

ChatGPT Empowers Smart Education: Potential, Challenges and Prospects

Nana Zhang and Xiuming Li(✉)

Qinghai Minzu University, Xining, Qinghai, China
lixiumingwhs@163.com

Abstract. ChatGPT was launched in November 2022 and has received widespread attention from the education community. How school education should be changed and upgraded in the age of artificial intelligence has become a major issue we are facing. The use of artificial intelligence technology has both advantages and disadvantages for education, and a dialectical view of the technological advantages ChatGPT gives to the information age will inevitably better facilitate schools to create smart classrooms, develop smart education, and realize the task of the times of digital transformation of education. To deeply explore the technical means to promote the development of smart education, this paper introduces the potential and challenges of ChatGPT empowering smart education, designs a framework for a practical model of ChatGPT empowering smart education, and analyses the prospective advantages of ChatGPT entering the education field, with a view to providing some reference for the future development of ChatGPT in the education sector and the comprehensive popularization of smart education.

Keywords: ChatGPT · smart education · artificial intelligence

1 Introduction

In recent years, artificial intelligence has penetrated all walks of life, and education is no exception. It is common to see robots entering the classroom, not only enhancing the fun of the classroom but also helping teachers deal with tedious tasks. In fact, the era of intelligent, informative and digital education has arrived on November 30, 2022, the U.S. company OpenAI listed a robot called ChatGPT, which has attracted widespread attention from all walks of life.

Especially in the field of education, it has created an uproar. The development and use of technology has both advantages and disadvantages, and how to reasonably use the technical advantages of ChatGPT to make artificial intelligence better serve education is a common theme of research throughout the education community. Studies have noted that smart education will enter a full-scale popularization stage in 2022, the same year ChatGPT was introduced, which undoubtedly brings the development of smart education to a new level. Although scholars at home and abroad have very different attitudes toward ChatGPT, with some actively embracing it and others negatively resisting it, this paper argues that there is nothing wrong with the technology itself, but the key is in the people

J. Gan et al. (Eds.): CSEI 2023, CCIS 1899, pp. 26–41, 2024.
https://doi.org/10.1007/978-981-99-9499-1_3

who use it. Based on existing research, this paper summarizes the main concerns of ChatGPT in the Chinese education sector; in addition, this paper explains the risks faced by ChatGPT in the field of smart education from three aspects, designs a framework of a ChatGPT-enabled smart education practice model, and analyses the development prospects of ChatGPT-enabled smart education from both educators and learners. The development prospects of ChatGPT-enabled smart education are analysed from both educators and learners.

2 ChatGPT and Smart Education

2.1 Introduction of the ChatGPT

ChatGPT quickly exploded in the world as soon as it was launched. The reason is that it can answer the questions asked by humans with its own language system, giving correct answers that almost match human language habits. It is a technological crystallization in the era of artificial intelligence and a power engine to accelerate the informatization of human society [1]. ChatGPT undoubtedly refreshed people's understanding of artificial intelligence technology after its launch. In comparison with the emergence of traditional robots and AlphaGo, ChatGPT involves and other fields more widely, and the participating user groups are more extensive.

ChatGPT, as an artificial intelligence product, first appeared in the science fiction movie Star Trek in 2017, when ChatGPT was just a simple chatbot. Today, ChatGPT has entered the education sector. One school in the United States has reportedly created a special course for ChatGPT, where students use ChatGPT's abilities and information during classes. The University of Manchester in the UK has also introduced ChatGPT into the classroom, where students can use ChatGPT to select a course for themselves, through which students can learn skills such as math, programming and writing. The release of ChatGPT marks another landmark technological change after deep learning, which will bring a new "historical opportunity" for cognitive intelligence technologies centered on NLP (neurolinguistic programming) [2]. In addition, ChatGPT is one of the typical representatives of AI-generated content, and together with other generative AI, ChatGPT will revolutionize the traditional content production and information access model, enabling it to perform intellectual tasks as efficiently as humans, using efficient human–machine collaboration to disrupt the content production model of all intellectual industries, achieving efficient, high-quality, massive, real-time, diverse, and personalized content generation, which will have a significant and profound impact on the transformation of various traditional industries, including school education [3].

2.2 Features of ChatGPT

Tool Properties

Recall the source stream of AI exploration. Due to its lack of body, lack of motivation, cognitive closure and lack of subjectivity, ChatGPT is a dedicated AI system that is by nature a tool [4]. Therefore, ChatGPT intervention in education can be used as a tool to improve the quality of education, but its functions should not be exaggerated; otherwise, it will fall into the chasm of technological omnipotence and make education bound by technology (Fig. 1).

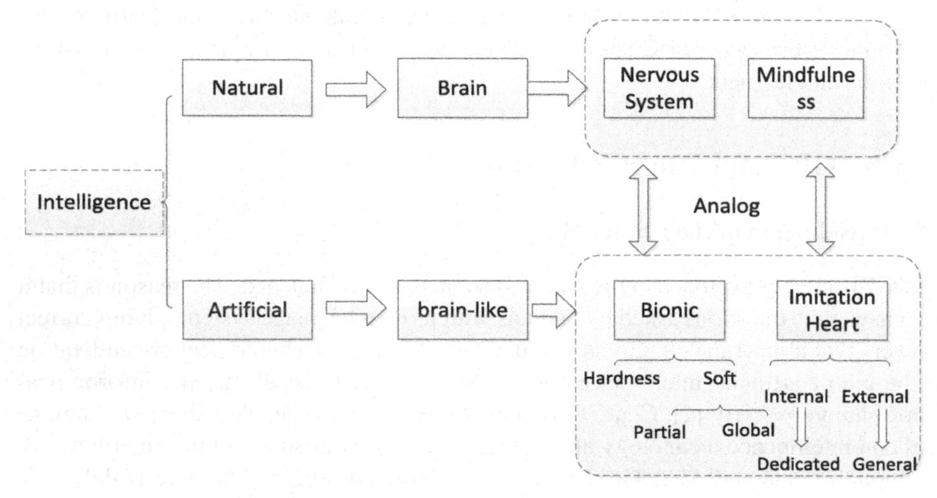

Fig. 1. Artificial Intelligence Exploration Schematic

Generativity

ChatGPT is an artificial intelligence language model that generates human-like answers based on textual content. In everyday life, it can converse with people and assist them with simple tasks. ChatGPT is a variation of the original GPT (Generative Pre-Trained Converter) language model, which is trained on massive text datasets from the Internet to enable it to produce human-like textual responses to various questions and prompts, with a generative model based on text that can generate human-like responses to user requests. As a conversational system, ChatGPT is able to understand the content of conversations and recognize the social and emotional needs of users during conversations. It mimics and interprets human communication, and ChatGPT's performance depends on the size and accuracy of its database, which means that a larger database size leads to

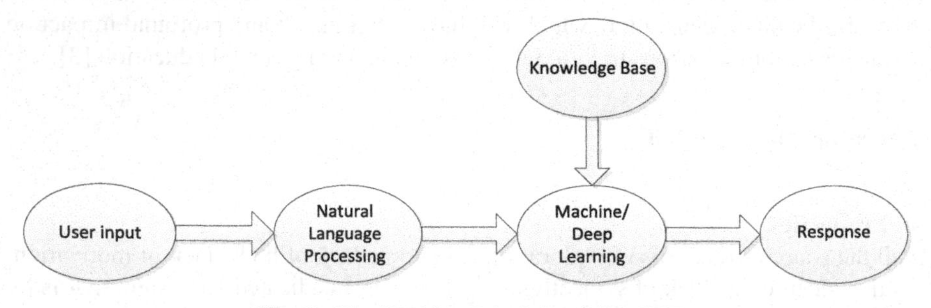

Fig. 2. The Working Principle of ChatGPT

better performance. Its creation involves the use of natural language processing (NLP), a technology that enables robots to understand, analyse, and interpret natural human language. Figure 2 illustrates how ChatGPT works.

2.3 Research on ChatGPT in the Chinese Educational Community

Artificial intelligence content generation technologies are rapidly evolving and have demonstrated amazing capabilities in mapping, programming, and writing and were selected by Science as one of the top 10 technological achievements of 2022. ChatGPT has attracted extensive attention from the Chinese education community since its introduction in the U.S. [5]. It is divided into the following six main research directions:

ChatGPT's Impact on Teaching
When ChatGPT first appeared, the focus of research was on its impact on the educational field. Since the introduction of ChatGPT, the main focus has been on its role in education. In the face of ChatGPT, we must take a proper view of its functional features, core values and the risks it may bring and adopt a cautious attitude to overcome the bias in the perception of the use of artificial intelligence in education. According to Professor Yang Zongkai, there are three potential effects of computer-assisted general-purpose technology on education. First, it will promote the change in education methods so that the dual structure of "teacher-student" will be transformed into the triadic structure of "teacher-student-robot". The first is that it will promote a change in the way education is delivered, from a dualistic "teacher-student" structure to a triadic "teacher-student-robot" structure [6]. According to Lee, its effect on education is mainly at the university level, where it can improve students' learning and research effectiveness, influence the evaluation and assessment of teaching and learning, and promote the direction of teaching to enhance students' academic innovation and thinking skills [7].

ChatGPT's Impact on the Education Ecology or the Risk of Entering the Education Field
The emergence of ChatGPT will inevitably have an impact on the education ecology, and what challenges this impact brings and how to deal with such challenges are the focus of scholars' research at this stage. According to Li Yuyang, while enjoying the technological dividend brought by ChatGPT, the risks it carries will also invade the education field along the way, and these risks include the risk of knowledge alienation, the risk of student subjectivity alienation, the risk of teaching process alienation, the risk of digital ethics and the risk of digital education governance [8]. Yomei Wang analysed the ethical risks of its application in teaching and learning, mainly in terms of data leakage and misuse, discriminatory and biased machine algorithms, dilution and destruction of teacher-student relationships, and dishonesty and imbalance in academic equity. Based on game theory, the optimal relationship between "education and ChatGPT" is analysed from an ethical perspective, and some suggestions are provided on how to avoid the ethical dilemma of ChatGPT in educational practice [9]. Wang Hongcai argued that a universal corpus helps students acquire knowledge but does not necessarily improve their knowledge. ChatGPT helps improve teachers' competence, but at the same time, there are problems such as data leakage, blind reliance and information distortion. The use of new

technological tools may make a direct change in the original way of learning, allowing educational activities to break through established spatial and temporal boundaries; therefore, the overall change in the form of education brought about is already on display in the world [10].

Advantages of ChatGPT's Entry into the Education Field
Scholars deeply appreciated the technological advantages of ChatGPT and discussed how to use ChatGPT to promote digital transformation in education. Professor Jiao Jianli analysed in depth linguistic text mapping and other generative AI technologies from six levels, especially their practical potential in driving the digitalization of school education; in addition, the application of ChatGPT in the education field was also explored in depth [2]. Based on ChatGPT's four core competencies, namely, inspiring content generation, conversational context understanding, sequential task execution, and procedural language parsing, Luu explored its potential educational applications in four areas: teacher teaching, learning process, educational assessment, and academic counselling [11].

Impact of ChatGPT on Structural Changes in School Education
Scholars are also investigating whether ChatGPT will give rise to structural changes in schools. According to Zhang Zhizhen, the current system structure of the subcurriculum system, class teaching system and teacher-led system is still relatively solid and has not been greatly affected by the existing intelligent teaching system and other resources such as catechism; automated teaching based on a large-scale language model still needs to make up for the "superstructure". In terms of basic education, the elements of the education system may change significantly, but the structure of the system is likely to remain the same [12].

The Impact of ChatGPT on Teachers
According to Li Zhengtao, what "disciplinary general theory" does not have is its irreplaceable, inextinguishable and unsurpassable value. For example, the value of human teachers' existence is irreplaceable and valuable in cultivating students' ideals and beliefs, values and meanings, thinking and emotions, will and courage, struggle and enterprise, reflection and self-reflection, and creativity and innovation [13]. According to Jiao, at the time of the emergence of generative AI applications such as ChatGPT, educators should keep pace with the times and embrace the changes in technology with an open mind; use new technologies, carry out creative teaching, and implement teaching according to the needs of the students; and the application of the tools in question should not be simply and brutally prohibited; on this basis, a new, more effective and efficient teaching method. Using AI tools to accomplish creative work and improve core competencies in high-tech contexts, AI for good, technology ethics, privacy protection, and the digital divide are hot issues of concern [14]. According to Yang Xianmin, in the era of AI, teachers urgently need to "cultivate" five core competencies, namely, the ability to collaborate and nurture people with machines, the ability to continuously reflect and learn, the ability to think critically and make choices, the ability to think creatively and innovate, and the ability to collaborate across disciplinary fields, to become qualified teachers in the era of AI teachers [15]. Wu Junqi, starting from the general background

of education digitization, analysed in depth the opportunities and challenges brought by ChatGPT to teachers' professional development in four dimensions: teachers' professional conception, professional knowledge, professional competence, and professional emotion, in the form of a case study, and on this basis, proposed five aspects of teacher education, including mechanism guarantee, environment creation, curriculum construction, method innovation, and assessment reform, for reform. In addition, ChatGPT has been used as a representative to establish an empowerment path for teachers' professional development based on ChatGPT and other artificial intelligence technologies [16]. In addition, human-computer collaboration is also a key area of interest. According to Yuanshang Li, at the level of "human-robot coeducation", teachers, students, and robots have a clear division of responsibilities, and the reasonable use of AI technology can achieve better education purposes. ChatGPT can provide teachers and students with personalized tutoring, interactive assistance, and innovative learning services in the process of "human-machine cocreation".

ChatGPT's Thinking About Education Teaching
Hao Yu, after analysing the application of ChatGPT technology in educational support systems and educational field scenarios, found that ChatGPT technology can help teachers teach more effectively to improve teaching quality and students learn more effectively to enhance their learning efficiency [17]. Zhou Ling pointed out that the theory of "comprehensive development" is important in promoting students' overall development, teaching according to their abilities, individualized teaching, and rebuilding dynamic classrooms [18]. Wang Shengyuan took the theory of "dialogue" as an entry point and elaborated the concept of "dialogue" teaching and the possibility of a "dialogue" learning community from the perspective of "dialogue". "The details include: the correction of "dialogue" elements, the "ChatGPT" tool in the classroom, the construction of "dialogue The course includes the construction of a "dialogue" learning community in the classroom, clarifying the logical connection between the five elements of "dialogue" and the "four stages", and analysing the four principles of a "dialogue" learning community. In this paper, we analyse the four principles of the "dialogue" learning community and use them as the basis for designing the "dialogue" model and applying it to the teaching of secondary school civics [19].

3 Potential of ChatGPT in the Field of Smart Education

In this paper, ChatGPT is considered to have the following applications in the field of smart education: it is an intelligent learning assistant; it can develop personalized learning programs; and it can generate and recommend educational content and conduct intelligent Q&A.

3.1 Intelligent Learning Assistant

ChatGPT can be used not only to answer students' questions but also to provide advice on learning strategies to help students learn better. For example, in the classroom, ChatGPT can help students create personalized study plans and provide personalized feedback on assignments and tests. In addition to providing advice, ChatGPT can help students better understand their learning progress. For example, when students perform exercises, ChatGPT can help them better understand their learning by analysing their answers to predict their next performance so that they can study in a more focused manner. In addition, ChatGPT can also be used for classroom interaction; for example, after students ask questions, ChatGPT can determine students' knowledge mastery based on their answers and then automatically generate interactive classroom answers for students' reference, thus improving the effectiveness of classroom interaction.

3.2 Set Personalized Learning Solutions

ChatGPT can accurately identify students' questions and knowledge mastery through intelligent language models and provide personalized learning solutions. In this program, students can choose the learning path that best suits them and set up personalized learning paths based on their learning abilities and preferences, thus enhancing their learning efficiency. With ChatGPT, students can not only choose a learning path that suits their learning level but also achieve targeted improvement by categorizing different knowledge points. In addition, students can analyse courses, knowledge points and question types to understand their learning situation and conduct targeted review and consolidation.

3.3 Intelligent Generation and Recommendation of Educational Content

ChatGPT not only has the ability to understand language, but in the field of education, ChatGPT can also automatically generate natural language text, such as recommended courses, exam topics, and essay abstracts. ChatGPT can automatically learn the teaching resources provided by teachers and provide students with personalized learning suggestions and can convert the teaching contents provided by teachers into text form and make personalized recommendations based on students' interests, hobbies and knowledge mastery to improve learning efficiency. ChatGPT can also automatically generate test questions based on students' learning to help students better consolidate their knowledge.

3.4 Conduct Intelligent Q&A

Based on its pretrained knowledge graph and powerful natural language processing capabilities, ChatGPT can generate an answer on its own based on the questions entered by users. For example, when a student asks "What is free will?" , ChatGPT can give the standard answer "Free will is a person's ability to decide his or her own behavior". Searching for answers to questions with common browsers often results in irrelevant content such as advertisements and spam; with ChatGPT, you can obtain more focused and accurate answers, avoiding the work of information screening and identification, which not only greatly improves the efficiency of question retrieval but also enhances the interest in learning smart learning.

4 Challenges of ChatGPT Development for Smart Education

Worldwide, many educators and local educational administrations have expressed concerns about the future of education, and many countries and regions have even begun to ban students from using ChatGPT technology. The article stands on the basis of previous studies to first analyse and summarize the challenges to teachers, learners and the whole educational ecology by the entry of ChatGPT into education and, second, to analyse what problems ChatGPT has in developing smart education based on previous studies.

4.1 Challenges for Teachers' Teaching

First, the value of the teacher may be in crisis; if ChatGPT is used in teaching, students will rely on asking questions about ChatGPT due to the novelty and better experience, so the teacher's role in the classroom will be weakened, so the value of the teacher may be reduced. Second, considering the duality of ChatGPT, the teacher's teaching dilemma is focused on physical weakness, skill limitations, and psychological blindness [20]. Again, it causes data leakage. The use of ChatGPT security and confidentiality has not yet been approved by national regulators, so the content of conversations with it may be leaked. Finally, blind reliance. The powerful language generation technology of ChatGPT can blind teachers to its use. However, ChatGPT is not a foolproof answer retrieval system; it can also suffer from information distortion, and OpenAI acknowledges that ChatGPT sometimes gives answers that seem reasonable but are incorrect or absurd.

4.2 Challenges to Student Learning

Risks such as shallowness of cognitive structure and homogenization of cognitive thinking. The phenomenon of bodily departure in the use of generic big models may engulf the learning community and make it difficult for learners to establish authentic and effective interactions with people and things around them. The conversational learning model of the Generic Big Model may bring risks such as the collapse of educational values, the rise of new digital authority systems, and the consciousness colonization of platform capital.

4.3 Challenges to Education Ecology

First, ChatGPT has uncertainty in ethical, technological and ideological aspects followed by the loss of the subject's ability to think under AI dependence, relational ethical issues in the teacher-student relationship, knowledge blindness and information cocoon, resource ethical issues, educational inequity and lack of clarity of power [21]. Second, there is a high randomness of answers to the same questions, lack of accuracy of answers, contamination of information, ethical and safety concerns, and possible knowledge plagiarism; finally, students' learning integrity is questioned, and the evaluation system is unbalanced [22].

In addition to the efficiency and convenience that ChatGPT brings to people, there are many ethical and technical challenges that need to be solved; in particular, ChatGPT, an AI technology model originating from the United States, hides many ideologies and uncertainties. Therefore, when we use ChatGPT to promote the development of smart education, we must have a clear mind and a discerning attitude toward this new emergence. In this paper, the potential and challenges of ChatGPT in teacher teaching, student learning, and educational ecology are summarized in the following table (see Table1).

Table 1. Challenges and Prospects of ChatGPT in Teacher Teaching, Student Learning and Educational Godliness

	The Challenges	Potential
Faculty Teaching	Crisis of values; Presenting dilemmas in education; Data breaches; Blind dependence; Alienation of the teacher-student relationship	Optimizing the quality of teaching and learning for teachers' intelligent education; Enriching digital teaching resources; Enhancing the intelligence and strategy of teaching strategies; Promoting the intelligence and interactivity of teaching feedback
Student Learning	Superficiality of cognitive structure and homogenization of cognitive thinking Overdependence; Alienation of the teacher-student relationship; Knowledge plagiarism	Intelligent learning assistants; Development of personalized learning programs; Intelligent generation of learning content; Intelligent Q&A and tutoring
Education Ecology	Lack of ethical awareness and difficulty in dealing with ethical risks; Inaccurate information transmission and restricted knowledge levels; Ethical and security issues and the risk of knowledge plagiarism challenges	ushering in a new definition of self-directed learning; New changes ushered in for teacher instruction; New challenges for school curricula; Talent development standards take a new turn

5 Prospect of ChatGPT-Enabled Smart Education

ChatGPT has good prospects for development, both in education and other industries. The following article analyses how ChatGPT has a promising future in empowering smart education. First, the framework of the ChatGPT-enabled smart education practice model is designed based on the working principle and characteristics of ChatGPT combined with the components of smart education (see Fig. 3). Second, the prospects of ChatGPT in students' learning are analysed. Finally, how teachers can use ChatGP for smart teaching in the future is discussed.

5.1 ChatGPT Empowering Smart Education Practice Model

According to available studies, smart education will be fully promoted from 2022 onwards [23]. The emergence of ChatGPT is undoubtedly a way to put the wings of technology on the smart education that is being fully popularized. The utilization of ChatGPT in school education should be in line with the connotation and characteristics of smart education to truly help its development. The introduction of ChatGPT in school education will be a change in education that integrates humans and machines. In smart education, ChatGPT technology can help achieve automated and interactive teaching and learning so that smart education can more easily grasp the individual needs of students and allow them to communicate more efficiently, improving the efficiency and quality of educators. The introduction of ChatGPT has brought a new perspective to education and brought opportunities to education in the history of education development. The popularity of smart education will be a major milestone.

ChatGPT Creates a Smart Learning Environment

With the support of convenient and intelligent technologies, the intelligent learning environment presents six characteristics: "interconnection", "perception", "interaction", "adaptation", "recording" and "integration". "Connected", "Perception", "Interaction", "Adaptation", "Recording", and "Integration". The "intelligent environment" is a technology-based, technology-based and ecological learning environment. The smart learning environment includes two categories: education cloud and "pedagogy-technology-culture". In Zhu's definition, the former is pedagogical intelligence, data intelligence, and cultural intelligence, from back to front: educational guidance, decision support, and action optimization. Using ChatGPT's dedicated AI system, a smart educational environment can be created. It is expected that in this learning environment, the cognitive load of learners can be effectively reduced and the connotation of knowledge generation, intelligence development and intelligent application can be improved through the design of various intelligent learning activities. It enhances students' self-directed and cooperative learning capabilities, expands the depth and breadth of learners' experiences, provides them with the most appropriate learning support, and increases the likelihood of their success.

ChatGPT Helps Teachers Adopt Smart Pedagogy

Smart pedagogy should embody at least one of the characteristics of "precision, individuality, optimization, collaboration, thinking, and creativity" and is divided into two aspects: smart pedagogical ecology and smart learning ecology. The two endpoints of the continuum are teacher-centered "instructional" teaching and student-centered "inquiry-based" learning. The "flipped classroom" is a new "knowledge-based" teaching model. By combining simulation learning, inquiry learning, debate learning, collaborative learning, and case study learning with advanced technology and equipment to enhance and empower them, intelligent teaching methods will favor creative learning.

However, in actual teaching, teachers cannot fully grasp the precise real intelligent teaching method, so they can use ChatGPT's powerful language generation system to provide advice and help teachers' teaching and promote teachers' precise teaching.

Wisdom Assessment

The evaluation mechanism of classroom teaching using ChatGPT is mainly reflected in three aspects. First, the teacher's assessment of students' learning performance focuses not only on students' performance in the learning process but also on the actual application of students in the learning process. Second, with the help of intelligent technology, implicit monitoring and measurement of the whole learning process can be realized. Through the mining of these big data and learning analyses, students' learning styles can be highlighted and presented to teachers and students in a visual way. Third, the prototype of "smart education" is beginning to emerge, and its goals, directions, composition and focus are clear: "smart education" is a new paradigm, a new field; its focus is on the importance of an intelligent environment to the cultivation of "smart people", with the goal of intelligent education and learning. From the technical point of view, in the big data environment, the design and implementation of smart education cannot be

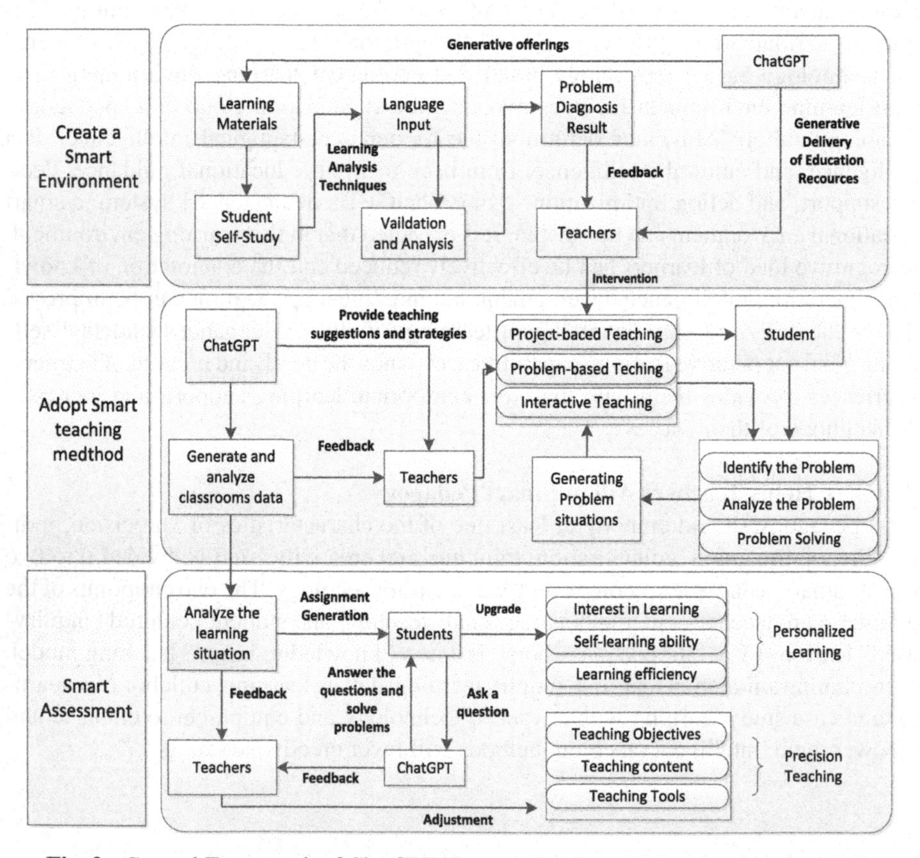

Fig. 3. General Framework of ChatGPT Empowering Smart Education Practice Mode

achieved without technologies such as statistical analysis, artificial intelligence and distributed computing. The ways, strategies and methods of implementing smart education still need to be explored.

5.2 Smarter Ways for Students to Learn

Smart Tutoring

Before the advent of ChatGPT, we needed students to spend a lot of time on tutoring, whereas now ChatGPT allows us to just conduct a simple Q&A. At the same time, we can use the information provided by ChatGPT to assist students so that they can master the relevant points in a short time. For example, ChatGPT can provide students with some suggestions about classroom learning to help them better understand the classroom content; ChatGPT can also help students understand some knowledge points so that they can better grasp the relevant content; ChatGPT can also help students improve their language skills and writing skills; and ChatGPT can also help students better understand scientific principles. In short, ChatGPT can easily be used as a "tutor" to help students solve problems and improve their academic performance. Smart tutoring will become an important way to tutor students. However, it is worth noting that ChatGPT is still in the development stage and cannot replace human teachers yet.

Smart Learning

It has been found that ChatGPT technology not only helps teachers transmit knowledge more efficiently but also improves their own standards and teaching quality and develops students' learning and information processing skills, thus improving their learning efficiency. In the traditional teaching process, students' learning style is mainly passive acceptance, and students acquire knowledge through teachers' explanations and classroom exercises. The emergence of ChatGPT provides students with a new way of learning, which can improve students' independent learning ability through continuous training. The emergence of ChatGPT makes intelligent learning an auxiliary way of learning, and students in ChatGPT are a vivid and interesting way for students to absorb knowledge, broaden their horizons and further enhance their self-efficacy.

5.3 Teachers' Teaching Ushered in New Changes

Optimize the Teaching Quality of Teachers' Wisdom Education

Smart education requires teachers to use smart teaching methods. ChatGPT can provide teachers with teaching guidance and suggestions and help teachers flexibly use new teaching methods such as interactive teaching methods, problem-based teaching methods and project-based teaching methods, thus reducing teachers' pressure to prepare lessons and the burden of innovation, devoting more time to the classroom and improving teaching quality and standards.

Make Classroom Teaching More Intelligent

Smart education requires a smart classroom, which requires the support of technology. ChatGPT enters the field of smart education and can act as another "teacher", forming a "dual teacher" collaborative classroom with human teachers, playing to their respective strengths and collaborating to complete The ChatGPT can act as another "teacher" and collaborate with human teachers to complete the teaching tasks. In addition, the emergence of ChatGPT lays the foundation for future classroom intelligence, which is "smart" because of its interactive, generative, dynamic, and contextual characteristics, better helping teachers to conduct intelligent classroom teaching, three-dimensional classroom interaction, intelligent inquiry learning, and efficient classroom management (see Fig. 4). As shown in Fig. 4, ChatGPT is involved in all aspects of classroom teaching and learning, which is conducive to further building a smart classroom and promoting intelligent and smart teaching points. Teachers should keep mentioning information literacy in such a teaching environment. In the future, ChatGPT in the classroom will become a powerful assistant for teachers.

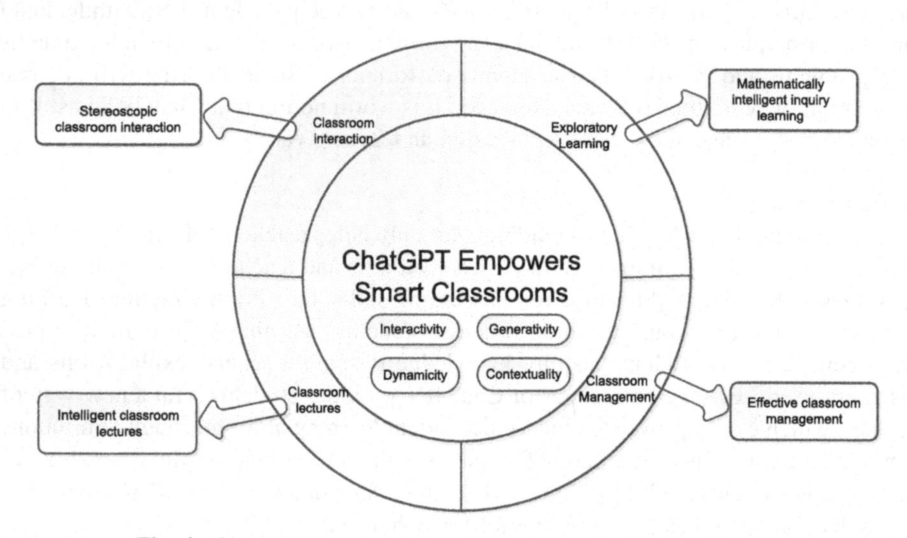

Fig. 4. ChatGPT Empowers Smart Classroom Application Context

Enhance the Intelligence and Teaching Strategies

First, ChatGPT will help teachers improve their teaching efficiency. In education and teaching, teachers have two main jobs: one is to teach students, and the other is to instruct students in learning. With the development of education technology, teachers can teach in many ways. Examples include using speech recognition and speech synthesis technologies to identify and correct students' pronunciation, providing students with rich learning resources through learning platforms, and providing teachers with learning suggestions through data collection and analysis of students' learning processes. However, these tasks often require teachers to invest much time and effort to accomplish. In these cases, ChatGPT can provide teachers with more scientific and efficient teaching services. First, it can help teachers identify and correct students' pronunciation through speech recognition technology. For example, ChatGPT can identify and correct students' pronunciation so that students can master pronunciation skills in a shorter time. Second, ChatGPT can provide students with rich learning resources through the learning platform. These resources not only enrich students' knowledge base but also promote the transformation of students' learning style. Finally, ChatGPT can provide teachers with teaching suggestions by collecting and analysing learning data.

Promote Intelligent and Interactive Teaching Feedback
Teachers can also use ChatGPT to identify students' problems and provide targeted tutoring. For example, if some students have problems with concentration, teachers can use ChatGPT to find these students and provide them with targeted tutoring. In the future, teachers will be able to solve more problems with ChatGPT, thus increasing their productivity. In the traditional education field, teachers play a very important role; they have to make learning plans for students, give instruction, help students with homework, etc. However, teachers are not able to fully understand the problems of their students and the reasons for their problems, which makes it impossible for them to plan for their students' learning. With the advent of ChatGPT, teachers can use ChatGPT to provide more personalized, precise, and comprehensive tutoring solutions for students. Through the interaction between teachers and ChatGPT and students and ChatGPT, the interactivity between teachers and students is promoted more efficiently, making teaching more intelligent and interesting.

6 Conclusion

As the impact of AI on education becomes more profound and comprehensive, in the postepidemic era of teaching and learning, students, teachers, and intelligent machines will come together to form an intelligent learning ecosystem. In this collaborative process, the relationship between teachers and students will be reorganized by AI, and students will change from being a traditional receiver to an inquirer and discoverer. The teacher will change from a "teacher" and "provider" to a "guide" and "enabler". Technology in the contemporary "technological revolution" has provided students with new ways of learning and more opportunities for both students and teachers while at the same time laying the groundwork for the development of both students and teachers. How to use the technological advantages of ChatGPT to play an optimal role in smart education while avoiding technological risks is still an important topic for our future research. In this paper, we study the characteristics of ChatGPT and analyse the potential and challenges of ChatGPT-enabled smart education based on existing research in the education sector. Based on this, we also construct a framework for a practical model of ChatGPT-enabled smart education development and then discuss the prospect of using the advantages of ChatGPT technology to develop smart education from both educators and educated people, with a view to providing some reference for the future development of ChatGPT in the education sector and the comprehensive popularization of smart education.

Acknowledgements. This research is supported by the Research on the Status Quo and Countermeasures to Enhance the National Common Language Proficiency of Qinghai Farmers and Herdsmen under the Support of Information Technology, Qinghai Provincial Language Commission.(No.:QHYW-KY2023-12); This study was also supported by the Academic Symposium of Postgraduate Disciplines of Qinghai Minzu University Excellent Academic Achievement Project "ChatGPT Empowers Smart Education: Potential, Challenges and Prospects".

References

1. Lock, S.: What is AI chatbot phenomenon ChatGPT and could it replace humans? In: What is AI Chatbot Phenomenon ChatGPT and Could it Replace Humans? (2022)
2. Wang, H., et al.: Challenges and opportunities brought by ChatGPT to education (PEN). J. Soochow Univ. (Educ. Sci. Edn.) 1–14
3. Wang, Y.: Taking advantage of ChatGPT to accomplish educational goals. China Soc. Sci. J. 03–31 (2023)
4. Liu, K.: Dual paradigm change in the integration of artificial intelligence and pedagogy. Open Educ. Res. 4–18 (2023)
5. Roopa, D., Prabha, R., Senthil, G.A.: Revolutionizing education system with interactive augmented reality for quality education. Mater. Today Proc. (2021)
6. Yang, Z., Wang, J., Wu, M.,Chen X.: Exploring the impact of ChatGPT/generative artificial intelligence on education and coping strategies. J. East China Normal Univ. (Edu. Sci. Edn.) **41**(07), 26–35 (2023)
7. Li, C.M.: Analysis of the nature of ChatGPT and its impact on education. China Educ. Inf. 12–18 (2023)
8. Li, Y.: Impact of ChatGPT on education ecology and coping strategies. J. Xinjiang Norm. Univ. (Philos. Soc. Sci. Edn.) 102–112 (2023)
9. Wang, Y.M., Wang, D., Liang, W.Y., Liu, C.C.: Ethical risks of ChatGPT educational applications and the way forward to avoid them. Open Educ. Res. 26–35 (2023)
10. Jiao, J.L., Chen, L., Wu, W.W.: The question of education raised by ChatGPT: possible impact and response. China Educ. Inf. 19–32 (2023)
11. Lu, Y., Yu, J.L., Chen, P., Li, M.: Educational applications and prospects of generative artificial intelligence-taking ChatGPT system as an example. China Dist. Educ. 24–31+51 (2023)
12. Chang, C.J., Chang, L.L., Mi, T.Y., Yau, S.P.: Will large-scale language modeling spawn structural change in schools? A prospective analysis based on ChatGPT. China Distance Edu. 32–41(2023)
13. Li, Z.: Facing ChatGPT directly, how can teachers survive?. Shanghai Educ. 18–21 (2023)
14. Jiao, J.: ChatGPT boosts the digital transformation of school education: what to learn and how to teach in the age of artificial intelligence. China Dist. Educ. 16–23 (2023)
15. Yang, X., Zheng, X.: Generative artificial intelligence reshapes education and teachers' response. Inf. Technol. Educ. Primary Second. Schools 8–10 (2023)
16. Wu, J., Wu, F., Wen, S., Zhang, M., Wang, J.: ChatGPT empowers teachers' professional development: opportunities, challenges and paths. China's e–learn. 15–23+33 (2023)
17. Li, Y., Zhang, Z., Wang, Y.: ChatGPT-based human-computer coteaching, coeducation and cocreation model. China Med. Educ. Technol. 1–8 (2023)
18. Yu, H., Zhang, W.: Should ChatGPT be banned by academics deep thoughts on teaching and learning. Shanghai Educ. Res. 6–11+29 (2023)
19. Zhou, L., Wang, F.: The educational inspiration of generative artificial intelligence: let each person become himself. China e-learn. 9–14 (2023)

20. Wang, S., Wang, Y.: Design and implementation of classroom learning community based on ChatGPT-like artificial intelligence-a perspective based on dialogue teaching theory. China Med. Educ. Technol. 1–8 (2023)
21. Yang, D., Chen, S., Wang, W., Zhu, X.: "ChatGPT" empowering teacher education: mechanisms, dilemmas, and breakthroughs. Continuing Educ. Res. 14–18 (2023)
22. Xu, G., Xiong, X., Zhang, Y., Wei, Q.: ChatGPT boosts digital transformation of educational examinations: opportunities, applications and challenges. China Exam 19–28 (2023)
23. Lv, J.C.: ChatGPT phenomenon and future-oriented talent cultivation. Chin. J. Opt. Sci. Technol. 42–43 (2023)
24. Gu, X., Du, H., Peng, H., Zhu, Z.: Theoretical framework, practical path, development and future picture of smart education. J. East China Norm. Univ. (Educ. Sci. Edn.) 20–32 (2021)

The Impact of Peer Feedback on Student Learning Effectiveness: A Meta-analysis Based on 39 Experimental or Quasiexperimental Studies

Chenfang Li[1], Zhijun Yang[2], and Ying Yang[1](✉)

[1] Information College of Yunnan Normal University, Kunming, China
1758401848@qq.com

[2] Key Laboratory of Yunnan Normal University, Kunming, China

Abstract. Peer feedback can help students construct learners' knowledge and is one of the most important ways to enhance the effectiveness of learning. This study used a meta-analytic approach to comprehensively sort, analyse, and evaluate 39 domestic and foreign experimental or quasiexperimental studies on the effects of peer feedback on student learning outcomes. Through coding statistical analysis, it was found that (1) the random effects model showed a combined effect value of 0.651 and reached a statistically significant level, indicating that peer feedback has a moderate to above positive impact on improving student learning and has a greater impact on cognitive dimensions than on noncognitive dimensions. (2) The effectiveness of peer feedback was moderated to varying degrees by school section, experimental period, class size, grouping principle, group size, feedback method, feedback type, and anonymity, with a significant moderating effect of the grouping principle on the effectiveness of peer feedback.

Keywords: Peer Feedback · Learning Effectiveness · Meta-analysis

1 Introduction

In pedagogical activities, peer feedback refers to the use of learners as a source of information and feedback and assumes roles and responsibilities usually performed by formally trained teachers, reviewers or editors [1]. In peer feedback activities, learners have two identities at the same time, i.e., the feedback giver and the feedback recipient. As feedback providers, learners can objectively analyse and evaluate their peers' work based on the evaluation criteria and judge and reflect on the quality of their work to compensate for their shortcomings. As feedback recipients, learners receive feedback from their peers to help themselves improve the quality of their work and perfect their cognition. To investigate the effectiveness of peer feedback, scholars in China and abroad have conducted a large number of experimental studies, but the findings vary widely. On the cognitive dimension, some studies have concluded that peer feedback is beneficial for enhancing students' academic performance and comprehensive abilities [2]. It has

J. Gan et al. (Eds.): CSEI 2023, CCIS 1899, pp. 42–52, 2024.
https://doi.org/10.1007/978-981-99-9499-1_4

been argued that peer feedback allows people to become more critical [3]. Taylor argued that peer feedback helps improve learners' problem-solving skills [4]. However, some scholars have argued that peer feedback fails to have a positive effect on teaching effectiveness or even has a negative impact [5, 6]. In the noncognitive dimension, Fanrong Weng concluded in his study that peer feedback can improve learners' motivation to write and increase learners' self-confidence [7]. However, some research suggests that the role of peer feedback in teaching should not be overstated and that not implementing peer feedback does not affect the "enjoyment" and "empathy" students experience from group activities [8]. Yu suggests that the effectiveness of peer feedback may be influenced by a combination of moderating variables [9].

From a meta-analytic perspective, Jianfeng Wu et al. confirmed that peer feedback has a significant moderate positive effect on the effectiveness of foreign language teaching and learning [10]. However, this study was limited to the field of foreign language teaching. Hongli Li et al. conducted a meta-analysis of the effectiveness of peer feedback, and the results demonstrated that peer feedback had a significant positive contribution to students' learning effectiveness [11]. However, this study covered articles from 1950 to 2017, the findings of the literature included in the meta-analysis may lack currency and representativeness, and the moderating variables considered in this study were not comprehensive, such as the grouping principle of peer feedback and group size.

To address this practical problem, this study uses meta-analysis to systematically review and analyse empirical studies on the effects of peer feedback on student learning outcomes at home and abroad, to investigate the effects of peer feedback on student learning outcomes and the differences in the effects of different moderating variables on student learning outcomes, and to further reveal the teaching situations in which peer feedback is applicable.

2 Methodology

2.1 Research Methods and Tools

Meta-analysis is a method of reanalysing the results of previous studies, which is an analytical method that uses statistical tools to synthesize data from several related independent experimental or quasiexperimental studies on a topic and systematically analyse and evaluate the overall effect of the study by obtaining its average effect value [12]. Comprehensive Meta-Analysis (CMA) 3.0 software was used as a meta-analysis tool in this study. Due to the small sample size of this study, Hedges' g (hereafter referred to as the g value) was used as the final effect value.

2.2 Research Process

Literature Search Process. In this study, domestic and international databases such as the China Knowledge Network (CNKI), Web of Science, Springer, and Elsevier were used as the scope of the literature search, supplemented by a search with Google Scholar. To ensure the timeliness and advancedness of the study, the search time was set to the last decade, that is, from 2013 to 2023. The study was conducted using "peer feedback", "peer review", "peer assessment", and the terms "experimental study", "learning performance", "effect", "learning achievements" as keywords to search the database.

Literature Screening and Inclusion Criteria. Since not all of the retrieved literature met the requirements, the literature needed to be screened, and the criteria for inclusion were as follows: (1) The research was experimental or quasiexperimental, and review articles and theoretical articles were excluded. (2) This paper studies the learning effect of peers, so the article should report the learning effect index (learning performance or work evaluation), and articles without the learning effect are excluded. (3) This paper should compare the effect of peer feedback and no peer feedback on learning effect, so the literature should have an experimental group and control group, and literature without (4) This paper explores the influence of peer feedback on students' learning effectiveness, so the research subjects of the paper need to be school students. (5) The literature provided sufficient data to calculate the experimental effect value, and the literature that could not calculate the effect value was excluded. (6) Duplicates were excluded, and if the same article was published in different journals or different forms, only one of them was taken. After the sample screening was completed, a total of 39 papers meeting the criteria were included, including 25 papers in Chinese and 14 papers in English. There were 80 effect values (13 studies with multiple effect values in the sample).

Literature Coding. To conveniently calculate the effect value at a later stage, the sample literature needs to be coded for eigenvalues. The independent variable in this study was peer feedback, and the dependent variable was learning effectiveness. The dependent variables were coded as cognitive (academic performance, independent learning ability, information processing ability, critical thinking ability, interpersonal skills, practical skills, etc.) and noncognitive (motivation, interest in learning, attitude toward learning, learning experience, learning anxiety, mental health, etc.

Meanwhile, this study extracted several eigenvalues from the literature for coding and used them as moderating variables, which can be classified into two categories, namely, peer feedback contexts and peer feedback forms. The feedback contexts include the following: (1) School sections: the sections are divided into elementary school, junior high school, high school, and university (specialist, undergraduate, and graduate). (2) Experimental period: The experimental period was divided into 0–1 month, 2–3 months, 4–6 months, and more than 6 months. (3) Class size: The experimental groups were divided into small class sizes (0–30 students), middle-class sizes (31–50 students), and large class sizes (more than 50 students) according to their numbers. Because several classes were studied as experimental groups at the same time, the average of the experimental group size was taken when coding class sizes. (4) Grouping principle: According to the principle of combining cooperative groups in the experimental group, they are divided into heterogeneous grouping and random grouping. Heterogeneous grouping means that with about the differences in students' gender, learning ability, performance, personality, etc., they are grouped into a group according to the principle of heterogeneity within the group and homogeneity between groups; random grouping means that students are randomly divided into various groups by sampling. (5) Group size: The experimental group was divided into 1–3, 4–6, and more than 6 people according to the number of cooperative groups. The feedback forms include (1) The type of feedback, which will be divided into ratings, comments, and a combination of ratings. (2) The feedback method is divided into written feedback, oral feedback, and a combination of written and oral feedback. (3) Anonymity: the experimental groups were classified as anonymous or not anonymous according to whether the identity of the other party was known at the time of the two sides of the review. In addition, this study coded the authors, year of publication, and sample size of the literature. The Cohen Kappa consistency coefficient for the study sample was 0.83, indicating that the eigenvalue coding was valid.

3 Results

3.1 Publication Bias and Heterogeneity Tests

Publication Bias. Publication bias refers to the fact that the retrieved literature is not representative of the research in the field as a whole, which makes it likely that the study will draw incorrect conclusions and affect its accuracy and reliability, so it is necessary to conduct publication bias tests and analysis [13]. This study used the funnel plot method and Egger's test for a comprehensive assessment of publication bias in the study sample. Figure 1 shows the funnel plot obtained using CMA 3.0. From the figure, it can be seen that the points on the funnel plot are evenly and symmetrically scattered around the combined effect values and are concentrated in the upper middle, which is initially judged not to have publication bias. However, the disadvantage of the funnel plot is that it is more subjective and prone to error based on the visual observation of the researcher alone. The Egger test allows for quantitative determination of publication bias; when $P < 0.05$, it indicates that there is publication bias in the study and vice versa. The results of the Egger test in this study showed that $P = 0.0512 > 0.05$, so there was no publication bias in this study, which indicates that the combined effect values obtained in this study are relatively robust.

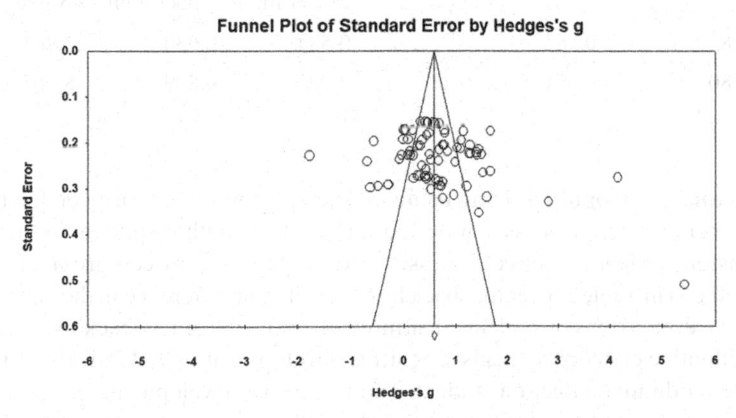

Fig. 1. Study samples were published for bias funnel testing

Heterogeneity Test. When the heterogeneity of the study was large, a random-effects model was used for analysis; when the heterogeneity of the study was small, a fixed-effects model was used for analysis [14]. The common methods used for qualitative tests are the Q test and the I2 test, and Higgins et al. pointed out that the criteria for classifying high and low I2 values are I2 statistics of 25%, 50%, and 75%, representing low, medium, and high degrees of heterogeneity, respectively [15]. The results of the heterogeneity test in this study showed that $Q = 849.143$, $P = 0.000 < 0.001$, and $I2 = 90.696\%$, indicating that approximately 90% of the heterogeneity was derived from the true differences in effect values. Therefore, the random effects model was chosen to assess the effect of peer feedback on student learning outcomes in this study.

3.2 The Overall Impact of Peer Feedback on Student Learning Outcomes

Overall Effect Value of Peer Feedback. The effect value is an indicator to assess the strength of the effect and the degree of association of the test. According to the effect size criteria proposed by Cohen, when the effect value $ES < 0.2$, it is a small effect, when $0.2 < ES < 0.8$, it is a medium effect, and when $ES > 0.8$, it is a large effect [16]. According to the combined effective values of the study (Table 1), the effect values of both the fixed and random effect models reached a statistically significant level ($P < 0.001$), and peer feedback had a positive effect on student learning outcomes. From the random effects model selected for this study ($g = 0.651$), peer feedback had a moderately positive effect on student learning outcomes. As a whole, it can be concluded that peer feedback has a positive contribution to student learning and helps to enhance learning outcomes.

Table 1. The overall impact of peer feedback on learning effectiveness.

Model	Sample size	Effect size (Hedges's g)	95%confidence interval		Test of null (2-Tail)	
			Lower limit	Upper limit	Z value	P value
Fixed	80	0.582	0.534	0.630	23.901	0.000
Random	80	0.651	0.493	0.809	8.065	0.000

Cognitive and Noncognitive Dimensions. The specific effects of peer feedback on students' learning effectiveness can be seen in terms of both cognitive and noncognitive dimensions of learning effectiveness. According to the between-group effect ($Q = 8.117$, $P < 0.05$) in Table 2, peer feedback has a significant difference in the cognitive and noncognitive dimensions of students' learning outcomes. Peer feedback had a moderate to high facilitative effect on students' cognitive development ($g = 0.781$, $P < 0.001$) and a moderate facilitative effect on students' noncognitive development ($g = 0.274$, $P > 0.05$) however, the statistics for the noncognitive dimensions were not statistically significant, indicating that the facilitative effect of peer feedback on students' noncognitive development was not significant.

Table 2. The effect of cooperative learning on the learning effectiveness of cognitive and noncognitive dimensions.

Learning effects	Sample size	Effect size (Hedges's g)	95% confidence interval		Test of null (2-Tail)		Between-group effects
			Lower limit	Upper limit	Z value	P value	
Cognitive	60	0.781	0.599	0.962	8.438	0.000	Q = 8.117 P = 0.004
Noncognitive	20	0.274	−0.024	0.572	1.800	0.072	

3.3 The Effects of Different Moderating Variables of Peer Feedback on Student Learning Effectiveness

To investigate the differences in the effects of peer feedback on student learning outcomes in different instructional contexts, this study was conducted on the moderating variables in peer feedback contexts and forms of peer feedback, which are shown in Table 3.

The effect of moderating variables in peer feedback contexts on student learning outcomes.

School Section. As shown in Table 3, the between-group effect of the school section ($Q = 0.592, P > 0.05$) was not statistically significant, indicating that peer feedback had an equal effect on the learning outcomes of students in each school band. In terms of specific effects, the order of effect size was elementary school ($g = 0.648, P < 0.001$), college ($g = 0.543, P < 0.001$), middle school ($g = 0.508, P < 0.001$), and high school ($g = 0.469, P > 0.05$), indicating that peer feedback had a moderate to high facilitation effect in elementary school, college, and middle school and a moderate to high facilitation effect in high school. Moderate facilitation effect in high school. However, the statistics at the high school level were not statistically significant, indicating that peer feedback had a less significant effect on students' learning at the high school level.

Teaching Periods. The data in the table show that the between-group effect of the instructional period did not reach a statistically significant level ($Q = 1.196, P < 0.05$), indicating that peer feedback had a positive effect on student learning outcomes and was correlated with the instructional period. Specifically, peer feedback had a higher degree of significant effect on student learning outcomes at 2–3 months ($g = 0.883 > 0.8$, $P < 0.001$) and 0–1 month ($g = 0.857 > 0.8, P < 0.001$), with the most significant effect at 2–3 months. Peer feedback at the 4–6 month ($g = 0.562, P < 0.001$) instructional cycle produced a moderately higher positive effect, and peer feedback at the more than 6 month ($g = 0.373, P < 0.05$) instructional cycle produced a moderately lower positive effect.

Class Sizes. In terms of between-group effects ($Q = 0.645, P > 0.05$), the three class sizes contributed equally to student learning outcomes. Specifically, peer feedback had a moderately positive effect on medium ($g = 0.569, P < 0.001$), large ($g = 0.513, P < 0.001$), and small classes ($g = 0.437, P < 0.01$). In contrast, peer feedback had a greater impact on learning outcomes in middle-class instruction.

Table 3. The effects of different moderating variables on student learning effectiveness.

	Encoded object	Type	Sample size	Effect size (Hedges's g)	95% confidence interval		Test of null (2-Tail)		Between-group effects
					Lower limit	Upper limit	Z value	P value	
Peer feedback contexts	Section	Elementary	22	0.648	0.341	0.955	4.131	0.000	Q = 0.592 P = 0.898
		Junior high school	3	0.508	0.308	0.709	4.975	0.000	
		High school	2	0.469	−0.372	1.311	1.097	0.274	
		University	53	0.543	0.358	0.728	5.756	0.000	
	period	0-1month	7	0.857	0.593	1.157	6.075	0.000	Q = 1.196 P = 0.524
		2–3months	28	0.883	0.582	1.184	5.753	0.000	
		4–6months	38	0.562	0.344	0.780	5.042	0.000	
		More than 6month	7	0.373	0.003	0.743	1.977	0.048	
	Class size	Small	32	0.437	0.150	0.724	2.988	0.003	Q = 0.645 P = 0.724
		Middle	40	0.569	0.399	0.739	6.560	0.000	
		Large	8	0.513	0.370	0.648	7.491	0.000	
	Grouping principle	Heterogeneous	15	0.811	0.490	1.131	4.959	0.000	Q = 6.963 P = 0.026
		Randomization	39	0.599	0.347	0.852	4.647	0.000	
	Group sizes	1–3 people	18	0.573	0.156	0.991	2.690	0.007	Q = 1.779 P = 0.620
		4–6 people	25	0.756	0.498	1.014	5.744	0.000	
		More than 6 people	6	0.491	0.185	0.798	3.141	0.002	
Peer feedback form	Feedback method	Written	51	0.616	0.397	0.835	5.522	0.000	Q = 1.595 P = 0.450
		Oral	2	0.300	-0.514	1.113	0.722	0.470	
		Both	27	0.745	0.551	0.939	7.522	0.000	
	Feedback type	Comments	31	0.703	0.409	0.998	4.680	0.000	Q = 3.751 P = 0.153
		Rating	6	0.613	−0.008	1.233	1.966	0.053	
		Both	43	0.710	0.535	0.885	7.948	0.000	
	Anonymity	Anonymous	25	0.593	0.312	0.873	4.140	0.000	Q = 0.247 P = 0.884
		Not anonymous	37	0.681	0.417	0.944	5.066	0.000	

Grouping Principles. Grouping is an essential step before peer feedback activity can take place. The two main forms of grouping currently available are heterogeneous grouping and random grouping. A total of 54 valid effect sizes were obtained in this analysis after excluding articles that did not explicitly report the grouping principle. As shown in Table 3, peer feedback had a high positive effect of heterogeneous grouping ($g = 0.811$, $P < 0.001$) on students' school effectiveness and a moderate positive effect of random grouping ($g = 0.599$, $P < 0.001$) on learning effectiveness. The between-group effect ($Q = 6.963$, $P < 0.05$) reached a statistically significant level, indicating that the implementation of different grouping principles in peer feedback had a significant effect on students' learning outcomes.

Group Sizes. As the basic component unit of a feedback group, group size can have a significant effect on the effectiveness of peer feedback. A valid effect size of 49 was obtained after excluding articles that did not report group size. From the data in the table, we know that the between-group effect ($Q = 1.779$, $P > 0.05$) did not reach a statistically significant level, indicating that peer feedback played a significant positive role in promoting student learning effectiveness at different group sizes. Specifically, peer feedback had a moderately positive effect for 1–3 ($g = 0.573$, $P < 0.001$), 4–6 ($g = 0.756$, $P < 0.001$), and 6 + ($g = 0.491$, $P < 0.01$) students. Taken together, peer feedback had the highest effect values between 4 and 6 students and had the best effect on student learning.

The effect of moderating variables in the form of peer feedback on student learning effectiveness.

Peer Feedback Method. As shown in Table 3, the between-group effects of the three feedback methods ($Q = 1.595$, $P > 0.05$) did not reach a statistically significant level, indicating that the different feedback methods all had a positive contribution to students' learning outcomes. Specifically, the combination of verbal and written feedback ($g = 0.745$, $P < 0.001$) and written feedback only ($g = 0.616$, $P < 0.001$) had a moderate to high facilitation effect on learning outcomes, and verbal feedback only ($g = 0.300$, $P > 0.05$) had a moderate facilitation effect on learning outcomes; however, the effect was not statistically significant, indicating that the effect of verbal-only peer feedback on students' learning was not significant.

Peer Feedback Type. As seen from the data in the table, the three types of feedback had an equal degree of positive impact on students' learning outcomes ($Q = 3.751$, $P < 0.05$). Specifically, the feedback types of rating only ($g = 0.703$, $P < 0.001$), rating only ($g = 0.613$, $P > 0.05$), and rating and rating combined ($g = 0.710$, $P < 0.001$) all had a moderate to positive effect on learning outcomes. However, the statistics for the rating-only feedback type were not statistically significant, indicating that the effect of the rating-only feedback type on learning effectiveness was not significant. The effect values for the three types show that the feedback type with a combination of ratings and rubrics had the best effect on learning.

Anonymity. After excluding the articles that did not report anonymity, a total of 62 valid effect sizes were obtained. As seen from the data in the table, the between-group effect of anonymity and nonanonymity ($Q = 0.247$, $P > 0.05$) did not reach a statistically significant level, indicating that peer feedback in both cases had an equal effect on students' learning outcomes. In particular, peer feedback in the anonymous case ($g = 0.593$, $P < 0.001$) and in the nonanonymous case ($g = 0.681$, $P < 0.001$) had more than moderate facilitative effects on learning outcomes. In comparison, the effect value of not anonymous is higher, which indicates that peer feedback in the case of not anonymous is more effective for student learning.

4 Conclusion

The results of the meta-analysis showed that peer feedback enhanced students' learning effects overall, with positive facilitative effects on both cognitive and noncognitive dimensions and higher effects on cognitive dimensions than on noncognitive dimensions. The moderating variables all had different degrees of positive effects on student learning outcomes, with significant differences in the effects of peer feedback on student learning across different grouping principles.

4.1 Peer Feedback Has a Positive Impact on Student Learning Outcomes

The results of the meta-analysis indicate that peer feedback can contribute to the improvement and enhancement of students' learning outcomes. The mechanism of peer feedback can be understood as follows: peer feedback is a learning activity based on social constructivist theory, based on adequate communication and interaction among peers, so that students can purposefully process the feedback they receive, thus allowing this feedback to guide the improvement of the quality of their work and achieve the effect of improving their learning outcomes [1, 17, 18]. In terms of specific effects, peer feedback had a significant facilitative effect on students' cognitive dimensions and a positive effect on noncognitive dimensions, but the effect was not significant. This suggests that peer feedback has a more positive contribution to students' academic performance, independent learning ability, information processing ability, critical thinking ability, interpersonal skills, and practical skills.

4.2 Different Moderating Variables of Peer Feedback Have Positive Effects on Student Learning Outcomes

Peer Feedback Contexts. The results of the study showed that the effectiveness of peer feedback at the secondary level was slightly lower and less applied than at the primary and university levels, possibly because secondary school students were under pressure to advance to higher education and were under time constraints to effectively conduct peer feedback activities.

From the length of the experiment, the best learning effect was observed for the teaching period of 2–3 months. It can be seen that the effect of using peer feedback is influenced by the teaching period, but it does not mean that the longer the period, the better the effect. This may be because along with the increased familiarity of students with peer feedback, the enthusiasm and novelty of learning decreases, and the engagement in learning decreases.

Is random grouping or heterogeneous grouping better? Statistics show that different grouping principles have significant differences in the effectiveness of peer feedback, which indicates that heterogeneous grouping can coordinate the balance within and between groups so that the strengths complement each other, give full play to the individual abilities of group members, and maximize the group effect. Compared with random grouping, heterogeneous grouping is more relevant and adaptive and promotes the overall learning effect [19].

In terms of numbers, class size and moderate group size work best for peer feedback, suggesting that teachers should not only focus on the heterogeneity of group members but also consider the number of group members when forming learning communities. With a moderate number of learning community members, a good group effect can be formed, producing a higher level of engagement in learning [20]. At the same time, it is easy for teachers to pay attention to each student's learning situation in classroom teaching and communication discussions, which is conducive to teachers' supervision and guidance, thus enhancing students' learning effectiveness.

Peer Feedback Form. The results showed that there was no significant difference in student learning outcomes between different forms of feedback. Specifically, combining the two forms of feedback is better for students than using a single form of feedback alone.

The use of a nonanonymous mechanism means that both reviewers know their identities and students give peer feedback conscientiously and responsibly, but students are susceptible to interpersonal interference when reviewing each other [21]. Anonymous feedback can effectively mitigate the negative effects of interpersonal relationships and enable learners to pay more attention to their peers' work itself, but anonymous feedback may lead to a slacker mentality among students, which may result in low engagement in mutual evaluation. The present study showed that the use of anonymous or nonanonymous mechanisms in peer feedback positively contributed to students' learning outcomes, but the difference between the two was not significant, and further validation of the application of anonymous mechanisms to peer feedback is needed.

Acknowledgements. This research was financially supported by Yunnan Province Professional Degree Postgraduate Teaching Case Base Construction Project "Information Technology and Discipline Curriculum Integration Case Base", China, 2022.

References

1. Nicol, D.: From monologue to dialogue: improving written feedback processes in mass higher education. Assess. Eval. High. Educ. **35**(5), 501–517 (2010)
2. Chien, S.Y., Hwang, G.J., Jong, M.S.Y.: Effects of peer assessment within the context of spherical video-based virtual reality on EFL students' English-speaking performance and learning perceptions. Comput. Educ. **146**, 103751 (2020)
3. Siow, L.F.: Students' perceptions on self-and peer-assessment in enhancing learning experience. Malay. Online J. Educ. Sci. **3**(2), 21–35 (2015)
4. Crouch, T., Moore, J.C.: Effect of peer-review on development of students' problem-solving abilities. In: Proceedings of the Physics Education Research Conference, pp. 71–74 (2019)
5. Wihastyanang, W.D., Kusumaningrum, S.R., Latief, M.A., et al.: Impacts of providing online teacher and peer feedback on students' writing performance. Turk. Online J. Dist. Educ. **21**(2), 178–189 (2020)
6. Au, H.Y.C., Bardakçi, M.: An analysis of the effect of peer and teacher feedback on EFL learners' oral performances and speaking self-efficacy levels. Int. Online J. Educ. Teach. **7**(4), 1453–1468 (2020)

7. Weng, F., Ye, S.X., Xue, W.: The effects of peer feedback on L2 students' writing motivation: an experimental study in China. Asia-Pac. Educ. Res. 1–11 (2022)
8. Cheng, Y.: Analysis of the effect of peer mutual evaluation in the perspective of experiential foreign language teaching. China Foreign Lang. **20**(01), 81–88 (2023)
9. Yu, S., Lee, I.: Peer feedback in second language writing (2005–2014). Lang. Teach. **49**(4), 461–493 (2016)
10. Wu, J.F., Zhang, L.Y., Lu, C.F., et al.: A meta-analysis of the impact of peer assessment on the effectiveness of foreign language teaching. Mod. Foreign Lang. **45**(04), 539–551 (2022)
11. Li, H., Xiong, Y., Hunter, C.V., et al.: Does peer assessment promote student learning? A meta-analysis. Assess. Eval. High. Educ. **45**(2), 193–211 (2020)
12. Glass, G.V.: Primary, secondary, and meta-analysis of research. Educ. Res. **5**(10), 3–8 (1976)
13. Rothstein, H.R., Sutton, A.J., Borenstein, M.: Publication bias in meta-analysis. Publication bias in meta-analysis: prevention, assessment and adjustments, pp. 1–7 (2015)
14. Borenstein, M., Hedges, L.V., Higgins, J.P.T., et al.: Introduction to Meta-analysis, pp. 311–319. Wiley, Hoboken (2009)
15. Higgins, J.P.T., Thompson, S.G., Deeks, J.J., et al.: Measuring inconsistency in meta-analyses. BMJ **327**(7414), 557–560 (2003)
16. Cohen, J.: Statistical Power Analysis for the Behavioral Sciences. Academic Press, New York (2013)
17. Ajjawi, R., Boud, D.: Researching feedback dialogue: an interactional analysis approach. Assess. Eval. High. Educ. **42**(2), 252–265 (2017)
18. Carless, D.: Trust and its Role in Facilitating Dialogic Feedback, 1st edn. Feedback in Higher and Professional Education, Routledge Press (2012)
19. Gillies, R.M.: Cooperative learning: Review of research and practice. Aust. J. Teach. Educ. (Online) **41**(3), 39–54 (2016)
20. Wang, W., Dong, Y.Q., Yang, M.: The effect of cooperative learning on students' learning effects–a meta-analysis based on 48 experimental or quasiexperimental studies. Shanghai Educ. Res. (07), 34–40+59 (2020)
21. Strijbos, J.-W., Wichmann, A.: Promoting learning by leveraging the collaborative nature of formative peer assessment with instructional scaffolds. Eur. J. Psychol. Educ. **33**(1), 1–9 (2018)

A Multilabel Classification Method for Chinese Book Subjects Based on the Knowledge Fusion Model ERNIE-RCNN

Yunqing Lu[1], Tingting Chen[1], and Tianwei Xu[2](✉)

[1] School of Information Science and Technology, Yunnan Normal University, Kunming, China
[2] Key Laboratory of Educational Information for Nationalities, Yunnan Normal University, Kunming, China
xutianwei@ynnu.edu.cn

Abstract. At present, my country's education modernization and university discipline construction plans have been carried out in major universities across the country. Classifying books according to the subject catalog can play an important role in promoting the discipline construction of universities, and it is also an important link in the construction of smart libraries. The traditional book classification work mainly relies on manual classification of books according to the Chinese Library Classification and some machine learning book classification algorithms, but it relies on domain experts to formulate rules, making migration difficult. This paper proposes a method of using the knowledge fusion model ERNIE-RCNN for multilabel classification of Chinese book subjects and constructs a Chinese book data set containing 82 subject labels to solve the problem that the current book subject label data sets are fewer and the classification effect is not good. Question. In the experimental results, the micro-F1 of the ERNIE-RCNN model is 0.8091, which has achieved a good classification effect. This study is helpful to realize the classification and organization of books according to the subject catalog and has a positive effect on the high-quality subject service provided by university libraries.

Keywords: University Library · Deep Learning · Natural Language Processing · Subject Classification

1 Introduction

The strategic task of accelerating the transformation of education in the information age is pointed out in "China Education Modernization 2035", which requires vigorously promoting the modernization of education concepts, systems, contents, methods and governance [1] and puts forward higher quality requirements for the construction of learning resources and precise knowledge services. The Implementation Measures for Coordinating the Construction of World-Class Universities and First-Class Disciplines (Provisional) jointly issued by the three ministries points out the important position of discipline construction in the high-quality development of universities [2]. Libraries are the treasure house of learning resources in universities and the main place for knowledge

J. Gan et al. (Eds.): CSEI 2023, CCIS 1899, pp. 53–64, 2024.
https://doi.org/10.1007/978-981-99-9499-1_5

services in universities, and they should actively respond to the call for modernization of education and contribute to the high-quality development of universities. Books are an important way for knowledge dissemination and the main way for university libraries to provide knowledge services, and the information management and use of books has become an important part of knowledge services. The classification method of book resources commonly used in China is "Chinese Library Classification" (fifth edition) (hereinafter referred to as "Chinese Library Classification"). The effectiveness of the Chinese Library Classification has been tested for many years, but the Chinese Library Classification classification categories do not match the existing subject catalogs, and there will be many problems in using the Chinese Library Classification in subject services. There is an urgent need for libraries to provide high-quality subject services to organize books according to subject catalogs. In the discipline construction of universities, it plays a significant part in promoting and is also an important link in the construction of smart libraries. However, there are currently many subject classification systems, each evaluation system is not the same [3], and each book should not be limited to one subject category. The large number of books and subject types does not rely on manual classification of book subjects. With th4e development of text classification research based on deep learning, many book classification models based on deep learning algorithms continue to emerge. However, the current book classification model mainly uses the Chinese library classification method to classify books with single-label numbers and multisubject labels for books. The method of classification is lacking, and multilabel classification has more labels than single-label classification, which requires the model to obtain more information from the text to support the prediction of multiple labels. Therefore, constructing a relatively accurate multilabel classification model for Chinese book subjects is particularly important.

In recent years, deep learning has made a breakthrough in the field of text feature representation, and various models have emerged in an endless stream. Based on the in-depth study of traditional models, a multilabel classification model is proposed for Chinese books based on ERNIE-RCNN in this paper, which is used for more effective multilabel classification of Chinese books. Compared with the traditional BERT [4], ERNIE [5] has increased the pretraining of information entities and can obtain more potential information in the text by adding external knowledge. To a certain extent, the model's ability to predict multilabels has been improved, the problem of overreliance on a single data source for classification has been effectively alleviated, the scalability and robustness of the model have been improved, and an idea for solving the practical application of library subject classification has been provided.

2 Related Work

2.1 Book Classification

Single-Label Classification. Book classification is the process of feature extraction and fusion after expressing the text information of book labels using vectors. Its essence is to extract and classify the information contained in the label data. Therefore, the current model applied to book classification is constantly developing with the model in the field of text classification. Traditional text classification is mainly based on feature engineering and feature selection. In the field of feature engineering, the most commonly used feature is the word bag feature, but there are also some more complex features, such as parts of speech markers and noun phrases [6]. The purpose of feature selection is to reduce the noise in the data and improve the classification accuracy of the model. Deletion of stops is the most common method, along with more complex methods such as mutual information, information gain [7], or L1 regularization [8], to select useful features. The machine learning models used are mainly naive Bayesian, support vector machine, logistic regression, etc. However, these traditional machine learning methods require considerable time-consuming and laborious feature engineering. Moreover, these methods or models usually do not consider the natural structure of the text corpus, such as the subject–verb-object structure, which makes it difficult for the model to have the ability to learn semantic information between words, so there are some data sparsity problems.

Multilabel Classification. The main difference between multilabel classification problems and traditional multicategory problems is that in multicategory problems, the labels of each category are independent of each other, i.e., an instance belongs to only one category, whereas in multilabel problems, the labels of each category are not in opposition to each other, and there may be interrelationships.

Common multiclass classification algorithms include Adabost, BP neural networks and SVM algorithms. The advantage of algorithm-based multilabel classification algorithms is that they do not change the structure of the data set, but the main problem is that in order to apply a specific multiclass problem algorithm to a multilabel problem, a complex optimization problem, i.e., a large-scale quadratic programming problem, is usually derived, which usually has a high computational complexity. For this reason, a growing number of scholars have been applying decomposition strategies to algorithmic extensions of multilabel classification algorithms, each with its own advantages.

2.2 Deep Neural Network

Compared with traditional machine learning, the deep learning model saves many manual steps. Through continuous training, iteration and optimization of the deep learning network, text learning can be carried out automatically, and rich semantic features can be learned from it. Long Short Term Memory (LSTM) [9] was improved based on RNN, allowing the model to learn to forget information at the right time to mitigate the problem of RNN gradient disappearance or gradient explosion. Later, Huan et al. [10] proposed a nonequilibrium Bi-LSTM classification model based on feature enhancement, which uses a hierarchical attention mechanism to distinguish important features from unimportant features. Compared with the traditional RNN, this model can better extract feature information of long texts and is therefore widely used in various classification models for feature extraction.

CNNs focus more on pixel-to-pixel spatial information than RNNs that focus on sequence information, which is expressed as word-to-word structural information in text classification. Kalchbrenner et al. [11] proposed a CNN-based text classification model DCNN (Dynamic CNN), which obtains the relational features of sentences through a dynamic k-Max global pooling operation to represent text information. Kim et al. [12]

proposed TextCNN, a convolutional neural network model applied to text classification, to simplify the convolutional layer of CNN and accelerate the training process in text classification tasks. As research progressed, researchers found that text features could not be well extracted and fused using only one network structure. TextRCNN [13] combined the sequence feature extraction of RNN with the structure of CNN to better obtain text features.

In 2017, Vaswani et al. proposed the Transformer model [14], which is entirely based on the attention mechanism, opening up a new line of research, and various pretraining models based on this have been proposed one after another. The Transformer-based BERT model, with its own huge volume, with its large volume and massive corpus training, has made a major breakthrough in the field of text representation. With the emergence of various pretraining models, some researchers have gradually developed more powerful uses of BERT, trying to introduce information from knowledge graphs into the BERT model for knowledge enhancement so that BERT can learn the coding of background knowledge or common sense contained in the text. ERNIE, a language representation model enhanced by the knowledge masking strategy proposed by Baidu in April 2019, proposes a multistage knowledge masking strategy, adding the knowledge of phrases and entities to the language representation to learn the complete semantic representation of a larger semantic unit.

Therefore, based on the previous research results, this paper combines the advantages of TextRCNN and ERNIE model, and applies it to the multilabel classification task of books to achieve better classification results.

3 Data Sets and Models

3.1 Construction of a Multilabel Data Set for Chinese Book Subjects at the First Level

Data Preprocessing. Since there is no publicly available Chinese book data set, this paper uses some book data from the library collection of Yunnan Normal University and book data collected from the China Higher Education Literature Assurance System (CALIS) Joint Catalogue Centre database and others through web crawlers as experimental data. After the book information is crawled from the library as well as the web, due to the nonuniform information format of the book fields, manual checking and screening is required to eliminate useless and redundant words in the integrated data and correct the wrong information, finally completing the data preprocessing process.

Disciplinary Multilabel Annotation. As the library collection does not have subject label attributes, it is necessary to obtain book subject label data from the Joint Catalogue Centre database of the China Higher Education Literature Assurance System (CALIS). A total of 4099 multidisciplinary label book data were finally selected from the library collection of Yunnan Normal University, and 6012 single subject label book data and 3122 multidisciplinary label book data were crawled through the web, totalling a total of 13,233 books. The book data contained the following tags: (i) title; (ii) author; (iii) publisher information; (iv) publication date; (v) content introduction; (vi) subject term; and (vii) ISBN. Eighty-two primary subject tags were used in the experimental data, with a maximum of three primary subject tags for a single book.

3.2 ERNIE-RCNN Model

In this paper, we propose a book classification model ERNIE-RCNN with a mixture of a knowledge fusion pretraining model and a deep learning network. Using the ERNIE series pretraining model as a book feature extractor, it can obtain more information related to books to provide to the book classifier for multilabel classification, and using the TextRCNN network as a book classifier, it integrates the advantages of RNN and CNN and combines temporal and local information together, which can better perform multilabel prediction. The structure diagram of the ERNIE-RCNN model is shown in Fig. 1.

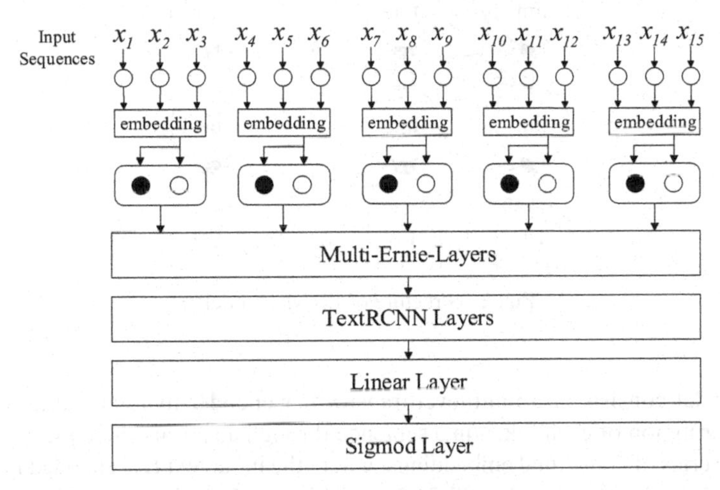

Fig. 1. ERNIE-RCNN Model

The x-sequence in the figure is a text sequence consisting of the book title, author, content summary and subject line encoded by ERNIE's encoder, as ERNIE adds a pretraining task of mask prediction at the entity level to the training process so that information can be extracted from the entities in the sequence in the encoder. The identification of entity information can make good use of the information in several fields of the book for feature extraction; for example, the author field was not obvious in the model previously encoded in characters, but after encoding it as an entity, the author information can be obtained. Although author information alone cannot be used to determine the subject label, the author's field and author's writing style can help determine the attribution of the subject label to achieve a better book classification effect. Afterwards, the book feature vectors extracted by the ERNIE model will be used as input to the TextRCNN book classifier, and after multiple layers of feature association and extraction, the feature vectors associated with the multilabel categories will be finally output. Finally, the feature vectors will be expressed as multilabel prediction probabilities through simple linear mapping and sigmoid activation to obtain the subject multilabel prediction of books.

Ernie Model. The ERNIE series model is a BERT-based knowledge fusion model proposed by the Baidu AI team, which is improved on the basis of the BERT model for pretraining tasks. Similar to BERT in terms of model architecture, the model is trained and modelled by introducing a large amount of Chinese corpus during pretraining, using words as semantic knowledge units, and adding two new task entity masks and phrase masks for knowledge integration. The architecture of the ERNIE model is shown in Fig. 2.

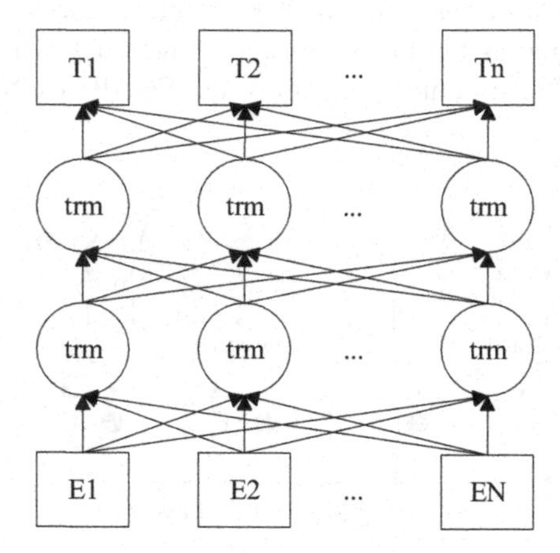

Fig. 2. Structure of ERNIE model

The model consists of a multilevel transformer encoder that can capture the contextual information of each token in a sentence through a self-attentive mechanism and generate a series of contextual embeddings, where the input text E is encoded in multiple layers to obtain the text encoding T. ERNIE uses prior knowledge to enhance the pretrained language model using a multilevel knowledge masking strategy that integrates the external knowledge of phrases and entities into the language representation rather than directly adding knowledge embedding. Thus enabling the model to learn rich entity and phrase representations from external knowledge. The different masking levels of the sentence are shown in Fig. 3.

Sentence	马	克	思	主	义	政	治	经	济	学	基	础	理	论	研	究
Basic-level Masking	马	[MASK]	思	主	义	政	[MASK]	经	济	[MASK]	基	础	理	论	研	[MASK]
Entity-level Masking	[MASK]	[MASK]	[MASK]	主	义	政	治	[MASK]	[MASK]	[MASK]	基	础	理	论	研	究
Phrase-level Masking	马	克	思	[MASK]	[MASK]	政	治	经	济	学	[MASK]	[MASK]	理	论	[MASK]	[MASK]

Fig. 3. Different masking levels for sentences

As shown in Fig. 3, this is the masked form of a book's title when mask training is performed. According to the external knowledge base, the "Marx" and "economics" entities in the title are extracted, and the corresponding entities in the title are masked and then input to the ERNIE model for prediction training, so that the ERNIE model can learn about the entity "Marx" and "economics" feature information. These two entities are richer in information content than a single character, and are more conducive to the subject multi-label prediction of books. The book information is extracted and learned through a 12-layer transformer layer, resulting in a feature vector of length 768 as the output of the ERNIE model.

ERNIE 2.0 [15] introduces a continuous training task to help models effectively learn lexical, syntactic, and semantic representations. ERNIE 3.0 [16] adds two networks, autoregressive and self-coding, to the BERT framework so that the model can carry out different tasks through zero sample learning, less sample learning or fine tuning. The ERNIE series models possess better contextual inference capability through knowledge fusion, enabling the models to accurately encode Chinese corpora from different sources and with different features to solve the problems of poor recognition of Chinese semantic concepts and weak Chinese representation capability of BERT models. After experimental screening, this model is selected as a feature extractor for book classification, which can extract the information embedded in book titles, authors, content profiles and keywords to a greater extent and better serve the multilabel classification of book subjects.

TextRCNN Model. TextRCNN combines the superior features of RNN and CNN. The network first uses a two-way cyclic network to collect the associated information of the features. Compared with the window-based network in traditional CNN, it can reduce the noise in the features and perform text features. The word order can be preserved in a large range during extraction, and then the key information in the text can be screened by using the maximum pooling layer to automatically select the features that play a more obvious role in book classification, which can deal well with the characteristics of rich book information. The model architecture of TextRCNN is shown in Fig. 4.

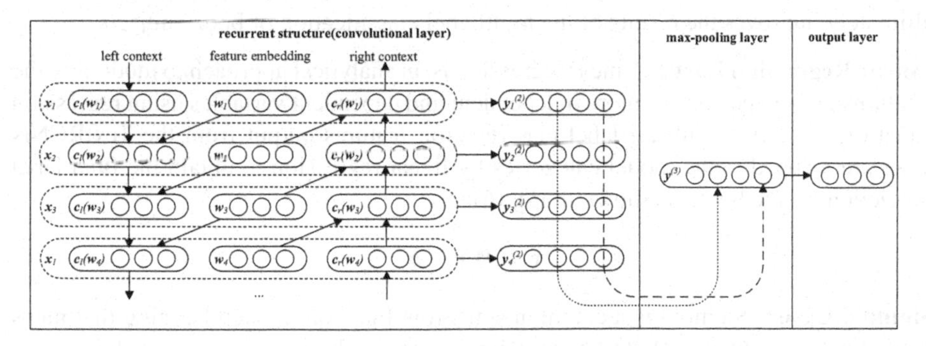

Fig. 4. TextRCNN Model Architecture

The feature embedding layer in Fig. 4 re-encodes the ERNIE output book feature vector w. After that, Bi-LSTM is used to obtain the associated feature information c_l and c_r between different features of the book, and the calculation process is shown in Eq. (1) and Eq. (2):

$$\boldsymbol{c}_l(w_i) = f\left(W^{(l)}\boldsymbol{c}_l(w_{i-1}) + W^{(sl)}\boldsymbol{e}(w_{i-1})\right) \tag{1}$$

$$c_r(w_i) = f\left(W^{(r)}c_r(w_{i+1}) + W^{(sr)}e(w_{i+1})\right) \tag{2}$$

The two calculated book feature information are then stitched together with the book feature code to obtain a representation x of the associated book feature information, as shown in Eq. (3):

$$x_i = [c_l(w_i); e(w_i); c_r(w_i)] \tag{3}$$

Then, x undergoes a linear transformation and tanh activation function to obtain the final representation of book association feature information $y_i^{(2)}$, at which point $y_i^{(2)}$ contains the feature information related to the book subject category for subsequent multilabel prediction, which is calculated as shown in Eq. (4):

$$y_i^{(2)} = \tanh(W^{(2)}x_i + b^{(2)}) \tag{4}$$

Finally, the output of the convolutional layer $y_i^{(2)}$ is then passed through the maximum pooling layer to select the significant features in the book information and transform the feature vector to a fixed length, as shown in Eq. (5):

$$y^{(3)} = \max_{i=1}^{n} y_i^{(2)} \tag{5}$$

In this paper, the dropout value in the TextRCNN convolutional layer (Bi-LSTM layer) is improved by raising the dropout value from 0.1 to 0.2 so that the convolutional layer has better generalization to different text inputs, improves the applicability of book association information to better identify the commonality between books, provides the output vector with more comprehensive feature information for the splicing layer, and ultimately improves the results of the multilabel classification of book subjects.

Linear Regression Layer. Linear regression is an analytical approach to modelling the relationship between one or more independent and dependent variables using regression equations. The book subject label classification features output from the TextRCNN layer are mapped to the model categories by linear regression to obtain the final label prediction for the book, as shown in Eq. (6):

$$y = Wx + b \tag{6}$$

Sigmoid Layer. Sigmoid is a common activation function in deep learning that maps predictions to between (0, 1) and can be used to make probabilistic predictions of classification labels with the following equation:

$$f(x) = \frac{1}{1 + e^{-x}} \tag{7}$$

Its function image is shown in Fig. 5, which converts the label values of the classifier output to probability values between (0, 1), facilitating subsequent loss calculation and model evaluation.

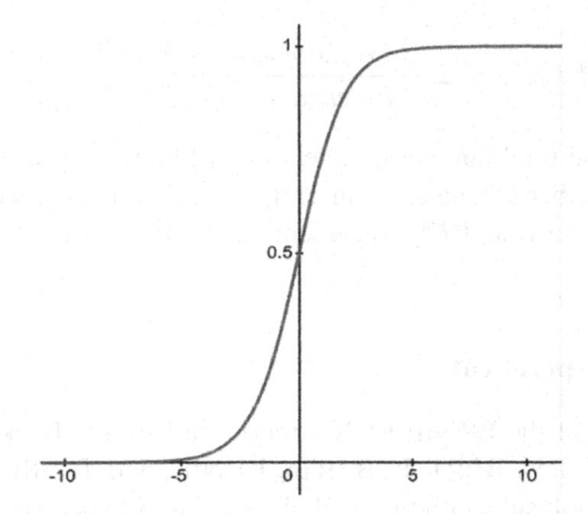

Fig. 5. Sigmoid function image

4 Experiments and Results

4.1 Experimental Data Set

The 13,233 pieces of book data that have been annotated with first-level subject labels in the book data set are used as experimental data. To ensure the scientific nature of the research, 70% of the test data were randomly selected as the training set, 15% as the verification set and 15% as the test set, and the data of each label were randomly allocated in proportion to the three data sets.

4.2 Model Loss Function

The experimental task was multilabel classification, and the final labels were multilabel tagged with a unique thermal encoding, so BCELoss was chosen as the loss function of the model, and the operation is shown in Eq. (8):

$$\text{Loss}(\boldsymbol{x}_i, \boldsymbol{y}_i) = -w_i\left[\boldsymbol{y}_i \log \boldsymbol{x}_i + (1 - \boldsymbol{y}_i)\log(1 - \boldsymbol{x}_i)\right] \tag{8}$$

4.3 Model Evaluation Index

Micro-F117 [17] was used as the evaluation index for the performance of the classification algorithm, and microprecision and microrecall were important reference indexes for the analysis of the experimental results. These three metrics are defined as follows:

$$Precision_{micro} = \frac{\sum_{i=1}^{N} TP_i}{\sum_{i=1}^{N} TP_i + \sum_{i=1}^{N} FP_i} \tag{9}$$

$$Recall_{micro} = \frac{\sum_{i=1}^{N} TP_i}{\sum_{i=1}^{N} TP_i + \sum_{i=1}^{N} FN_i} \tag{10}$$

$$F1_{micro} = 2 \times \frac{Precision_{micro} \times Recall_{micro}}{Precision_{micro} + Recall_{micro}} \tag{11}$$

where N represents the total number of categories of tags, i represents the class i tags, TP_i represents the number of true cases in sample i, FP_i represents the number of false positive cases in sample i, and FN_i represents the number of false negative cases in sample i.

4.4 Comparative Experiment

To verify the validity of the ERNIE-RCNN model in Chinese book subject multilabel classification, four models, BERT, RoBERTa, ERNIE, and TextRCNN, were selected to conduct Chinese book subject multilabel classification experiments. RoBERTa is an improved model with sufficient pretraining based on the BERT model, and their Micro-F1, Micro-Precision and Micro-Recall metrics on Chinese book data sets were compared. The three pretrained models are then combined with RNN, CNN and RCNN networks, and the results are compared to verify the effect of the knowledge fusion pretraining model in book classification.

4.5 Experimental Results

The classification results of each model on the multilabel data set of Chinese book subjects are shown in Table 1. It can be seen from the table that the accuracy and recall rate of the ERNIE-RCNN model are higher than those of ERNIE and TextRCNN alone, indicating that the combination of the two can improve the classification of books. The F1 score of the model is also higher than that of other pretraining models, indicating that the model has excellent performance in the multilabel classification task of Chinese books and has the best classification effect. The performance of ERNIE is also better than that of traditional BERT, which indicates that the pretraining of knowledge enhancement by using an external knowledge base in ERNIE has obtained certain effects in book classification. The experimental results of combining the pretraining model with RNN, CNN and RCNN show that the effect of combining with RNN and CNN is not as good as that of combining with RCNN, indicating that RCNN can make use of the advantages of the two complementary models to achieve a better classification effect. The effect of BERT-RCNN and RoBERTa-RCNN is similar to that of using BERT and RoBERTa alone. It is speculated that the reason for this phenomenon is that the information extraction effect of the TextRCNN network is not obvious because the book information extracted by BERT is insufficient. Therefore, using the knowledge fusion model ERNIE can better extract the feature information of books to obtain a better book classification effect.

Table 1. Comparative experimental results of multilabel classification models for Chinese books

Models	Micro-F1	Micro-Precision	Micro-Recall
BERT	0.7815	0.8138	0.7517
RoBERTa	0.7882	0.8258	0.7540
ERNIE	0.7958	0.8321	0.7517
TextRCNN	0.7707	0.7910	0.7514
BERT-CNN	0.7783	0.8140	0.7456
RoBERTa-CNN	0.7885	0.8308	0.7503
ERNIE-CNN	0.7921	0.8214	0.7650
BERT-RNN	0.7687	0.8431	0.7065
RoBERTa-RNN	0.7719	0.8452	0.7103
ERNIE-RNN	0.7645	**0.8528**	0.6929
BERT-RCNN	0.7799	0.8345	0.7320
RoBERTa-RCNN	0.7807	0.8352	0.7329
ERNIE-RCNN	**0.8091**	0.8469	**0.7747**

5 Conclusion

The efficient and accurate classification of Chinese books with first-level subject labels is not only a contribution to the construction of subjects but also an important part of the construction of smart libraries, contributing to the provision of high-quality subject services in libraries and providing a good basis for making recommendations based on book information. Therefore, this paper proposes a multilabel classification method for Chinese books based on the knowledge fusion model ERNIE-RCNN, using the characteristics of the ERNIE model that can identify entity information, applying it to the field of book multilabel classification and verifying its classification effect.

Through comparison experiments, we found that the ERNIE-RCNN model has improved the classification effect compared with the BERT model, RoBERTa model, original ERNIE model, ERNIE-CNN model, ERNIE-RNN model and TextRCNN model, indicating the effectiveness of the feature extraction method of knowledge fusion in the field of multilabel classification of book subjects, which can provide new ideas for book classification. The classification effect of the current model in some subject categories is not ideal. The next step is to analyse the reasons and introduce a new method to further optimize the classification effect of the model.

References

1. The Central Committee of the Communist Party of China and the State Council issued the China Education Modernization 2035. Bulletin of the Ministry of Education of the People's Republic of China, no. Z1, pp. 2–5 (2019)
2. Ministry of Education, Ministry of Finance, National Development and Reform Commission. Implementation Measures for Coordinating and Promoting the Construction of World-Class Universities and First-Class Disciplines (Provisional). http://www.moe.gov.cn/srcsite/A22/moe_843/201701/t20170125_295701.html. Accessed 5 Apr 2023

3. Huizhen, X.: Research on the influence of disciplinary classification on the discipline evaluation service of university library. LIS **64**(2), 85–93 (2020)
4. Devlin, J., Chang, M.W., Lee, K., et al.: BERT: pretraining of deep bidirectional transformers for language understanding. arXiv preprint arXiv:1810.04805 (2018)
5. Sun, Y., Wang, S., Li, Y., et al.: ERNIE: enhanced representation through knowledge integration. arXiv preprint arXiv:1904.09223 (2019)
6. Lewis, D.D.: An evaluation of phrasal and clustered representations on a text categorization task. In: SIGIR, pp. 37– 50 (1992)
7. Cover, T.M.: Elements of Information Theory. Wiley, Hoboken (1999)
8. Ng, A.Y.: Feature selection, L 1 vs. L 2 regularization, and rotational invariance. In: Proceedings of the Twenty-First International Conference on Machine Learning, p. 78 (2004)
9. Sherstinsky, A.: Fundamentals of recurrent neural network (RNN) and long short-term memory (LSTM) network. Phys. D **404**, 132306 (2020)
10. Huan, H., Yan, J., Xie, Y., et al.: Feature-enhanced nonequilibrium bidirectional long short-term memory model for Chinese text classification. IEEE Access **8**, 199629–199637 (2020)
11. Kalchbrenner, N., Grefenstette, E., Blunsom, P.: A convolutional neural network for modelling sentences. arXiv preprint arXiv:1404.2188 (2014)
12. Kim, Y.: Convolutional neural networks for sentence classification. In: Proceedings of the 2014 Conference on Empirical Methods in Natural Language Processing. Doha, Qatar: EMNLP, pp. 1746–1751 (2014)
13. Lai, S., Xu, L., Liu, K., et al.: Recurrent convolutional neural networks for text classification. In: Proceedings of the AAAI Conference on Artificial Intelligence, vol. 29, no. 1 (2015)
14. Vaswani, A., Shazeer, N., Parmar, N., et al.: Attention is all you need. In: Advances in Neural Information Processing Systems, vol. 30 (2017)
15. Sun, Y., Wang, S., Li, Y., et al.: ERNIE 2.0: a continual pretraining framework for language understanding. In: Proceedings of the AAAI Conference on Artificial Intelligence, vol. 34, no. 05, pp. 8968–8975 (2020)
16. Sun, Y., Wang, S., Feng, S., et al.: ERNIE 3.0: large-scale knowledge enhanced pretraining for language understanding and generation. arXiv preprint arXiv:2107.02137 (2021)
17. Chicco, D., Jurman, G.: The advantages of the Matthews correlation coefficient (MCC) over F1 score and accuracy in binary classification evaluation. BMC Genom. **21**, 1–13 (2020)

Chinese Book Information Extraction Based on Bert and Rule Matching

Tingting Chen[1], Yunqing Lu[2], and Tianwei Xu[2](✉)

[1] School of Information Science and Technology, Yunnan Normal University, Kunming, China
[2] Key Laboratory of Educational Information for Nationalities, Yunnan Normal University, Kunming, China
xutianwei@ynnu.edu.cn

Abstract. Extracting book-related information from length texts is of great importance as the basis for downstream tasks in the field of graphical intelligence. Book texts are characterized by prominent information features and simple sentences, but few studies have been conducted on the information extraction of book texts. Based on this, this paper proposes an information extraction model that combines entity extraction and rule matching using a BERT pretrained model. The BERT-wwm-ext+CRF model is used as the basis for extracting entities and formulating specific rules for book texts to match the relationships between entities so that the book information can be output as a result of a triplet. Through this method, there are 5 types of entities that can be finally recognized and 4 types of information extracted, which can match the common basic information of books and meet the basic requirements of book information processing. After experimental comparison, the method has good performance in extracting book information and can extract entities and identify entity relationships and attributes from text data more accurately. The final triplets obtained by the model can pave the way for tasks such as building knowledge graphs, thus serving smart libraries.

Keywords: Book Information · Information Extraction · Entity Extraction · Bert Model · Rule Matching

1 Introduction

Smart services for libraries, driven by users' needs, involve smart mobile services, smart Q&A services, knowledge services, etc. [1]. Knowledge Graph (KG) [2] Organizes data in a structured form that can yield application value in intelligent services such as smart search and smart Q&A. Information extraction (IE) [3], also called knowledge extraction, is the most basic and critical step in building a knowledge graph. Facing the massive amount of text data, we want the computer to help to extract the related information in the text, rather than extracting some unrelated keywords.

IE is the extraction of structured information from natural language text and involves knowledge related to natural language processing and machine learning. It includes Antity Extraction [4], Attribute Extraction [5] and Relationship Extraction [5] Subtasks,

J. Gan et al. (Eds.): CSEI 2023, CCIS 1899, pp. 65–75, 2024.
https://doi.org/10.1007/978-981-99-9499-1_6

etc., and IE can transform massive amounts of text into structured data. IE has an essential application and driving role in today's digital era.

In recent years, Zixuan Tian et al. [6] used the BERT-CRF model to detect Chinese events. Hongfei Xu et al. [7] used the BERT model to achieve the extraction of entity relationships in power safety regulation data. Qiuying Zhang et al. [8] extracted information from scholars' homepages based on a BERT-BiLSTM-CRF model, and the experiments showed that the introduction of the BERT pretraining model helped the model's ability to extract information. Liang et al. [9] constructed an accident causation lexicon with a sample library of reports of heavy gas explosion accidents in coal mines and proposed an algorithm for accident causation information extraction based on rule patterns, which can quickly extract coal mine accident causation information from text. Yang Yanyun et al. [10]. Used a sequence annotation strategy combined with optimized extraction rules to complete the joint extraction of TCM entity relations by combining the characteristics of TCM texts, and the experimental results show that the model is more effective compared with the traditional pipeline method as well as other methods. Zhang W et al. [11] and Sun Zhetao et al. [12] proposed combining rule matching with lexical annotation or deep learning models to extract the information in the text for enterprise information text and fishery information text, respectively, and the experiments showed that both achieved the expected results.

Book information focuses on the book entity. With the book entity as the center-piece, important information commonly found in the text is author, publisher, publication date, subject category, etc.However, at present, few people have conducted relevant research in the field of graphical information oriented to the characteristics of book information and how to extract book information from text, and further in-depth research and exploration are needed.

Using the BERT model yields sentence-level semantic representations, and subsequent model tasks can better understand the text, resulting in better performance.With the rise of pre-training techniques, many variants and improved versions of BERT models have emerged that aim to optimize the performance of BERT models, adapt to specific tasks or languages, and provide better language representation capabilities.BERT-wwm (Whole Word Masking) is an improved model based on BERT.In the original BERT version, Chinese phrases are split into individual words for pre-training, while BERT-wwm adopts the "whole word masking" approach.It retains the complete Chinese phrase as input in the pre-training process instead of slicing it into individual words, which can better capture the semantic and contextual information of the text.BERT-wwm-ext extends the vocabulary list of the original BERT-wwm model and uses larger pre-training to enable it to cover more Chinese words, further improving the quality and richness of the language representation.

In this paper, we propose an information extraction method based on the BERT pretraining model for entity extraction, combined with rule matching to extract the relationship and attribute information of book entities. After experimental comparison, the BERT-wwm-ext-CRF model is finally used for entity extraction, and then custom rules for book information are written for matching entity relationships and entity attributes for the simple structure and obvious information features of the book text dataset to extract the information about books contained in the text and obtain the triad. To pave the way for tasks such as building a knowledge map of the book field and advancing the work of intelligent library services.

2 Model Design and Methodology

The overall research work in this thesis requires first obtaining the text dataset and then inputting it to the model training after sequential annotation of the dataset, i.e., first annotating the entities in the text by entity recognition, based on which regular rules for extracting book information are applied to extract the relationships between entities or the attributes of book entities, and finally outputting the triplet.

2.1 Data Annotation

The entities contained in the dataset and their annotations according to the BIO tagging method are as follows (Table 1).

Table 1. Entity and entity labelling.

Label	Label meaning
B-xxx	The start position of the xxx entity
I-xxx	The end position of the xxx entity
O	Indicates that not belong to any entity

When extracting the book information in the text, the types of information that can be extracted to the book entity as the center are shown in Table 2.

Table 2. IE mapping.

Extraction category	Information category	Tags
Relationships	Writed	RE_Write
Relationships	Published	RE_Press
Attributes	Published	AB_Date
Attributes	Belongs to	AB_Subject
Other	Unrecognized	ERR

2.2 BERT-CRF Based Entity Extraction Model

In this paper, after comparison experiments, the BERT-CRF model is finally used for entity annotation, and the specific model structure is shown in Fig. 1. The word in the

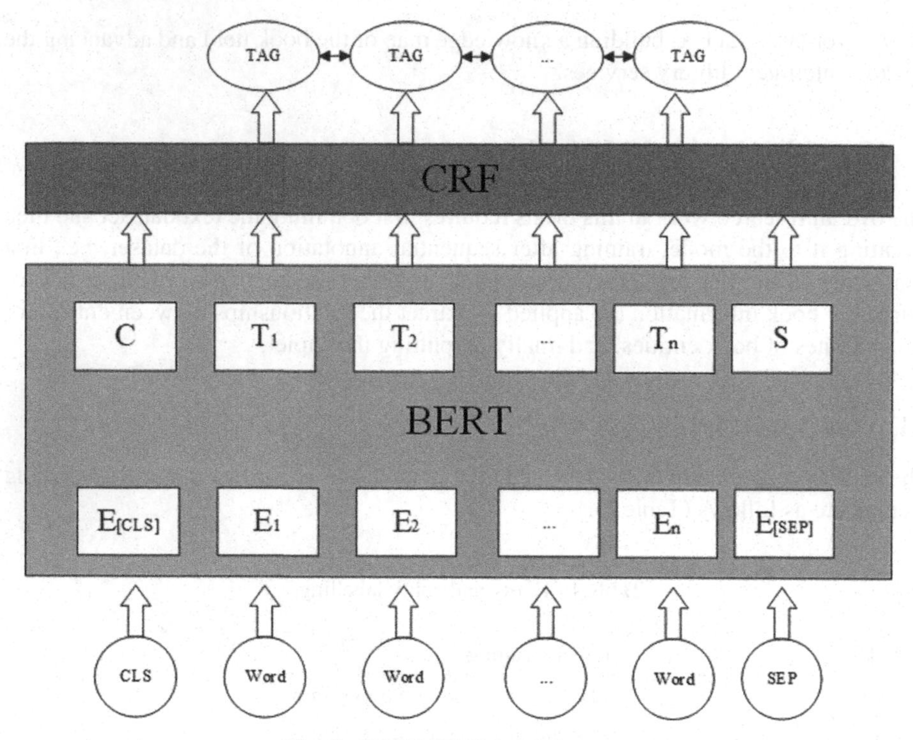

Fig. 1. BERT-CRF Model Structure

figure denotes the word of the input sequence, Ei denotes the i-th word embedding vector, and Ti denotes the feature vector obtained from the i-th word after the BERT model. TAGi is the label of entity recognition finally obtained after the CRF layer.

BERT Pretraining Model. Bidirectional Encoder Representation from Transformers (BERT) [13] is a pretrained model proposed on the basis of Transformer [14], which can achieve the effect of creating state-of-the-art models for a wide range of tasks, such as QA, by adding an additional output layer for fine-tuning.

Using BERT as the embedding layer of the sequence annotation model can generate a semantic representation vector with rich contextual semantic features based on the input sentence sequence, so we use the BERT layer to obtain the embedding of the word and learn to the sequence state.

The Transformer model structure is divided into encoder and decoder parts, but it is unidirectional and loses contextual information. The BERT model is designed as a bidirectional model by stacking multiple encoders, allowing the network to use contextual information more efficiently. The input of BERT consists of three embeddings, namely, token embeddings, position embeddings and segment embeddings [15], and represents participle information, clause information, and location information. In this paper, the word vector is used to split the sentences by adding [CLS] and [SEP] at the beginning and end of each text sentence, respectively. Each layer of the encoder consists of multihead attention, layer normalization, and feedforward.

There are two tasks in the pretraining phase of the BERT model: masked LM (MLM) [16] and next sentence prediction (NSP) [17]. MLM is the ability to train the model to capture contextual relationships by masking some random words in the input text and predicting the words from contextual information. BERT-base The model masks the token in the text sequence. The token in English refers to each word, but there is a large difference between words and characters in Chinese.

BERT-wwm (BERT-whole word masking) [18] is a pretraining model proposed for Chinese word separation, mainly improving the MLM strategy in the pretraining phase, masking by word instead of word, and the corpus used is from the Chinese wiki. In addition, there is BERT-wwm-ext, the difference being that the corpus used is much larger and richer.

CRF Layer. By using the BERT layer to obtain a vector representation of each word in the text incorporating the sequence semantic information, if another layer of softmax is added, the label prediction of each word can be obtained. However, its performance is not satisfactory, and its predicted tag sequences will have obvious errors. For example, for the identified entity tags, the sequence "B-PERSON I-PERSON" can appear, but the sequence "B-BOOK I-ORG" is not possible. The beginning of the entity should be "B-" instead of "I-", and both "I-" should belong to the same entity category. If these useful constraints are learned, the sequence of errors predicted by the model will be greatly reduced. For the sequence labelling problem of text, the "softmaxt" classifier does not consider the dependencies between labels in the sequence labelling task but simply learns the sequence state [6]. Therefore, we thought of adding a CRF layer on top of the BERT layer.

CRF (Conditional Random Fields) [19] has two types of eigenfunctions, one for the correspondence between observation sequences and states and one for interstate relations [20]. Relying on the BERT layer to vectorize each word and input it into the CRF layer, the constraints of each label are learned by the CRF layer, and finally, the label sequence with high accuracy can be obtained.

If the input text sequence $X = (x_1, x_2, ..., x_n)$, n is the length of the sequence, the corresponding label prediction result is $Y = (y_1, y_2, ..., y_n)$, , and the total score of the label sequence is calculated as in Eq. (1):

$$\text{Score}(\text{X}, y) = \sum\nolimits_{i=1}^{n} T[y_i, y_{i+1}] + \sum\nolimits_{i=1}^{n} P[i, y_i] \tag{1}$$

Eq: $T\left[y_i, y_{i+1}\right]$ denotes the fraction transferred from label y_i to label y_{i+1}, and $P\left[i, y_i\right]$ denotes the fraction for which the i th sequence is labelled y_i.

Rule Matching. After the BERT-CRF model, the entity annotation sequence in the text is obtained, and the book information in the text can be extracted by rule matching on the basis of the entity. The overall process is shown in Fig. 2.

The effect of rule-based information extraction is very dependent on the quality of the rule string, and each category of target information requires a specific rule string, requiring the user to be very skilled in the use of regular expression syntax [11]. Text with book information has obvious features and simple syntax, which is suitable for using rule matching. Rule matching is performed using regular expressions, and the relationships between entity pairs are further determined based on the extracted entity pairs.

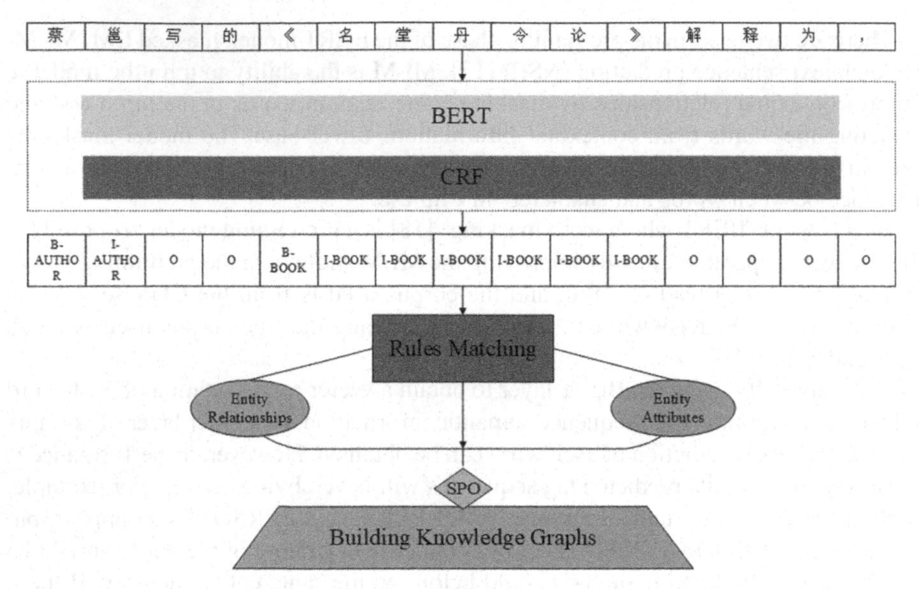

Fig. 2. Instantiation process

After the text has been extracted by entities, the entity pairs are obtained. Although the entities have been classified, the relationship between different entity types is not certain; for example, in the text "Harry Potter and the Sorcerer's Stone is a children's fantasy novel written by British author J.K. Rowling about the adventures of an orphan Harry Potter in the wizarding world". The entity 'Harry Potter and the Sorcerer's Stone' extracted after the BERT-CRF layer belongs to the BOOK class, while 'J.K. Rowling' and 'Harry Potter' are both classified as the PERSON class, and it is necessary to further determine the relationship between the three.

By organizing and summarizing, it was found that the various attributes and relationships of the book entities have regular positions and characteristics in the sentences where they appear. For example, if you extract to PERSON and BOOK entities, if they have an RE_Write relationship between them, generally speaking, keywords such as 'author' and 'writing' will be matched between the two entities. Similarly, if you want to extract information about publication date or publisher, you often need to match to keywords such as 'publish', 'release', etc. Therefore, we make different regular rules for different relationships and attributes. Each piece of information is matched by matching keywords, and the matching rules are shown in the Table 3.

In addition to keyword matching, the rules of matching also use proximity matching and keyword matching. The use of the proximity principle can be a good solution to the problem of overlapping relationships between multiple pairs of entities extracted in the text [21]. As in the 'Harry Potter' example listed above, the match between the 'Harry Potter and the Sorcerer's Stone' BOOK entity and the 'J.K. Rowling' PERSON entity to the keyword 'write', and the keyword is further away from 'Harry Potter', so the judgment is < 'Harry Potter and the Sorcerer's Stone', RE-Write,J.K. Rowling > and < 'Harry Potter and the Sorcerer's Stone', ERR, Harry Potter >. Considering

Table 3. Matching rules.

Entity vs.	Keywords	Tags	Other rules
BOOK\PERSON	Authors, Publications, Writings, Representative Works	RE-Write	Proximity principle If the word match is unsuccessful, the word match
BOOK\ORG	Publishing, Distribution, Production	RE-PRESS	Proximity principle
BOOK\DATE	Publishing, Distribution, Production	AB-Date	Proximity principle
BOOK\SUBJECT	Belongs to, Class, About	AB-SUBJECT	Proximity principle

that keywords have limitations, continuing to use keyword matching in keywords after unsuccessful use of keyword matching improves the robustness of matching. If no match succeeds after the above rules, the entity pair is judged to have no relationship with each other and marked as ERR.

With the book entity as the center and matching by the above rules, the final triad can be used to build a knowledge graph for other applications.

3 Experiments and Results

3.1 Data Acquisition and Labelling

At present, there is no publicly available Chinese book text dataset in the field of graphical intelligence. The flow chart of data processing for the experiments in this paper is shown in Fig. 3. The datasets used in this study were obtained from Dangdang.com and the Union Catalogue Public Access System (CALIS OPAC). The standard data within the website are crawled through the Python Selenium package, and the final book information obtained is the book title, book author, publisher, publication date, subject classification and content summary. The content profile is text data, and the other information is tabular data. For the text experimental work, we need the text to contain the book title and at least one other kind of information. In the crawled content profile, the book information is embedded into the text by rule matching for data that do not satisfy the experimental conditions for this experiment. For example, for the book title information, book pronouns such as 'this book' and 'the whole book' in the introduction are replaced with the book title and marked. The author information is matched by keywords, and then the author name is inserted into the sentence and marked.

The final constructed and labelled dataset consisted of a total of 10,946 articles, of which 7,662 were used as the training set, and the rest of the data were divided into validation and test sets at a ratio of 7:2:1. When labelling, each text is divided by line break '\n', each text is line break by word, and each line consists of words and entity labels, separated by spaces, saved as txt format for reading. The relationship tag exists in a separate txt file.

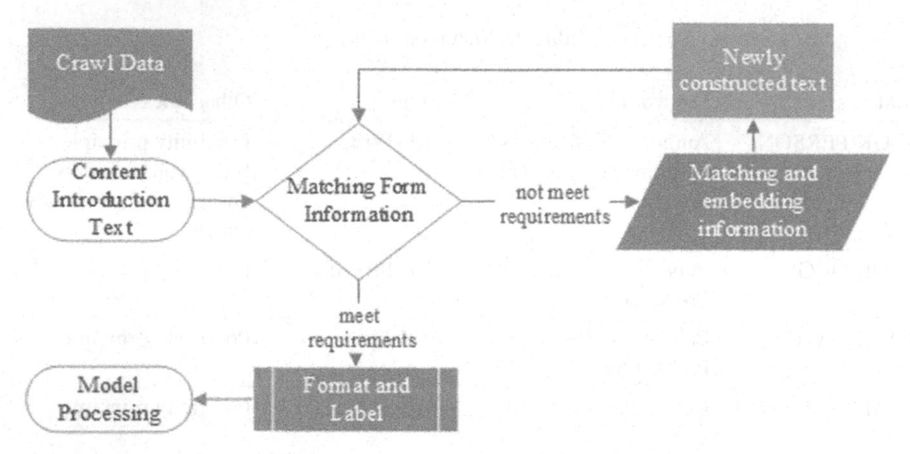

Fig. 3. Data sources and processing flow

3.2 Experimental Parameters and Evaluation Indexes

In the original paper [13], the size of the BERT model is divided into BERT-large with 24 layers of encoder and 16 attention layers and BERT-base with 12 layers of encoder and 12 attention layers. In the experimental part of this paper, it is sufficient to use BERT-base.

The models used in this paper are written using the PyTorch deep learning framework. In this experiment, the optimizer is set to Adam, 30 epochs are iterated, the batch size is 64, dropout is set to 0.5, the learning rate of pretrained model fine-tuning is set to 5e−05, and the learning decay rate of CRF is 5e−02. The experiment uses the precision (P), recall (R) and F1 values as the evaluation metrics for the experiments.

3.3 Experimental Effects and Analysis

With other experimental conditions set the same, comparing only the CRF model and only the BERT_base model provided by Google [13], only the Harbin Institute of Technology Xunfei Joint Lab is used to release the BERT-wwm model [18], only the BERT-wwm-ext model is used [18] and CRF layers are added separately for entity extraction (NER). The subsequent information extraction (IE) results after rule matching are shown in Table 4.

The results show that BERT-wwm-ext performs better in the pretrained model because it obtains word vectors incorporating word information, and no type of BERT plus CRF layer will improve the model prediction ability.

Based on this paper, we use the BERT-wwm-ext+CRF model for entity extraction. After extracting the entity pairs using rule matching to further extract the information, the results obtained are shown in Table 5.

The experiments show that the model in this paper performs well in extracting each relationship and attribute, in which the F1 values of the publisher relationship and publication date attribute of book entities are above 80%, and can extract relevant information correctly. The main reason is that the information characteristics of the publisher and

Table 4. NER experimental comparison and results.

Model	P	R	F1
CRF	0.7464	0.7692	0.7576
BERT-base+Softmax	0.7392	0.7666	0.7527
BERT-wwm+Softmax	0.7520	0.7714	0.7616
BERT-wwm-ext+Softmax	0.7629	0.7632	0.7630
BERT-base+CRF	0.7533	0.7817	0.7672
BERT-wwm+CRF	0.7677	0.7888	0.7781
BERT-wwm-ext+CRF	**0.7825**	**0.7981**	**0.7902**

Table 5. The results.

Extraction type	P	R	F1
RE_Write	0.7154	0.7036	0.7094
RE_Press	0.8361	0.8341	0.8301
AB_Date	0.8524	0.8719	0.8620
AB_SUBJECT	0.7396	0.7254	0.7324

publication date are obvious, and common expressions can be matched by the rules in this paper.

4 Conclusion

In this paper, we propose a model combining entity extraction and rule matching to extract the book information contained in the text, which is characterized by simple sentences and outstanding features of book text. The entity classes that can be extracted are BOOK, PERSON, ORG, DATE and SUBJECT. There are four types of information that can be extracted around the entity: writing, publisher, release date, and subject category.

Through comparison experiments, it is found that the wwm-based BERT pretraining model works better than the traditional BERT, and the use of a larger corpus during pretraining also improves the model learning ability. Of course, there are also many labelled sequences obtained by pretraining models alone that defy common sense, and CRF can compensate for this drawback.

The model in this paper uses the BERT-wwm-ext pretraining model to obtain the vectorized representation of each word in the sequence and then inputs it into the CRF layer, which is used to constrain the tagging sequence to obtain the book-related entity pairs in the text, judges the relationship between the entity pairs by rule matching, and finally obtains the triad that can be used to construct the knowledge graph. The current model does not have sufficient rules for information extraction and can be expanded.

References

1. Wu, C., Yang, X.: Research and practice of intelligent libraries in China. Libr. Intell. Work **65**(04), 20–27 (2021)
2. Xu, Z., Sheng, Y., He, L., et al.: A review of knowledge graph technology. J. Univ. Electron. Sci. Technol. **45**(04), 589–606 (2016)
3. Fader, A., Soderland, S., Etzioni, O.: Identifying relations for open information extraction. In: Conference on Empirical Methods in Natural Language Processing. Edinburgh, UK, pp. 1535–1545. SIGDAT (2011)
4. Liu, L., Wang, D.: A review of named entity identification research. J. Intell. **37**(03), 329–340 (2018)
5. Guo, J., Li, Z., Yu, Z., et al.: Extraction of domain ontology concept instances, attributes and attribute values and relationship prediction. J. Nanjing Univ. (Nat. Sci. Edn.) **48**(04), 383–389 (2012). https://doi.org/10.13232/j.cnki.jnju.2012.04.015
6. Zihan, T., Xin, L.: Research on Chinese event detection method based on BERT-CRF model. Comput. Eng. Appl. **57**(11), 135–139 (2021)
7. Xu, H., Li, Y.: Entity relationship extraction in electric power safety regulation data using Bert model. Power Sci. Eng. **39**(01), 44–51 (2023)
8. Zhang, Q.-Y., Fu, L., Wang, X.-B.: BERT-BiLSTM-CRF based information extraction from scholars' homepages. Comput. Appl. Res. **37**(S1), 47–49 (2020)
9. Liang, J.J., Lei, H.R., Wu, B., Cai, Z.J., Li, J.: Rule-based model of gas explosion accident information extraction technique. Coal Mine Saf. **54**(02), 239–245 (2023)
10. Yang, Y.Y., Du, J.Q., Nie, B., et al.: A deep learning joint extraction method of entity relations for TCM texts. Comput. Appl. Softw. **40**(03), 217–222+234 (2023)
11. Zhang, W., Pan, X.M., Zhang, H.B., He, X., Bo, J., Qin, S.L.: An information extraction method based on a combination of lexical annotation and rules. Comput. Technol. Dev. **31**(10), 215–220 (2021)
12. Sun, Z., et al.: A method for extracting fishery standard form information based on rule matching and deep learning AB Transformer. J. Dalian Ocean Univ. **38**(01), 140–148 (2023)
13. Devlin, J., Chang, M.W., Lee, K., et al.: BERT: pretraining of deep bidirectional transformers for language understanding. arXiv preprint arXiv:1810.04805 (2018)
14. Vaswani, A., Shazeer, N., Parmar, N., et al.: Attention is all you need. In: Advances in Neural Information Processing Systems, vol. 30 (2017)
15. Rahman, W., Hasan, M.K., Lee, S., et al.: Integrating multimodal information in large pretrained transformers. In: Proceedings of the conference. Association for Computational Linguistics Meeting, vol. 2020, p. 2359. NIH Public Access (2020)
16. Salazar, J., Liang, D., Nguyen, T.Q., et al.: Masked language model scoring. arXiv preprint arXiv:1910.14659 (2019)
17. Shi, W., Demberg, V.: Next sentence prediction helps implicit discourse relation classification within and across domains. In: Proceedings of the 2019 Conference On Empirical Methods in Natural Language Processing and the 9th International Joint Conference on Natural Language Processing (EMNLP-IJCNLP), pp. 5790–5796 (2019)
18. Cui, Y., Che, W., Liu, T., Qin, B., Yang, Z.: Pre-training with whole word masking for Chinese BERT. IEEE/ACM Trans. Audio Speech Lang. Process. **29**, 3504–3514 (2021). https://doi.org/10.1109/TASLP.2021.3124365
19. Lafferty, J., McCallum, A., Pereira, F.: Conditional random fields: probabilistic models for segmenting and labelling sequence data. In: Proceedings of the18th International Conference on Machine Learning, Williamstown, USA, pp. 282–289 (2001)

20. Xie, T., Yang, J.A., Liu, F.: Chinese entity recognition based on BERT-BiLSTM-CRF model. Comput. Syst. Appl. **29**(07), 48–55 (2020). https://doi.org/10.15888/j.cnki.csa.007525
21. Hoffman, R., Zhang, C.H., Ling, X., et al.: Knowledge-based weak supervision for overlapping relational information extraction. In: Proceedings of the 49th Annual Meeting of the Association for Computational Linguistics: Human Language Technologies, pp. 541–550 (2011)

Research on flow Game Educational Game Design Framework to Promote flow Experience – A Case Study of "The Mystery of Binary Principle"

Mingfan Wang[1], Min Xie[1,2](✉), and Yuhao Ma[1]

[1] School of Information Science and Technology, Yunnan Normal University, Kunming 650500, China
294611018@qq.com

[2] Key Laboratory of Education Informatization for Nationalities, Ministry of Education, Yunnan Normal University, Kunming 650500, China

Abstract. In educational game design, there is still a lack of systematic research and framework on how to design an educational game that can promote learners' flow experience. To this end, this paper integrates gamified learning experience and flow theory to build an educational game design framework that promotes students' flow experience – the Flow Game Framework. This paper introduces in detail the three dimensions, six design steps and nine design principles of the Flow Game framework and takes the design of "The Mystery of Binary Principle" of educational games as an example to demonstrate the educational game design process under the guidance of the Flow Game framework to provide theoretical and practical references for the design of educational games to promote learners' flow experience.

Keywords: Educational Games · Gamified Learning Experience · Flow Theory · Design Framework · Flow Game

1 Introduction

Educational games are playing an increasingly important role in promoting student learning and improving educational outcomes [1]. Educational games are designed with the goal of improving students' learning outcomes by stimulating their interest and initiative. In educational game design, the question of how to facilitate students' access to a state of mind-flow and improve their learning outcomes has been a matter of great interest. The flow experience, when students are fully engaged and highly focused in an activity, is one of the best states of experience [2]. By facilitating students' mind-flow experiences, educational games can enhance students' motivation and engagement and improve learning outcomes. Specifically, facilitating a student's flow experience can have the following benefits: Improved student learning outcomes; in a mind-flow state, students are more focused and engaged and are able to better master knowledge and

J. Gan et al. (Eds.): CSEI 2023, CCIS 1899, pp. 76–90, 2024.
https://doi.org/10.1007/978-981-99-9499-1_7

skills; Enhances students' motivation and engagement in learning; In a mindful flow state, students will feel the joy of learning and will be more motivated and interested in learning; and promote students' self-growth and self-realization. In the state of flow, students can feel the pleasure of self-realization, which is helpful to cultivate students' confidence and positive attitude. It can be seen that the design of educational games should focus on promoting students' flow experience, which will help achieve a better learning experience and teaching effect.

However, there is still a lack of a systematic design framework for research and guidance on how to design an educational game that promotes learners' flow experience. This paper integrates flow theory and gamified learning experience to build an educational game design framework - the Flow Game framework. Then, on the basis of the Flow Game framework, educational game design principles that promote students' flow experience are proposed. Taking the "Binary Principles Exploration" game as an example, the design practice process guided by the Flow Game framework is demonstrated. This paper aims to construct an educational game design framework to promote learners' flow experience and demonstrates the Flow Game framework to guide the educational game design practice of promoting students' flow experience with game cases.

2 Theoretical Basis

2.1 Flow Experience and Flow Theory

Flow experience was first proposed by Professor Csikszentmihalyi (1975) in the field of positive psychology, and he defined it as the best emotional experience that occurs when an individual focuses on solving a problem or participating in a certain activity [3]. Flow experience refers to the extreme state of forgetting time and oneself when people are invested in an activity that they are interested in and have comparable abilities. In this state, people experience pleasure and happiness [4].

Flow theory refers to people's focus and pleasant experience. It is a popular theoretical framework to understand people's continuous use of information technology tools, and its core is flow experience [5]. According to flow theory, the structure of individual flow experience in the game is divided into nine dimensions: "balance of skills and challenges", "clear goals", "timely feedback", "high concentration", "sense of control", "integration of action and perception", "time warp", "loss of self-awareness", and "embodied experience" [6]. Relevant studies have shown that flow experience is more likely to stimulate personal motivation and achieve positive results [7]. Since the theory of flow was proposed, it has received attention in various fields, and its main application fields include the fields of sports and education, art creation, IT, etc. [8].

In educational game design, flow theory can be used to design game challenges and tasks suitable for learners to maximize learners' interest and engagement in learning. Massimini et al. proposed an eight-interval flow experience model, believing that when "challenge" and "skill" are balanced, learners will enter the flow state and generate a strong flow experience [9]. Thus, the design of the game should also consider the skill level of the learner to ensure that the difficulty of the game challenge matches the learner's ability level and to avoid overly challenging or overly easy situations. In this way, learners can have a flow experience in a gamified learning environment, thus improving learning effectiveness and satisfaction. In conclusion, flow theory provides a powerful practical tool to help educational game designers design more effective and engaging gamified learning experiences, thereby promoting learners' learning outcomes and interest in learning.

2.2 Gamified Learning Experience

Gamified learning experience is the application of game elements and mechanisms in education and learning to enhance students' learning motivation and enthusiasm and improve learning effects and outcomes [10]. Gamified learning realizes efficient learning through multiple interactive methods, including physical activity, intelligent crowdfunding, competition and situational experience, to create interdisciplinary, multisensory and interactive learning experiences and to achieve changes in cognition, emotion, attitude or behavior [11]. Zhang Lu et al. proposed the framework of gamified learning experience from the perspective of learning experience and believed that the content of gamified learning experience should include learners' acquisition of tacit knowledge in the game environment, the experience of embodied cognition, and the elements and feedback mechanism of games that can stimulate learning motivation [12]. In the framework of gamified learning experience constructed by Zhang Lu et al., gamified learning experience is divided into three categories: situational cognitive experience, collaborative social guidance and motivation-based subjective experience [13].

Context-based cognitive experience is a learning style based on a gamified learning environment, which is characterized by providing learning situations with cognitive authenticity [14]. The design of such experiences is usually based on the theories and methods of learning science to help learners achieve a more scientific and effective cognitive experience. In this experience, learners improve their cognitive abilities by engaging in tasks, challenges and problem solving in a gamified learning environment. Social experience based on collaboration refers to gamified learning situations in which learners need to cooperate with other peers to complete tasks to obtain instructive information and exercise collaborative ability [14]. This kind of experience can not only enhance learners' learning motivation but also promote their social skills and cooperation spirit. Motivation-based subjective experience refers to the important role of emotion and motivation in the learning process, and the gamified learning environment should assist learners in metacognitive reflection [14]. This kind of experience can not only enhance learners' learning motivation but also promote them to reflect and evaluate their own learning state and learning effect. These three types of gamified learning experience are interrelated and interact with each other, which together constitute the main content of the learning experience. In addition, gamified learning can guide learners to devote themselves to the learning process with the help of game mechanisms, enhance their flow experience, and enable them to actively learn and construct knowledge in the game process [15].

3 Build the Flow Game Framework

Based on mind-flow theory and gamified learning experiences, this paper constructs the Flow Game framework.

Fig. 1. Flow game framework

As shown in Fig. 1, the paper integrates the three categories of gamified learning experience (context-based cognitive experience, collaboration-based social experience and motivation-based subjective experience) developed by Zhang Lu et al. with the nine dimensions of mind flow experience (balance of skills and challenges, clear goals, timely feedback, high concentration, sense of control, integration of action and perception, time distortion, loss of self-awareness and embodied experience) to form a theoretical framework. Are integrated to form a theoretical framework. This framework develops six design ideas from three dimensions: (1) designing game scenarios and characters; (2) providing immediate guidance and feedback; (3) providing appropriate opportunities for social interaction and collaboration; (4) reward and point mechanisms; (5) clear goals, challenging tasks and activities; and (6) setting game levels that progressively increase in difficulty. The detailed analysis of the educational game design ideas of the Flow Game framework in three dimensions and six steps to promote students' flow experience is as follows.

3.1 Context-Based Cognitive Experience

Step 1: Designing game scenarios and characters:

In the context-based cognitive experience, the primary goal is to design game scenarios and characters. By creating game scenarios, the learning content can be integrated with real-life situations, enabling learners to better understand and grasp the learning material. Simultaneously, well-designed game scenarios can foster a sense of closeness and passion for the learning content, enhancing learner engagement. Designing game characters can provide learners with an immersive learning experience, allowing them to better experience the learning material and further improve learning outcomes. Learners can also create a learning character relevant to themselves within the game, increasing the attractiveness and affinity of the learning content.

The design of game scenarios and game characters can increase learners' engagement and motivation. The design of game scenarios can provide a challenging learning environment for learners and stimulate their interest and enthusiasm. The design of game characters can provide learners with an interesting role-playing experience, increasing learners' engagement and motivation. Therefore, in educational game design, the focus on game scenarios and game character design is to create a realistic, immersive, fun and challenging game-based learning experience that enhances learners' learning effectiveness and motivation.

3.2 Collaboration-Based Social Experience

Step 2: Providing immediate guidance and feedback:

In the design of educational games, immediate instruction and feedback can help students understand the rules and knowledge of the game more quickly, thus improving learning. By catching students' mistakes and correcting them in time, it can help students avoid unnecessary mistakes and save learning time. Educational games are often more fun than traditional teaching methods. Immediate feedback allows students to experience the game more quickly and stimulates their interest and motivation to learn. Immediate instruction and feedback can help students identify their shortcomings and improve during the game. By correcting mistakes in real time and giving timely rewards, students' learning can be enhanced, and their motivation boosted.

When learners receive continuous immediate instruction and feedback during the game, they can understand the rules and knowledge of the game more quickly and continue to improve their skill level. This continuous feedback helps learners enter a state of mind-flow, i.e., full engagement and immersion in the task at hand, thus enhancing the learning and experience.

Step 3: Providing appropriate opportunities for social interaction and collaboration:

In educational games, opportunities for social interaction and collaboration can engage students, increase their interest and motivation, and thus motivate them to learn. By interacting and collaborating with others, students can feel that learning is fun and meaningful. By interacting and collaborating with others, students can work together to solve problems, discuss learning content and share experiences and knowledge, thus enhancing learning. By interacting and collaborating, students can gain different perspectives and ideas and discover their own shortcomings, thus improving their own learning. Social interaction and collaboration opportunities can help students develop social skills such as collaboration, communication, communication and coordination, which play an important role in students' future development and career planning. Social interaction and collaboration opportunities in educational games can add to the fun and interactivity of the game, and when learners learn through social interaction and collaboration, they can feel more motivated and accomplished. This helps them to enter a state of mind flow' and thus become more engaged and enjoy the learning process.

3.3 Motivation-Based Subjective Experience

Step 4: Reward and point mechanisms:

In educational games, reward and point mechanisms can be used to motivate students to learn and make them more active in the game. Students can earn rewards and points for completing tasks, answering questions correctly and participating in interactions, thus gaining a sense of achievement and satisfaction and motivating them to keep exploring and learning. The rewards and points mechanism can also help students better understand the game content and knowledge points and deepen their memory and understanding of the learning content. Students can earn more points and rewards by continuously exploring and learning, thus enhancing their learning effectiveness. The rewards and points mechanism can enhance the fun and attractiveness of the game and make students enjoy participating in the game more. Students can gain a sense of achievement and satisfaction by continually earning rewards and points, thus making them more willing to participate in the game. The rewards and points mechanism can also promote students' sense of competition and cooperation. Students can show their strengths and abilities by gaining more points and rewards, and they can also enhance their sense of cooperation by gaining more rewards and points through cooperation and mutual help.

When students earn rewards and points in the game, they feel a greater sense of achievement and self-confidence, which leads to a state of mind-flow and engagement in the game. At the same time, these mechanisms can also motivate students to keep exploring and challenging themselves.

Step 5: Clear goals, challenging tasks and activities:

The aim of educational games is for students to learn knowledge and skills through play, so the games need to be engaging and interesting enough for students to want to participate and continue learning. By setting clear objectives, challenging tasks and activities, students can feel that the game is challenging and fulfilling and therefore more willing to participate. Setting clear objectives in the game helps students establish clear learning goals, so they know what they need to accomplish and achieve in the game. This helps students learn more purposefully, focus more on the learning tasks in the game and improve their learning outcomes. The challenging tasks and activities in the game can motivate students to learn and make them more active in learning through the game. By completing challenging tasks and activities, students can gain a sense of achievement and satisfaction, which makes them more willing to engage in play-based learning. Tasks and activities in educational games require students to solve a variety of issues and problems, which helps students improve their problem-solving skills. In educational games, students are required to use their knowledge and skills to explore and solve problems, which helps to develop creative thinking and problem-solving skills. Learners feel more motivated and accomplished when they are given clear goals and faced with challenging tasks and activities in games. This helps them to enter a state of mind-flow and thus better engage and enjoy the learning process.

Step 6: Setting game levels that progressively increase in difficulty:

Game level setting can make learning more fun and challenging, which can increase students' motivation and engagement. Students will feel a sense of achievement after completing a less difficult level, which can motivate them to continue learning. By gradually increasing the level of difficulty, educational games can help students to gradually acquire knowledge and skills, giving more focus and depth to the learning process. Each level guides students to master a specific point of knowledge or skill and prepares them for the next level. The game's level setting helps teachers to assess students' learning outcomes and mastery. By observing students' performance in completing the levels, teachers can understand how well students are learning and further tailor their teaching to their needs.

When learners are faced with multiple levels and progressively increasing difficulty in the game, they feel a sense of achievement and challenge, which leads to a state of mind-flow. At the same time, automatic difficulty adjustment allows learners to feel moderately challenged and supported, helping them to better engage with and enjoy the learning process.

3.4 Principles of Educational Game Design Based on the Flow Game Framework

To facilitate learners' mind-flow experiences in educational games, there are many factors to consider in educational game design. According to the flow game framework, the design of educational games takes into account the cognitive experience of the context, the social experience of collaboration, and the subjective experience of motivation. In the Flow Game framework, more detailed educational game design ideas are designed with the three dimensions of cognitive experience of context, social experience of collaboration, and subjective experience of motivation as the main focus. However, to design an educational game that facilitates students' mind-flow experience and allows them to learn through the game, it is not enough to follow the ideas of this framework, but it is necessary to develop corresponding educational game design principles based on it. Therefore, based on the three dimensions of the Flow Game framework and the six design ideas, this study has developed the following nine educational game design principles to assist in the design of educational games that facilitate students' mind-flow experiences (Table 1).

Table 1. Principles of educational game design based on the Flow Game framework

The dimensions of the Flow Game framework	Educational Game Design Principles
Context-based cognitive experience (CC)	CC1: Game scenarios and characters should be appropriate to the theme and objectives of the game in order to capture the interest and attention of the player
	CC2: Scenarios and characters should present realistic situations so that players can better understand and apply the concepts and skills in the game
	CC3: Game scenarios and characters should stimulate curiosity and exploration in order to promote learning and growth

(continued)

Table 1. (*continued*)

The dimensions of the Flow Game framework	Educational Game Design Principles
Collaboration-based social experience (CS)	CS1: Games should provide immediate guidance and feedback to help players understand how they are performing and how they are progressing
	CS2: Games should provide appropriate opportunities for social interaction and collaboration to encourage players to interact and work with others to achieve game goals
	CS3: Games should encourage players to share their experiences and knowledge so that other players can benefit from them
Motivation-based subjective experience (MS)	MS1: The game should provide rewards and points to motivate players to continue to participate and progress
	MS2: Games should set clear goals, challenging tasks and activities to give players a sense of achievement and satisfaction
	MS3: Games should have levels of play that progressively increase in difficulty to allow players to continually challenge themselves and improve their abilities

In summary, the design of educational games should focus on three aspects, context, collaboration and motivation, to help players learn and grow better. In addition, the objectives and tasks of the game should match the theme of the game and the learning needs of the players to enhance the educational effectiveness of the game. In educational game design, it is important to promote learners' mind-flow experience from multiple dimensions and follow certain design ideas and design principles.

4 Educational Game Design Based on the Flow Game Framework

This study is based on the design principles and educational game design principles of the Flow Game framework. By utilizing Scratch as the development tool, an educational game called 'The Mystery of Binary Principle' was created. The game presents binary knowledge in a gamified manner and consists of four mini-games: 'Guess What', 'Binary Cards', 'Binary Abacus' and 'LED Dots'.

Among them, "Guess What" is to play the deformed digital bomb game in a human-computer interaction way, mainly from the two different perspectives of humans and computers, to carry out step-by-step disassembly exercises on the conversion steps between binary and decimal. The "Binary Cards" game mainly exercises the computing ability of learners in binary and decimal conversion. The "Binary Abacus" game mainly provides learners with binary and decimal conversion as a cognitive aid for verification. The "LED Dots" game mainly introduces the application of binary knowledge transfer

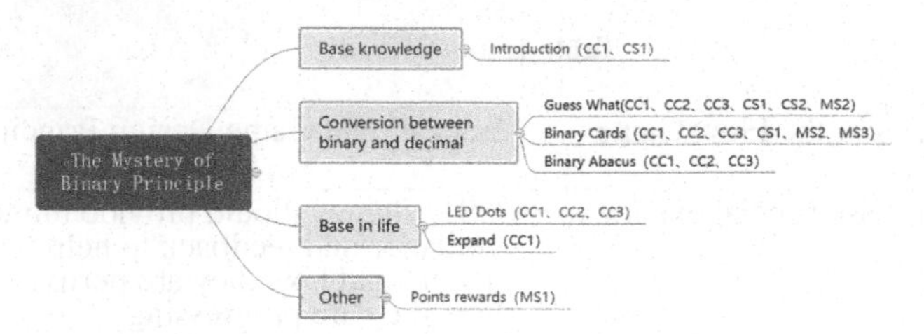

Fig. 2. Functional structure diagram of 'The Mystery of Binary Principle'.

to life for learners so that learners can understand the binary knowledge contained in the LED panel. In addition, the software provides a basic introduction and expansion of binary knowledge to help learners understand the relevant concepts in depth. The software functional structure is shown in Fig. 2.

The nine design principles mentioned above provide theoretical support for the "binary principles exploration" game design. First, game scenes and characters should be designed to align with the theme and goals of educational games (CC1). Second, game scenes and characters should present realistic situations (CC2). At the same time, the game scene and characters should also stimulate the player's curiosity and desire to explore (CC3). In terms of providing immediate guidance and feedback (CS1), games should give players timely guidance and feedback to help them understand their performance and progress so that they can adjust their learning strategies and improve their skills. To promote social interaction and cooperation (CS2), games should provide opportunities for players to communicate and collaborate with others to achieve game goals. This enhances players' social skills and teamwork skills. Encouraging players to share experience and knowledge (CS3) is another important principle. To motivate player engagement and progress (MS1), games should provide reward and point mechanisms that give players a sense of accomplishment and keep them motivated. Clear objectives, challenging tasks, and activities (MS2) can make players feel fulfilled and satisfied. Finally, the game should set up game levels and gradually increase the difficulty (MS3). By gradually increasing the difficulty, the game allows players to constantly challenge themselves, improve their abilities, and gradually improve their learning level.

Step 1: Designing game scenarios and characters (Fig. 3).

There are few characters and scenes available in the Scratch development tool. Therefore, to design the scenes and characters for the game "The Mystery of Binary Principle", it was necessary to find much material on the internet. In this game, a large number of materials related to plants and animals are used to design the scenes and characters, giving the learners an atmosphere of exploring the forest. The scenario is forest themed, and the characters are all animals. The audience for this game is students who are new to IT, mostly primary and junior high school students, so they will be more interested in games with this theme. Many students are more interested in playing games, especially in boring studies, and having an educational game that interests them will greatly increase their enthusiasm and thus stimulate learners' interest in learning.

Step 2: Providing immediate guidance and feedback.

In the "The Mystery of Binary Principle" game, learners can choose their own game or knowledge based on the cards in the game interface. For learners who are new to binary

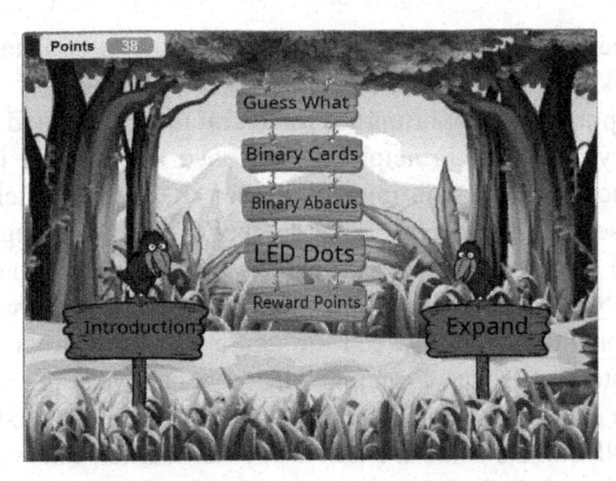

Fig. 3. Main game interface.

knowledge and may not be familiar with it, learners can choose the level 'Introduction to Binary' to learn about it. Learners can also select the games directly, where there are NPCs to guide them, and they can easily understand how to play the games. At the same time, learners can also understand the principles of the game at the end of the game so that they can understand the points. For example, in the game 'Guess what', the learner clicks in and is guided by an NPC. After following the instructions, the learner can click on 'Game principles' to learn about the principles behind the game and the relevant knowledge points (Fig. 4).

Fig. 4. "Guess what" game interface.

In educational games, immediate feedback allows learners to know quickly if the results they have made are correct. If the learner fails in the game, it allows the learner to know why they failed as soon as possible, which also allows the learner to understand the point. In the "The Mystery of Binary Principle" game, positive feedback is set up so that if the learner gets the correct answer in the 'Binary Cards' game, an animal pops up in the interface and says "Right! ". This feedback gives learners a sense of achievement, which not only increases their confidence but also shows them how they obtained the correct answer, and the repetitive positive feedback helps them to enter a state of mindfulness and understand the knowledge behind the game.

Step 3: Providing appropriate opportunities for social interaction and collaboration:

In "The Mystery of Binary Principle" game, once in the game interface, learners can select content according to their interests. When the learner touches a character or level with the mouse, the interface gives the learner a sense of being touched, and the interaction between the interface and the learner lets the learner know what they are clicking on. In the 'Guess What' game, there are also scenes where NPCs talk to the learner, allowing for interaction between the game and the learner. In several of the games in "The Mystery of Binary Principle", learners can work together to understand the principles of the game and the rules of binary and decimal conversion by having one learner imitate the NPC in the game and talk to another learner. This will enable learners to understand the principles of the game and the rules for converting between binary and decimal.

Step 4: Reward and point mechanisms:

"The Mystery of Binary Principle" game has a detailed point system that allows learners to earn points in a variety of ways. Learners can click on 'Reward Points' on the game screen to determine the rules and redeem their accumulated points for music to play. In "The Mystery of Binary Principle" game, each time a learner completes the game, one point is added to their score. "The Mystery of Binary Principle" game also includes a length of time online test, which adds 1 point for every 90 s the learner is online. At the same time, if you are online for more than 30 min, the game will indicate that you have been online for 30 min and force you to pause the game and take a break to relax before continuing. During the 30-min boost, the interface also has a posture correction chart to prompt learners to adjust their sitting posture. Once the learner has accumulated some points, they can redeem them for music to play, with 5 points being spent for each song played. In "The Mystery of Binary Principle" game, there are not only rewards such as increased points but also a time limit to play. When a learner is in the middle of playing a game and is abruptly stopped, the learner is left wanting more, thus arousing their interest in playing the game again.

Step 5: Clear goals, challenging tasks and activities:

In "The Mystery of Binary Principle" game, 'Guess What' and 'Binary Cards', there is a clear objective to obtain the correct result. It is also clear to learners what the objective of these two games is as soon as they click on them. In the 'T Guess What' game, the objective is to mentally think of an integer from 1 to 30 and then follow the instructions. After thinking of an integer from 1 to 30 and following the game's prompts, the learner finds that the NPC has guessed the number he or she thought of. The game. As the game is repeated, the learner not only enters a state of mind-flow but also gradually understands the principles of the game and then the knowledge.

In the game 'Binary Cards', the learner's objective is to convert a randomly given decimal integer into a binary number by flipping the card. Once the learners have been prompted to do this, they can choose to increase the level of difficulty themselves. In progressively more challenging games, learners are more likely to enter a state of mindfulness. When learners are in a state of mental flow, it is easier for them to translate the principles of the game into knowledge that they can accept.

Step 6: Setting game levels that progressively increase in difficulty:

In "The Mystery of Binary Principle" game, four mini-games are designed so that learners can choose which game to play, similar to how learners choose their own levels in a game. With more choices, learners will continue to play the remaining games once they have played one. In "The Mystery of Binary Principle" game, although there are four mini-games, the core content of the game is related to binary knowledge, so learners gradually understand and even master binary knowledge as they continue to play the game.

In the 'Binary Cards' game, there are many prompts at the beginning of the game that make it easy for learners to complete the game. After playing the game, learners can choose to increase the difficulty of the game as they become more aware of the rules and principles of the game. With this variation in difficulty, the learner is motivated to enter a state of mental flow.

5 Key Technologies

Scratch uses an event-driven programming model, where in-game behaviors and interactions are driven by the triggering of events. Use event-driven programming in "The Mystery of Binary Principle" game to respond to events such as user clicks on cards, timer updates, and more to enable game interaction and logic. Scratch provides data management and variable functions, using variables in the "The Mystery of Binary Principle" game to track the status, score, timing and other information of the game and make logical judgments and game control based on the value of the variables. In addition, Scratch provides a rich library of media resources, including graphics, sounds, and animations, using the graphics resources provided by Scratch to draw the appearance of the cards in "The Mystery of Binary Principle" game, using sound resources to add sound effects, and using animation resources to enhance the visual effects of the game.

In the 'Binary Cards' game, the above technologies are used comprehensively, so the algorithm of the game is displayed, and the specific implementation refers to the following algorithm:

Algorithm 1 The algorithm for setting the initial state of the game

Input: None

1: If set the image background = "Binary Cards"=True：

2： Show cards {"1", "2", "4", "8", "16"}

3： Displays the role {"Refresh Target Score", "Return to Main Interface", "Game Tip 2", "Advance"}

4： Initial value settings for integral variables: Target score = Random numbers (1：31)， My card score = 0

Algorithm 2 "card. Clicked" message response algorithm

Input: None

Output: Pop

1: Play sound effect = "Pop"

Algorithm 3 "card. Flip" message response algorithm

Input：My card score =0, Card total =0

1: card1 =1, card2 =2, card3 =4, card4 =8, card5 =16 #The values of the five cards are 1, 2, 4, 8, 16

2: Variable "Card total" = sum of clicked "card" constants

3: My card score == My card score + Card total

4: if My card score == Target score:

5： broadcast ="dance"

6： Show Role = "Dance", Role "Dance". Size = 10

Algorithm 4 Broadcast the "dance" message response algorithm

Input: None

1: Play sound effect = "Magic Spell"

2: points += 1

3: Repeat 30 times：# Make text appear longer

4： Display text ="Correct"

5: Wait 2 seconds

6: Hide Role = "Correct"

Algorithm 5 "Advance. Clicked" message response algorithm

Input: None

1: Hide variable = "My card score" # Advanced mode, increase difficulty, hide hints

2: Hidden text hints = "Card hints"

Algorithm 6 "Refresh Target Score" message response algorithm
Input: None
1: Initial value setting of integral variables: Target score = random number (1:31)
2: Display Text = "Target Score Refreshed"

Algorithm 7 "Game Tip 2.Clicked" message response algorithm
Input: None
1： If set image background="Game Tip"=True:
2： Display text = "Game Rules"

Algorithm 8 "Return to Main Interface."
Input: None
Output: Main interface
1： return Main interface ()

6 Conclusion

By introducing the concepts of flow theory and gamification education, the ideas and principles of educational game design based on the flow game framework are discussed, and the practical application of "the mystery of binary principles" is carried out. The results show that flow theory and gamified experience can be integrated into educational game design to promote educational games for students' flow experience. In the design of educational games, if the factors of gamified learning experience and flow experience are not considered at the same time, it will be difficult to get learners to engage in the game to learn knowledge. Otherwise, if learners cannot enter the flow state in the educational game, the educational game will not be able to attract students, and then the designed educational game will have no practical value.

Although this paper has performed relevant theoretical research and practical application to educational game design, there are still shortcomings. Due to the limitations of the selected application cases, all the design principles in the theoretical framework could not be applied to game design, so the designed educational game could only partially reflect the ideas of the Flow Game framework. In future research, the theoretical framework can be applied to different educational game designs to comprehensively test the guiding nature of the design framework. In addition, the developed educational game allows learners to experience it for themselves, investigate the actual experience of learners after playing the game, and then continuously modify and improve the educational game and design framework according to the survey results.

Acknowledgements. Project funding: 1. Yunnan Key Laboratory of Smart Education.2. Ideological and Political Construction of the Course "Research on Artificial Intelligence Education in Primary and Secondary Schools". Yunnan International Joint R&D Center of China-Laos-Thailand Educational Digitalization, Project No.: 202203AP140006.

References

1. Junfei, Y., Jianxia, Z.: Educational games and learning: concepts, theories and applications. J. Educ. **12**, 14–19 (2018). https://doi.org/10.16215/j.cnki.cn44-1371/g4.2018.12.004
2. Ryan, R.M., Deci, E.L.: Self-determination theory and the facilitation of intrinsic motivation, social development, and well-being. Am. Psychol. **55**(1), 68–78 (2000)
3. Zhenyu, L., Yujing, L., Jihui, Z.: How self-efficacy affects learning outcomes in a desktop virtual reality environment: the mediating role of mind-flow experience. J. Dist. Educ. **40**(04), 55–64 (2022). https://doi.org/10.15881/j.cnki.cn33-1304/g4.2022.04.005
4. Chang, L.: Exploration of a positive psychology-oriented mental health education curriculum system for college students. Fujian tea **41**(06), 165–166 (2019)
5. Ruxue, L., Youqun, R.: Research on mind-flow experience and empathy effect in immersive virtual environment. Electrochem. Educ. Res. **40**(04), 99–105 (2019). https://doi.org/10.13811/j.cnki.eer.2019.04.013
6. Csikszentmihalyi, M.: Flow: The Psychology of Optimal Experience. Harper Collins, New York (1990)
7. Zhang, P., Finneran, C.: Flow in computer-mediated environments: promises and challenges. Soc. Sci. Electron. Publ. **15**(4), 82–101 (2013)
8. Ya-jie, Z.H.O.U., Sha-na, W.A.N.G.: A case study of app interface design based on mind flow theory. Electron. Technol. **50**(11), 20–24 (2021)
9. Winchao, Z., Lei, Y., Ruoxiong, Y., Hang, Y.: From gamified learning to learning metaverse: a new framework for immersive learning and the essentials of practice. J. Distance Educ. **40**(04), 3–13 (2022). https://doi.org/10.15881/j.cnki.cn33-1304/g4.2022.04.004
10. Xu, J., Yang, W.C., Li, M.L., Ma, Y.M.: International hotspots of game-based learning research in China and its implications and implications for China–an analysis based on the articles contained in computers & education (2013–2017). J. Distance Educ. **36**(06), 73–83 (2018). https://doi.org/10.15881/j.cnki.cn33-1304/g4.2018.06.008
11. Li, C.-B.: Embodied cognition and gamified learning:the return and innovation of adult training. Adult Educ. **37**(06), 10–14 (2017)
12. Lu, Z., Junjie, S.: Research on the theory of gamification learning based on the perspective of learning experience. Electrochem. Educ. Res. **39**(06), 11–20+26 (2018). https://doi.org/10.13811/j.cnki.eer.2018.06.002
13. Zhang, L., Ruonan, H., Jialing, Z., Junjie, S.: How to design scientific, effective and interesting educational games–a study on the design of mathematical games from the interdisciplinary perspective of learning science. Electrochem. Educ. Res. **42**(10), 70–76 (2021). https://doi.org/10.13811/j.cnki.eer.2021.10.010
14. Lu, Z., Mingyu, H., Junjie, S.: A qualitative analysis study of gamified learning experience. China Distance Educ. **542**(03), 35–41+80–81 (2020). https://doi.org/10.13541/j.cnki.chinade.2020.03.005
15. Guoshuai, L., Jiazai, W., Chunyu, H., Yi, Z., Yuting, H., Xiaoli, Z.: The learning metaverse empowers education: constructing a new model of smart+ educational applications. J. Dist. Educ. **40**(02), 35–44 (2022). https://doi.org/10.15881/j.cnki.cn33-1304/g4.2022.02.003

Construction and Research on Learning State Analysis in Classroom Teaching

Qingquan Zhou[1], Xiner Shen[2], Xiaoyu Du[1](✉), Daojun Han[3], and Baojun Qiao[1]

[1] College of Computer and Information Engineering, Henan University, Kaifeng 475004, China
dxy@henu.edu.cn

[2] Department of Government and Public Administration, The Chinese University of Hong Kong, New Territories, Hong Kong Special Administrative Region, Hong Kong, China

[3] Henan Engineering Laboratory of Spatial Information Processing, Kaifeng 475004, China

Abstract. The learning state of students in the classroom is affected by many aspects of influence. According to the neural network and equation of state, this paper analyzes effect of classroom in the University. This paper first puts forward the improvement scheme of classroom teaching and constructs a simplified mathematical model of the students' brain in the classroom, then points out the main information and its description signals in the classroom, and finally under the stimulation of these signals, mathematical language was used to qualitatively describe the excited state of the brain. According to the analysis of the mathematical model, this paper summarizes the teaching scheme of tacit cooperation between teachers and students to improve the effect.

Keywords: Neural network · Learning state · Classroom teaching · Mathematical modeling

1 Introduction

"Students should play the main role with the dominance of teachers"is the basic requirement for the comprehensive implementation of quality education [1], which is reflected in classroom teaching, that is, teachers teach knowledge in a planned, purposeful, creative and step-by-step manner based on the textbooks; Students concentrate, think positively, and absorb knowledge in a timely manner. Students absorb knowledge, which is closely related to the excited state of the brain, and the teacher's teaching is full of interest and willing to accept linear correlation. Only when the two sides cooperate tacitly, can satisfactory results be achieved [2–4]. Therefore, it should be the most basic and important topic in teaching research to explore the excited state of students' brains in the classroom and the teaching methods of teachers. This paper firstly uses the

J. Gan et al. (Eds.): CSEI 2023, CCIS 1899, pp. 91–100, 2024.
https://doi.org/10.1007/978-981-99-9499-1_8

method of mathematical modeling to construct a simplified mathematical model of the brain for students' classroom learning, and then selects several kinds of information that often affect classroom teaching and describes them with signals. The main information description signals of these classes are divided into three categories: incidental information, interference incidental information and prior knowledge information. It shows the excited state of the brain in these cases, that is, the solution of the volume-resistance system. Finally, based on these analyses, suggestions are given for the establishment of excellent classrooms for college students, such as grasping the key points of lectures, encouraging students to ask questions, and starting or leaving classes on time.

2 Simplified Mathematical Model of the Brain

2.1 The Magical Brain

It is generally believed in the scientific and technological circles: "The human brain is the most sophisticated and reliable 'machine' formed by biological evolution in nature" [5]. It is a perfect information processing center, information storage center and command control center. The brain is estimated to contain about 86 billion neurons, divided into hundreds of different types. In 1943, the first neural network model McCulloch-Pitts neuron was proposed by McCulloh and Pitts, which is a logic unit with a delay function with multiple inputs and one output. The number of inputs is arbitrarily large, but finite; the outputs are only two states: excitation and inhibition. Assume that exactly one time beat elapses from the moment the input acts to the moment when the neuron is excited or inhibited, and assumes that the time beat is the same for all different types of neurons. Then, a neuron is essentially equivalent to an inseparable combination of a logic unit and a delay unit whose delay time is one beat, so that a temporal logic equation with a uniform beat can be used to describe a neural network composed of multiple neurons. The input and output of a finite number of neurons constitute a state component, and the excitation or inhibition of the neuron output determines the value of the state component. Therefore, a neural network composed of S neurons can have at most 2^S states. Figure 1 shows a simple neural network:

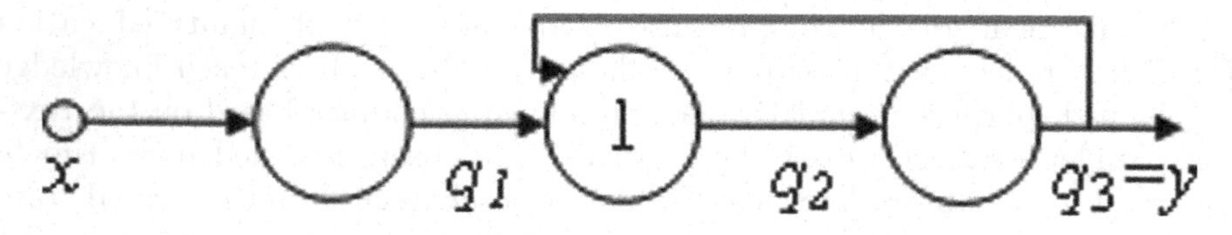

Fig. 1. Simple neural network diagram.

The simple neural network shown above has a state space expression of:

$$
\begin{aligned}
y(k) &= q_3(k) \\
q_3(k) &= q_2(k-1) \\
q_2(k) &= q_1(k-1) + q_3(k-1) \\
q_1(k) &= x(k-1)
\end{aligned} \tag{1}
$$

The brain has 86 billion neurons, which can form a huge number of simple and complex neural networks, so the state space expression is very complex, and the state space expression only shows the input-output relationship of the neural network. Since about 1015 binary bits of brain information are not included in the state space expression, the understanding of the brain is still at a preliminary stage. Therefore, well-known science and technology leaders Qian Xuesen and Song Jian pointed out:"Understanding the principles of thinking activities and specific structural functions of the human brain is always a most fascinating and scientifically significant subject" [6].

2.2 A Simplified Math Model of the Brain for Students' Classroom Learning

According to existing research results, such as McCulloch-Pitts neurons, that is, a combination of logic units with multiple inputs and one output and delay units delayed by one beat. The input and output ports of the neurons in the brain are connected in a certain way to form a neural network with the function of simulating students' classroom learning. For this neural network, only when the number of excitatory inputs is at least h more than the number of inhibitory inputs, it is in an excitatory state, where h is a finite value. These h or more synthesis can be called input ports. This is the physical reason why the brain works with high reliability. Each neuron contains a delay unit, and the input signal at any moment needs to go through a time beat to get a response at the output. Then, the neural network contains a limited number of m delay time beats, and these m delay time beats represent the response time of people receiving information (transactions). In this way, the brain can be thought of as a receptacle for receiving knowledge, and reaction times indicate resistance to receiving knowledge. Therefore, it is appropriate to use a volume-resistance system to describe students' brains during classroom learning. Differential equations describing capacity-resistance systems.

$$
\tau \frac{dy(t)}{dt} + y(t) = x(t) \tag{2}
$$

in the formula:

x(t)-The input signal of the neural network;

y(t)-The output signal of the neural network;

τ-Reaction time of neural network.

Under the zero-initial condition, perform Laplace transform on (2), and obtain the transfer function *w(s)* that indicates the input-output relationship.

$$w(s) = \frac{y(s)}{x(s)} = \frac{1}{\tau s + 1} = \frac{\frac{1}{\tau}}{s + \frac{1}{\tau}} \quad (3)$$

3 Main Messages in Class and Their Descriptive Signals

There are many factors that affect classroom teaching. This article selects several that occur frequently and play an important role, mark them, and describe them with signals. The strength of various signals is not the same. For the convenience of analysis, the unit signal is always used.

3.1 Teacher Teaching

In the classroom, teachers use the pronunciation of each word, the words form phrases, the phrases form sentences, and the sentences are connected to express the meaning of the story. Although the pronunciation is discrete, the explanations that students receive are carried out continuously according to the meaning. Of course, teachers have cadence and other speaking skills in their lectures, but the volume fluctuates and the time interval is not large. Naturally, there are differences in the lectures of different teachers [7]. Ignoring the nuances of the teacher's lecture, the signal of the lecture can be represented by the unit step signal *u(t)*.

$$u(t) = \begin{cases} 0, t < 0 \\ 1, t >= 0 \end{cases} \quad (4)$$

Use *u(t)=1(t)* to replace the above formula.

3.2 Incidental Information

This kind of information will happen by chance, but it is common, such as the teacher's questioning; making and speaking behaviors and language that interest students, etc. Due to the short time, the time of occurrence is also random, using Dirac function representation.

$$\begin{cases} \int_{-\infty}^{+\infty} \delta(t)dt = 1 \\ \delta(t) = 0, t \neq 0 \end{cases} \quad (5)$$

Shift the time domain of $\delta(t)$ to ζ_{i2}.

$$\delta_{1,\zeta_{i2}}(t) = \delta(t - \zeta_{i2}) \quad (6)$$

The subscript 1 represents the unit of the Dirac function $\delta(t)$; ζ is a set of i random time variables, i represents the number of occurrences of ζ_i, ζ_{i2} represents the moment when the signal occurs, i = 0,1,2,3. . . .

3.3 Interfere with Occasional Information

In the classroom, it may happen to individual people, such as students whispering, yawning loudly, etc. Outside the classroom, like loud noises, calling sounds, etc. This kind of information is called interfering incidental information, and it also happens by chance. The signal properties are similar to formula (6). Since it is interference, the formula (6) is reversed along the time axis, and the occurrence time is represented by ζ_{2i}.

$$\delta_{1,\zeta_{2i}}(t) = \delta(t - \zeta_{2i}) \tag{7}$$

The subscript annotation class is used in equation (6), and ζ_2 is used to distinguish it from ζ_1.

3.4 Prior Knowledge Information

Brief brain excites are bound to occur every class. Obviously, there are two kinds of excitement at the beginning of the class and when the teacher enters the classroom to give a lecture, and the time difference between them is very short, which can be represented by the same Dirac function.

$$\delta_{1,0}(t) = \delta(t) \tag{8}$$

Translate the Eq. (8) by δ in the time domain, and then reverse the fold along the vertical axis, then

$$\delta_{1,\delta}(t) = \delta(-t + \delta) \tag{9}$$

This formula expresses excitement near the end of class, where δ represents the time of a class, and the rest of the subscripts of Eq. (8) and Eq. (9) are similar to Eq. (6).

3.5 Analysis of Students Sleeping and Lack of Con-Centration in Class

In both cases, students are not able to accept the knowledge taught by the teacher when they are sleeping and their thoughts are not concentrating in class, and they will continue for a period of time, which can be represented by a rectangular pulse, and the duration is set to b.

$$G_{1,b}(t) = \begin{cases} 1, 0 \le t \le b \\ 0, t < 0, t > b \end{cases} \tag{10}$$

The time domain of $G_{1,b}(t)$ is shifted to ζ_{3i}, and the rectangular pulse signal after deconvoluted along the time axis is expressed as:

$$G_{1,b\zeta_{3i}}(t) = -[u(t - \zeta_{3i}) - u(t - \zeta_{3i} - b)] \tag{11}$$

In the formula: ζ_{3i} is the moment when either of the above two situations occurs, and it is also a random amount of time. In the classroom, there may be more than one person who sleeps and lack of concentration, and there may be more than one person, and the number of occurrences *i=0,1,2,3....*

3.6 Mental Fatigue

The brain accounts for only 2% of the body weight, but the blood demand accounts for 15% of the cardiac output, and the oxygen consumption accounts for 25% of the whole body. It can be seen that the workload of the brain is the heaviest among the various organs of the human body, and the brain is the most easily fatigued. After a period of time, people will involuntarily want to rest and sleep, that is, the brain is in a state of inhibition. As mentioned earlier, the brain is only in the excited state when there are h more neurons in the excited state than in the inhibitory state. Over time, the number of neurons in the excited state will gradually decrease. As long as there are no less than h, the brain is still in a state of excitement, when there are less than h, the brain is in a state of inhibition. This is a process of change from gradual change to qualitative change. This process varies from person to person. Most students can be excited for the entire class; some students are sluggish and even sleep [8].

At the beginning, the student is in a highly excited state, that is, the initial value $y(t)|_{t=0} \neq 0$ of the excited state is set to $y(0$. Since the energy of $y(0)$ is very small, it will be quickly consumed in the capacity-resistance system, and it is regarded as a Dirac function$\tau(t)$, and the change of the excited state is observed under the condition of zero input, that is, $x(t) = 0$. Change τ in formula (2) to k, and do Laplace transform:

$$kys(s) - y(0) + y(s) = 0 \tag{12}$$

$$y(s) = \frac{\frac{y(0)}{k}}{s + \frac{1}{k}} \tag{13}$$

In the formula, k is the time that the brain experiences from the excited state to the inhibitory state, and do the inverse Laplace transform:

$$y(t) = \frac{y(0)}{k} e^{-\frac{1}{k}t} \tag{14}$$

As explained earlier, the brain output only has two states of excitation and inhibition. The above formula represents the change of the excited state, then the inhibitory state caused by mental fatigue can be expressed as:

$$y^*(t) = \frac{y(0)}{k} [1 - e^{-\frac{1}{k}t}] \tag{15}$$

Expand $e^{-\frac{1}{k}t}$ into a Taylor series, since $\frac{1}{k}$ is a relatively small quantity, the high-order terms above the second order can be omitted.

$$y^*(t) = \frac{y(0)}{k} t \tag{16}$$

Relative to the excited state, it is unfolded along the time axis as

$$\bar{y}(t) = -\frac{y(0)}{k} t \tag{17}$$

It can be seen from Eq. (17) that the decrease in the excitation state caused by mental fatigue is relatively slow. During a class time, the vast majority of people are still able to learn in a state of excitement.

4 The State of the Brain Receiving Knowledge in the Classroom

In Sect. 2, the main information description signals of the classroom can be divided into three categories. Among them, the formula (17) has already shown the decrease in the excitation state of the brain caused by mental fatigue. Only for the other two types of situations, the excited state of the brain under the excitation of the signal is explained, that is, the total solution of the volume-resistance system is sought. Equations (4) and (10) are both unit step signals, but the time of occurrence is different. The change of the brain excitation state caused by the excitation of the unit step signal $u(t)$ at time zero.

$$y(t) = 1 - e^{-\frac{1}{\tau}t} \tag{18}$$

This is the case when the teacher's lecture stimulates changes in the brain's excitation. Using the time domain transfer characteristics of the unit impulse function $\delta(t - t_0)$, Eq. (18) can be moved to any specified time position.

$$f(t) * \delta(t - t_0) = f(t - t_0) \tag{19}$$

The brain excitation state change caused by Eq. (10) is:

$$y(t) = -(1 - e^{-\frac{1}{\tau}t})[u(t - \zeta_{3i}) - u(t - \zeta_{3i} - b)] \tag{20}$$

That is, the changes in the brain's 'excited' state caused by students sleeping and lack of con-centration in the classroom. Equations (5), (7), and (9) in Sect. 2 are all Dirac functions (unit impulse signal Eq. (5)). There are simultaneous occurrences, the excitement at the beginning of the class and the excitement when the teacher gives a lecture, which can be expressed by the formula (5), which is like the function $x(s) = L[\delta(t)] = 1$. The excited state of the brain caused by it:

$$\bar{y}(t) = L^{-1}[w(s) \times 1] = L^{-1}[\frac{\frac{1}{\tau}}{s + \frac{1}{\tau}}] = \frac{1}{\tau}e^{-\frac{1}{\tau}t} \tag{21}$$

The transmission coefficient will be affected by many factors. For the convenience of analysis, if it is set to 1, then

$$y(t) = e^{-\frac{1}{\tau}t} \tag{22}$$

The rest all occurred at different times. Also, using the time domain transfer characteristics of the unit impulse signal $\delta(t-t_0)$, the brain excitation state caused by the unit impulse signal excitation expressed by Eqs. (6), (7), and (9) is expressed as:

$$y(t) = e^{-\frac{1}{\tau}t}u(t-\zeta_{i2}) \tag{23}$$

$$y(t) = e^{-\frac{1}{\tau}t}u(t-\zeta_{2i}) \tag{24}$$

$$y(t) = e^{-\frac{1}{\tau}t}u(-t+\delta) \tag{25}$$

The capacity-resistance system represented by formula (3) is a simplified mathematical model of the brain, which belongs to a linear system. One of its extremely important and invaluable properties applies the principle of selection and addition, and is represented by an image function:

$$y(s) = w(s)[\sum_{j=1}^{8} x_j(s)] = \sum_{j=1}^{8} x_j(s)w(s) \tag{26}$$

The changes in the brain excitation state caused by the chronological order of the excitation effects are listed in Table 1. The excited state of the brain in a class is shown in (27), when the occasional disturbance does not occur, there is no item y_6; when there is no student sleeping or thinking drifting apart, there is no item y_7.

$$\begin{aligned} y(t) &= \sum_{j=1}^{8} y_j \\ &= e^{-\frac{1}{\tau}t} + e^{-\frac{1}{\tau}t} + (1-e^{-\frac{1}{\tau}t}) - \frac{y(0)}{k}t + e^{-\frac{1}{\tau}(t-\zeta_{i2})} - e^{-\frac{1}{\tau}(t-\zeta_{2i})} \\ &- (1-e^{-\frac{1}{\tau}t}[u(t-\zeta_{3i}) - u(t-\zeta_{3i}-b)] + e^{-\frac{1}{\tau}(-t+\sigma)} \\ &= 1 + e^{-\frac{1}{\tau}t} - \frac{y(0)}{k}t + e^{-\frac{1}{\tau}(t-\zeta_{i2})} - e^{-\frac{1}{\tau}(t-\zeta_{2i})} \\ &- (1-e^{-\frac{1}{\tau}t})[u(t-\zeta_{3i}) - u(t-\zeta_{3i}-b)] + e^{-\frac{1}{\tau}(-t+\sigma)} \end{aligned} \tag{27}$$

Table 1. List of brain excitation states and related signals

Motivating Effect		Changes in brain excitation	
Excited of classes begin	$\delta_1(t)$	y_1	$e^{-\frac{1}{\tau}t}$
Excited of lecture begin	$\delta_2(t)$	y_2	$e^{-\frac{1}{\tau}t}$
Teacher lecture	$u(t)$	y_3	$1-e^{-\frac{1}{\tau}t}$
Mental fatigue	$y(0)$	y_4	$-\frac{y(0)}{k}t$
Beneficial occasional signal	$\delta_{\zeta_{i2}}(i=0,1,2...)$	y_5	$e^{-\frac{1}{\tau}(t-\zeta_{i2})}$
Interfering occasional signals	$\delta_{\zeta_{2i}}(i=0,1,2...)$	y_6	$-e^{-\frac{1}{\tau}(t-\zeta_{i2})}$
Sleep and mind desertion	$\delta_b = -[u(t-\zeta_{3i}) - u(t-\zeta_{3i}-b)]$	y_7	$-(1-e^{-\frac{1}{\tau}t})[u(t-\zeta_{3i}) - u(t-\zeta_{3i}-b)]$
Excited at the end of class	$\delta_3(t)$	y_8	$e^{-\frac{1}{\tau}(-t+\sigma)}$

5 Conclusion

According to the previous analysis, it can be seen that the teaching effect of a class is affected by many aspects. The final output $y(t)$ is directly related to the teacher's lecture, the status of the students, and the length of time. Therefore, the following suggestions are made for excellent classrooms in universities:

(1) Entertaining and entertaining, using vivid language and visual actions will generate incentives that are conducive to learning, and follow the good guidance, so that students will be full of interest and attentive to the class, which will significantly improve the effect of classroom teaching.
(2) Study textbooks, often talk about often new. Not only memorize the content of the textbook, but also summarize the characteristics of the course, the organic connection and key points of the content, for example, the key to the circuit lies in Kirchhoff's laws: KCL and KVL. For what is inappropriate and wrong, it is necessary to make rigorous and thorough arguments and have unique opinions. It is best to do it by yourself according to the topic of the lecture, then read the textbook, learn from each other's strengths, and write in-depth lesson plans. The great Mao Zedong once criticized: The teacher who copied the content of the book on the blackboard and then let the students copy from the blackboard to the notes is the most incompetent. For courses that have been taught 1–2 times, still take seriously.
(3) Lecture content is substantial and concise. For the content that students can understand at a glance, simply explain it, and for the key and difficult content, do in-depth analysis and explain in detail. And there should be signs to remind students to review to deepen memory. To be detailed and appropriate, focused.
(4) At the beginning, the students are full of energy. Briefly describe the content. After that, take the time to teach new content, and don't spend too long on reviewing the relevant learned content. Timely reminders can be given for students to recall and review after class. Make students connect new knowledge with original knowledge. The more connections, the deeper the understanding and the stronger the memory. Towards the end of the class, summarize the content of the lesson in time. At this time, it is also the high excitement point of the student's brain, which can enhance the effect of the lecture.
(5) In the classroom, teachers should have sufficient participation and avoid a single way of laying out directly, so as to prevent students from being uninterested, resulting in fatigue, drowsiness, or even sleep, which seriously affects the effect of listening to the class. Once there is a student sleeping in class, don't wake him up immediately, let him sleep for a few minutes and then wake up, it can make the student more awake, and it is worth it instead of being groggy throughout the class.
(6) Get to and from get out of class on time, don't delay the end of get out of class, and have plenty of breaks in between. Do not take two classes in a row. Brain fatigue will increase linearly in a short period of time. After a long period of time, it will increase exponentially, and fatigue will increase rapidly.

The famous American educator Jeannette Vos put forward: "In all learning process, intermittent rest is necessary". "...the more breaks you take, the more 'beginning' and 'ending' highlights you'll have."

(7) Encourage students to ask questions, be willing to discuss problems with students, and communicate with each other. When encountering problems that own have not thought of and cannot answer, can study and solve them together. Don't say no, don't deal with it casually. This situation is a sign of deep thinking for students and should be happy. Teachers should be able to guide, motivate, and facilitate students' learning. Han Yu, an advocate of the ancient prose movement in the Tang Dynasty once said: teacher is the one who could propagate the doctrine, impart professional knowledge, and resolve doubts.

Acknowledgements. This research was supported by This research was supported by Henan Province Higher Education Teaching Reform Research and Practice Project (2021SJGLX080,2019SJGLX044); Henan Province Teacher Education Curriculum Reform Research Project (2022-JSJYYB-025); Henan Province New Engineering Research and Practice Project (2020JGLX011); Henan University undergraduate teaching reform research and practice project (HDXJJG2018-04, HDXJJG2019-10, HDXJJG2020-13, HDXJJG2021-047, HDXJJG2021-116); Henan University Graduate education and Teaching Reform Research and Practice Project (YJSJG2022XJ056); Postgraduate Cultivating Innovation and Quality Improvement Action Plan of Henan University(SYLAL2022018, SYLKC2022022).

References

1. Peng, Q., Wang, B.: Thematic analysis of the research on the relationship between teachers and students in the past 70 years in my country [J]. Curr., Teach. Mater. Method **39**(02), 19–26 (2019)
2. Chvátal, V., et al.: McCulloch-Pitts brains and pseudorandom functions. Neural Comput. **28**(6), 1042–1050 (2016)
3. Lu, F., Wei, L.: The construction and application of an intelligent analysis system for classroom learning status. J. Yancheng Teach. Univ.(Humanities & Social Sciences Edition) **39**(06), 99–103 (2019)
4. Zhang, M.: Research on classroom behavior state analysis based on natural environment[D]. Central China Normal University (2020)
5. Li, H., Wen, Z.: Introduction to Natural Science [M]. Nanjing University Press, 2019.01.267
6. Liu, S.: A Study of Howard Gardner's Educational Thought [D]. Harbin Normal University (2016)
7. Deng, H., Liang, J.: Research on the influence of college teachers' body language on students' classroom engagement. High. Educ. Sci. **01**, 75–80 (2021)
8. Huang, Y., Liu, X.: A study on the learning behavior of higher vocational students in mathematical modeling classroom. Occupation **24**, 93–94 (2020)

On the Teaching Innovation Mode of "One Center, Two Closed Loops and Three Drives" from the Perspective of Curriculum Ideology and Politics

Huamei Qi[1,2], Yisu Jin[2], Dan Cao[2], Xiaoyan Kui[1], and Fei Tang[3](✉)

[1] School of Computer Science and Engineering, Central South University, Changsha, China
[2] Teacher Development Center, Central South University, Changsha, China
[3] School of Electrical Engineering and Automation, Wuhan University, Wuhan, China
tangfei@whu.edu.cn

Abstract. Through the analysis of the current situation of ideological and political teaching in professional courses, find the pain points in the current teaching mode, put forward the teaching innovation mode of "one center, two closed loops and three drives, and give the "data structure" of the basic course of the School of Computer Science as an example to practice cases of the reform planning to provide reference for the ideological and political construction of the curriculum.

Keywords: Innovative teaching mode · Curriculum ideological and political · Closed-loop and driven

1 Introduction

In 2020, the Ministry of Education will further promote universities to accelerate the pace of innovation and do a good job in training leading innovation talents. In the same year, the Ministry of Education issued the Guiding Outline for Ideological and Political Construction in Institutions of Higher Learning. The Outline points out that colleges and universities should deepen the reform of education and teaching, fully tap the ideological and political resources of various courses, give full play to the educational role of each course, and comprehensively improve the quality of talent training [2]. It can be seen that "ideological and political" not only provides an opportunity for the development of higher education in the new era, but also inspires college teachers' thinking and exploration for the future development of higher education. The comprehensive implementation of curriculum ideological and political education is an important measure of ideological and political education in the new era. The fundamental problem of "who to cultivate, how to train people and who to cultivate people" has also become an urgent problem to be solved.

This paper first analyzes the construction situation of "ideological and political" and finds the "pain points" in the process of ideological and political teaching. Discuss the innovative teaching mode of "one center, two closed loop and three driven" under

J. Gan et al. (Eds.): CSEI 2023, CCIS 1899, pp. 101–107, 2024.
https://doi.org/10.1007/978-981-99-9499-1_9

the ideological and political perspective of the course: student-centered, teaching design and ideological and political closed loop, interest driven, goal driven and mission driven. Finally, practice it in the data structure course and make continuous improvement.

2 The Dilemma in Computer Subject Teaching

As a typical major of engineering, the teaching of computer science comes from production practice and mainly analyzes the objective development law of things. Because the courses are closely related to mathematics, physics and other science knowledge, the "ideological and political" education is more difficult than the humanities and social science courses. The existing problems are:

A. **Students' lack of interest and motivation in learning**

Some students lack professional identity and professional confidence, are not very interested in learning, and lack of learning motivation. In the traditional classroom teaching mode, students are in the position of passively accepting knowledge, which also causes the phenomenon of truancy and phubbers. Students have no desire for active learning, generally enjoy passive acceptance of knowledge, after class active learning and exploration is insufficient.

B. **Students' practical ability is not strong, lack of team and innovation consciousness**

Computer subjects have many course experiments, the practice is complex, and students are prone to fear of difficulties. Students emphasize self-development and lack a sense of collaboration. Students can't really understand the connotation and application. In classroom learning, they are used to copying things in the course, are not good at solving problems through their own problems, tend to seek the help of teachers, and lack of innovative consciousness.

C. **Students have a weak sense of mission**

Students in the ivory tower of the university, can not feel the needs of the society, the sense of professional mission is very weak, always feel that the construction of the motherland is too early, still do not need to consider.

3 Teaching Innovation Mode of "One Central Loop, Two Closed Loop and Three Drives"

Education in the new era advocates the student-centered construction concept, cultivates correct values to develop talents in an all-round way, and cultivates interdisciplinary innovative talents with international competitiveness. Combined with the above pain points of "ideological and political" education in teaching, the teaching innovation mode of "one center, two closed loop and three drive" is designed. That is, the student-centered teaching design of "learning situation analysis, teaching objectives, teaching content, teaching implementation, teaching evaluation and teaching reflection", and the ideological and political closed loop of "height, depth, heat, correlation, temperature and achievement". On this basis, "interest-driven, goal-driven and mission-driven" are used to promote students to learn knowledge, ability and value well. The specific scheme of the construction is shown in Fig. 1.

One center is student-centered. Reconstruction teaching and discussion modules to ensure the ideological and political guidance and gender of learning content. Consider students' preferences and habits, and make full use of various information resources and platforms. While "case teaching" and "problem solving" are taken as the main line of learning and research activities, "collaborative learning" is emphasized, and process evaluation is considered.

The two closed loops include "teaching design closed loop" and "ideological and political six-degree closed loop". Teaching design closed loop is: "learning situation analysis-teaching objective-teaching content-teaching implementation-teaching evaluation-teaching reflection"; ideological and political six degree closed loop is: "height, depth, heat, correlation, temperature and achievement".

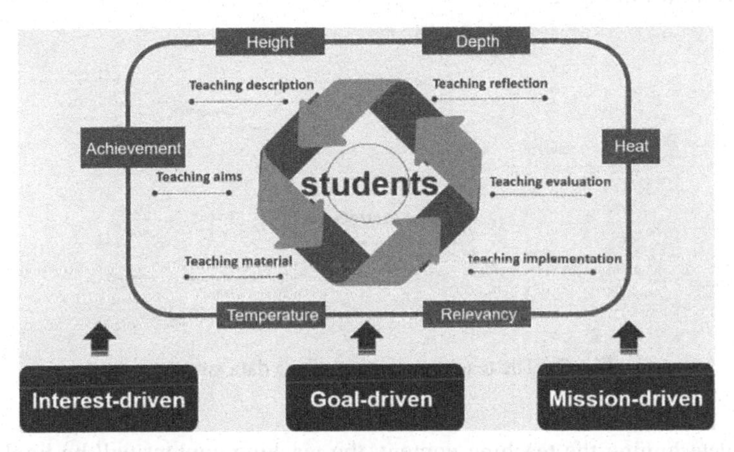

Fig. 1. Construction idea of "one center, two closed loops and three drives"

The three drivers include: interest driven, goal driven and mission driven. Interest-driven students enjoy it, be fully online and deeply involved in learning; goal-driven clear goals, motivate students, diagnose teaching, and make continuous improvement; mission-driven to cultivate professional responsibility and promote engineering thinking.

The teaching innovation mode of "one center, two closed-ops and three drives" takes students as the implementation object, creates the implementation path with "teaching design closed-loop", and tests the implementation effect with "ideological and political six-degree closed-loop". Then with three drive as a push force, let the students happy to learn, learn, learn fine.

4 Innovative Practice of the "Data Structure" Course

According to the requirements of "innovative teaching mode", as a basic course of computer science, the "data structure" course changes the previous teaching goal of only knowledge education, formulates the 3H new teaching goal, and deeply penetrates the "ideological and political" into the course teaching. The practice process is elaborated in detail below.

By analyzing the foundation of mathematics and programming of the "data structure" course, To conduct the study situation analysis, To determine the teaching objectives of the course according to the situation analysis, Including knowledge objectives: to explain the logical structure and storage structure of linear tables, trees and graphs, Can analyze various data structure algorithms, Can display the sorting and finding algorithms; Ability objective: Ability to select and construct appropriate data structures and design appropriate algorithms, Ability to prepare and debug programs correctly using the programming language, Be able to use professional knowledge to contribute to national key core technologies; Quality objective: Good political literacy, Strong sense of mission and responsibility, Good professionalism, Strong teamwork ability, Have a good materialist dialectical literacy, Strong innovation and practical ability. The teaching content is determined according to the teaching objectives. The teaching content of the data structure is shown in Fig. 2.

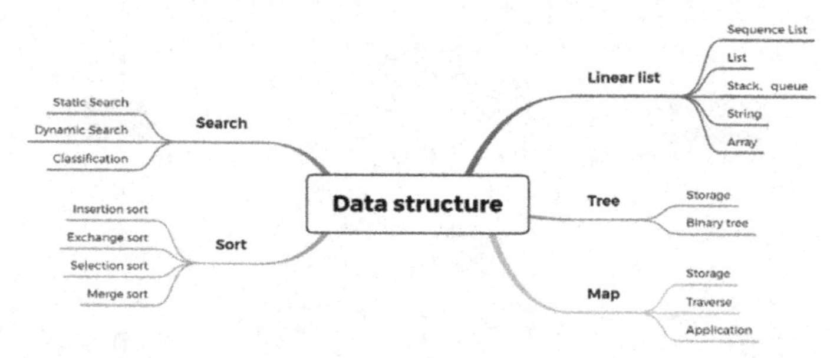

Fig. 2. The teaching content of the data structure

After determining the teaching content, the teaching content will be implemented from the two aspects of cooperation and practice to highlight the quality objectives of the curriculum. As shown in Fig. 3.

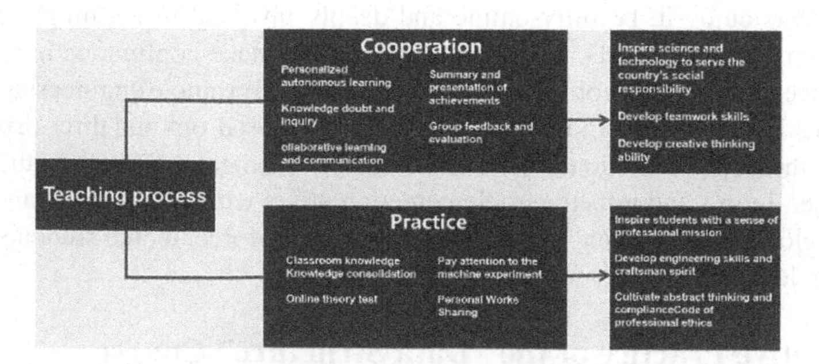

Fig. 3. The quality objectives of the curriculum

The whole course is implemented through Before Class, During Class and After Class. In order to achieve the teaching objectives of the above course, the curriculum design is shown in the Fig. 4 [9]. Through the implementation of each link, the "ideological and political thinking" is explored and integrated.

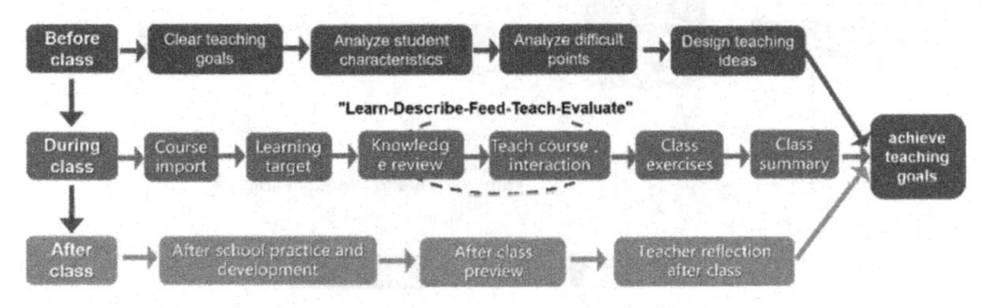

Fig. 4. Curriculum Teaching design

In the whole implementation process, the data structure course summarizes three ideological and political directions, namely, political quality, professional quality and materialist dialectical quality. Political literacy mainly expounds the mission and responsibility, professional quality focuses on teamwork and teamwork spirit, and materialist dialectical literacy focuses on innovation and practical ability. At the same time of construction, the six-degree ideological and political closed-loop should be achieved, as shown in Fig. 5.

In the process of teaching implementation, the course is carried out before, during and after class. Before class, through the visual platform and MOOC preview, homework statistics, on the one hand, consolidate the previous knowledge, preview new knowledge, on the other hand, also exercise students' self-study ability. Lesson: This teaching design consists of six closed links: course introduction, learning objectives, reviewing old and knowing new, course teaching and interaction, application of learning, and course summary. Through the introduction of story, game-style interaction, attract students' attention, stimulate interest. Inform the students of their learning objectives and clarify the purpose of the class. At the same time, the above content is pretested to analyze the students' preview (preview is based on the MOOC of Chinese universities). When teaching and interaction, fully mobilize the enthusiasm of students, take students as the center, use case type, enlightening guidance and problem oriented to guide students to actively participate in the classroom. What you learn to use is a classroom practice, insert the blackboard design, students performance board, on the computer, interaction, to deepen the understanding of knowledge points. The course summary adopts the formula summary, and uses the way of mind mapping to summarize the knowledge points. In the course, the ideological and political points of the course are added to cultivate students' socialist core values and sense of professional mission.

After class, students 'innovative thinking and critical thinking ability are cultivated through homework and expanded thinking, as well as teachers' after-class reflection. Students' after-class exercises are used for consolidation and improvement, which refers to completing homework and thinking questions according to the after-class expansion reference materials given by the teacher, realize the data structure system, participate in

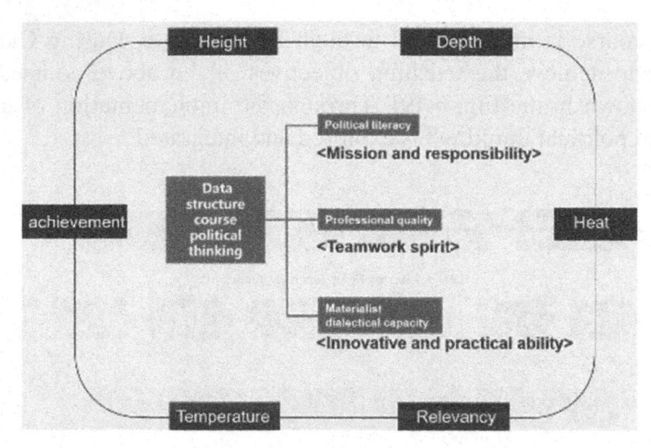

Fig. 5. The six-degree ideological and political closed-loop

projects or competitions, serve the industry, and preview the content of the next class. The teacher's after-class reflection is the teaching postscript, used to correct the teaching.

Finally, through the evaluation and feedback, reflection and improvement. Course cases should come from life, reflecting the correlation, temperature and heat of ideological and political affairs. For example, teaching is close to current affairs such as "epidemic transportation, medical supplies path planning", "looking for the most economical gas transmission network" and so on. Students' practical ability and ideological and political ability are integrated to achieve the effect of education and reflect the depth of thinking and politics. Make full use of information teaching tools and platforms, to provide rich curriculum resources, homework expansion to meet the high order and challenges, reflect the height of ideological and political. From the learning situation analysis, teaching design, evaluation, reflection to form a closed-loop ideological and political feedback mode, reflect the degree of ideological and political achievement. Of course, the ideological and political evaluation rules need to be further improved.

5 Conclusion

Social development requires colleges and universities to cultivate outstanding talents with international vision and innovation ability, and "ideological and political development" requires the training of high-quality talents with responsible responsibilities. The paper constructs the innovative teaching mode of "one center, two closed loop and three drives", expounds from "teaching design closed loop" to "ideological and political six closed loop", sets up the curriculum framework with "teaching design closed loop", tests the construction effect with "ideological and political six closed loop", and practices it in the "data structure" course. The current practice is still preliminary, and there are still a wide range of areas to be explored in the future. According to the development requirements of The Times, we should further strengthen the construction of teachers, accumulate rich experience in education, and implement the mission of "cultivating people by virtue". Through the implementation of the innovation mode of "one center, two closed loop and three drive", we will cultivate outstanding innovative talents with an international vision for the motherland.

References

1. Pengfei, Q.: Fully realize the same direction of ideological and political courses and ideological and political courses. High. Educ. China (13), 3 (2020)
2. Xianmin, P., Ying, W.: Ideological and political teaching reform and practice in new engineering courses——Taking the computer network technology course as an example. Educ. Cult. Forum **5**, 120–125 (2021)
3. Li, Y., Zhongdao, C.: Case design and implementation of course ideology and politics under the background of "new engineering" ——Taking the course of "digital image processing" as an example. Ind. Inf. Technol. Educ. (03), 33–36 + 41 (2021)
4. Jun, N., Dancheng, L.: The exploration and practice of curriculum ideology and politics in computer courses. China Univ. Teach. **3**, 47–51 (2021)
5. Song, Z., Shuhua, D.: Problems and path optimization of ideological and political construction of college curriculum. Sch. Party Build. Ideol. Educ. **649**, 58–60 (2021)
6. The connotation, characteristics, difficulties and coping strategies of curriculum ideology and politics in the new era. J. Xinjiang Norm. Univ. Philos. Soc. Sci. Edition **41**(2), 9 (2020)
7. Lei, C., Yang, S., Bo, H.: The value orientation of curriculum ideological and political construction, realistic dilemma and its practice transcendence. Sch. Party Build. Ideol. Educ. **14**, 3 (2020)
8. Xinjie, Y.: Curriculum ideology and politics in core courses of science and engineering—Why and how to do it. China Univ. Teach. **9**, 56–60 (2019)
9. Huamei, Q., Xiaoyan, K., Ping, Z., et al.: Study on the application of learner's output-oriented Feynman-five-energy method in computer teaching. In: 2021 16th International Conference on Computer Science & Education (ICCSE 2021), pp. 258–261 (2021)

A Model for Dividing Comment Users in Weibo Hot Topic Under Entity Extraction and Sentiment Analysis

Fenghua Tian[1] and Bin Wen[1,2](✉)

[1] School of Information Science, Yunnan Normal University, Kunming, China
ynwenbin@163.com
[2] Key Laboratory of Educational Informatization for Nationalities, Yunnan Normal University, Kunming, China

Abstract. This paper proposes a division model to solve the problem of user classification in Weibo hot topics and to address the issue of inconsistent entity syntax and entity naming diversity in Weibo named entity recognition. Entity extraction is performed by combining part-of-speech analysis, word frequency statistics, and word vector similarity calculation. K-means is used to cluster entities, and entity sentiment analysis is performed using sentiment dictionaries. Finally, user groups are divided based on entity-sentiment categories. The user group division model proposed in this paper divides users into 18 categories, and the evaluation index CA value is 79.5%. This model has certain requirements for the comment corpus. According to the research results, the rationality of the model construction and feature selection in this paper is demonstrated. In addition, the user group accuracy obtained by using this model is high, and users with similar opinions can be well clustered together.

Keywords: ENTITY EXTRACTION · SENTIMENT ANALYSIS · USER GROUP PARTITION · K-MEANS CLUSTING

1 Introduction

As social media has advanced, Weibo has grown to become a vital platform for individuals to gather information and engage in social interaction. The comments under hot topics contain a large amount of valuable social and emotional in-formation, so analysing Weibo comments has important re-search value. However, extracting effective information and emotional content from comments and effectively classifying and dividing comments are still challenging tasks.

At present, research on Weibo user group division is mainly based on factors such as user personal information, social relationships, and Weibo content. Weibo user group division based on user personal information mainly includes using gender, age, region, occupation, and education level and ma-chine learning methods such as clustering analysis and classifiers for group division. These methods have objectivity and clarity, but

J. Gan et al. (Eds.): CSEI 2023, CCIS 1899, pp. 108–121, 2024.
https://doi.org/10.1007/978-981-99-9499-1_10

they also face data quality issues. Weibo user group division based on social relationships mainly uses in-formation such as follow relationships, forwarding relation-ships, and comment relationships and uses methods such as social network analysis and network clustering for division. However, there are challenges in data quality and scale, algorithm efficiency, and interpretability. Weibo group division based on Weibo content mainly includes sentiment analysis, topic modelling, entity recognition, and hybrid methods.

The text uses Weibo content-based group division and com-bines entity extraction technology and sentiment analysis technology to design a novel comment user group division model. Specifically, in view of the problems of inconsistent entity syntax and entity naming diversity in Weibo comments, the method for entity recognition is improved. Entity extraction is performed by combining part-of-speech analysis, word frequency statistics, and word vector similarity calculation. Experiments were conducted to test and validate the effectiveness and practicality of the model. The application of this model will provide more accurate and detailed research methods and means for social information and sentiment analysis, helping to better understand social changes and development trends.

2 Related Work

Users post a large number of comment texts on Weibo to express their views and emotions about events and the people or organizations involved in them on the internet. Based on these views and emotions, these users can be classified to better understand them. Currently, entity extraction has attracted much attention and research from scholars [1–3]. Text sentiment analysis has also been studied extensively by researchers, including sentiment analysis of different modal data. For example, some scholars extract users' emotions from images [4, 5], some conduct emotion mining on audio data [6], and some perform multimodal sentiment classification on text, audio, and tags [7].

2.1 Entity Extraction Research in Social Media

Named entity recognition (NER), also referred to as entity extraction, holds great significance in the domain of natural language processing because it involves identifying and categorizing named entities in text. Its goal is to identify named entities with specific meanings, such as person names, place names, and organization names. Significant progress has been made in NER in recent years thanks to the rapid development of deep learning technology. Many scholars have studied named entity recognition on social media platforms. Zheng Honghao et al. improved the traditional Transformer encoder's inability to obtain relative position information based on the XLNET-TransformerP-CRF model [8]. Gustavo et al. proposed a novel multitasking approach to address the inherent noise problem of named entity recognition on social media by adopting a more general named entity (NE) segmentation subtask and a main task of fine-grained NE classification [9].

For social media platforms such as Weibo, text data are often grammatically inconsistent and consist mostly of phrases, and there is also the problem of multiple naming variations for the same entity, which poses a great challenge to named entity recognition. To address this problem, Wang Hao et al. [10] proposed a Weibo text named entity recognition model that incorporates part-of-speech information. While the use of part-of-speech information and word embedding vectors in a bidirectional long short-term memory neural network can potentially address grammatical irregularities, it may not fully resolve the issue of inconsistent entity naming. In this paper, we use a method that combines part-of-speech tagging, word frequency statistics, and word vector models. This method not only solves the problem of grammatical inconsistencies but also addresses the problem of multiple naming variations for the same entity.

2.2 Sentiment Analysis Research in Social Media

Text sentiment analysis is a technique for automatically categorizing text by its emotional tone, including positive, negative, or neutral sentiment. Text sentiment analysis finds broad applications across various domains, including natural language processing, information retrieval, and social sciences. This analysis can be classified into two categories: rule-based methods and machine learning-based methods.

The rule-based text sentiment classification method relies on a predefined set of rules based on linguistic and sentiment analysis knowledge. It uses features such as keywords, syntactic structure, and context to determine the sentiment category of the text. These rules can be manually written and adjusted to suit specific domain and task requirements. Advantages: 1) Strong interpretability: Since the rules are manually defined, the classification results can be intuitively explained. 2) Adjustability: Rules can be adjusted and optimized based on specific needs and domain knowledge, resulting in more desirable classification results. Disadvantages: 1) Dependency on manual rules: Writing and adjusting rules requires human involvement and can be labor-intensive. 2) Inability to capture complex expressions: Rule-based methods may fail to capture some complex sentiment expressions, as sentiment expressions often exhibit diversity and context dependency. Machine learning-based text sentiment classification methods use training datasets to learn models and automatically extract patterns and features for sentiment classification. These methods can employ various machine learning algorithms, such as Naive Bayes, Support Vector Machines, Decision Trees, Deep Neural Networks, etc. Advantages: 1) Automatic feature and pattern learning: Machine learning methods can automatically learn features and patterns from data without the need for manual rule definition. 2) Wide applicability: Machine learning-based methods are applicable to different languages and domains, and can handle complex and diverse sentiment classification tasks. Disadvantages: 1) Requirement of labeled data: Machine learning methods require a significant amount of labeled data for training, which can be time-consuming and resource-intensive for data collection and annotation. 2) Data dependency: The performance of the model heavily re-lies on the quality and coverage of the training data. 3) Model complexity: Some machine learning methods may require complex model structures and parameter tuning, increasing the complexity of development and debugging.

Weibo comment text analysis belongs to the category of text sentiment analysis, but Weibo comment text sentiment analysis differs from traditional text due to its short length, diverse composition, and sometimes inconsistent use of language. To address these issues, scholars have proposed various methods. Huang et al. proposed a short text sentiment analysis model that can be used to process various types of short text data, such as Weibo text and movie review text [11]. For sentiment lexicon methods, the quality of the lexicon needs to be considered for the impact on sentiment classification results. Park et al. expanded the lexicon by collecting synonyms and antonyms and used it for text classification [12]. With the evolution of social culture, the emergence of a large number of new words has brought some difficulties to sentiment analysis, especially for social media such as Weibo, which contains a large number of new network words. To solve this problem, some scholars have proposed various models to extract new words and determine their sentiment polarity to enhance the accuracy of sentiment analysis [13, 14]. Some scholars also choose other methods for text sentiment analysis to improve the efficiency and accuracy of analysis [15]. In this paper, we use a sentiment lexicon-based method for sentiment analysis, and the selected sentiment lexicons include the open-source HowNet Chinese sentiment lexicon and the Taiwan University Simplified Chinese sentiment polarity lexicon, negative adverb lexicon, degree adverb lexicon, and network sentiment lexicon collected from platforms such as Baidu and Weibo.

2.3 Research on Weibo User Grouping

Research on Weibo user grouping is mainly based on user personal information, social relationships, and Weibo content. User personal information on Weibo mainly includes gender, date of birth, number of followers, number of fans, Weibo level, and authentication information. Chi Xuehua et al. collected basic user information and user tag information from Weibo and manually classified user tags according to the user tag classification system [16]. Wu Shufang et al. fused user tag information and user relationships to calculate user similarity [17].

The user's following information and follower information reflect the user's social relationships. Li Yidan conducted community relationship mining based on Weibo user behavior and content features. Weibo content mining is a common method for user grouping that mainly analyses Weibo themes, calculates theme preferences, and performs group classification based on the results [18]. Wang Zhigang et al. used LDA models to mine preferred themes in user comments, obtained the probability distribution vectors of user preference themes, calculated user similarity based on them, and used multidimensional scaling to classify user groups [19]. Sun Jingjing used the BTM topic model based on short text to mine user topic interests and calculate user background information similarity, user social information similarity, and user topic interest similarity to perform group classification [20]. This paper also mines Weibo content and uses entity extraction combined with sentiment analysis to perform group classification. Compared with theme analysis, entity extraction can more accurately represent user evaluation focus and opinions, and combined with sentiment analysis, it can make user group classification more accurate.

3 Research Approach

First, data cleaning and data preprocessing are performed on the downloaded dataset. Data cleaning mainly involves deleting meaningless text, and data preprocessing involves word segmentation and stop-word removal. Second, Gensim's word2vec model is used to train word vectors on the processed text corpus, and the trained word vector model is saved. Then, Hanlp is used to perform part-of-speech tagging on the tokenized text and filter out the nouns. The top 50 high-frequency nouns are then counted, and the entities with actual meanings are selected along with their entity words with a word vector similarity greater than 0.65. K-means clustering is used to cluster the entities based on their word vector similarity.

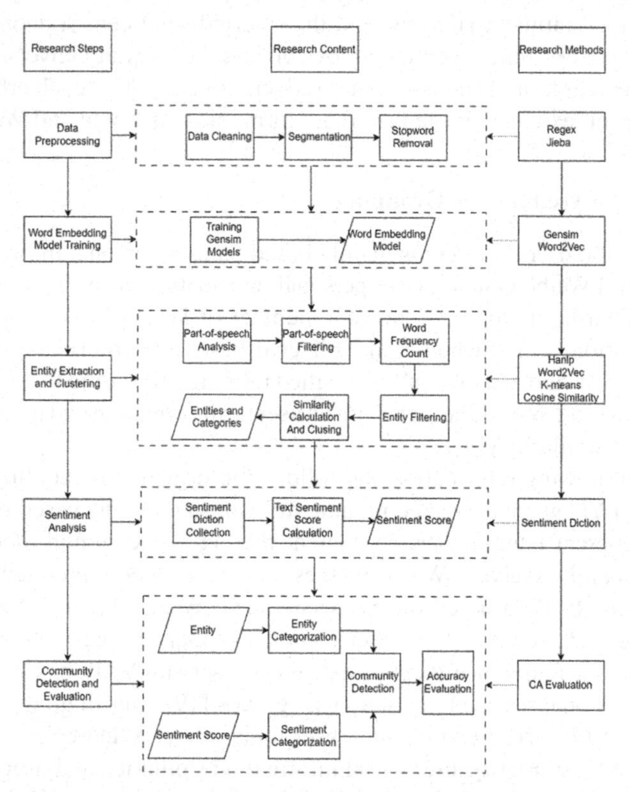

Fig. 1. Research framework of the group dividing model

Finally, for each user, entity extraction and sentiment analysis are performed, the extracted entities and sentiment polarities are classified into entity-sentiment categories, and the users are grouped based on the category. Based on the above analysis, the text research framework is shown in Fig. 1, including data preprocessing, word vector model training, entity extraction and clustering, sentiment analysis, and community detection and evaluation.

3.1 Data Preprocessing

Data preprocessing mainly includes data cleaning, segmentation, and stop word removal. For user comments that only contain punctuation marks, such as the comment "?????" from the user "in their twenties," they should be removed. In Weibo, some symbols have certain rule meanings, such as using "@" followed by a user nickname to mention that user or using "#" at the beginning and end to represent a topic. These texts do not have much meaning and should be deleted. The built-in re module in Python can be used for cleaning using regular expressions. For segmented texts, the Jieba segmentation tool is used for segmentation, and stop words are removed based on this. The stop word table used is the one from Harbin Institute of Technology.

3.2 Word Vector Model Training

Since Weibo comments contain a large number of internet words, using a pretrained word vector model directly may lead to poor accuracy and ineffective calculation of word correlations. Therefore, it is necessary to retrain a suitable word vector model based on actual text data. Gensim is a Python library for natural language processing that includes many tools and algorithms for processing text data. Its main features are high efficiency and ease of use. Word2vec is a word vector training model that can represent each word as a vector while preserving the semantic relationship between words. This article uses Word2vec from the Gensim library for word vector training, and the corpus used is the user comment text that has already been segmented and stop words removed.

3.3 Entity Extraction and Clustering

The entities contained in Weibo comments have strong ambiguity and nonstandardization. Conventional named entity recognition often fails to extract them. To address this issue, this paper uses a combination of part-of-speech analysis, word frequency statistics, and word vector models for entity extraction. First, Hanlp is used for part-of-speech analysis on the segmented data to select nouns with the part-of-speech NR (proper noun) and NN (common noun excluding proper nouns and time nouns). Then, word frequency statistics are performed to obtain the top 50 most frequent nouns, followed by filtering out the nouns with entity meaning. These filtered nouns are used to calculate their similarity with other words using the pretrained word vector model, and those with a similarity score greater than 0.65 are selected as related entity words. Finally, the entity words are clustered based on their similarity using K-means clustering, and the number of clusters is determined using the silhouette coefficient method, which is calculated using Formula (1). The silhouette coefficient (s(i)) of a given data point is determined by its average distance from other points in the same cluster (a(i)), as well as its average distance from the nearest neighboring cluster (b(i)). In other words, s(i) represents a measure of how well the data point fits within its assigned cluster, taking into ac-count the distances to other clusters.

$$s(i) = \frac{b(i) - a(i)}{max(a(i), b(i))} \tag{1}$$

Clustering algorithms are a category of unsupervised learning algorithms used to partition data samples into different groups or clusters, where samples within the same cluster have high similarity, while samples across different clusters have low similarity. Here are some common clustering algorithms. K-means clustering: It divides data samples into K clusters, each represented by a centroid. The algorithm iteratively assigns data points to the cluster whose centroid is closest to them; Hierarchical clustering: It is a hierarchical-based clustering method that can follow either an agglomerative (bottom-up) or divisive (top-down) strategy. This algorithm constructs a clustering tree by calculating the similarity or distance between samples and gradually merging or splitting samples; Density-based clustering: It partitions clusters based on the density of data points. One commonly used density-based clustering algorithm is DBSCAN (Density-Based Spatial Clustering of Applications with Noise), which categorizes data points as core points, boundary points, and noise points and constructs clusters based on density reachability. The advantages and disadvantages of the K-Means clustering algorithm: 1) Simplicity and efficiency.The implementation of the K-Means algorithm is relatively simple and easy to understand. It also exhibits good computational efficiency, even with large-scale datasets. 2) Scalability. K-Means is suitable for handling large datasets and can effectively handle high-dimensional data. 3) Interpretability of results: The cluster assignments produced by the K-Means algorithm are relatively intuitive. Each cluster is represented by a centroid, which can be interpreted as the average features of the samples in that cluster. Based on the advantages mentioned above and considering the specific context of this article, it is appropriate to use the K-Means algorithm.

3.4 Sentiment Analysis

The text sentiment analysis calculation adopts a method based on a dictionary and rules. The sentiment lexicon includes open-source sentiment lexicons, network sentiment lexicons, negative adverb lexicons, degree adverb sentiment lexicons, etc. Among them, the open-source sentiment lexicon includes the HowNet Chinese sentiment lexicon and the Taiwan University Simplified Chinese sentiment polarity lexicon, which have a clear distinction between emotions. The network sentiment lexicon selects new network words from the Baidu and Sohu engines and collects popular network languages with good coverage of network terms. The negative adverb and degree adverb are self-annotated. When calculating the sentiment value of entities in comment text, it suffices to compute the sentiment score of the text segment containing the respective entity. Each text segment is divided by "," "?" "," ".", and "!" as boundaries. The calculation method for the y-th sentiment word v_y in the text segment is shown in Formula (2). Here, w represents the weight of v_y, j represents the polarity of v_y, neg represents the number of negative words before v_y, and deg represents the weight of the degree adverb before v_y.

$$v_y = w \times j \times (-1)^{neg} \times deg \quad (2)$$

3.5 Grouping and Model Evaluation

Based on the previously extracted entities and the analysed sentiment values, these two indicators are classified. Entity categories can be divided into no entities, single entities, and multiple entities, and single entities can be further divided based on the meaning of the entities. The classification of sentiment categories is based on the polarity of the sentiment, with positive and negative sentiment classes being the two main categories. Users are first grouped based on the same entity category and then further grouped based on sentiment polarity, resulting in different user groups.

Finally, the CA value is calculated to evaluate the accuracy of the grouped entities and validate the model's usability. The accuracy of the clustering model is evaluated using cluster accuracy (CA) as the evaluation standard, which selects new network words from the Baidu and Sohu engines and collects popular network languages with good coverage of network terms to ensure accuracy. Formula (3) illustrates the CA calculation method, which determines the quality of the clustering effect. A higher calculated CA value indicates a better clustering outcome.

$$CA = \frac{\sum_{i=1}^{n} \delta(t_i, r_i)}{n} \quad (3)$$

The formula utilizes variables such as 'n', which refers to the overall number of users, 't_i', which represents the actual category, and 'r_i', which denotes the category assigned to the user after clustering. δ is an indicator function, the specific expression of which is shown in Formula (4)

$$\delta(x, y)\begin{cases} 1 & x = y \\ 0 & x \neq y \end{cases} \quad (4)$$

4 Experimental Process

4.1 Data Preprocessing

This study used the public dataset of the RNG S8 8-strong tournament apology post with 5000 level-one comments un-der the official Weibo account, which was provided by Ali Tianchi. The obtained data content includes Weibo user ID (user_id), Weibo username (user_name), Weibo personal verification (1-yes, 0-no), Weibo VIP level (vip_rank), com-ment content (content), comment time (comment_time), etc. As the classification is based on Weibo comments, only the user ID, user name, and comment content are needed. After preprocessing the comment content, the dataset contains 4833 items.

4.2 Word Vector Model Training

The comment data were segmented and then used to train a word vector model using the Word2Vec algorithm in the Gensim library. The word vector dimension is set to 100, the word frequency threshold is set to 5, and the window context size is set to 5. The trained model is saved.

4.3 Entity Extraction and Clustering

Word frequency statistics are performed on the segmented and stop-word-removed data to obtain some of the words, as shown in Table 1. Words such as "rng", "bp", "coach", and "coaching staff" have high word frequencies, appearing 276, 189, 121, and 98 times, respectively. These words are all closely related to the people and events involved in this event. Figure 2 displays the results obtained from the silhouette coefficient method, depicting the number of clusters and the corresponding change in the silhouette coefficient. The optimal number of clusters for achieving the best classification result appears to be 7. Therefore, it is recommended to divide the single entity category into seven distinct categories. The categories and the entities they contain are shown in Table 2.

Table 1. Entity word frequency table.

word	word frequency	word	word frequency
rng	276	bp	189
Coach	121	coaching staff	98
Obama	55	uzi	51
g2	51	lpl	50
lol	48	Lu Xun	36
ig	32	Royal Club	28
League of Legends	25	Xiang Guo	21
edg	18	Little Dog	18

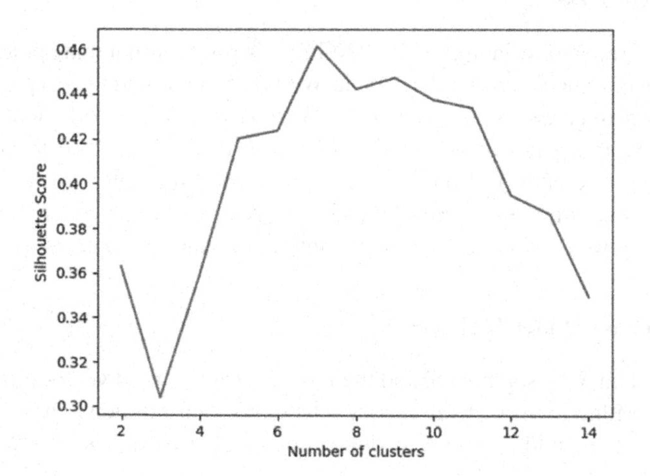

Fig. 2. Changes in cluster number and silhouette coefficient.

Table 2. Entity categories and related entity word table.

Clustering	Entity words
loser team	RNG,XiaoIG, China, IG, edg, Royal Club
winning team	g2, the opponent side
failure reason	Coaching staff, coach, banpick, bp, Sun Dayong, Hart, Heart
game character	O'Maba, Lu Xian, Obama, Lu Xi, Lusian
player Liu Shiyu	Liu Shiyu, teacher, Karsa, mlxg, Xiang Guo, life-and-death match
player uzi	Uzi, Little Dog, and Gouzi
race game	Game, League, League of Legends, retire from the game, LOL, LPL

4.4 Sentiment Analysis

The sentiment of the text segment where the entity is located is analysed, and the numbers of positive and negative senti-ments obtained are shown in Table 3. It can be seen from the table that the negative sentiment of the comment data ac-counts for the vast majority, and the overall sentiment is negative, which is consistent with the fact that the RNG team lost the game.

Table 3. Number of sentiment categories table.

total comments	positive comments	negative comments
4648	262	3854

4.5 Grouping and Model Evaluation

Entities are classified into no entities, single entities, and multiple entities. No entities are classified into one category, single entities are divided into seven categories based on the clustering results, and multiple entities are divided into one category. Sentiment is divided into positive and negative sentiment categories based on sentiment values greater than or less than 0, respectively. Based on the above description, users are finally divided into 18 groups, including 9 entity categories and 2 sentiment categories. The experimental results are shown in Fig. 3, where class number –1 represents the multiple entity category, class number 0 represents the no entity category, and class number 1–7 represents the entity categories related to the defeated team, the entity categories related to the victorious team, the entity categories related to the reason for the defeat, the entity categories related to game roles, the entity categories related to team member Liu Shiyu, the entity categories related to team member Uzi, and the entity categories related to the game. The number of users in each category is shown in Table 4. Finally, the results of the grouped users are shown in Table 5.

Finally, the clustering results are evaluated based on the CA calculation method. The CA value of entity-sentiment grouping is calculated to be 79.5%. The accuracy of entity grouping is 92.7%, and the accuracy of sentiment grouping is 82.2%.

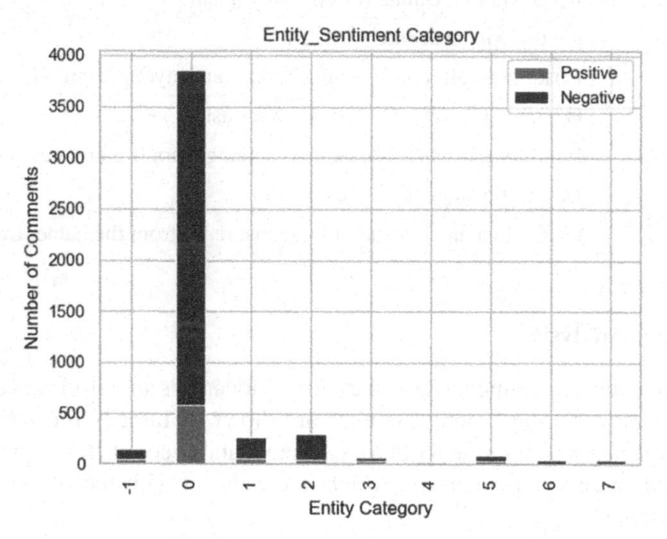

Fig. 3. Entity-Sentiment category.

Table 4. User classification quantity table.

class number	user count	number of users with positive sentiment	number of users with negative sentiment
−1	143	48	94
0	3854	578	3276
1	262	60	202
2	293	41	252
3	66	40	26
4	22	2	20
5	95	33	62

Table 5. Users and their comments by category table.

entity class number	sentiment	user id	comment content
−1	positive	5846470587	Little Dog has fallen. Let us go IG, EDG, and cheering for C9
	negative	6332405132	Does BP underestimate G2, who are also in the quarterfinals?
0	positive	5712031509	Take a good rest, you have worked hard. Let us do our best next year
	negative	5651482450	Now I think the expressions on your faces during the draw were truly ironic
1	positive	2602886531	RNG never gives up! Keep going!
	negative	3058531687	Dead from arrogance, goodbye RNG
2	positive	5767041898	Congratulations to the coach on getting rich!
	negative	5964144313	What kind of BP is so bloated?
3	positive	3187454032	Lu Xian is truly fun to play
	negative	1731509965	Four-protect-one with Lu Xian, it is one's own fault for seeking death
4	positive	5495662869	Feel sorry for Xiang Guo
	negative	1869564274	Let Karsa leave!
5	positive	5303534816	Royal Club never give up! Keep going!
	negative	5904372918	Did losing after staying up all night to play today? I do not even want to play LoL anymore
6	positive	5726863432	Congratulations to G2!
	negative	6055183688	What were they playing? How could they lose to G2?
7	positive	1785907785	Keep going next year, Uzi. I will always support you
	negative	6447928106	Uzi retires

5 Conclusion

This paper classifies users based on entity extraction and sentiment analysis of comments under popular topics on Weibo. To solve the problem of the grammatical and naming diversity of entities in Weibo comments, this paper combines part-of-speech analysis, word frequency statistics, and word vector similarity calculation to extract entities. First, Hanlp is used to perform part-of-speech analysis on the segmented data, and words with NR (proper noun) and NN (noun except for proper nouns and time nouns) are selected. Then, word frequency statistics are performed to obtain the top 50 nouns ranked by frequency, and words with entity meaning are screened. These screened words are then used as queries to retrieve related words from a pretrained word vector model using cosine similarity, and words with a similarity greater than 0.65 are considered related to the entity. The K-means clustering algorithm is utilized to cluster entity words according to their degree of similarity. The clustering algorithm's cluster number is determined using the silhouette coefficient method, and the experimental results show that the entity classification accuracy reaches 92.7%, indicating that the entity extraction effect is excellent. However, the sentiment classification accuracy is only 82.2%, which affects the overall accuracy of 79.5%, indicating that more work is needed to improve the accuracy of sentiment analysis. Furthermore, since the feature entity category clustering depends on the word vector models' similarity calculation, the quality of the word vector model's training is critical, which is determined by the corpus. If the corpus data are scarce or there are many interfering words, it will indirectly lead to unsatisfactory clustering results. Future research will focus on improving entity extraction for Weibo comments and reducing the dependence on word vector models.

Acknowledgements. The research is supported by the Key Laboratory of Education Informalization for Nationalities of Ministry of Education, Yunnan Key Laboratory of Smart Education, Key Laboratory of Digital Learning Supporting Technology, Department of Education of Yunnan Province, and Yunnan International Joint R&D Center of China-Laos-Thailand Educational Digitalization.

References

1. Fangcong, Z., Qiuli, Q., Yong, J., et al.: Research on named entity recognition of Chinese electronic medical records based on RoBERTa-WWM-BiLSTM-CRF. Data Anal. Knowl. Discov. **6**(Z1), 251–262 (2022)
2. Li, L., Zhou, H., Guo, X., et al.: Named entity recognition of Chinese crop pests based on multisource information fusion. J. Agric. Mach. **52**(12), 253–263 (2021)
3. Wang, J., Yu, L., Xia, W., et al.: Named entity recognition meth-od for power grid dispatch domain based on ERNIE-IDCNN-CRF model. Electr. Power Inf. Commun. Technol. **20**(10), 1–8 (2022)
4. Yang, S., Liu, J., Wu, T.: Research on emotional classification of art images based on deep features and attention mechanism. Intell. Comput. Appl. **12**(02), 126–132 (2022)
5. Wang, L., Wang, W., Cheng, X.: Speech-text bimodal emotion recognition model combining Bi-LSTM-CNN. Comput. Eng. Appl. **58**(04), 192–197 (2022)
6. Qiao, D., Chen, Z., Deng, L., et al.: Chinese speech emotion recognition method based on improved speech processing and convolutional neural network. Comput. Eng. **48**(02), 281–290 (2022)
7. Jia, N., Zheng, C.: Multimodal emotion recognition based on audio, text, and facial expressions. J. Appl. Sci. **41**(01), 55–70 (2023)
8. Zheng, H., Yu, H., Li, S.: Chinese named entity recognition based on improved transformer encoder. J. Netw. Inf. Secur. **7**(05), 105–112 (2021)
9. Aguilar, G., Maharjan, S., López-Monroy, A.P., et al.: A mul-titask approach for named entity recognition in social media data, arXiv preprint arXiv:1906, 04135 (2019)
10. Hao, W., Yuxue, S., Gaojun, L., et al.: Named entity recognition of Weibo texts with joint Part-of-Speech features. J. North China Univ. Technol. **31**(05), 90–96 (2019)

11. Huang, Z., Zhao, Z., Liu, Q., et al.: An unsupervised method for short-text sentiment analysis based on analysis of massive data. In: Proceedings of the 2015 International Conference of Young Computer Scientists, Engineers and Educators (ICYCSEE), Harbin, China, pp. 169–176 (2015)
12. Park, S., Kim, Y.: Building thesaurus lexicon using dictionary-based approach for sentiment classification. In: Proceedings of the 2016 IEEE 14th International Conference on Software Engineering Research, Towson, MD, USA, pp. 39–44 (2016)
13. Li, W., Guo, K., Shi, Y., et al.: Improved new word detection method used in tourism field. Procedia Comput. Sci. **108**, 1251–1260 (2017)
14. Yan, L.W., Bai, B., Chen, W., et al.: New word extraction from Chinese financial documents. IEEE Signal Process. Lett. **24**(6), 770–773 (2017)
15. Zhang, Y., Zheng, J., Huang, G., et al.: Weibo sentiment analysis based on dual attention model. J. Tsinghua Univ. (Sci. Technol.) **58**(02), 122–130 (2018)
16. Chi, X., Zhang, Y., Gao, X., et al.: Research on differences in user tagging behaviors in different disciplines: taking Sina Weibo user tags as an example. Libr. Tribune **36**(09), 112–120 (2016)
17. Wu, S., Xu, J., Wu, X.: Measuring similarity of Weibo users based on user tags and relationships. J. Intell. **33**(12), 170–173+126 (2014)
18. Li, Y.: Research and Implementation of User Relationship Network Mining System Based on Weibo, Beijing University of Posts and Telecommunications (2020)
19. Wang, Z., Qiu, C.: Research on user profile of government Weibo comments based on topics. J. Intell. **41**(03), 159–165 (2022)
20. Sun, J.: Research on Weibo Group User Profile Based on BTM Topic Model. Yanshan University (2019)

A Summary Research of the Current Status, Hot Spots and Trends in STEM Education

Visual Analysis Based on Relevant Literature Published in CNKI Database

Xiaobo Shi, Bingying Zhao(✉), Ningning Li, Weiwei Lian, and Gongli Li

Key Laboratory of Artificial Intelligence and Personalized Learning in Education, Big Data Engineering Lab of Teaching Resources & Assessment of Education Quality, College of Computer and Information Engineering, Henan Normal University, Xinxiang, China
2208283033@stu.htu.edu.cn

Abstract. In the context of the publication of the "Thirteenth Five-Year Plan for Educational Informationization," and China's entry into the era of education informatization, the integration of information technology and STEM education has become research hot topic. This article uses visualization tools to analyze STEM education literature from 2016 to 2023, summarizes the current status of STEM education research in China, and identifies four research hotspots: research on the application of information technology to broaden the sources and design forms of STEM courses, research on the adaptability of STEM teachers to educational technology reforms, research on the mutual learning of STEM education and maker education under the background of "Internet+". And research on the transition from STEM Education to STEAM Education in the era of Educational Informatization. It also identifies five research trends: research on the participation of the whole people in promoting the Development of STEM Education, research on promoting the Integration of STEM Education and Creator Education, research on the Integration of STEM Education and Deep Learning assisted by emerging Technologies, research on two-way empowerment of STEM education and artificial intelligence, research on STEM Teachers' Professional Development to meet the needs of Educational Information era. Finally, development suggestions are proposed for the problems existing in the development of STEM education under the background of educational informatization, which can provide references for the reform and innovation of STEM education in the future.

Keywords: STEM education · Educational informatization · Information technology

1 Introduction

STEM was first proposed by Yakman, a scholar at Virginia Tech University in the United States, at the National Science Foundation (NSF) in 1990. It is an abbreviation of the English initials of the four disciplines of Science, Technology, Engineering and

J. Gan et al. (Eds.): CSEI 2023, CCIS 1899, pp. 122–139, 2024.
https://doi.org/10.1007/978-981-99-9499-1_11

Mathematics [1]. STEM education organically integrates the four disciplines of science, technology, engineering and mathematics, creates real problem situations for students, and stimulates students' interest in learning based on project-based learning [2].

In recent years, STEM education has also attracted the attention of the domestic education community because of its characteristics of integrating multi-disciplinary knowledge, cultivating innovative spirit and practical ability. In 2016, China officially wrote STEM education into "the 13th Five-Year Plan" for Educational Informatization, emphasizing the improvement of students' information literacy, innovation consciousness and innovation ability through interdisciplinary STEM learning combined with information technology [3]. The Outline of the 14th Five-Year Plan and 2035 Vision Goals clearly put forward that innovation plays a core role in the overall situation of China's modernization construction, and STEM education is an important way to cultivate young people's innovative spirit and practical ability [4]. This series of policies proves that the country pays more and more attention to STEM education development. Although STEM education started late in China, under the background of the country's strong promotion of education informatization, many scholars have realized that the use of emerging technologies to explore STEM education has made STEM education develop rapidly, and breakthroughs have been made in practice and application research. Through the search of core journals, it was found that previous research on STEM education was carried out from different perspectives, and there was a lack of systematic review research on the development of STEM education under the background of informatization in China. Based on this research status, this study uses CiteSpace visualization software, bibliometrics method, content analysis method and interdisciplinary research method to focus on STEM education research under the background of education informatization, analysis research hotspots and possible future trends, clarify the main problems existing in STEM education in China, and propose to increase financial support. Reasonable use of network resources to promote the regional balanced development of STEM education, support by big data technology, realize the scientific development of STEM education quality evaluation, improve teachers 'comprehensive ability, and build a professional team of STEM teachers in the education information age, so as to promote the healthy and sustainable development of STEM education in the future.

2 Research Data and Methodology

2.1 Data Sources

In this study, the China National Knowledge Internet (CNKI) database was used as the source of literature samples, and the subject of the search condition was "STEM education" when conducting the advanced search. In order to enhance the credibility of the research content, only well-known core journals at home and abroad, such as SCI, EI, Peking University Core and CSSCI, were selected as the source of literature. The search period was 2016–2023, and the database was updated until 18 March 2023. 585 relevant documents were retrieved, and after manual screening, 522 were identified as valid documents, and these 522 documents were used as the research sample for this paper.

2.2 Research Tools and Methods

The main tool used in this study is Citespace, which is a scientific literature analysis tool jointly developed by Dr. Chaomei Chen, a British-Chinese scholar, and the WISE laboratory of Dalian University of Technology. It is mainly a software that measures literature in a specific field and generates a visual map to present the research structure and development trend of a subject field [5]. The version used in this study is CiteSpace 6.1. R6 (64-bit). This paper mainly uses the research methods of bibliometrics, content analysis, interdisciplinary research and other research methods, combined with visual analysis and literature reading, to grasp the research status, hotspots and trends in the field of STEM education in recent years.

3 Analysis of the Current State of Research

3.1 Analysis of the Current Status of Annual STEM Education Publication Volume

In order to understand the output of research results in the field of STEM education, this paper counts the number of articles published in recent years and the publication time of the literature is statistically processed, which is finally presented in the form of a line graph to help us understand the changing trend of the literature in this field from 2016 to 2013, combined with Fig. 1, we can divide the research related to STEM education into two stages: the rapid development stage(2016–2019) and the flat advancement phase (2020–2023).

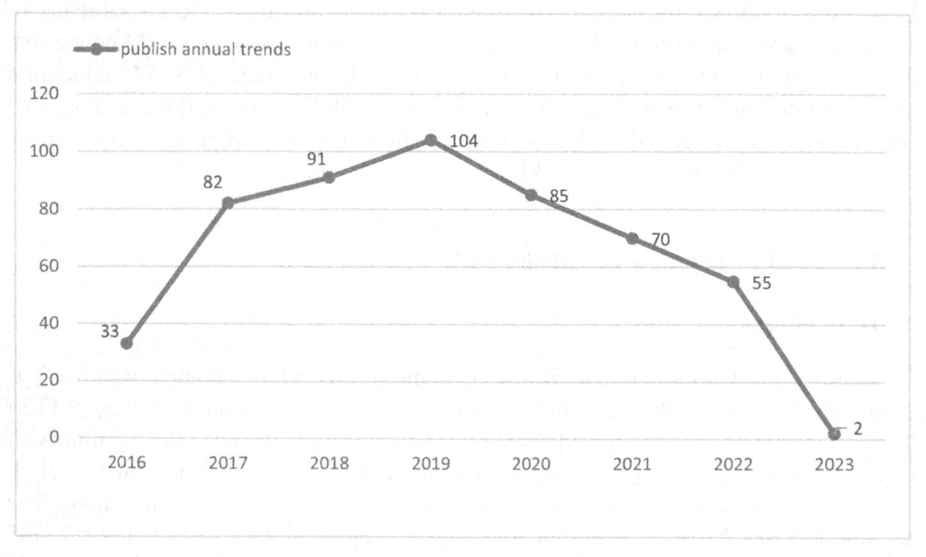

Fig. 1. The change trend of STEM education research publications in China from 2016 to 2023

3.1.1 The Rapid Development Stage (2016–2019)

China's STEM education began to develop when the 13th Five-Year Plan for Educational Informationization issued by the Ministry of Education in 2016 year. it was clearly pointed out that the effective use of information technology to promote the construction of "mass creation space", explore new education models such as STEM education and maker education, cultivate students' information awareness and innovation awareness, develop the habit of digital learning, and abide by the literacy of ethics and laws and regulations in the information society [2]. To some extent, this has promoted the attention of Chinese scholars to STEM education and tried to use technology to promote STEM education reform and innovation. In 2017, the Ministry of Education promulgated the Science Curriculum Standards for Compulsory Primary Education, which advocates STEM education and interdisciplinary learning approaches. In the same year, STEM, STEAM and STEM+ education also appeared in curriculum standards for various subjects in general high schools, which emphasize the concept of STEM education or STEAM education as a guide, the use of open sources hardware for project learning, and the development of students' awareness and ability to use information technology for problem solving and innovative design. Since then, the number of literatures related to STEM education has shown a trend of rapid growth. As can be seen from Fig. 1, the number of published papers reached 91 in 2018, and reached a peak of 104 in 2019.STEM education has grown rapidly during this period.

3.1.2 The Flat Advancement Phase (2020–2023)

The number of publications declined slightly between January 2020 and March 2023 (possibly due to the impact of COVID-19). But generally speaking, the popularity of STEM education continues to show a steady rising trend, which can be called the stage of peaceful promotion. According to the annual trend graph generated by CNKI on STEM education publication, it is predicted that the number of STEM education publications will reach 53 in 2023.

On the whole, STEM education started late in China. It began to rise in 2016, began to show an active state in 2017, and then showed a developing trend. At the same time, it has produced a number of achievements in practice and application. Therefore, STEM education becomes an inseparable field of Chinese education study.

3.2 Analysis of the Characteristics of High-Impact Authors

In recent years, 232 scholars in China have published papers related to the field of STEM education, and the top ten authors in terms of the number of papers published are shown in Table 1. Huichen Zhao and Yi Song are the most prolific STEM authors with seven papers. According to the theory of Price's law, the number of papers published by core authors is $N = 0.749(\eta max)1/2$ and above, where ηmax indicates the number of papers published by the most prolific authors, N is the critical value of the number of papers published by the group of authors, and the authors with the number of papers published greater than N are core authors [6]. According to the formula, the number of core authors in the field of STEM education can be calculated as $N \approx 3$. Through CiteSpace statistical analysis, there are 32 core authors who have published 3 papers or more, and the core authors have published a total of 132 papers, accounting for 25% of the total number of papers published. According to Lipes' law, the number of papers published by core authors should account for half of the total number of literatures in the field. This shows that the field has not yet formed a core team of authors.

Table 1. The top 10 authors by number of publications

Serial number	Author	Number of articles issued
1	Hui-Chen Zhao	7
2	Yi Song	7
3	Zhao-Ning Ye	6
4	Wei Zhao	6
5	Qiang Jiang	6
6	Rong Zhou	5
7	Yuan-Kui yang	5
8	Lei Yuan	5
9	Ye-Ping Li	5
10	Hong-Jia Ma	5

Take the author as the node, the co-occurrence analysis of posting authors was carried out to obtain a visualisation of the co-occurrence of authors in STEM education, as shown in Fig. 2. Each node represents an author, and the size of the name indicates the volume of the author's postings. The larger the name, the more the number of publications. A line between nodes indicates a cooperative relationship between authors. Among all the researchers, Huichen Zhao and Yi Song led, followed by Zhaoning Ye, Wei Zhao and Qiang Jiang, who carried out in-depth research in the field of STEM education and made achievements, As can be seen in Fig. 2, there are also scattered nodes, which indicates that there are many scholars who are concerned about it. But many of whom have published only one paper and have not continued to conduct further research.

4 Analysis of STEM Education Research Hotspots

Keywords are representative words or phrases chosen by the author to reflect the core content of the paper [7]. The co-occurrence of keywords helps us to quickly grasp the current research hotspots in the field and the relationships between them. Figure 3 shows the keyword co-occurrence map of STEM education using CiteSpace. The whole co-occurrence network is based on stem education, other research hotspots include steam education, science education, maker education, stem teacher, stem curriculum, and artificial intelligence, which all focus on stem education to carry out.

Fig. 2. Author co-occurrence graph

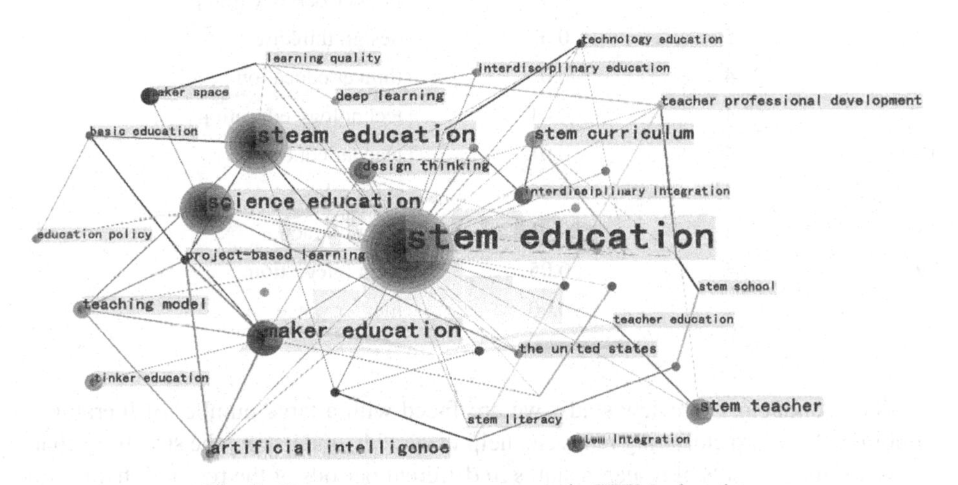

Fig. 3. Keyword co-occurrence map in STEM education

The centrality indicates the importance of a keyword in a certain field, and by collating the frequency and centrality of keywords in the sample literature of STEM education, we get Table 2. The frequency of research hotspots such as steam education and science education are high, and so is their centrality. At the same time, there are some other areas with relatively high citation frequency but low centrality, such as marker education, teacher professional development and deep learning, which indicate a mismatch between the attention and influence, and these areas will be the focus of further research in STEM education. These aspects will be the focus of further research in STEM education.

Table 2. Keyword frequency and centrality statistics for STEM fields, 2016 to 2023

Serial number	Frequency	Centrality	Keywords
1	177	0.99	stem education
2	25	0.11	steam education
3	18	0.04	maker education
4	16	0.09	science education
5	10	0.04	stem curriculum
6	9	0.05	artificial intelligence
7	9	0.06	stem teacher
8	6	0.03	teaching model
9	5	0.03	deep learning
10	5	0.04	teacher professional development
11	5	0.02	the united states
12	5	0.01	project-based learning
13	5	0.02	design thinking
14	4	0.02	thinker education
15	4	0.01	technology education
16	4	0.01	teacher education
17	4	0.00	stem school
18	4	0.01	stem literacy
19	4	0.05	stem integration
20	4	0.00	marker space

When conducting a review study, we are faced with a large number of literatures. Combining keyword clustering maps can help us quickly understand the structural characteristics and hotspots of research status in different periods of the research field. This study obtained a keyword clustering map as shown in Fig. 4. Based on the results shown in Fig. 4, nine keyword clustering labels were generated, representing nine relatively hot research topics in the STEM education field.

Based on a comprehensive analysis of the high-frequency co-occurrence and clustering of keywords in China's maker education research, combined with literature reading, we summarized the four hot topics of STEM education in China: First, the study of using information technology to broaden the sources and design of STEM courses; second, the adaptability of STEM teachers to educational technology changes; third, the research on the interaction between STEM education and maker education in the context of "Internet Plus"; fourth, the study on the transformation of STEM education to STEAM education in the era of educational informatization.

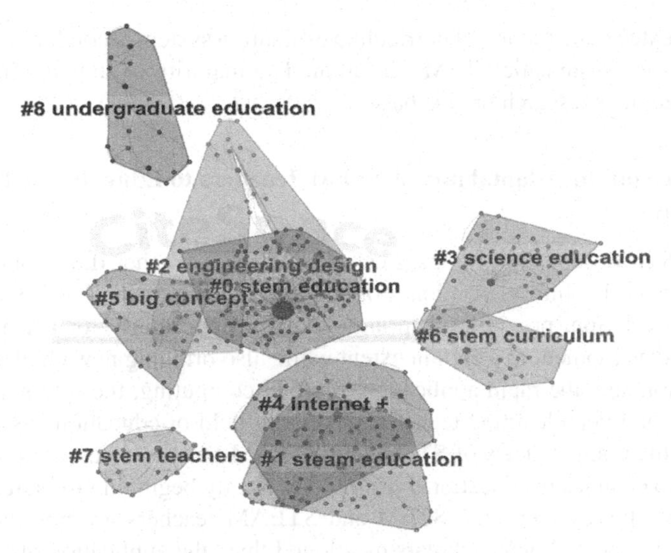

Fig. 4. Keyword clustering mapping in STEM education

4.1 Research on the Application of Information Technology to Broaden the Sources and Design Forms of STEM Courses

The sources and forms of STEM curriculum resources supported by information technology in education are becoming more and more diverse: on the one hand, advanced information devices can visually present STEM research scenarios and activate students' enthusiasm for learning; on the other hand, information resources include materials and technical software tools in the fields of science, technology, engineering and mathematics needed for STEM education, broadening the resources for STEM interdisciplinary thematic learning courses [8]. China has been exploring the integration of modern information technology and STEM curriculum in recent years, and has made initial achievements. Information technology plays an important role in the construction and development of STEM curricula. Technological innovations represented by the construction of smart campuses, the development of online education, big data and learning analytics provide strong support for the restructuring of curriculum content, which in turn leads to changes in the entire education system [9, 10]. In Beijing, a STEM robotics curriculum for primary and secondary schools has been developed based on robotics technology and has been implemented and improved in more than ten schools in Haidian and Xicheng districts [11]. The STEM curriculum is the vehicle for the implementation of STEM education, and project-based learning is the main way in which the STEM curriculum is practised. The project-based learning is the main way to implement STEM curriculum. Hailong Men has conducted research on collaborative web-based project learning, and designed and organised project-based learning activities based on the open source Atutor web-based course management platform [12]. The STEM curriculum is built on the open source Atutor web-based course management platform. The scientific evaluation system of STEM courses has a significant role in the construction and development of the courses, and is a key focus and a challenge. The use of big data technology, based on evidence-oriented construction of curriculum evaluation system is conducive to promote the scientific and systematic STEM education. The majority of scholars in China can further deepen their research on this basis.

4.2 Research on the Adaptability of STEM Teachers to Educational Technology Reforms

The rise of STEM education brings great challenges to teacher development. STEM education, driven by Informatization 2.0, has ushered in a new wave of information technology revolution, providing a springboard and opportunity for teachers' STEM professional development to a certain extent while also bringing new challenges [9]. In the information age, the rapid application of cloud computing, the Internet of Things, robotics, 5G, and deep learning technologies in the field of education has placed new demands on the competencies of STEM and STEAM teachers. Research on teachers' adaptability to changes in educational technology is only beginning to increase in 2019 in China, and studies show that STEM and STEAM teachers are not yet fully prepared [13]. Peng Di and other scholars mentioned that "the application of 5G+STEM" technology is an important foundation for education informatization, while 5G information technology promotes the upgrading of STEM teaching environment and hardware equipment, it requires teachers to have stronger learning and adaptation ability, teachers should change the concept of STEM education and transfer the knowledge-based learning to the updating of concepts and the improvement of information processing ability, the development of technology and the progress of concepts are occurring in tandem [14]. Wu et al. studied the impact of remote access labs on pre-service teachers' STEM competency enhancement and found that STEM learning experiences in remote access labs can serve as scaffolding for pre-service teachers to teach STEM subjects later. The Education Informatization 2.0 Action Plan suggests that information literacy, such as "artificial intelligence", should be included in the information literacy enhancement system for teachers. STEM teachers should have not only traditional interdisciplinary literacy, but also network literacy and media literacy in the information age.

4.3 Research on the Mutual Learning of STEM Education and Maker Education Under the Background of "Internet+"

Since its inception, creator education has had varying degrees of influence on STEM education, innovation education and quality education, which in turn have influenced creator education [15]. There are a strong body of research on the interplay between traditional STEM education and maker education. There are prominent research findings on the mutual learning between traditional STEM education and creator education. Wang et al. argue that maker education can enhance students' interest in participating in STEM courses, while integrating STEM education into maker education can facilitate the development of maker education [16]. On this basis, the study of the integration of STEM education and maker education, which is a new form of education in the era of "Internet+", has become a focus of research in recent years. This is a major focus of research in recent years. The emergence of creative courses ("interactive media technology, Arduino creative robotics courses", etc.) and STEM education concepts and practices are integrated, providing a platform for innovation and stimulating students' enthusiasm for creativity and comprehensive STEM literacy [17] This is the first time that we have been able to do this. Based on this, Wang Xuqing constructs a creative education model for STEM education from six aspects: basic concept, learning environment, teaching objectives, teaching content, teaching strategies, and evaluation methods, and the study concludes that this education model is an innovative model to adapt to the digital information age and cultivate talents with innovative thinking and comprehensive abilities [15]. Creative education in the context of "Internet+" creates a creative space for students' innovative practice, collaborative cooperation and resource sharing, and cooperates with STEM interdisciplinary education to promote students' comprehensive development in innovative practice, and "creative education + STEM education" has now become the direction of IT curriculum reform [18]. In addition, many scholars have proposed the use of maker education with the characteristics of the Internet and the rapid development of information technology to promote the development of STEM education to a newer form.

4.4 Research on the Transition from STEM Education to STEAM Education in the Era of Educational Informatization

The promulgation of a series of policy documents such as the National Medium and Long-term Education Reform and Development Plan (2010–2020) and the Education Informatization 2.0 Action Plan indicates that China is now in the era of education informatization [19, 20]. Education informatization refers to the application of modern information technology in education. Informatization in education refers to the application of modern information technology to the field of education, to promote educational reform and development, to develop students' comprehensive application ability, and to cultivate integrated and innovative talents who can adapt to the requirements of society. STEM education focuses on mathematical and scientific education, neglecting the cultivation of humanistic and artistic qualities of students, and cannot achieve the fundamental goal of whole-person education [21]. This is the fundamental goal of whole-person education. In response to this drawback, the educational concept of STEM + Arts = STEAM has gradually emerged, and STEAM education was introduced in China in 2017. Hetland et al. provide a model for the successful interface between arts and STEM education with studio thinking, Bresler provides the necessary support and structure for the integration of arts into STEM education, and Li Gang and other scholars put forward a proposal based on this Li Gang and other scholars have proposed three main ideas to facilitate a smooth transition from STEM education to STAEM education: emphasising the broad interdisciplinary concept, emphasising arts-based practices, and creating an arts atmosphere based on appropriate educational resources [22–24]. Feng Zhengdong and other scholars have constructed a STEAM education action space that integrates the fun of science, the meticulousness of technology, the rigour of engineering, the logic of mathematics and the humanity of art and culture, exploring a new path for the development of STEM education to STEAM education [25]. The Information Technology Curriculum Standards for General High Schools (2017 Edition) proposes to use the STEM and STEAM education concepts as a guide to carry out project learning using open source hardware, allowing students to experience the fun of research and creation in the education process, and to develop students' ability to use information technology to solve problems, innovative design and interrogative thinking, etc. [26]. China has written STEM education and STEAM education into the curriculum standards, expecting the in-depth integration of the arts to balance the disadvantages of STEM education, which is dominated by science and technology learning, with a preference for logical thinking and less attractiveness, in order to cultivate high-quality talents who can adapt to the information age.

5 Analysis of STEM Education Research Trends and Development Suggestions

5.1 Trends in STEM Education Research

In order to more deeply explore the development trends and cutting-edge dynamics of STEM education, this study used CiteSpace software to obtain a keyword emergence map of the STEM education research field through the application of vocabulary detection and analysis technology. Keyword emergence refers to the sudden increase in the frequency of certain keywords in a field during a certain period of time. The trend of keyword emergence can reflect the development and evolution of the research in the field, and provide a certain basis for judging future development trends. From Fig. 5, it can be seen that deep learning, artificial intelligence education are research hotspots from 2021 to 2023. This study predicts the future development trend of STEM education through comprehensive reading of literature in this field and combining Table 3 and Fig. 5.

Top 8 Keywords with the Strongest Citation Bursts

Keywords	Year	Strength	Begin	End	2016 - 2023
maker education	2016	2.37	**2016**	2018	
maker space	2016	1.69	**2016**	2017	
content analysis	2017	1.06	**2017**	2018	
tinker education	2019	0.92	**2019**	2021	
teaching model	2019	0.92	**2019**	2021	
stem curriculum	2016	2.25	**2020**	2021	
deep learning	2021	1.85	**2021**	2023	
artificial intelligence education	2021	1.39	**2021**	2023	

Fig. 5. Keyword emergence map for the STEM education sector

5.1.1 Research on the Participation of the Whole People in Promoting the Development of STEM Education

STEM education involves personnel training, social activities, all kinds of education at all levels and other aspects, so the implementation of STEM education activities depends on the participation of many parties. In the promotion of STEM education in the United States, in addition to the strong support of the government, a group of civil organizations led by the "Change Equation" have played an extremely important role in the process of STEM education, which is a bridge between the government, social forces and school education. The Finnish National STEM Education Cooperation Network aims to promote and support national and international cooperation around STEM education among all educational institution education administrations from kindergarten to university, museums, media, students, parents and any other relevant organizations and individuals. China's STEM education has entered a stage of vigorous development, combining the needs of the country and society, bringing together the power of all walks of life, and constantly exploring the practical path of STEM education, but the author believes that there are still more possibilities for collaborative participation in STEM education activities. For example, manufacturing enterprises are encouraged to participate in STEM education, explore a set of "government-led, enterprise operation, and college implementation" STEM education model, combine theory and practice, cultivate innovative talents, and achieve a win-win situation between enterprises and schools.

5.1.2 Research on Promoting the Integration of STEM Education and Marker Education

STEM education is an interdisciplinary education mainly based on scientific disciplines and promoted by engineering practice, while the development of engineering practice requires the use of technical tools and equipment. Traditional STEM education often focuses on hands and lacks the support of technical tools, resulting in rough products and failing to meet the purpose of verifying the corresponding scientific principles. Both maker education and STEM education are regarded as the forces to promote educational change. Similar to STEM education, the learning content involves multiple disciplines such as science, technology, engineering and mathematics, and it is also interdisciplinary learning. One of the major advantages of maker education is the application of technical tools and equipment in engineering practice. The effective combination of 3D printing, robotics, virtual reality, visual programming and other emerging information technologies has spawned maker activities and maker education, but its shortcomings lie in the relative lack of attention to scientific concepts and principles. The two are complementary. If the two can be integrated together, their respective shortcomings can be converted into their respective advantages, so as to achieve further interdisciplinary integration of maker education and science education, and at the same time provide a favorable technical lever for STEM education, realize engineering practice in the true sense, and effectively promote the sustainable development of STEM education and maker education. Therefore, integrating STEM education and maker education will become a major research direction in the future.

5.1.3 Research on the Integration of STEM Education and Deep Learning Assisted by Emerging Technologies

The American Association for College and University Education Informatics released the document "2020 EDUCAUSE Horizon Report: Teaching and Learning Edition", which identifies XR (AR, VR, MR) as an emerging technology for education reform

[27]. China began researching the use of emerging technology tools to facilitate the integration of STEM education and deep learning in 2021 and has shown an accelerating trend, with research momentum only increasing to date. Qin Jinruo based on primary and secondary schools to verify the use of virtual reality technology can create a three-dimensional STEM learning environment, break through the traditional two-dimensional display of learning resources, bringing students a rich observation experience, emotional interaction experience, practical operation experience, to promote students deep learning is of great significance [28]. It is important to promote students' deep learning. Deep learning, in its occurrence, relies on authentic environments, interdisciplinary integration of ideas and knowledge transfer capabilities, and is intrinsically coupled with STEM education, so it is necessary to study the relationship between STEM education and deep learning. In the context of education informatization, information technology support brings a new perspective to the integration of the two. In this process, technology can play three roles: firstly, as a medium to diversify the presentation of tasks and stimulate students' enthusiasm; secondly, as a supporting environment and tool to break the constraints of time and space and enhance students' experience; and thirdly, as an aid to process evaluation, which gives teachers and students feedback by describing students' learning process through a large amount of data. At present, the use of emerging technologies to promote the integration of deep learning and STEM education at all stages of education has become a major trend, not only to facilitate the training of talents in the information age, but also to open up new perspectives for the study of STEM education and to find "new soil" for the occurrence of deep learning.

5.1.4 Research on Two-Way Empowerment of STEM Education and Artificial Intelligence

Research on artificial intelligence in STEM education is focused on 'artificial intelligence education' and 'artificial intelligence technology'. AI education focuses on the process of advanced cognitive thinking based on learning knowledge, effectively promoting deeper learning and enhancing students' computational, programming and innovation skills, which coincides with the goals of STEM education. The promotion of STEM-based AI programmes in primary and secondary schools is now a new direction in education research, which is conducive to enhancing students' comprehensive ability to use technology to solve problems based on real-life scenarios and to develop intelligent talents. Artificial intelligence technology and STEM education are complementary. On the one hand, the use of artificial intelligence technology can create a more optimal teaching and learning environment for students. In a review of the relevant literature, it was found that the support of AI technology for STEM education can be summarised in six areas: firstly, creating an adaptive learning environment; secondly, intelligent guidance; thirdly, resource recommendation, fourthly, knowledge sharing; fifthly, monitoring and feedback, and sixthly, real-time record tracking. On the other hand, the development of STEM education can drive the advancement of artificial intelligence technology. The STEM learning experience provides feedback for the development of artificial intelligence technology and further optimises it. In the context of education informatization, with the continuous optimization of new information technologies such as network technology and artificial intelligence technology, how to better promote the future development of STEM education with the help of new technologies and promote the effective integration between STEM interdisciplinary disciplines into will become the focus of education research. With the advent of the age of intelligence, there is a long way to go for both AI technology to help STEM education and the popularisation of AI education and STEM education. We will definitely make a breakthrough if we recognise the direction of development and study the pathway, so we expect all scholars to keep trying and exploring for the innovation and popularisation of STEM education and AI in the future.

5.1.5 Research on STEM Teachers' Professional Development to Meet the Needs of Educational Information Era

The Ministry of Education's Opinion on the Implementation of the National Primary and Secondary School Teachers' IT Application Capacity Enhancement Project 2.0 emphasises the importance of strengthening the training of STEM teachers, generalist teachers and "dual-teacher teachers". Professional development for STEM teachers only received attention in China in 2019, and 2020 is on a rapid upward trend, with the total number of articles published to date accounting for the fourth largest number of all articles published in the field of STEM education. Although on the rise, the output on STEM teacher outcomes is mismatched with the rapidly developing information age. In the study, it was found that the quality of today's teacher personnel hardly meets the needs of STEM education development. In the context of educational informatization, conceptually, STEM education puts forward some new views on parenting, teaching and resources that teachers may have never been exposed to before; in terms of teaching behaviour, STEM emphasizes creating STEM learning spaces, organizing teams to develop works, using information technology to teach intelligently, and coordinating resources inside and outside schools, which are very different from traditional teaching behavior. Therefore, the professional level of STEM teachers needs to be improved. The Ministry of Education's Department of Teacher Work proposes the digitalisation of the teaching force and the strengthening of big data to support the modernisation of teacher governance and other development measures to improve teachers' professionalism and information literacy.

5.2 Recommendations for the Development of STEM Education

Through exploration and research, it has been found that there are still imbalances and inadequacies in the development of STEM education in China during the era of education informatization, mainly in three areas: uneven regional development, lack of a scientific STEM education evaluation system, and inadequate STEM teacher skills. To promote the improvement of the equity and quality of STEM education in China in the era of informatization and the healthy and sustainable development of STEM in the future, the following recommendations are proposed to address the above issues.

5.2.1 Increase Financial Support and Rationalize the Use of Network Resources to Promote the Balanced Regional Development of STEM Education

The study found that STEM education research in China pays more attention to urban areas than rural areas, and pays more attention to Jiangsu, Beijing, Shanghai, Shaanxi, Northeast and other regions than Yunguichuan in the west and south, and there are significant differences in the quantity and quality of STEM education research. The western and southern Yunguichuan regions of China do not attach importance to the development of STEM education, and the fundamental reason is that due to the influence of economic strength, China should increase capital investment in the region, build STEM education space, and introduce emerging technologies to promote the sustainable development of regional STEM education; At the same time, increase policy support to create a good STEM education cultural environment and atmosphere in the region, so as to promote STEM education in the region to keep pace with the development and updating of STEM education in the context of informatization. Emerging technologies such as AR, drones, 3D printing, and intelligent robots are emerging to provide key support for the development of STEM education, which may be familiar to urban students but relatively unfamiliar to children in rural areas. STEM education objectively requires software and hardware support, but this does not mean that rural schools that do not have the conditions are not suitable for STEM education, and we can start by developing STEM education with rural characteristics. The overall improvement of the level of education informatization has pushed the distance education learning shared by the network to the depths, thereby promoting resource sharing, improving the quality of education, and promoting educational equity, which is conducive to better playing the role of urban driven rural STEM teaching. Secondly, rural schools can also be led to jointly carry out STEM teaching activities through live broadcast software, recording software and other forms, so that students can experience the charm of technology in STEM education, and rural teachers can also obtain and update STEM education concepts and teaching methods in a timely manner. In this way, STEM education with rural characteristics will be developed, the gap between urban and rural areas will be narrowed, and educational equity will be promoted.

5.2.2 Scientific Development of STEM Education Quality Evaluation Supported by Big Data Technology

STEM education activities often adopt real problem-based and project-based learning, which is extremely open and flexible, diverse, and pays more attention to cultivating students 'innovation and research spirit. Therefore, the process evaluation is generally adopted for the quality evaluation of STEM education. Chinese scholars' research on STEM education quality evaluation is often based on classroom observation combined with scales with certain reliability and validity, which is faced with problems such as high cost of process data collection and lack of certain scientificity and accuracy. The development of big data technology has broadened the source path of data, and it can collect the all-round and whole process learning behavior and results of students and teachers in the real state, as well as the interaction data between teachers and students.

For example, the VR system is used to create a three-dimensional STEM learning environment, and the interaction data between students and VR in this environment are automatically recorded in the form of log files. The process learning behavior of learners is monitored and the data is collected, which saves time and effort. Then, based on the collected multivariate data, learning analytics, artificial intelligence algorithms and other technologies were used to simultaneously characterize and predict learners 'learning outcomes, which strongly supported teachers 'transformation from traditional experience-based teaching to evidence-based teaching, and promoted STEM education evaluation to move forward in the direction of scientific and systematic.

5.2.3 Improving Teachers' Comprehensive Capacity and Building a Professional STEM Teaching Force in the Era of Education Information Technology

Building a professional team of STEM teachers is an important starting point to improve teaching quality and implement STEM education. With the rapid development of information technology today, the combination of technology and STEM education has become the general trend. As a new education model, STEM education in the information age requires teachers to adapt to it in new educational concepts, methods and educational literacy that keep pace with The Times. At present, STEM teachers are still in short supply in China. There are still some concepts such as "teacher-centered" and "teaching for the test" that are extremely inconsistent with STEM education and the development of The Times, or teachers' STEM literacy and ability are insufficient, and they do not pay attention to emerging educational technology. Therefore, in the future education research, we should not only establish a perfect STEM teacher training system to cultivate teachers 'professional ability and comprehensive quality, such as the establishment of online and offline STEM teacher training system, especially to radiate to schools in remote mountainous areas or set up special normal majors for training STEM teachers in colleges and universities, but also explore new education concepts. To train teachers to keep pace with The Times, receive new educational concepts and new technologies in time, and adapt to the new needs of STEM teachers in the Internet era. In the process of STEM teaching, teachers should pay attention to individual students, cultivate students 'interdisciplinary thinking and ability, encourage students to combine in-school and off-school learning, change learning methods, and look at problems with a development perspective. In the future, training STEM teachers, exploring new educational concepts, and changing students 'learning styles to diversity will be a focus of STEM education.

Acknowledgements. Thanks for the support of the 2022 Ministry of Education Industry-University Cooperation Collaborative Education Project "Artificial Intelligence Boosts Teacher Team Construction, 220604515170027".

Thanks for the support of the Higher Education Teaching Reform research and practice project in Henan Province (2021GLX110).

References

1. Martín-Páez, T., Aguilera, D., Perales-Palacios, F.J., et al.: What are we talking about when we talk about STEM education? A review of literature. Sci. Educ. **103**(4), 799–822 (2019)
2. Qin, J., Fu, G.: STEM education: interdisciplinary education based on real problem scenarios. China Audio-Vis. Educ. (4), 67–74 (2017)
3. Ministry of Education on the issuance of Education Informatization 13th Five-Year Plan notice. http://www.moe.gov.cn/srcsite/A16/s3342/201606/t20160622_269367.html. Accessed 7 June 2016
4. The 14th Five-Year Plan for National Economic and Social Development of the People's Republic of China and the Outline of the Long-term Goals for 2035. http://www.gov.cn/xinwen/2021-03/13/content_5592681.htm. Accessed 13 Mar 2021
5. Chen, Y., Chen, C., Liu, Z., et al.: The methodology function of CiteSpace mapping knowledge domains. Stud. Sci. Sci. **33**(02), 242–253 (2015)
6. Li, X., Zhang, X., Li, Z., et al.: A bibliometric analysis on business models. Syst. Eng. Theory Pract. **36**(2), 273–287 (2016)
7. Duan, N., Duan, L., Lu, H.: Visual analysis of domestic research in the field of learning analysis in the past ten years. J. Guangxi Coll. Educ. (4), 181–186 (2022)
8. Li, Y., Wang, K., Xiao, Y., et al.: Research and trends in STEM education: a systematic review of journal publications. Int. J. STEM Educ. **7**(1) (2020)
9. Xu, Y.: Research on the construction of STEAM education ecosystem under the background of education informatization 2.0. China Educ. Technol. Equip. (9), 36–38+44 (2020)
10. Yang, Z.: Comprehensively promoting education modernization by informationization: the historical responsibility of educational technology specialty. Res. Audio-Vis. Educ. **39**(1), 5–11,35 (2018)
11. Wang, X.: Innovation and Practice of STEM education: research on the construction of robotics curriculum in primary and secondary schools. Educ. Sci. Res. **11**, 91–95 (2022)
12. Men, H., Liu, J., Han, J.: Application research of open source network course management platform atutor. Mod. Educ. Technol. **20**(S1), 113–116 (2010)
13. Zhang, N., Song, N., Huang, X., et al.: Research Hotspots and development trends of International STEAM teachers: bibliometric analysis based on VOSviewer. Open Educ. Res. **26**(5), 78–87 (2020)
14. Peng, D., Yang, J., Wei, J.: The Future application Path and reflection of '5G+STEM' technology teaching and learning. China Educ. Inf. (19), 11–14+36 (2020)
15. Mustafa, S., Didem, S.: Augmented reality in STEM education: a systematic review. Interact. Learn. Environ. **30**(8), 1556–1569 (2020)
16. Fu, X., Zheng, Y., Ma, Y.: Research status, hotspots and trends of maker education in China – based on the visual analysis of related literature published in China national knowledge infrastructure database. Mod. Distance Educ. **6**, 42–50 (2018)
17. Wang, Z., Li, F., Zhuo, Z.: The integration of maker education and STEM education in American universities: ideas, paths, and inspirations. Fudan Educ. Forum **14**(04), 101–107 (2016)
18. Wang, X.: Research on the maker education model oriented to STEM education. China Audio-Vis. Educ. (08), 36–41 (2015)
19. Li, X., Gao, H., Zou, J., et al.: The transition from STEAM education to maker education under the background of "Internet +" – from project-based learning to the cultivation of innovation ability. Distance Educ. J. **34**(1), 28–36 (2016)
20. Bao, G.: Analysis of the necessity and feasibility of educational informationization and educational technology promoted to the first-class discipline first-class discipline – the experience of learning the outline of the national medium and long term education reform and development plan (2010–2020). Res. Audio-Vis. Educ. **02**, 11–15 (2011)

21. Yang, Z., Wu, D., Chen, M.: Emerging technology helps education ecological reconstruction. China Audio-Vis. Educ. **2**, 1–5 (2019)
22. Fan, W., Zhang, W.: STEAM education: development, connotation and possible path. Mod. Educ. Technol. **28**(03), 99–105 (2018)
23. Liora, B.: The subservient, co-equal, affective, and social integration styles and their implications for the arts. Arts Educ. Policy Rev. (5), 31–37 (1995)
24. Hetland, L., Winner, E., Veenema, S., et al.: Studio Thinking: The Real Benefits of Arts Education, 128–130. Teachers College Press, New York (2007)
25. Li, G., Lv, G.: From STEM education to STEAM education: an analysis of the role of arts. China Audio-Vis. Educ. (09), 31–39+47 (2018)
26. Feng, Z., He, L., Jing, L.: Building STEAM education space with school personality. People's Educ. **07**, 63–65 (2022)
27. EDUCAUSE.2020 ECUCAUSE Horizon Repor. https://library.educause.edu/resources/2020/3/2020-educause-horizon-report-teaching-and-learning-edition. Accessed 2 Mar 2020
28. Qin, J.: Review and thinking of STEM education from the perspective of deep learning. Educ. Theory Pract. **42**(07), 58–63 (2022)

Research on the Current Situation and Enhancement Strategies of Information Technology Teaching Ability of Teachers in Rural Teaching Points

Shanshan Li(✉), Yunge Gao(✉), Kebu Wang, Ruiqing Liu, and Xia Liu

Sanya Aviation and Tourism College, Sanya 57200, Hainan, China
515157293@qq.com, 1976186489@qq.com

Abstract. In this study, a combination of literature research, surveys, interviews, and observation, as well as quantitative and qualitative analysis methods was used to investigate the differences in teaching ability between 10 rural teaching points and 6 urban central schools in Xian an Test Area. The study identified several problems in the development of our target teaching competencies, including the need for an improved IT environment in schools, the lack of specialized training for qualified teachers, the inadequate assessment system without incentives, the relatively poor initiative and continuity in information technology teaching program, the rather conservative teaching mode, and, the single professional development path and ineffective teaching training programs. Based on previous investigations and analyses, this study suggests that in order to improve the teaching ability of our targets, it is of vital importance to optimize their development environment, together with enhancing their motivation for development, providing multi-level teacher training, encouraging independent exploration, as well as guiding them to form a regular, professional development model that combines urban and rural areas under virtual situations.

Keywords: educational information technology · teaching points · central schools · teacher's teaching ability · promotion

1 Introduction

The issue of uneven educational development has long been a major concern for China's education sector and has adversely affected both the quality and efficacy of education. Achieving a balanced development of compulsory education is thus, one of a key element in China's educational developments current research area. However, as an important aspect of rural education, the poor quality of education at teaching points remains to be a persistent obstacle to the progress of basic education in China [1].

The development of a high-quality teaching strength is critical to improving the overall quality of education in China [2]. As social progress and educational advancement continues to accelerate, there is a growing need for equitable and effective education [3].

J. Gan et al. (Eds.): CSEI 2023, CCIS 1899, pp. 140–157, 2024.
https://doi.org/10.1007/978-981-99-9499-1_12

Therefore, improving the teaching capacity of educators in rural teaching institutions has become an imperative to improve education in these areas. The National Medium- and Long-Term Education Reform and Development Plan (2010–2020) also emphasizes the importance of stringent teacher qualification and skill enhancement to develop a skilled and professional teaching strength [4].

The rapid progress of educational informatization imposes not only stern challenges and higher standards to rural teachers, but also requires innovative teaching theories, scientific teaching methods, and what's more, first-class teaching materials [5]. As such, it provides new perspectives for enhancing teaching abilities of instructors and new opportunities for improving education in rural teaching centers. With this purpose in mind, a survey upon teachers' teaching ability in urban center schools and rural teaching sites in Xian an, Hubei Province, as our experimental area, was conducted and practically explored, with the aim of providing some reference for improving teachers' teaching ability and thus the overall quality of education in rural teaching points.

2 Research Design

2.1 Objectives and Data Sources

Six central schools and ten rural teaching points in Xian an district, Hubei Province were selected for this study. Relevant data were obtained through questionnaire surveys, in-depth interviews and classroom observations. The purpose was to compare and analyze the teaching abilities of teachers from central schools and teaching points, to identify existing problems and causes, and to provide targeted strategies and suggestions based on the analysis.

2.2 Distribution of Questionnaires and Reliability Testing

The survey questionnaire consists of three main parts: teachers' teaching attitudes, teaching cognition, and teaching behavior skills, each of which has been further divided into three dimensions. The ratings were based on a Likert 5-point scale. Additionally, the survey questionnaire included basic information about the teachers and external factors related to the information development environment. A total of 16 schools were surveyed, including 6 central schools and 10 rural teaching points located in Xian an district. Among the 10 teaching points, 27 questionnaires were distributed and collected with an effective rate of 100%. For the six central schools, 130 teacher questionnaires were classified into different groups. Among them, 124 valid questionnaires were collected, with an efficiency rate of about 95.4%. All the data of the collected valid questionnaires were statistically analyzed with the help of SPSS 22 software.

The reliability and validity of the questionnaires was analyzed and the Cronbach's α coefficient of the questionnaires and scales used in this study was 0.913 (as shown in Table 1). Hence, the questionnaire had a high reliability with strong stability and consistency for specific analysis and research purposes.

Furthermore, the questionnaire was developed by thoroughly reviewing a significant amount of related literature and incorporating indicators that had been extensively adopted in relevant studies. As a result, the questionnaire used in this study possesses a reasonable level of validity.

Table 1. Reliability Analysis of the Scale

Reliability statistical data		
Cronbach's α	Cronbach's α based on standardized items	number of items
.913	.910	62

3 Analysis of The Teaching Ability of Teachers Between Urban Center Schools and Rural Teaching Points in Xian An District

3.1 Analysis of Differences in Teacher Basic Information

Table 2 shows that teachers in teaching points are lower than teachers in central schools in all dimensions, except for the number of young teachers in the age structure. Only 27.8% of those in the former have more than 20 years of teaching experience, which is 26.9% lower than that of those in the latter. Meanwhile, the proportion of teaching points teachers who received non-teacher education is 27.8%, which is 18.3% higher than that of central school's teachers. The proportion of teaching points teachers who teach subjects that do not match their majors is 44.4%, which is 18.2% higher than that of central schools' teachers. This suggests that experienced teachers are relatively scarce at teaching points and that many teachers have not received appropriate training. Moreover, a large proportion of staff teaches subjects that do not match their educational background. These issues need to be addressed and further mitigated.

Table 2. Description and Statistics of Basic Teachers Information in Urban Central Schools and Rural Teaching Points

Basic information		Teachers in urban central schools	Teachers in rural teaching points
Gender	Male	28.6%	27.8%
	Female	71.4%	72.2%
Age	Under 25 years old	9.8%	11.1%
	25–35 years old	26.2%	33.4%
	35–45 years old	39%	22.2%
	Over 45 years old	25%	33.3%
Teaching experience	0–5 years	4.8%	33.3%
	5–10 years	16.7%	16.7%
	10–20 years	23.8%	22.2%
	Over 20 years	54.7%	27.8%

(*continued*)

Table 2. (*continued*)

Basic information		Teachers in urban central schools	Teachers in rural teaching points
Academic qualifications	Junior college or lower	38.4%	55.6%
	Undergraduate	61.6%	44.4%
	Master's Degree	0.0%	0.0%
	Doctoral degree or higher	0.0%	0.0%
Type of education	Teacher education programs	90.5%	72.2%
	Non-teacher education programs	9.5%	27.8%
Teaching subject and Major studied	Matching	73.8%	55.6%
	Not matching	26.2%	44.4%

3.2 Analysis of Differences in Teacher Development Environment

3.2.1 Multimedia Equipment Provision

According to the survey, all classrooms in the central schools are equipped with multimedia devices, while only 1–2 classrooms in teaching points are equipped with multimedia devices. Regarding the availability of common teaching software such as was, Office and Photoshop, 64.5% of the teachers in the central school said "basically available", while only 11.1% of the teachers in the teaching sites reported the same. Besides, none of the teaching points have a dedicated multimedia manager while the central schools have specialized multimedia management personnels who are able to solve any problems timely and ensure regular updates. In contrast, problems with multimedia equipment at teaching points are often not addressed timely, and also, rarely updated. The specific details are shown in Table 3.

Table 3. The Multimedia Equipment Allocation in Urban Central Schools and Rural Teaching Points

Variable		Urban central schools	Rural teaching points
The installation status of electronic whiteboard	Already installed	100%	100%
	Not installed	0.0%	0.0%
Number of multimedia classrooms	Zero	0.0%	0.0%
	1–2	0.0%	100%
	3–5	0.0%	0.0%
	6–10	0.0%	0.0%
	All	100%	0.0%

(*continued*)

Table 3. (*continued*)

Variable		Urban central schools	Rural teaching points
educational software	All have	0.0%	0.0%
	Mostly have	64.5%	11.1%
	Some have	35.5%	81.5%
	Almost none	0.0%	7.4%
	All none	0.0%	0.0%
management personnel	Yes	100%	0.0%
	part-time employees	0.0%	0.0%
	None	0.0%	100%

3.2.2 Teacher Training

The frequency with which schools organize teacher training for teaching and learning is compared in Table 4. The results show that 57.3% of teachers in central school report that their school organizes information technology training frequently, whereas only 15.6% of teachers in teaching points agreed. In terms of the frequency of off-campus teaching and research activities organized every school year, 44.8% of central school's teachers say that they had many opportunities, while teachers at teaching sites have no such opportunities. Additionally, a strikingly high proportion (i.e., up to 84.9%) of teachers in teaching points, claim that they rarely participate in off-campus teaching and research activities.

Table 4. Teachers Training Status of Urban Central Schools and Rural Teaching Point

Variable		Urban central schools	Rural teaching points
Information Technology Teaching Training	Frequently	57.3%	15.6%
	Sometimes	40.3%	73.3%
	Rarely	2.4%	11.1%
	Never	0.0%	0.0%
The frequency of extracurricular teaching and research activities	Frequently	44.8%	0.0%
	Sometimes	48.1%	15.1%
	Rarely	7.1%	84.9%
	Never	0.0%	0.0%

3.2.3 Analysis of Differences in Teachers' Attitudes Towards Teaching

As shown in Table 5, an independent sample t-test was conducted to compare the teaching attitudes of central school's teachers and teaching points teachers. The total average score for teaching attitudes among central school's teachers was M = 4.4484, with a Standard Deviation of SD = 0.18222. For teaching points teachers, the total average score and Standard Deviation of SD was 4.2426 and 0.36954, respectively. The t-test results confirm T = 1.224 and P = 0.249 > 0.05, indicating that there was no significant difference in teaching attitudes between the two groups of teachers.

More specifically, it was found that there was no significant difference in the mean scores of teachers' attitude towards teaching between teaching sites and central schools on the three dimensions of IT education, IT teaching, and teaching evaluation. All corresponding p-values were greater than 0.05, indicating that there were no differences in attitudes between the two groups. Nevertheless, there were significant differences in IT students' perceptions ($p = 0.000 < 0.05$) and attitudes towards teaching innovation ($p = 0.029 < 0.05$), suggesting the need for teachers at the teaching points to strengthen students' sense of self-directed learning and innovation. Although no significant differences were observed in the perception of teaching differences ($p = 0.911 > 0.05$), the mean scores of both groups were relatively low. This reveals that both groups performed poorly in this area.

Table 5. T-test for Differences in Teaching Attitudes between Urban Central Schools and Rural Teaching Points

Dimension	Teachers in urban central schools		Teachers in rural teaching points		T-value	P-value
	Average value	Standard Deviation	Average value	Standard Deviation		
Lifelong learning awareness	4.6905	.46790	4.6667	.48507	.179	.859
Enhancing capability awareness	4.6429	.48497	4.6111	.50163	.230	.819
Enhancing capability awareness	4.4048	.49680	4.2333	.48507	.514	.609
Information-based teaching awareness	4.3810	.49151	4.2222	.42779	1.189	.239
Proactive awareness of information teaching	4.3571	.57685	4.0556	.23570	2.135	.037
Continuous awareness of information teaching	4.2143	.51965	3.6667	.48507	3.813	.000

3.2.4 Analysis of Differences in Teachers' Cognitive Perception of Teaching

According to the results of the independent t-test in Table 6, the overall mean of teachers' perceptions of teaching in the central school is M = 4.1135 with a Standard Deviation of SD = 0.39659. By comparison, among teaching points teachers, the corresponding values are M = 3.8889 and SD = 0.50062, respectively. The t-test for the overall cognitive perception of teaching between the two groups yielded a T-statistic of 0.861 and P = 0.409 > 0.05, proving that there is no significant difference in the overall cognitive perception of teaching between the two groups.

A closer look at the mean scores for the dimensions of perceptions of IT teaching, perceptions of IT teachers, and perceptions of teaching assessment show the smallest differences between the two groups. Furthermore, the P values for all three dimensions are much greater than 0.05, indicating no significant differences and a shared attitude. However, there are a significant difference between them on the perception of student-centered learning and teaching innovation dimensions, with p-values of 0.000 and 0.029, respectively, both less than 0.05. Thus, teaching points teachers should focus on strengthening their innovation consciousness and promoting student-centered learning. Despite the P value for perceived differences in teaching is 0.911, which is greater than 0.05, the mean scores of both groups are relatively low, which indicates that both groups performed poorly on this dimension.

Table 6. T-test of Teaching Cognitive Differences between Urban Central Schools and Rural Teaching Points

Dimension	Teachers in urban central schools		Teachers in rural teaching points		T-value	P-value
	Average value	Standard Deviation	Average value	Standard Deviation		
Information technology teaching perspective	4.4762	.50549	4.4444	.51131	.222	.825
Information technology teacher perspective	4.4762	.50549	4.3889	.50163	.614	.541
Information technology student perspective	4.1429	.35417	3.5556	.61570	4.664	.000
Teaching differentiation perspective	3.4286	.50087	3.4444	.51131	-.112	.911
Teaching evaluation perspective	4.2381	.48437	4.1667	.51450	.514	.609
Teaching innovation perspective	3.9190	.49151	3.3333	.48507	2.071	.029

3.2.5 Analysis of Differences in Teacher Teaching Behavior Skills

3.2.5.1 Teachers' Basic IT Operational Skills

Based on the data presented in Table 7, there is a significant difference considering the overall level of their basic IT operational skills. The total average score of basic operation skills of information technology for central school's teachers is M = 4.1778 with a Standard Deviation of SD = 0.38602, while the total average score of teaching points teachers is M = 3.4167 with a Standard Deviation of SD = 0.62038. The t-test results between the two groups are t = 2.551 with p = 0.029 < 0.05, further confirming the significant difference in the proficiency of basic IT skills.

These findings suggest that there is room for improvement in the ability of the teachers at the teaching sites to use IT effectively in the classroom. Teachers in central schools have a higher level of mastery of the required skills and may be more capable of integrating technology into their teaching practices.

Since the P-values for each dimension are all less than 0.05, this indicates that the two groups are significantly different on each dimension. Based on the average values of each dimension, it is evident that there is a significant disparity between teaching points teachers and central school's teachers, requiring more emphasis on learning and training. Although the center school teachers score higher on average than the teaching site teachers in image processing and audiovisual processing skills, these two dimensions also score the lowest in their own skills. This implies that both groups need to focus on learning and enhancing their image processing and audio-visual processing skills.

Table 7. T-test for Differences in Basic Information Technology Operation Skills Between Teachers in the Urban Central Schools and Rural Teaching Points

Dimension	Teachers in urban central schools		Teachers in rural teaching points		T-value	P-value
	Average value	Standard Deviation	Average value	Standard Deviation		
Information retrieval skills	4.5000	.59469	4.0556	.23570	3.057	.003
Resource downloading skills	4.5238	.50549	3.9444	.53930	3.988	.000
Text editing skills	4.4286	.50087	3.8333	.51450	4.185	.000
PPT production skills	4.2143	.41530	3.2778	.48507	6.198	.000
Image processing skills	3.7190	.58236	2.7222	.82644	4.800	.000
Audio and video processing skills	3.6810	.66083	2.6667	.68599	3.794	.000

3.2.5.2 Teachers Selection and Utilization of Teaching Resources

In Table 8, the average score for central school's teachers' selection and utilization of teaching resources is M = 3.8968, with a Standard Deviation at SD = 0.42073. The average score for teaching points teachers is M = 3.0741, with a Standard Deviation at SD = 0.64278. The results of T-test show that T = 2.623 with P = 0.025, which is below the level of significance of 0.05. Therefore, there is a significant difference in the ability to select and utilize teaching resources between the two groups, and the P-values for all dimensions are less than 0.05, indicating significant differences in each dimension.

Specifically, teachers at the teaching sites score very low on communication, handling, development and sharing of resources, which indicates their poor performance in this area. Additionally, teachers in central schools need to continuously improve in this area.

Table 8. T-test for Differences in Teaching Resource Selection and Utilization Skills Between Teachers from Urban Central Schools and Rural Teaching Points

Dimension	Teachers in urban central schools		Teachers in rural teaching points		T-value	P-value
	Average value	Standard Deviation	Average value	Standard Deviation		
Ability to communicate resources	3.9286	.46291	3.0000	.59409	6.528	.000
Ability to acquire resources	4.4762	.59420	3.9444	.41618	3.444	.001
Ability to select resources	4.2857	.55373	3.7778	.42779	3.467	.001
Ability to process resources	3.7381	.66478	2.7222	.75190	5.215	.000
Ability to develop resources	3.3810	.66083	2.3889	.50163	5.694	.000
Ability to share resources	3.5714	.70340	2.6111	.69780	4.857	.000

3.2.5.3 Teachers' Ability in Lesson Planning

Table 9 reveals that the average score for teachers' ability in lesson planning among central school's teachers is $M = 4.0131$ with a Standard Deviation at $SD = 0.23701$. In contrast, the average score for lesson planning ability among teaching points teachers is $M = 3.6778$, with a Standard Deviation at $SD = 0.51129$. Notably, the T-test results indicate that there is no significant difference in the overall ability in lesson planning between teaching points and central school's teachers, with $T = 1.330$ and $P = 0.220 > 0.05$. Nevertheless, the P-values for the ability in selecting teaching methods and design teaching media are both 0 and less than 0.05. Thus, there exist significant differences between these two groups in these areas. Furthermore, the scores in these two areas are lower than the other three areas, demonstrating that both groups need to emphasize and strengthen these two areas in their daily teaching programs.

Table 9. T-test for Differences in Teaching Design Ability Between Teachers in Urban Central Schools and Rural Teaching Points

Dimension	Teachers in urban central schools		Teachers in rural teaching points		T-value	P-value
	Average value	Standard Deviation	Average value	Standard Deviation		
Teaching needs analysis skills	4.1667	.53723	4.0556	.53930	.733	.466
Teaching content analysis skills	4.3095	.56258	4.2222	.42779	.588	.559
Teaching objective analysis skills	4.0476	.43909	3.8333	.51450	1.645	.105
Teaching method selection skills	3.7857	.56464	3.1111	.67640	3.994	.000
Teaching media design skills	3.7619	.48437	3.1667	.61835	4.008	.000

3.2.5.4 Teachers' Teaching Implementation Ability

In accordance with Table 10, the average score for teachers' ability in teaching implementation among central school's teachers is M = 4.0088, with a Standard Deviation of SD = 0.23200. In comparison, the overall average score for teachers' teaching implementation ability in teaching points is M = 3.5555, with a Standard Deviation of SD = 0.54141. The T-test indicates that there is no significant difference in the overall ability in teaching implementation between teaching points and central school's teachers, as T = 1.721 and P = 0.124 > 0.05.

However, there are significant differences between the two groups in the dimensions of class introduction, teaching methods application, and integration of teaching and technology, all with P-values of 0. These results suggest that there are significant discrepancies between the two groups in these three areas, and the average scores also indicate an obvious gap. Therefore, it is highly recommended to prioritize and promote improvement in these areas in their daily teaching.

Table 10. T-test for the Differences in Various Dimensions of Teaching Implementation Ability Between Teachers in Urban Central Schools and Rural Teaching Points

Dimension	Teachers in urban central schools		Teachers in rural teaching points		T-value	P-value
	Average value	Standard Deviation	Average value	Standard Deviation		
Classroom introduction skills	3.9762	.41249	3.2778	.66911	4.943	.000
Lesson implementation skills	4.1429	.41739	4.0556	.41618	.743	.460
Teaching content explanation skills	4.3333	.57027	4.2222	.42779	.741	.462
Teaching method application skills	3.8059	.55163	3.1667	.70711	3.794	.000
Integration of teaching and technology skills	3.7857	.56464	3.0556	.72536	4.207	.000

3.2.5.5 Teachers' Teaching Evaluation Ability

According to Table 11, the average score of teachers' teaching evaluation ability among central school's teachers is M = 3.8929, with a Standard Deviation of SD = 0.31014. In comparison, the overall average score of teachers' teaching evaluation ability among teaching points teachers is M = 3.2222, with a Standard Deviation of SD = 0.72156. The T-test indicates that there is no significant difference in the overall teaching evaluation ability between teaching points and central school's teachers, as T = 1.708 and P = 0.139 > 0.05. However, there are some significant differences between the two groups in terms of procedural evaluation ability and information-based procedural evaluation ability, with P-values of 0 for both dimensions. These results indicate that there are significant differences between the two groups in procedural evaluation ability and informational evaluation ability, and the mean scores also indicate a significant gap between the teaching site teachers and the central school's teachers. The findings suggest that teaching points teacher pay little attention to procedural evaluation of students in the teaching process and do not use informational tools to evaluate teaching. On the other hand, the difference evaluation ability scores of the teaching site teachers are higher than those of the central school's teachers, implying that the teaching points teachers performed better in evaluating students' differences.

Table 11. T-test for Differences in Teaching Evaluation Ability Between Teachers from Urban Central Schools and Rural Teaching Points

Dimension	Teachers in urban central schools		Teachers in rural teaching points		T-value	P-value
	Average value	Standard Deviation	Average value	Standard Deviation		
Process evaluation skills	3.9524	.49151	2.8333	.70711	7.052	.000
Information-based process evaluation skills	3.7857	.60630	2.4444	.51131	8.208	.000
Summative evaluation skills	4.2857	.45723	4.0556	.63914	1.580	.120
Differential evaluation skills	3.4476	.59274	3.5556	.61570	−.047	.963

3.2.5.6 Reflection Ability of Teachers' Teaching

According to Table 12, it is evident that the average value of the reflective ability of teachers' teaching among central school's teachers is $M = 3.7917$, with a Standard Deviation of $SD = 0.08558$. The average value of the reflective ability of teachers' teaching among teaching points teachers is overall $M = 2.8611$, with a Standard Deviation of $SD = 0.28144$. T-test results indicate that there is a significant difference in the reflective ability of teaching between teaching points and central school's teachers, where $T = 6.327$ and $P = 0.001 < 0.05$.

Further analysis reveals that the P-values of all three dimensions are 0, revealing that there are significant differences between the two groups on each dimension. Based on the scores, it can be seen that teaching points teacher pay the least attention to reflection on teaching methods and teaching activities, followed by reflection on teaching goals.

Table 12. T-test for Differences in Teaching Reflective Ability Between Teachers from Urban Central Schools and Rural Teaching Points

Dimension	Teachers in urban central schools		Teachers in rural teaching points		T-value	P-value
	Average value	Standard Deviation	Average value	Standard Deviation		
Reflective ability on teaching objectives	3.8095	.55163	2.9444	.53930	5.603	.000
Reflective ability on teaching methods	3.7381	.62701	2.6111	.60768	6.438	.000
Reflective ability on teaching activities	3.7143	.55373	2.6667	.59409	6.572	.000
Reflective ability on teaching outcomes	3.9048	.57634	3.2222	.80845	3.710	.000

3.2.5.7 Teachers Selection and Utilization of Teaching Reflection Ability of Teachers' Teaching

According to the data in Table 13, it is evident that central school's teachers possess a higher level of teaching innovation ability (average value of $M = 3.7500$ and a Standard Deviation of $SD = 0.08415$) compared to teaching points teachers (an average value of $M = 2.5556$ and a Standard Deviation of $SD = 0.07856$). Additionally, T-test analysis indicates a significant difference in teaching innovation ability between the two groups with $T = 14.674$ and $P = 0.005 < 0.05$.

Furthermore, it is worth noting that there are highly significant differences in both dimensions of teaching content innovation and teaching method innovation, with a p-value of 0. This suggests that teaching points teachers should focus on enhancing their ability to cultivate an awareness of innovation and utilize information technology more effectively to promote the development of innovative teaching content and teaching methods.

Table 13. T-test for Differences in Teaching Innovation Ability Between Teachers from Urban Central Schools and Rural Teaching Points

Dimension	Teachers in urban central schools		Teachers in rural teaching points		T-value	P-value
	Average value	Standard Deviation	Average value	Standard Deviation		
Innovative ability in teaching content	3.8095	.55163	2.6111	.69780	7.111	.000
Innovative ability in teaching methods	3.6905	.56258	2.5000	.61835	7.292	.000

4 Analysis of Problems and Causes in the Development of Teaching Ability of Teachers in Rural Teaching Points

4.1 School's Efforts in Information Technology Have Achieved Some Positive Results, but there is Still Room for Improvement

In recent years, there have been great progress in education information reform Xian an district, and the information environment in rural teaching centers has been improved. To facilitate information-based teaching, the local government and education bureau have provided multimedia classrooms and installed electronic whiteboards in each teaching center. These measures have greatly benefitted teachers and students alike.

However, based on interviews conducted, it is found that despite the current improved teaching environment with IT teaching aids, the network or multimedia equipment is often interrupted due to natural or human factors, resulting in disruptions in the normal conduct of the classroom. Firstly, network connectivity is often affected by weather, road repairs, and other external factors. Secondly, due to the lack of technical managers for IT teaching aids at the teaching sites, teachers have no choice but to report to the central school, which notifies the equipment company or higher management. This results in a delay in the timely repair of equipment malfunctions.

4.2 The Issues of Low Academic Qualifications and Professional Mismatch Among Teachers are Particularly Prominent

Based on the survey of 27 teachers in 10 teaching sites, it is found that only 44.4% of them had attained a bachelor's degree or higher, a percentage 17.2% lower than that of the central school. Furthermore, 27.8% of the teachers graduated from non-teacher training institutions, implying that they lack the necessary systematic learning and training. Most notably, many teachers in these points are assigned to teach subjects that do not align with their academic specialization, and they often play multiple roles simultaneously.

Essentially, there are two main reasons for this phenomenon. First, new teachers tend to opt for teaching environments and conditions that is conducive to their development, which are typically found in urban schools. As a result, they are often deterred from working in rural teaching sites, which are known to have relatively inferior teaching environments and living conditions. Secondly, teacher mobility usually involves the relocation of highly qualified rural teachers to urban schools, while relatively few teachers from urban schools relocate to rural schools. As a consequence, recruitments of new teachers in rural areas often depend on enrolling non-specialist university graduates with diverse backgrounds, many of whom have not went through any training program.

4.3 The Imperfect Teacher Evaluation System and the Lack of Incentive Mechanisms is Important Problems for Teachers' Teaching Ability Improvement in the Context of Information Technology

The current evaluation for teaching quality and ability is mainly based on a result-oriented approach, which primarily depends on students' final learning outcomes without due consideration of the other efforts made by teachers in the educational process.

One of the crucial reasons for the inadequate evaluation system of teachers in rural teaching centers is the low level of attention and recognition given to these teachers by the local education authorities compared to schools in urban centers. Furthermore, the emotional and psychological needs of rural teachers are neglected. Additionally, the majority of students in rural teaching centers are left-behind children who are looked after by older family members, revealing that they lack the public opinion monitoring and evaluation capacity of families in urban centers with respect to education.

4.4 Teachers at Teaching Sites Have a Strong Identification with IT Teaching, although they Lack Initiative and Continuity in Its Implementation

The survey indicates that teachers at these sites generally possess an objective understanding of information technology teaching and exhibit a high level of recognition. However, there is still room for improvement in terms of initiative and continuity when implementing information technology in teaching practices. Although synchronous blending of classes with central schools through multimedia classrooms is common, the integration of multimedia devices in daily instruction remains limited.

There may be two factors contributing to this phenomenon. On one hand, teachers at the teaching site often have incomplete knowledge of multimedia device functions. Although they are aware of the operation and use of multimedia equipment during synchronous hybrid classes, other functions may remain unknown to them. On the other hand, the untimely and inconvenient maintenance of the equipment caused teachers' concerns and prevented them from using the equipment autonomously and consistently.

4.5 Teachers at Teaching Sites Use Outdated Teaching Models and Have a Low Level of Integration Between Subject Teaching and IT

Currently, teachers at these sites continue to rely on traditional lecture-style teaching, with little interaction or communication among students, and minimal opportunities for independent and collaborative exploration. Interviews with these teachers also revealed that they tend to rely heavily on resources downloaded from digital platforms in their daily instruction, and rarely customize or develop their own materials.

Main reasons for the conservative pedagogical model at these sites are the teachers' age, limited IT skills, and lack of pedagogical innovation Moreover, given the limited resources and heavy teaching loads at these sites, teachers often find it difficult to devote sufficient time and energy to learning and innovation and therefore find it difficult to simply fulfill their teaching responsibilities. Hence, more support and resources are required to help strengthen teaching practices and foster innovation at these sites.

4.6 Inadequate Access to Teachers' Professional Development Has Led to Poor Results in their Training

Presently, local education departments organize centralized or online training for teachers at teaching sites annually. However, many teachers report that this training has little positive impact and dwarfs the frequency of their training compared to central school's teachers.

Part of the reason for this situation may be attributed to the fact that local education departments do not place as much emphasis on improving the teaching capacity of teachers at the teaching sites as they do on teachers in central schools. It is also due to the limited number of teachers at the teaching sites, most of which have only one or two staffs. If they attend training courses, they will inevitably not be able to take teaching tasks. Therefore, many of them chose not to attend and the education authorities did not enforce it.

5 Strategies and Suggestions for Improving the Information-Based Teaching Ability of Teachers in Rural Teaching Sites

5.1 Optimizing the Environment for Teacher Development and Enhancing Teachers' Motivation for Professional Growth

The availability of IT hardware and software in schools is a basic prerequisite for improving teachers' teaching ability. Local educational authorities ought to arrange for specialist personnel to periodically conduct thorough inspections of the hardware and software teaching equipment in teaching points, and assign technical support personnel to the teaching points, with the aim of improving the efficiency of using or repairing hardware and software equipment and minimizing their disruptive effects on regular teaching program [6].

Unequal distribution of resources is also one of the main reasons for the huge gap in teaching capacity between central and satellite schools to address this issue, a number of measures can be taken. To start with, it is important to strive for a balanced allocation of teachers and to recruit more young, highly qualified, and professional teachers. Then, a sound teacher mobility mechanism should be established to allow rural teachers to move to urban schools and urban teachers to move to rural schools. Such a mechanism will encourage and motivate teachers to learn and grow. Finally, multi-level incentive mechanisms should be developed at the regional, school, and subject levels to improve teachers' teaching enthusiasm and to promote the upgrading of their teaching abilities in a comprehensive way.

5.2 Develop Multi-Level Teacher Training to Guide Teachers to Change their Concepts and Roles

Establishing a multi-level teacher training system is crucial to promote teachers' attitude and role change in integrating information technology into teaching [7]. The first stage is to improve teachers' awareness of information technology in education through training in information technology application skills. This process will equip them with basic skills apply IT while gradually developing the habit of using IT for teaching and learning.

The second stage involves TPACK knowledge and skill training, which will be facilitated through various approaches, such as showcasing exemplar teaching cases, practical teaching observation, and teaching seminars, which aims to provide a comprehensive guidance so that they can seamlessly integrate subject knowledge, technology knowledge and teaching skills.

In the third stage, teachers will be organized to participate in practical exercises in information technology teaching, such as selecting and showcasing their achievements in the application of information technology, and conducting hands-on activities to deepen their experience in teaching scenarios. The objective is to encourage teachers to actively apply information technology in teaching and to facilitate the normalization of information technology in teaching.

In the fourth stage, specialized personnel will be assigned to guide the effectiveness of teacher training and information technology teaching practice, and to organize research and reflective discussions for all trainers.

5.3 Encourage Teachers to Conduct Independent Exploration and Improve their Teaching Abilities through Reflective Practice

Action research are an efficient educational research approach. Conducting action research in the actual teaching environment means "research in education and education in research" [8], it is performed in practical educational contexts to address teaching issues. The improvement strategies acquired from research are then implemented in teaching practice. Through continuous critical thinking and reflection on their own classroom teaching, teachers can improve their teaching styles and strengthen their teaching abilities [9].

Teachers in information-based education need to improve their face-to-face collaborative communication skills in addition to the effective use of information technology to develop collaborative communication skills in the online environment. Moreover, teachers can leverage their professional development platforms, teacher forums, and other resources to communicate and learn from renowned teachers and experts, thereby promoting self-learning and self-reflection on teaching practices and ultimately improving their teaching capabilities.

5.4 Form a Regular Pattern of Teacher Professional Development through a Combination of Urban and Rural Contexts, and the Integration of Theoretical and Practical Knowledge

An urban-rural teacher community is a collaborative and learning-based organization established by teachers to transcend geographic barriers and support each other. With shared resources, teachers engage in teaching and learning activities and work together in equal and harmonious partnership to address educational and pedagogical challenges. This process promotes the Co-development of urban and rural educators [10].

In the context of urban-rural teacher communities, it is crucial to encourage collaborative and reciprocal research-based activities between teachers from both urban and rural areas. Participation in group learning can enhance their sense of self-development and foster a voluntary commitment to improving their own teaching skills [11]. Such activities may involve opportunities to facilitate teacher observation and exchange, as well as collective lesson evaluations. However, it can be challenging to organize face-to-face seminars due to geographical limitations. The use of information technology, such as the creation of QQ or WeChat groups, or the use of online teacher communities and forums to ships resources and conduct research activities, are of vital importance in this regard.

References

1. Wang, S., Bao, J.: Empowering the co-governance of urban and rural compulsory education with digital technology—theoretical mechanisms and implementation pathways. China Educ. Technol. **575**(12), 26–34+83 (2022)
2. Notice on the Release of the "New Era Strong Teachers Plan for Basic Education" by the Ministry of Education and Eight Other Departments Homepage. https://www.gov.cn/gongbao/content/2022/content_5697984.htm. Accessed 21 July 2023

3. Yang, L.: How rural teaching points promote teachers' professional growth. Learn. Wkly. (08), 81–82 (2018)
4. State Council. National Medium-and Long-Term Education Reform and Development Plan Outline (2010–2020) (2010)
5. He, W., He, W., Jiang, H.: Issues and solutions of teacher team building for compulsory education in rural areas in the new stage —a case study of Chongqing. J. Chongqing Univ. Arts Sci. (Soc. Sci. Edition) **41**(03), 117–129 (2022)
6. Li, R., Cheng, L., Tang, Z.: Research on hot topics, fields and trend of rural teachers' professional development—an analysis on science knowledge map of CiteSpace. J. Teach. Educ. **6**(3), 21–30 (2019)
7. Xiao, Y.: Study on the evaluation index system of school education informatization — the perspective of primary and secondary school principals. China Educ. Technol. **265**(02), 25–29 (2009)
8. Bai, Y.: Research on the professional development of English teachers under the background of high school curriculum reform in China. Master's thesis, Inner Mongolia Normal University, p. 23 (2017)
9. Deepening the Reform of Precision Training Enables Teacher Professional Development — The Second Academic Roundtable of Teacher Professional Development in the Digital Era and the Press Conference of China Teacher Training Development Report (2022) — Precision Training Perspective was held. Chin. J. Distance Educ. **43**(07), 77 (2023)
10. Zuo, M., Lu, Q. Lei, L.: Confusion and breakthrough—a study on regional teachers' information technology teaching ability training practice. China Educ. Technol. (05), 104–111 (2016)
11. Zhang, L., Liang, K., Liu, X., et al.: Name teacher classroom from the perspective of symbiosis: essence, realistic predicament, and solutions. China Educ. Technol. **44**(05), 44–50+59 (2023)

Research on User Profile of Game Products Based on Self-determination Theory

Zhongyuan Liu[1] and Bin Wen[1,2(✉)]

[1] School of Information Science, Yunnan Normal University, Kunming, China
ynwenbin@163.com

[2] Key Laboratory of Educational Informatization for Nationalities, Yunnan Normal University, Kunming, China

Abstract. As the global technology competition intensifies, the technological and cultural value of the game industry has been seen more and more, and countries have also increased their investment in the game industry. This paper proposes a method that combines self-determination theory and user profile to provide a new approach for establishing user profiles in the gaming field. Based on research related to self-determination theory, we build an automatic division algorithm by division metrics and Fisher-Jenks clustering algorithm to profile users of sample products. We found that users who seek audiovisual experiences are the core users of the platform where the sample of products are located. These users exhibit high levels of activity, payment levels, and influence. Additionally, the sample products excel in two specific content areas, which attract the majority of their users.

Keywords: User Profile · Fisher-Jenks Clustering · Self-Determination Theory · Group Division

1 Introduction

As global technological competition becomes increasingly fierce, countries are investing more and more in the gaming industry. The public has gradually begun to realize and explore the diverse social values of gaming, particularly its technological and cultural values. By 2022, the gaming industry became a strong engine for stimulating cultural consumption potential and promoting the development of the digital economy. The actual sales revenue reached 296.5 billion yuan, the user scale reached 666 million, and the number of related enterprises reached more than 390,000. The gaming industry has also become an important field for exploring digital technology innovation and application and promoting innovation in external industries. Research and development investment in digital engines, image rendering, cloud computing, virtual reality, motion capture, digital humans, and other fields has increased year by year. And some of these specialties have reached world-leading levels. As of now, the contribution of the gaming industry to technological progress in chips, high-speed communication networks, and the AR/VR industry has increased to 14.9%, 46.3%, and 71.6%, respectively. At the same time, gaming has become an effective carrier for inheriting and promoting excellent

J. Gan et al. (Eds.): CSEI 2023, CCIS 1899, pp. 158–171, 2024.
https://doi.org/10.1007/978-981-99-9499-1_13

traditional Chinese culture and telling China's story to the world. Chinese gaming users overseas have rated China's national image more than 20% higher than nongaming users, and 68% of overseas gaming users widely recognize and accept the Chinese cultural elements contained in games. This research proposes a method that combines self-determination theory with user profiling, and is applied to the gaming industry. The method to profile users to understand product's user characteristics, and provide a new approach for researching gaming user profile. This method is helpful for small enterprises and independent developers without data mining departments to understand user characteristics. And then, to adjust development content and promotional strategies based on the characteristics.

2 Related Work

2.1 User Profile

User profiles refer to the characterization of user characteristics through direct or indirect data [1]. Through user profiling, user needs can be better understood. In the business field, user profiling can provide personalized services for users, achieve precision marketing [2], and serve as a tool for personalized recommendations [3].

When profiling users, different researchers may use different data. The common indicators include user names, time, and text content. An et al. extracted user features based on the time of user tweets or participation in discussions according to the life cycle theory [4]. Guo et al. used the TF-IDF algorithm to extract keywords from user comments as user tags [5]. Common user profiling methods include statistical analysis [6], clustering analysis, and topic modelling methods. Wang et al. used statistical analysis, social network analysis, natural language processing technology, and LDA topic clustering to construct a multidimensional user profiling tag system [7]. Ying et al. proposed a multilevel variable weight clustering method to complete property profiling, effectively identifying short-term rental properties [8]. Wu et al. used the BERT method for short text comment clustering and mining content themes of self-presentation [9].

The current domestic and foreign research on user portraits is mostly focused on social, e-commerce, statistics and other fields. There are fewer studies applied to the game field. Zhang combines communication theory to derive the communication patterns of game players through user profiling [10]. Chen creates user profile based on user behaviour data in gaming products, which helps in iterative optimization of the product [11]. Yang utilizes the LDA topic model to create user profile based on user's comments, reflecting the design information of the game product [12].

2.2 Self-determination Theory

Deci E. L. et al. proposed self-determination theory (SDT) in 1985 [13], which suggests that when an individual's autonomy, competence, and relatedness needs are met, internal motivation will dominate their behaviour. The behaviour guided by internal motivation is more autonomous, positive, and long-lasting than that guided by external motivation.

This theory has opened up a new perspective in the field of behavioural motivation research and has been widely applied in psychology, management, sociology, information science, and other fields. Chen et al. verified through empirical research that the impact of need satisfaction and frustration is the same in four countries with different cultural backgrounds, demonstrating the universal applicability of basic psychological needs under cross-cultural conditions [14]. This theory can effectively explain the process of formation, transformation, and evolution of user behaviour motivation in information systems. With the explanation, system designers and managers can explore how to cultivate user initiative, maintain long-term system operation, and guide healthy and positive system usage behaviour.

Liu et al. found that current research mainly focuses on education, sports, physiology, and psychological. And the research content mainly includes the interaction mode between the environment and individuals, the mediating role of psychological needs, the internalization of motivation, and individual goal expectations [15]. Peng et al. found that selective role customization and growth plans, as well as players' self-selection rights in game branches, can meet their autonomy needs, bring greater game fun, stronger experiential motivation, stronger recommendation intentions, and enable games to receive higher ratings [16]. Ryan et al., the proponents of SDT, found that game products can gain user support because they can provide content that satisfies users' autonomy, competence, and relatedness needs [17].

3 Research Methods

The construction of group user profiles generally involves two main processes: first, the realization of user group division. And second, the use of reasonable methods to extract the characteristics of each user group and build group user profiles.

Our methods are as follow. First, we collected the introductory information, content tags, and user data of game products. Next, we expanded the content tags of the game products based on the introductory information, and classified the expanded content tags according to self-determination theory. Then, the user preference features are obtained based on the classified content tags and user data. After the main preferences in the preference features are preliminarily grouped, the Fisher-Jenks algorithm and the degree of user attention to the main preferences are used to set a threshold to determine the optimal number of groups for each preliminary group division through one-dimensional clustering. Finally, the data are integrated, the characteristics of each user group are extracted, and group user profiles are constructed for analysis.

3.1 User's Needs Classification Based on SDT

Ryan et al. applied self-determination theory to the gaming industry in his 2006 study [17], which analysed the factors that influence users' support for gaming products based on the theory. As shown in Fig. 1, based on the conclusions of this study and its extended research [18], as well as some concepts of gaming products, the following conclusions regarding the application of self-determination theory to the gaming industry were summarized: 1) Intrinsic motivation and presence can affect users' support for gaming products. 2) The satisfaction of autonomy, competence, and relatedness needs can promote intrinsic motivation. 3) The degree of satisfaction of autonomy, competence, and relatedness needs is positively correlated with presence. 4) Intuitive control affects the expression of the three needs and is a necessary but insufficient condition for achieving psychological needs satisfaction. 5) Presence is characterized by physical presence, narrative presence, and emotional presence. The former one refers to the audio-visual experience users obtain from the game, while the latter two reflect users' sense of participation in the story of the gaming product and their emotional investment.

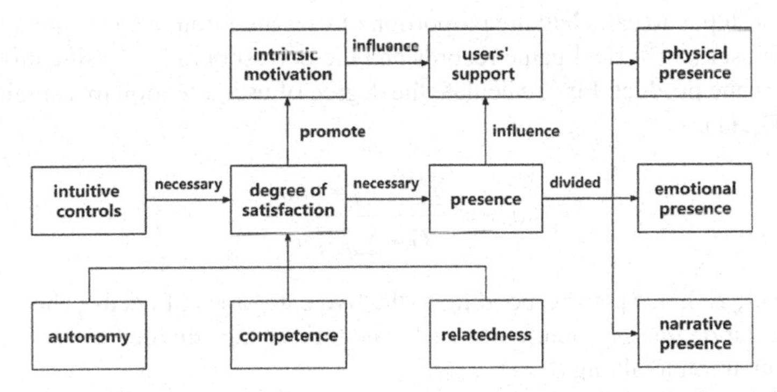

Fig. 1. The relevant conclusions of applying self-determination theory to the gaming field.

Based on the above conclusions, users can be divided into two major categories: those who seek psychological satisfaction (more concerned with the three basic psychological needs) and those who seek immersive experiences (lower requirements for the three basic psychological needs). Further subdivision can classify users' needs into five categories, which are as follows:

Autonomy needs. This category is reflected in the power of user's choice and whether the user feels restricted or controlled within the game product.
Relatedness needs (social needs). This category is reflected in the product's ability to provide users with interaction and contact with other users.
Competence needs. This category is reflected in the balance between the user's abilities and the game difficulty. Difficulty and numerical systems are highly related, and those related to numbers and difficulty can be classified into this category.
Physical. This category is reflected in the visual and music of the game.
Emotional presence. This category is reflected in the world view, story, characters, and the user's role in the story about the game product.

3.2 Game Product User's Preference Characteristics

Game products seek user support by providing relevant content to meet the five categories of user needs. Due to cost, technical level or development goals, the content emphasis of game products is a nonempty subset of the five categories of needs. The content tag of the game product is a summary of the important content within the game product. Therefore, by using classification standards to screen and divide content tags into five categories, the classification content tag of the game product can reflect which category of needs the product focuses on satisfying for players.

We define user's preference characteristics as the degree of attention they pay to these five categories of needs. The set of needs that a user is highly attentive to is a subset of the five categories of needs, and this set is defined as the user's preference. Through the user's historical game records and the corresponding classification content tags of game products, the user's preference characteristics can be reflected to some extent. To more accurately express the user's preference characteristics, this study processed the data in three steps.

The first step is to calculate the proportion of user attention to each category of tags through the user's historical game records and the corresponding classification content tags of the game product. First, calculate the degree of user attention to a single tag i, as shown in Eq. (1).

$$tag_i = \frac{\sum_{j=1}^{3} w_j * num_j}{G * \sum_{j=1}^{3} w_j} \tag{1}$$

where $n \in [1, 2, 3, 4, 5]$, corresponding to the five categories of needs. The meaning is the sum of the degree of attention to each category of tags divided by the sum of the degree of attention to all tags.

Since the proportion of each category of content tags for all game products on the platform is not evenly distributed, this proportion cannot accurately reflect the user's preferences. Therefore, it needs to be measured using the proportion of each category of tags on the platform as a standard, as shown in Eq. (2).

$$\overline{Rate_n} = \frac{\sum Tag_n}{\sum Tag} \tag{2}$$

where Tag is the sum of the appearance of all tags on the platform, and Tag_n is the sum of the appearance of the corresponding category tags. The formula represents the probability of the appearance of each category tag in a game product.

In the third step, the user's preference characteristics are calculated based on the proportion of user attention to each category of needs using the proportion of each category of tags on the platform as a standard, as shown in Eq. (3).

$$need_n = \frac{rate_n - \overline{Rate_n}}{\overline{Rate_n}} \tag{3}$$

The resulting $need_n$ reflects the user's degree of attention to that type of need, that is, the user's demand for that type of need. Each ten percent can be used as a level to convert the degree of attention to a demand level, as shown in Eq. (4).

$$level(n) = \begin{cases} \lfloor 10 * need_n \rfloor, & need_n > 0 \\ \lceil 10 * need_n \rceil, & need_n \leq 0 \end{cases} \tag{4}$$

The demands with a demand level greater than zero are the user's preferences, and the preference with the highest demand level is the user's main preference.

3.3 Group Division

After obtaining the user's preference characteristics, the user groups can be divided based on these characteristics. Firstly, users are preliminarily divided into five groups based on their main preferences. After that, each group is further divided based on the user's degree of attention to their main preference. This study uses the level accuracy of attention as an index to quantify the effectiveness of group division and determine the optimal number of groups.

The level accuracy of attention is the probability that the user's main preference demand level is similar to the main preference demand level of the group, and it is calculated as shown in Eq. (5).

$$LA(K) = \sum\nolimits_{k=1}^{K} \frac{\sum\nolimits_{p=1}^{P_k} Count\_level(p)}{P_k} \tag{5}$$

where K is the number of groups, and P_k is the number of users in the k-th group. $Count\_level(p)$ means that whether the difference between user p's and the group's is not greater than one value. It is calculated as shown in Eq. (6).

$$Count\_level(p) = \begin{cases} 1, |level(p) - Level| \leq 1 \\ 0, |level(p) - Level| > 1 \end{cases} \tag{6}$$

where $level(p)$ represents the user's main preference demand level. And $Level$ represents the group's main preference demand level.

The degree of attention to the user's main preference is one-dimensional data, so two methods can be used: k-means algorithm and natural breaks algorithm. The Fisher-Jenks algorithm is one of the natural breaks algorithm, which is more computationally efficient. Therefore, the Fisher-Jenks algorithm was adopted in this study. By focusing on the accuracy of classification and reasonable thresholds, an automatic algorithm for user division can be achieved, as shown in Fig. 2.

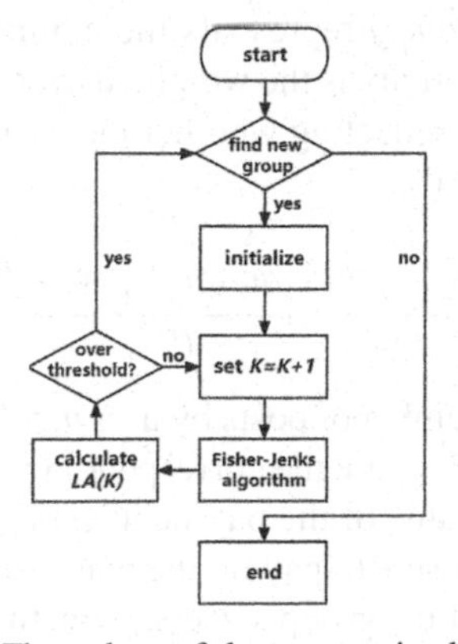

Fig. 2. Flow chart of the automatic algorithm

3.4 Representation of the Characteristics of User Groups in Game Products

After the user groups are segmented, high-interest content tags, product tag responsiveness, average game activity, average platform activity, average platform payment level, and average influence are extracted based on the division results of each group. High-interest content tags are the most popular content tags among the group, which can reveal the content tags that the group is interested in. The average value of the group's attention to each tag is calculated by Eq. (7) to obtain the top few tags with the highest values as the high-interest content tags of that group.

$$Tag_i = \frac{\sum_{p=1}^{P} tag_{p,i}}{P} \tag{7}$$

where $tag_{p,i}$ represents the attention of user p to tag i, and P represents the number of users in the current group. Product tag responsiveness is the degree to which the group is interested in the content tags of the sample product, and a higher value indicates that the group is more likely to be interested in the sample product. It is calculated by summing the average attention of the group to the content tags of the sample product, as shown in Eq. (8).

$$Rsp = \frac{\sum_{r=1}^{R} Tag_r}{R} \tag{8}$$

where R is the number of content tags of the sample product, and Tag_r is the average attention to the corresponding content tag of the sample of products. The average game activity is the weighted average of the number of games played, games reserved, and games purchased by the group's users, which can reflect whether the group frequently uses the gaming products of the platform. It is calculated as shown in Eq. (9).

$$GA = \frac{\sum_{j=1}^{3} w_j * \sum_{p=1}^{P} num_{p,j}}{P} \tag{9}$$

where w_j is the weight, and $num_{p,j}$ represents the number of games corresponding to user p. The average platform activity is the weighted average of the number of posts and followers of the group's users, reflecting whether the users frequently use the platform. It is calculated as in formula (10).

$$PA = \frac{\sum_{p=1}^{P} w_1 * action_p + w_2 * follow_p}{P} \tag{10}$$

where $action_p$ represents the number of posts by user p, $follow_p$ represents the number of followers of user p, and w_1 and w_2 are the corresponding weights. The average platform payment level is the average value of the payment level of the group's users, reflecting the willingness of the group's users to pay on the platform. The average influence is the average number of followers of the group's users, reflecting how many users the group's users can influence on average.

4 Experimental Process

4.1 Data Source

In this study, the data of the Bilibili platform and Bilibili gaming platform were collected through Octopus Collector. The game product *China without regrets* on this platform was selected as the research sample, and all relevant data of the comment users of the product were collected, including the users' historical game records, reserved game records, purchased game records, platform posts, platform followers, platform fans, and platform payment level, as well as the introduction data and content tag data of all gaming products on this platform.

4.2 Content Tag Classification and User Preference Characteristics Calculation

Firstly, we expand the content tags based on the introduction data. The introduction data and tag data both contain information about the content and focus of gaming products. Therefore, in the case of sparse and incomplete content tags, expanding them with introduction information is effective. The expansion steps are as follows: first, we use the jieba word segmentation tool to segment, remove stop words, and filter by word type for all introduction data. Second, we count the frequency of appearance of all vocabulary in the introduction and remove low-frequency or nonoriginal content tag vocabulary. Third, we remove meaningless vocabulary that is not content tags manually, and merge the final result with the original content tags. The expansion's result as shown in Table 1.

Table 1. The expansion's result

Game name	Tags before	Tags After
Romance of Three Kingdoms	strategy, hardcore, social, three kingdoms, Chinese style	strategy, hardcore, social, three kingdoms, Chinese style, war, history, art, simulation, romance, management, sandbox
China without regrets	strategy, history, management, Chinese style	strategy, history, management, Chinese style, three kingdoms, card, construction, exploration

Subsequently, the expanded content tags were classified based on the conclusions of relevant studies on self-determination theory. Some classification results are shown in Table 2, where 1 represents autonomy, 2 represents relatedness, 3 represents competence, 4 represents physical presence, and 5 represents emotional presence.

Finally, user preference features were calculated based on the classified content tags. When calculating the attention to tags in the first step, the weights in the formula were subjectively set to 0.3, 0.2, and 0.5, indicating that the tag appearing in the purchased game has the greatest impact on attention, while the tag appearing in the reserved game has the smallest impact.

Table 2. The expansion's result

Tag	Category	Tag	Category
turn-based	1	challenging	3
freedom	1	achievement	3
friends	2	ink painting	4
cooperation	2	scenery	4
social	2	history	5
hardcore	3	narrative	5

4.3 Group Division of Game Product Users

After obtaining the user preference features, the automatic group division algorithm will automatically complete the group division based on the preference features as input data and setting the threshold of LA without manually adjusting. The threshold in this study is set to 0.8, meaning that when the LA of each group is greater than 0.8, the division stops. The number of clusters and corresponding LA values for each group are shown in Table 3, indicating that five groups will be further divided into 2, 5, 6, 4, and 3 groups, respectively, for a total of 20 groups.

Table 3. Number of clusters and LA values for each group

K	Autonomy	Relatedness	Competence	Physical	Emotional
2	***0.960**	0.466	0.359	0.548	0.786
3	0.995	0.607	0.424	0.690	***0.933**
4	0.995	0.684	0.583	***0.847**	0.986
5	1	***0.821**	0.738	0.887	0.976
6	1	0.939	***0.874**	0.949	0.986

4.4 Construction of the User Profile of the Game Product

According to the results of group division, Table 4 is obtained. The Table 4 include the top 7 content tags of attention, the responsiveness of these content tags to the sample product's content tags, and the number of people in each group. It can be seen that the need for physical presence for this product is the highest. Since the content tags of the sample product that belong to this type of demand have a relatively low proportion, it can be found that the platform's users mainly prefer the need for physical presence. If considering releasing products on this platform, it is necessary to satisfy players' basic audio-visual experience. Meanwhile, as the level of demand for preferences increases,

Table 4. High-attention content tags of groups

Preference	Degree	The high attention content tags	Respon-sivity	People
1	1	Exploration (0.54), Strategy (0.48), Card (0.34), History (0.30), Management (0.28)	2.6	131
1	4	Strategy (0.65), Exploration (0.62), Card (0.47), Management (0.43), History (0.41)	3.6	65
2	3	Exploration (0.37), Strategy (0.37), Adventure (0.26), Card (0.24), RPG (0.23)	1.8	389
2	6	Strategy (0.34), Exploration (0.32), Adventure (0.24), RPG (0.20), History (0.19)	1.5	421
2	9	Strategy (0.40), Exploration (0.37), Adventure (0.26), Team (0.23), Card (0.20)	1.8	253
2	13	Strategy (0.46), Exploration (0.44), Adventure (0.28), Team (0.24), Card (0.22)	2.1	119
2	21	Adventure (0.32), Strategy (0.30), Exploration (0.26), Sports (0.26), Battle (0.25)	1.0	22
3	3	Strategy (0.37), Exploration (0.36), Card (0.24), Adventure (0.22), Storyline (0.20)	1.8	196
3	6	Exploration (0.36), Strategy (0.33), Action (0.26), Collection (0.23), Storyline (0.21)	1.6	183
3	9	Strategy (0.42), Exploration (0.41), Action (0.28), Collection (0.25), Adventure (0.22)	1.9	138
3	13	Exploration (0.47), Strategy (0.37), Action (0.34), Collection (0.29), Pixel (0.25)	1.8	100
3	16	Exploration (0.57), Action (0.43), Collection (0.41), Rogue-like (0.37), Skill (0.35)	2.3	56
3	24	Collection (0.48), Exploration (0.45), Action (0.42), Skill (0.41), Rogue-like (0.40)	1.5	32
4	4	Strategy (0.28), Exploration (0.26), Adventure (0.21), RPG (0.20), Storyline (0.20)	1.3	1788
4	7	Strategy (0.26), Anime style (0.24), Exploration (0.23), Storyline (0.21), RPG (0.20)	1.1	2242

(*continued*)

Table 4. (*continued*)

Preference	Degree	The high attention content tags	Respon-sivity	People
4	10	Anime style (0.31), Strategy (0.26), Storyline (0.24), Exploration (0.22), Seiyu (0.22)	1.2	1179
4	17	Anime style (0.54), Seiyu (0.37), Storyline (0.35), Anime (0.34), Beautiful girls (0.30)	1.3	173
5	2	Strategy (0.38), Exploration (0.34), Card (0.33), History (0.32), Storyline (0.30)	2.0	279
5	5	Storyline (0.41), Card (0.34), Strategy (0.33), History (0.31), RPG (0.31)	1.9	179
5	9	Storyline (0.50), RPG (0.42), Card (0.37), Adventure (0.31), Text (0.26)	1.5	46

the overall number of people in each group shows a downwards trend, but the proportion of people for physical presence is still not low. This also indirectly confirms the point.

The responsiveness of each group to the product's content tags is highest for autonomy and lowest for the need for physical presence. The lowest responsiveness is for relatedness users with a demand level of 21, who have the least number of people compared to other similar users and are more interested in content tags such as competition, battle and teamwork.

Most groups' high attention content tags include *strategy* and *exploration*, both of which are also content tags for the product. Most users of this product are attracted by its strategic content and exploration content.

As the level of demand increases, the attention of each group to various high-attention content tags shows an upwards trend, indicating that users with lower demand levels tend to have more dispersed attention to content, while those with higher demand levels tend to have more concentrated attention.

The calculation results of four characteristics, including game activity, platform activity, platform payment level, and influence of different groups, as shown in Table 5. From Table 5, it can be found that the physical presence group generally has high characteristics, especially in game activity, platform activity, and platform payment level. This indicates that physically present users are indeed the core and main users of the platform. Game products that focus on audio-visual experience can be promoted on this platform.

Among the major groups, the group with the highest demand level generally has low game activity. The demand level reflects to a certain extent the user's demand for game products. These groups are all heavy game users. The platform's game products are not very rich, which cannot fully meet the needs of these users. The main game product platform for these users is not the sample platform, so the game activity on the sample platform is relatively low.

The group with high game activity is mainly concentrated in the physical presence group, while the group with high platform activity is mainly composed of relatedness,

Table 5. Other characteristics of groups

Preference	Degree	Game activity	Platform activity	Pay	Influence
1	1	8.7	311	0.73	138
1	4	4.1	161	0.49	51
2	3	20.4	419	0.95	201
2	6	20.2	424	0.90	450
2	9	12.0	314	0.77	25
2	13	7.9	367	0.55	85
2	21	4.3	203	0.23	367
3	3	19.9	315	0.85	61
3	6	17.4	340	1.14	70
3	9	10.9	285	0.62	90
3	13	7.5	277	1.01	23
3	16	5.3	188	0.50	18
3	24	4.5	262	0.47	32
4	4	46.3	409	1.14	100
4	7	56.6	411	1.18	140
4	10	43.9	338	1.11	484
4	17	12.5	208	0.94	26
5	2	13.2	323	0.91	20
5	5	8.0	308	1.04	465
5	9	4.2	262	1.00	23

physical presence and emotional users. The group with a high platform payment level is mainly concentrated in physical presence and emotional users. The group with high influence includes the group with a demand level of 6 and 21 in the relatedness category, the group with a demand level of 10 in the physical presence category, and the group with a demand level of 5 in the emotional category. The difference in influence between these groups and other groups is very large, so these groups may include bloggers of the sample platform.

5 Conclusion

Based on the conclusions of research related to self-determination theory, this research extracts the preferred characteristics of game product users. By the characteristics we divides users into groups, and summarizes the characteristics of each group. The experimental results show that users who prefer audio-visual experiences are the core users of the platform, and these users generally have higher characteristics in the four aspects. The strategy and exploration content of the product *China without regrets* are at a higher level, and most of the users of this product are attracted by this content. The research results are helpful for game product developers to understand the characteristics of platform users, product user characteristics, and excellent product content. These can provide some assistance for the development and promotion of products by developers. Based on the main preferences of users, this research divides users into groups, and other methods can be used for user profiling in the future. In future research, the method of comment mining can be used to explore more users' opinions on product content.

Acknowledgements. The research is supported by Key Laboratory of Education Informalization for Nationalities of Ministry of Education, Yunnan Key Laboratory of Smart Education, Key Laboratory of Digital Learning Supporting Technology, Department of Education of Yunnan Province, and Yunnan International Joint R&D Center of China-Laos-Thailand Educational Digitalization.

References

1. Liu, H., Sun, J., Zhang, Y., et al.: Research on user portrait and information dissemination behavior in online social activities. Inf. Sci. **36**(12), 17–21 (2018)
2. You, Z., Si, Y., Zhang, D., Zeng, X., et al.: A decision-making framework for precision marketing. Expert Syst. Appl. **45**(7), 3357–3367 (2015)
3. Wu, J., Xu, M.: Personalized recommendation based on user portrait and video interest tags. Inf. Sci. **39**(01), 128–134 (2021)
4. An, L., Zhou, Y.: Portrait and comparison of weibo information and comment users under the context of terrorist events. Inf. Sci. **38**(04), 9–16 (2020)
5. Guo, Y., Sun, Z., Liu, W., et al.: Research on UGC user portrait of mobile library based on data-driven method. Inf. Stud. Theory Appl. **45**(01), 30–37 (2022)
6. Xu, G., Zhang, Y., Zhou, X.: Towards user profiling for Web recommendation. In: Zhang, S., Jarvis, R. (eds.) AI 2005. LNCS (LNAI), vol. 3809, pp. 415–424. Springer, Heidelberg (2005). https://doi.org/10.1007/11589990_44
7. Wang, R., Yan, C., Guo, F., et al.: Research on user churn prediction of online health community based on user portrait. Data Anal. Knowl. Discov. **6**(Z1), 80–92 (2022)
8. Ying, D., Liu, F., Xin, J.: Identification of prepaid electricity customers based on property status portrait. Smart Power **50**(01), 68–74 (2022)
9. Wu, J., Liu, T., Liu, Y.: Portrait of online community users and theme mining of self-presentation: taking netease cloud music community as an example. Data Anal. Knowl. Discov. **6**(07), 56–69 (2022)
10. Zhang, Y.: A study on user profiles of tactical competitive games from the perspective of communication studies. Master, Heilongjiang University (2020)
11. Chen, R.: Research on fine-grained user portrait construction of online games based on user behavior. Master, East China Normal University (2022)
12. Yang, M.: Construction of game product profiles and sentiment analysis based on online game reviews. Master, Dalian University of Foreign Languages (2021)
13. Deci, E.L., Ryan, R.M.: Intrinsic Motivation and Self-Determination in Human Behavior, pp. 3–9. Springer, New York (1985). https://doi.org/10.1007/978-1-4899-2271-7
14. Chen, B., Vansteenkiste, M., Beyers, W., et al.: Basic psychological need satisfaction, need frustration, and need strength across four cultures. Motiv. Emot. **39**(2), 216–236 (2015). https://doi.org/10.1007/s11031-014-9450-1
15. Liu, J., Zhong, B., Si, G.: Application of self-determination theory in the Chinese population. Adv. Psychol. Sci. **21**(10), 1803–1813 (2013)

16. Peng, W., Lin, J.H., Pfeiffer, K.A., et al.: Need satisfaction supportive game features as motivational determinants: an experimental study of a self-determination theory guided exergame. Media Psychol. **15**(2), 175–196 (2012)
17. Ryan, R.M., Rigby, C.S., Przybylski, A.K.: The motivational pull of video games: a self-determination theory approach. Motiv. Emot. **30**(4), 344–360 (2006). https://doi.org/10.1007/s11031-006-9051-8
18. Przybylski, A.K., Rigby, C.S., Ryan, R.M.: A motivational model of video game engagement. Rev. Gen. Psychol. **14**(2), 154–166 (2010)

Knowledge Graph Embedding Based on Triple Multilayer Perceptron

Zhihou Hou[1], Junxiang Zhou[2], and Tianwei Xu[2](✉)

[1] School of Information Science and Technology, Yunnan Normal University, Kunming, China
[2] Key Laboratory of Educational Information for Nationalities, Yunnan Normal University, Kunming, China
xutianwei@ynnu.edu.cn

Abstract. The knowledge graph is a structured semantic knowledge base, that can organize the information in the Internet at the minimum cost and can be applied to many downstream fields at the same time. However, knowledge graphs in the real world are mostly incomplete, and the idea of knowledge graph embedding is proposed to solve this problem. In the early days, the translation series model was used for knowledge graph embedding, but it was only suitable for modelling some simple relations. The neural network-based model has more advantages in capturing complex features, so it has more advantages in link prediction than traditional translation models. This paper proposes a model called TMLPE (Triple Multiplayer Perceptron Embedding), the main body of which is composed of three MLP modules, one of which is used to capture the interaction features between head entities and relations, and one MLP model is used to capture the characteristics of the head entities and relations themselves. An MLP is used to project the tail entities into a vector space similar to that of the head entities and relations. Experiments show that TMLPE exhibits good link prediction performance on two benchmark datasets.

Keywords: Knowledge Graph Embedding · Perceptron · Residual Connection · Attention Mechanism

1 Introduction

In recent years, as a kind of human structured knowledge, knowledge graphs has attracted the attention of many researchers. A knowledge graph is a conceptual network that can be stored in a directed graph. The nodes in the graph are entities in the real world, and the edges in the graph represent the relationship between entities. The original intention of knowledge graph creation is to improve the quality of answers returned by search engines, but with its continuous development, it not only changes the existing information retrieval methods but is also widely used in other fields, such as semantic matching [1], intelligent question answering [2] and recommendation systems [3].

It can be seen from many studies related to knowledge graphs that the problem of missing triples exists in almost all knowledge graphs, even the two most commonly used

J. Gan et al. (Eds.): CSEI 2023, CCIS 1899, pp. 172–181, 2024.
https://doi.org/10.1007/978-981-99-9499-1_14

datasets (WordNet [4] and Freebase [5]) in the field of knowledge graphs. When a more complete knowledge map is applied downstream, it often has better results. Therefore, research on knowledge map completion is important. Knowledge graph embedding uses supervised learning to learn embeddings and low-dimensional vector representations of nodes and edges and then predicts missing entities, which is one of the current research hotspots in the field of knowledge graph completion.

In the early days, some distance-based models were used for knowledge graph embedding, such as TransE [6] and TranH [7]. In recent years, deep learning models have been used for knowledge graph embedding, such as ConvE [8], AcrE [9], DeepE [10]. The core of the KGE is the scoring function. Compared with simple models such as TransE, the deep learning model can capture more complex features. However, in the knowledge graph, a large part of the relationship is a simple linear relationship, and a simple model can be well scored. As the number of layers increases, the deep learning model may not be as good as the simple model in the learning effect of simple relationships. To ensure that the learning effect is lost as the number of layers increases, this article refers to the DeepE model using residual connections to solve this problem.

Although the neural network model has great advantages in capturing complex features, most current neural network-based knowledge graph embedding models only consider capturing the interaction features between entities and relationships for scoring and ignore the impact of the characteristics of the entities and relationships on the results, which will lead to the loss of the characteristics of the entities and relationships, thus affecting the prediction effect. To solve this problem, this paper proposes a triple MLP-based model-TMLPE. The main body of the TMLPE model is three MLP modules, two of which are used to capture the interaction characteristics between entities and relations as well as the characteristics of entities and relations themselves. In this way, we can ensure that our model learns the interaction features between entities and relationships, and will not lose the basic features of entities and relationships themselves; the third MLP module is used to project the label vector to the output vector of the first two modules in a similar vector space. The final experimental results show that the TMLPE model based on three MLP modules has better link prediction performance than the current baseline model results show that the TMLPE model based on three MLP modules has better link prediction.

2 Related Work

2.1 Knowledge Graph Embedding (KGE)

As a widely used knowledge representation method, knowledge graph embedding is mainly applied to solve the problem of knowledge graph completion. The computational complexity can be greatly reduced. The models embedded in the knowledge map can be roughly divided into three types: distance-based models, bilinear models, and neural network-based models. In this paper, it is divided into non-neural network models and neural network-based models.

2.2 Nonneural Network KGE

TransE is based on pioneering work in distance models where relations are considered as translations between head entities to tail entities. Later, many extended models such as TransH, TransR [11], etc., were proposed. Bilinear models use similarity-based scoring functions, and Rescal [12], RotatE [13], DisMult [14], and ComplEx [15] are all bilinear models. Rescal mainly uses the idea of three-dimensional tensor. Each relationship corresponds to a slice (that is, a matrix) in the three-dimensional tensor, which is equivalent to representing the adjacency matrix of the graph, and stores whether there is such a relationship between each pair of entities DisMult The model is an improvement of Rescal, which limits the relationship matrix to a diagonal matrix, which can reduce the parameters of the bilinear matrix to the same as TransE. The ComplEx model extends the DisMult model by introducing more complex vectors. The RotatE model also introduces Complex spaces, while utilizing the properties of dihedral angle groups, can support various properties such as symmetry and inversion. The nonneural network KGE model is not inferior to the neural network-based model for simple relationship modelling, but it cannot be compared with the neural network-based model in terms of complex relationship modelling.

2.3 Neural Network KGE

In recent years, neural networks and deep learning have become research hotspots in the field of artificial intelligence, and many researchers have begun to try to use neural networks to solve the problem of knowledge graph embedding. The ConvE model applies two-dimensional convolution to KGE for the first time; the AcrE model applies hollow convolution to allow the filter to have a larger field of view without increasing parameters; the ConEx [16] model combines the ComplEx and ConvE models to compensate for the ComplEx model The disadvantage is that it is unable to model the transfer relationship; the InteractE [17] model uses circular convolution while setting and reshaping features and enhances ConvE through the above three core ideas; DeepE uses the ideas of DNN and ResNet to model. Overall, applying the neural network model to KGE has become a hot spot in the field of KGE. Additionally, many neural network-based KGE models exhibit better predictive performance than nonneural network KGE models.

3 Methodology

3.1 Overall Architecture

This paper proposes the TMLPE model with reference to the architecture of the DeepE model and the BCFNet [18] model. The architecture of TMLPE is shown in Fig. 1. TMLP consists of four modules, named interactive feature capture module, basic feature capture module, feature projection module and output module. The knowledge graph is defined as $G = \{(h, r, t)\} \subseteq \mathbb{R}^{\mathcal{E}\times\mathcal{R}\times\mathcal{E}}$, the relationship is defined as $r \in \mathbb{R}^{\mathcal{R}}$, the head entity is defined as $h \in \mathbb{R}^{\mathcal{E}}$, and the tail entity is defined as $t \in \mathbb{R}^{\mathcal{E}}$.

First, project and embed the entity h and relation r to obtain a low-dimensional vector $h, r \in \mathbb{R}^{d}$, where d is the embedding dimension; the weight of the embedding layer is

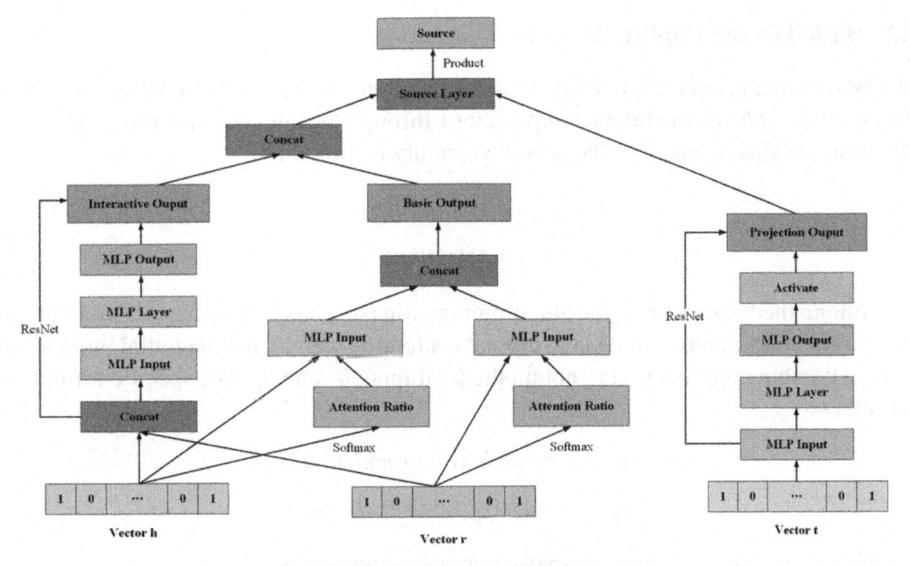

Fig. 1. TMLPE Architecture

obtained as the label vector $t \in \mathbb{R}^{\mathcal{E}}$. Then h and r are used as inputs to the interactive feature capture module and the basic feature capture model respectively to obtain the output of the interactive feature capture module $v_1 \in \mathbb{R}^d$ and the output of the basic feature capture module $v_2 \in \mathbb{R}^d$. Take t as input and input it to the feature projection module to obtain the output $t' \in \mathbb{R}^{\mathcal{E}}$. Then first combine v_1 and v_2 to obtain the output v, use v and t' as input, and input it to the output module to obtain the final score as score(h, r, t).

3.2 Interactive Feature Capture Module

As shown in Fig. 1, the interactive feature capture module consists of an MLP and a residual connection, where each MLP layer has a BN (batch normalization) layer, a dropout layer and an activation function layer (the activation function used here is ReLU) between each MLP layer. Taking h and r as input, input the interactive feature capture module is input to obtain the output v_1, denoted as $f(h, t)$. The specific definition is given to formula 1:

$$f(h, t) = BN([h \| t] + MLP([h \| t])) \tag{1}$$

Among them, $\|$ represents the concatenation operation, BN is batch normalization, and MLP is a multilayer perceptron. The specific definitions are given in formula 2:

$$MLP^{(1)}(x) = \sigma((Dropout(BN(W_1 x)))) \tag{2}$$

where W_1 is the weight matrix, and σ is the activation function (ReLU is used here). The above picture shows a single-layer MLP structure, and the real situation may be a multilayer MLP structure.

3.3 Basic Feature Capture Module

The basic feature capture model consists of an attention layer and an MLP. First, pass the head vector h and the relationship vector r through the attention layer to obtain their attention weights α_h and α_r. The specific formula is formula 3:

$$\begin{aligned} \alpha_h &= Attention(h) \\ \alpha_r &= Attention(r) \end{aligned} \tag{3}$$

Among them, attention is the attention function (softmax is used here). After obtaining the attention weights of h and r, input the attention weight and the initial input h and r into a combination function to obtain the final input h_1 and r_1. The specific formula is formula 4:

$$\begin{aligned} h_1 &= concat(h, \alpha_h)\ or\ mul(h, \alpha_h) \\ r_1 &= concat(r, \alpha_r)\ or\ mul(r, \alpha_r) \end{aligned} \tag{4}$$

The merge function is concatenation or vector dot product.

Then input the final inputs h_1 and r_1 are input the MLP layer to obtain the final output v_2. The specific formula of the MLP layer is formula 5:

$$MLP^{(2)}(x) = Dropout(BN(\sigma(W_n(\ldots W_1 x)))) \tag{5}$$

The MLP structure of the basic feature capture model is slightly different from that of the interactive feature capture model, which only adds dropout, BN and activation functions to the linear layer of the last layer. In summary, the basic feature capture model is denoted as $g(h, t)$, and the specific definition is given in formula 6:

$$g(h, t) = MLP(Attention(h) \| Attention(r)) \tag{6}$$

Here, the merge function is concatenation as an example, and $\|$ represents the concatenation operation.

3.4 Feature Projection Module

The final output v is obtained through a series of nonlinear functions. To make v and t as close as possible to the space, t needs to be projected, that is, let it go through an MLP layer to obtain the final output t'. The specific definition is given in formula 7:

$$\phi(t) = \sigma(BN(t + MLP(t))) = t' \tag{7}$$

The MLP layer structure here uses the same structure as the interactive feature capture module. Unlike the interactive feature capture module, an additional activation function layer is added to the feature projection layer.

3.5 Output Module

After the interactive feature capture module and the basic feature capture module obtain the output v_1 and v_2, the two output vectors must first be merged into one vector. Here, concatenation or vector addition is selected for merging. After obtaining the final input v, perform an inner product operation with the feature projection module t′ to obtain the final score. The specific formula is as in formula

$$\begin{aligned} score(h, r, t) &= \left[f(h, t) \| g(h, t)\right] \cdot \phi(t) \\ &= v \cdot t' \end{aligned} \tag{8}$$

Here, the merge operation is concatenation as an example, and || represents the concatenation operation.

3.6 Loss Function

This article, similar to most KGE methods based on neural networks, uses a binary cross-entropy loss function, the specific formula is as in formula 9:

$$L = -\frac{1}{N}\sum_{i=1}^{N}\left[t_i \log(p_i) + (1 - t_i) \cdot \log(1 - p_i)\right] \tag{9}$$

Among them, t_i is the label of triplet i, and its elements indicate whether there is a relationship between two entities, and it is 1; otherwise, it is 0; p_i is the corresponding score; N indicates the number of entities in the knowledge graph.

4 Experiments and the Results

4.1 Dataset

This paper uses one of the two most common datasets in the KGE field, FB15K-237 and WN18RR. These two datasets are subsets of the FB15K and WN18 datasets. In the ConvE model paper, it is mentioned that there is an inverse relationship between the two original datasets, which leads to data leakage, so the subset is used as the experimental dataset. The specific data statistics of the dataset are shown in Table 1:

Table 1. Dataset Statistics

	WN18RR	FK15K-237
#Relations	11	237
#Entities	40943	14541
#Train	86834	272114
#Valid	3033	17534
#Test	3136	20448

4.2 Evaluation Metrics

This paper uses Mean Rank (MR), Reciprocal Mean Rank (MRR), Top 10 Percentage (Hit@10), Top 2 Percentage (Hit@3) and Top 1 Percentage (Hit@1) as evaluation metrics. Among them, MR indicates the average number in the predicted sequence to match the correct missing entity; MRR indicates the ranking of the correct retrieval result value in the retrieval; Hit@1, Hit@3 and Hit@10 indicate the top 1, 3, The probability that the correct missing entity exists among the 10 predictions. In summary, in the experiment, the smaller the MR value, the larger the values of MRR and Hit@N, the better the embedding effect of the model.

4.3 Experimental Settings

The range of hyperparameters used in this paper is as follows: Dropout {0.1, 0.2, 0.3, 0.4, 0.5} of the interactive feature extraction module, Dropout {0.1, 0.2, 0.3, 0.4, 0.5} of the basic feature extraction module, and Dropout of the feature projection module {0.1, 0.2, 0.3}; embedding sizes {200, 250, 300, 350, 400}; batch sizes {500, 1000, 1500}.

The parameters that must be learned are the weights of the embedding layer and the MLP layer of each module. The optimizer uses Adam and SGD, where the momentum of SGD is {0.1, 0.3, 0.5, 0.7, 0.9}, and the weight decay of Adam is $\{5 \times 10^{-4}, 5 \times 10^{-5}, 5 \times 10^{-6}, 5 \times 10^{-7}, 5 \times 10^{-8}\}$. The learning rate is updated regularly. When training the WN18RR dataset, the learning rate is initially 1×10^{-3}. If the performance of the model does not improve every 5 epochs, the learning rate becomes the current 0.5, and the lowest learning rate is 1×10^{-5}. For the FB15K-237 dataset, the initial learning rate is 3×10^{-3}. If the performance of the model does not improve every 5 epochs, the learning rate becomes the current 0.6, and the lowest learning rate is 1×10^{-6}. On the WN18RR dataset, approximately 300 epochs are trained to obtain the best prediction effect, and on the FK15K-137 dataset, approximately 1000 epochs are trained to obtain the best prediction effect.

4.4 Performance Comparison

Table 2 shows the experimental results of the TMLP model on the two datasets WN18RR and FB15K-237 and compares them with the experimental results of other baseline models. The entries marked in bold indicate the best experimental results in all tables. From the experimental results, we can see that the TMLPE model has achieved good link prediction performance on both datasets and achieved the first or second best results in all indicators. In summary, the TMLPE model proposes three MLP modules for interactive feature capture, basic feature capture, and feature projection. Better predictive performance than other baseline models.

On the WN18RR dataset, the five indicators of the TMLPE model are better than those of the other baseline models. On the four indicators of MRR, hit@10, hits@3 and hit@1, the prediction effect is slightly improved, while in the MR indicator on the other hand, its prediction effect has been greatly improved, from 2337 to 1774 (relative improvement of approximately 24%). On the FB15K-237 dataset, although no five evaluation indicators are better than the baseline indicators, it is better than all baseline models in hit@1, hit@3 and MR indicators, while in hit@10 and MRR indicators is also only slightly lower than the state-of-the-art baseline model ConEx.

Table 2. Link Prediction. The results of TMLPE

	WN18RR					FB15K-237				
	Hit@1	Hit@3	Hit@10	MRR	MR	Hit@1	Hit@3	Hit@10	MRR	MR
TransE	–	–	0.501	0.226	3384	–	–	0.465	0.294	357
ComplEx	0.39	0.44	0.49	0.43	5110	0.155	0.263	0.419	0.241	254
ConvE	0.40	0.46	0.51	0.43	4187	0.237	0.358	0.501	0.325	244
RotatE	0.428	0.492	**0.571**	0.476	3340	0.241	0.375	0.533	0.338	177
HypER [19]	0.436	0.477	0.522	0.465	5798	0.252	0.376	0.520	0.341	250
InteractE	0.43	–	0.528	0.463	5202	0.263	–	0.535	0.354	172
ConEx	0.448	0.493	0.55	0.481	–	0.271	0.403	**0.555**	**0.366**	–
AcrE	0.422	0.473	0.532	0.459	–	0.266	0.393	0.545	0.358	–
JointE [20]	0.438	–	0.537	0.358	4655	0.262	–	0.543	0.356	177
G2SKGE [21]	0.424	0.467	0.493	0.447	–	0.253	0.375	0.515	0.342	–
DeepE	0.445	–	0.567	0.487	2337	0.266	–	0.544	0.358	161
TMLPE	**0.449**	**0.506**	**0.571**	**0.489**	**1774**	**0.272**	**0.404**	0.551	0.361	**151**

5 Conclusion

In this paper, a new knowledge map embedding model TMLPE based on triple MLP module is proposed, which mainly consists of three modules, namely interactive feature capture module, basic feature capture module and feature projection module. The interaction feature capture module can effectively capture the interaction features between entities and relationships; the basic feature capture module can well capture the basic features of entities and relationships; the feature projection model projects vector t into a vector space similar to vector v. Experiments show that the TMLPE model based on the triple MLP architecture achieves the best or second best results in the two standard datasets WN18RR and FB15K-237, among which the MR index on the WN18RR dataset has achieved a greater improvement, demonstrating the effectiveness of the TMLPE model in KGE.

The TMLPE model uses three MLP structures to capture features, and in the research of deep learning-based knowledge map embedding, the CNN model and the GNN model are also research hotspots and have also achieved good link prediction results, which can be considered in the future Replace the MLP structure in TMLPE with a CNN or GNN structure.

References

1. Yuxiang, W., Arijit, K., Tianxing, W., et al.: Semantic guided and response times bounded top-k similarity search over knowledge graphs. In: International Conference on Data Engineering, Dallas, United States, April 2020, pp. 445–456 (2020)
2. Maheshwari, G., Trivedi, P., Lukovnikov, D., Chakraborty, N., Fischer, A., Lehmann, J.: Learning to rank query graphs for complex question answering over knowledge graphs. In: Ghidini, C., et al. (eds.) ISWC 2019. LNCS, vol. 11778, pp. 487–504. Springer, Cham (2019). https://doi.org/10.1007/978-3-030-30793-6_28
3. Xiang, W., Xiangnan, H., Yixin, C., et al.: KGAT: knowledge graph attention network for recommendation. In: International Conference on Knowledge Discovery and Data Mining, New York, United States, August 2019, pp. 950–958 (2019)
4. Miller, G.: WordNet: a lexical database for English. Commun. ACM. ACM **11**(38), 39–41 (1995)
5. Bollacker, K., Evans, C., Paritosh, P., et al.: Freebase: a collaboratively created graph database for structuring human knowledge. In: Proceedings of the 2008 ACM SIGMOD International Conference on Management of Data, vol. 7, pp. 1247–1250 (2009)
6. Antoine, B., Nicolas, U., Alberto, G., et al.: Translating embeddings for modelling multi-relation data. In: Advances in Neural Information Processing Systems, vol. 12, no. 2, pp. 2787–2795 (2013)
7. Zhen, W., Jianwen, Z., Jianlin, F., et al.: Knowledge graph embedding by translating on hyperplanes. In: Twenty-Eighth AAAI Conference on Artificial Intelligence, Quebec, Canada, July 2014, pp. 1112–1119 (2014)
8. Tim, D., Pasquale, M., Pontus, S., et al.: Convolutional 2D knowledge graph embeddings. In: Thirty-Second AAAI Conference on Artificial Intelligence, February 2018, pp. 1811–1818 (2018)
9. Feiliang, R., Juchen, L., Huihui, Z., et al.: Knowledge graph embeddings with atrous convolution and residual learning. In: International Conference on Computational Linguistics, Barcelona, Spain, November 2020, pp. 1532–1543 (2020)
10. Danhao, Z., Si, S., Shujian, H., et al.: DeepE: a deep neural network for knowledge graph embedding. arXiv preprint arXiv:2211.04620 (2022)
11. Lin, Y., Liu, Z., Sun, M., et al.: Learning entity and relation embeddings for knowledge graph completion. In: AAAI Conference on Artificial Intelligence, Texas, United States, January 2015, pp. 2181–2187 (2015)
12. Nickel, M., Tresp, V., Kriegel, H.P.: A three-way model for collective learning on multirelational data. In: International Conference on Machine Learning, Washington, United States, June 2011, pp. 809–816 (2011)
13. Sun, Z., Deng, Z.H., Nie, J.Y., et al.: Rotate: knowledge graph embedding by relational rotation in complex space. arXiv preprint arXiv:1902.10197 (2019)
14. Yang, B., Yih, W.T., He, X., et al.: Embedding entities and relations for learning and inference in knowledge bases. arXiv preprint arXiv:1412.6575 (2014)
15. Theo, T., Johannas, W., Sebastian, R., et al.: Complex embeddings for simple link prediction. In: International Conference on Machine Learning, New York, United States, June 2016, pp. 2071–2080 (2016)
16. Demir, C., Ngomo, A.-C.: Convolutional complex knowledge graph embeddings. In: Verborgh, R., et al. (eds.) ESWC 2021. LNCS, vol. 12731, pp. 409–424. Springer, Cham (2021). https://doi.org/10.1007/978-3-030-77385-4_24
17. Shikhar, V., Soumya, S., Vikram, N., et al.: InteractE: improving convolution-based knowledge graph embeddings by increasing feature interactions. In: Proceedings of the AAAI Conference on Artificial Intelligence, vol. 3, no. 34, pp. 3009–3016 (2020)

18. Hu, Z., Huang, J., Deng, Z., Wang, C., et al.: BCFNet: a balanced collaborative filtering network with attention mechanism. arXiv preprint arXiv:2103.06105 (2021)
19. Balažević, I., Allen, C., Hospedales, T.M.: Hypernetwork knowledge graph embeddings. In: Tetko, I.V., Kůrková, V., Karpov, P., Theis, F. (eds.) ICANN 2019. LNCS, vol. 11731, pp. 553–565. Springer, Cham (2019). https://doi.org/10.1007/978-3-030-30493-5_52
20. Zhehui, Z., Can, W., Yan, F., et al.: JointE: jointly utilizing 1D and 2D convolution for knowledge graph embedding. Knowl.-Based Syst. **240**, 108100 (2022)
21. Weidong, L., Xinyu, Z., Yaqian, W., et al.: Graph2Seq: fusion embedding learning for knowlegde graph completion. IEEE Access **10**(7), 157960–157961 (2019)

Research on Recognition of Official Script in Natural Environment

Xinya Shu, Xiaofeng Gao, Yanqing Wang(✉), and Niu Man

Nanjing Xiaozhuang University, Nanjing 211171, Jiangsu, China
wyq0325@126.com

Abstract. The domestic dual collaborative education system is becoming increasingly mature, and the computer industry is a hot spot. Aiming at problems such as the absence of a dataset and the complicated recognition of pictures containing multiple characters, this paper mainly studies the preprocessing, data augmentation, word positioning and cutting methods of text pictures in a natural environment. First, image processing and data augmentation functions are used to create datasets; then, a CNN convolutional neural network model is built for training; finally, the method combining horizontal projection and vertical projection is used to locate and cut the word of multi-word graphs. The training accuracy was 96% and the test accuracy was 94%. The results show that the preprocessed image is in line with expectations, and the effect of the cutting monogram has a certain applicability.

Keywords: Image Processing · Ancient Character Recognition · Dataset

1 Introduction

The domestic dual collaborative education system is committed to integrating school and social education resources to provide diversified learning opportunities. This research focus is mainly reflected in the establishment of interdisciplinary and cross-institutional educational partnerships to promote the sharing of high-quality resources and cross-border integration [1]. For example, online and offline cross-school courses are set up, and educational resources are shared using Internet technology. According to the Ministry of Education, the Internet access rate of primary and secondary schools (including teaching sites) has reached 100%; more than 75% of schools are covered by wireless networks, and 99.5% of schools have multimedia classrooms. Currently, the national Smart Education platform for vocational education has access to 1014 national and provincial professional teaching resources and 6628 high-quality online open courses. With the emergence of new technologies, society has increasingly more requirements for the training of computer network professionals [2].

For historical researchers and archaeologists [3], it is inevitable to deal with ancient Chinese characters on historical sites in the process of work, but the translation of a large number of documents is time-consuming. Children learning calligraphy often have to copy ancient Chinese characters [4]. If they did not know the meaning of ancient Chinese

J. Gan et al. (Eds.): CSEI 2023, CCIS 1899, pp. 182–191, 2024.
https://doi.org/10.1007/978-981-99-9499-1_15

characters, the learning effect was small. At present, the products on the market are neither significant nor convenient in the field of ancient character recognition. Therefore, this paper studies official script recognition technology in a natural environment.

The main research contents of this paper include the production of a dataset, construction of a CNN model, and positioning and clipping of text in pictures.

In the making of dataset, due to the difficulty of data acquisition, and there are generally spots, folds and other noise points in the acquired data that affect the recognition [5], it is necessary to not only grayscale and binarize the image so that the image style is black characters on the white background to reduce noise interference, but also to flip and rotate the image to increase the amount of data.

In the construction of CNN model, the network structure and parameters were adjusted many times to obtain better accuracy.

The purpose of studying text positioning and cutting is to identify pictures containing multiple clerical texts. This paper introduces a method of combining horizontal and vertical projections. The intersecting part of the projection is regarded as the area containing text in the picture, and the coordinates of this part are recorded and cut using the image crop function in PIL module.

This research provides help for historians to inquire ancient characters and calligraphy lovers to learn calligraphy, and promote traditional Chinese culture [6].

2 Experiment

First, image processing and data augmentation functions were used to create datasets. Subsequently, a convolutional neural network model was built for training. Finally, a method combining horizontal and vertical projections was used to locate and cut the words of multi-word graphs (Fig. 1).

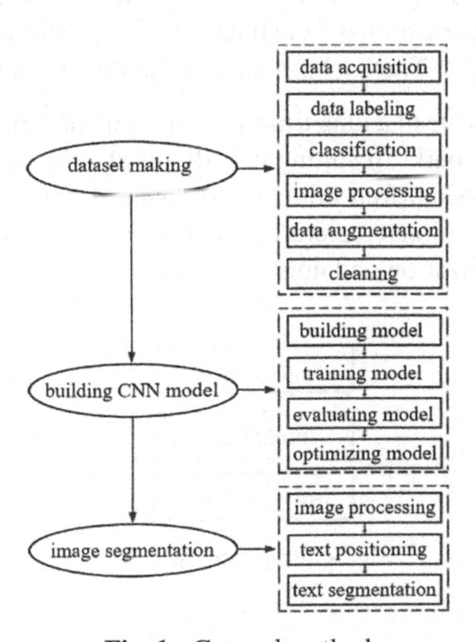

Fig. 1. General method

2.1 Dataset Making

Image dataset making includes data acquisition, data labeling, classification, image processing, data augmentation, and cleaning (Fig. 2).

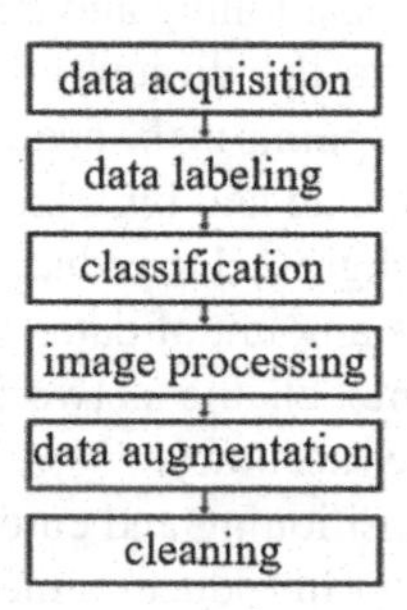

Fig. 2. Dataset making steps

There are approximately 100,000 Chinese characters [7], and the corresponding official scripts are also very large. In contrast to document text recognition, text recognition in natural environment faces challenges such as a complex background, low resolution, diverse fonts, and random text distribution. In order to make the dataset better reflect the characteristics of the natural environment, the data adopts pictures of Chinese characters of official script text taken in the natural environment. At the same time, there is no suitable dataset for the official script, so the experiment needs to build its own dataset. In this paper, 80 commonly used characters ware selected as the data object. As more data are available in the neural network experiment, the experimental effect will be better. Therefore, the data need to be amplified, that is, data augmentation. Find at least 4 pictures of each character from the Internet as raw materials, including the official script text in ancient books. The backgrounds of the images in the data were varied.

Image Preprocessing. Due to a long time, ancient official script paper has mixed color. There are also spots and marks, resulting in difficult identification. Considering that the text may be unclear, missing, font diluted and have different picture brightness in the natural environment, the collected pictures were preprocessed [8]. Image preprocessing includes grayscale, binarization and noise reduction (Fig. 3).

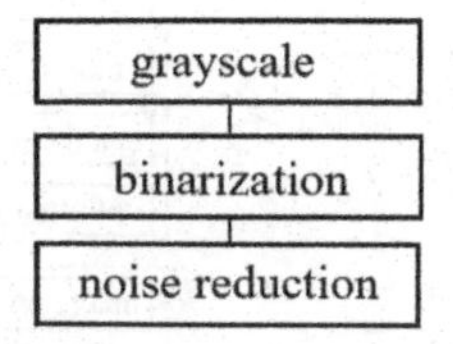

Fig. 3. Preprocessing steps

Gray Processing. The position of each pixel in the image matrix is expressed as (n, m). The color of a pixel is represented by three color variables: red, green, and blue.

The color of a pixel can be changed by assigning values to these three variables. Image graying equalizes the value of the red variable, the value of the green variable, and the value of the blue variable, which is called the gray value. The general image-graying method assignment formula is as follows:

$$\begin{cases} R'_{ij} = 0.3 \times R_{ij} + 0.59 \times G_{ij} + 0.11 \times B_{ij} \\ G'_{ij} = 0.3 \times R_{ij} + 0.59 \times G_{ij} + 0.11 \times B_{ij} \\ B'_{ij} = 0.3 \times R_{ij} + 0.59 \times G_{ij} + 0.11 \times B_{ij} \end{cases} \tag{1}$$

R_{ij}, G_{ij}, B_{ij} represent the values of the red, green, and blue variables, respectively, of the pixel point in row i and column j before graying. R'_{ij}, G'_{ij}, B'_{ij} represent the values of red, green, and blue variables of pixel point in row i and column j after graying.

Image Binarization. Binarization makes the entire image appear black and white. The color distribution of different pictures is very different. Therefore, an appropriate threshold can be customized. The part of the gray value greater than the threshold becomes 0, that is, it becomes black; the part whose gray value is less than the threshold becomes 255, that is, it becomes white. The calculation formula for pixel points after binarization is as follows:

$$C_{ij} = \begin{cases} 0, & Gr_{ij} > T \\ 255, & Gr_{ij} < T \end{cases} \tag{2}$$

T represents the threshold. Gr_{ij} represents the gray value of pixel points in row i and column j, $Gr_{ij} = R'_{ij} = G'_{ij} = B'_{ij}$. C_{ij} represents the value of pixel points in row i and column j after binarization.

Image Denoising. There are many methods for image denoising, such as mean filtering, median filtering, and bilateral filtering.

In this experiment, the cv2.medianBlur function was used to realize the median filtering method for image denoising. Median filtering is a nonlinear smoothing technique, that replaces the value of a point in the image matrix with the median value of each point in the neighborhood of the point to weaken the noise in the image (Table 1).

Data Augmentation. The image was first changed to the same size, so that the CNN model could be built later. Using the flip and rotation method on the denoised images, at least 40 images can be added to each word, which can effectively alleviate the overfitting problem of deep learning model caused by insufficient training data and further improve the accuracy of the model. Consider the following figure as an example. The amount of data after preprocessing is 3200 (Table 2).

Flip includes horizontal flip, vertical flip and horizontal vertical flip (Figs. 4 and 5).

Table 1. Image preprocessing effect

Original	After graying	After binarization	After denoising

Table 2. Functions used for data augmentation

Effect	Function used
resize image	cv2.resize
flip image	cv2.flip
rotate image	cv2.getRotationMatrix2D cv2.warpAffine

Fig. 4. Original image

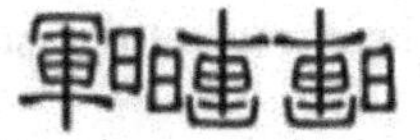

Fig. 5. The Flipped Image

The image is regarded as a matrix, and the upper-left corner of the matrix is represented as (0, 0). For image flip, the relationship between the position of the original pixel (i, j) and the position of the target pixel (I, J) can be expressed by the following formula:

$$\begin{cases} I = i \\ J = n - j \end{cases}, \text{ horizontal flip} \quad \begin{cases} I = n - i \\ J = j \end{cases}, \text{ vertical flip} \quad \begin{cases} I = n - i \\ J = n - j \end{cases}, \text{ horizontal vertical flip} \tag{3}$$

The getRotationMatrix2D function is used to obtain the rotation matrix of the image around a certain point, and the cv2.warpAffine function is used to obtain the rotation of the image (Fig. 6).

Fig. 6. The Rotated Image

For an image with counterclockwise rotation around the image center point, the relationship between the position of the original pixel point (i, j) and the position of the target pixel point (I, J) can be expressed by the following formula:

$$\begin{cases} I = \frac{n}{2} - \left(j - \frac{n}{2}\right)\sin\theta + \left(i - \frac{n}{2}\right)\cos\theta \\ J = \frac{n}{2} + \left(i - \frac{n}{2}\right)\sin\theta + \left(j - \frac{n}{2}\right)\cos\theta \end{cases} \tag{4}$$

θ represents the anticlockwise rotation angle of the image.

2.2 CNN Module

CNN, convolutional neural networks [9], is one of the most classic algorithm models of deep learning, which has a more obvious effect than other neural networks when processing image or video data.

There are three important network layers in the CNN model: convolution, pooling, and fully connected layers. The convolutional layer is composed of several convolution units that have the ability to learn features. The pooling layer further screens the feature output [10]. The fully connected layer maps the results after deep learning to a fixed dimension vector.

When choosing the network model, we should not only retain the features to the greatest extent, but also reduce the changes to the features. Increasing the network depth can improve the network performance, but the increase in the number of parameters not only makes the network easier to overfit but also increases the demand for computing resources [11]. Therefore, the network depth should be neither too small nor too large, and an appropriate depth should be obtained experimentally.

The input is a 50 by 50 size picture. In the convolution layer, the value of the convolution kernel matrix can be changed based on the training effect. In the pooling layer, the max-pooling operation is performed. In the dropout layer, dropout = 0 is set first. After training was completed, the fitting of the training and test dataset was compared. If an underfit occurred, the structure of the model was adjusted. If an overfit occurs, the value of dropout is changed, and training is repeated to select the optimal model (Fig. 7).

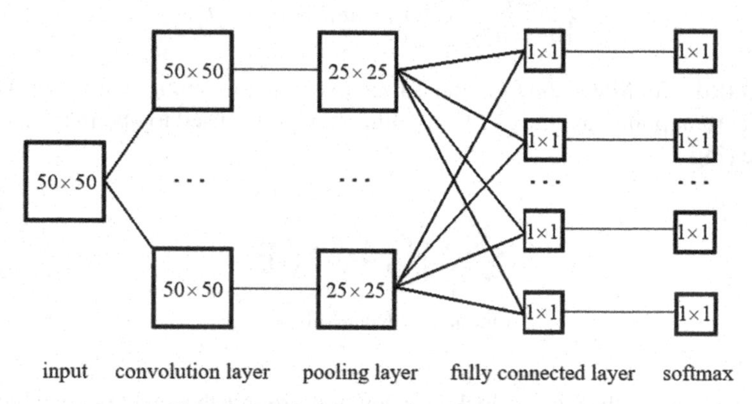

Fig. 7. CNN basic network model structure

Finally, the dataset was divided into training dataset and test dataset according to the ratio of 4:1. After training, it is necessary to compare whether the accuracy of training meets the expectation, and finally retains the model with the highest accuracy.

After comparison, we chose a lightweight network model architecture that includes two-layer convolution, two-layer pooling, two-layer full connection, one softmax and dropout layer. The training accuracy was 96% and the test accuracy was 94%.

2.3 Image Segmentation

To facilitate the identification of pictures containing multiple words, we must locate and segment the text area to obtain a single word. This paper used a combination of horizontal and vertical projection [12] to determine text areas.

First, cv2.imread function is used to read the images that need text positioning. Then, the images are grayscale successively. And the binary processing is performed by changing the black character to white and the white background to black. Then create an array with the same length as the height of the image, use the for loop and count the number of white pixels in each row of the preprocessed image. Finally, the position is recorded and the difference between matrix values is compared to determine the horizontal segmentation position. Similarly, the vertical segmentation position can be obtained (Figs. 8, 9 and 10).

報 得 三 春 暉

Fig. 8. Multiword image

Fig. 9. Horizontal projection

Fig. 10. Vertical Projection

The image.crop function in the PIL module is used to cut the image according to the obtained horizontal and vertical projection positions, and the one-word graph shown below is obtained (Fig. 11).

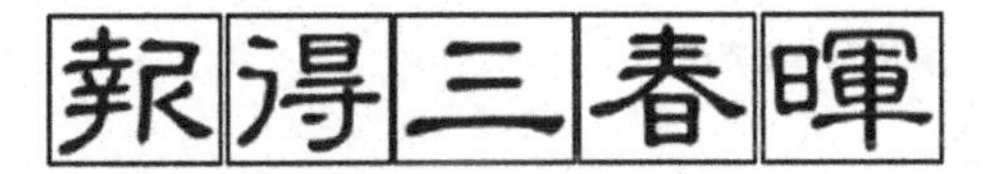

Fig. 11. Cutting Effect

In the experiment, both the horizontal and vertical diagrams had similar effects, but sometimes insufficient or excessive segmentation occurred. In this case, the positional parameters must be adjusted prior to cutting.

3 Demo Effect

After clicking the official script image for uploading, image is processed for grayscale, binarization and denoising; then, the text area is positioned and divided by the method of vertical projection and horizontal projection; finally, recognize it, and the result is printed on the interface. Because of the different lengths and widths of different pictures, some are too wide and some are too high, so each uploaded picture should be adjusted to an appropriate size through the resize function and then placed into the interface (Figs. 12 and 13).

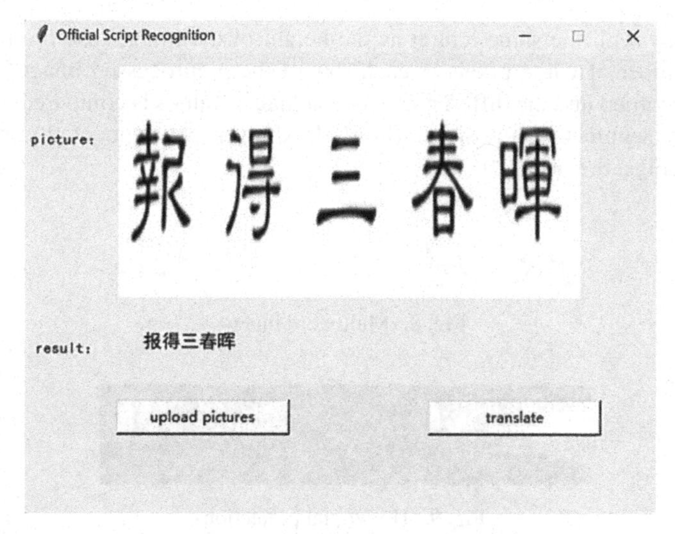

Fig. 12. Effect Demonstration

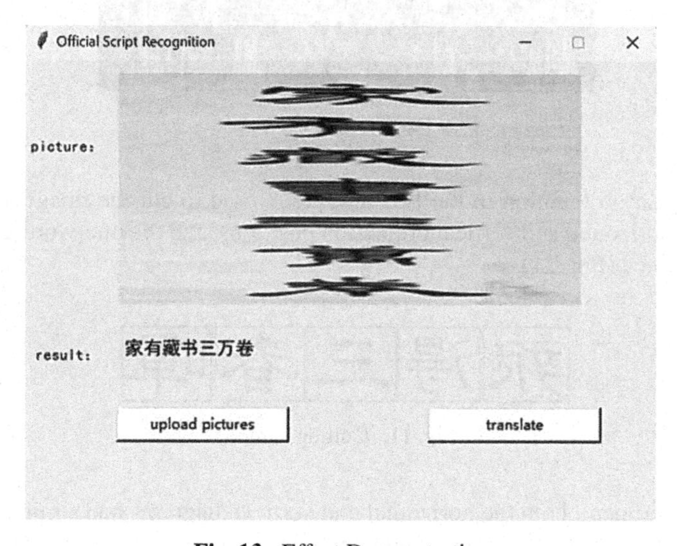

Fig. 13. Effect Demonstration

4 Summary

This paper mainly studies image preprocessing and data augmentation when datasets are created, as well as the locating and cutting of text in pictures. This experiment has a good application effect and popularization, as it can be used to build other ancient script datasets.

Of course, there are many areas that require improvement. The further research will focus on the further expansion of the dataset, more optimization and modification of the CNN model structure and neuron-related parameters to improve the accuracy of the model. In addition, at present, only single-column or single-line uploaded text can be translated in word order. The real Chinese text sometimes needs to be read vertically from the right and sometimes from left to right. For this, the corresponding command function can be set to choose text-reading order recognized when running the program.

References

1. Sun, T.: An analysis of the "dual" cooperative education model of vocational education and enterprises in the new era. Educ. Teach. Forum **458**(12), 391–392 (2020)
2. Xu, X.: Research and practice of "dual" education mode of schools and enterprises—taking the computer network technology of Changjiang Polytechnic as an example. Educ. Teach. Forum **564**(13), 173–176 (2022)
3. Miao, D.: Chinese language and literature (ancient writing direction): a combination of history and writing. Friends High Sch. Students **560**(03), 10–11 (2023)
4. Shang, Q.: On the development of Chinese calligraphy and the inheritance of Chinese character culture. Identif. Appreciation Cult. Relics **224**(05), 151–153 (2022)
5. Yang, X., Wu, S., Song, J., et al.: An adaptive image enhancement and AlexNet ancient character recognition algorithm. Inf. Technol. Informatization **274**(01), 212–216 (2023)
6. Dai, W.: The modern application of Chinese paleography. J. Xiangnan Univ. **42**(03), 75–81 (2021)
7. Li, C., Zhang, Q., Xu, H., et al.: Ancient Chinese characters research based on artificial Intelligence technology. Jilin Univ. J. Soc. Sci. Ed. **63**(02), 164–173+238–239 (2023)
8. Feng, T., Shi, C., Wang, Y.: Method of deep reinforcement learning autonomous driving strategy based on heterogeneous fusion features. Comput. Digit. Eng. **50**(09), 1929–1934 (2022)
9. Zhang, S., Gong, Y., Wang, J.: The development of deep convolution neural network and Its applications on computer vision. J. Comput. Sci. **42**(03), 453–482 (2019)
10. Wang, J.: Chinese text classification based on CNN and Bi-LSTM hybrid model. Software **22**(01), 158–164 (2023)
11. Zhang, K., Feng, X., Guo, Y., et al.: Overview of deep convolutional neural networks for image classification. Chin. J. Image Graph. **26**(10), 2305–2325 (2021)
12. Jiao, H.: Research on character segmentation of license plate Image based on vertical projection segmentation. J. Anhui Vocat. Tech. Coll. Electron. Inf. **20**(06), 17–20 (2021)

Research on Information Literacy Evaluation Framework and Its Indicator Interaction Relationship

Chunhong Liu[1(✉)], Zhengling Zhang[2], Wenfeng Li[1], Congpin Zhang[1], and Dong Liu[1]

[1] Henan Key Laboratory of Educational Artificial Intelligence and Personalized Learning, Xinxiang, Henan, China
lch@htu.edu.cn

[2] Henan Normal University, Xinxiang, Henan, China

Abstract. In the information society, information literacy is significant to students' success, but the existing evaluation frame is far from satisfying. To address this issue, this paper introduces disciplinary literacy into the evaluation system and constructs an evaluation framework for normal university students of computer science and technology from the three modules of disciplinary development, general level and teaching orientation. Then, typical features of each module are extracted by the canonical correlation analysis method, and correlations between typical features are assessed by the Pearson correlation coefficient. With the support of 139 students' data, we have already obtained the following conclusions. First, the general level is a bridge between disciplinary development and teaching orientation. Second, there are two groups of moderate positive correlations here, one between computational thinking attitude and information knowledge and the other between teaching belief and information ethics, with coefficients of 0.62 and 0.53, respectively. Moreover, there is a strong positive correlation between teaching integration and information ability, with a coefficient of 0.72.

Keywords: Information Literacy Evaluation Framework · Normal University Students · Canonical Correlation Analysis · Pearson Correlation Coefficient

1 Introduction

In 2018, the Ministry of Education issued the Action Plan for Revitalizing Teacher Education (2018–2022) and the Action Plan for Education Informatization 2.0 [1, 2]. The documents clearly pointed out that the reform of teaching methods centring on normal university students should be advanced and deep integration of education and information technology ought to be continuously strengthened. By formulating a reasonable information literacy evaluation index system, normal universities can better improve students' abilities. In this environment, appropriate evaluation of information literacy for normal university students and comprehensive construction of an evaluation framework have become research focuses in education informatization.

J. Gan et al. (Eds.): CSEI 2023, CCIS 1899, pp. 192–206, 2024.
https://doi.org/10.1007/978-981-99-9499-1_16

Good information literacy has a positive impact on students' academic and career performance [3]. Many studies have emphasized that information literacy education could improve students' information technology skills, help them adapt to the digital learning environment and ultimately form lifelong learning ability [4]. In early studies, information literacy was often understood as the ability to utilize information technology and data resources [5]. However, subsequent studies indicated that information literacy also included the ability to obtain, identify, process and transmit information [6]. Namely, information literacy is a synthetic ability to use information to solve practical problems and make innovations [7]. Empirical studies have shown that people with higher information literacy are more able to recognize when they need information and have the ability to discover, retrieve, evaluate and utilize the required information [8]. The discoveries widely advance the development of information literacy assessment.

Establishing a universal evaluation framework for information literacy is an important way to measure students' abilities and optimize training programs. In addition, it is also the premise of making student promotion plans [9]. In this context, the most authoritative Information Literacy Framework for Higher Education, released by the American Association for College and Research Books (ACRL), has been exploring the new information literacy ecosystem for many years. Later, Zhu et al. [9] and Na et al. [10] proposed evaluation frameworks for information literacy from different perspectives. In summary, although there are many differences in the expression of evaluation frameworks of home and abroad, they all focus on the four aspects of information awareness, information knowledge, information ability and information ethics.

With the dual identity of social learner and future educator, normal university students should not only cultivate the four aspects mentioned above. It has been found that they need to not only have the information technology ability to analyse students' needs but also apply information technology, manage classroom instruction and reflect on themselves [11]. However, current research on information literacy mostly focuses on the assessment of information literacy ability in primary and secondary schools [12] and the bridging education of information literacy from high school to university [13]. These studies seriously ignore the importance of information literacy in higher education [14] and its vital role in accelerating education informatization. To solve these problems, some scholars have begun to shift their research focus to normal university students [15]. For example, Li et al. [16] produced a study on the evaluation index system from the perspective of education informatization 2.0 but did not consider the different cultivation modes of different majors. In addition, Guo et al. [17] constructed an evaluation framework based on mathematics subjects but neglected the role of learners in the information society.

Computer science and technology is a major that cultivates high-level engineering talents with independent consciousness and innovation capacity, combining science with engineering. Students in this major can maintain high informational awareness and proficiently apply information technology to classroom instruction. Meanwhile, they are disseminators of emerging technologies as well. Therefore, computer science and technology majors should be given priority in the assessment of information literacy ability for normal university students.

Ultimately, we build the following three main research questions by analysing the existing information literacy evaluation frameworks. First, the framework of information literacy indicators for normal college students of computer science and technology is constructed from the three aspects of disciplinary development, general level and teaching orientation. Second, taking our university of Grade 20 students as an example, the typical features of three modules are extracted by using the canonical correlation analysis method. Third, we calculate the Pearson correlation coefficient to measure the correlation between typical features and explore the relationship between indexes.

2 Methodology

2.1 Hypothesis Model

Information Literacy Evaluation Index System for Accounting Computer Science and Technology Normal College Students. As having the dual roles of learners and future teachers, the information literacy ability of teacher-training students is directly related to the process of China's education informatization reform. Because of their double identity, their information literacy cannot be measured by the standards of ordinary in-service teachers but should have special standards and evaluation systems. The training of accounting computer science and technology teacher trainees, who are both computer and normal college students, should also focus on the disciplinary development of computer science. Based on this, the paper referred to the information literacy evaluation framework of normal college students in the era of education informatization 2.0 proposed by Li et al. [16]. Moreover, we have presented an information literacy evaluation index system for computing normal college students from disciplinary development, general level and teaching-oriented perspectives.

Interaction Relationships of Disciplinary Development, General Level and Teaching-Oriented. To measure the interactions between each module, we plan to extract the typical features of the indicators and analyse the correlation between the features using intelligent algorithms. First, we collected a total of 36 tertiary indicators through questionnaires to investigate the three information literacy modules of disciplinary development, general level and teaching orientation. Then, using the two methods of weighting and principal component analysis, we reduced the dimension from 36 tertiary indicators to 9 secondary indicators. With the help of canonical correlation analysis, we screened the typical features of 9 secondary indicators that could represent the three modules. Finally, the Pearson correlation coefficient was used to calculate the correlation between typical features to obtain a reliable conclusion. The specific process is shown in Fig. 1.

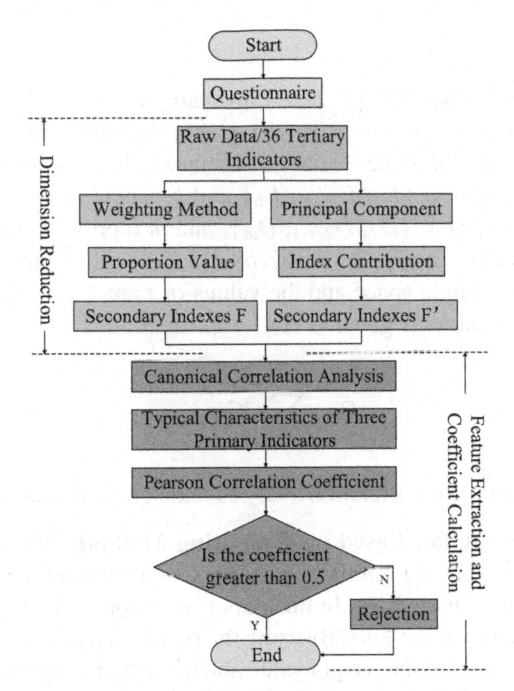

Fig. 1. Typical feature extraction and relationship analysis of the proposed indexes.

2.2 Sample and Instruments

Participants. We chose 147 normal college students of computer science and technology in Grade 20 at our school. Among them, 78 students' data came from Class one, accounting for 53.10% of the total data. Meanwhile, 69 students were from Class 2, accounting for 46.90%. All of the above students obtained the appropriate right to know before the experiment and agreed to us obtain the corresponding information data to complete the follow-up work.

Questionnaire Design. To explore the interactions among the information literacy modules, we designed an information literacy questionnaire based on the index framework constructed above. The questionnaire was divided into three main components: subject development, generic level and teaching-oriented. At the same time, each module was designed with corresponding questions according to relevant indicators, and each question was assigned a score using a five-level Likert scale for subsequent data processing.

Data Collection. After distributing the questionnaire to 20th grade accounting normal college students, we obtained data from 147 students. After cleaning, filtering abnormal data and removing incomplete student information, we eventually obtained 139 valid data points. The effective recovery rate of this questionnaire is approximately 94.56%, which indicates that the content of the questionnaire is designed more reasonably and can lead to reliable conclusions.

2.3 Data Analysis

Given a decision system $NDT = \{X, D, F\}$, the sample space is $X = \{X_1, X_2,\ldots, X_n\}$. For any $i \in n$, we have $X_i = \{x_{i1}, x_{i2},\ldots, x_{ia}\}$. Among them, n is the total number of people in this survey, and a is the number of tertiary indicators. Assume that the set of secondary indicators is $F = \{F_1, F_2,\ldots, F_b\}$ and b denotes its number. Similarly, the primary indicator set is $D = \{D_1, D_2,\ldots, D_m\}$, and m represents its total number. The range of a is also specified as $\{1, 2,\ldots, 36\}$, b is $\{1, 2,\ldots, 8, 9\}$, and m is $\{1, 2, 3\}$.

Suppose X is the sample space and the values of t are $\{2, 4, 3\}$. If any $i \in |t|$, then the set of primary indicators is given as (1):

$$D = \sum_{i=1}^{|t|} CCA(F_i) \tag{1}$$

where CCA is the canonical correlation analysis and $|t|$ denotes the number of arrays t.

Typical Feature Extraction Based on Weighting Method. The method reveals the structural relationships among multiple variables by calculating the weights or proportions of similar items in the whole. In this paper, we adopt the approach to reduce the data dimension of tertiary indicators. By using the proportion of each index as the weight value, we take the product of the weight value and the actual value as the comprehensive value of each secondary index. Eventually, b secondary indicator data are obtained.

Assume that X is the sample space and the value of s is $\{3, 5, 4, 6, 6, 3, 2, 2, 5\}$. If any $i \in |s|$, the secondary indicators are defined as:

$$F = \sum_{i=1}^{|s|} W_i \tag{2}$$

where W_i is the combined weight value of each tertiary indicator and $|s|$ represents the number of arrays s.

If X is the sample space, for any $i \in |s|$ and $j \in s_i$, the comprehensive weight value can be transformed as follows:

$$W_i = \frac{X_i}{\sum_{j=1}^{s_i} X_j} \tag{3}$$

Typical Feature Extraction Based on Principal Component Analysis. This method is used to reduce the dimension of high-dimensional data and extract the components of the main features. The paper utilizes SPSS software to extract the typical features of the original for a tertiary index. Finally, we obtain b secondary index.

Suppose X is the sample space and the value of s is $\{3, 5, 4, 6, 6, 3, 2, 2, 5\}$. For any $i \in |s|$, we can obtain the secondary indicators as shown in Eq. (4):

$$F' = \sum_{i=1}^{|s|} PCA(X_i) \tag{4}$$

Among them, *PCA* symbolizes the principal component analysis method, and $|s|$ denotes the number of arrays s.

After data dimension reduction by the above method, 36 three-level indicators are converted into 9 second-level indicators. The specific results are shown in Table 1.

Table 1. Secondary indexes extracted by *PCA*.

Tertiary indicators	Secondary indicators
Emotional attitude and values	Thinking attitude
Decomposing task ability	Thinking skills
Sensitive awareness	Info-awareness
Tool knowledge	Info-knowledge
Psychological control ability and Bad info-filtering ability	Info-ability
Network intellectual property	Info-ethics
Student center	Teaching belief
Equipment operation	Teaching technology
Resource preparation	Teaching integration

Typical Feature Correlation Analysis Based on the Pearson Correlation Coefficient. The coefficient is widely used to measure the degree of correlation between two variables. We use it to explore the correlation between typical features. Suppose X is the sample space. For any P and Q belonging to the typical feature set H, the correlation coefficient formula is as follows:

$$\rho_{P,Q} = \frac{E[(P - \mu_P)(Q - \mu_Q)]}{\sigma_P \sigma_Q} \tag{5}$$

The Pearson correlation coefficient is viewed as the quotient of covariance and standard deviation between two variables.

3 Results

3.1 Information Literacy Assessment Framework for Computer Science and Technology Normal College Students

Combined with the characteristics of actual roles, literature in the field of information literacy was consulted and referenced. Then, we build an information literacy evaluation framework for computer science and technology normal college students from the perspectives of discipline development, information society learners and future teachers. The results are shown in Fig. 2.

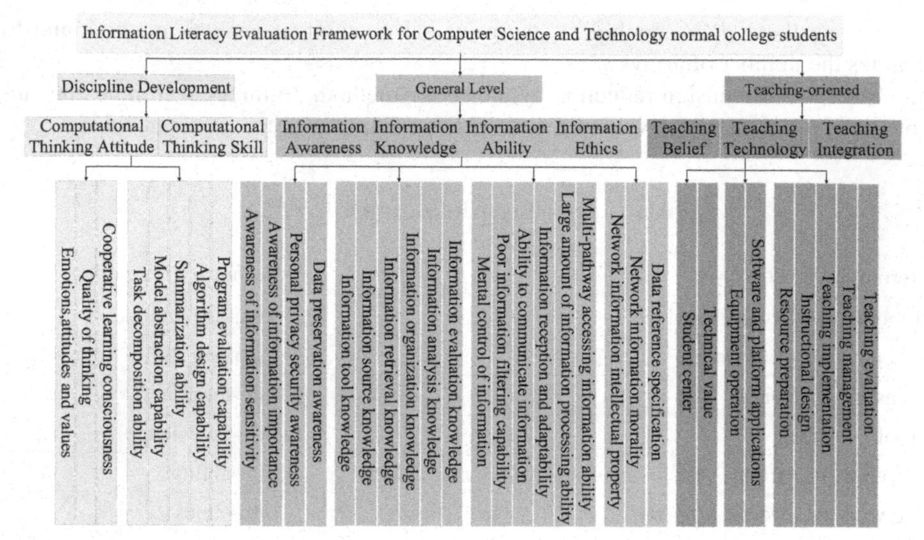

Fig. 2. Design of information literacy evaluation index for computer science and technology normal university students.

Development Information Literacy. In May 2019, UNESCO stated in its Artificial Intelligence Education Report that computational thinking has emerged as one of the key competencies that will enable learners to flourish in an AI-driven society. Yadav et al. began an early exploration in 2014 and elaborated on its connotation [18]. By deconstructing its elements and attempting to integrate it with other disciplines, it was found that computational thinking is a universal competency that should be included as part of students' learning in school and added to their daily development. In recent years, the cultivation of computational thinking in China has been entrusted to computer science [19]. Presenting the core content in specific information technology courses is either biased to programming languages or to technical tool applications. This method may lead to students' narrower understanding and make it difficult to form computational thinking skills.

Based on the above views, we found that the disciplinary development of computer science and technology should focus on the cultivation of students' computational thinking [20]. Computational thinking is an important thinking skill for individuals to adapt to the survival of digital society. Therefore, it can expand students' cognitive world and problem-solving abilities and help them think about problem solutions from the level of principles and methods [21]. This finding also suggests that computational thinking is a manifestation of both problem-solving skills and the cognitive-psychological ability of individuals to adapt to changes in digital technology [22]. Hence, we chose "computational thinking attitude" and "computational thinking skills" as two secondary indicators under the "disciplinary development module".

General Level Information Literacy. In the digital age, information literacy has become a basic information-related awareness and competency that a global citizen needs to possess. Its connotation has undergone several changes, shifting from the emphasis on the technology itself and the use of skills to comprehensive literacy and interdisciplinary literacy [23]. It has been suggested that [24] information literacy includes but is not limited to information awareness, information acuity, information processing, information sharing, and information security. Liu [25] believed that information literacy is a collection of integrated abilities, including discovering information, understanding information production and value, using information to create new knowledge, and participating in community learning.

Empirical studies by Kim et al. [26] and Greenberg et al. [27] have shown that college students already have basic information retrieval skills, information judgment abilities, and the ability to share or collaborate with each other on social platforms. Therefore, students need to continuously enhance their awareness of big data, information knowledge and skills, and data ethics in the process of general education and professional development [28]. Therefore, to further cultivate students' ability to handle massive data and organize large-scale projects, our paper extracts "information awareness", "information knowledge", "information competence", and "information ethics" as four secondary indexes under "general-level information literacy".

Teaching-Oriented Information Literacy. As the main source and reserve strength of future teachers, the information technology teaching ability of normal college students is directly related to the development of education in China. Their cultivation needs to be given high priority. However, the current traditional education system did not give their information literacy the status it deserves, resulting in a lack of competence, experience, and preparation of some teachers in using information technology to implement instruction [29]. In this context, normal colleges also need to promote teachers' exemplary role in teaching normal university students and take the initiative to guide them to use information technology in classroom instruction. Through continuous teaching practice, their information literacy ability can be enhanced. Thus, Wang et al. [30] argued that teachers should possess information quality, information knowledge and information ability in the "Internet+" era. Huang [31] believed that teachers should also have attitudes and beliefs about the integration of information technology into education. Based on this, we extract "teaching belief", "teaching technology" and "teaching integration" as three secondary indicators under "teaching-oriented information literacy".

3.2 The Interaction Between Disciplinary Development, General Level and Teaching-Oriented Information Literacy

To explore the correlation between the three modules, our paper first uses the Pearson coefficient to calculate the correlation between any two modules. Then, partial correlation analysis is chosen to eliminate the influence of other modules. Based on this idea, the correlations between the explored modules in this paper are shown in Table 2.

As shown in the table below, when the effect of other modules is ignored, any two modules of disciplinary development, general level and teaching-oriented are significantly correlated at a confidence level of 99%. The coefficients are 0.67, 0.80 and 0.51, respectively.

Table 2. The results of Pearson Correlation Coefficient and Partial Correlation Analysis.

Variable setting	Pearson correlation	Each module	
		Partial correlation	P
Subject-General	0.67	0.50	0.00
Teaching-General	0.80	0.72	0.00
Teaching-Subject	0.51	−0.05	0.54

Considering the influence of other factors, we try to calculate the partial correlation coefficient after controlling the corresponding modules. After isolating the role of teaching orientation, when the confidence level is 99%, the coefficient of disciplinary development and general level is 0.50. By excluding the effect of disciplinary development, we find that the coefficient is 0.72 at a confidence level of 99%. Finally, it is found that there is no correlation between teaching-oriented and disciplinary development with 90% confidence ($P = 0.50 > 0.1$) through controlling the general level. Based on the conclusion, our paper will subsequently explore two aspects of work. One is to study the relationship between disciplinary development and the general level. The other is to discover the relationship between teaching-oriented and general levels.

The Results of Typical Feature Extraction for Disciplinary Development and General Level. To improve the accuracy of the data and reliability of the conclusion, two methods of weighting and principal component analysis were introduced to reduce the dimension of the data. Later, we carried out canonical correlation analysis on the reduced data to extract typical features.

After using the weighting method, there are two pairs of typical variables between disciplinary development and general level at the 99% confidence level ($P = 0.000 < 0.01$ and $P = 0.005 < 0.01$). The correlation coefficient of the 1st pair of typical variables is 0.72, and that of the 2nd pair is 0.30. By dimension reduction by principal component analysis, with a confidence level of 99% ($P = 0.000 < 0.01$), there is a pair of typical variables between two modules, and the correlation coefficient is 0.67. The results of canonical correlation analysis after dimension reduction by both methods are shown in Table 3.

According to the acquired data, we can draw the following conclusions in the weighting method. In the first pair of loading coefficients of typical variables, computational thinking attitude and information knowledge have the largest absolute value. Two values indicate that the typical characteristics of disciplinary development and general level are computational thinking attitude and information knowledge, respectively. In the second pair of loading coefficients of typical variables, the absolute value of computational thinking skills and information awareness is the largest. The above data show that the typical characteristics of disciplinary development and general level are computational thinking skill and information awareness, respectively.

Table 3. Typical feature extraction results of two methods in disciplinary development and general level modules.

Variable	Weighting method		Principal component
	Typical load 1	Typical load 2	Typical load
Thinking attitude	**−0.94**	−0.35	−0.73
Thinking skills	−0.93	**0.38**	**−0.95**
Info-awareness	−0.83	**−0.49**	−0.77
Info-knowledge	**−0.91**	−0.09	**−0.87**
Info-ability	−0.89	0.30	−0.58
Info-ethics	−0.61	−0.21	−0.60

In the principal component analysis method, based on the first pair of loading coefficients of typical variables, computational thinking skills and information knowledge have the largest absolute value. Therefore, we know that the typical characteristics of disciplinary development and general level are individual computational thinking skills and information knowledge.

The Results of Typical Feature Extraction for Teaching-Oriented and General Level. Similarly, referring to the processing method in Sect. 3.2.1. By using the weighting method to process the data, there is one pair of typical variables between teaching-oriented and generic levels with a correlation coefficient of 0.82 at a confidence level of 99% ($P = 0.000 < 0.01$). With the help of principal component analysis, the correlation coefficient of teaching-oriented and general level is 0.70 with a confidence level of 99% ($P = 0.000 < 0.01$). The canonical correlation analysis results from the two methods are shown in Table 4.

Table 4. Typical feature extraction results of two methods in teaching-oriented and general level modules.

Variable	Weighting method	Principal component
	Typical load	Typical load
Teaching belief	−0.44	**−0.90**
Teaching technology	−0.21	−0.82
Teaching integration	**−0.46**	−0.77
Info-awareness	−0.21	−0.74
Info-knowledge	−0.32	−0.51
Info-ability	**−0.41**	−0.75
Info-ethics	−0.21	**−0.87**

As shown above, in the weighting method, based on the loading coefficients of typical characteristics, the absolute value of teaching integration and information competence is the largest, which indicates that the typical feature of the teaching-oriented module is teaching integration and the general level module is information ability. With the aid of principal component analysis, we find that teaching belief and information ethics have the largest absolute value. The outcomes reveal that the typical feature of teaching orientation is teaching belief and that the general level is information ethics.

The Results of Correlation Analysis Based on the Pearson Correlation Coefficient. With the support of the above two methods, we use canonical correlation analysis to extract typical features of the three modules under different situations. To calculate the correlation between each typical feature, the Pearson correlation coefficient is introduced in this paper. The specific results are shown in Table 5.

Table 5. Correlation analysis results of typical features.

Modules	Features	Coefficient
Subject-General	Thinking attitude and Info-knowledge	0.62
	Thinking skill and Info-awareness	0.49
	Thinking skill and Info-knowledge	0.39
Teaching-General	Teaching integration and Info-ability	0.72
	Teaching belief and Info-ethnics	0.53

As shown above, we obtained the following Pearson correlation coefficients under the two modules of disciplinary development and general level. In the weighting method, computational thinking attitude and information knowledge are 0.62, and computational thinking skills and information awareness are 0.49. Under the principal component analysis method, the Pearson correlation coefficients for computational thinking skills and information knowledge are 0.39. Accordingly, some conclusions would be found in both teaching-oriented and general-level modules. First, the coefficient for teaching integration and information competence is 0.72 in the weighting method. Second, the teaching belief and information ethics coefficient is 0.53 in the principal component analysis approach. (Define feature groups as features 1 to 5 in the order of the rightmost column in Table 5.)

By reviewing the relevant literature, the empirical rules for the magnitude of the correlation coefficient are described slightly differently in different research areas, but the overall direction is generally consistent. Since Mukaka [32] explains the correlations between variables in more detail, we would like to choose his rule for the subsequent screening exercise. Set the feature groups in the rightmost column of Table 5 to be 1 to 5 in the order. Combining Mukaka's rule of thumb, we can gain the results shown in Table 6.

Table 6. The results of feature selection by empirical rules.

Size of correlation	Relevance	Results	
		Feature groups	Factor
0.90 to 1.00	Very high		
0.70 to 0.90	High	Feature 4	0.72
0.50 to 0.70	Moderate	Feature 1 and Feature 5	0.62 and 0.53
0.30 to 0.50	Low	Feature 2 and Feature 3	0.49 and 0.39
0.00 to 0.30	Negligible		

From the table above, we have found that when the correlation coefficient is greater than 0.50, the two features belong to medium strength correlation. This means that there is a significant relationship between the variables. Based on the theories, we extracted 3 groups of more reliable conclusions, namely, feature group 1, feature group 4 and feature group 5. Therefore, we can hold the following conclusions. First, there was a positive medium correlation between computational thinking attitude and information knowledge. Thus, teaching belief and information ethics have a positive medium correlation. In the end, there is a strong positive correlation between teaching integration and information ability.

4 Conclusion

4.1 The General Level is a Bridge for Disciplinary Development and Teaching-Oriented

After excluding the effect of the general level module, there is no significant correlation between disciplinary development and teaching orientation. At a confidence level of 90.00% ($p = 0.54 > 0.10$), the partial correlation coefficient was −0.05, which was almost negligible. However, the Pearson correlation coefficient between the two modules is $0.50 < 0.51 < 0.70$ without shielding the influence of other factors, which is a positive moderate correlation. According to the above analysis, we have summarized that the general-level module plays a bridging role in the transition between disciplinary development and teaching orientation.

4.2 Significant Facilitation Between Computational Thinking Attitude and Information Knowledge

With the help of canonical correlation analysis, we have found that computational thinking attitude is a typical feature of disciplinary development. Simultaneously, information knowledge is a typical characteristic of the general level. According to the Pearson correlation coefficient, the coefficient of the two modules is 0.62, between 0.50 and 0.70, which indicates a positive moderate correlation relationship. Based on this conclusion, our paper has inferred that when students have a strong belief in managing information and active thoughts about understanding and using data, it would advance the understanding and mastery of information knowledge. That is, the more positive the computational thinking attitude, the smoother the learning of information knowledge.

4.3 Vital Motivational Effects Between Teaching Belief and Information Ethics

With the help of canonical correlation analysis, we found that teaching belief is a typical feature for teaching orientation and that information ethics is a typical characteristic at the general level. According to the Pearson correlation coefficient, the coefficient of the two modules is 0.53, greater than 0.50, which is a positive moderate correlation relationship. As a result, we have suspected that when normal college students establish a firm attitude to promote the development of students' rational use of information, it would continuously expand and extend the connotation of information ethics and promote the development of information security. That is, the stronger the teaching belief, the richer the information ethics content.

4.4 A Clear Drive Between Teaching Integration and Information Ability

By means of canonical correlation analysis, we found that teaching integration is a typical feature of teaching orientation and that information competence is a typical characteristic at the generic level. Based on the Pearson correlation coefficient, the coefficient for the two modules is 0.72, between 0.70 and 0.90, which is a positive and strong correlation relationship. In summary, we know that when normal college students have the ability to prepare teaching resources, design teaching content and create a classroom environment with the support of information technology, it would advance the improvement of students' information competence. That is, teaching integration ability is closely related to information competence.

Acknowledgements. We would like to thank the Henan Provincial Higher Education Teaching Reform Research and Practice Project Foundation for supporting the study [number: 2021SJGLX355]. We are supported by the 2021 special research project of Wisdom Teaching in General Undergraduate College and University of Henan Province, the Tracking of Group Intelligent Learning Knowledge Integrated with Learning Emotion, Personalized Guidance and Effectiveness Research. Simultaneously, we are honestly grateful to Grade 20 computer science and technology normal students of Henan Normal University for allowing us to use questionnaires to obtain relevant information literacy data.

References

1. Action Plan for Revitalizing Teacher Education. http://www.moe.gov.cn/srcsite/A10/s7034/201803/t20180323_331063.html. Accessed 23 Mar 2018
2. Notice of the Ministry of Education on Printing and Distributing the Education Informatization 2.0 Action Plan. http://www.moe.gov.cn/srcsite/A16/s3342/201804/t20180425_334188.html. Accessed 25 Apr 2018

3. Mohagheghzadeh, M.S., Mortazavi, S.M.J., Ghasempour, M., et al.: The impact of computer and information communication technology literacy on the academic achievement of medical and dental students at Shiraz University of Medical sciences. Eur. Sci. J. **10**(9), 273–280 (2014)
4. Zhong, Z.X.: Lifelong learning: the connotation, evolution and standard of information literacy. Distance Educ. China (8), 21–29+95 (2013)
5. Zhang, Q.W.: Information literacy and information literacy education. E-Educ. Res. (2), 9–14 (2001)
6. Na, R., Wu, X.W., Lv, J.H.: Research status and prospect of information literacy standards at home and abroad. Libr. Inf. Work **54**(3), 32–35 (2010)
7. Zhou, J., Wang, Y., Iris, X.: Generation characteristics, changes of information environment and innovation of information literacy education for college students. J. China Libr. **41**(4), 25–39 (2015)
8. Luo, M., Wang, Z.H.: Research on the influencing factors of students' information literacy based on ISM and AHP. China Educ. Technol. (4), 5–11 (2018)
9. Zhu, S., Wu, D., Yang, H., et al.: Research framework of student information literacy evaluation based on ECD. China Educ. Technol. (10), 88–96 (2020)
10. Na, R., Wu, X.W., Lv, J.H.: Network information literacy evaluation based on AHP and fuzzy comprehensive evaluation. Inf. Mag. **30**(7), 81–84 (2011)
11. Markauskaite, L., Goodwin, N., Reid, D., Reimann, P.: Modelling and evaluating ICT courses for pre-service teachers: what works and how it works? In: Mittermeir, R.T. (ed.) ISSEP 2006. LNCS, vol. 4226, pp. 242–254. Springer, Heidelberg (2006). https://doi.org/10.1007/11915355_23
12. Dolenc, K., Sorgo, A.: Information literacy capabilities of lower secondary school students in Slovenia. J. Educ. Res. **113**(5), 335–342 (2020)
13. Gerrity, C.: The new National School Library Standards: implications for information literacy instruction in higher education. J. Acad. Librarianship **44**(4), 455–458 (2018)
14. Bury, S.: Learning from faculty voices on information literacy. Ref. Serv. Rev. **44**(3), 237–252 (2016)
15. Tu, P.: Information literacy survey and curriculum system construction of normal students in ethnic areas. Comput. Educ. **326**(2), 17–21 (2022)
16. Li, Y., He, S.W., Qiu, L.H.: Research on the evaluation index system of normal university students' information literacy in the era of educational informatization 2.0. China Educ. Technol. **401**(6), 104–111 (2020)
17. Guo, J.C., Miu, L., Chen, Q.H.: Construction and investigation of evaluation framework of mathematics teachers' information literacy. Res. Mod. Basic Educ. **44**(4), 32–40 (2021)
18. Yadav, A., Mayfield, C., Zhou, N., et al.: Computational thinking in elementary and secondary teacher education. ACM Trans. Comput. Educ. **14**(1), 1–16 (2014)
19. Ren, Y.Q., Sui, F.W., Li, F.: How is digital indigenous possible—on the necessity and possibility of computing thinking in information technology education in primary and secondary schools. China Educ. Technol. (1), 2–8 (2016)
20. David, W., Elham, B., Michael, H.: Defining computational thinking for mathematics and science classrooms. J. Sci. Educ. Technol. **25**, 127–147 (2016). https://doi.org/10.1007/s10956-015-9581-5
21. Xiao, G.D., Huang, R.H.: Problems in the implementation of high school information technology curriculum and consideration of the new curriculum standard. China Educ. Technol. (12), 10–15 (2016)
22. Li, F., Wang, J.Q.: Computational thinking: an intrinsic value of information technology curriculum. China Educ. Technol. (8), 19–23 (2013)
23. Shi, G.: The connotation and cultivation of digital literacy of primary and secondary school students. Curriculum Textbook Teach. Method **36**(7), 69–75 (2016)

24. Sang, G.Y., Dong, Y.: On the connotation evolution of teachers' information literacy and its promotion strategies in the internet plus era. E-Educ. Res. **37**(11), 108–112 (2016)
25. Liu, H.: Analysis of the concept and content elements of paninformation literacy. Books Inf. (4), 67–73 (2020)
26. Kim, K.S., Sin, S.C.J.: Perception and selection of information sources by undergraduate students: effects of avoidant style, confidence, and personal control in problem-solving. J. Acad. Librarianship **33**(6), 655–665 (2007)
27. Greenberg, R., Bar-Ilan, J.: Information needs of students in Israel—a case study of a multicultural society. J. Acad. Librarianship **40**(2), 185–191 (2014)
28. Meng, X.B., Li, A.G.: Research on scientific data literacy education in foreign university libraries. J. Univ. Libr. **32**(3), 11–16 (2014)
29. Song, J., Liu, W., Liu, L.S.: Analysis on the current situation of online teaching and training needs of teachers during the epidemic prevention and control period—based on the results of a sampling survey of 100 primary and secondary schools nationwide. Res. Teach. Educ. **32**(3), 1–9 (2020)
30. Wang, Y., Shi, W.L., Cui, Y.H.: Research on young teachers' information literacy in the internet plus era. China Educ. Technol. (3), 109–114 (2017)
31. Huang, Y.X.: Research on the development of primary and secondary school teachers' literacy in the internet plus environment. Teach. Manag. (27), 59–61 (2018)
32. Mukaka, M.M.: A guide to appropriate use of correlation coefficient in medical research. Malawi Med. J. **24**(3), 69–71 (2012)

Evolutionary Game Analysis to Promote the Improvement of Youth Digital Literacy from the Perspective of Multiple Collaboration

Mingxin Wang[1], Yingxuan Tian[1], and Saidong Lv[2](✉)

[1] School of Information, Yunnan Normal University, Kunming, China
[2] Network and Information Center, Yunnan Normal University, Kunming, China
15938338917@163.com

Abstract. Improving the digital literacy of young people and nurturing qualified digital citizens is a crucial issue in the digital age. The improvement of youth digital literacy requires the joint efforts of multiple subjects, and the game relationship between different subjects is the key to promoting the improvement of youth digital literacy. From the perspective of multiple collaborations, this paper constructs a three-way evolutionary game model of "government-school-family" with the help of evolutionary game methods, which provides data support for effectively improving adolescents' digital literacy ability and provides a theoretical basis for the implementation of relevant policies.

Keywords: Adolescent · Digital Literacy · Evolution Game

1 Introduction

In the digital age, with the rapid development of information technology, digital technology has gradually penetrated into human production and life. According to the 50th Statistical Report on Internet Development in China released by the China Internet Network Information Center, as of June 2022, there were 186 million Internet users under the age of 19 in China, accounting for 17.7% of the total Internet users [1]. While the number of juvenile netizens has increased, juvenile digital literacy has also become a national strategic competitiveness that is widely valued by countries around the world. To promote the development of digital literacy, the European Union implemented the "Digital Literacy Project" in 2011, which established a digital literacy framework that includes five "literacy domains": information domain, communication domain, content creation domain, security awareness domain and problem solving domain [2]. For example, on November 14, 2022, Minister of Education Huai Jinpeng once again stressed at the symposium on education digitalization that it is necessary to "promote the strategic action of

[Funds] Youth Fund of the General Project of Humanities and Social Science Research of the Ministry of Education, "Research on the Spatial Structure Characteristics and Coordinated Development of Compulsory Education in Ethnic Areas from the Perspective of Urban Agglomeration" (22YJC880053)

J. Gan et al. (Eds.): CSEI 2023, CCIS 1899, pp. 207–216, 2024.
https://doi.org/10.1007/978-981-99-9499-1_17

education digitalization in depth" and "focus on improving the digital literacy and ability of teachers and students". Young people are the new force for comprehensively building a modern socialist country with Chinese characteristics, and strengthening youth digital literacy education is an effective way to popularize and improve the digital literacy of all people [3].

Although the hardware of information technology in China has developed rapidly and the information literacy of the people has also been greatly improved, the development of digital capabilities of schools and teachers is very uneven, and according to China's situation and development needs, it is urgent to vigorously improve teachers' digital literacy and formulate a national teacher digital ability improvement plan [4]. Most teenagers cannot distinguish between real and false information on the Internet, and the multitasking mode of the information age also makes people more distracted and difficult to filter irrelevant information, which will lead to difficulties in processing basic information [5]. A large number of homogeneous information pushes under algorithm manipulation cause minors to only contact people with the same or similar opinions as themselves, adopt views that meet their expectations, and form an "echo chamber".

Effect, and strengthen the cognitive bias of minors [6]. From the perspective of the future development of higher education and the development of teachers themselves, Yin Bingshan proposed that to better adapt to changes in teaching and learning, teachers need to reflect and adjust their teaching role positioning and improve their digital literacy [7]. E. Adomi proposed that an evaluation system involving the respondents' own evaluation, computer use, and frequency of software should be established to help schools improve students' digital skills and develop teaching plans based on students' needs [8]. G. Soldativa et al. constructed digital ability indicators based on the digital competency literacy model of multiple psychologists, investigated the digital ability of Russian 12- to 17-year-old adolescents and their parents, and identified the problems of adolescents and parents in digital ability motivation [9].

At present, most of the research in the field of adolescent digital literacy is qualitative, and there are few quantitative studies on the evolutionary game process of digital literacy improvement. In the evolutionary game, the subject is bounded rationality, and by constantly improving and modifying the existing strategy, all the subjects may eventually tend to choose a stable strategy that will not change, gradually approach the Nash equilibrium, and the system will reach a stable state [10]. As a systematic scientific research methodology, game theory can help explore the gains and losses of multiple subjects, and provide a theoretical reference for the improvement of adolescents' digital literacy ability.

Therefore, under the framework of bounded rationality, this study uses game theory and is based on the multisubject collaboration of government, family and school to establish a three-group asymmetric evolutionary game analysis model for the improvement of adolescent digital literacy, analyses the decision-making behavior strategies of each subject, and proposes an effective development mechanism and practical optimization suggestions for the policy-oriented trinity to participate in the improvement of adolescent digital literacy.

2 Build a Game Model

2.1 The Subject of the Game

The improvement in youth digital literacy is the result of the participation of multiple stakeholders in the evolutionary game, of which the government, family, and school are the three main stakeholders. Parents mainly supervise the implementation of the school and the government, the government is responsible for implementing relevant policies and supervising the implementation of the school, and the school is the basic governance and enforcement unit for students' digital literacy improvement. The relationship between the three stakeholders is manifested in: the active supervision of adolescent parents under the top-level design, and the evolutionary game between government supervision and school implementation. Family, government and school are regarded as participants in the process of the game, and the degree of active supervision of the family, the degree of supervision of the government and the degree of implementation of the school are the influencing factors, and the participants will play with each other over time.

2.2 Government

The government, as the implementer and regulator of policies, should follow central documents to cultivate young people's digital literacy capabilities, supervise schools under its jurisdiction during the implementation process, and reward schools with outstanding performance. The government will choose passive supervision based on local economic income, and will also choose active supervision due to the pressure of public opinion and the credibility of the government. Assuming the probability of the government choosing positive regulation is $x(0 < x < 1)$, the probability of negative regulation is $1 - x$.

School

Schools are the basic implementing units, and under the guidance of the government, they carry out school-based digital literacy improvement work for teenagers. Schools will choose to implement actively or passively based on the documents issued by the government, and the choice will result in various factors, such as financial pressure and reputation. Assuming that the probability of a school choosing positive execution is $y(0 < y < 1)$, the probability of negative execution is $1 - y$.

Family

Families are third-party active supervisors of the government and schools, and after the policy is issued and publicized, families choose to understand the specific content of the policy according to the degree of attention, actively supervise the implementation of the government and schools, and choose passive supervision if they do not pay attention to the cultivation of digital literacy among adolescents. The probability of the family choosing to actively implement active supervision is $z(0 < z < 1)$; then, there is a $1-z$ probability that the family chooses passive supervision.

2.3 Basic Assumptions

According to the above analysis, the basic hypothesis of the evolutionary dynamic model of adolescent digital literacy ability improvement is given, and the relevant parameters are set.

Hypothesis 1: Assume that the participants in promoting the improvement of youth digital literacy include the government, schools, and families, and the three participants are all limited and rational, and adjust their own strategies to achieve the best stable strategy according to the game information they obtain.

Hypothesis 2: Information asymmetry hypothesis: In the process of choosing whether to actively implement, the school cannot predict whether the government will actively supervise and whether the family will actively supervise, the government cannot predict whether the school will actively implement and whether the family will actively supervise in the process of supervision, and the family cannot predict whether the school will choose to actively implement and whether the government will actively supervise.

Hypothesis 3: The variables that influence local government behavior strategies are as follows: The government provides basic financial subsidies for schools are M. When the government actively supervises, schools also actively implement the public opinion orientation triggered by teaching, which will enhance the government's image and credibility, and the potential benefits are S_1. The benefits of government regulation are L_1. The results of negative government regulation are L_2. The cost of active government regulation is A_1. The cost of negative regulation by the government is A_2. When the government actively regulates it, the policy is not coordinated by the school, and the potential harm to the families of adolescents is the same W.

Hypothesis 4: The variables affecting school behavior strategies are as follows: the cost of manpower and material resources for introducing teachers and equipment when the school actively implements it is C_1; the basic cost of passive implementation by schools is C_2; the potential benefits brought by the students attracted by the school because of its characteristic teaching when the school chooses to actively implement it are S_2; the government's punishment for schools when they are negatively enforced is P; and when the school actively implements it, it will give a certain subsidy to the families of students involved in the improvement of information literacy as J.

Hypothesis 5: The variables influencing the family behavior strategy of adolescent students are as follows: the time, money and other costs of adolescent students' families when choosing active supervision are $\boldsymbol{C}_3$; the benefits of families of adolescent students when they choose active supervision are $\boldsymbol{S}_3$; families of adolescent students choose to actively supervise, but passive implementation in schools can call into question the quality of teaching and credibility of the government, which in turn will lead to losses and $\boldsymbol{D}$ and $\boldsymbol{H}$, respectively.

According to the above model assumptions, the return matrix of the three-way game between the government, the school, and the student's family is obtained, as shown in Table 1.

Table 1. Payoff matrix of tripartite

Government	School	Family	
		Active supervision	Negative supervision
Positive regulation	Active execution	$S_1 - M - A_1 S_2 + M - C_1 - JS_3 + J - C_3$	$S_1 - M - A_1$ $S_2 + M - C_1$ 0
	negative execution	$P - A_1 - H - M$ $M - P - D$ $S_3 - C_3 - W$	$P - A_1 - M$ $M - P$ 0
Negative regulation	Active execution	$L_2 - A_2 - M$ $S_2 + M - C_1 - J$ $S_3 + J - C_3$	$L_2 - A_2 - M$ $S_2 + M - C_1$ 0
	negative execution	$L_2 - A_2 - M - H$ $S_2 + M - C_1 - D$ $S_3 - C_3$	$L_2 - A_2 - M$ $S_2 + M - C_1$ 0

3 Dynamic Analysis of the Evolution of Game Participants

3.1 Evolutionary Equilibrium Analysis of Government

Suppose the expected return of the government choosing an active regulatory strategy is V_{11}, the expected return of choosing a negative regulatory strategy is V_{12}, and the average return is V_1.

$$\begin{aligned} V_{11} =& yz(S_1 - M - A_1) + y(1-z)(S_1 - M - A_1) + (1-y)z(P - A_1 - H - M) \\ &+ (1-y)(1-z)(P - A_1 - M) \end{aligned} \tag{1}$$

$$\begin{aligned} V_{12} =& yz(L_2 - A_2 - M) + y(1-z)(L_2 - A_2 - M) + (1-y)z(L_2 - A_2 - M - H) \\ &+ (1-y)(1-z)(L_2 - A_2 - M) \end{aligned} \tag{2}$$

$$V_1 = xV_{11} + (1-x)V_{12} \tag{3}$$

If $V_{11} - V_{12} > 0$, the expected benefits of the government's choice of active regulation are greater than the expected benefits of choosing a negative regulatory strategy, and the government prefers the positive regulatory strategy. If $V_{11} - V_{12} < 0$, the government chooses a negative regulatory strategy with greater benefits, and the government will tend to choose a negative regulatory strategy.

The dynamic equation for the replication of government policy evolution is:

$$\begin{aligned} F_1(x) &= \frac{dx}{dt} = x(V_{11} - V_1) = x(1-x)(V_{11} - V_{12}) \\ &= x(1-x)[A_2 - A_1 + P - L_2 + y(S_1 - P)] \end{aligned} \tag{4}$$

Derivation of $F_1(x)$ yields:

$$\begin{aligned} &F_1'(x) = (1-2x)[A_2 - A_1 + P - L_2 + y(S_1 - P)] \\ &A_2 - A_1 + P - L_2 + y(S_1 - P) = 0 \\ &\text{So, } y_0 = \frac{A_1 - A_2 + L_2 - P}{S_1 - P}, F_1(x) = 0 \end{aligned} \tag{5}$$

At this point, all are in an evolutionary steady state. When $A_2 - A_1 + P - L_2 + y(S_1 - P) \neq 0$, let $F_1(x) = 0$, and obtain the two equilibrium points of $x = 0$ and $x = 1$. At this point, it is divided into two situations:

When $A_2 - A_1 + P - L_2 + y(S_1 - P) < 0$, that is, when $y < \frac{A_1 - A_2 + L_2 - P}{S_1 - P}$, there is $F_1'(x)|_{x=0} < 0$, $F_1'(x)|_{x=1} > 0$, where $x = 0$ is the evolutionary dynamic equilibrium point. That is, when the probability of active implementation by the school is less than $\frac{A_1 - A_2 + L_2 - P}{S_1 - P}$, the government chooses a negative regulatory strategy.

When $A_2 - A_1 + P - L_2 + y(S_1 - P) > 0$, that is, when $y > \frac{A_1 - A_2 + L_2 - P}{S_1 - P}$, there is $F_1\prime(x)|_{x=1} < 0$, $F_1\prime(x)|_{x=0} > 0$, where $x = 1$ is the evolutionary dynamic equilibrium point.

That is, when the probability of active implementation by the school is greater than $\frac{A_1 - A_2 + L_2 - P}{S_1 - P}$, the government chooses the active regulatory strategy.

3.2 Evolutionary Equilibrium Analysis of Schools

Suppose the expected payoff for schools choosing an aggressive execution strategy is V_{21}, the expected payoff for choosing a passively executing strategy is V_{22}, and the average payoff is V_2.

$$\begin{aligned} V_{21} = &xz(S_2 + M - C_1 - J) + x(1-z)(S_2 + M - C_1) + z(1-x)(S_2 + M - C_1 - J) \\ &+ (1-x)(1-z)(S_2 + M - C_1) \end{aligned} \tag{6}$$

$$\begin{aligned} V_{22} = &xz(M - P - D) + x(1-z)(M - P) + z(1-x)(S_2 + M - C_1 - D) \\ &+ (1-x)(1-z)(S_2 + M - C_1) \end{aligned} \tag{7}$$

$$V_2 = yV_{21} + (1-y)V_{22} \tag{8}$$

If $V_{21} - V_{22} > 0$, then the expected return of the school choosing active execution is greater than the expected return of choosing a negative execution strategy, and the school tends to choose active execution. If $V_{21} - V_{22} < 0$, then the school tends to choose a passive execution strategy.

The replication dynamic equation for the evolution of family strategy is:

$$\begin{aligned} F_2(y) &= \frac{dy}{dt} = y(V_{21} - V_2) = y(1-y)(V_{21} - V_{22}) \\ &= y(1-y)[z(D - J) + x(S_2 + P - C_1)] \end{aligned} \tag{9}$$

Deriving $F_2(y)$, we obtain:

$$F_2'(y) = (1-2y)[z(D - J) + x(S_2 + P - C_1)] \tag{10}$$

When $z(D-J)+x(S_2+P-C_1)=0$, then $x_0=\frac{z(J-D)}{S_2+P-C_1}$. There is $\frac{dy}{dt}=0$, at which point all y is in an evolutionarily stable state.

When $z(D-J)+x(S_2+P-C_1)\neq 0$, let $F_2(y)=0$ to obtain the two equilibrium points of $y=0$ and $y=1$.

At this point, it is divided into two situations:

When $z(D-J)+x(S_2+P-C_1)<0$, that is, when $x<\frac{z(J-D)}{S_2+P-C_1}$, there is $F_2\prime(y)|_{y=0}<0$, $F_2\prime(y)|_{y=1}>0$, where $y=0$ is the evolutionary dynamic equilibrium point. That is, when the probability of active government regulation is less than $\frac{z(J-D)}{S_2+P-C_1}$, the school chooses a passive enforcement strategy.

When $z(D-J)+x(S_2+P-C_1)>0$, that is, when $x>\frac{z(J-D)}{S_2+P-C_1}$, there is $F_2\prime(y)|_{y=0}>0$, $F_2\prime(y)|_{y=1}<0$, where $y=1$ is the evolutionary dynamic equilibrium point. That is, when the probability of active government regulation is greater than $\frac{z(J-D)}{S_2+P-C_1}$, the school chooses to actively implement the strategy.

3.3 Evolutionary Equilibrium Analysis of The Family

Suppose the expected payoff for households choosing an active surveillance strategy is V_{31}, the expected payoff for choosing an inactive surveillance strategy is V_{32}, and the average payoff is V_3.

$$\begin{aligned}V_{31}=&xy(S_3+J-C_3)+x(1-y)(S_3-C_3-W)+y(1-x)(S_3+J-C_3)\\&+(1-x)(1-y)(S_3-C_3)\end{aligned}\tag{11}$$

$$V_{32}=0\tag{12}$$

$$V_3=zV_{31}+(1-z)V_{32}\tag{13}$$

If $V_{31}-V_{32}>0$, then the expected benefit of families choosing active supervision is greater than the expected benefit of choosing a nonactive supervision strategy, and families tend to choose an active supervision strategy. If $V_{31}-V_{32}<0$, then the family tends to choose not to actively supervise.

If $V_{31}-V_{32}>0$, then the expected benefit of families choosing active supervision is greater than the expected benefit of choosing a nonactive supervision strategy, and families tend to choose an active supervision strategy. If $V_{31}-V_{32}<0$, then the family tends to choose not to actively supervise.

The replication dynamic equation for the evolution of family strategy is:

$$\begin{aligned}F_3(z)=\frac{dz}{dt}&=z(V_{31}-V_3)=z(1-z)(V_{31}-V_{32})\\&=z(1-z)[S_3-C_3+yJ+x(yW-W)]\end{aligned}\tag{14}$$

Deriving $F_3(z)$, we obtain:

$$F_3'(z)=(1-2z)[S_3-C_3+yJ+x(yW-W)]$$

When

$$S_3 - C_3 + yJ + x(yW - W) = 0, x_0 = \frac{C_3 - S_3 - yJ}{yW - W}$$

There is $\frac{dz}{dt} = 0$, at which point all z is in an evolutionarily stable state.

$S_3 - C_3 + yJ + x(yW - W) \neq 0$, let $F_3(z)$ to obtain the two equilibrium points of $z = 0$ and $z = 1$.

At this point, it is divided into two situations:

When $S_3 - C_3 + yJ + x(yW - W) < 0$, that is, when $x < \frac{C_3 - S_3 - yJ}{yW - W}$, there is $F_3'(z)|_{z=0} < 0$, $F_3'(z)|_{z=1} > 0$, where $z = 0$ is the evolutionary dynamic equilibrium point. That is, when the probability of active government regulation is less than $\frac{C_3 - S_3 - yJ}{yW - W}$, the family chooses the passive supervision strategy.

When $S_3 - C_3 + yJ + x(yW - W) > 0$, that is, when $x > \frac{C_3 - S_3 - yJ}{yW - W}$, and $F_3'(z)|_{z=0} > 0$, $F_3'(z)|_{z=1} < 0$ where $y = 1$ is the evolutionary dynamic equilibrium point. That is, when the probability of active government regulation is less than $\frac{C_3 - S_3 - yJ}{yW - W}$, the family chooses the passive supervision strategy.

Through the evolutionary game process, it can be seen that the "government-school-family" game will not converge on a certain set of strategies, the whole process of the three parties is constrained by various factors, and the change in any one factor will affect the strategic choice of the subject.

4 Conclusions and Revelations

Based on evolutionary game theory, this paper establishes an evolutionary game model between the three subjects of government, school and family, and draws the following conclusions by referring to the evolutionary model of the above three subjects:

The government's strategic choices are related to regulatory costs, public opinion and credibility. When the government realizes the importance of strengthening supervision to the guidance of public opinion and the credibility of the government, the government tends to choose "regulation"; when the government increases the rewards and punishments of schools under its jurisdiction, schools tend to actively implement policies to obtain rewards and avoid punishment, thereby ensuring the credibility of the government. The choice of school strategy is related to its implementation cost (including the introduction of excellent teachers, technology and construction of hardware infrastructure, etc.), image benefits. Schools tend to actively implement policies when they believe that the image benefits of active implementation are higher than the cost of implementation. Similarly, when the cost of active execution is too high for schools to obtain the expected benefits, they will gradually choose an evolutionary strategy of passive execution.

The strategic choice of families is related to parents' attention, awareness and school subsidies for the improvement of the digital literacy of adolescents, and the school's lack of attention to the harm caused by digital literacy improvement to adolescents is also a key factor affecting whether families choose to actively supervise. Under government supervision and active family supervision, schools can improve youth digital literacy under the stated policy goals, and the government's credibility can be enhanced.

In addition, schools and families are important participants in the process of improving youth digital literacy, and the government is an important leader in the collaborative governance of schools and families. Coordinating the three parties is conducive to improving young people's digital literacy, so based on the results of evolutionary game analysis, the following suggestions are summarized:

4.1 Improve Systems, Actively Supervise, and Broaden Channels for Supervision and Feedback

As far as the government is concerned, active supervision of schools under its jurisdiction is fundamental to ensuring the effective implementation of policies. Therefore, at the macro level, the government needs to improve supervision and supervision policies and reasonably set up reward and punishment systems. Reward schools that actively implement policies, reasonably guide opportunistic or perfunctory schools, and punish schools when necessary. In the middle of the world, encourage exchanges and cooperation between schools to learn excellent cases together and facilitate the promotion of schools with poor policy implementation results. At the micro level, broadening supervision and feedback channels, and improving the digital literacy of adolescents requires the joint efforts of the three parties to guide schools and families to participate in the supervision process, create multichannel supervision channels, and encourage feedback and suggestions.

4.2 Introduce Teachers and Technology, Strengthen Interschool Exchanges, and Improve Infrastructure Construction

As far as schools are concerned, actively participating in the improvement of youth digital literacy is conducive to building a positive school image and promoting the long-term development of schools. Therefore, schools need to set up overall planning, have an overall grasp of the overall digital literacy situation of the school, actively create relevant courses and activities, and actively learn from excellent schools with advanced experience. In terms of teachers, schools need to introduce high-level digital literacy teachers under the premise of reasonable planning of capital costs and carry out digital literacy capacity improvement training for teachers in schools. In terms of students, guide students to actively participate in the learning of digital literacy courses, encourage participation in various digital literacy related competitions (such as intelligent robot development, computer design competitions, etc., and increase students' autonomy and choice in digital literacy development.

4.3 Actively Participate in Process and Results Monitoring and Encourage Recommendations and Evaluations

Regarding the family, the family is the supervisor of school policy implementation and government supervision, and passive school implementation and government supervision can lead parents to question the school's teaching level and the government's credibility. Positive family supervision can effectively reduce the occurrence of such problems, so families are encouraged to participate in the process and outcome monitoring of youth digital literacy, establish a multifaceted governance system between government, school and family, and collaborate to improve youth digital literacy.

References

1. China Internet Network Information Center: The 50th Statistical Report on Internet Development in China [EB/OL]. Accessed 01 Sept 2022
2. Ren, Y., Sui, X., Liu, X.: Research on the framework of digital literacy in the European Union. Modern Distance Educ. Res. (05), 3–12 (2014)
3. Zhao, G., Zhong, B.: Improving youth digital literacy and cultivating qualified digital citizen. Educator (49), 38–39 (2022)
4. Yuan, Z.: J. East China Normal Univ. (Educ. Sci. Edn.) **41**(03), 1–11 (2023)
5. Lin, L., Yan, T.: Research on the relationship between minors and digital technology from the perspective of digital literacy. China Educ. Inf. (2022)
6. OECD: Trends shaping education spotlights No.13: citizens with a say [EB/OL], 15 October 2017. Accessed 07 July 2021
7. Yin, B., Gao, Q.: Technology, education and society: integrated development in collision---interpretation of the 2017 higher education edition of the new media alliance horizon report. Open Educ. Res. (2), 222–234 (2017)
8. Adomi, E.E., Anie, S.O.: An assessment of computer literacy skills of professionals in Nigerian university libraries. Libra y Hi Tech News **23**(2), 10–14 (2006)
9. Soldativa, G., Rasskazova, E.: Assessm hent of the digital competence in Russian adolescents and parents: digital competence index. Psychol. Russia State Art **4**, 65–74 (2014)
10. Niu, Q., Zhang, R.: Evolutionary game analysis of school-community cooperation to promote school sports development from the perspective of multisubject collaboration. Phys. Educ. Res. **01**, 102–112 (2023)

Research on Construction of Student Academic Early Warning Model Based on Ensemble Learning

Xiao Li(✉) and Chen Li

School of Management, Capital Normal University, Beijing 100048, China
lixiao@cnu.edu.cn

Abstract. The educational data mining technology could support teaching management and it has received more and more attention. This paper focuses on the prediction problem of student academic performance and constructs the ensemble learning based early academic warning model to make accurate prediction. This paper collects students' behavioural data from different campus systems, i.e., teaching system, online learning system, education and research system, library system and campus e-card consuming system, and make standardization processing for the original data. By utilizing the educational big data, this paper constructs an ensemble learning based early academic warning framework to predict students' academic performance. The framework contains three modules, Correlation analysis and Potential Features Selection, Data Reduction and Ensemble Learning based Academic Performance Prediction. Correlation analysis and Potential Features Selection module first analyses the correlation relationship between independent variables (i.e., indicators) and dependent variable (i.e., students' academic performance) through Apriori algorithm and then selects indicators which have strong correlations with students' academic performance as potential features. In order to identify accurate features from potential features, the PCA method is utilized for Data Reduction. In the Ensemble Learning based Academic Performance Prediction module, an ensemble learning-based model is constructed to make accurate academic performance prediction, which aggregates Random Forest Classifier, XGBoost Classifier, BP Neural Network as the base classifiers and takes multinomial logistic regression classifier as the meta classifier. The prediction results could provide support for educational administrators and teachers, and give early warning for students.

Keywords: Educational Data Mining · Academic Early Warning · Ensemble Learning · Prediction Model · Data Reduction

1 Introduction

With the development of big data, Smart Campus and Digital Campus play increasing importance role in many colleges. Students produce data in their study life every day, the corresponding platforms generate a large number of tracking records which could

J. Gan et al. (Eds.): CSEI 2023, CCIS 1899, pp. 217–228, 2024.
https://doi.org/10.1007/978-981-99-9499-1_18

reflect students' actual learning situation. At the same time, the research and application of educational big data mining is becoming the hot topic [1–3]. Students' study situation which is the focus of educational administrators, teachers and parents, is an important application of educational data mining [4–7]. In this paper, we focus on students' academic performance problem and analyse students' learning behaviour by utilizing their history tracking records through multiple campus platforms. In particular, we propose to utilize data mining technology to produce accurate academic performance and academic early warning, which could provide support for educational administrators, teachers and students.

Most traditional researchers study students' learning behaviour analysis by using questionnaire surveys. This type of methods costs a lot of time and produces a large number of invalid data. Moreover, since there are many human factors in the process of devising questionnaire surveys and collecting data through questionnaire surveys, the results of this type of methods are not objective enough. Some researchers utilize fuzzy rule-based and frequent pattern algorithm for the academic performance prediction [8–10].

Recently, some researchers focus on student's learning behaviour analysis and performance prediction problem. Some researchers utilize students' reading behaviour and e-book consuming records for study academic performance [11, 12]. Some studies propose prediction models by integrating the data mining technology, machine learning technology and artificial intelligence technology [13–22]. Based on artificial intelligence, Zhang et al. design an online learning early warning model [14]. Shi et al. collect students' borrowing data during 2016/01–2020/09 from a school, study the correlation between student academic performance and book borrowing behaviour and propose a BP neural network based academic early warning model [15]. They found that student performance and student borrowing behaviour have greater correlations. Their devised BP neural network algorithm could predict student academic performance accurately and provide valuable talent training direction for students. Liu et al. propose a decision trees algorithm for the academic early warning prediction [18]. Cheng et al. propose a random forest algorithm for solving the problem [19]. Moreover, some studies adopt the deep learning technology [20, 21], such as deep neural network and convolutional neural network for solving the academic performance prediction problem.

Although some researches have integrated educational data and artificial intelligence technology and carried out in-depth study and exploration on students' academic performance prediction problem, there are still some problems in the educational data mining based academic early warning prediction.

Single Data Source. Most existed researches focus on students' campus educational data from single system, such as library systems in campus. In fact, there are multiple campus platforms could collect students' records data which have high correlation with student academic performance, such as teaching system, online learning systems and campus e-card consuming system. Thus, it is necessary to collect and aggregate students' educational data from multiple systems.

Prediction Accuracy Not Enough. How to analyze the correlation between students' multiple behaviours and academic performance, construct important factors which affect students' academic performance, and devise an accurate prediction model is still a challenging problem.

Therefore, in this paper, we collect campus students' behavioural data from multiple campus systems, i.e., teaching system, online learning system, education and research system, library system and e-card consuming system. Based on standardized processing, we select important indicators which could affect students' academic performance through Apriori algorithm. In order to capture key features, we make data reduction for the potential features by using PCA method. Finally, we construct an ensemble learning based early academic warning model for accurate prediction which takes captured features as the input, and aggregates multiple machine learning methods (i.e., random forest, XGBoost, and BP neural network). The constructed student academic early warning model could provide targeted intervention and guidance for students, which has high practical value and realistic significance.

2 Educational Data Collection and Data Processing

In this paper, we collect students' behavioural data from multiple systems and make pre-processing for the original collected data. The data source and pre-processing are shown in Fig. 1.

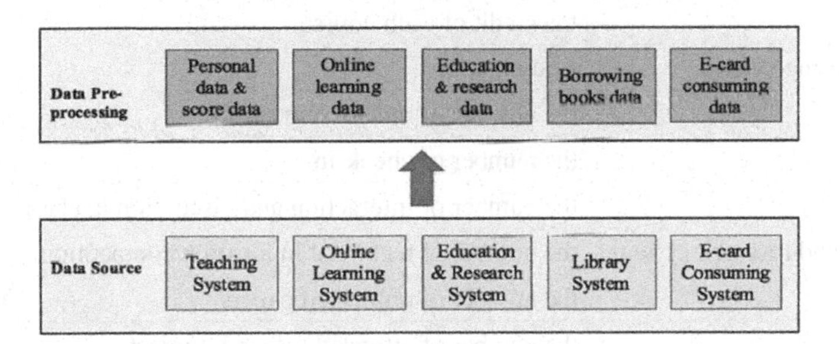

Fig. 1. The data source and data pre-processing

2.1 Educational Data Collection

With the support of institutions, we collect educational data from multiple campus systems. We summarize students' information collected from different systems in Table 1.

1) **Teaching system**. This system records students' personal information (containing student number, major and gender), test score of each course (containing final exam score, Mid-term score and in class score) and the course credit information.
2) **Online learning system**. This system records students' online behavioural data during the classroom teaching process, containing study hours, the number of missed homework, the number of check-in and the number of interaction and discussion in class.

3) **Education and research system**. This system records the number of students' entered technical innovation competition times, the number of published papers, the number of attended research projects and the number of applied patents.
4) **Library system**. This system records students' borrowing history, containing the reading hours of borrowing books and the total number of borrowing books.
5) **E-card consuming system**. This system records students' e-card consuming history, containing the amount of e-card consuming per day in campus canteen, consuming frequency per day in campus canteen.

Table 1. Data source and students' detailed information

Data source	Detailed information
Teaching system	student number
	major
	gender
	final exam score
	mid-term score
	in class score
	the credit of each course
Online learning system	study hours
	the number of missed homework
	the number of check-in
	the number of interaction and discussion in class
Education and research system	the number of technical innovation competition
	the number of published papers
	the number of attended research projects
	the number of applied patents
Library system	the reading hours of borrowing books
	the total number of borrowing books
E-card consuming system	the amount of e-card consuming per day in campus canteen
	consuming frequency per day in campus canteen

2.2 Educational Data Pre-processing

The Pre-processing of Dependent Variable. Since students take a variety of courses in their professional field and outside their major field of study, there are multiple dimensional score data. In order to reduce the high dimension, we pre-process student's academic comprehensive score (i.e., the dependent variable) by using the following equation,

$$y = \frac{\sum_{i=1}^{n} credit_i * score_i}{\sum_{i=1}^{n} credit_i}, \quad (1)$$

$$score_i = \alpha_1 score_{ic} + \alpha_2 score_{mid} + \alpha_2 score_f, \quad (2)$$

where y denotes the academic comprehensive score of a target student, n denotes the number of his selected courses, $credit_i$ denotes the credit of course i, $score_i$ denotes the score of course i which can be computed by the student's weighted average of in-class score, mid-term score and final score, $score_{ic}$ denotes the in-class score, $score_{mid}$ denotes the mid-term score and $score_f$ denotes the final exam score of course i. After we compute each student's academic comprehensive score, we standardize computed scores as five levels, i.e., *Excellent, Good, Fair, Pass and Poor.* The standardization rules are that if the academic comprehensive score of a student is in range 90–100, we categorize this student as *Excellent*. Similarly, 80–90 as Good, 70–80 as Fair, 60–70 as Pass, and under 60 as Poor, which are shown in Table 2.

Table 2. Student academic performance pre-processing results

Student score, y	Corresponding performance level
$y >= 90$	Excellent
$80 <= y < 90$	Good
$70 <= y < 80$	Fair
$60 <= y < 70$	Pass
$y < 60$	Poor

The Pre-processing of Independent Variables. Based on the five campus systems, we capture 14 independent variables to represent 14 dimensions' data. Since different dimension has different scale, we need to make standardized process for the captured data. For each independent variable x, we take the standardized process based on the equation as follows,

$$x^* = \frac{x - \mu}{\sigma}, \quad (3)$$

where x^* denotes the standardized value of the independent variable x, μdenotes the average value of x, andσdenotes the standard deviation of x.

3 Correlation Analysis and Data Reduction for Student Academic Early Warning

In this paper, the student academic early warning problem is to classify student academic performance into five categories, i.e., Excellent, Good, Fair, Pass and Poor. Since many factors may affect student academic performance, we need to first identify the important features from multiple campus systems and then devise an accurate prediction model to predict student academic performance and give early warning for students. Therefore, the student academic early warning problem is formulated as, given multi-dimensional data collected from multiple campus systems, the student academic performance in terms of the categories (i.e., Excellent, Good, Fair, Pass and Poor) is identified by using the prediction model. In order to solve this problem, we construct the ensemble learning based student academic early warning model which contains three modules, i.e., correlation analysis and potential feature selection, data reduction and the ensemble learning based academic prediction model. We give the overall framework of the student academic early warning model in Fig. 2. In this section, we describe the correlation analysis and potential feature selection module and the data reduction module in detail.

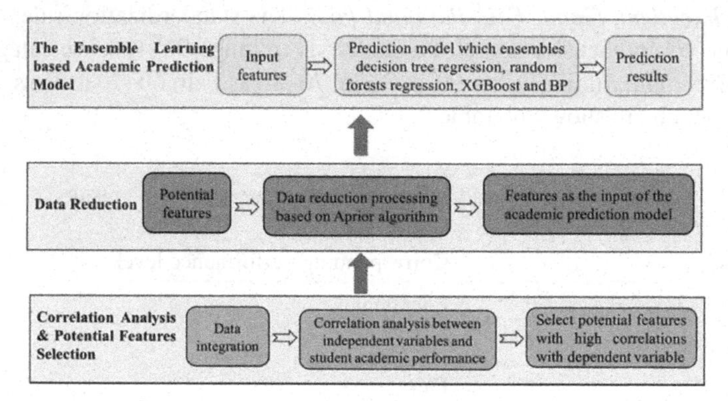

Fig. 2. The overall framework of the student academic early warning model

3.1 Correlation Analysis and Potential Features Selection

Based on students' multiple data collected from multiple systems in campus, we derive 14 independent variables (i.e., 14 dimensional data). We devise the correlation analysis and potential features selection module to evaluate the correlation between independent variables and student academic performance (i.e., dependent variable). In particular, we devise the Apriori algorithm for the correlation analysis.

The Apriori Algorithm. Apriori algorithm is a typical association rule mining algorithm, which utilizes the iteration way to find out potential correlations for the large data. Apriori algorithm is also called frequent pattern mining algorithm and is commonly used to analyse the relationship whether two objects (or more objects) are related to each other. Apriori algorithm contain three concepts, i.e., support, confidence and lift. In this paper, we first calculate the value of support, confidence and lift based on the following equation, and then identify frequent item sets with minimum support, minimum confidence and lift greater than 1.

$$Support(X) = \frac{The\ number\ of\ occurrences\ of\ item\ set\ X\ in\ the\ total\ set}{Total\ number\ of\ records\ in\ the\ total\ set}, \quad (4)$$

$$Confidence(X \rightarrow Y) = \frac{Support(X, Y)}{Support(X)}, \tag{5}$$

$$Lift(X \rightarrow Y) = \frac{Confidence(X \rightarrow Y)}{Support(Y)}. \tag{6}$$

Correlation Analysis between Independent Variables and Student Academic Performance. In order to compute the correlation relationship between each independent variable and the dependent variable (i.e., academic performance), we process each variable based on the clustering algorithm. Specifically, based on each student's value on this independent variable, we adopt classification algorithm to classify students. For example, for the independent variable *"consuming times per day in campus canteen"*, we classify students to 3 levels shown in Table 3. For the independent variable "the number of interaction and discussion in class", we classify students to 3 levels shown in Table 4. Note that, the dependent variable in this paper is student academic performance which is also a classification variable (i.e., Excellent, Good, Fair, Pass, Poor). Finally, we utilize the Apriori algorithm to find independent variables as potential features, which have strong correlation with student academic performance.

Table 3. Consuming level classification rules

Consuming frequency per day in campus canteen, m	Corresponding consuming level
$m >= 2$	A
$m = 1$	B
$m = 0$	C

Table 4. Interaction and discussion level classification rules

The number of interaction and discussion in class, n	Corresponding interaction and discussion level
$n >= 15$	A
$7 <= n < 15$	B
$0 <= n < 7$	C

3.2 Data Reduction

Based on the correlation analysis and potential feature selection module, we could obtain potential features which have strong correlation with student academic performance. However, the dimension of the potential features is high, and they may have slight correlation relationship between each other. In order to solve this problem and improve the prediction accuracy, we construct the data reduction module to reduce the dimension of independent variables, remove the unimportant potential features (and noisy data) and select the most related variables as features which are the input of the prediction model. In the data reduction module, we utilize Principal Components Analysis (i.e., PCA) method to realize data reduction.

The PCA Method. PCA method is a common method used in data compressing. It extracts key features through linear transformation. PCA could obtain the principal components (i.e., eigenvector) and the corresponding weights (i.e., eigenvalues), through feature factorization for the covariance matrix.

PCA-Based Data Reduction. In this part, we utilize the PCA method for data reduction to obtain key features. The input of the PCA method is the multiple potential features which are obtained from the correlation analysis and Potential feature selection module. We assume the dimension of the potential features are t, and there are p students in our training data. The main steps of the PCA method is shown as follows.

Construct the matrix X which is $t*p$.

Standardize X as X^*.

Calculate the covariance matrix C.

Calculate the eigenvector and eigenvalues of matrix C.

Take the top-k eigenvectors whose corresponding eigenvalues are top-k to construct matrix P ($k*p$).

Compute matrix $Z=PX$ and matrix Z is the reduced k-dimensional data, which is the selected features as the input of the prediction model.

4 The Ensemble Learning Based Academic Prediction Model

In order to predict student academic performance and provide academic early warning, we construct the ensemble learning based academic prediction model which takes features selected from data reduction module as the input. The prediction model ensembles Random Forest, XGBoost, BP Neural Network as base classifiers and uses multinomial logistic regression classifier as the meta classifier, and takes advantages of these models to make accurate prediction.

4.1 Theory Related to Random Forest Algorithm, XGBoost Algorithm and BP Neural Network Algorithm

Random Forest Algorithm. Random forest algorithm is a classifier algorithm which ensembles multiple decision trees. It first randomly selects m samples from the original data to generate m training data. Then, it trains m decision tree models based on the m training data. Specifically, in each iteration, each decision tree model selects the best feature to split based on the information gain and Gini coefficient. Finally, it constructs random forests by using the m decision trees and produces the final classification results based on the voting method. Since random forests model ensembles results of multiple decision trees, it could produce good classification accuracy.

XGBoost Algorithm. XGBoost is an efficient Gradient Boosted Decision Tree algorithm which improves the GBDT algorithm. It adopts the Boosting way to integrate multiple weak learners to strong learner. Since there are several algorithmic optimizations, XGBoost algorithm has good scalability. In particular, the novel tree learning algorithm makes XGBoost capable for sparse data.

The Optimization objective function of the XGBoost algorithm is defined as follows,

$$L(\emptyset) = \sum_{i} l(\widehat{y_i} - y_i) + \sum \Omega(f_k), \tag{7}$$

$$\Omega(f_k) = \gamma T + \frac{1}{2}\lambda||\omega||^2, \tag{8}$$

where L is the loss function and it denotes the difference between predicted value $\widehat{y_i}$ and real ground-truth value y_i. T denotes the number of leaves of each tree. ω denotes the predicted value of leaves. The second term $\sum \Omega(f_k)$ is the penalty term, which restricts the complexity of the tree functions. The regularization term helps to smooth the learned weights to avoid the overfitting.

BP Neural Network Algorithm. BP neural network is a commonly used artificial neural network. It contains three layers, i.e., input layer, hidden layer and output layer. The weights of the neural network between two layers denote the strengths between any two neurons. The input of the input layer is the features of the dataset, the input of the hidden layer is the output results of the input layer and the input of the output layer is the output results of the hidden layer. BP neural network algorithm learns weights of the network via the background propagation, and outputs the prediction result. Since BP neural network has the nonlinear ability, it receives more accurate results.

4.2 The Ensemble Learning Based Academic Performance Prediction Model

In this paper, in order to utilize abilities of different machine learning models, we construct an ensemble learning based academic performance prediction model which ensembles random forests algorithm, XGBoost algorithm and BP neural network algorithm. Our prediction model is a stacking model which includes base classifiers and a meta classifier. The base classifiers integrate Random Forests classifier, XGBoost Classifier and BP Neural Network Classifier and the input of the base classifiers is the features of original data generated from the data reduction module. The meta classifier is the multinomial logistic regression classifier and the input of the meta classifier is the prediction results of the base classifiers. The constructed ensemble learning based academic performance prediction model is shown in Fig. 3.

Based on the ensemble learning based performance prediction for each student and identify their predicted performance level, i.e., Excellent, Good, Fair, Pass and Poor. Finally, teachers could grasp each student's study situation in real time. For the student whose predicted performance level is Poor, teachers could make an early warning, talk with the student and find the reasons. Moreover, teachers need to play a guiding role in helping the student for improving their grades. The overall flow chart of the student academic early warning model is shown in Fig. 4.

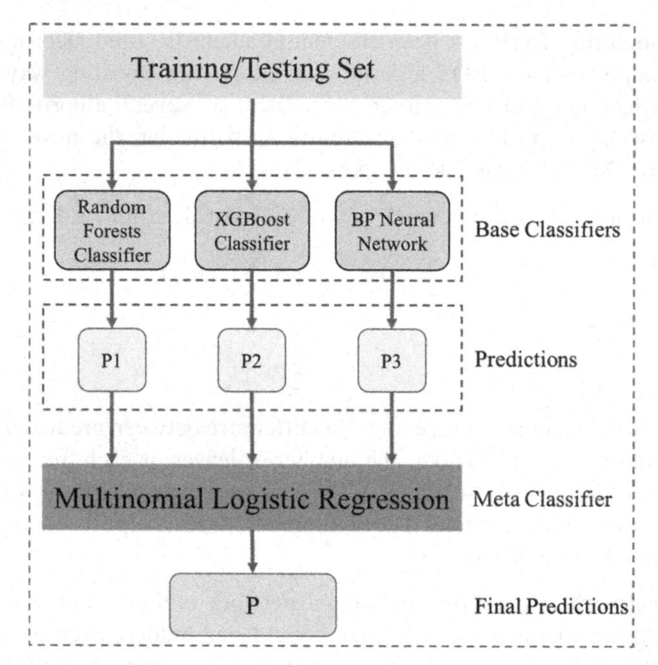

Fig. 3. The ensemble learning based performance prediction model

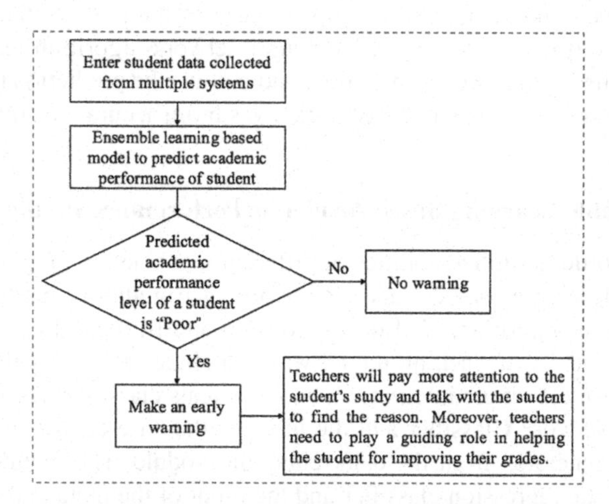

Fig. 4. The flow chart of the student academic early warning model

5 Conclusion

This paper constructs a student academic early warning model which utilizes students' information data collected from multiple campus systems, i.e., teaching system, online learning system, education and research system, library system and e-card consuming system, and provides early academic guiding and helping for students. Firstly, in order to remove the noise data and improve the prediction accuracy, the collected data is pre-processed by using the standardization method. Specifically, the student academic performance is categorized to five levels, i.e., Excellent, Good, Fair, Pass and Poor, which are based on student's grades. Secondly, the Apriori algorithm is adopted to analyze the correlation relationship between the academic performance and multiple independent variables. The potential features are selected from independent variables which have strong correlations with academic performance. Thirdly, the PCA based data reduction model is utilized to reduce the dimension of potential features and find the key features which are the input of the prediction model. Finally, the ensemble learning based prediction model is proposed to predict student academic performance. The prediction model ensembles Random Forest, XGBoost and BP Neural Network as the base classifiers and takes the multinomial logistic regression classifier as the meta classifier. Since the prediction model utilizes different machine learning models, it could take advantages of these models and make accurate academic prediction. Finally, the student academic early warning model could help teachers make an early warning for students whose predicted performance levels are Poor, talk with the students and guide these students for improving their academic performance.

Acknowledgments. This work is supported by the Beijing Municipal Social Science Foundation (No. 21SRC015).

References

1. Wang, Z., Zhu, C., Ying, Z., Wang, B., Jin, X., Yang, H.: Design and implementation of early warning system based on educational big data. In: International Conference on Systems and Informatics (ICSAI), pp. 549–553. IEEE (2018)
2. Yang, P., Ming, Y.: Research on the management model of university students academic early warning based on big data analysis. In: International Conference on Communications, Information System and Computer Engineering (CISCE), pp. 639–642. IEEE (2019)
3. Akçapınar, G., Arif, A., Petek, A.: Using learning analytics to develop early-warning system for at-risk students. Int. J. Educ. Technol. High. Educ. **16**(1), 1–20 (2019)
4. Bañeres, Rodríguez, M.E., Guerrero-Roldán, A.E., Karadeniz, A.: An early warning system to detect at-risk students in online higher education. Appl. Sci. **10**(13), 4427 (2020)
5. Raffaghelli, J.E., Rodríguez, M.E., Guerrero-Roldán, A.E., Baneres, D.: Applying the UTAUT model to explain the students' acceptance of an early warning system in higher education. Comput. Educ. **182**, 104468 (2022)
6. Veerasamy, A.K., D'Souza, D., Apiola, M.V., Laakso, M.J., Salakoski, T.: Using early assessment performance as early warning signs to identify at-risk students in programming courses. In: IEEE Frontiers in Education Conference (FIE), pp. 1–9. IEEE (2020)
7. Hu, Y.: Using few-shot learning materials of multiple SPOCs to develop early warning systems to detect students at risk. Int. Rev. Res. Open Distrib. Learn. **23**(1), 1–20 (2022)
8. Chen, S.: Improved fuzzy algorithm for college students' academic early warning. Math. Probl. Eng. **2022**, 5764800 (2022)
9. Zhao, Q., Zhao, Q., Wang, J.L., Pao, T.L., Wang, L.Y.: Modified fuzzy rule-based classification system for early warning of student learning. J. Educ. Technol. Syst. **48**(3), 385–406 (2020)
10. Zhang, J., Zhang, J., You, C., Huang, J., Li, S., Wen, Y.: Research on application of frequent pattern growth algorithm in academic early warning. In: Proceedings of the International Conference on Information and Education Technology, pp.116–121 (2020)

11. Flanagan, B., Majumdar, R., Ogata, H.: Early-warning prediction of student performance and engagement in open book assessment by reading behavior analysis. Int. J. Educ. Technol. High. Educ. **19**(1), 1–23 (2022)
12. Akçapınar, G., Hasnine, M.N., Majumdar, R., Flanagan, B., Ogata, H.: Developing an early-warning system for spotting at-risk students by using eBook interaction logs. Smart Learn. Environ. **6**(1), 1–15 (2019)
13. Chung, J.Y., Lee., S.: Dropout early warning systems for high school students using machine learning. Children Youth Serv. Rev. **96**, 346–353 (2019)
14. Zhang, T., Xiao, W., Hu, P.: Design of online learning early warning model based on artificial intelligence. Wirel. Commun. Mob. Comput. **2022**, 3973665 (2022)
15. Shi, C., Tan, Y.: A BP neural network-based early warning model for student performance in the context of big data. J. Sens. **2022**, 2958261 (2022)
16. Wang, J., Zhang, Z., Luo, H., Liu, Y., Chen, W., Wei, G.: Research on early warning model of college students' psychological crisis based on genetic BP neural network. Am. J. Appl. Psychol. **8**(6), 112–120 (2019)
17. Han, J., Wang, G.: Application of data mining in academic early warning. In: International Conference on Machine Learning, Big Data and Business Intelligence (MLBDBI), pp. 28–31. IEEE (2020)
18. Liu, W., Wu, J., Gao, X., Feng, K.: An early warning model of student achievement based on decision trees algorithm. In: International Conference on Teaching, Assessment, and Learning for Engineering (TALE), pp. 517–222. IEEE (2017)
19. Cheng, X., et al.: A novel learning early-warning model based on random forest algorithm. In: Nkambou, R., Azevedo, R., Vassileva, J. (eds.) Intelligent Tutoring Systems. ITS 2018. LNCS, vol. 10858, pp. 306–312 Springer, Cham (2018). https://doi.org/10.1007/978-3-319-91464-0_32
20. Tao, T., Sun, C., Wu, Z., Yang, J., Wang, J.: Deep neural network-based prediction and early warning of student grades and recommendations for similar learning approaches. Appl. Sci. **12**(15), 7733 (2022)
21. Yang, Z., Yang, J., Huang, J.L.: Using convolutional neural network to recognize learning images for early warning of at-risk students. IEEE Trans. Learn. Technol. **13**(3), 617–630 (2020)
22. Nam, S., Samson, P.: Integrating students' behavioral signals and academic profiles in early warning system. In: Isotani, S., Millán, E., Ogan, A., Hastings, P., McLaren, B., Luckin, R. (eds.) Artificial Intelligence in Education. AIED 2019. LNCS, vol. 11625, pp. 345–357 Springer, Cham (2019). https://doi.org/10.1007/978-3-030-23204-7_29

Generating One-Turn Dialogue from Given Keywords Based on GPT-2(Chinese) for Oral Chinese Teaching

Haigang Lin, Huizhou Zhao(✉), and Boqian Zhang

Information Science School, Beijing Language and Culture University, 15 Xueyuan Road, HaiDian District, Beijing 100083, China
zhaohuizhou@blcu.edu.cn

Abstract. Pedagogical materials are the basis for carrying out teaching and learning activities. Compared to inefficient manual organization or retrieving methods limited in data scale, text generation technique, aiming to generate readable text, has shown promising potential in automatic generation of pedagogical materials. For purpose of satisfying the need that vocabulary teaching in oral Chinese teaching should expose to more relevant dialogue pedagogical materials, this work builds a model focusing on generating one-turn dialogue from given keywords. The model is built under fine-tuning paradigm and large-scale pre-trained generative language model, GPT-2(Chinese), both of which have not been yet explored in related work, topic-to-essay (TEG) and poetry generation. And this work introduces dialogue role embeddings technique from dialogue system to model topic transfer in one-turn dialogues. Evaluation results show that our model can achieve sufficient quality and diversity simultaneously with comparative novelty in general text generation ability and have the ability to generate one-turn dialogue from given keywords for oral Chinese teaching. Case study hardens the evaluation results. The results provide implications in generating multi-turn dialogue from given keywords.

Keywords: Pedagogical Materials · Oral Chinese Teaching · GPT-2(Chinese) · Role Embeddings Technique · One-Turn Dialogue

1 Introduction

Pedagogical materials are the basis for carrying out teaching activities. Traditional pedagogical materials are difficult to provide more references for teachers and students. Manual organization of relevant pedagogical materials lacks economy and efficiency. The data sources of existing e-learning recommendation systems are mostly Internet corpus, cannot be used as pedagogical materials directly. No matter how advanced their retrieval technologies are, e-learning recommendation systems cannot provide pedagogical materials high relevant to those teaching points out of databases. With the advancement of text generation technology, to overcome the problems above, automatic generation of pedagogical materials is a new way worth exploring. For instance, poetry learning can be assisted by poetry generation.

J. Gan et al. (Eds.): CSEI 2023, CCIS 1899, pp. 229–238, 2024.
https://doi.org/10.1007/978-981-99-9499-1_19

Oral language teaching plays an important role in teaching, and key vocabulary teaching needs more dialogue examples. Its essence is that, given a keyword group, a dialogue text covering most words of this keyword group or a dialogue text that is highly related to the keyword group in topic should be output. This work focuses on generating one-turn dialogue given keyword group for further research on generating multi-turn dialogue. In spite of identical input form, the distinct character to topic-to-essay (TEG) and Poetry Generation, both output of whose are none-dialogue, dialogue role transfer appearing in the expected one-turn dialogue output sets a barrier for this work. Aiming to promote research on automatic generation of pedagogical materials, this work builds a model based on pre-trained large-scale generative model, GPT-2(Chinese), under the fine-tune paradigm, both of which have not yet been explored in most related work, TEG and poetry generation, and introduces the role embeddings technique to facilitate modeling dialogue role transfer as several dialogue system work do [1–3].

2 Related Work

2.1 Topic-to-Essay (TEG) and Poetry Generation

TEG aims to generate high-quality and diverse paragraph-level text given multiple topic words. This task is first proposed by Feng et al. [4], who utilize the coverage word vector to integrate topic information. Additional commonsense knowledge information has been introduced into TEG [5–7]. Qiao et al. [5] inject sentiment tags into the generator to control the sentiment of the generated short text.

Furthermore, the task of generating readable poetry given a number of subject words also models the mapping of topic words to text. Zhang et al. [8] propose a memory-augmented neural model to balance the requirements of linguistic consistency and aesthetic innovation. Li et al. [9] combine adversarial training and a CVAE framework to generate diverse poems. Yang et al. [10] propose a hybrid decoder to generate Chinese poems. Reinforcement learning algorithms have been used to directly increase the diversity of poetry [11].

2.2 Dialogue System and Dialogue Role Embeddings

Compared with non-dialogue text output of TEG and poetic text output of poetry generation, dialogue role transfer modeling is a key issue that has to be considered due to one-turn dialogue output of this work. Dialogue system, designed to give human-like response to dialogue context which is extremely different from input form of this work. However, the output of this work contains a flow between adjacent dialogue turns as dialogue system. And role embeddings technique draws our attention for dialogue role transfer modeling. In the chitchat dialogue system, role embeddings are applied to facilitate modeling dialogue role transfer [1]. In the task-oriented dialogue system, if the system is regarded as a dialogue role, the token-type embeddings are employed to distinguish different dialogue roles for modeling dialogue role transfer [2, 3]. Essentially, both make use of role embeddings to boost modeling dialogue role transfer, allowing the model to generate more relevant conversational responses. Although our task form is different from the dialogue response task, the expected output of our task is a one-turn dialogue, so we introduce role embeddings into this work to build our model.

2.3 Pre-training and Fine-Tuning

Recently, pre-trained large-scale language models, such as BERT [12], GPT-2 [13] and fine-tuning paradigm, have achieved prominent success in natural language processing [13–15]. GPT-2 [13], pre-trained large-scale generative model, sheds light on the tasks of natural language generation, like dialogue generation [16–18] after further pretraining or fine-tuning.

Whether it is the work that does not incorporate commonsense knowledge graph [4], or those works that introduce additional commonsense knowledge [5–7], the TEG models are based on the RNN architecture (LSTM, GRU), initializing the model word embeddings with the 200-dimensional pretrained word embeddings provided by Song et al. [19].

Zhang et al. [8] and Li et al. [9] don't introduce pre-trained word embeddings into poetry generation. Yang et al. [10] pre-train Chinese character embeddings on Chinese poem corpus (CPC) to promote generation of Chinese classical poems. Yi et al. [11] use the pretrained word2vec word embeddings. These works are also based on the RNN (LSTM, GRU) architecture.

In short, the paradigm of fine-tuning on pre-trained models based on Transformer architecture has not yet been explored on tasks related to this work.

Different from related works, this work follows the idea of fine tuning pre-trained models to boost downstream tasks, introduces role embeddings technique from the dialogue system to model dialogue role transfer, and builds our model based on the generative pre-trained language model GPT-2(Chinese), realizing the generative mapping of a given keyword group to a one-turn dialogue for oral Chinese teaching.

3 Methodology

3.1 Problem Formulation

The input of our model is a set of words, $InWs = (w_1, w_2, \cdots, w_i, \cdots, w_m)$, where w_i refers to i-th word and m is the number of words.

The output expected, *Out1Dia*, is a one-turn dialogue covering most of words in *InWs* or highly consistent to the topic expressed by *InWs*, containing utterance A, a natural conversational text, and uttrance B, a natural response to utterance A. *OutDia* is formulated as $(x_1, x_2, \cdots, x_j, \cdots, x_m, \text{[SEP]}, y_1, y_2, \cdots, y_k, \cdots, y_N)$, where [SEP] is a special token separating the two utterance, x_j is the j-th token in utterance A and y_k is the k-th token in utterance B.

3.2 Model Description

In our model, there are two elements: *InWs*, prompt to guide dialogue generation, and *Out1Dia*, target output, denoted as P and O for simplicity, respectively.

The goal of our model is to learn a function f parameterized as Θ to well estimate the probablistic distribution $p(O|P)$.

$$p(O|P) = f(P; \theta) \tag{1}$$

$$\theta^* = \mathrm{argmax}_\theta f(P;\theta) \tag{2}$$

where Θ^* is the maximum likelihood estimation of Θ and given the P, the O can be estimated as

$$\log(p(O|P)) = \sum \log(p(O_t|P, O_{<t})) \tag{3}$$

where, O_t represents the t-th word of O, $O_{<t}$ denotes the first t-1 words of O and N is the length of O.

Since the conditioned generation process depicted by formula (3) is a language modeling process, NLL loss, widely adopted, is embraced in optimizing our model to find out good-enough Θ so as to well estimate $p(O|P)$:

$$L_{NLL} = -\mathrm{E}(\log(p(O|P))) \tag{4}$$

where L_{NLL} is the negative expected log probability of observing O given P.

3.3 Input Representation

For P to O modeling, elaborate designs have been made on the input representation in this work. The input embedding of each token is the sum of corresponding token, role (only token in O will be assigned) and position embeddings. One visual example is shown in Fig. 1, details are described in the following.

Fig. 1. Input representation. The input embedding is the sum of token, role and position embedding.

The input is the concatenation of P and O. [CLS] token, whose final hidden state (i.e., output of the last transformer block) is used to predict the first token of O during generation, is used to separate P and O. Since O consists of two utterances corresponding to role A and role B, respectively, [SEP] token is appended to the end of utterance A for separating the two utterances. And we add [PAD] as the end mark of every input.

Role embeddings are applied to differentiate the characters evolved in the dialogue in O. The role embedding E_A is added for the character of role A in O. And role embedding E_B is used for the character of role B. In Fig. 1, empty block in Role Embeddings represents a zero vector added to those characters not belong to role A and role B.

Position embeddings are added according to the token position in the input.

4 Experiments

4.1 Dataset

Listening dialogue texts of Hangyu Shuiping Kaoshi (HSK) are collected as our raw corpus. Any one-turn dialogue in each text and the keyword group extracted from it by jieba make up a data pair of our dataset. Due to practicality, those data pairs, whose keywords number is less than 1 or more than 5, are filtered out. The length of a one-turn dialogue is between 10 and 65. The training set and the test set contain 3020 samples and 756 samples, respectively. For hyper-parameters tuning, we set 50% of test set as the validation set.

4.2 Baselines

This work can be viewed as a subtask of TEG in a broad sense since no exact matching task, so we compare our model with the following typical TEG methods.

MTA [4] maintains a topic coverage vector to guarantee that the semantic of all the topic words are expressed during decoding.

CTEG [6] enhances TEG generation with external commonsense knowledge and improve generation performance resorting to adversarial training.

TEGKE [7] employs a topic knowledge graph encoder to integrate multi-hop knowledge structural and semantic information to facilitate essay generation and introduces a discriminator by the adversarial training based on the Wasserstein distance to improve generation.

4.3 Evaluation Metrics

In this paper, we adopt Bleu, Dist-1, Dist-2, Novelty for evaluating general text generation capacity following the baselines we choose. Apart from metrics above, we set three special metrics, not been used in TEG, the most related task of this work, since the output form of this work is one-turn dialogue.

Metrics for evaluating general text generation capacity (Metrics A) are listed as follows:

Bleu [20]: The BLEU score is widely used in text generation tasks (e.g., dialogue generation and machine translation). It could measure the generated texts' quality by computing the overlapping rate between the generated texts and the ground truth texts.

Dist-1, Dist-2 [21]: The Dist-1 and Dist-2 scores are the proportion of distinct unigrams and bigrams in the generated texts, respectively, which measure the diversity of the generated texts.

Novelty [6]: The novelty is calculated by the difference between the generated texts and the ground truth texts with similar topics in the training set. A higher score means more novel texts would be generated under similar topics.

Special metrics set for our task (Metrics B) are listed as follows:

One-turn dialogue-like results percentage (1tDiaLiRe_Per): The proportion one-turn dialogue-like texts among all generated texts on our test corpus. Since the expected output form of this work is one-turn dialogue, the higher one-turn dialogue-like texts percentage, the stronger the ability of our model to generate one-turn dialogue. In addition, this metric also indicates a model's capacity to model contextual relevance and dialogue role transfer required for generated dialogue-like texts. All one-turn dialogue.

Keyword coverage percentage (KwCoPer): The proportion given keywords covered by keywords of output texts. For vocabulary teaching, any given keyword is supposed to be expressed in the generated text as keyword. For any generated text, we extract its keywords as we do on our dataset.

Topic Consistency (To-Con): It is difficult to include all words in a given keyword group in the generated text as keywords, however the generated text should be consistent to the given keyword group in topic at least. We sum the word embedding cosine similarity of any word in given keyword group and any word in the keyword group of the generated text as the Topic-Consistency score. Any word in given keyword group or the keyword group of the generated text obtain its word embedding from Tencent AILab Chinese Word Embedding [19].

4.4 Experimental Results

Evaluation Results. The evaluation results over generated texts on Metrics A are shown in Table 1, the evaluation results over generated texts on Metrics B are shown in Table 2.

Results and analyses on Metrics A. On the Bleu score, our model outperforms the best baseline TEGKE by 0.40, revealing that the potential of our model to generate high-quality texts in spite of different dataset and different output form. Our model achieves 0.8528, 0.9815 on Dist-1 score and Dist-2 score on our dataset respectively, much higher than the performance of MTA, CTEG, TEGKE shown in Table 1, demonstrating splendid ability of our model in diverse lexical expression. On the Novelty score, our model is near to CTEG which is in the middle of all baselines in this metric. That is, the generated texts from our model would be different-enough from texts with similar inputs in the training corpus. In general, by finetuning GPT-2(Chinese) on our training corpus, our model can achieve sufficient quality and diversity simultaneously with comparative novelty, showing the potential and validity of transferring the outstanding generation ability of GPT-2(Chinese) to our task.

Results and analyses on Metrics B. The 1tDiaLiRe_Per of our model is 22.75%. That is about one in five generated texts of our model is one-turn dialogue-like texts. This result shows that integrating role embeddings technique, our model in deed has the ability to perceive dialogue role transfer and generate one-turn dialogue from given keywords for oral Chinese teaching. And there is still space for improving the ability. The KwCoPer of our model is 22.56% in overall. The KwCoPer score corresponding to 1 keyword to 5 five keywords is 50.77%, 23.04%, 18.73%, 10.48%, 5.53%, respectively. Our model performance in this metric drops sharply as the number of keywords in input increase, showing that On To-Con score, our model achieves 0.2841. The To-Con score corresponding to input containing 1 keyword to input containing 5 five keywords is 0.4852, 0.2657, 0.2733, 0.2099, 0.2841. Although when the number of keywords in the input is 2, 3, 4, the To-Con score is generally stable, but the performance is far worse than that when the number of keywords in the input is 1. The trends of the KwCoPer score and To-Con score show that the ability of our model to express multiple keywords in the generated texts and generate high relevant texts to given keywords when the input is multiple keywords are relatively poor and in deed need to improve in further study.

Table 1. The evaluation results over generated texts on Metrics A.

Method	Bleu	Dist-1	Dist-2	Novelty
MTA	10.79	5.58	28.11	80.18
TEG	7.09	2.24	11.70	70.68
TEKG	9.72	5.19	20.29	**75.71**
Our Model	**11.15**	**85.28**	**98.15**	75.22

Table 2. The evaluation results over generated texts on Metrics B.

Method	1tDiaLiRe_Per	KwCoPer	To-Con
MTA	×	×	×
TEG	×	×	×
TEKG	×	×	×
Our Model	22.75	22.56	0.2841

Case Study. We observe all generated texts on our test corpus, and focus on one-turn dialogue-like texts.

In general, the one-turn dialogue-like texts are fluent and coherent. Three Cases in Fig. 2, each of which contains an input of several keywords and a one-turn dialogue output, show the capacity of our model to generate one-turn dialogue highly relevant to given keyword group in topic. Meanwhile, these cases demonstrate that our model' s potential to express any word in a given keyword group in the generated one-turn dialogue as a keyword. To further improve current task performance and facilitate the task that generating multi-turn dialogue from given keywords, the typical drawbacks of our model in generating one-turn dialogue from keywords have also been observed and grouped into three categories, each of which occupies a row of Fig. 3 and contains a name, an example and a brief description of the example, providing implications for further generating multi-turn dialogue in whole word expression, multiple keywords expression, expression of core subject words.

Case1	Case2	Case3
Input: 椅子	Input: 医生，医院，工作	Input: 帽子，漂亮
Output:	Output:	Output:
A：你说的是哪个椅子？左边的？	A：您妻子在哪儿工作？	A：你看，这个帽子怎么样？
B：不是，是右边的这个。	B：医院，她是医生。	B：很漂亮。

Fig. 2. Three cases on test corpus, each input and output of which is highly relevant on topic.

Name	Example	Description
drawback in whole word expression	Input: 好喝，牛奶，香蕉 Output: A：怎么样？好喝不好喝？ B：很好喝，你是放糖吧。	Only one keyword in input is expressed in the generated one-turn dialogue.
drawback in multiple keywords expression	Input: 想要 Output: A：你在想什么呢？ B：我在想要不要帮助他。	The two characters in word "想要" are assigned to two "想" and "要不要" in the generated result.
drawback in expression of core subject words	Input: 小马，结婚，听说 Output: A：听说你要去国外读书？ B：是，下周五的飞机。	Two keywords in the three keywords are expressed in the one-turn dialogue, but the core keyword "结婚" is not expressed.

Fig. 3. Typical drawbacks of our model in generating one-turn dialogue from keywords.

4.5 Parameter Settings and Required Hardware Resources.

The model was implemented with pytorch. We tuning the hyperparameter values manually. Parameters of main part of our model were initialized using GPT-2(Chinese). Parameters of the extra role embeddings were randomly initialized over a normal distribution with mean of 0 and standard deviation of 0.02. The model was trained on single 24 GB NVIDIA TITAN RTX GPU machine for 1000 with optimizer Adam [22], where the minibatch was set to be 128 and the learning rate was set to 2e–3. Besides, the dropout schedule followed GPT-2-small. We apply greedy search during decoding and average length of generated text is 28.

5 Conclusion

This work fine tunes GPT-2(Chinese) to generate one-turn dialogue from given keywords aiming to providing more pedagogical materials for oral Chinese teaching. Role embeddings technique is introduced from dialogue system to model the topic transfer in one-turn dialogues so as to sharpen the ability of our model in generating more one-dialogue-like text from given keywords. Experimental results demonstrate that our model achieves sufficient quality and splendid diversity simultaneously with comparative novelty in general text generation capacity and has great potential in generating one-turn dialogue from given keywords for oral Chinese teaching.

Acknowledgements. The research is supported by Science Foundation of Beijing Language and Culture University (supported by "the Fundamental Research Funds for the Central Universities")(22YJ080013); the Fundamental Research Funds for the Central Universities, and the

Research Funds of Beijing Language and Culture University (22YCX081); Major Program of National Social Science Foundation of China (18ZDA295); 2020 Beijing Higher Education Undergraduate Teaching Reform and Innovation Project "Reform and Practice of the Training Mode of Language Knowledge Engineering Innovative Talents Based on Emerging Engineering Education".

References

1. Bao, S., He, H., Wang, F., Wu, H., Wang, H.: PLATO: pre-trained dialogue generation model with discrete latent variable. arXiv preprint arXiv: 1910.07931 (2019)
2. Ham, D., Lee, J.-G., Jang, Y., Kim, K.-E.: End-to-end neural pipeline for goal-oriented dialogue system using gpt-2. In: ACL, pp. 583–592 (2020)
3. Peng, B., Li, C., Li, J., Shayandeh, S., Liden, L., Gao, J.: Soloist: few-shot task-oriented dialog with a single pre-trained auto-regressive model. arXiv preprint arXiv:2005.05298 (2020)
4. Feng, X., Liu, M., Liu, J., Qin, B., Sun, Y., Liu, T.: Topic-to-essay generation with neural networks. In: IJCAI, pp. 4078–4084 (2018)
5. Qiao, L., Yan, J., Meng, F., Yang, Z., Zhou, J.: A sentiment-controllable topic-to-essay generator with topic knowledge graph. In: EMNLP: Findings, pp. 3336–3344 (2020)
6. Yang, P., Li, L., Luo, F., Liu, T., Sun, X.: Enhancing topic-to-essay generation with external commonsense knowledge. In: ACL, pp. 2002–2012 (2019)
7. Liu, Z., Wang, J., Li, Z.: Topic-to-essay generation with comprehensive knowledge enhancement. arXiv preprint arXiv:2106.15142 (2021)
8. Zhang, J., et al.: Flexible and creative Chinese poetry generation using neural memory. In: ACL, pp. 1364–1373 (2017)
9. Li, J., et al.: Generating classical Chinese poems via conditional variational autoencoder and adversarial training. In: EMNLP, pp. 3890–3900 (2018)
10. Yang, X., Lin, X., Suo, S., Li, M.: Generating thematic Chinese poetry using conditional variational autoencoders with hybrid decoders. In: IJCAI, pp. 4539–4545 (2018)
11. Yi, X., Sun, M., Li, R., Li, W.: Automatic poetry generation with mutual reinforcement learning. In: EMNLP, pp. 3143–3153 (2018)
12. Devlin, J., Chang, M.-W., Lee, K., Toutanova, K.: BERT: pre-training of deep bidirectional transformers for language understanding. In: NAACL-HLT (2019)
13. Alec Radford, Jeffrey Wu, Rewon Child, David Luan, Dario Amodei, and Ilya Sutskever. 2019. Language models are unsupervised multitask learners. OpenAI blog (2019)
14. Du, Z., et al.: GLM: general language model pretraining with autoregressive blank infilling. arXiv preprint arXiv:2103.10360 (2021)
15. Jiang, H., He, P., Chen, W., Liu, X., Gao, J., Zhao, T.: SMART: robust and efficient fine-tuning for pre-trained natural language models through principled regularized optimization arXiv preprint arXiv:1911.03437 (2019)
16. Budzianowski, P., Vulić, I.: Hello, It's GPT-2 - how can i help you? Towards the use of pretrained language models for task-oriented dialogue systems. arXiv preprint arXiv:1907.05774 (2019)
17. Hosseini-Asl, E., McCann, B., Wu, C.-.S., Yavuz, S., Socher, R.: A simple language model for task-oriented dialogue. arXiv preprint arXiv: 2005.00796 (2020)
18. Donghoon, H., Jeong-Gwan, L., Youngsoo, J., Kee-Eung, K.: End-to-end neural pipeline for goal-oriented dialogue systems using GPT-2. In: ACL, pp. 583–592 (2020)
19. Song, Y., Shi, S., Li, J., Zhang, H.: Directional skip-gram: explicitly distinguishing left and right context for word embeddings. In: NAACL, pp. 175–180 (2018)

20. Papineni, K., Roukos, S., Ward, T., Zhu, W.J.: BLEU: a method for automatic evaluation of machine translation. In: ACL, pp. 311–318 (2002)
21. Li, J., Galley, M., Brockett, C., Gao, J., Dolan, W.B.: A diversity-promoting objective function for neural conversation models. In: NAACL, pp. 110–119 (2016)
22. Kingma, D.P., Ba, J.: Adam: a method for stochastic optimization. In: International Conference on Learning Representations (2015)

Exploring the Establishment and Implementation of a Teaching Evaluation System Based on Value-Added Assessment

Li Yang[1], Gang Chen[2], Jie Chang[1], Xiangzi Li[1], Nan Wan[1], and Ying Liu[1(✉)]

[1] School of Medical Information, Wannan Medical College, Wuhu, People's Republic of China
liuyingwuhu@wnmc.edu.cn

[2] School of Information and Artificial Intelligence, Anhui Business College, Wuhu, People's Republic of China

Abstract. Value-added assessment (VAA) can effectively solve the existing problems of the excess of outcome-oriented evaluations and the lack of teaching evaluation feedback mechanisms in higher education, which plays an essential role in the innovative development of higher education. Taking the course of "Database Technology and Applications" as an example, this paper introduces a VAA concept into the teaching process, designs a VAA model and explores the performance of VAA in enhancing the quality of training information talent in higher education from three perspectives, i.e., students' comprehensive development and professional and curriculum construction.

Keywords: Value-added Assessment · Teaching Evaluation · Database Technology and Applications

1 Introduction

A reasonable education assessment system is an important means to ensure the quality of talent training. However, there are some problems in current higher education assessment, such as the excess of outcome-oriented evaluations and the lack of teaching evaluation feedback mechanisms in higher education, which seriously hinders the effectiveness of education assessments [1–3]. In 2018, the Ministry of Education of the People's Republic of China issued the "Opinions on Accelerating the Construction of High-Level Undergraduate Education and Improving the Comprehensive Ability of Talent Training" (Jiao Gao [2018] No. 2) [4], which proposed deep reform of the evaluation system for teachers in universities and colleges. It also suggested implementing teacher classification management and evaluation mechanisms and setting evaluation content and methods according to the characteristics of different types of institutions and different teaching positions. Additionally, it emphasized the assessment of teachers' abilities to educate and practice.

Against this background, in June 2020, the State Council designed the top-level reform of education evaluation, issuing the "Overall Plan for Deepening the Reform

J. Gan et al. (Eds.): CSEI 2023, CCIS 1899, pp. 239–251, 2024.
https://doi.org/10.1007/978-981-99-9499-1_20

of Education Evaluation in the New Era" [5], which clearly stated the importance of adhering to scientific and effective methods, improving outcome evaluations, strengthening process evaluations, and exploring value-added assessments. The plan aims to establish the guiding principles of education assessments and eliminate the currently existing chronic problems in higher education assessments. For the first time, "value-added assessment" appeared in national education policy documents and is now widely adopted.

Value-added assessment (VAA) is an evaluation mechanism for the academic progress of students during a certain period of time. VAA has two main characteristics: (1) VAA evaluates the comprehensive qualities of students' academic progress, including knowledge, skills, mindset, and beliefs. (2) VAA is a developmental evaluation mechanism that focuses on the entire process of students' learning. Therefore, VAA can take into account students of different levels, encourage students to enjoy the learning process, experience a sense of achievement, and enhance their intrinsic motivation to learn. Therefore, VAA can help achieve comprehensive education and improve the quality of talent training.

2 Current Status of VAA Development

In the 1980s, William et al. [8] first introduced the concept of VAA in teaching evaluation reforms in Tennessee, USA. To examine the net contribution of college teachers to students' academic progress by comparing students' scores before and after their enrollment in college. The difference between the two scores represents the net contribution of teachers, which is used to assess the teacher's effectiveness. With the development of statistical techniques, the VAA model has been continuously improved. In the 1990s, the Tennessee Value-Added Assessment System (TVAAS) [9] was officially launched in Tennessee. TVAAS was then promoted to other states (North Carolina, Ohio, and Pennsylvania.) in the USA and to other countries (UK and the Netherlands) [10].

In China, Jiang et al. [11] first introduced the theory of VAA, pointing out that for teacher evaluations, we should not only consider teaching outcomes but also the students' existing intellectual level. Based on [11], Wang et al. [12] further elaborated on the connotation and development status of VAA in Europe and America and explored the feasibility of localizing value-added assessment. Ma et al. [13] conducted empirical research on VAA effectiveness in several ordinary high schools in China. The empirical results showed that, for these students from different high schools, there was a significant difference between the college entrance examination scores and their value-added scores, thus confirming the huge difference between VAA and traditional assessment.

However, significant differences between courses make a single VAA model no longer applicable to all courses. Thus, educators have focused on the application of VAA in specific courses. Wang et al. [14] applied VAA to the teaching reform of the "Java Object-Oriented Programming" course, reconstructing the teaching objectives, contents, and methods of the course from the perspective of cultivating students' professional qualities. Chen et al. [15] adopted the concept of VAA in the "Physical Education and Health" course, analysing the value of VAA from five aspects, i.e., emphasizing students' comprehensive development, improving their classroom participation, enhancing their emotional and volitional commitment, highlighting their physical fitness, and showing an increase in their longitudinal academic achievement. Practical teaching has shown that VAA helps to improve students' autonomy, self-discipline, and self-motivation in learning.

With the localization of VAA, many educators have focused on the difficulties in the application of VAA in Chinese schools. Zhou et al. [7] conducted empirical research on 26 universities in Jiangsu Province and found that the application of VAA still faced many problems. First, it is difficult to balance the multiple subjects of VAA. Second, the selection of VAA models is difficult. Third, the utilization rate of VAA results is low. Zhou et al. [16] believe that a VAA model seems simple, but how to use the model is complex, especially in data collection and analysis. Li et al. [17] noted that the performance of VAA depends on the selection of VAA models, and a biased VAA model may lead to improper evaluation results.

Current research on VAA mainly focuses on teaching evaluation at the school or course level and lacks theoretical and practical research from the perspective of promoting discipline and curriculum development. This paper explores the implementation of VAA to improve teaching quality and information talent cultivation quality by conducting empirical research on the application of a chosen VAA model in the evaluation process of "Database Technology and Application", as shown in Fig. 1.

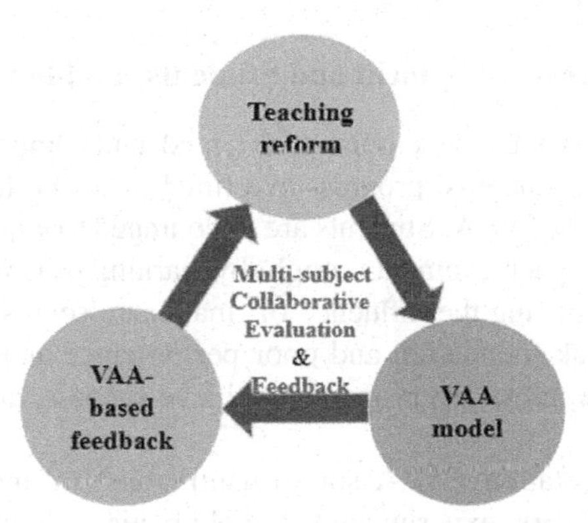

Fig. 1. VAA-based teaching evaluation system is a cyclic structure. The system includes three parts, i.e., VAA-based teaching reform, a VAA model and a VAA-based feedback mechanism.

3 VAA-Based Teaching Reform

Teaching evaluation, as an important means of achieving teaching objectives, is an indispensable part of the teaching process. VAA as a developmental evaluation mechanism can embody the teaching philosophy of student-oriented and development-oriented education. By taking VAA as an opportunity, the teaching quality of the course "Database Technology and Applications" can be enhanced in teaching objectives, teaching methods, student participation, and fairness.

3.1 Modifying Teaching Objectives and Teaching Methods

"Database Technology and Application", as a basic course for information majors, plays a major supporting role in the development of students' professional quality and students' job competency training, providing essential database knowledge and skills for information talent.

Based on the VAA concept, the course objectives are designed from three aspects, i.e., knowledge, ability, and values. For specific chapters of the teaching content, chapter teaching objectives need to be further designed in detail. Based on chapter teaching objectives, teaching content is optimized while suitable teaching methods are chosen. The specific reform content includes the following:

- Chapter course objectives are divided from three views, i.e., knowledge, ability and values.
- Course content is divided into basic content and expanded content. All students should master the basic content, and the expanded content is aimed at students of higher level. The division of teaching content can meet the needs of students at different levels;
- Appropriate teaching methods are chosen according to the type of teaching content, such as classroom lectures for conceptual knowledge, project-based teaching for applicable knowledge, and self-study or group discussion for popular science knowledge.

3.2 Focusing on Process Assessment and Students' Fulfillment

To realize the student-oriented, development-oriented, and comprehensive teaching philosophy, acknowledging students' progress in a timely manner during the learning process is an important goal of VAA. Students are encouraged to enjoy the learning process and experience a sense of achievement brought by learning progress. Strengthening process assessment and reducing the influence of final exam scores on students is helpful for students with a weak foundation and poor performance and facilitates the goal of "everyone can make progress, everyone can achieve success, and everyone can stand out".

During the implementation of VAA, some quantifiable VAA indicators are set, including exam scores, homework, experimental, social practice, class performance, rewards and punishments, attendance, and professionalism. Two points are worth noting. First, for all VAA indicator assessment content, teachers need to set points for each VAA indicator and inform students of all assessment content and indicators during process assessment. Second, the assessment subjects should be diversified. For example, the assessment subjects for attendance and homework performance indicators are teachers, while the assessment subjects for class performance and group discussion should include group members.

3.3 Rewarding Progress, Penalizing Regression and Balancing Fairness

The essence of educational equity lies in focusing on individuals, recognizing individual differences, and promoting the comprehensive development of all individuals. VAA emphasizes the progress of students' academic performance, which is highly consistent with the concept of educational equity. "Reward progress and penalize regression" refers to rewarding students who have made significant progress and punishing those who have shown significant regression, further inspiring and urging students through exemplary effects. Specifically, for the "Database Technology and Application" course, in the assigned experimental project of "Complex Query", students are required to demonstrate their ability to identify innovative query methods while distinguishing them from erroneous query methods. After completing the project, the students who have successfully completed the project are praised, and the mistakes are pointed out. This approach serves to motivate students to learn and to excel, thus creating a positive learning atmosphere in the classroom.

4 VAA-Based Multisubject Collaborative Evaluation and Feedback Mechanism

This mechanism involves multiple subjects working together to evaluate and provide feedback on students' academic progress during a certain period of time. Each subject is responsible for evaluating a specific aspect of student's academic progress, and their evaluations are combined to provide a comprehensive assessment. The feedback provided is constructive and aims to highlight areas for improvement and promote continuous learning. Overall, this mechanism encourages collaboration, accountability, and continuous improvement.

4.1 Construction of a Multisubject Collaborative VAA Mechanism

Taking the "Database Technology and Application" course as an example, a VAA mechanism should closely revolve around the course objectives to assess the added value of students by designing evaluation contents and choosing evaluation subjects. Single evaluation subjects are limited by personal subjective emotions and are difficult to comprehensively, objectively, and dynamically evaluate the "added value" of student performance. To comprehensively reflect the added value of students in various dimensions of this course, including the knowledge, skills, and values of the course objectives, a total of eight evaluation indicators have been set as the evaluation contents.

- For the knowledge aspect, two evaluation indicators, namely, exam scores and homework, were set.
- For the skills aspect, two evaluation indicators, namely, experimental performance and social practice performance, have been set.
- For the values of the course objectives, three evaluation indicators, namely, classroom performance, rewards and punishments, and attendance, were set.
- Additionally, one evaluation indicator, professional quality, has been added to reflect students' employment capabilities of mastering database knowledge.

Regarding the eight evaluation indicators, teachers, students, teaching administrators, and employers were chosen as the evaluation subjects. The corresponding relationships between the evaluation subjects and evaluation indicators are shown in Table 1.

Different evaluation methods were used to objectively quantify each evaluation indicator, as shown in Table 1. For four indicators (classroom performance, rewards and punishments, social practice performance, and professional quality), the scale evaluation method was used. In detail, the Scale 4 table shown in Table 2 is used for the indicator of "professional quality". After students independently completed the experimental project "design of student course selection database" in groups. Professional personnel from employers, teachers, and students evaluate the research objects based on the Scale 4 table.

Table 1. Multisubject collaborative evaluation indicators

VAA Indicators	Evaluation Subject				Evaluation Method
	Teacher	Student	Teaching Management Personnel	Employer	
Exam Scores	√				Examination Paper
Class Performance	√	√			Scale 1
Attendance	√				Attendance Record
Homework	√				Homework
Experiment	√	√			Experimental Process
Rewards & Punishments	√		√		Scale 2
Social Practice			√		Scale 3
Professionalism	√	√		√	Scale 4

Table 2. Classroom Performance Evaluation Scale (Scale 4)

Evaluation Content (100 points)	Specific Performance	Teacher Evaluation	Employer Evaluation	Student self-Evaluation	average
Planning and Organization (20points)	Project planning, division of labor, and organization	–	–	–	–
Database Knowledge(30points)	Mastery and application of basic knowledge	–	–	–	–
Database Skills(30points)	Mastery and use of various skills and tools	–	–	–	–
Team Work(10points)	Communication among team members	–	–	–	–
Innovative Thinking(10points)	Project characteristics and innovation	–	–	–	–
total					–

4.2 Construction of a Multisubject Collaborative VAA Feedback Mechanism

Based on a multisubject VAA, a feedback mechanism has been constructed. The feedback mechanism can provide personalized guidance and suggestions for improvement, promote communication and cooperation between teachers, students, parents, and employers, and ultimately help students achieve their learning goals and career development. The multisubject collaborative feedback mechanism is helpful in identifying deficiencies in the teaching process, mobilizing the initiative of all subjects in teaching and learning, and creating a good educational atmosphere.

To maximize the effectiveness of VAA, a multisubject collaborative feedback mechanism was established from the views of the college or teaching research office, as shown in Fig. 2. On the one hand, the college or teaching research office should promptly convey the results of VAA to all subjects and analyse the results to provide corresponding suggestions to each subject. For example, based on the analysis of the results, the phenomenon that the VAA scores of higher-level student groups are significantly lower than those of other student groups indicates that the teacher's teaching content no longer meets the needs of higher-level student groups. In this case, the latest knowledge of database technologies should be provided. On the other hand, based on the VAA results, each evaluation subject provides feedback to the college or teaching research office, such as students' learning reports, teachers' teaching reflections, and parents' teaching opinions. For example, some lower-level students have given feedback in their learning reports that they find it difficult to judge whether their complex data query experiments are correct. Based on this feedback, teachers carefully designed the content of the data query and provided it to the students when assigning complex data query experiments.

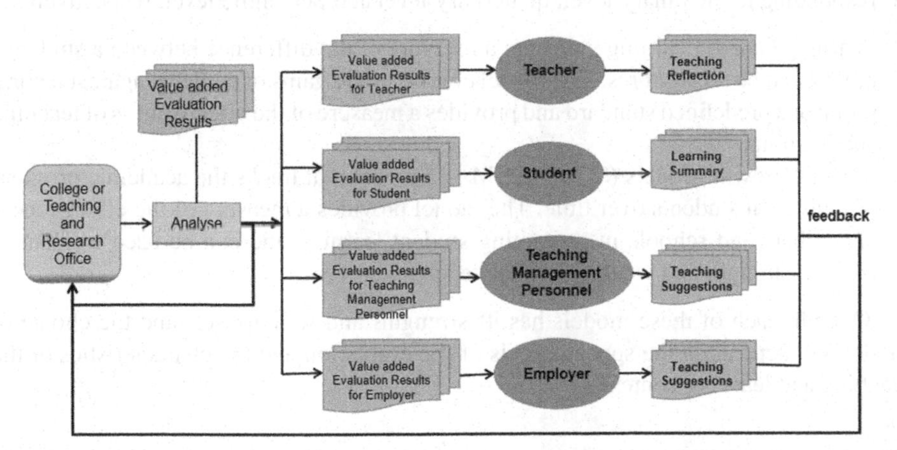

Fig. 2. Feedback mechanism based on multisubject collaborative evaluation. The figure shows a circular diagram of a feedback mechanism based on multisubject collaborative evaluation.

5 Establishment and Implementation of the VAA Model

5.1 Common Value-Added Evaluation Models

Establishing a reasonable and feasible VAA mechanism is the core of realizing the VAA concept. There are several commonly used value-added evaluation models in the field of education, including:

- Student Growth Percentiles (SGP): SGP is a model that compares the academic growth of students against the growth of similar students. The model is based on a statistical analysis of student achievement data and provides a measure of how much progress students have made over a certain period of time. The formulation of the fractional regression model is shown in Eq. (1)

$$Q_y(\tau|x) = argmin \sum_{i=1}^{n} p_\tau(y_i - x_i\beta) \tag{1}$$

where x denotes the individuals in the same group. x_i and y_i denote the initial score and the final score of the i-th individual in the same group. β denotes the regression coefficient, and p_τ is a piecewise linear loss function shown in Eq. (2).

$$p_\tau(w) = \begin{cases} w\tau, w \geq 0 \\ w(\tau - 1), w < 0 \end{cases} \tag{2}$$

τ represents the level of segmentation with the value range of (0,1). The number of its values corresponds to the number of groups. The common values are 2, 4, and 100, corresponding to the binary level, quaternary level and percentile level, respectively.

- Learning Gains: Learning gains are a measure of the difference between a student's pretest and posttest scores. The model compares the gains of students against a norm group or a predefined standard and provides a measure of the effectiveness of teaching and learning.
- Student Growth Models (SGM): SGM is a model that tracks the academic progress of individual students over time. The model provides a measure of the effectiveness of teachers and schools in promoting student learning and can be used to identify areas of strength and weakness in the teaching process.

Overall, each of these models has its strengths and weaknesses, and the choice of model will depend on the specific goals of the evaluation and the characteristics of the teaching and learning context.

5.2 Reasons for Choosing SGP in the Database Technology and Applications Course

Taking Wannan Medical College as an example, the course "Database Technology and Application" is lectured for students who major in medical information engineering and intelligent medical engineering. Two characteristics exist when the course is lectured. First, the number of students in each class is small, approximately two to three hundred per session. Second, the level of students varies. In the past two years, the proportion of excellent grades in the final exam of the course is 7.3%, while the proportion of failing grades is 5.3%. The total number of students at the top and bottom ends accounts for 12.6%.

The use of SGP as a VAA model in the "Database Technology and Applications" course is supported by its comparative analysis approach, flexibility, accessibility, and alignment with course goals.

- Comparative analysis: SGP compares the academic growth of students against the growth of similar students, which can effectively avoid extreme value disturbances and ensure high prediction accuracy even with a small sample size, making it suitable for courses with a small number of students such as "Database Technology and Application".
- Flexibility: SGP can be used to evaluate student growth in a wide range of courses and grades, including the "Database Technology and Application" course. SGP can effectively overcome the "ceiling" and "floor" effects of VAA. The core idea of SGP is to compare the progress of students within the same group and unify the degree of value-added to the same scale, which can effectively evaluate students at both ends of the performance spectrum.
- Accessibility: SGP is relatively easy to understand and implement, which makes it accessible to educators and administrators with varying levels of statistical expertise.
- Alignment with course goals: SGP can align with the goals of the "Database Technology and Applications" course, which may include developing students' technical skills in database design, programming, and optimization.

5.3 Empirical Research on the Application of SGP in the "Database Technology and Applications" Course

An empirical research study was conducted to evaluate the effectiveness of SGP as a VAA model for the "Database Technology and Applications" course. The study involved collecting data on the academic growth of students in the course and analysed these data using SGP to determine the extent to which students had improved in their database technology skills.

A total of 329 students majoring in medical information engineering and intelligent medical engineering at Wannan Medical College were chosen as the research objects. The increase in academic achievement of the "Database Technology and Application" course in the second semester of the 2022–2023 academic year was collected. Since the course had not finished, in-class quizzes were used instead of the final exam indicator, and other assessment indicators remained unchanged. The specific implementation process is as follows:

- Calculation of academic initial scores and academic stage scores. The academic initial score is set as the comprehensive score of all courses in the previous semester. The academic final score is obtained by the multisubject joint VAA, consisting of eight weighted evaluation indicators, and the specific indicators and weights are as follows: exam scores (50%), homework (10%), experiment (10%), social practice (10%), class performance (5%), rewards & punishments (5%), attendance (5%), and professionalism (5%).

- Division of groups. Due to the small number of research objects, according to the academic initial score (0–100 points), 10 different groups were divided. The academic initial scores, academic initial average scores, and size of research objects in each group are shown in Table 3.
- Calculation of growth percentile level. The growth percentile levels of the four groups were calculated using the score percentile regression equation in the SGP package in R software. Table 4 shows the comparative analysis on the growth percentile level and the average score changes of groups. Figure 3 shows the trend of group growth percentile levels and score changes. This demonstrates that the growth percentile levels of different groups are basically consistent with the score changes.

Table 3. Classification of Similar Groups

Group division	Academic Starting Point Score Range	Average Academic Starting point score	Size
Group 1	0–59	57.5	16
Group 2	60–66	63.2	38
Group 3	67–71	69.4	39
Group 4	72–77	74.8	39
Group 5	78–81	79.6	38
Group 6	81–83	81.9	39
Group 7	84–86	85.1	37
Group 8	87–90	88.7	36
Group 9	91–93	91.9	37
Group 10	94–100	95.4	10

The results also show the difficulty of judging students' learning progress solely based on score changes. For example, for group 1, the score change is only 0.1, but the average growth percentile is 44, indicating that the learning progress is negative. On the other hand, for group 10, the score change is -0.1, but the average growth percentile is 56, indicating that the learning progress is positive. In addition, the overall average growth percentile of the group shows that lower-level students' progress lags behind that of higher-level students during the teaching process. Teachers can adjust their teaching strategies in a timely manner based on VAA results, such as paying more attention to lower-level student groups, strengthening the teaching of basic database theory knowledge, and emphasizing key knowledge repeatedly.

The results of the study showed that using SGP as a VAA model was effective in measuring student progress in the course. The comparative analysis approach of SGP allowed for a more accurate measure of student growth, as it took into account the growth of similar students. The flexibility and accessibility of SGP also made it a suitable model for evaluating student growth in the "Database Technology and Applications" course.

Table 4. Comparative Analysis of Average Growth Percentile Grades and Score Changes

Group	Average Academic Starting Point Score	Academic Stage Average	Scores Change	Average Growth Percentile Grades
Group 1	57.5	57.6	0.1	44
Group 2	63.2	62.9	−0.3	43
Group 3	69.4	70.1	0.7	51
Group 4	74.8	75.7	0.9	72
Group 5	79.6	79.5	−0.1	53
Group 6	81.9	83.4	1.5	73
Group 7	85.1	86.2	1.1	70
Group 8	88.7	89.1	0.4	67
Group 9	91.9	92.1	0.2	61
Group 10	95.4	95.3	−0.1	56

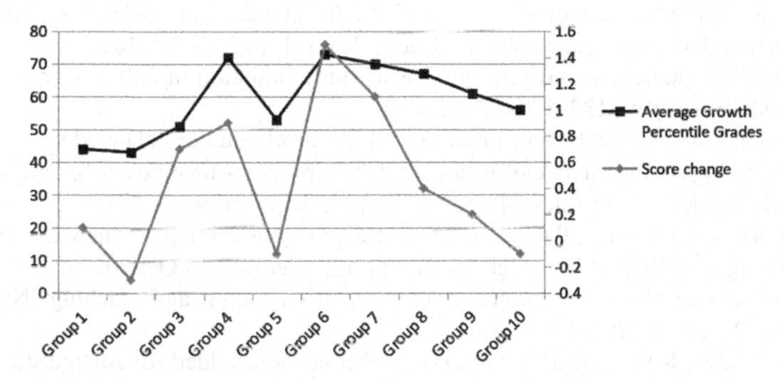

Fig. 3. Group Growth Percentage Rank and Score Change Trend Chart

Overall, the empirical research study provided support for the use of SGP as a value-added evaluation model in the "Database Technology and Applications" course. The study demonstrated that SGP was an effective tool for measuring student progress and identifying areas for improvement, and it could be used to align teaching practices with course goals.

6 Conclusion

The VAA concept still faces several challenges in practice, such as the unreasonable setting of evaluation indicators [16], unscientific value-added evaluation models [17], and the lack of VAA-based feedback mechanisms [7]. However, as long as the evaluation indicators are set reasonably, appropriate evaluation models are selected, and effective evaluation feedback mechanisms are constructed, VAA will undoubtedly become an important means of comprehensive education and a key guarantee for improving the quality of talent cultivation.

Acknowledgements. The key project of the research on higher education teaching reform of Wannan Medical College (project No. 2022jyxm08); Anhui Provincial Humanities and Social Science Foundation of China (project No. SK2021A0466); The major project of teaching reform and research in higher education of Anhui provincial (project No. 2021jyxm1605); The online and offline hybrid and social practice course project of Wannan Medical College (project No. 2022xsxxkc03); Teaching Demonstration Course Project in Anhui Province (project No. 2020–2459); The teaching quality and teaching reform project of Wannan Medical College (project No. 2022xskc01), The key research fund project of Wannan Medical College (project No. WKS2022Z01); The science project of Anhui Provincial Education Department (project No. 2022AH051203); School Enterprise Cooperative Practical Education Base of Wannan Medical College (project No. 2022xqhzsjjd01); Doctoral research start-up fund of Wannan Medical College (project No. WYRCQD2023011). The Education and Teaching Research Program of Anhui Vocational and Adult Education Society in 2021 (Project No. Azcj2021130).

References

1. Yu S.:Reflection on the reform of college teacher assessment and evaluation in the new era, Beijing Education (Higher Education), no. 06, pp 54–55 (2022)
2. Guo, M.: Research on the status quo and mechanism innovation of teacher teaching evaluation in local applied undergraduate colleges. Educ. Obser. 11(07), 5–10 (2022)
3. Xiang, X.: The status quo and reform of academic evaluation in colleges and universities. Think Tank Times (46), 123–124+126 (2019)
4. 'Opinions on accelerating the construction of high-level undergraduate education and comprehensively improving talent cultivation ability. http://www.moe.gov.cn/srcsite/A08/s7056/201810/t20181017_351887.html?isappinstalled=0, Accessed 8 Oct 2018
5. 'Overall plan for deepening the reform of educational evaluation in the new era',http://www.gov.cn/zhengce/2020-10/13/content_5551032.htm, Accessed 13 Oct 2018
6. Xu, N.: Application of value-added evaluation in education and teaching. Neijiang Sci. Technol. (12), 29–30 (2021)
7. Zhou, J., Wu, X., Kuang, Y.: Evaluation of academic value added for college students: basic attributes, practical dilemmas, and practical approaches. Modern Educ. Manage. (12), 10 (2021)
8. Hanushek, E., Rivkin, S., Review, A.E., et al.: Generalizations about using value-added measures of teacher quality. Am. Econ. Rev. **100**(2), 261–267 (2010)
9. Sanders, W.L., Horn, S.P.: Research Findings from the tennessee value-added assessment system (TVAAS) database: implications for educational evaluation and research. J. Pers. Eval. Educ. (3), 247–256 (1998)
10. Tennessee value-added assessment system: a brief overview. https://comptroller.tn.gov/content/dam/cot/orea/advanced-search/2013/2013_OREA_TVAASBrief.pdf, Accessed 31 Oct 2020
11. Jiang, W.: Value added evaluation: a new perspective of educational evaluation -- and evaluation of the quality of elementary language teaching. Jiangsu Educ. (5), 2 (2000)
12. Wang, B.: Teacher evaluation: value added evaluation method. Educ. Theor. Pract. (12), 20–23 (2005)
13. Ma, X., Peng, W., Sally, T.: Value added evaluation of school effectiveness: an empirical study of ordinary high schools in Baoding City. Educ. Res. (10), 77–84 (2006)
14. Wang, L.: Research and practice on the reform of teaching mode for value-added evaluation in higher vocational colleges -- taking the "Java object oriented programming" course for software technology majors as an example. J. Hunan Vocat. Tech. College Posts Telecommun. **21**(01), 45–49 (2022)

15. Chen, Z., Huang, Y., Li, H.: Application of value-added evaluation in physical education and health courses. Phys. Educ. Teach. Friends **44**(04), 18–20 (2021)
16. Zhou, Y., Chen, X.: Value added evaluation: core experience from tennessee. Prim. Secondary School Manage. (10), 11–15 (2020)
17. Li, S., Hong, Z., Hu, Z.: Reflection on value-added evaluation. Educ. Today (01), 14–18 (2021)
18. Chen, A., Guan, D.: Comparative analysis and empirical study of several value added evaluation methods. China Exam (09), 54–62 (2022)
19. Wang, X.: Common models and practical application considerations for value-added evaluation of teaching quality. Exam. Res. **16**(05), 11–16 (2020)
20. Chaoyuezi, L.: Empirical Study on the growth percentile hierarchy model. Basic Educ. Res. (09), 11–13 (2022)

Exploration and Practice of Operating System Curriculum Reform Based on the Integration of Science and Education

Lingli Li(✉)

Heilongjiang University, Harbin, China
lilngli@hlju.edu.cn

Abstract. Operating system (OS) is the core control of a computer, which serves as the command and management center of a computer, often referred to as the brain of a computer. Currently, operating systems are an important required course for computer science majors. Compared with other professional courses, the OS course is more abstract in concept, more theoretical, and difficult to practice, which is often considered as a "hard nut to crack" by many students. Many students often face difficulties in understanding concepts, mastering theories, and completing experiments. How to stimulate students' interest in learning this course, improve the low effectiveness of classroom teaching and the tedious and difficult nature of experiments is a problem that has been constantly explored in the teaching reform of operating system courses. Based on the characteristics of the knowledge system of operating systems and combined with heuristic teaching methods, this paper proposes a new approach to the reform of operating system courses through the integration of science and education.

Keywords: Operating System · Curriculum Reform · Integration of Science and Education

1 Introduction

The operating system is the core control center of the computer, serving as its command and management center, and is often referred to as the "brain" of the computer. It acts as a bridge between the user and the computer hardware, responsible for the translation of user commands, coordinating computer system resources, and ensuring that the internal workings of the computer run smoothly. The operating system controls the execution of other programs, manages system resources, and provides the most basic computing functions, such as managing and configuring memory, determining the priority of system resource supply and demand, and providing some basic service programs.

The operating system can be regarded as the "heart" of a computer, as all applications on a computer work under its support. In other words, whoever controls the operating system has access to all the operating information on the computer as long as it is connected to the internet. The operating system acts like a government, controlling other software while also providing them with various conveniences and constraints.

J. Gan et al. (Eds.): CSEI 2023, CCIS 1899, pp. 252–259, 2024.
https://doi.org/10.1007/978-981-99-9499-1_21

Currently, the operating system is an important mandatory course for computer science majors. Compared with other courses, the operating system course is abstract in concept, theoretical, and difficult in practical operation, making it a "hard nut to crack" for many students [1, 2].

During the learning process, most students often encounter problems such as unclear concepts, difficulty in understanding theories, and struggles in performing experiments. How to stimulate students' interest in the course, improve the low effectiveness of classroom teaching, and alleviate the dull and arduous nature of experiments have been issues discussed in the reform of operating system course teaching [3]. To avoid students becoming theoretical giants but practical midgets, and to address the issues of the outdated and shallow content, strong theoretical orientation, lack of practical training, and poor system capabilities in the existing operating system courses, this paper proposes a new approach to operating system course reform based on the characteristics of the operating system knowledge system, combining with heuristic teaching methods. We will carry out reforms in the following three aspects.

2 Integration of New Teaching Techniques

An operating system (OS) is a type of system software that manages a computer's hardware and software resources, and provides basic services such as file management, process management, memory management, and input/output management. To learn about operating systems, students need to understand these concepts, their implementation principles, and apply them in practice. Operating system courses are typically divided into theoretical and practical parts. The theoretical part introduces the concepts and principles of operating systems, while the practical part requires students to write and run operating system code to deepen their understanding and mastery of the subject [4]. As an important course in computer science, operating systems are a required subject for computer science majors.

However, many students encounter difficulties when studying operating systems. Firstly, the concepts of operating systems are abstract and difficult to understand, such as processes, threads, scheduling, and deadlocks. Secondly, operating systems are highly theoretical and require a foundation in computer architecture, compiler principles, data structures, and other courses. Thirdly, practical operations in operating systems are difficult and require students to master multiple programming languages and tools, such as C language, assembly language, GNU/Linux operating system, and so on. Due to the unique problems of operating systems courses, such as being highly theoretical and detached from practical operations, traditional teaching methods can no longer meet the requirements of classroom teaching. Reform is necessary to adapt to the development of this course. Integrating science and education is an effective teaching method that can help us better achieve teaching goals.

The integration of science and education refers to the combination of scientific research with education and teaching to improve the quality and effectiveness of teaching. By incorporating the knowledge areas that students need to learn from scientific research into the classroom, the gap between practice and theory can be bridged. We introduce scientific research projects into classroom teaching. During the teaching process, teachers can bring in some practical and applied scientific research projects related to the operating system and break them down into several small tasks for students to complete in the classroom. These tasks can be related to operating systems or application projects related to operating systems. By completing these tasks, students can gain a deeper understanding of the concepts and applications of operating systems, while also improving their practical and problem-solving abilities.

The heuristic teaching method is a teaching method based on exploration and discovery, which encourages students to actively participate and think, and improves learning effectiveness through practice and self-discovery. We believe that the heuristic teaching method is consistent with the essential characteristics of the operating system course, as practical operations in operating systems require students to explore and discover autonomously. Based on the concept of integrating science and education, we combine theoretical learning with practical operations and apply the heuristic method to the reform of the operating system course.

Using case-based teaching method can be an effective way to integrate the concepts and principles of operating system with practical cases, making it easier for students to understand and master. For instance, an actual process scheduling algorithm can be introduced, and students can design and implement it by themselves. Through comparing the advantages and disadvantages of different algorithms, students can have a deeper understanding of the principles behind process scheduling.

In addition, the experimental teaching method can be employed to allow students to master the knowledge of operating system in practice. For example, a simple operating system can be designed and implemented by students themselves, through which they can gain a deeper understanding of the principles and implementation of operating systems. Meanwhile, existing operating system experimental platforms such as QEMU, Bochs, etc. can also be utilized to enable students to practice operating system programming and debugging, thus improving their practical skills.

Moreover, group cooperative learning method can be adopted to enable students to work together in groups, exchange and cooperate with each other to complete the design and implementation of the operating system. Through group cooperative learning, students can interact and collaborate with each other, thus enhancing their learning effectiveness and interest.

Finally, we can also use information technology to assist in teaching the operating system course. For example, we can use online courses, virtual labs, and online discussions to enhance classroom interaction and effectiveness, making it easier for students to master and understand the knowledge of the operating system.

In addition to classroom teaching, we can also help students deepen their understanding of the application and development of operating systems through extracurricular activities. For example, organizing students to participate in operating system development competitions, operating system technology forums, and other activities, giving students the opportunity to exchange ideas, learn from each other, and share experiences with other professionals. Through these activities, students can not only learn about the latest developments in operating systems, but also apply theoretical knowledge to practice, and improve their practical and problem-solving abilities.

In conclusion, science-education integration is an effective teaching method that can not only improve students' interest and understanding but also help us achieve teaching goals. By using a variety of teaching methods, multimedia teaching, and strengthening practical teaching, we can cultivate high-quality talents with practical skills and innovative spirit, and make greater contributions to the development of computer science.

3 New Methods Introduction

Introducing new methods is crucial in operating system courses [5]. New methods, also known as cutting-edge methods, are an important driving force for the development of computer science and a crucial support for the continuous expansion of computer application areas. Therefore, in the teaching process of operating system courses, teachers can introduce the latest cutting-edge research results into the classroom and combine them with classroom teaching content. Introducing new methods can enable students to have a more comprehensive understanding of the application scenarios and development trends of operating systems, and also help them better grasp the latest development dynamics of computer science. By combining these cutting-edge research results with classroom teaching, students can gain a deeper understanding of the concepts and applications of operating systems, while also enhancing their practical ability and problem-solving skills.

For example, when teaching about memory management in operating systems, traditional teaching methods only introduce basic concepts and common memory management algorithms without exploring the relationship between memory management and new methods such as multicore processors and virtualization. However, using virtualization methods as a starting point in the course can help students better understand the relationship between memory management and new methods such as multicore processors and virtualization, thus gaining a better understanding of the practical applications of memory management.

Introducing new methods can also help students better understand and solve practical problems in the field of operating systems. For example, when teaching file systems, traditional methods often only focus on the basic concepts and storage methods of file systems, and rarely involve the fault-tolerance and performance optimization of file systems. However, in practical applications, the fault-tolerance and performance optimization of file systems are very important, especially in scenarios that require high reliability and performance. Therefore, by introducing some of the latest fault-tolerance and performance optimization methods as the entry point of the course, students can better understand and solve practical problems in the field of file systems, and at the same time, improve their practical skills and problem-solving abilities.

In addition, introducing new methods in the operating systems course can also help students better understand the working principles of computer systems. For example, when teaching process management, traditional methods often only briefly introduce the basic concepts and common process management algorithms, without in-depth discussion of the relationship between process management and new methods such as concurrent programming and multithreaded programming. By introducing concurrent programming, multithreaded programming, and other new methods as the entry point of the course, students can better understand the relationship between process management and new methods such as concurrent programming and multithreaded programming, and thus better grasp the practical applications of process management.

In addition to introducing new methods, the teaching methods of the operating system course can also be combined with practical application scenarios, introducing practical application cases to deepen students' understanding and interest, and better demonstrate the practicality and applicability of the operating system. For example, by introducing the application practice of operating systems in cloud computing, the Internet of Things and other fields, students can have a deeper understanding of the practical application and development trend of operating systems, while also cultivating their innovative thinking and practical operational skills. Additionally, teachers can also introduce the implementation of some large-scale application systems to help students better understand the application and practical value of new methods. In this way, students can not only learn theoretical knowledge but also understand practical applications, thereby better mastering the application scenarios and development trends of the operating system. Furthermore, the teaching methods of the operating system course can also be combined with actual engineering projects, allowing students to better understand and apply relevant knowledge and skills of the operating system through participation in actual engineering projects. This teaching method can not only improve students' practical skills but also allow them to better understand the organization and management of engineering projects, laying the foundation for their future work.

When education and scientific research are combined, we can find many new teaching resources and projects from scientific research. These projects not only help deepen students' understanding and mastery of course knowledge, but also enhance their hands-on ability and problem-solving skills, preparing them for future careers. For example, we can introduce research results on open-source operating systems to help students understand the latest developments in operating system technology, or introduce research results from well-known universities at home and abroad to help students have a deeper understanding of cutting-edge research in operating systems. In addition, students can be encouraged to innovate independently and conduct their own research projects on operating systems to improve their research and practical abilities.

In summary, introducing new methods, combining practical application scenarios and actual engineering projects, and other teaching methods in operating system courses can help students better understand and apply relevant knowledge and skills, have a more comprehensive understanding of the application scenarios and development trends of operating systems, and better grasp the latest developments in computer science. It can also improve students' practical abilities and problem-solving skills, enabling them to be more competitive and adaptable in the rapidly evolving field of computer science and technology.

4 New Projects Support

In addition to introducing new methods, the teaching of operating system courses should also focus on cultivating students' practical skills. Traditional teaching methods for operating systems often only focus on theoretical concepts, neglecting the importance of practical skills. However, operating systems are a very practical course with strong practicality and applicability, and only through practical operations can students better understand its concepts and applications. The traditional teaching of operating systems usually combines theory lectures with computer lab experiments, but this method is difficult to fully tap into students' initiative and creativity, and also challenging to cultivate their practical skills and problem-solving abilities. Therefore, we need to reform the operating system course, incorporate scientific research projects into the practical process of the course, and improve students' comprehensive qualities and practical abilities. Teachers can improve students' practical skills through practice, such as setting up computer lab experiments, project training, etc., to help students gradually master practical application skills of operating systems.

In the integration of science and education teaching, the role of teachers also needs to be emphasized. Teachers not only need to have solid disciplinary knowledge and rich teaching experience but also need to have certain scientific research and innovation capabilities. They should be able to transform scientific research results into teaching resources to provide students with a better teaching experience. At the same time, teachers also need to actively participate in students' scientific research projects, guide them in completing research tasks, and cultivate their scientific research and teamwork abilities.

Firstly, we need to integrate scientific research projects into the practical process of the course. In terms of practical operation, computer lab experiments are very important in the operating system course. Through these experiments, students can operate the computer system hands-on, gaining a deeper understanding of the concepts and applications of operating systems. Lab experiments should include practical and applicable tasks to help students gradually master the practical application skills of operating systems. For example, tasks such as setting up virtual machines, configuring networks, and implementing multi-process management can help students better understand the application scenarios and development trends of operating systems, while also improving their practical and problem-solving abilities.

In addition to lab experiments, project training is also an important way to improve students' practical ability [6, 7]. In the operating system course, teachers can set up some operating system-related projects for students to practice their knowledge and skills. For example, students can be tasked with developing a simple operating system and implementing some basic operating system functions. These projects can help students better understand the concepts and applications of operating systems, while also exercising their practical and problem-solving abilities.

In the operating system course, we not only want students to master the theoretical knowledge of operating systems, but also to cultivate their practical and problem-solving abilities. Therefore, we can integrate scientific research projects with practical course content. For example, when discussing process management, we can introduce a scientific research project that is practical and applicable, such as a graphical process manager, into the classroom. In class, we can have students design and implement a graphical process manager. By completing this project, students can gain a deeper understanding of process management concepts and applications, while also improving their practical and problem-solving abilities.

To further promote the integration of scientific research projects into the teaching process of the operating system course, we need to establish a scientific research project database. In this database, we can collect some scientific research projects with practicality and applicability and update and maintain it regularly. Through this project database, we can provide students with richer learning resources and promote the integration of scientific research and teaching by teachers.

In addition to cultivating practical abilities, the operating system course should also focus on cultivating students' innovation abilities. In the field of computer science, innovation ability is very important, and only people with innovation ability can play a greater role in the field of computer science. Therefore, in operating system teaching, teachers can guide students to conduct scientific research and exploration, allowing them to continuously discover problems, solve problems, innovate and improve, and cultivate their innovation ability and creativity.

By using the above methods, we can integrate scientific research projects into the teaching process of the operating system course to improve students' comprehensive quality and practical abilities. At the same time, we can also establish a scientific research project database to provide students with richer learning resources and promote the integration of scientific research and teaching by teachers, and promote the integration of scientific research projects.

The integration of science and education can also promote the cooperation between schools and industry. Schools can invite industry experts to participate in science and education integration teaching, allowing students to understand the current needs and applications of operating system technology in enterprises and learn about the latest technologies and development trends in the industry, providing reference and guidance for students' employment and entrepreneurship. At the same time, schools can also organize students to participate in relevant industry exhibitions and competitions, allowing them to showcase their operating system research results to society and the industry, and expand their exchange and influence.

5 Conclusion

As computer technology continues to advance, the operating system technology is constantly updating, and incorporating new knowledge and content into operating system courses is essential. This article proposes a new approach to operating system course teaching reform based on the integration of scientific research and education and heuristic teaching methods, which addresses the characteristics of concept abstraction, strong theoretical content, and difficult practical operations in operating system courses. The introduction of scientific research and education into operating system teaching is committed to providing updated and more valuable course knowledge, breaking the outdated teaching content, and stimulating students' interest. The proposed practical solution provides a novel and friendly approach to integrating scientific research project subproblems into students' practical content, combining teaching with practice and avoiding the disconnection between theory and practice. Practical results have shown that this teaching reform plan has achieved good results in stimulating students' learning interest, improving classroom teaching quality, and cultivating students' practical abilities.

In future teaching processes, teachers can further improve teaching methods and strategies to better adapt to the characteristics of operating system courses. For example, teachers can increase investment in laboratory environments, simplify the setup and maintenance of laboratory environments, and reduce the difficulty of practical operations for students. Additionally, teachers can establish a good communication mechanism with students, timely understand students' learning needs and difficulties, and provide personalized guidance and assistance to students.

References

1. Lifang, S.: Exploration on curriculum reform of operating system based on mixed teaching mode. Adv. Educ. Technol. Psychol. **5**, 218–222 (2021)
2. Li, T., Sanmin, L.: Practical analysis of teaching reform of operating system principle course based on OBE concept. Comput. Knowl. Technol. **18**(34), 146–148 (2022)
3. Liping, F., Chunnan, Z., Jing, Z.: Operating system classroom teaching practice based on demand development theory. Softw. Guide (Educ. Technol.) **17**(03), 33–35 (2018)
4. Niu, J., Hu, Z., Xiao, X.: Study on curriculum reform of computer operating system. In: International Workshop on Education Technology and Computer Science (2009)
5. Hui, Y.: Exploration of operating system curriculum reform. In: International Academic Exchange Symposium on Smart City and Informatization Construction II. [Publisher unknown], p. 61 (2016)
6. Xiaobing, L., Jie, Y., Xiaowu, L., et al.: Reform and exploration of curriculum system and teaching content under the background of new engineering: taking the course of "Operating System" as an example'. J. Hunan Univ. Sci. Technol. **42**(03), 105–107 (2021)
7. Wen, J., Jie, Z., Shulin, S.: Discussion on the reform method of college operating system curriculum under output-driven assumption. China Mod. Educ. Equipment **341**(13), 81–84 (2020)

Teaching Quality Evaluation of Online Courses Based on Cloud Model and Entropy Weight

Fang Yang[1] and Mingjing Tang[2](✉)

[1] School of Fine Art and Design, Kunming University, Kunming, China
[2] Yunnan Key Laboratory of Smart Education, Yunnan Normal University, Kunming, China
tmj@ynnu.edu.cn

Abstract. Quality evaluation is essential to measure the effectiveness of online course teaching. The existing research mainly focuses on qualitative methods and lacks a set of scientific, objective, and applicable quantitative evaluation methods. This paper uses the Delphi method to construct the quantitative evaluation index system, uses the cloud model and entropy weight to construct the quantitative evaluation model, and makes an empirical analysis combining with specific cases. The empirical results show that this approach can solve the problems of index weight allocation and qualitative index quantification and achieve good feasibility and effectiveness.

Keywords: Online courses teaching · Quality evaluation · Cloud model · Entropy weight

1 Introduction

With the continuous in-depth application of information technology in the field of education, online course teaching has become an important teaching mode with its characteristics of open learning mode, flexible form, rich teaching resources and multiple evaluation methods, which promotes educational equity and brings profound changes in the field of education and teaching. However, it is these characteristics that lead to the problems of high enrollment rate, high dropout rate and low completion rate in online course teaching practice, which seriously affect the quality of online course teaching.

Evaluating the quality of online course teaching is essential to measure and manage online course teaching activities. It helps identify problems and deficiencies in the process of online course teaching and improve its effectiveness [1].

To address the problem of evaluating the quality of online course teaching, researchers have carried out multi-dimensional research from different evaluation perspectives and achieved a lot of research results. However, there are still issues in the following areas. With regard to the evaluation mechanism, the research work mainly focuses on the result, lacks the process evaluation, and the evaluation is not scientific and accurate [2]. In terms of evaluation methods, qualitative analysis is used to construct evaluation index system, but quantitative analysis and feasibility verification are lacking, so the credibility of evaluation results is low [3]. In terms of evaluation content, the

J. Gan et al. (Eds.): CSEI 2023, CCIS 1899, pp. 260–269, 2024.
https://doi.org/10.1007/978-981-99-9499-1_22

evaluation indexes and weights are not standardized, with more qualitative indexes and less quantitative indexes, more subjective opinions and less objective criteria [4]. In the terms of evaluation feedback, the form is single, the degree of information is not high, and it is not convenient to promote the improvement of the work [5]. Thus, it is essential to establish a set of scientific, objective, and feasible measurement and evaluation methods that take into account the characteristics of online course teaching to improve its quality.

Motivated by above problems, this paper proposes a method for evaluating the quality of online course teaching based on cloud models and entropy weight, and verifies the method with practical cases. The primary contributions of this paper are as follows:

1) The factors that affect the quality of online course teaching are identified and sorted out. The Delphi method is used to construct a set of evaluation index systems for online course teaching quality.
2) A quantitative evaluation model of online course teaching is proposed based on cloud models and entropy weight theory, and an empirical analysis is conducted based on practical cases.
3) The empirical analysis results demonstrate that this method effectively addresses the problem of index weight allocation and qualitative index quantification, achieves good feasibility and effectiveness.

The rest of this paper is structured as follows: Sect. 2 introduces the construction of online course teaching quality evaluation index system. Section 3 elucidates each module of the proposed approach in detail. Section 4 presents the extensively empirical analysis results and discussions. Section 5 draws the main conclusion of this paper.

2 Construction of Evaluation Index System

Evaluation factor analysis and index identification are the basis of teaching quality evaluation of online courses. The construction of online course teaching quality evaluation index system should follow scientific principles and consider the combination of points and aspects, orientation and operability, qualitative and quantitative analysis, and objective and process. This will improve the functional effectiveness of online course teaching quality evaluation.

In view of this, this paper combines the requirements of online course teaching, and uses the Delphi method to construct the evaluation index system of online curriculum teaching quality. First, we will select 15 experts who have been working in the course teaching for more than 10 years. Then, the potential factors influencing the teaching quality of online courses are summarized from the aspects of course organization, course content, course implementation and teaching effect, and the boundary value method is used to screen the indicators. After 3 discussions of consultation, opinions on various indicators of experts tend to be consistent, and a quantitative evaluation index system of online course teaching quality covering 4 first-level indicators and 11 s-level indicators is constructed, as shown in Fig. 1.

Among them, the index of Course organization F_1 includes three second-level indexes: teaching objective f_1, teaching team f_2 and teaching platform f_3. The index

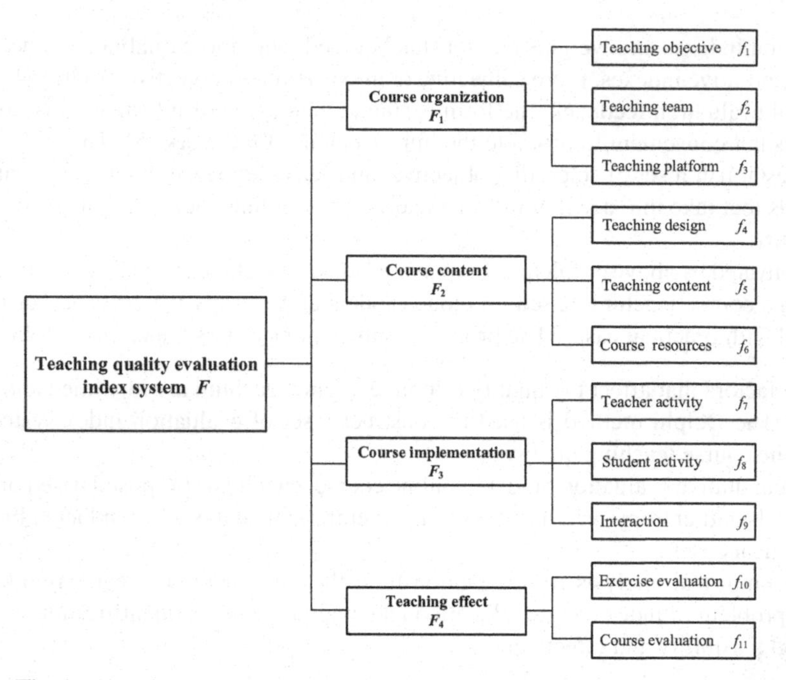

Fig. 1. Quantitative evaluation index system of online course teaching quality

of Course content F_2 includes three second-level indexes: teaching design f_4, teaching content f_5 and course resources f_6. The index of Course implementation F_3 includes three second-level indexes: teacher activity f_7, student activity f_8 and interaction f_9. The index of Teaching effect F_4 includes two second-level indexes: exercise evaluation f_{10} and course evaluation f_{11}.

The above second-level indexes of online course teaching quality evaluation also include relevant evaluation observation points, which are explained in detail as follows:

1. Teaching objective. Teaching objectives affect the organization of teaching activities and teaching evaluation, which is very important for the development of online course teaching. This index focuses on whether the teaching objectives are clear, scientific and reasonable, whether meet the needs of the industry, and whether meet the cognitive level of students.

2. Teaching team. This index mainly examines the teaching level, academic level, scientific research ability and teaching team composition of the course presenter.

3. Teaching platform. This index mainly examines the influence of online teaching platform, whether the function meets the demand, and whether the operation is humanized.

4. Teaching design. This index mainly examines whether the course content is appropriate, whether the total course hours are appropriate, and whether the schedule is reasonable.

5. Teaching content. This index mainly examines whether the difficulty setting is reasonable, whether the length of the video is reasonable, whether the content is rich and varied, and whether the content meets the needs of the industry.

6. Course resources. This index mainly examines whether the teaching videos are standardized, and whether ppt courseware, reading materials, bibliography, homework library and test library are equipped.
7. Teacher activity. This index mainly examines whether the knowledge explanation is prominent and clear, whether the classroom organization is proper, and whether the teaching state is natural and inspirational.
8. Student activity. This index mainly examines the number of course visits and the length of course study.
9. Interaction. This index mainly examines teacher-student interaction channels, discussion and Posting.
10. Exercise evaluation. This index mainly examines the difficulty of exercise design, whether the types of exercise are diverse, exercise correction, exercise completion rate and exercise qualification rate.
11. Course evaluation. This index mainly examines the course completion rate, course qualification rate, course excellence rate and so on.

3 Proposed Method

3.1 The Introduction of Cloud Model and Entropy Weight Theory

Li proposed the cloud model in 1995 to enable the conversion between quantitative value and qualitative language. The model better solves the correlation between fuzziness and randomness in the evaluation process [6]. The cloud model realizes the transformation of qualitative concepts and quantitative characteristics through the digital characteristics of the cloud. The digital characteristics of the cloud are expressed as Expectation (Ex), Entropy (En) and Hyper-entropy (He). The Expectation (Ex) represents the expectation of the spatial distribution of cloud droplets in the domain of discourse. Entropy (En) represents the degree of uncertainty and measurability of qualitative concepts. The larger the entropy value is, the larger the span in the cloud image is, and the higher the degree of recognition of qualitative concepts is. Hyper-entropy (He) represents the uncertainty of entropy and the randomness of samples. The higher the degree of acceptance of qualitative concepts, the smaller the value of Hyper-entropy, and vice versa [7].

$$Ex=\overline{x} = \frac{1}{n}\sum_{i=1}^{n} xi \tag{1}$$

$$En = \sqrt{\frac{\pi}{2}} \times \frac{1}{n}\sum_{i=1}^{n} |xi - Ex| \tag{2}$$

$$He = \sqrt{S^2 - En^2} \tag{3}$$

$$S^2 = \frac{1}{n-1}\sum_{i=1}^{n} (x_i - \overline{x})^2 \tag{4}$$

where, n is the number of samples; x_i is the value in the sample; $\overline{x}$ is the sample mean; S^2 is the sample variance.

The concept of entropy comes from physics and is introduced into information theory by Shannon, the founder of information theory. It is used to measure the uncertainty or information quantity of a random variable. Entropy weight method is a method to assign weights to evaluation indexes. The weight of each evaluation index is determined by calculating the information entropy of evaluation results [8]. Compared with other weighting methods, entropy weight method uses the variation degree among variables to determine the objective weight of each index and avoids the influence of subjective factors, so it has strong objectivity, accuracy and practicability. When the entropy value of an evaluation index is smaller, the degree of variation of its variables will be greater, more information will be provided for evaluation reference, and the weight of the index will be greater. Conversely, the greater the entropy value of an index, the smaller the variation degree of its variables, the less information to provide evaluation reference, and the smaller the weight of the index.

3.2 Teaching Quality Evaluation Based on Cloud Model and Entropy Weight

There are many qualitative indexes in the evaluation index system of online course teaching quality, and human factors have great influence. The teaching quality evaluation method of online course based on cloud model and entropy weight can realize the mutual transformation of qualitative and quantitative evaluation, and the evaluation index weight assignment is more objective, so as to improve the correctness and effectiveness of evaluation results. The following steps describe the method:

1. Determine the index domain. There are n indexes in the evaluation index system, then the evaluation domain is $C = \{c_1, c_2, c_3, \cdots, c_n\}$.

2. Calculating index weights. The entropy weight method is used to calculate the weight of the teaching quality evaluation index of online courses. The weight assignment steps are as follows:

First, the initial matrix of evaluation index is constructed. There are m experts to evaluate n evaluation indexes for the teaching quality evaluation of online courses, and the initial matrix is:

$$A = \left[A_{ij}\right]_{m\times n} \tag{5}$$

Among them, A_{ij} is the evaluation value of the j-th index by the i-th expert. Then normalize the initial matrix **A** to get the standard matrix **B**:

$$B = \left[B_{ij}\right]_{m\times n} \tag{6}$$

Then, calculate the entropy value H_i of the i-th index according to the formula of information entropy:

$$H_i = -\frac{1}{\ln(n)}\sum_{j=1}^{m} p_{ij}\ln p_{ij} \tag{7}$$

$$p_{ij} = \frac{B_{ij}}{\sum\limits_{j=1}^{m} B_{ij}} \tag{8}$$

Finally, the entropy weight of the i-th index is calculated:

$$q_i = \frac{1 - H_i}{\sum_{n-1}^{n} (1 - H_i)} \tag{9}$$

3. Calculating the digital eigenvalues. The digital eigenvalues of the cloud model are calculated according to formula (1) - (4): Expectation (Ex), Entropy (En) and Hyper-entropy (He).

4. Establish a standard evaluation cloud. The digital eigenvalues of the standard evaluation cloud model are calculated by combining the evaluation index system and the computing rules of cloud model. The standard evaluation cloud is constructed by the forward cloud generator. In this paper, the teaching quality evaluation of online courses is divided into five standard grades: "Excellent", "Good", "Qualified", "Basically qualified" and "Unqualified". The corresponding evaluation intervals are: [2–5], [0, 1]. The calculation formula of standard evaluation cloud is as follows:

$$\begin{cases} Ex = (\alpha_{\min} + \alpha_{max})/2 \\ En = (\alpha_{\max} - \alpha_{\min})/6 \\ \mathrm{He} = \mathrm{k} \end{cases} \tag{10}$$

where, α_{max} and $\alpha_{\min}$ are respectively the upper and lower limits of the evaluation interval; k is a constant and 0.25 is taken in this paper.

5. Establish a comprehensive evaluation cloud. According to the index weight q and index digital eigenvalues, the cloud digital eigenvalues and comprehensive evaluation cloud chart of online course teaching quality evaluation are obtained by using weighted average calculation.

$$Ex = \sum_{i=1}^{n} qiEx_i \tag{11}$$

$$En = \sum_{i=1}^{n} qiEn_i \tag{12}$$

$$He = \sum_{i=1}^{n} qiHe_i \tag{13}$$

4 Empirical Analysis

The following is an empirical analysis based on the online course teaching of university in Yunnan Province, and the practical application of the model is introduced in detail. The specific process is as follows:

The teaching quality of online courses was evaluated using a Likert scale-based evaluation table designed according to the constructed evaluation index system. 15 experts in the field of course teaching were invited to evaluate and score, and the score interval of each index was [0, 5].

1. Determine the index domain. According to the index system of online course teaching quality evaluation constructed above, the index domain can be obtained as follows: $C = \{c_1, c_2, c_3, \cdots, c_{11}\}$.

2. Calculating index weights. According to the data of the evaluation table and formula (7) - (9), the weights of each index and dimension are calculated, as shown in Table 1.

Table 1. The weight of evaluation index.

Dimension	Index	Weight of index	Weight of dimension
Course organization F_1	teaching objective f_1	0.0560	0.1878
	teaching team f_2	0.0773	
	teaching platform f_3	0.0545	
Course content F_2	teaching design f_4	0.1285	0.3551
	teaching content f_5	0.1012	
	course resources f_6	0.1254	
Course implementation F_3	teacher activity f_7	0.0765	0.2062
	student activity f_8	0.0281	
Teaching effect F_4	interaction f_9	0.1016	
	exercise evaluation f_{10}	0.1736	0.2509
	course evaluation f_{11}	0.0773	

3. Establish a standard evaluation cloud. According to the standard evaluation cloud construction algorithm and formula (10), the digital eigenvalues of the standard evaluation cloud are calculated, as shown in Table 2.

Table 2. The digital eigenvalues of the standard evaluation cloud.

Evaluation level	Ex	En	He
Excellent	4.5	0.167	0.25
Good	3.5	0.167	0.25
Qualified	2.5	0.167	0.25
Basically qualified	1.5	0.167	0.25
Unqualified	0.5	0.167	0.25

According to the digital eigenvalues of the standard evaluation cloud in Table 2, the matlib drawing interface of Python is called to obtain the cloud chart of the standard evaluation cloud, as shown in Fig. 2.

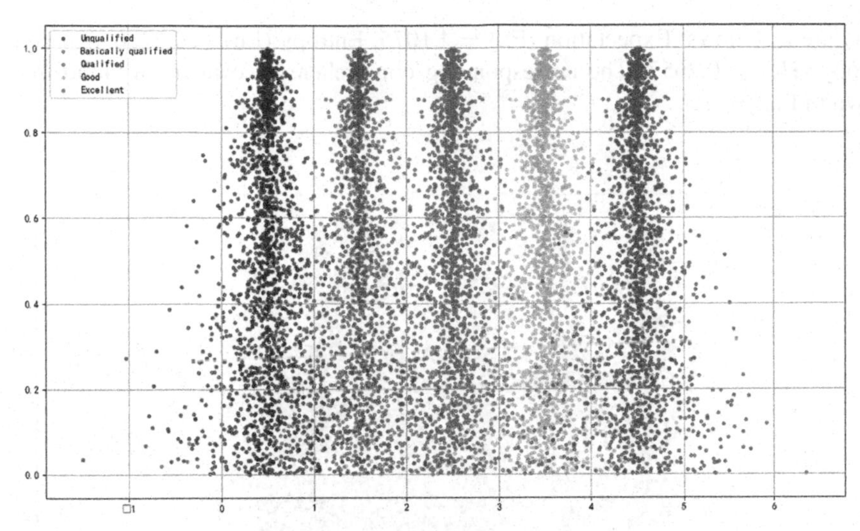

Fig. 2. Standard evaluation cloud chart

4. Establish a comprehensive evaluation cloud. Firstly, according to the evaluation table data and formula (1)-(4), the digital eigenvalues of each index of online course teaching quality evaluation are calculated, and the results are shown in Table 3.

Table 3. The digital eigenvalues of each index of online course teaching quality evaluation.

Index	Ex	En	He
teaching objective f_1	4.2	0.6684	0.1419
teaching team f_2	4.2	0.8021	0.2888
teaching platform f_3	4.3333	0.7798	0.3453
teaching design f_4	3.9333	0.7798	0.1122
teaching content f_5	3.9333	0.6238	0.2702
course resources f_6	3.8	0.6684	0.1419
teacher activity f_7	4.0	0.5013	0.3856
student activity f_8	4.067	0.6239	0.4542
interaction f_9	3.9333	0.6239	0.2701
exercise evaluation f_{10}	4.5333	0.6239	0.3746
course evaluation f_{11}	4.2	0.8021	0.2888

Secondly, combined with the evaluation index weights and corresponding digital eigenvalues obtained by the above calculation, the cloud digital eigenvalues and comprehensive evaluation cloud chart of online course teaching quality are calculated according to formula (11) - (13). Finally, the digital eigenvalues of the comprehensive evaluation cloud are as follows: Expectation (Ex) = 4.1075, Entropy (En) = 0.6786, and Hyper-entropy (He) = 0.2657. The corresponding comprehensive evaluation cloud map is shown in Fig. 3.

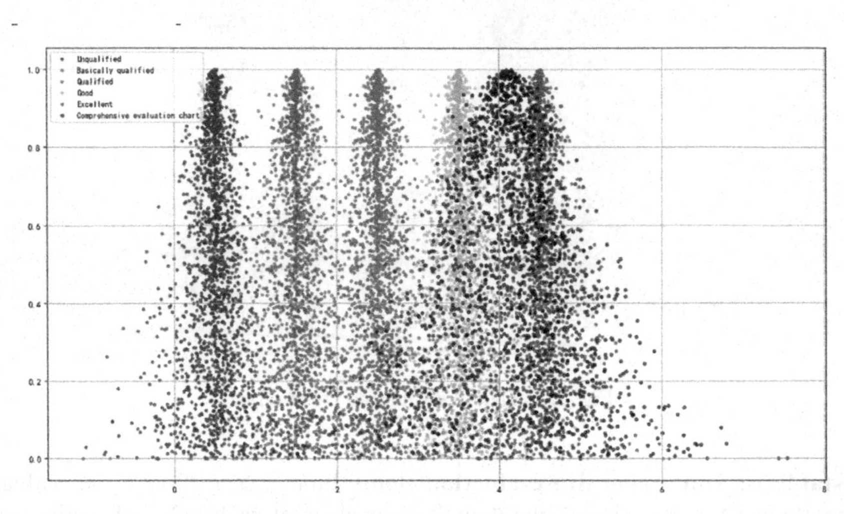

Fig. 3. Comprehensive evaluation cloud chart

The actual evaluation result of the comprehensive evaluation cloud chart of online course teaching quality is represented by the black part in Fig. 3. Compared with the standard evaluation cloud chart, it can be found that the teaching effect of this course is between the "excellent" level and "good" level, and there is much overlap with the "good" level, and the comprehensive evaluation result is "good". The evaluation results match the actual situation, indicating that the method combined with cloud model and entropy weight has good feasibility.

5 Empirical Analysis

Online course teaching quality evaluation is a necessary means to promote the Internet + education work, which is helpful to promote the improvement of online teaching effect. However, in the process of evaluation practice, some evaluation indexes are difficult to quantify and lack of objective evaluation, which affects the scientific, refined and standardized evaluation of online course teaching quality. In this paper, Delphi method is used to construct the evaluation index system of online course teaching quality from the aspects of course organization, course content, course implementation and teaching effect. To avoid the influence of human subjective factors, a quantitative evaluation model based on cloud model and entropy weight are proposed to solve index weight allocation and qualitative index quantification. The empirical analysis shows that this method is scientific, reasonable and feasible. It provides a new way for evaluating online course teaching quality.

Acknowledgements. We thank the anonymous reviewers and the editors for their suggestions. This work is supported by the Yunnan International Joint R&D Center of China-Laos-Thailand Educational Digitalization (Grant no. 202203AP140006).

References

1. Yang, Z.: The application of AHP in the quality evaluation of online teaching in colleges and universities. Theory Pract. Innov. Entrepreneur. **3**(17), 61–62 (2020)
2. Cheng, Y., Tan, A.: The construction and application of evaluation index system for online open course learning quality. Contemp. Vocat. Educ. **1**, 62–69 (2020)
3. Lai, Y., Jiang, S.: Study on the evaluation index system of online course teaching quality in university libraries. J. Xichang Univ. (Nat. Sci. Ed.) **36**(4), 111–123 (2021)
4. He, S., Mei, L.: Teaching quality evaluation of MOOC based on Kirkpatrick model. Logist. Eng. Manage. **43**(9), 209–212 (2021)
5. Ying, L., Li, X., Zhao, J.: Construction of teaching quality evaluation system for civil engineering online open courses. J. Archit. Educ. Institut. High. Learn. **31**(6), 25–34 (2022)
6. Ye, Q., Li, S., Zhang, Y., Shu, X., Ni, D.: Cloud model and application overview. Comput. Eng. Design **32**(12), 4198–4201 (2011)
7. Wang, Y., Han, X., Xiong, K.: Risk evaluation of PPP projects based on cloud model and entropy weighting method. J. Eng. Manage. **34**(6), 66–70 (2020)
8. Fan, H., He, J., Tian, S.: Robust evaluation method of integrated energy system based on variable step simulation and improved entropy weight method. J. Shanghai Jiaotong University **28**, 1–17 (2023)

University Engineering Education

Curling Strategy Teaching Case Design Based on Deep Reinforcement Learning

Guojun Liu(✉), Qi Zhou, and Ye Jin

Faculty of Computing, Harbin Institute of Technology, Harbin, China
hitliu@hit.edu.cn

Abstract. Reinforcement learning is becoming more and more important in the field of artificial intelligence. Compared with traditional supervised learning and unsupervised learning, reinforcement learning has wider application scenarios and higher flexibility. As a reinforcement learning problem in continuous space, curling has a good representative significance in the field of reinforcement learning, students can have a deeper understanding of the principles and applications of deep learning and reinforcement learning, thinking deeply about the differences and relationships between artificial intelligence and human intelligence. The reinforcement learning algorithm in curling uses the Monte Carlo tree search method, which covers many basic theoretical knowledge of computer science, such as machine learning, mathematics, algorithms, and data structures. In this paper, we propose a case study of reinforcement learning teaching based on digital curling. First, we designed and implemented a digital curling simulator and made a visual interface. Then, to make the algorithm more understandable, we implement a visual explanation of Monte Carlo search trees. Additionally, we have also provided the digital curling competition mode, so that students can realize the competition of different algorithms. Students can effectively improve their understanding of reinforcement learning by using their own algorithms to fight against digital curling.

Keywords: Curling Strategy · Reinforcement Learning · Digital Curling · Monte Carlo Tree Search · Teaching Case

1 Introduction

Reinforcement learning is a branch of machine learning that aims to learn how to make optimal decisions through the interaction of an agent with the environment [11]. In reinforcement learning, the agent obtains feedback from the environment (reward or punishment) by trying different actions, and learns from it the optimal policy, that is, the sequence of actions that maximizes the long-term reward in a given environment [6].

Reinforcement learning is becoming more and more important in the field of artificial intelligence, and it is one of the hot spots in current artificial intelligence research. Compared with traditional supervised learning and unsupervised learning, reinforcement learning has wider application scenarios and higher flexibility.

J. Gan et al. (Eds.): CSEI 2023, CCIS 1899, pp. 273–284, 2024.
https://doi.org/10.1007/978-981-99-9499-1_23

Reinforcement learning can be applied to control of autonomous agents, game design, natural language processing, computer vision, robot control, autonomous driving, and many other fields. At the same time, reinforcement learning is also widely used in practical applications. Projects such as DeepMind's AlphaGo [18] and AlphaZero [19] are based on reinforcement learning algorithms. Fawzi et al. discovered a faster algorithm for matrix multiplication by reinforcement learning [7]. Chen et al. use deep reinforcement learning (DRL) to control the real-world atom manipulation process [5]. Cao et al. present a dynamic confidence-aware reinforcement learning (DCARL) technology for guaranteed continuous improvement [4]. The technology was demonstrated and evaluated on the vehicle at the 2022 Beijing Winter Olympic Games. In the development of deep learning, reinforcement learning has become one of the important branches, and deep reinforcement learning combines the advantages of deep learning and reinforcement learning, and has achieved a series of important successes. With the continuous exploration of its application scenarios and the continuous improvement of algorithm theory, reinforcement learning will continue to play an important role in the future development.

With the explosive development of artificial intelligence in recent years, people's expectations for using AI to solve practical production and life problems are getting higher and higher [12,13]. Therefore, accelerating the improvement of the artificial intelligence education and teaching system is of great significance for cultivating students majoring in computer science and other information technology-related majors. A good teaching case is very important to help students improve their learning interest, exercise their hands-on ability and experience the real application scenarios of artificial intelligence algorithms. It can effectively make up for the dullness and tediousness brought about by simple artificial intelligence-related theoretical explanations. It is both entertaining and educational. Let students acquire knowledge while enjoying entertainment, thereby improving learning efficiency and effectiveness.

In recent years, some artificial intelligence teaching application cases have been proposed to help students better learn various artificial intelligence technologies. Yuyan Qiu et al. [21] designed a simple reinforcement learning maze environment to help students better understand and practice the iterative process of SARSA algorithm and Q-learning algorithm, and help students master the essence of the two algorithms through the comparison of the two methods. Zhiyuan He [10] built 21 deep learning projects to help beginners in artificial intelligence learn the application scenarios and implementation process of deep learning. Through these application cases, students can be freed from simple boring theory, so that students can personally practice the application scenarios of artificial intelligence algorithms. However, the interest and comprehensiveness of these cases need to be improved, and there is not enough space for students to play freely in these cases, so it is difficult to develop students' creativity.

This paper proposes that using digital curling as an application case and practical scene in reinforcement learning teaching can fully reflect the particularity of curling in reinforcement learning. At the same time, the digital curling environment we built has more realistically restored the process of curling, and students can experience the fun of curling during the learning process. Students can test, compete and learn different algorithms in our digital curling simulator. Through different algorithms, students can experience the similarities and differences between artificial intelligence and human thinking. At the same time, curling is a competitive sport, and digital curling can help publicize and popularize this sport, making it easier for students to understand the rules, techniques and historical origins of curling. The visual explanation of the Monte Carlo tree search method can help students better understand the execution process of the algorithm and realize how the MCTS algorithm improves the strategy level step by step through the game tree.

The remainder of this paper is organised as follows. Section 2 introduces the basic rules of curling and models the curling process. In Sect. 3, we explain the detailed flow of the Monte Carlo tree search algorithm used in teaching, and demonstrate how to abstract curling into a Markov Decision Process. In Sect. 4, we design the digital curling teaching system. Section 5 presents how students implement their own algorithms in digital curling and illustrates how they are implemented. Finally, Sect. 6 concludes the paper.

2 Curling Environment

Curling is a beloved Winter Olympic sport. In curling game, two teams of four players each take turns throwing their stone with the goal of getting their stone as close to the center mark as possible. The game is divided into multiple ends, and the number of throwing rounds in each round is variable, usually 8 to 10 ends. At the end of each round, the score will calculate which team has the most curling stones near the center mark, and that team will get the score for that end, and the team with the most points wins [17]. During the curling competition, players need to complete their own decision-making or overdraft operations within a limited time, which deeply tests the player's thinking speed and flexibility, so curling is also called "chess on ice".

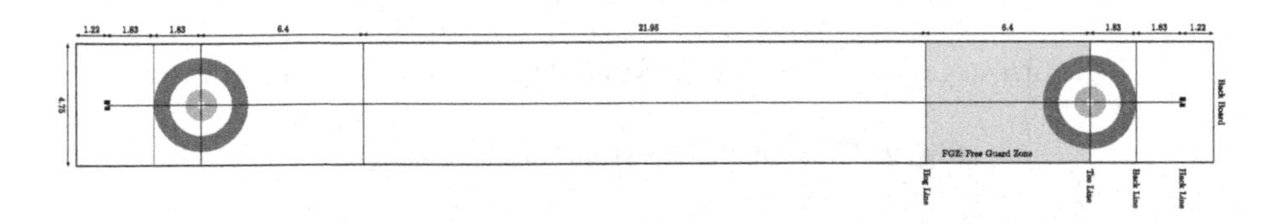

Fig. 1. Detailed specification of curling ice surface.

The curling field is generally composed of a special ice surface with a length of 44.5 m and a width of 4.75 m. Figure 1 shows the detailed specification of curling ice surface. The curling stone is made of special marble with a mass of 19 kg. The friction between curling and ice is special, and the friction between curling stones and ice is still a hot research field. Until now, people have no mathematical equations that can accurately predict the trajectory of curling stones, and can only be approximated by simulation [14,15].

In order to simplify the model and highlight the characteristics of the unique curling trajectory of curling stones, we divide the curling process into three stages [9]. In the first stage, the curling stone runs at a faster speed, and there is intense friction between the bottom of the stone and the ice surface, and the ice surface will melt briefly to form a liquid film. At this time, the friction between the ice surface and the bottom of the stone is small, and the trajectory of the stone basically runs along a straight line. In the second stage, the speed of the stone has decreased. At this time, there will still be a short-term liquid film between the bottom of the stone and the ice surface due to friction. In the third stage, the movement speed of the stone is low, and the rotation speed is relatively high. At this time, it is difficult to form a liquid film between the bottom of the stone and the ice surface. At the same time, the rapid rotation causes the force of the stone to be deflected, and the trajectory of the curling will be greatly deflected. This stage is also the main stage for the deflection of the curling stone trajectory. According to the analysis of these three stages, we carry out physical simulation of the curling stone movement process, and construct a digital curling operating environment. Using digital curling, we can build various algorithms on this basis to help students better understand reinforcement learning.

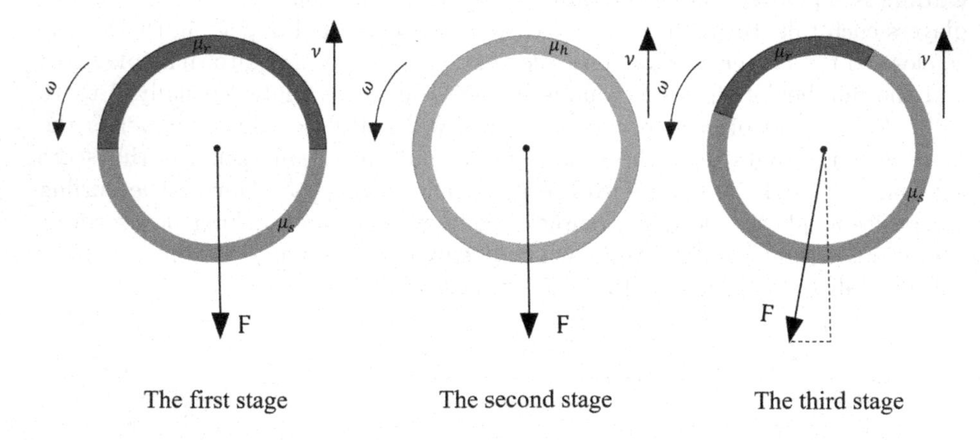

Fig. 2. Force of curling stone in three stages.

Figure 2 explains the three stages mentioned above. The variables in Fig. 2 represent the following meanings. F in the figure represents the resultant force on the stone. v represents the direction of the stone speed. w represents the direction of the angular velocity of the stone. μ_r , μ_s and μ_h are the coefficient of friction between the bottom of the stone and the ice surface.

3 Monte Carlo Tree Search Algorithm

All reinforcement learning problems can be abstracted as a Markov Decision Process (MDP) [20], and MDP is also the most basic problem in reinforcement learning. The simplest MDP generally includes four basic elements $< A, S, R, P >$, which represent A: Action space, the collection of all legal actions that can be taken; S: State space, the collection of all states is called the state space; R: Reward, which can be positive reward, negative reward or zero; P, state transition probability matrix, the probability of the state transitioning from s to s' after performing action a.

The interaction process of the agent in reinforcement learning is shown in Fig. 3. The agent gives the corresponding action a_t and executes the action according to the current state s_t. Afterwards, the environment state will be converted from s_t to s_{t+1}, and the corresponding r_{t+1} will be given, and then the agent will further give new actions according to the new state s_{t+1} and reward r_{t+1}. This cycle goes on and on until the environment reaches the terminal state s_T and finally forms a Markov chain, as shown in equation (1).

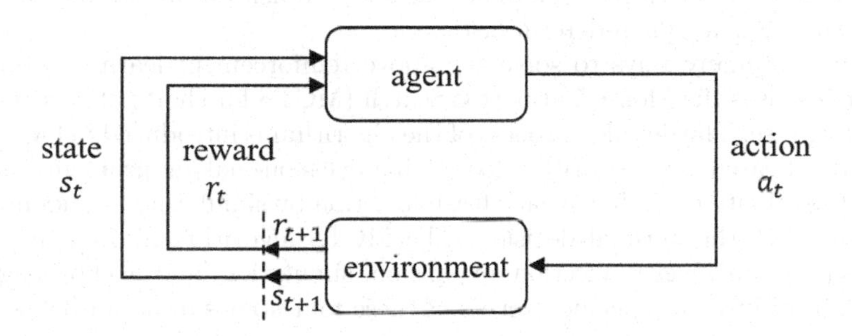

Fig. 3. The interaction process between the agent and the environment.

$$S_0 \xrightarrow[r_1]{a_1} S_1 \xrightarrow[r_2]{a_2} S_2 \cdots \xrightarrow[r_T]{a_T} S_T \tag{1}$$

Go is a very classic reinforcement learning problem [16]. In order to allow computers to play chess like humans, countless scientists have come up with various methods to improve the intelligence of computers. Until the appearance of AlphaGo, it really proved that the computer can reach the intelligence beyond the human level by virtue of its powerful computing ability. Go can be described as the following Markov decision process: A: All legal positions, as the game progresses, more and more positions will be occupied, and the action space will decrease accordingly; S: The collection of all possible states of the game is inexhaustible; R: lose, win or draw at the end; P: A chess piece placed at a certain position will cause a fixed state transition, and the state transition function is deterministic.

Table 1. Differences between Go and Curling as Markov Decision Processes.

	Go	Curling
Action Space	Discrete	Continuous
State Space	Discrete	Continuous
Reward	Loss, Win or Draw	Loss, Win or Draw
Transition	Deterministic	Non-Deterministic

For digital curling, we can also abstract it as a Markov Decision Process, and each element can be embodied in the following way. A: The set of all initial velocities, angles and rotation directions is a range value and is continuous. S: There are infinitely many representations for the position of each curling stone, so the state space is continuous. R: The return value is determined by the final loss, win or draw. P: In actual curling game, the state transition probability matrix is non-deterministic. Due to various reasons, the speed and trajectory of the planned curling stone always have errors with the actual speed and trajectory. In order to be closer to the real scene, the state transition probability matrix of digital curling is also non-deterministic.

There are many ways to solve the above reinforcement learning problems. This article uses the Monte Carlo Tree Search (MCTS for short) algorithm [3] as a teaching case. The detailed process of the algorithm is introduced below. Monte Carlo Tree Search is an algorithm for solving decision-making problems. Its core idea is to evaluate the value of each feasible action by simulating a random game, so as to select the optimal decision. The MCTS algorithm divides the search process into four stages: selection, expansion, simulation, and backpropagation. We will introduce the specific process of these four stages in detail below.

Selection: In the selection phase, the MCTS algorithm traverses the search tree from the root node, and selects an incompletely explored child node for expansion according to a certain strategy. Commonly used strategies include UCB1 algorithm and PUCB algorithm [3]. Both strategies are derived from the multi-armed bandit problem, which ensures that the algorithm maintains a balance between exploration and exploitation [1]. The UCB1 algorithm is a commonly used Upper Confidence Bound (UCB) [8] strategy. When selecting a child node, it considers the winning rate and the number of explorations of the node, and adopts the following equation.

$$UCB_i = \frac{w_i}{n_i} + c\sqrt{\frac{lnN}{n_i}} \tag{2}$$

Among them, UCB_i represents the UCB value of the child node i, w_i represents the number of victories of the child node i, and n_i represents the number of explorations of the child node i, N represents the total number of explorations of the current node, and c is a constant.

Expansion: After the selection phase ends, the MCTS algorithm will expand according to the selected child nodes, that is, add one or more child nodes to the next layer of the current node. These new child nodes represent all possible actions in the current state.

Simulation: After the expansion phase ends, the MCTS algorithm evaluates the value of each feasible action by simulating a random game. This process is often referred to as "rollout" or "playout". During the simulation, the MCTS algorithm starts from the current state and randomly selects actions until the end of the game. This evaluates the odds of winning for each feasible action and updates the corresponding statistics for the nodes in the search tree.

Backpropagation: After the simulation phase ends, the MCTS algorithm updates statistics from the simulation results, feeding back the simulation results to each node in the search tree. This process is called backtracking or backpropagation. Specifically, the MCTS algorithm will backtrack upwards from the simulated leaf node, and update the number of victories and the number of explorations of each node. If the current node is the victory node of player i, the number of victories w_i will be increased by 1; At the same time, the number of explorations n_i of the current node is increased by 1. This updates the win rate estimates for each node, providing a reference for subsequent selection and expansion phases.

During the backpropagation process, the MCTS algorithm also needs to update the action value of each node for use in the next selection of child nodes. Action value refers to the contribution to the player's winning rate from the current node and the actions passing through the node. Specifically, the MCTS algorithm calculates the average win rate and action value of each node, and combines them to calculate the action value. This provides more precise information for the subsequent selection and expansion phases.

Through the four stages of iterative selection, expansion, simulation and backpropagation, the MCTS algorithm can gradually deepen the search space and continuously improve the accuracy and efficiency of decision-making. This enables the MCTS algorithm to obtain good running results in complex digital curling environments.

In the actual operation of the MCTS algorithm, thousands of times of cyclic search are often required to obtain a relatively good result. Generally speaking, the more times you search, the better the strategy you get, and the higher the expected score. By adjusting the number of searches, students can observe how the MCTS algorithm extracts a better strategy step by step from a poor strategy distribution; By adjusting the hyperparameters of the MCTS algorithm, students can observe the different construction processes of the tree structure, thereby deepening their understanding of the MCTS algorithm; By comparing the MCTS-based deep reinforcement learning method with the general reinforcement learning method, students can more intuitively feel the convergence process of the neural network in reinforcement learning and the reasons for the convergence.

In the teaching case, we used the Monte Carlo tree search algorithm based on deep reinforcement learning. Figure 4 show the path of backpropagation in MCTS of curling after selection, expansion and simulation. In the figure, we use the red box to circle the node path we selected for this search. In the fourth layer, we circled one of the nodes we expanded, and did not draw the other newly expanded nodes. In the simulation phase, we use a deep neural network to obtain this value estimate instead of using a "rollout" strategy. Finally, according to the value obtained in the simulation stage, wake up the backpropagation according to the path shown in the Fig. 4.

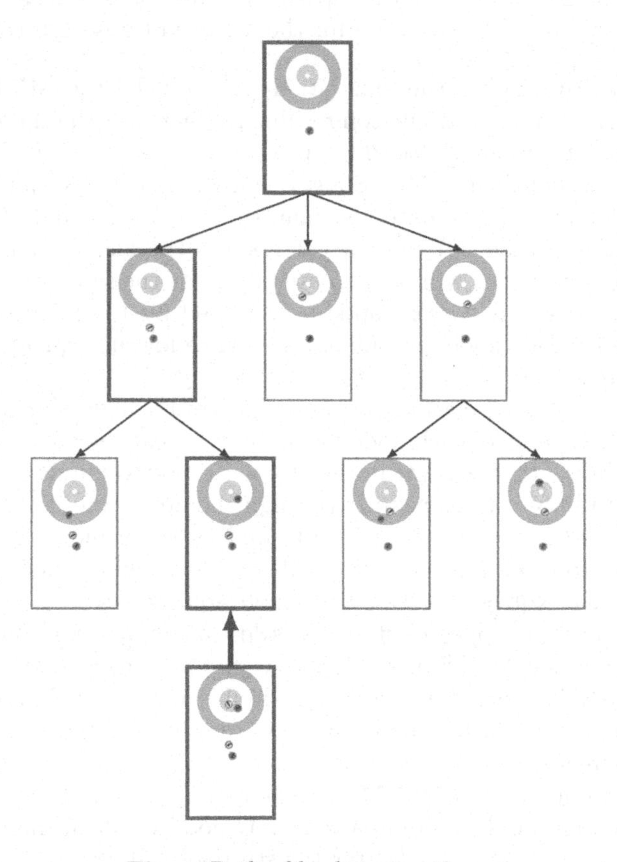

Fig. 4. Path of backpropagation.

4 Simulation Environment of Digital Curling

In order to better realize the teaching link of intensive learning, we design a digital curling environment. The overall digital architecture is shown in Fig. 5. The core of digital curling is the curling simulation module. According to the three-stage principle, this module uses the physics engine Pymunk [2] to simulate the curling process, and the simulation results are basically consistent with the real curling skating process. The specifications of the entire digital curling are designed strictly according to the size of the standard curling field, and it is also equipped with a rendering interface, Through the interface, students can see the trajectory and process of curling in real time, and can better feel the impact of throwing strategies on the current situation in curling game. In order to prevent students from tampering with the digital curling environment and affecting the design of the algorithm, only some interfaces of the program are reserved for students to write corresponding algorithms.

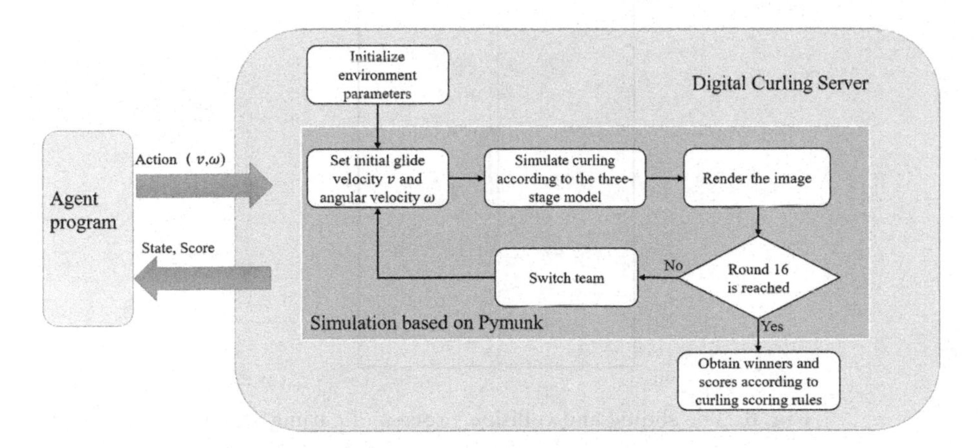

Fig. 5. Digital curling teaching environment design. Students can test and verify their algorithms by interacting with the server through the interface.

Students can use their own programs to compete with other curling algorithms through a specific interface, and count the results, so as to test the performance of different algorithms. Through these competitions, students' enthusiasm for debugging algorithms can be effectively mobilized. At the same time, it can help students understand the rules of curling game and enhance the influence of curling game. It can also improve students' algorithm level through competitions and enhance students' enthusiasm for learning algorithms.

In the digital curling we built, the curling stones can spin, curl and collide like curling stones in real curling game. Figure 6 demonstrates the spin, curl, and collision of a thrown curling stone. As shown in Fig. 6, since both the rotation speed and the sliding speed are not 0, when the yellow curling stone is sliding in our simulator, the motion trajectory also curls. Then the yellow curling stone collided with the red curling stone, and after the collision, the yellow curling stone continued to slide while curling slightly. The red curling stone is the one that is hit, and its rotation speed is always 0, so the red curling stone slides along a straight line for a period of time after being hit and then stops in the field.

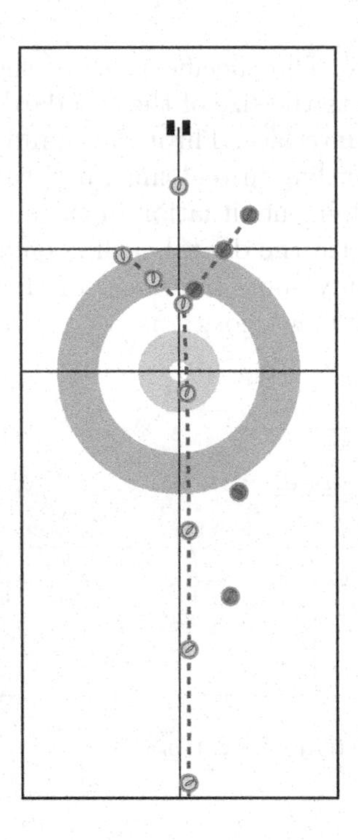

Fig. 6. The sliding and collision process of curling stones.

5 Battle Modes with Different Algorithms

In order to highlight the algorithm part of the teaching example in this paper, we also package and standardize the digital curling simulator. Specifically, we set a unified standard interface to realize the interaction between the algorithm and the digital curling simulator. In this way, on the one hand, it can reduce the difficulty for students to use digital curling. On the other hand, it can also hide the implementation process and important variables of digital curling to prevent data tampering. In addition, in order to facilitate students to test, compare and compete with different algorithms on a unified platform, we also built a digital curling server. Digital curling is used as the server side, and various curling Strategy algorithms are used as the client side, so that the two can realize real-time message transmission through socket or network. Each interface on the server side adopts a unified data format, and any client request that does not use the specified data format will be rejected by the server side.

Through the digital curling server, students can implement various program execution algorithm battles and compare the algorithm performance of different algorithms. For example, students can develop a simple rule-based curling strategy algorithm and an MCTS-based curling strategy algorithm, and then connect to the digital curling server and compete. After the game, students can analyze the difference between the two algorithms by counting the game time, score and other results. By using the server-side as the battle platform, students save the trouble of installing different algorithm operating environments, and at the same time, the server can ensure the fairness of the battle between different algorithms. This greatly facilitates the development of teaching activities.

6 Conclusion

In short, as a competitive sport, curling game is a test of the participants' brain power, and digital curling inherits this feature of curling game. In order to use deep learning to implement the curling strategy algorithm, there are many algorithms that can be selected, among which the MCTS algorithm based on deep learning used in this paper can effectively implement a high-level curling strategy algorithm. At the same time, MCTS is a method that integrates multiple fields such as data structure, mathematics, machine learning, deep neural network, and reinforcement learning, and can effectively integrate various knowledge learned by students. It can also enable students to recognize and understand the classroom knowledge contained in practical problems, and help students establish the thinking habit of integrating multidisciplinary knowledge to solve practical problems.

As a classic problem of uncertain state transition function in continuous action space, digital curling can replace most reinforcement learning problems and become the baseline of some algorithm experiments. This paper uses digital curling as an actual case of algorithm teaching, which can improve students' practical ability on the one hand. Due to the strong interaction of curling game, students can understand the advantages and disadvantages and differences of algorithms by researching and comparing different algorithms, and promote students' cooperative learning and communication. On the other hand, curling, as a sport, has a rich cultural background and historical origin, which can stimulate students' interest and spirit of exploration, and promote students' in-depth understanding and learning of artificial intelligence. At the same time, digital curling has a certain degree of entertainment, which can fully mobilize the enthusiasm of students, so that students can learn happily.

Acknowledgements. This work is supported by the National Natural Science Foundation of China (61976071), the Natural Science Foundation of Heilongjiang Province of China (LH2020F012), the Key Research and Development Plan Task of Heilongjiang Province (GA21C031), and the National Key Research and Development Plan Task of China (2021YFF0307903).

References

1. Auer, P., Cesa-Bianchi, N., Fischer, P.: Finite-time analysis of the multiarmed bandit problem. Mach. Learn. **47**, 235–256 (2002)
2. Blomqvist, V.: pymunk (2023). http://www.pymunk.org/
3. Browne, C.B., et al.: A survey of monte Carlo tree search methods. IEEE Trans. Comput. Intell. AI Games **4**(1), 1–43 (2012)

4. Cao, Z., Jiang, K., Zhou, W., Xu, S., Peng, H., Yang, D.: Continuous improvement of self-driving cars using dynamic confidence-aware reinforcement learning. Nature Mach. Intell. **5**(2), 145–158 (2023)
5. Chen, I.J., Aapro, M., Kipnis, A., Ilin, A., Liljeroth, P., Foster, A.S.: Precise atom manipulation through deep reinforcement learning. Nat. Commun. **13**(1), 7499 (2022)
6. Dayan, P., Niv, Y.: Reinforcement learning: the good, the bad and the ugly. Curr. Opin. Neurobiol. **18**(2), 185–196 (2008)
7. Fawzi, A., et al.: Discovering faster matrix multiplication algorithms with reinforcement learning. Nature **610**(7930), 47–53 (2022)
8. Garivier, A., Moulines, E.: On upper-confidence bound policies for switching bandit problems. In: Kivinen, J., Szepesvári, C., Ukkonen, E., Zeugmann, T. (eds.) ALT 2011. LNCS (LNAI), vol. 6925, pp. 174–188. Springer, Heidelberg (2011). https://doi.org/10.1007/978-3-642-24412-4_16
9. Haikuo, Z.: Research on digital curling strategy based on reinforcement learning (2021)
10. He, Z.: 21 Projects to Play with Deep Learning - Detailed Explanation Based on TensorFlow Practice. Publishing House of Electronics Industry (2018)
11. Kaelbling, L.P., Littman, M.L., Moore, A.W.: Reinforcement learning: a survey. J. Artif. Intell. Res. **4**, 237–285 (1996)
12. Liu, G., Tang, X., Cheng, H.D., Huang, J., Liu, J.: A novel approach for tracking high speed skaters in sports using a panning camera. Pattern Recogn. **42**(11), 2922–2935 (2009)
13. Liu, G., Tang, X., Huang, J., Liu, J., Sun, D.: Hierarchical model-based human motion tracking via unscented Kalman filter. In: 2007 IEEE 11th International Conference on Computer Vision, pp. 1–8. IEEE (2007)
14. Nyberg, H., Alfredson, S., Hogmark, S., Jacobson, S.: The asymmetrical friction mechanism that puts the curl in the curling stone. Wear **301**(1–2), 583–589 (2013)
15. Nyberg, H., Hogmark, S., Jacobson, S.: Calculated trajectories of curling stones sliding under asymmetrical friction. In: Nordtrib 2012, 15th Nordic Symposium on Tribology, 12–15 June 2012, Trondheim, Norway (2012)
16. Pumperla, M., Ferguson, K.: Deep Learning and The Game of Go, vol. 231. Manning Publications Company Shelter Island, NY, USA (2019)
17. Feng, S., Xiaoyi Yuan, H.X.: Knowledge of winter olympics-curling. Youth Sports (12), 24–25 (2018)
18. Silver, D., et al.: Mastering the game of go with deep neural networks and tree search. Nature **529**(7587), 484–489 (2016)
19. Silver, D., et al.: Mastering the game of go without human knowledge. Nature **550**(7676), 354–359 (2017)
20. Wagenmaker, A.J., Chen, Y., Simchowitz, M., Du, S., Jamieson, K.: Reward-free RL is no harder than reward-aware RL in linear markov decision processes. In: International Conference on Machine Learning, pp. 22430–22456. PMLR (2022)
21. Qiu, Y., Xinle Gao, F.W.: Case design of experimental teaching of reinforcement learning algorithms based on temporal difference learning. J. Anqing Normal Univ. **28**(01), 109–115 (2022)

Improving Programming Education Based on Programming Contest Problems: The Algorithm Implementation for the Constructive Proof of Euler Graph

Yonghui Wu[1,2](✉)

[1] Fudan University, Shanghai 200433, China
yhwu@fudan.edu.cn

[2] Quanzhou University of Information Engineering, Quanzhou 362000, China

Abstract. "Set and Graph Theory" is the theoretical foundation for computer science and technology. We construct joint experimental curriculums for set and graph theory and programming curriculums based on programming contest problems, to improve students' skills solving problems by programming and comprehensively applying knowledge. The paper specifies a joint experimental curriculum for set and graph theory and data structure "the algorithm implementation for the constructive proof of Euler graph". A programming contest problem solving Eulerian circuit and its analysis constitute the experiment. Students are required to finish the constructive proof of Euler graph based on DFS, and realize the proof is the algorithm finding the Eulerian circuit. Solving the problem by programming requires students to comprehensively apply DFS, Union-Find Set used to determine graph connectivity, graph modeling, and so on.

Keywords: Programming · Set and Graph Theory · Euler Graph · DFS · Constructive Proof · Union-Find Set · Graph Modeling

1 Introduction

"Set and Graph Theory" is the theoretical foundation for computer science and technology. The curriculum includes set, graph theory and Combinatorics. The goal for "Set and Graph Theory", on the one hand, is to lay the theoretical foundation of students' computer professional knowledge system, and polish students' thinking mode in mathematical way; on the other hand, it shows the relationships between Set and Graph Theory and other curriculums, makes students understand the knowledge system of computer science and technology better, and apply theoretical knowledge to solve practical problems.

The current programming curriculums in universities, programming languages, data structure, algorithm analysis and design, and set and graph theory, have been experienced curriculum construction many years, and there are many classic textbooks. However, on the one hand, these curriculums are relatively independent from each other; and on the

J. Gan et al. (Eds.): CSEI 2023, CCIS 1899, pp. 285–291, 2024.
https://doi.org/10.1007/978-981-99-9499-1_24

other hand, programming curriculums are mainly classroom-teaching models, and focus on teaching contents. Students' skills solving problems by programming can hardly be polished. And set and graph theory does not make the students realize the relationships between the theoretical foundation and other curriculums in computer field well, nor does it make the students' ability to solve practical problems with theory well.

Programming contests are contests solving problems by programming. A large number of programming contest problems have been accumulated these years. And if these problems are used in education, students' programming skills solving problems can be improved greatly.

In teaching material construction based on programming contest problems, the book series "Collegiate Programming Contests and Education" has been compiled and published [1–5].

Based on the book series, curriculums are constructed [6, 7]. In these curriculums, case teaching is widely used as the teaching model, and online judge systems and virtual online programming contests are widely used as the informatization technologies.

The paper specifies a joint experimental curriculum for set and graph theory and data structure "the algorithm implementation for the constructive proof of Euler graph". First, union-find set used to determine graph connectivity is introduced. The experiment of union-find set is also a joint experimental curriculum of set and graph theory and data structure. Second, the experiment "the algorithm implementation for the constructive proof of Euler graph" is showed. The algorithm calculating Euler circuit is given based on the constructive proof of Euler graph. A programming contest problem "The Necklace" and its analysis and solution constitute the experiment and show comprehensively applying DFS, Union-Find Set used to determine graph connectivity, and graph modeling to solve the programming contest problem "The Necklace".

2 Union-Find Sets Used to Determine Graph Connectivity

In reality, there is a relationship of "Birds of a feather flock together", which is defined as follows:

Definition 1(Partition, Block). Suppose S is a set. $S_i \subseteq S$, $S_i \neq \emptyset$, $i = 1,2, \ldots, n$. If $S_1 \cup S_2 \cup \ldots\ldots \cup S_n = S$, and $S_i \cap S_j = \emptyset$, where $i, j = 1, 2, \ldots, n$, and $i \neq j$, then $\pi = \{S_1, S_2, \ldots, S_n\}$ is a partition for S, and each S_i is a block for π.

Because such problems are more about set operations for union and search, $\pi = \{S_1, S_2, \ldots, S_n\}$ is called union-find sets.

Union-find sets $\pi = \{S_1, S_2, \ldots, S_n\}$ are disjoint sets, where set S_i has an element $rep[S_i]$, called the representative for S_i. There are three specific set operations for union-find sets.

1. *Make_Set*(x): For union-find sets $\pi = \{S_1, S_2, \ldots, S_r\}$, a set only containing one element $\{x\}$ is added into π, and its representative $rep[\{x\}] = x$, where x is not in any S_i, $1 \leq i \leq r$. Initially, for each element x, *Make_Set*(x) is called and constitute π.

2. *Join*(x, y): For union-find sets $\pi = \{S_1, S_2, \ldots, S_r\}$, the union of two different sets S_x and S_y containing x and y respectively is denoted by *join*(x, y). That is, S_x and S_y are deleted from π, and $S_x \cup S_y$ is joined into π.

3. *Set_find*(x): For union-find sets $\pi = \{S_1, S_2, \ldots, S_r\}$, element x is in Set S_x, and *set_find*(x) returns representative *rep*[S_x] for Set S_x.

A set S_i in union-find sets $\pi = \{S_1, S_2, \ldots, S_r\}$can be represented as a tree, where the root is the representative for the set. It is showed as Fig. 1.

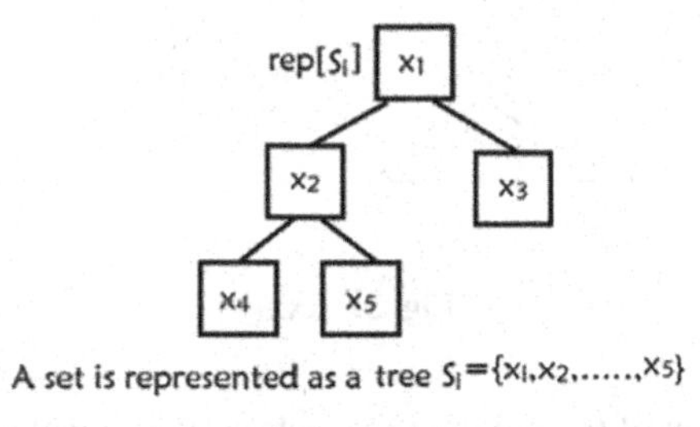

Fig. 1. Xxx.

In the tree representing a set in union-find sets, each vertex p has a pointer *set*[p] pointing to its parent. If *set*[p] < 0, p is the root. Initially, one element constitutes a set, that is, for each element p, *set*[p] < 0.

In the search operation for union-find sets, the search should be with "path compression" to reduce the depth of the tree. It is showed in Fig. 2(a). If element y_2 in the set is required to search, then the search path is y_2-y_3-y_1-x_1 and the representative is x_1. The search path is compressed and set pointers for y_2, y_3, and y_1 should point to x_1. It is showed in Fig. 2(b).

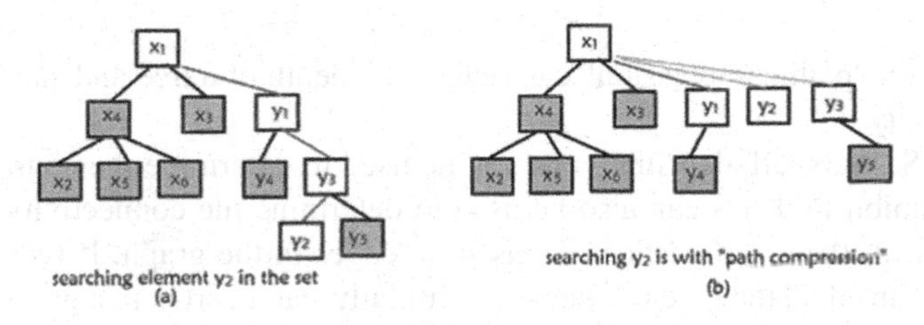

searching element y2 in the set
(a)
searching y2 is with "path compression"
(b)

Fig. 2. Xxx.

The program segment of the search operation for union-find sets is as follows. First, from vertex x, through set pointers the root of the tree f (*set*[f] < 0) is found. Then set pointers for each vertex on the path from x to f point to f to compress the path. The search operation is implemented by a recursive function *set_find*.

```
int set_find(int p)
{
    if (set[p]<0)
        return p;
    return set[p]=set_find(set[p]);
}
```

The union of two different sets in union-find sets is to connect roots for the two corresponding trees. Suppose one set contains element x, and its representative is fx; and the other set contains element y, and its representative is fy. The union of two different sets is to let the set pointer for fx point to fy (Fig. 3).

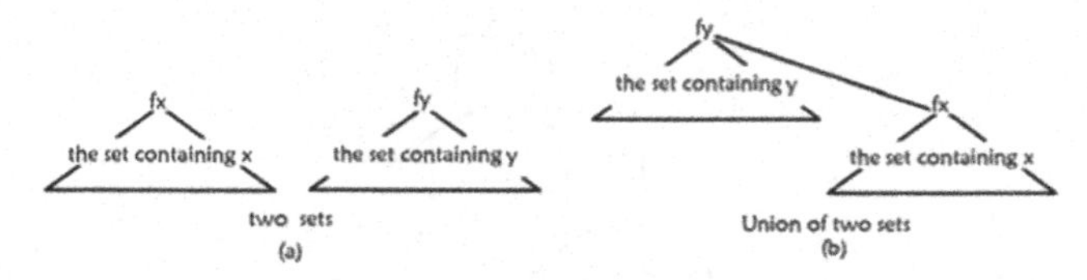

Fig. 3. Xxx.

The program segment of the union of two sets containing elements p and q in union-find sets is as follows. First, search representatives for union-find set containing p and q. If representatives are equal, then p and q are in the same union-find set; else the set containing p is joined into the set containing q, that is, the set pointer for p points to q:

```
void join(int p, int q)
{
   p=set_find(p);
   q=set_find(q);
   if (p!=q)
      set[p]=q;
}
```

Search with "path compression" can reduce the depth of a tree and can improve the time complexity.

BFS, DFS, Warshell algorithm, etc. can be used to determine the connectivity of a graph. And union-find sets can also be used to determine the connectivity of a graph: The partition for the set of vertices is based on edges in the graph. If two vertices are connected by an edge, they are in a same set. Initially, each vertex in a graph constitutes a set. Then, input the edges in the graph. If the two vertices are associated with an edge, and are in two different sets, then the two sets should be merged. Repeat the above process to get the partition of the set of vertices. Finally, if all vertices are in a same set, the graph is connected; otherwise, the graph is not connected, and each partition for the set of vertices is a connected component of the graph.

3 The Algorithm Implementation for the Constructive Proof of Euler Graph

3.1 The Constructive Proof of Euler Graph Based on DFS

Definition 2(Euler Circuit, Euler graph). A circuit in a graph G containing all edges is called an Euler circuit of G. And graph G is called Euler graph.

The theorem and the constructive proof of Euler graph based on DFS is as follow.

Theorem 1. Graph G is connected. Graph G is an Euler graph if and only if degrees for all vertices are even.

Proof. If graph G is an Euler graph, G must has an Euler circuit $x_1\ x_2\ \ldots\ x_m$, where $x_1 = x_m$. Vertex x_i occurs k times in Euler circuit $x_1\ x_2\ \ldots\ x_m$, $1 \leq i \leq m$-1. Therefore, the degree for vertex x_i is an even number $2k$. Therefore, degrees for all vertices are even.

Because G is connected and degrees for all vertices are even, DFS can be used to find a circuit C in G. If C=G, then C is an Euler circuit of G. Else C doesn't contain all edges in G, in C there must be a vertex v_k, whose degree in G is larger than the degree in C. From v_k a cuicuit C' whose edges aren't in C can be founded by DFS. If $C \cup C'$=G, then $C \cup C'$ is an Euler circuit. Else DFS is recursively used to find a new circuit whose edges aren't in $C \cup C'$. Repeat the above process until the Euler circuit is found. ■

Obviously the proof for necessity is also the algorithm finding the Euler circuit.

3.2 The Experiment for the Algorithm Implementation for the Constructive Proof of Euler Graph: The Necklace

In the experiment, students are required to solve a programming contest problem "the necklace" by programming. The program should pass the official test data or online judge systems within the time and memory limits.

The problem description is as follow.

A girl has a necklace made of colorful beads. Two successive beads in the necklace shares a common color at their meeting point. Figure 4 shows a segment of the necklace:

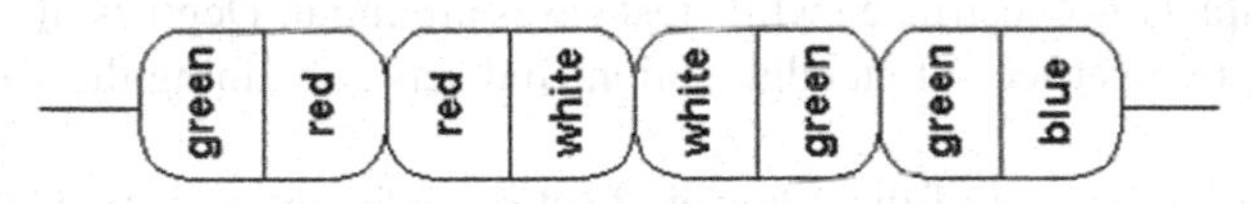

Fig. 4. Xxx.

One day, the necklace was torn and the beads were all scattered over the floor. The girl recollects beads from the floor, but she is not sure whether she was able to collect all beads. She asks me whether she can to make a necklace using beads she collects. That is, two successive beads in the new necklace also shares a common color at their meeting point.

Please write a program to give the answer.

The input contains several test cases. The first line of the input gives the number of test cases T.

For each test case, the first line shows an integer N ($5 \leq N \leq 100$), the number of beads that the girl recollects. For the next N lines, each line shows two integers representing colors of a recollected bead. Colors are represented by a integer interval, [1, 50].

For each test case, first output the test case number as shown in the sample output. Then if beads that the girl recollects can't constitute the necklace, output recollects "some beads may be lost" on a line. Otherwise, output N lines and each line represents a bead with two integers showing the colors of its two ends. For $1 \leq i \leq N$-1, the second integer on line i must be the same as the first integer on line $i + 1$. Additionally, the second integer on line N must be equal to the first integer on line 1.

Output a blank line between two successive test cases.

3.3 Analysis and Solutions to the Experiment: Data Structure + Algorithm = Program

Graphs provides a natural structure. Graph models are suitable for almost all fields of science (natural science and social science), if we need study objects and relationships among objects in this field.

The most important thing for creating a graph model is: in the graph, what are vertices (objects)? What are edges (relationships among objects)?

For the experiment "the necklace", if we take an intuitive approach, beads are represented as vertices, and if two beads can be connected, there is an edges between the two beads, the graph can't represent the problem well. For example, there are three beads (red | green), (red | white) and (red | red), the circuit (green | red) (red | white) (red | red) can be gotten in the graph. Obviously, the graph can't represent objects and relationships among objects.

A graph $G(V, E)$ is created. Each color is represented as a color, $V = \{ v_1, v_2, \ldots\ldots, v_m\}$. And each bead is represented by an edge. If there is a bead ($c1$, $c2$), there is an edge $\{v_{c1}, v_{c2}\}$. Therefore, the problem whether a necklace can be made from collected beads is the problem whether there is a Euler circuit in a graph.

The algorithm is as follow.

Step 1: Graph G is constructed while test cases are input. Degrees of all vertices are calculated. For two vertices of an edge, union-find sets containing the two vertices are merged.

Step 2: Search the root of the union-find set of each vertex: if two vertices belong to different union-find sets, graph G is not connected, and Euler circuit does not exist. Otherwise,

Step 3: If there is a vertex with odd degree, Euler circuit does not exist. Otherwise,

Step 4: DFS is used to search an Euler circuit.

4 Conclusion

The paper shows a joint experimental curriculum for Set and Graph Theory "The Algorithm Implementation for the Constructive Proof of Euler Graph". The experiment is as an example. Through it we show our work improving programming education based on programming contest problems: Programming contest problems and their analysis constitute experiments, and experiments are basic for our teaching materials and curriculums. Students solve problems by programming and comprehensively applying knowledge.

The work is financially supported by following projects: Research projects for Computer Education from Association of Fundamental Computing Education in Chinese Universities, and China Machine Press (HZ Books) (2022-AFCEC-028); and from

Association of Fundamental Computing Education in Chinese Universities, and Xidian University Press (2022-AFCEC-029); Fudan Good Practice Program of Teaching and Learning (FD2022A106), and Ministry of education – Aliyun collaborative education project (220500643282258, 220600643265604).

References

1. Wu, Y., Wang, J.: Data Structure Practice: for Collegiate Programming Contest and Education. 3rd edn. China Machine Press, Beijing (2021)
2. Zhou, J., Wu, Y.: Preliminary Programming Practice: for Collegiate Programming Contest and Education. 1st edn. China Machine Press, Beijing (2021)
3. Wu, Y., Wang, J.: Algorithm Design Practice: for Collegiate Programming Contest and Education. 2nd edn. China Machine Press, Beijing (2020)
4. Wu, Y., Wang, J.: Algorithm Design Practice: for Collegiate Programming Contest and Education. 1st edn. CRC Press, Orlando (2018)
5. Wu, Y., Wang, J.: Data Structure Practice: for Collegiate Programming Contest and Education. 1st edn. CRC Press. Orlando (2016)
6. Wu, Y.: The implementation for polishing students' programming skills solving problems. In: Proceedings of the 2021 International Conference on Diversified Education and Social Development, pp. 92–97. Atlantis Press, Beijing (2021)
7. Wu, Y.: Promoting students' programming skills in constructions for teaching materials and curriculums: experiments for comprehensive application of programming methods. In: Proceedings of 2022 Global Conference on Robotics, Artificial Intelligence and Information Technology (GCRAIT), pp. 770–773. IEEE CPS (2022)

Research on the Teaching Model of Interdisciplinary Computational Thinking Cultivating from the Perspective of Problem-Solving

Gongli Li[1,2], Xixi Liu[1,2](✉), and Jingwen Hou[1,2]

[1] Computer and Information Engineering, Henan Normal University, Xinxiang, China
XXLLL0419@163.com

[2] Big Data Engineering Lab of Teaching Resources and Assessment of Education Quality, Xinxiang, Henan, China

Abstract. Computational thinking is a thinking process related to formal problems and their solutions, and the development of students' computational thinking skills is one of the important objectives of basic IT teaching. This paper explores the feasibility of developing computational thinking skills through mathematical problem solving using Python programming. To accomplish this, we conducted a literature review spanning the past ten years, focusing on the keywords "IT computational thinking" and "mathematical problem solving" in basic education. The analysis of the literature allowed us to assess the current state of research. We generated keyword clusters to uncover the intrinsic link between IT computational thinking and mathematics in problem solving. Based on this analysis, we developed a model that integrates the sub-competencies of computational thinking and the elements of mathematical problem solving. Furthermore, we designed teaching activities and provided targeted teaching suggestions to promote the development of learners' computational thinking in various aspects. Our intention is to offer new perspectives and research ideas for the advancement of computational thinking education.

Keywords: Computational Thinking · Information Technology · Mathematical Problem Solving · Interdisciplinary

1 Introduction

Since the concept of computational thinking was introduced, it has received widespread attention and great importance from scholars in various countries. It is also regarded as an essential literacy and survival skill for citizens in the 21st century [1]. Computational thinking helps students to better understand the information world, to use and create

This paper is supported by the Higher Education Teaching Reform research and practice project in Henan Province (2021GLX110)

J. Gan et al. (Eds.): CSEI 2023, CCIS 1899, pp. 292–303, 2024.
https://doi.org/10.1007/978-981-99-9499-1_25

technology effectively, and to apply computational thinking to solve problems. Therefore, it plays an important role in the K12 education system. In fact, 12 European Union countries have included computational thinking in their compulsory education curriculum. In addition, China's "Information Technology Curriculum Standards for General High School (2017 Edition)" and "Information Technology Curriculum Standards for Compulsory Education (2022 Edition)" both explicitly propose computational thinking as a core literacy in the subject of information technology. The core of this curriculum is reflected in the development of students' computational thinking and points to the problem-solving process.

With its long history as a traditional subject, mathematics has undergone extensive research and exploration to foster students' logical thinking abilities. It is primarily focused on equipping students with problem-solving skills, characterized by its high level of abstraction, rigorous logic, and broad practical applications [2]. Recognized as a fundamental IT competency that has garnered significant attention in recent years, computational thinking raises the question of whether there exists an inherent relationship between these two disciplines and if they can mutually enhance each other's development. To address this query, this paper begins by analyzing the current state of research on both fields based on the essential concepts found in the CNKI database. Next, by utilizing CiteSpace software, keyword clusters are created to explore the interconnections between the inherent elements of mathematics and computational thinking, as well as the feasibility of integrating them within the discipline. Lastly, by combining the attributes of problem-solving processes present in both disciplines, a model for interdisciplinary integration is proposed, aimed at cultivating computational thinking. This model includes the design of teaching activities and offers recommendations for the teaching process, ultimately fostering the development of computational thinking across different academic subjects.

2 Conceptual Cognition

In 2006, Professor Yi-Zhen Zhou proposed that "computational thinking is a thinking activity that uses computer science to solve problems, design systems and understand human behaviour, not by thinking like a computer, but by thinking like a computer scientist [3]. Since then, scholars have delved into the concept of computational thinking from two major perspectives: "thinking skills theory" and "process elements theory." The "thinking skills theory" asserts that computational thinking is a way of thinking that includes characteristics of creative thinking, engineering thinking, design thinking, mathematical thinking, and other ways of thinking. It is considered a problem-solving skill that everyone must possess. The "process element theory" asserts that computational thinking is the process of systematically dividing a problem into different levels and solving each problem at different levels [4].

Modern scholars have expanded the understanding of mathematical problem solving beyond extensive training in mathematical exercises. They have focused on the development of learners' strategies and thinking in the process of problem solving. Cognitive scientists define problem solving as purposeful and directed problem solving, falling under the category of thinking activities. From the learner's perspective, mathematical problem solving involves mental activity, using mathematical knowledge and methods to solve practical problems, and promoting the development of human thinking. From the educator's perspective, mathematical problem solving serves as a pedagogical goal, evaluating pedagogical outcomes based on problem-solving skills and the quality of mathematical thinking. It also serves as a pedagogical tool emphasizing the development of problem-solving skills and the quality of mathematical thinking through students' learning of the knowledge embedded in problem conditions [5].

Computational thinking, in the context of problem solving, is concerned with the behavior of specified objects and explains and points to behavior of a general nature. On the other hand, mathematical problem solving focuses on problems within the mathematics curriculum. Despite these nuances, problem solving involves a process of logic, reasoning, and abstraction, which are integral to computational thinking [6]. Therefore, mathematical problem solving represents a concrete manifestation of the problem-solving model of computational thinking in the field of mathematics.

3 Current Status of Research

The article uses the bibliometric method in the CNKI database from January 2012 to December 2022 to explore the current status of research on IT computational thinking and mathematical problem-solving in the field of education. The scope of the research is limited to the basic education stage. A total of 230 articles were retrieved using the keyword "IT computational thinking", while 665 articles were retrieved using the keyword "mathematical problem solving". The trend of the number of articles published in the last decade or so was plotted as shown in Fig. 1.

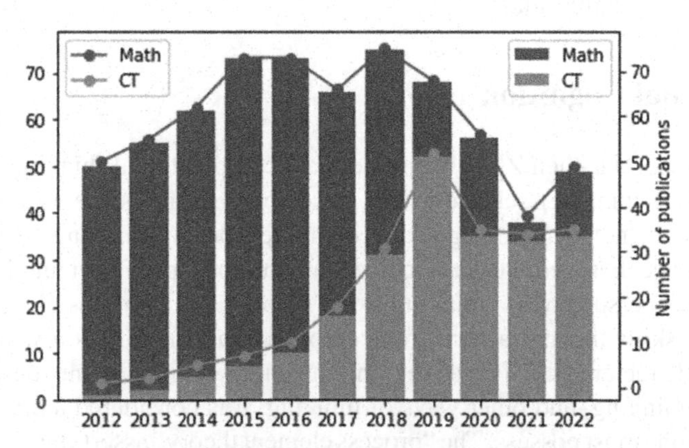

Fig. 1. Trends in postings over the last decade.

The annual publication volume of literature is a mapping of research content in time, and it is important to predict the development trend. In the early stage, the number of articles published on mathematics problem solving is larger and less volatile than that of IT computational thinking. This is due to the advantage of mathematics as the main subject of basic education. On the other hand, IT computational thinking had a slow increment in the early stage but started to increase significantly in 2017. The reason for this is the promulgation of the "General High School Information Technology Curriculum Standards (2017) Edition", which includes "computational thinking" as one of the four core literacies and the core problem-solving method of the IT curriculum. From the beginning of the search in 2012 to 2022, the gap between the number of computational thinking and mathematical problem solving studies in information technology was large in the early period. However, now the gap between the number of articles published has been narrowing, indicating that computational thinking has received more and more attention from researchers in recent years. It has become a hot spot for educational research, with greater research significance and value.

4 Keyword Clustering Analysis

Keyword clustering analysis can help to understand the evolutionary relationship of knowledge structures and research hotspots in a particular research area. CiteSpace version 6.2.R2 was used to cluster the keywords in slices of 1 year in the last decade or so of articles selected. It measures the degree of affinity and association between subject terms, which are clustered into different categories. The size table indicates the volume of keywords included, and clustering with a size greater than 10 is considered more effective. Silhouette, which indicates the similarity between documents, is another measure. A higher value suggests a greater similarity within the cluster, with a silhouette value greater than 0.7 indicating efficient and convincing clustering. Additionally, the year of the citation peak is noted as the year in which the cluster is most cited [7].

4.1 IT Computational Thinking Keyword Clustering

As shown in Table 1. In the "#1 Classroom Teaching" cluster up to 2017, the integration of computational thinking with the subject of mathematics in primary and secondary school international technology classrooms was observed. However, the new high school international technology standards have influenced the emergence of IT computational thinking in clusters such as "#0 Information Technology", "#3 Teaching Programming", "#4 Programming Education" and "#5 Problem Solving, with a focus on teaching strategies, pedagogy, and development. The use of teaching methods like "visual programming", "flow charting", "mind mapping" and "microlecturing" has formed a training system with international technology subject characteristics. Further exploration is needed to better implement these methods in teaching. The "#6 Thinking Development" cluster emphasizes abstract problem decomposition, algorithm development, and computational skill improvement in teaching computational thinking. The "#7 Grade" cluster highlights learning attitude and feedback from student learning results. Teachers should consider individual students' physical and mental characteristics and learning enthusiasm during reflection, training, and calculation thinking.

Table 1. Clustering Keywords of IT computational thinking research from 2012 to 2022

Cluster	Size	Silhouette	Year	Top Terms
#0 Information Technology	55	0.972	2019	Information technology (13.56); Teaching strategies (7.22); Computational thinking (4.36); Information technology curriculum (4.2); Senior secondary information technology (3.92)
#1 Classroom Teaching	35	0.914	2016	Classroom teaching (10.665); Mathematics (9.81); Lower secondary education (7.08); Primary and secondary schools (7.08); Current status survey (7.08)
#2 Core Literacy	25	0.910	2018	Information society responsibility (9.81), Teaching practice (8.36); Curriculum standards (8.35); Information awareness (6.38); Digital practicability (4.17)
#3 Teaching Programming	15	0.906	2017	Programming teaching (11.07); Programming thinking (11.07); Information literacy (10.22); Competency development (7.381); Primary and secondary articulation (5.51)
#4 Programming Education	14	0.852	2018	Programming education (13.62); Primary (11.93); Thinking maps (8.22); Problem exploration (5.93); Visual programming (5.93)
#5 Problem solving	12	0.952	2018	Problem solving (16.14); Flow charting (10.7); Programming (9.68); Microlearning (5.32); Task-driven approach (5.32)
#6 Thinking Development	12	0.973	2017	Development of thinking (14.55); Abstraction (14.55); Arithmetic (7.37); Decomposition (7); Numeracy (7.2)
#7 Grade	4	0.956	2021	Grade (9.4); Achievement (9.4); Attitude towards learning (9.4); Primary school students (9.4); Information technology (0.85)

4.2 Clustering of Mathematical Problem Solving Keywords

As shown in Table 2. The cluster "#0 Problem Solving" is the largest with a size of 44 and requires an understanding of students' metacognition and the creation of problem situations prior to the problem-solving process. "#5 Ways of Thinking" displays markers such as thinking echoes, mathematical literacy, and mathematical modeling closely related to the characteristics of the subject of mathematics. The clustering identifier of "#7 Mathematical Thinking" integrates various types of thinking, including thinking ability, logical thinking, divergent thinking, computational thinking, and others. The clustering labels "#1 Primary School Mathematics" and "#2 High School Mathematics" indicate that basic education levels emphasize analyzing students' learning situations and training by levels. In contrast, clusters "#3 Mathematics Teaching", "#6 Mathematics Knowledge", "#8 Teaching Methods", and "#9 Images" focus on the process of mathematical problem-solving. Teaching should prioritize students' interest in learning and the application of mathematical knowledge, cooperative learning, and the rational arrangement of teaching content, with visual representations to aid understanding.

Both IT computational thinking and mathematical problem solving exhibit integration between the two disciplines, as evidenced by the presence of identifiers such as visual programming, flowcharting, mind mapping, and function images. These identifiers reflect the shared emphasis of both disciplines on cultivating visual approaches to comprehend abstract subject knowledge, and they highlight the close connection between computer science and mathematics in terms of their approach to education. However, there are certain distinctions between the two. Mathematical problem solving heavily relies on human cognitive abilities, while IT computational thinking leans more towards programming. Mathematical problem solving focuses on exploring the internal laws of mathematics itself, emphasizing theoretical thinking and the development of deductive reasoning skills in students. On the other hand, computational thinking centers around the problem-solving process, involving the gradual decomposition and summarization of ideas for problem-solving, which continuously enhance students' abstract and logical thinking abilities [8]. Computational thinking equips students with the confidence and competence to tackle complex, open-ended problems, employing a step-by-step approach that aligns with their cognitive process when acquiring new knowledge and understanding the unknown. This training process enhances students' ability to solve complex problems.

Table 2. Clustering of mathematical problem solving research keywords from 2012 to 2022

Cluster	Size	Silhouette	Year	Top Terms
#0 Problem Solving	44	0.95	2017	Problem solving (47.28); Pupils (14.57); Metacognition (9.91,); Problem situations (9.915)
#1 Primary School Mathematics	32	0.868	2017	Primary mathematics (64.06); Diversity (23.92); Teaching strategies (23.92); Core literacy (20.47); Information technology (17.03)
#2 High School Mathematics	26	0.916	2016	Senior secondary mathematics (36.93); Problems (16.85); Teacher-student interaction (11.2); Causal stereotypes (11.2); Learning difficulties (11.2)
#3 Mathematics Teaching	26	0.907	2015	Mathematics teaching (37.64); Secondary mathematics (21.18); Development (10.53); Application problems (10.53); Classroom teaching (9.4)
#4 Questions	21	0.812	2016	Problems (37.06); Strategies (36.77); Middle School Mathematics (31.21); Multimedia (10.29); Problem Solving (10.16)

(*continued*)

Table 2. *(continued)*

Cluster	Size	Silhouette	Year	Top Terms
#5 Ways of Thinking	17	0.956	2016	Approach to Thinking (13.37); Thinking Echoes (13.37); Strategic Awareness (9.62); Mathematical Literacy (9.62); Mathematical Modelling (9.62)
#6 Mathematical knowledge	13	0.929	2016	Mathematical Knowledge (15.67); Humanities (15.67); Cooperative Learning (7.78); Statistics and Probability (7.78); Content Arrangement (7.78)
#7 Mathematical Thinking	12	0.877	2014	Mathematical Thinking (24.03); Thinking Skills (19.57); Logical Thinking (7.89); Computational Thinking (7.89); Divergent Thinking (7.89)
#8 Teaching Methods	10	0.936	2014	Teaching methods (16.68); Mathematical thinking (11.19); Students (8.27); Learning applications (8.27); Interest in learning (8.27)
#9 Images	5	0.945	2013	Images (9.87); Periodicity (9.87); Inequalities (9.87); Segmentation functions (9.87)

5 Building a Model for Teaching the Development of Computational Thinking with Interdisciplinary Integration

As the grade level increases, mathematical problems become more difficult and students face many difficulties in learning and developing logical thinking. Mathematics is an abstract and logical subject. In view of this, computational thinking enables complex problems to be broken down and abstracted for solution one by one. Computational thinking can be used as the underlying thinking into the problem-solving process to analyze the problem, with the help of programming tools to solve it with a computer perspective. In mathematics teaching activities, it is important to extract representative knowledge points and create mathematical problem-solving situations. By incorporating computational thinking into the problem-solving process, students can experience the convenience of computer solutions to mathematical problems, which enhances their computational thinking skills [9]. This will enable students to develop more targeted thinking training by linking IT computational thinking and mathematical problem-solving skills, thus improving the quality of students' learning in mathematics and shaping and cultivating logical thinking.

5.1 Analysis of the Elements of Computational Thinking and Mathematical Problem Solving Processes

Problem solving from the perspective of different disciplines has precipitated the formation of their unique problem solving methods over a long period of development. The study analyses the process elements and connotations involved in IT computational thinking problem solving and mathematical problem solving according to the characteristics of problem solving in the disciplines as follows:

Computational thinking for problem solving involves several key steps, including decomposing abstraction, algorithm design, debugging optimization, and assessment summary. Decomposing abstraction entail breaking down complex data and processes into more manageable and simpler problems, while also removing irrelevant details and extracting essential features. Algorithm design requires careful consideration of the decomposed problem and the development of a corresponding algorithm that is aligned with the problem's unique characteristics. Debugging optimization involve identifying and fixing any errors or issues in the algorithm to ensure that the program functions correctly and efficiently. Lastly, assessment summary allows for a better understanding of the algorithm's code, including its strengths, weaknesses, and applicability to a broader range of problems.

To make the problem-solving process clearer and more organized, it can be divided into four essential elements based on the characteristics of mathematics: analysis of the problem, mathematical modeling, verification of solution, and communication evaluation. Analysis of the problem involves understanding the background and conditions of the problem to identify key information. Mathematical modeling involves converting the problem into abstract mathematical models and language, aiding in better comprehension and finding solutions. Verification of solution includes calculations, reasoning, and validation to ensure the correctness of the answers. Communication evaluation requires students to communicate and evaluate the process and results of problem-solving, share methods and strategies, seek feedback, and foster critical thinking and communication skills.

To summarize, computational thinking and logical mathematical thinking both employ a problem-solving process that centers around "disassembly." They also utilize a distinctive thinking approach to resolve the decomposed sub-problem [10].

5.2 Interdisciplinary Integration of Computational Thinking Development Model Design

The study aims to develop computational thinking by using mathematical problem solving as an entry point. It focuses on integrating the development of computational thinking with mathematical problem solving. This is based on the process elements involved in computational thinking problem solving and the characteristics of the mathematical problem solving process. The final model of computational thinking development with an interdisciplinary integration design is shown in Fig. 2.

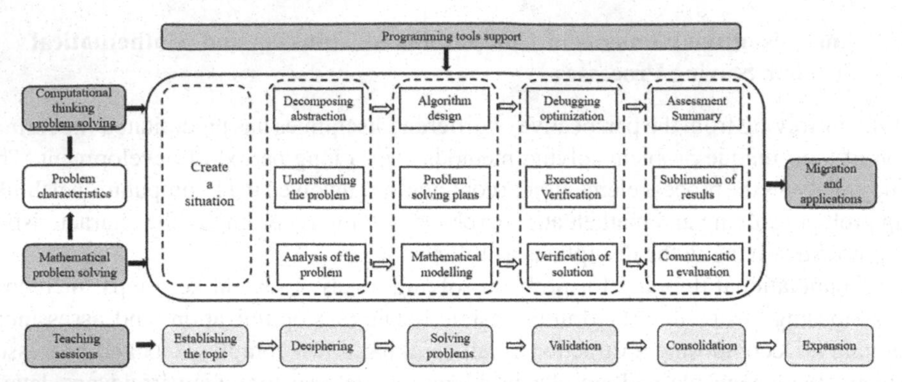

Fig. 2. A model for teaching the development of computational thinking with interdisciplinary integration

The interdisciplinary design of the Computational Thinking development model allows for a deeper analysis of the problem when decomposing it, with the methods of observation, analysis, comparison and modelling provided by mathematical problem solving, and then abstracting the common features of the problem to identify the problem and solve it. Computational thinking provides unique algorithmic skills to work with mathematical problem solving before and after judgement and reasoning to introduce solution steps. Assessment and synthesis can be effective in helping students to consolidate their knowledge [11]. Finally, generalization leads to knowledge expansion and transfer of application.

6 Design of Teaching Activities for the Development of Computational Thinking with Interdisciplinary Integration

The interdisciplinary teaching model provides a systematic and coherent teaching framework for developing students' computational thinking, and the design of teaching cases based on the teaching model can maintain a consistent logical structure and teaching style throughout the learning process. In this study, an example of a teaching activity was designed using the "random dot method to find pi", as shown in Fig. 3. The target group is the senior class. In the IT classroom, the teacher creates a situation to solve the mathematical problem of calculating the circumference of a circle as a starting point, and follows the teaching process and the development of computational thinking in the teaching model. Students will not only learn programming techniques, but also be able to acquire more in-depth mathematical knowledge and concepts in the process of solving mathematical problems, develop their computational thinking skills and experience the ease of using computers to solve complex problems.

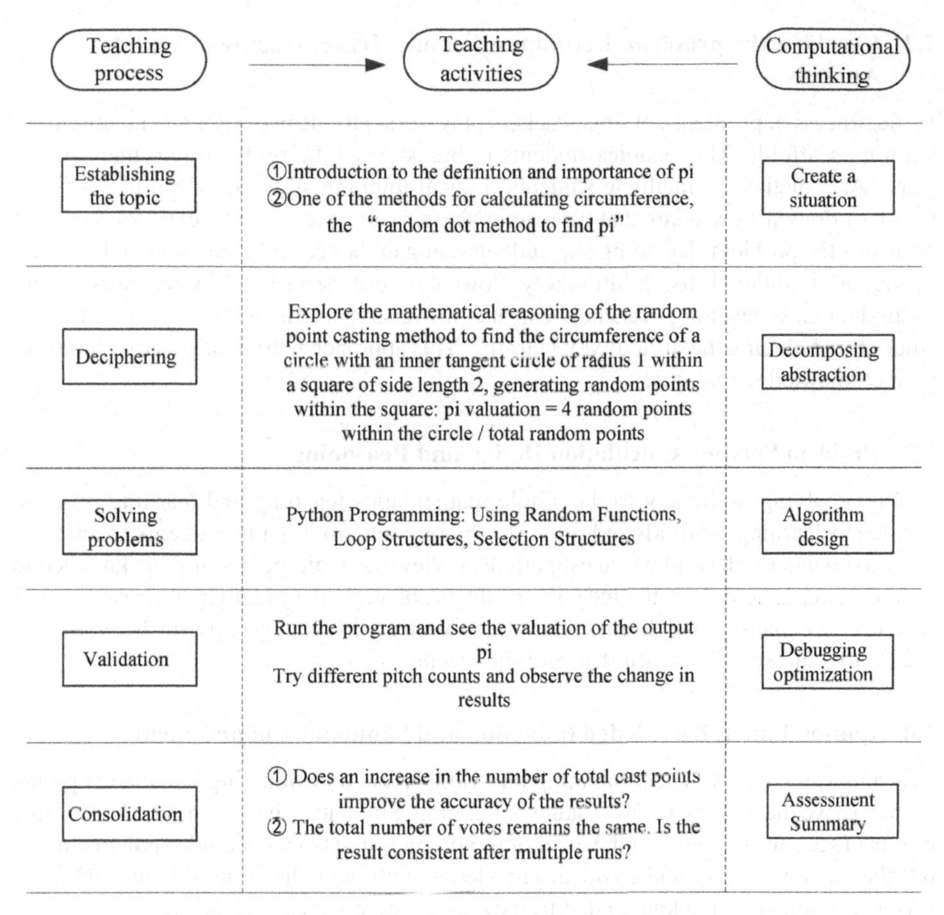

Fig. 3. Teaching activities for finding pi by random point casting

7 Teaching Suggestions

The development of computational thinking revolves around problem solving, making it an essential component of computational thinking. The key to enhancing students' problem solving skills lies in their ability to design clear solutions. To cultivate students' computational thinking, the introduction of mathematical problems, coupled with the use of programming tools, can be implemented pedagogically in the following ways.

7.1 Setting up a Topic, Creating a Context and Clarifying the Problem

At the beginning of the teaching process, it is important to set up a topic, create a context, and clarify the problem. Contextualization helps to enliven the classroom atmosphere and stimulate students' interest and curiosity. The problems should be based on real-life situations, analyzing the relevant knowledge and the students' actual level of thinking. By asking questions, the teacher can build a learning scaffold and guide students to explore the problems.

7.2 Cracking the problem, Decomposition and Transformation, Abstract Analysis

In the process of problem-solving, teachers play a crucial role in designing and providing learning scaffolds. This enables students to break down the problem into manageable steps. As a method to facilitate students' logical thinking skills, they can use pen and paper to draw a flow chart that represents the solution process and extracts the main points of the problem. By doing so, students can gain better understanding and training in logical thinking skills. Additionally, flowcharts can be utilized by teachers during individual class teaching. Teachers can use flowcharts to fill in the blanks and assist students in reducing the difficulty of learning. This approach helps students to effectively extract knowledge features.

7.3 Problem Solving, Calculation Design and Reasoning

Problem solving is the key to the whole mathematics teaching and learning process. Guided by learning scaffolds and supported by problem flow charts, students are encouraged to conduct independent investigations, review the main points of their knowledge to make connections with the meaning of the problem, make judgmental reasoning and then list the equations and discuss them collaboratively in small groups, further verifying their correctness under the guidance of the teacher.

7.4 Consolidation, Knowledge Induction and Summary Enhancement

Learning is a process of accumulating knowledge, and consolidating knowledge points helps to pave the way for the next stage of learning. Students can list complex knowledge points in sections to mark out the level of importance, and teachers guide students to sort out the main points of mathematical knowledge with the help of mind maps and other forms to summarize the knowledge framework of the course.

7.5 Extend, Debug and Optimize, Migrate and Apply

Once knowledge has been summarized, the application process should learn to iterate and update in order to transfer the application of knowledge. Knowledge exchange and sharing is organized in the classroom to further expand knowledge in conjunction with problems, with effective cooperation and clear division of labor formed between group members and communication and sharing between groups at the end of problem exploration. The teacher provides timely evaluation feedback on their learning process and discussion results to help students internalize their knowledge.

8 Conclusion

The integration of computational thinking development in the mathematical problem solving process and the realization of problem solving with the help of programming tools focuses on the development of the learner's steps and thinking in the problem-solving process. While traditional mathematical problem solving is limited to mathematical exercises and emphasizes the outcome of the solution, the abstract, logical, and derivative nature of solving mathematical problems also contributes to the enhancement of computational thinking skills. Moreover, primary and secondary school students are trained in mathematical and logical thinking earlier and are in their prime thinking years. Therefore, the study uses IT computational thinking as the underlying thinking and typical mathematical problems as the base point for the development of convergent thinking. This approach breaks the barriers to developing students' thinking in a single discipline and uses programming to solve problems, not only improving the efficiency of problem solving but also helping students master the main points of mathematical and IT knowledge and promoting the formation of good thinking skills. However, there are limitations to the research, as it only considers teaching activities designed in terms of modeling practice. Thus, classroom implementation is still needed to conduct a holistic analysis of the integration of mathematical problems into programming learning for the development of computational thinking.

References

1. Xiaohua, Y., Meiling, W.: How far is the road to developing computational thinking? Based on the perspective of computational thinking assessment. Open Educ. Res. **26**(01), 60–71 (2020)
2. Shiyin, M.: Extending the logic chain: clarifying the path of mathematics learning for students' deep thinking. Xueyuan Education (16), pp.82–83+86 (2022)
3. Wing, J.M.: Computational thinking. Commun. ACM **49**(3), 33–35 (2006)
4. Yun, Z.X.: Research on the Development of Kittenblock Curriculum for Primary School Students. Nanchang University (2021)
5. Hongxiang, Q.: Mathematical problem solving: evolution, connotation and practical path. Shanghai Educ. Res. **402**(11), 88–92 (2020)
6. Weintrop, D., Beheshti, E., Horn, M., et al.: Defining computational thinking for mathematics and science classrooms. J. Sci. Educ. Technol. **25**(1), 127–147 (2016)
7. Xinyan, L.: Analysis of hotspots and trends of STEM education research in China in the past decade. J. Educ. **07**, 29–35 (2022)
8. Ge, X.: A comparative study of computational thinking and mathematical thinking in problem solving. China Inf. Technol. Educ. **10**, 52–55 (2020)
9. Vallance, M., Towndrow, P.A.: Computational thinking and interdisciplinary learning: time to focus on pedagogy. Int. J. Learn. Technol. **15**(2), 180–200 (2020)
10. Yaqin, L.: Research on the Design and Application of an Interdisciplinary Problem-Driven Learning Environment for the Development of Computational Thinking. Jiangnan University (2020)
11. Jing-Hua, Y.: Analysis of the feasibility of integrating information technology into the teaching of mathematics. Test Res. **12**, 165–166 (2021)

Design and Development of Digital Circuit Simulation Software Based on Virtual Reality Technology

Lianshuan Shi(✉), Xiao Han, and Xiaochen Bian

Tianjin University of Technology and Education, Tianjin, China
shilianshuan@sina.com

Abstract. In order to improve teachers' teaching efficiency, stimulate students' interest in learning, increase students' initiative and consciousness of learning, break through the limitation of physical environment conditions, design and develop digital circuit simulation experiment software based on virtual reality technology. On the basis of the analysis of the learning characteristics of college students, the teaching design was carried out in combination with the characteristics of the course of digital circuit and logic design, and the modeling tool 3ds Max and the immersive game engine Unity 3d were used to develop the digital circuit simulation experiment teaching software. The virtual simulation experiment teaching software is convenient for students to conduct experiments independently, and teachers can verify the theoretical knowledge in class.

Keywords: Virtual simulation software · Digital circuit · Unity 3d · 3ds Max

1 Introduction

"Digital Circuits and Logic Design" course is the electrical engineering, automation, electricity class specialized, such as computers, and other related main technical foundation courses, professional courses is an important part of the training, mainly contains the basic logic functions of the digital circuit, the working principle of integrated circuit, logic circuit analysis and design, testing and validation methods, typical application of the device, etc. With the development of electronic technology and the adjustment of talents training objectives in colleges and universities, it is not only the pilot basic course for many subsequent professional courses, but also a discipline to cultivate students' excellent qualities such as respect for practice, courage to explore and active innovation [1]. Students can understand the basic principles of digital circuits and improve their logical thinking ability.

In the course of learning Digital Circuit and Logic Design, experiments occupy a large proportion. Through experimental operation, students can verify the theoretical contents in the books, deepen their understanding of theoretical knowledge, and also clarify the practical application value of the knowledge they have learned [2]. The study of digital circuit course requires the combination of theory and experiment, and the

J. Gan et al. (Eds.): CSEI 2023, CCIS 1899, pp. 304–314, 2024.
https://doi.org/10.1007/978-981-99-9499-1_26

connection of circuits on the operating table in the laboratory. According to the existing research results, the following problems in the digital logic circuit experiment teaching: first, in the process of experiment teaching is still a "teacher with the students to do", or the teacher the experiment method and the process writing into a laboratory manual, ignore students' initiative and initiative [3],the students to take by laboratory experiment content [4]complete regulation; Secondly, due to high cost,students often cause damage to experimental equipment due to operation mistakes [5]. Third, students' learning interest and efficiency are low. Students spend a lot of energy on boring trivia such as connection and error checking in the experimental process, which reduces students' learning interest and efficiency and affects the experimental teaching effect [6]. Fourth, the lack of stereo and visualization, such as Proteus ISIS and other software can be used to simulate digital logic circuits, the way of presentation is planar, lack of visualization. Combining virtual reality technology and experiment course content, developed a simulation software based on virtual reality technology and application [7]in the course of teaching, using the virtual simulation experiment teaching software to solve the above problem has incomparable advantages: first, without the restrictions of time and place, as long as the students can be equipped with the appropriate software and hardware independent experiment, for play to students' initiative; Second, the experimental cost is significantly reduced. Third, the experimental interaction is good, the feedback is real-time, the operation is simple, and the acceptance of students is high; Fourth, the scene image is realistic. Virtual simulation experimental teaching software can meet the diverse needs of the modernization of experimental teaching, teachers in the process of explaining theoretical knowledge using software to demonstrate, can directly verify the experimental results,can help students to understand the logic and function of digital circuits.

2 Design of Digital Circuit Simulation Experiment Software

2.1 Teaching Design

1. Learner Analysis

College students in the early adult stage, distinct personality, intelligence tends to be stable, logical thinking ability is strong, can adapt to professional knowledge learning, strong curiosity. College students have a strong ability to accept new knowledge, dare to explore, dare to innovate, have unique intuition and keen perception of advanced technology, and are good at using appropriate technological means to acquire knowledge [8]. As the "digital natives" and through the middle school information technology courses, college students have the basic computer operation ability, these conditions for the learners to carry out experimental operation to lay the foundation.

2. Analysis of Experimental Content

In the experimental part of digital circuits and logic design course, the teaching content ranges from the use and conversion of basic gate circuits and the representation of logic diagrams to the analysis and application of common logic devices. Learners have mastered the basic concepts and laws of digital circuits in the course of physics in junior and senior high schools, and have the ability of logical thinking. Digital circuit starts from the logic analysis of basic circuits that are easy to understand, then proceeds to the analysis and design of combinative logic circuits, and then to the functions and applications of various common devices. In this way, learners can gradually absorb new knowledge on the original basis. Before the beginning of the experimental course, students have learned the theoretical knowledge of digital circuit and have mastered the relevant theoretical knowledge.

3. Analysis of Experimental Objectives

This virtual simulation experimental teaching software selects six experiments of the course "Digital Circuits and Logic Design", which are logic function test of gate circuit, analysis and design of combinatorial logic circuit, data selector and decoder, trigger, analysis and application of sequential logic circuit and register. The design of experimental objectives is shown in Table 1.

Table 1. Design of experimental objectives

Experiment Title	Experiment Objectives
Experiment 1 Circuit Logic Function Test	1. Familiar with the functions of each part of digital circuit experimental unit, and master the use of basic gate circuit; 2.Master the test method of logic function of common integrated gate circuit; 3.Master the conversion between gate and circuit, and can draw logical diagram according to the expression; 4. Master how to use multimeter and oscilloscope
Experiment 2 Analysis and Design of Combinatorial Logic Circuit	1. Master the analysis method of combinatorial logic circuit; 2. Master the design method of combinatorial logic circuit; 3. Master the test and verification methods of combinatorial logic circuits
Experiment 3 Data Selector and Decoder	1. Master the logic function of data selector; 2. Master the working principle and logic function of the medium-scale integrated circuit decoder
Experiment 4 Trigger	1. Master the logic functions and test methods of basic RS flip-flop, JK flip-flop and D flip-flop; 2. Be familiar with the conversion method of logic function between each trigger; 3. Learn to use integrated triggers correctly
Experiment 5 Analysis and Application of Sequential Logic Circuit	1. Master the analysis and testing methods of timing circuit; 2. Mastering the test method of integrated shift register logic function and its application
Experiment 6 Register	1. Further master the logic function of D trigger; 2. Learn to use D trigger to form synchronous digital register and shift register; 3. Master the method of using shift register to form loop counter and torsion ring counter

4. Analysis of Teaching Resources

The experimental part of the traditional course of digital circuit and logic design is realized through the circuit board of the operating platform in the laboratory of the school. However, due to the limitation of practical conditions, teachers cannot demonstrate the theoretical knowledge to students in the process of explaining it in the classroom. Therefore, the digital circuit simulation software based on virtual reality technology can be applied in the classroom as the teaching resources of teachers in the process of theoretical course explanation.

5. Analysis of Learning Environment

Firstly, the digital circuit simulation software based on virtual reality technology can be applied to the study of theoretical courses in the classroom. Secondly, it can be used as a supplement to the experimental course. Students can use this software to continue learning after class if they can't finish the tasks in the experimental class. Again, in the face of the outbreak, teachers generally online teaching, using the digital circuit simulation software based on virtual reality technology, can very good help teachers in the process of theoretical explanation for real-time demonstration experiment, students to install this software, as long as have the software and hardware conditions, can be anywhere at any time for experimental courses, breakthrough the limitation of time space, promote the students' understanding of knowledge.

6. Evaluation

The evaluation criterion for learning results is whether learners have internalized knowledge [9]. After the initial completion of instructional design, the design content should be accurately implemented, and various positive or negative feedbacks should be recorded in the process to continuously modify and improve the entire instructional design [10].

2.2 Software Design

1. Software Function Module Design

The definition and refinement of software functions can provide clear guidance for software development and improve development efficiency. Modularization is an indispensable step in software development. Dividing the whole software into specific modules can also avoid the coupling between different processes and reduce the probability of error [11]. This software is mainly designed to help students learn the experimental process. It mainly designs the experimental operation module, the equipment display module and the experimental help module. The experimental operation module is the key module, as shown in Fig. 1.

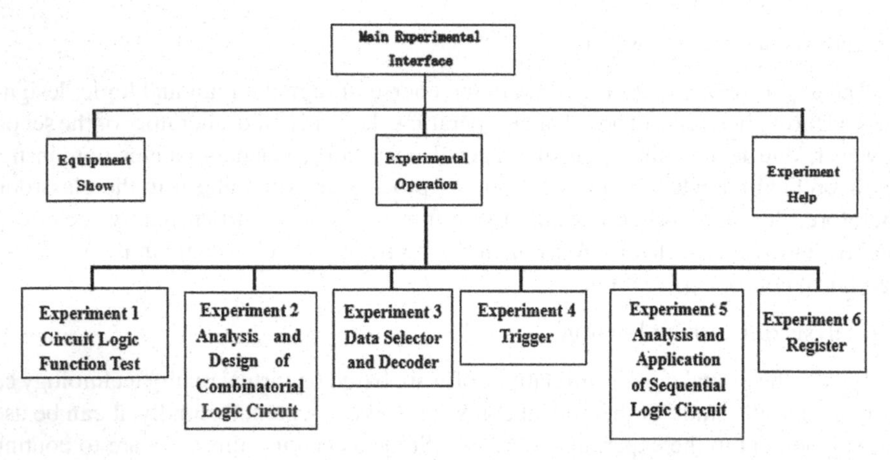

Fig. 1. Software Function Module Diagram

2. Interface Design

The interface design of virtual simulation software should bring students comfort and convenience. According to cognitive load theory, software interface design can affect the external cognitive load in information processing. Interface design should follow the principle of consistency, using a unified, simple, clear interface structure, the use of conventional standardized interface elements. In addition, the software should minimize the jumps between pages and establish clear navigation, which can reduce the external cognitive load of students in the learning process and reduce the interference of irrelevant factors [12]. Virtual digital circuit experiment operation module is the core part of the software, the interface circuit board according to the actual size, according to certain proportion relationship, a strong sense of reality of the interface is more intuitive, image close to the real experimental environment, is helpful for students to learn the meaning of content construction, stimulate interest in learning, enhance learning motivation, as shown in Fig. 2.

3. Interaction Design

In the virtual simulation experimental software, students need to complete experiments by operating virtual experimental equipment with input devices. Friendly and smooth interaction design can bring students a relaxed and good operation experience.

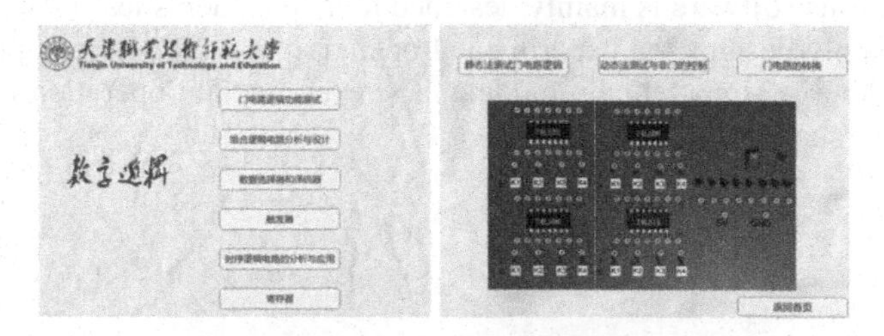

Fig. 2. Interface Design Effect Diagram

The interaction of this software mainly uses the mouse stand-alone way, simple and fast, students through the stand-alone experiment selection, the connection between the equipment, switch closure, etc.

4. Feedback Design

In the experiment, what students pay most attention to is the experimental results, and real-time feedback is crucial, so that students can know the experimental results in time and whether the operation is correct or not. The feedback of virtual simulation software is mainly expressed by the state of electronic devices. In virtual experiment platform, such as light-emitting leds expressed as on and off the effect of two kinds of state, as shown in Fig. 3, the left side to the status of light-emitting leds dies, the leds lit up when the status is on the right and the students can be judged by destroy the light of the light emitting diode experiment correctly or not, to facilitate students to adjust the experimental process.

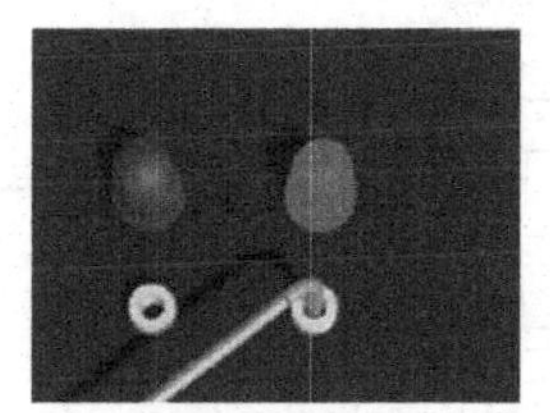

Fig. 3. Light-Emitting Led Extinguishing and Lighting Effect

3 Development of Digital Circuit Simulation Experiment Software

3.1 Software Development Tools

Digital circuit simulation software based on virtual reality technology is developed using modeling tool 3ds Max and immersive game engine Unity 3D.

1. 3ds Max 3D Modeling Tool

3ds Max is Autodesk company development based on the PC has been applied to the three dimensional animation and model making and rendering software, with its low requirements for PC system configuration, good compatibility, strong ability of role animation advantages is widely used in interior design, 3d animation, advertising, games, auxiliary teaching, and engineering visualization in areas such as [13]. 3ds Max has advanced rendering and simulation capabilities, a powerful set of drawing, texturing and modeling tools, and a smooth multi-application workflow [14]. Devices used in digital circuit simulation software, such as simulation circuit board, switches, indicator lights, corresponding components, etc., are modeled, mapped and set up background lights by 3ds Max software, so that these models look close to the real texture. Some of them need different materials or colors to distinguish different states. 3ds Max has a strong compatibility and will import the model with maps into the Unity 3D software for further development.

2. Unity 3D Game Development Tools

Unity 3D engine is currently the mainstream 3D interactive software development engine, widely used in game production, virtual reality, augmented reality and other aspects [15]. It has the advantages of cross-platform release, strong compatibility, simulation of many effects in the real world, support for C# and JAVA Script programming languages, and powerful functions, which can meet the development of digital circuit simulation software based on virtual reality technology.

3.2 Software Development Process

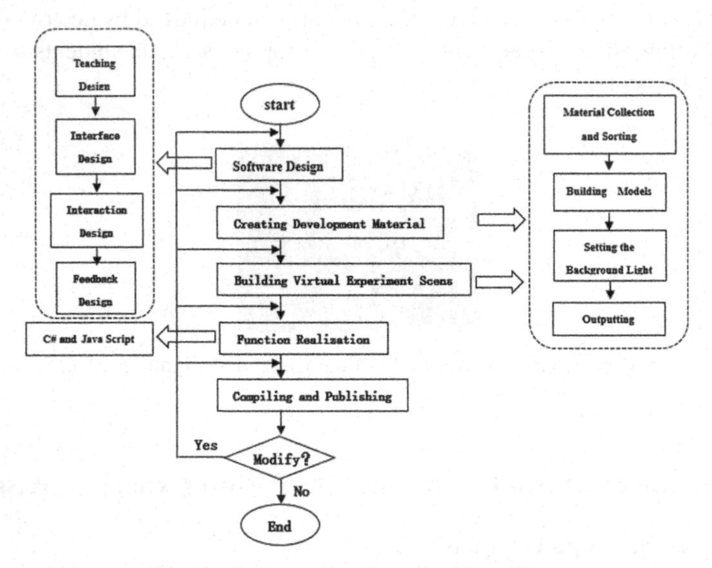

Fig. 4. Software Development Flow Chart

As can be seen from the development flow chart of the virtual simulation software in Fig. 4, the development of the virtual simulation software mainly includes the following steps:

1. Software Design

Mainly including teaching design, interface design, interaction design, feedback design, the previous has been described in detail.

2. Making Models of Electronic Devices needed for the Experiment

Material collection and sorting: collect the prototype of the electronic device to be modeled, and determine the size and proportion. Make the texture image and Photoshop the image to prepare the texture.

Building Models: according to the size of the prototype has been determined, according to the corresponding proportion, the use of polygon, facet and nurbs modeling way to establish the model.

Setting Background Light: lighting is a key part of the scene, but also an important auxiliary tool for model and material performance. The effect of background light directly affects the final rendering effect of the scene.

Outputting: select the corresponding renderer, set the resolution, frame number and other key parameters, it can render output.

3 Building Virtual Experiment Scens

Including the main interface and three function module scenes.

4. Function Realization

The corresponding function implementation needs to be written through C# and Java Script to achieve the interaction.

5. Compiling and Releasing Software

Go to "Build Settings" in the Unity software menu and set the appropriate Settings to release the software.

After the release of the software, the trial, according to the existing problems, the corresponding modification, until the software no problem, the end of the software development.

3.3 Experiment 4 "Trigger" Case Realization

The digital circuit software based on virtual reality technology uses Unity 3D as the development tool to present the content of the experimental part in a virtual form. This paper takes the content of Experiment 4 trigger as an example to briefly introduce the development idea and process.

Flip-flop is a basic unit circuit with memory function and is one of the basic units that constitute the sequential logic circuit. The flip-flop has two stable states. Under the action of appropriate trigger signal, the state of the flip-flop will flip. When the input trigger signal disappears, the state of the flip trigger remains unchanged [16].

Basic RS logic function test, using a 74LS00 device. The basic RS trigger has three functions: set "1", set "0" and "hold". Usually called $\overline{\mathrm{S}}$ set "1" side, namely $\overline{\mathrm{S}}=0$ ($\overline{\mathrm{R}}=1$) when the trigger is set "1"; $\overline{\mathrm{R}}$ as "0", namely $\overline{\mathrm{R}}=0$ ($\overline{\mathrm{S}}=1$) when the trigger is set "0"; When $\overline{\mathrm{S}}=\overline{\mathrm{R}}=1$ state keep; When $\overline{\mathrm{S}}=\overline{\mathrm{R}}=0$, the trigger condition, should avoid the situation [17].

74LS00 is four groups of 2-input terminal and non-gate, and its pin figure [18] is shown in Fig. 5.

The basic RS flip-flop consists of two Nand gates connected end to end, as shown in Fig. 6.

The rendering effect in the digital circuit system based on virtual reality technology is shown in Fig. 7. The upper right corner is the master switch. When the switch is opened, the indicator light next to it is on, and the whole circuit board is powered up, simulating the master switch on the operating table. "5V" and "GND" in the lower right corner are positive and negative terminals, which can be used normally only when the positive and negative terminals of the chip are connected correctly; The bottom six terminals correspond to six toggle switches, the initial state is 0, when the mouse click, it will

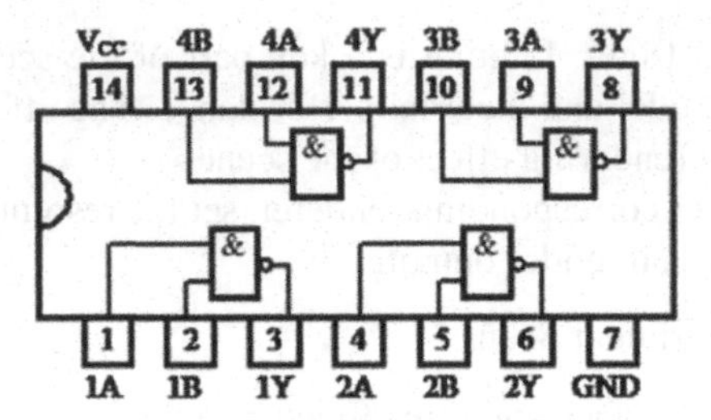

Fig. 5. Pin Diagram of 74LS00

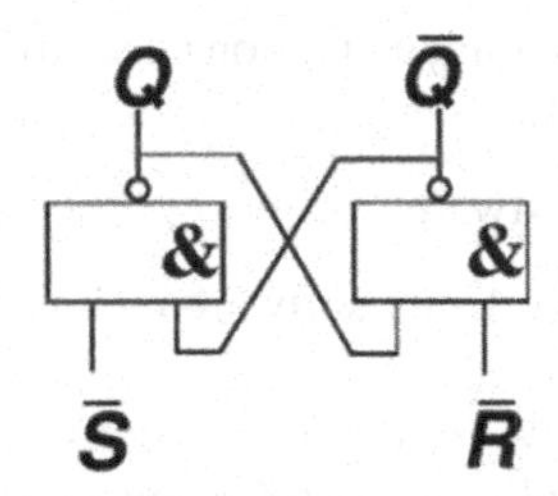

Fig. 6. Basic RS Flip-flop Line Connection Diagram

change to 1, control the state of the terminals; The chip is in the middle position, and there are 14 pins in total. Pin 14 of the 74LS00 chip is connected to the positive pole of the power supply, and pin 7 is connected to the negative pole of the power supply. Among them, 1, 2,4, 5,9, 10,12 and 13 are the input ends of four groups of nand gate, and 3, 6, 8 and 11 correspond to the output ends of the nand gate. On the top of the circuit board, there are 8 indicator lights and the corresponding terminal. The indicator lights show the status of the terminal.

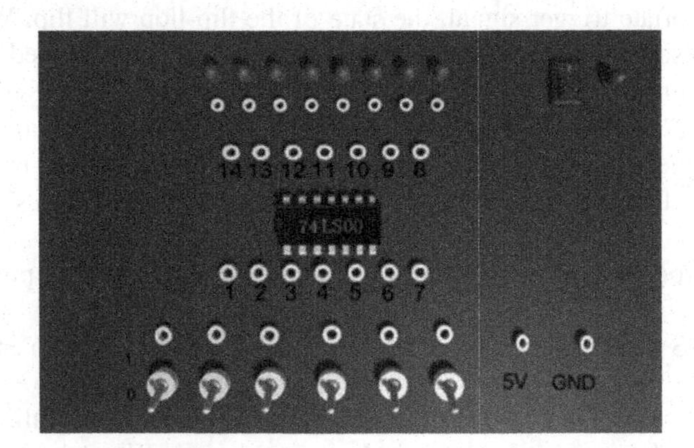

Fig. 7. Basic RS Flip-flop Experiment Virtual Circuit Board

Are used in this experiment, two groups of nand gate 1, 2, 3, 8, 9, and 10 (any two group), according to the Fig. 6, you can connect the circuit diagram is shown in Fig. 8, the pin 1 in Fig. 4–2 $\overline{S}$, pin 9 in Fig. 4–2 $\overline{R}$, pin 3 Q in Figs. 6, 8 as in Fig. 6 $\overline{Q}$ pins.

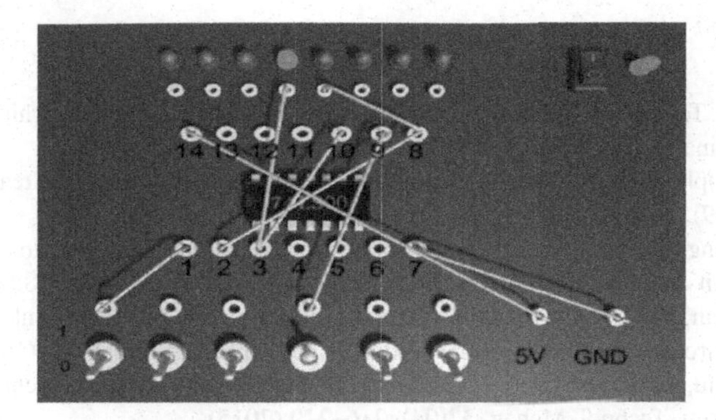

Fig. 8. Experimental Test of Basic RS Trigger

Through the experiment, the results are obtained as shown in Table 2:

Table 2. Basic RS Trigger Test Results

$\overline{S}$	$\overline{R}$	Q	$\overline{Q}$
0	1	Keep	Keep
0	1	0	1
0	1	1	0
0	0	/	/

4 Conclusion

Based on virtual reality technology, a digital circuit virtual simulation experiment teaching software is developed by using 3ds Max and Unity 3D software. After the software development is completed, the software is tried out and evaluated. Most learners think that the software is convenient, the knowledge structure is relatively complete, and it can simulate the real experimental environment. The learners are happy to use the software to learn, which shows that the software has a certain positive significance for solving the problems existing in the current digital circuit experimental teaching. The practice shows that the teaching software can help students to learn and master the knowledge of digital circuit and improve their ability of circuit design. Subsequent research will continue to improve the interactive and immersion of the experimental teaching software, enhance the immersion of learners, and further improve the learning effect of learners.

References

1. Qiaoyan, Z.: Teaching reform of digital circuit and logic design course “learning as the center". Western China Quality Educ. **6**(10), 193–194 (2020)
2. Zhou, J.: Application of multisim10 simulation software in digital circuit teaching. Practical Electron. (09), 114+79 (2013)
3. Yin, J., Huang, Q., Yin, L., et al.: Reform and practice of bilingual experimental teaching of digital circuit and logic design. Res. Exploration Laborat. **39**(08), 183–188 (2020)
4. Zhao, Q., Han, Y., Qin, X., et al.: Reform and exploration of new experimental teaching mode of “digital circuit experiment” course. Industry Informat. Technol. Educ.(10), 54–58 (2019)
5. Sheng, J., Liu, S., Wang, Y., et al.: Research on reform of experimental technology of digital logic. Experim. Technol. Manag. **32**(04), 216–219 (2015)
6. Xian, J., Lai, X.: Based on multisim simulation digital logic experiment teaching reform. Res. Explorat. Laborat. **38**(09), 228–232+297 (2019)
7. Ying, G.: Application of multisim10 software in teaching digital circuit. Comput. Modern. **07**, 162–165 (2010)
8. What are the characteristics of contemporary college students? [EB/OL].https://wenku.baidu.com/view/c475d8af33687e21ae45a927.html
9. Meina, W.: Teaching Design, pp. 236–238. Higher Education Press, Beijing (1998)
10. Li, E., Shi, L.: Instructional design model and analysis of elderly health knowledge learning system under the theory of contextual learning. In: Tianjin University of Technology and Education, 14th International Conference on Computer Science and Education, ICCSE 2019, pp. 448–453 (August 2019)
11. Shi, Y.: Research on the development and application of virtual experiment system in higher vocational colleges based on unity 3d -- taking computer networking as an example. Shaanxi Normal University (2018)
12. Qi, Y., Xiong, C.: The application research of cognitive load theory in the design of multimedia software. J. Dist. Educ. **03**, 51–53 (2009)
13. Zhi, L., Xiaofeng, Q.: Chinese version of 3ds Max 2014 basic training course [M], pp. 5–8. Posts and Telecommunications Press, Beijing (2015)
14. 3dsMax[EB/OL].https://baike.baidu.com/item/3ds%20max/272324?fromtitle=3dmax&fromid=3236629&fr=aladdin
15. Zhang, K., Zhang, X.: Design and development of subway safety education software based on Unty3D. J. Safety Sci. Technol. **15**(S1), 156–162 (2019)
16. Morris, M., Mano, C.R.: Digital Logic and Computer Hardware Design Basis. Beijing: Beijing Electronic Industry Press (2002)
17. Xian, L.: Multisim is used to analyze the uncertain state of RS trigger. In: Electronic Technology Teaching Research Association of Higher Education in North China (2004)
18. Yan, S.: Fundamentals of Digital Electronic Technology. Higher Education Press, Beijing (1998)

An Empirical Study on the Influence of Phonetic Annotation Methods on New-Character Words Learning of Children in Senior Grade of Primary School

Zhuo Yang and Hua Zhang(✉)

School of International Study, Ningbo Tech University, Ningbo 315100, People's Republic of China
zhanghua201061@163.com

Abstract. This study investigated the accurate labelling of Pinyin to enhance the acquisition of new-character words by fourth-grade students and to facilitate scientific annotation of supplementary reading materials for children. Using E-Prime 2.0, we examined the effect of different Pinyin presentation methods on the reading performance of elementary school students. The main findings indicated that (1) marking only new-character words with Pinyin significantly enhances students' reading speed, compared to reading sentences with full-sentence annotation; (2) the placement of Pinyin above or below the Chinese character has no effect on students' reading speed.

Keywords: Pinyin Presentation Methods · New-Character Words Learning · Cognitive load

1 Introduction

Children have accumulated a large amount of oral vocabulary and established the "sound-meaning" connection before they entered school. One of the main tasks of Chinese class in elementary school is to transform spoken vocabulary, which is only used for listening and speaking, into written vocabulary that can be read, and to establish the "form-sound-meaning" connection. As a kind of ideograph [4], Chinese characters are weak in their ability to represent sounds, and that makes Pinyin the most important tool for acquiring words and phrases.

Previous studies have shown that the presentation method of Pinyin is an important factor in the effectiveness of children's word acquisition [1–3, 9, 10], and it is moderated by multiple factors, one of which is the conceptual familiarity of the word. The role of Pinyin in first- and second-grade children's reading was examined [2]. It was found that when the conceptual familiarity of the word was high, the accuracy of sentences with the full text marked with Pinyin was significantly higher than that of sentences without Pinyin; while when the conceptual familiarity of the word was low, whether Pinyin was marked or not did not affect the accuracy of sentence reading. The second factor is

J. Gan et al. (Eds.): CSEI 2023, CCIS 1899, pp. 315–322, 2024.
https://doi.org/10.1007/978-981-99-9499-1_27

teacher's involvement. Wu et al. studied first grade students and found that in independent reading, test scores were best in the full-text with Pinyin condition compared to the Pinyin-only and full-text without Pinyin; while in shared reading with some teacher's involvement, test scores were best in the full-text without Pinyin condition [9]. The third factor is the number of new Chinese characters contained in new-character words. Shu et al. chose first- and second-grade students as subjects, and found out that the effect of Pinyin was not significant when children were learning new words containing only one new character, but the effect of Pinyin was significant when learning new words containing two new characters [2]. In addition, the strength of children's language ability was also found to be an important factor, but the relationship between Pinyin's role and children's language ability was inconsistent. Shu et al. found that first- and second-grade students with high language ability were able to acquire new words better using Pinyin annotation, while annotation mode had a smaller effect on students with lower ability in terms of the effectiveness of vocabulary learning [2]. Wu et al. found that the higher the language ability of first-grade children, the less dependent the role of Pinyin is [9]. Shu et al.'s study focused on independent reading [2], while Wu et al.'s study focused on shared reading with teacher's involvement which can replace the role of Pinyin [10]. Thus, the annotation method has a greater impact on texts or extracurricular reading materials that require self-study. The above study compares the effect on vocabulary acquisition or reading when Pinyin, which is marked over the Chinese character, varies (either the whole sentence is marked, or only the new word is marked, or no marker).

Other studies have focused more on the cognitive processing of Pinyin or Chinese characters during the reading of the annotated text. Examining grade 2 children's eye movements during reading of Pinyin-annotated texts, Yan et al. found that reading speed was slower for full-Pinyin condition and new-word-Pinyin condition than for no-Pinyin condition, and the providing of Pinyin reduced reading efficiency. However, there was no significant difference in the number and duration of children's gazing at new words between the full-Pinyin and new-word-Pinyin conditions, and only the numbers they gazed at the Pinyin of new word was significantly higher than the numbers they gazed at Pinyin of familiar word [8]. Xu and Jiang examined the eye movements of second language (L2) learners of different Chinese language levels while reading sentences with Pinyin, it was found that the gaze time on Pinyin decreased and the reading efficiency of sentences with Pinyin increased as the L2 learners' Chinese language level increased, and even the L2 learners of elementary level did not show any inclination to spend more time on Pinyin and less on Chinese characters [5]. Both studies examined the reading process itself, but the relationship between the indicators of gaze duration or gaze number during reading and the effect of vocabulary acquisition is yet unknown [5, 8].

With the development of international Chinese education, some Chinese textbooks at home and abroad have begun to label Pinyin below the Chinese characters. For example, in the Chinese text *Happy Partner*, which is the second book of Grade 4 in Singapore, Pinyin is labelled below the Chinese characters. Lee and Kalyuga found that the learning effect was better when Pinyin and English meanings were horizontally to the right of the Chinese characters for the elementary level Chinese learners than when Pinyin and English meanings were placed vertically below them [7]. Therefore, placing Pinyin under the Chinese character may be one of the options for Pinyin labelling.

Building upon previous studies, this paper introduces the position of Pinyin as a new factor to be considered. The study investigates the impact of various methods of presenting Pinyin on the acquisition of new-character words by fourth-grade elementary school students. Specifically, four Pinyin presentation methods are examined, based on the content of the annotation and the position of Pinyin: full-Pinyin above the character, new-character-Pinyin above the character, full-Pinyin below the character, and new-character-Pinyin below the character. The aim of this research is to identify the most effective Pinyin presentation method for promoting the acquisition of new-character words. Effectiveness in this context is measured by the shortest learning time and the highest correct rate. The study evaluates which Pinyin presentation method enables participants to read Pinyin-annotated sentences that contain new-character words more quickly and to complete the task of selecting the correct Pinyin of the new-character words more quickly and accurately.

2 Experiment

2.1 Participants

In this study, 24 fourth-grade students with an average age of 10 years and 2 months, comprising 12 boys and 12 girls, were recruited from various elementary schools in Ningbo. The inclusion criteria for this study required the students to have normal vision or corrected-to-normal vision and pass the Pinyin ability test. The parents of the participants signed informed consent forms before the experiment, and received payment upon completion.

The Pinyin ability test was a paper-and-pencil test that consisted of 10 Pinyin-picture matching questions. The words related to the pictures used in the test were different from those used in the experimental materials. All participants demonstrated 100% accuracy in completing the Pinyin-picture matching test, indicating that they possessed normal Pinyin reading ability.

2.2 Experimental Materials

Fifty new two-character words were selected from the new word lists of Chinese textbooks for grades 5 and 6, which do not appear in the textbooks for grades 1–4. These words are frequently used in daily life and have high conceptual familiarity. To facilitate learning, participants would need to utilize the sound to establish the connection between the form and meaning of the new-character words with the help of Pinyin. The effect of different Pinyin presentation formats on new-character learning was then evaluated based on the experimental results.

To ensure high conceptual familiarity of the words, seven fourth-graders who didn't participate in the experiment completed a Pinyin-picture matching task. 50 simple and clear pictures were chosen to match new words, like "霹雳/thunderbolt" matched with a picture of thunderbolt. The new words were split into 5 groups of 10, with each group matched with 12 pictures, including 2 unrelated pictures to avoid exclusion method usage. Words with an error rate of 66% or more were excluded, leaving 40 words with high conceptual familiarity.

The remaining 40 new-character words were used as key words to create sentences, with each sentence consisting of 8–12 words and the word positioned as far back as possible to avoid using complex sentence structures and other new words. 63 non-language or psychology majors rated sentence fluency on a 5-point scale (1 = most fluent, 5 = incoherent). Scores ranged from 1.2–2.3, with an average of 1.5 across all sentences.

Referring to the presentation form of sentences with Pinyin in Chinese textbooks, the Pinyin is centered above or below the corresponding Chinese character. In this study, 160 sentences were presented to participants using four different Pinyin presentation methods. To ensure that each participant was exposed to all stimuli, a Latin square design was used to counter-balance the order of the four conditions, resulting in four versions of the stimuli, each containing 40 different types of sentences. Participants were randomly assigned to one of these versions.

2.3 Experimental Design

The study employed a within-subject, two-factor experimental design. The first independent variable was content marked Pinyin (Full sentence marked Pinyin, and new-character word marked Pinyin). The second independent variable was the position of the Pinyin (Pinyin labelled above the Chinese character, and Pinyin labelled below the Chinese character). The dependent variables were the reading time for sentences marked with Pinyin in 4 different ways, as well as the reading time and accuracy of responses to multiple choice questions. The control variables were the selection of the new-character words and their conceptual familiarity.

2.4 Experimental Tasks and Procedures

The participants were instructed to silently read the sentences with different Pinyin methods and selected accurate Pinyin for new-character words previously appeared in the sentence.

The experiment used E-prime 2.0, beginning with a 500 ms presentation of a red cross as a fixation point in the centre of the screen, followed by Chinese sentences with black Song font characters (30 × 30 pixels) and Pinyin (GB Pinyinok-B, 20 pixels) with 20 pixel vertical spacing. Pinyin was aligned as close as possible to the Chinese characters with equal distance between words in each sentence.

After silently reading a sentence, the participant was instructed to press the space bar. Following this, a multiple-choice question appeared, asking the participant to choose the correct Pinyin for a new-character word. The options included A and B, with A appearing at the top and B at the bottom. Questions with A as the correct answer constituted 50% of the total questions. Among all the incorrect answers, there are 10 cases of wrong initial consonants, 10 cases of wrong final consonants, 10 cases of wrong tones, and 10 cases of wrong both initial and final consonants. The font, size, and colour of the Chinese characters and Pinyin in the multiple-choice questions were the same as those presented on the previous screen. Participants were instructed to press F (labelled A on the keyboard) if they think A is the correct answer, or J (labelled B on the keyboard) if they choose B. After the participant made a choice, the correctness of their response was automatically displayed, followed by the next trial. An example of the sentence and the question are shown in the Fig. 1.

Tā zài shén xiàngqián jìng jìng de qí dǎo 祈祷
他在神像前静静地祈祷。 A、qí dǎo
B、qǐ dǎo

Fig. 1. An example of experimental sentences and questions

Prior to conducting the formal experiment, four practice trials will be administered to participants. These practice trials will encompass four distinct conditions. Notably, the practice sentences will be completely unrelated to the formal experiment materials. Each participant will be required to read 40 sentences arranged in a random order, and subsequently answer 40 multiple-choice questions. The experimental procedure is outlined in Fig. 2. The whole experiment took about 20 min. There was a break after 20 sentences in the experiment.

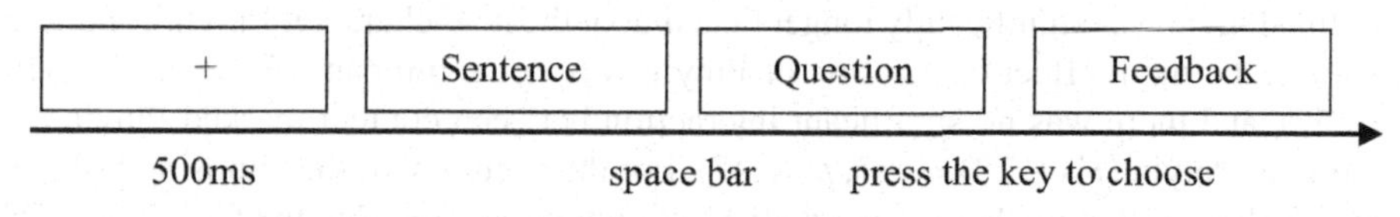

Fig. 2. Experimental flow chart

2.5 Experimental Results

All 24 participants in the study exhibited a correct response rate of at least 94% for four experimental conditions: full-Pinyin presented above the Chinese characters (FULL-UP), full-Pinyin presented below the Chinese characters (FULL-DOWN), new-character-Pinyin presented above the Chinese characters (NEW-UP), and new-character-Pinyin presented below the Chinese characters (NEW-DOWN). Furthermore, all participants were deemed valid for inclusion in the study.

Prior to statistical analysis, data were preprocessed to exclude a total of 45 responses that fell beyond ±2.5 standard deviations. The final response times of participants for reading sentences and making choices across all four conditions, as well as their accuracy in completing the task, were calculated, and are reported in Table 1 below.

A two-factor repeated measures ANOVA was conducted on the results of the study, with the factors being content marked Pinyin (full-Pinyin, new-character Pinyin) and position of Pinyin (above the character, below the character).

In terms of the REA RT, the analysis revealed a significant main effect of content marked Pinyin (F (1, 23) = 10.64, p = .003). Participants took significantly longer to read sentences that were marked with full-Pinyin than those marked with new-character Pinyin. However, the main effect of position of Pinyin was not significant (F (1, 23) = 3.15, p = .08), and there was no significant interaction between content marked Pinyin

Table 1. Means (SD) of reading time (REA RT), choice time (CHO RT), and accuracy (ACC)

Experimental Condition	REA RT M (SD)	CHO RT M (SD)	ACC M (SD)
FULL-UP	2801.57 (1317.63)	2854.05 (728.62)	.96 (.08)
FULL-DOWN	2981.29 (1664.26)	2857.37 (548.03)	.95 (.078)
NEW-UP	2312.12 (1029.8)	2673.60 (520.02)	.94 (.078)
NEW-DOWN	2503.02 (1126.34)	2588.08 (498.87)	.96 (.07)

and position of Pinyin (F (1, 23) = .00, p = .962). On the CHO RT, the ANOVA showed a significant main effect of content marked Pinyin (F (1, 23) = 8.43, p = .008), indicating that the time taken to make choices after reading sentences that were marked with full-Pinyin was significantly longer than that of the new-character Pinyin condition. However, the main effect of position of Pinyin was not significant (F (1, 23) = .419, p = .52), and there was no significant interaction between content marked Pinyin and position of Pinyin (F (1, 23) = .53, p = .47). For the accuracy of the choosing task, the ANOVA showed that neither the main effect of content marked Pinyin (F (1, 23) = .08, p = .78), nor the main effect of position of Pinyin (F (1, 23) = .35, p = .56), nor the interaction between content marked Pinyin and position of Pinyin (F (1, 23) = .68, p = .42) were significant.

3 Discussions

This study used E-Prime 2.0 to create an experimental program with Pinyin-marked sentences for children to read silently and choose the right pronunciation of new-character words accurately. The impact of Pinyin on children's vocabulary acquisition was measured by their reading speed, completion speed, and accuracy.

3.1 Only New-Character Word Marked Pinyin Facilitated New-Character Words Acquisition

The experiment found that using only Pinyin for new-character words can speed up participants' reading of sentences and their response time in choosing the correct Pinyin. This is especially helpful for primary four students who have a larger vocabulary, as it allows them to focus solely on the new-character word's Pinyin and accelerate their reading and choosing speed. In our research, the speed of the choosing task in only new-character words with Pinyin condition is significantly higher than that in full-sentence Pinyin condition. When reading full sentence with Pinyin, the participants need to pay equal attention to all words and Pinyin in the sentence. If cognitive information is dispersed across two or more sources, learners need to spread their attention to search and integrate various sources of information, thus generating a larger additional cognitive load [11]. Our result is contrary to the research results of Wu et al. [9, 10]. Wu et al. investigated the influence of Pinyin in Shared-book Reading on students' vocabulary acquisition [10]. Reading materials marked with Pinyin in different ways were used for share-reading in classroom. Two weeks later, the results of the new word naming test showed that the test scores of only new word with Pinyin condition were significantly worse than those of the full sentences with Pinyin condition, which may result from the unique novelty stimulus of Pinyin marked a new word. The students are reminded that this is a new word, which leads them to focus on Pinyin directly, which distracts their attention and processing of the character and hinders the establishment of the connection between the form and sound. In addition, the experiment of Wu et al. found that Pinyin has no influence on students' acquisition of words in the classroom teaching environment [9]. Both studies [9, 10] involved the participation of teachers, who could replace the role of Pinyin to a certain extent [7, 9]. In our study, children's independent reading was completely excluded from the role of teachers. Moreover, according to cognitive load theory, when Pinyin is a learning material that is not fully mastered, it requires more working memory to process [6, 12]. Pinyin, as the teaching content of grade 1, is still a relatively new content for grade 1 students. In the study of Wu et al. [9, 10], all the subjects were grade 1 primary school children. Compared with grade 4 students, grade 1 students may not be as proficient in Pinyin as grade 4 students. Therefore, when Pinyin is a unique novelty stimulus of new characters, it will distract grade 1 students' attention and processing of characters. For the fourth grade students, Pinyin, as a tool that has been able to be skillfully used, will not distract students' attention too much and affect the processing of new words. Finally, Wu et al. examined long-term memory of new words (tested two weeks later) [10], while this study examined short-term memory of new words (after reading the sentence). These are all possible reasons for the inconsistent results.

3.2 Position of Pinyin Had no Effect on New-Character Words Acquisition

Chinese textbooks typically label Pinyin above characters, but in our experiment, we found that placing Pinyin below characters had little effect on participants, despite the theoretical advantage for fourth graders in responding faster. This is different from what Lee & Kalyuga found in their experiment, in which they used Chinese L2 learners as subjects [7]. They found that Pinyin position has an effect on the acquisition of new words. The learning effect of new words when Pinyin and English definitions are placed vertically below new words is better than when Pinyin and English definitions are placed horizontally to the right of them. One possible reason is that fourth-grade students have become skilled in using Pinyin as a tool. As a non-specific material, processing Pinyin does not require too much attention and will not increase the burden of working memory [6]. Therefore, the transfer of Pinyin's location from the top to the bottom exerted little influence on extraneous cognitive load [7, 11], especially for native language learners. Unlike the horizontal layout with Pinyin next to the characters, whether you put Pinyin above the two-character words or below them, the reading material captures more or less the same amount of learners' attention because it does not cause split attention effect.

4 Conclusion

The finding of this study demonstrated that whether the Pinyin was placed above the two-character words or below them has little impact on the subjects. However, annotating only new-character words with Pinyin is clearly beneficial to the learning process of upper elementary grades. The experimental results also verified that the placement of Pinyin has an important impact on students' vocabulary learning. Although fourth graders already know many words, the limited attention and cognitive resources available to annotate learned words are still consumed by this unnecessary information. This leaves them with fewer cognitive resources to devote to the structure of Chinese characters and the pronunciation of new-character words. Evidence of this can be seen in their reaction speed when reading sentences and answering questions. Thus, when designing learning materials for upper elementary students, it is important to help students reduce unnecessary cognitive load in order to achieve the desired instructional outcomes.

References

1. Wang, A.P., Shu, H., Zhou, Y.X.: The role of captioning in children's accompanying learning. Psychol. Sci. **32**, 98–101+113 (2009)
2. Shu, H., Liu, B.X.: A study of the role of phonics in early reading for early elementary school children. Psychol. Dev. Educ. **3**, 11–15 (1994)
3. Shu, H., Zeng, H.M., Cheng, Z.: An experimental study on the use of pinyin to learn new-character words by children in the lower grades of elementary school. J. Psychol. Sci. **1**, 18–22 (1993)
4. Wang, H.Y.: A brief introduction to Chinese character annotation methods. J. Heilongjiang Ecol. Eng. Vocat. Coll. **27**, 127–129 (2014)
5. Xu, J.J., Jiang, X.: An eye-movement study on the reading of annotated texts by second language learners of different Chinese levels. World Chin. Lang. Teach. **35**, 548–561 (2021)
6. De Leeuw, K.E., Mayer, R.E.: A Comparison of three measures of cognitive load: evidence for separable measures of intrinsic, extraneous, and germane load. J. Educ. Psychol. **100**, 223–234 (2008)
7. Lee, C.H., Kalyuga, S.: Effectiveness of different pinyin presentation formats in learning Chinese characters: a cognitive load perspective. Lang. Learn. **61**(4), 1099–1118 (2011)
8. Yan, M., Miller, K.F., Li, H., Shu, H.: What is the place for pinyin in the beginning Chinese reading? Evidence from eye movements. In: Payner, K., Shen, D.L., Bai, X.J., Yan, G.L. (eds.) Cognitive and Cultural Influences on Eye Movements', pp. 344–360. Tianjin People's Publishing House (2008)
9. Wu, X.C., Li, H., Liu, Z.H.: The role of annotation style and teaching format in children's classroom Chinese character learning. Psychol. Behav. Res. **7**, 166–170 (2009)
10. Wu, X.C., Li, H., Shu, H., Anderson, R.C., et al.: The role of phonics in children's shared reading. Psychol. Sci. **5**, 548–551+639 (2002)
11. Jiang, X.G., Cui, M.: A study on the design strategy of online teaching resources. Health Occup. Educ. **40**, 12–14 (2022)
12. Diao, Y., Sweller, J.: Redundancy in foreign language reading comprehension instruction: concurrent written and spoken presentations. Learn. Instr. **17**, 78–88 (2007)

A Study on Personalized Learning Resource Recommendation Method Based on Association Rule Mining

Kun Nie and Hong Li(✉)

Yunnan Normal University, Kunming 650500, China
651035658@qq.com

Abstract. As the diversity of educational resources continues to grow, it is becoming increasingly important to provide learners with learning resources that meet their needs and interests. This paper proposes a personalized learning resource recommendation method based on association rule mining, aimed at providing learners with more accurate and personalized learning resource recommendations. Firstly, by analyzing the learners' historical learning behavior and resource usage, the interest model of the learners is extracted. Then, using association rule mining techniques, potential relationships between learning resources are discovered, generating recommendation rules. Finally, based on the learners' interest model and recommendation rules, personalized learning resource recommendations are provided for learners. Experimental results show that compared to traditional recommendation methods, this method can significantly improve the accuracy and satisfaction of recommendations.

Keywords: Association Rule Mining · Personalized Learning Resource Recommendation · Interest Model · Recommendation Rules

1 Introduction

With the rapid development of information technology and network technology, a large number of educational resources have been integrated into various online learning platforms. These rich resources provide great convenience for learners, but at the same time, they also bring about the problem of learning resource overload. Faced with such a massive resource library, learners often find it difficult to locate resources that best meet their needs and interests, which in turn affects their learning outcomes [1]. Therefore, researching how to provide personalized learning resource recommendations for learners has become an urgent need.

Association rule mining is a method for discovering the relationships between data items in large datasets, widely used in fields such as market analysis and medical diagnosis. In the field of education, association rule mining can help uncover potential relationships between learning resources, thereby providing more accurate and personalized

The research is one of the Yunnan Normal University results of the 2023 Graduate Research Innovation Fund Project (project number: YJSJJ23-B164).

J. Gan et al. (Eds.): CSEI 2023, CCIS 1899, pp. 323–332, 2024.
https://doi.org/10.1007/978-981-99-9499-1_28

learning resource recommendations for learners [2]. This paper proposes a personalized learning resource recommendation method based on association rule mining, which mainly consists of three steps: 1) extracting the interest model of learners; 2) using association rule mining techniques to discover potential relationships between learning resources; 3) providing personalized learning resource recommendations for learners based on their interest model and recommendation rules. This paper will detail the specific implementation methods of these three steps and verify the effectiveness of the proposed method through experiments.

2 Research Theoretical Foundation

2.1 Association Rule Mining

Association Rule Mining (ARM) is a widely applied technique in the field of data mining, aimed at discovering the latent relationships between items within a dataset [3]. These relationships are typically represented in the form of rules, such as "if item A is purchased, then item B is likely to be purchased," where A and B are data items. Association rule mining was first introduced by Agrawal et al. in 1993 to analyze shopping basket data, uncover patterns in customer purchasing behavior, and guide retailers in making decisions about product placement, promotions, and more. Since then, association rule mining techniques have been widely applied in various domains, such as market analysis, medical diagnosis, and network security.

The core problem in association rule mining is finding frequent itemsets. Frequent itemsets refer to sets of items that appear at a high frequency within a dataset. For a given dataset, frequent itemsets can be mined based on two threshold values: minimum support and minimum confidence. The minimum support represents the lowest frequency at which an itemset appears in the dataset, while the minimum confidence represents the lowest probability of a rule being valid. The Apriori algorithm was the first association rule mining algorithm proposed. It employs a bottom-up search strategy, generating candidate itemsets layer by layer to mine frequent itemsets. Subsequent researchers have continuously optimized the Apriori algorithm, developing algorithms such as FP-Growth and Eclat, which have improved the efficiency of association rule mining.

2.2 Personalized Learning Resource Recommendation

Personalized learning resource recommendation is one of the research hotspots in the field of education, focusing on how to recommend appropriate learning resources according to learners' needs and interests [4]. The purpose of personalized learning resource recommendation is to help learners find the resources that best meet their needs from a vast amount of resources, thereby improving learning outcomes and satisfaction. Personalized learning resource recommendation usually requires analyzing learners' historical learning behaviors, resource usage, knowledge levels, and other aspects of information to construct learners' interest models.

Personalized learning resource recommendation methods can be mainly divided into three categories: content-based recommendation, collaborative filtering recommendation, and hybrid recommendation.

(1) Content-based recommendation: This method recommends resources with similar content to learners based on the content of resources they liked in the past [5]. It requires feature extraction of resources, such as text analysis and keyword extraction, to construct the content representation of resources. Then, by calculating the similarity between the resources that learners like and the candidate resources, resources with higher similarity are recommended to learners. The advantages of content-based recommendation methods are simplicity and ease of implementation, and they do not depend on other users' behavior data; the disadvantages are that they may lead to poor diversity of recommendation results and difficulty in discovering learners' potential interests [6].
(2) Collaborative filtering recommendation: Collaborative filtering recommendation methods recommend resources that other similar learners like to learners based on the similarity between learners and other learners. Collaborative filtering recommendation can be divided into user-based collaborative filtering and item-based collaborative filtering. The former calculates the similarity between learners, while the latter calculates the similarity between resources. The advantages of collaborative filtering recommendation are that they can discover learners' potential interests and have higher diversity of recommendation results; the disadvantages are that they are subject to the cold start problem, which means it is difficult to make effective recommendations for new learners or new resources due to the lack of sufficient behavior data.
(3) Hybrid recommendation: Hybrid recommendation methods combine the advantages of content-based recommendation and collaborative filtering recommendation, integrating the recommendation results of both methods through various strategies [7]. The advantages of hybrid recommendation methods are that they can overcome the limitations of a single recommendation method, improving the accuracy and diversity of recommendations; the disadvantages are that they have higher implementation complexity and require adjusting multiple parameters to achieve the best results.

2.3 Application of Association Rule Mining in Personalized Learning Resource Recommendation

In recent years, association rule mining technology has received widespread attention in the field of personalized learning resource recommendation. Researchers have attempted to discover the potential relationships between learning resources through association rule mining, providing more accurate and personalized recommendations for learners. For instance, Sarwar et al. proposed a collaborative filtering recommendation method based on association rule mining, which generates recommendation rules by mining frequent itemsets from learners' behavior data [8]. Mobasher et al. applied association rule mining technology to content-based recommendation by analyzing learners' browsing behavior and resource content data, discovering the relationships between resource content, and recommending related resources based on learners' interest models. Meanwhile, researchers have also tried to combine association rule mining technology with other recommendation methods, proposing hybrid recommendation methods based on association rule mining [9]. For example, Wang et al. proposed a recommendation method that combines association rule mining and collaborative filtering, improving recommendation accuracy and diversity by mining learner behavior data and resource content information to discover potential relationships [10].

Despite the achievements of association rule mining in personalized learning resource recommendation, there are still some challenges and issues [11]. First, the efficiency and scale of association rule mining depend on the algorithm used, and selecting an appropriate algorithm to cope with massive learning resources and user data is a problem. Second, it is worth investigating how to adjust recommendation strategies based on the results of association rule mining to improve recommendation accuracy and satisfaction. Moreover, further research is needed on how to deal with data sparsity, cold start problems, and recommendation result diversity and novelty.

In summary, association rule mining has broad application prospects in the field of personalized learning resource recommendation. This paper will propose a personalized learning resource recommendation method based on association rule mining. By analyzing learners' historical learning behavior and resource usage, we will extract learners' interest models and use association rule mining technology to discover potential relationships between learning resources, thereby providing personalized learning resource recommendations for learners.

3 Implementation Process of Personalized Learning Resource Recommendation Method Based on Association Rule Mining

3.1 Overall Framework of the Method

Continuing the translation: The personalized learning resource recommendation method based on association rule mining mainly includes the following four steps:

(1) Data preprocessing: Clean and transform the raw learning behavior data to generate a standardized learning behavior matrix;
(2) Association rule mining: Use association rule mining algorithms to mine frequent itemsets and association rules in the learning behavior matrix;
(3) Interest model construction: Generate learners' interest models based on association rules;
(4) Recommendation strategy: Recommend personalized learning resources for learners based on their interest models and association rules.

3.2 Data Preprocessing

Data preprocessing is the first step in the personalized learning resource recommendation method, aiming to convert raw learning behavior data into a standardized format suitable for association rule mining. Data preprocessing includes the following sub-steps:

(1) Data cleaning: Remove invalid records, duplicate records, and noise data from the raw data to ensure data quality. Specific operations include removing invalid user IDs, resource IDs, and eliminating incomplete learning behaviors, etc.

(2) Data transformation: Convert the cleaned data into a standardized learning behavior matrix. The learning behavior matrix is a two-dimensional table, where each row represents a learner, each column represents a learning resource, and the elements in the matrix indicate the learners' usage of resources. Usually, a binary representation (0 for not used, 1 for used) or a rating representation (e.g., 1–5 points) can be used to represent the relationship between learners and resources. In this method, binary representation is adopted.
(3) Data discretization: To improve the efficiency of association rule mining, it is necessary to discretize the learning behavior matrix. The purpose of discretization is to convert continuous attributes (such as ratings, learning duration, etc.) into discrete attributes (such as used or not used). In this method, binarization is used, that is, the elements in the learning behavior matrix are converted into 0 or 1, indicating whether the learner has used the corresponding resource. After data preprocessing, a standardized learning behavior matrix is obtained, laying the foundation for subsequent association rule mining.

3.3 Association Rule Mining

Association rule mining is a method for discovering latent relationships between variables in a dataset. In this method, association rule mining techniques are used to mine the association relationships between resources used by learners. Association rule mining includes two stages: frequent itemset mining and association rule generation.

(1) Frequent Itemset Mining

Frequent itemsets refer to itemsets that appear in the dataset a number of times reaching the threshold. In this method, the Apriori algorithm is used to mine frequent itemsets in the learning behavior matrix. The Apriori algorithm is a classic association rule mining algorithm that generates frequent itemsets through layer-by-layer search based on prior knowledge. First, the algorithm scans the learning behavior matrix, calculates the support of each item (i.e., the probability of the item appearing in the dataset), and forms a 1-item frequent itemset from items with support greater than the given threshold. Next, the algorithm generates 2-item candidate itemsets by connecting 1-item frequent itemsets and calculates the support of candidate itemsets, forming 2-item frequent itemsets from candidate itemsets with support greater than the threshold. This process continues, and the algorithm generates k-item frequent itemsets layer by layer until no larger frequent itemsets can be generated.

(2) Association Rule Generation

Association rules refer to implications in the form of $X \rightarrow Y$, where X and Y are itemsets, indicating that transactions containing X are likely to contain Y as well. In this method, association rules are generated based on the mined frequent itemsets. Specifically, the following steps are taken: First, traverse each frequent itemset, decomposing it into several non-empty subsets X and Y (the union of X and Y equals the frequent itemset, and X and Y are disjoint). Then, calculate the confidence of $X \rightarrow Y$ (i.e., the probability of containing Y in transactions containing X) and add association rules with confidence greater than the given threshold to the association rule set.

Through association rule mining, the latent association relationships between learning resources are obtained, providing a basis for constructing learners' interest models and generating personalized recommendations.

3.4 Interest Model Construction

The interest model is a data structure that describes learners' interests and preferences, helping to understand their needs and recommend appropriate resources. In this method, learners' interest models are generated based on association rules. The specific steps are as follows:

(1) Initialize an empty interest model for each learner, containing resource categories and their weights;
(2) Traverse the learner's learning behavior data, and update the interest model based on the association rules. Specifically, if the learner has used the antecedent (i.e., X) in the association rule, increase the weight of the resource category corresponding to the consequent (i.e., Y) in the association rule;
(3) Normalize the interest model so that the sum of the weights of all resource categories equals 1.

Through the above process, an interest model is constructed for each learner, reflecting their preference levels for different resource categories.

3.5 Recommendation Strategy

The recommendation strategy is the process of recommending personalized learning resources for learners based on their interest models and association rules. In this method, the following recommendation strategy is adopted:

Based on the learner's interest model, recommend resource categories with higher weights; within the recommended resource categories, use association rules to recommend resources related to the resources the learner has already used. Specifically, traverse the learner's learning behavior data and recommend resources related to the used resources according to the association rules, taking into account the confidence and support of the association rules, prioritizing rules with higher confidence and support for recommendation;

To ensure the diversity and novelty of the recommended results, a certain proportion of popular resources and newly released resources can also be included in the recommended resources. Through the above recommendation strategy, a personalized learning resource recommendation list is generated for learners, which helps to improve their learning interest and effectiveness.

4 Experiment Verification and Analysis

To verify the effectiveness of the personalized learning resource recommendation method based on association rule mining, this chapter will evaluate the proposed method through experiments. The experiment is divided into three stages: first, introducing the experimental dataset and its characteristics; second, designing the experimental scheme, including evaluation metrics, comparison methods, and experimental settings; and finally, analyzing the experimental results and comparing them with other recommendation methods.

4.1 Experimental Dataset

This experiment uses the learning behavior data of an online education platform as the experimental dataset. The dataset contains the learning behavior records of several learners over a period of time, recording the learners' usage of various types of resources. The resources in the dataset include online courses, video tutorials, e-books, etc., covering multiple subject areas. To protect user privacy, the original data has been de-identified.

To evaluate the effectiveness of the recommendation method, the dataset is divided into a training set and a test set. The training set contains the learners' learning behavior records in the first 80% of the time period, used to construct interest models and association rules; the test set contains the learners' learning behavior records in the last 20% of the time period, used to evaluate the recommendation results.

4.2 Experimental Scheme

4.2.1. Evaluation Metrics. To comprehensively evaluate the performance of the recommendation method, the following four evaluation metrics are used:

(1) Precision: the proportion of correctly recommended resources in the total recommended resources;
(2) Recall: the proportion of correctly recommended resources in the actual resources of interest to users;
(3) F1-Score: the harmonic mean of precision and recall, used to comprehensively evaluate the performance of the recommendation method;
(4) Coverage: the proportion of different resources that can be recommended by the recommendation method to the total resources, used to evaluate the diversity of the recommendation method.

4.2.2. Comparison Methods. To demonstrate the superiority of the proposed method, it is compared with the following three recommendation methods: Random Recommendation: randomly recommend resources to users; Popularity Recommendation: recommend the most popular resources to users; Collaborative Filtering Recommendation: recommend resources to users based on the similarity between learners.
4.2.3. Experimental Settings. In the experiment, the following steps are performed:

(1) Data preprocessing: clean the raw dataset and convert its format to generate a standardized learning behavior matrix;
(2) Association rule mining: use the Apriori algorithm to mine association rules in the learning behavior matrix, setting minimum support and minimum confidence thresholds;
(3) Interest model construction: build an interest model for each learner based on the association rules;
(4) Recommendation strategy: generate personalized learning resource recommendation lists for learners based on their interest models and association rules;

(5) Recommendation result evaluation: use the test set to evaluate the recommendation results, calculating metrics such as precision, recall, F1-score, and coverage;
(6) Comparison experiment: conduct comparison experiments using random recommendation, popularity recommendation, and collaborative filtering recommendation methods to evaluate the performance of various methods.

4.3 Experimental Results Analysis

According to the experimental scheme, the evaluation metric results for various recommendation methods were obtained, as shown in Table 1.

Table 1. Evaluation metric results for various recommendation methods

Recommendation Method	Precision	Recall	F1-Score	Coverage
Association Rule-based Recommendation	0.65	0.61	0.63	0.72
Random Recommendation	0.15	0.17	0.16	0.45
Popularity Recommendation	0.52	0.48	0.50	0.35
Collaborative Filtering Recommendation	0.57	0.54	0.55	0.62

As can be seen from Table 1, the personalized learning resource recommendation method based on association rules outperforms the other three recommendation methods in terms of accuracy, recall, F1 score, and coverage. This indicates that the proposed method exhibits better performance in mining learners' interests and recommending personalized resources, providing more accurate and high-quality recommended resources for learners.

Through comparative experiments, it was also found that the recommendation method based on association rules is particularly outstanding in terms of coverage. This is attributed to the association rule mining technique's ability to discover the latent relationships between learning resources, which helps uncover learners' potential interest points, thereby improving the diversity of the recommended results.

In summary, the experimental results demonstrate that the personalized learning resource recommendation method based on association rule mining has good effectiveness, providing learners with accurate and diverse learning resource recommendations.

5 Conclusion and Discussion

Experimental validation reveals that the personalized learning resource recommendation method based on association rule mining achieves good results in terms of accuracy, recall, F1 score, and coverage. However, in practical applications, some other factors need to be considered to further improve the performance and practicality of the recommendation method.

(1) Dynamically update interest models: Learners' interests change over time. Therefore, it is necessary to regularly update learners' interest models to capture these changes. Specifically, a time window can be set, considering only the learners' behavior data within that window to update the interest model [12].
(2) Consider learners' background information: Learners' background information (such as age, gender, education, etc.) may affect their learning interests and needs. In practice, these background factors can be incorporated into the interest model construction process to improve the personalization level of the recommendation method [13].
(3) Resource quality screening: To ensure the quality of recommended resources, resources need to be screened and ranked. A feasible method is to introduce resource rating information, rank resources, and prioritize recommending resources with higher ratings.
(4) User feedback mechanism: User feedback on recommended results is an important basis for evaluating the performance of recommendation methods. In practice, a user feedback mechanism can be introduced, collecting user evaluations of recommended resources to optimize the recommendation method and improve the accuracy of recommended results [14].
(5) Explore other association rule mining algorithms: The Apriori algorithm used in this paper may have lower computational efficiency in the association rule mining process. In the future, other association rule mining algorithms, such as the FP-Growth algorithm, can be explored to improve the computational efficiency of the recommendation method [15].

In summary, through experimental validation and result discussion, it is believed that the personalized learning resource recommendation method based on association rule mining has good effectiveness. In future research, the recommendation method will be further optimized to meet the growing personalized learning needs of learners.

References

1. Wang, H., Fu, W.: Personalized learning resource recommendation method based on dynamic collaborative filtering. Mob. Netw. Appl. **26**, 473–487 (2021)
2. Li, H., Li, H., Zhang, S., et al.: Intelligent learning system based on personalized recommendation technology. Neural Comput. Appl. **31**, 4455–4462 (2019)
3. Telikani, A., Gandomi, A.H., Shahbahrami, A.: A survey of evolutionary computation for association rule mining. Inf. Sci. **524**, 318–352 (2020)
4. Raj, N.S., Renumol, V.G.: A systematic literature review on adaptive content recommenders in personalized learning environments from 2015 to 2020. J. Comput. Educ. **9**(1), 113–148 (2022)
5. Zhou, L., Zhang, F., Zhang, S., et al.: Study on the personalized learning model of learner-learning resource matching. Int. J. Inf. Educ. Technol. **11**(3), 143–147 (2021)
6. Joy, J., Raj, N.S.: An ontology model for content recommendation in personalized learning environment. In: Proceedings of the Second International Conference on Data Science, e-Learning and Information Systems, pp. 1–6 (2019)
7. Zhou, Y., Huang, C., Hu, Q., et al.: Personalized learning full-path recommendation model based on LSTM neural networks. Inf. Sci. **444**, 135–152 (2018)

8. Liu, Y., Li, J., Ren, Z., et al.: Research on personalized recommendation of higher education resources based on multidimensional association rules. Wirel. Commun. Mob. Comput. **2022** (2022)
9. Yu, X., Wei, D., Chu, Q., et al.: The personalized recommendation algorithms in educational application. In: 2018 9th International Conference on Information Technology in Medicine and Education (ITME), pp. 664–668. IEEE (2018)
10. Kardan, A.A., Ebrahimi, M.: A novel approach to hybrid recommendation systems based on association rules mining for content recommendation in asynchronous discussion groups. Inf. Sci. **219**, 93–110 (2013)
11. Chatti, M.A., Dakova, S., Thüs, H., et al.: Tag-based collaborative filtering recommendation in personal learning environments. IEEE Trans. Learn. Technol. **6**(4), 337–349 (2013)
12. Zhang, L., Tao, Q., Teng, P.Q.: An improved collaborative filtering algorithm based on user interest. J. Softw. **9**(4), 999–1006 (2014)
13. Chen, J., Wei, L., Zhang, L.: Dynamic evolutionary clustering approach based on time weight and latent attributes for collaborative filtering recommendation. Chaos Solitons Fractals **114**, 8–18 (2018)
14. Cai, B., Zhu, X., Qin, Y.: Parameters optimization of hybrid strategy recommendation based on particle swarm algorithm. Expert Syst. Appl. **168**, 114388 (2021)
15. Chen, J., Zhao, C., Chen, L.: Collaborative filtering recommendation algorithm based on user correlation and evolutionary clustering. Complex Intell. Syst. **6**, 147–156 (2020)

A Study on the Influence of Students' Expectation on the Quality Satisfaction of Online Courses from the Perspective of Quality Perception

Zhipeng Ou[1(✉)], Han Zhang[1], and Xia Liu[2]

[1] Sanya Aviation and Tourism College, Sanya 572000, Hainan, China
hainanozp@126.com
[2] Faculty of Humanities and Social Sciences, Macao Polytechnic University, Macao 999078, China
paolo_lx@qq.com

Abstract. The construction of online course resources has been rapid, but the satisfaction of online course learning among university students is not high, so how to improve online learning satisfaction has become a key issue. In this paper, we analyze the influence of the perceived quality of online courses on the realization of the value of online learning and satisfaction of university students from the perspective of online course quality, and build a research model based on the expectation confirmation theory. The research hypothesis was formulated, data were collected through questionnaires, and statistical analysis and hypothesis testing were carried out using SPSS and Smart PLS. The experimental results show that the expectation confirmation of university students' online learning affects their perception of the quality of online courses, and the quality of online courses significantly affects the value and satisfaction of university students' online learning, while the perceived value directly affects the satisfaction of online learning. The results of this study have important implications for improving the quality of online courses, enhancing the value of online learning, and increasing the satisfaction of students with online learning.

Keywords: Expectation Confirmation Theory · Online Learning Satisfaction · Quality Perception

1 Background of the Study

Based on the online catechism platform and the online teaching system, a large number of online course resources have been built at the faculty, university, provincial and national levels, playing a very important role in ensuring normal teaching and learning, and achieving the goal of "stopping classes without stopping learning and stopping classes without stopping teaching". Thus, the online course resources have become the main channel of independent learning for students during the epidemic prevention and control

J. Gan et al. (Eds.): CSEI 2023, CCIS 1899, pp. 333–345, 2024.
https://doi.org/10.1007/978-981-99-9499-1_29

period. Satisfaction with online courses is the key to students' persistence in completing online courses, and how to improve satisfaction with online courses has become a core concern of the platform and teachers.

Research on online learning satisfaction is mainly based on satisfaction theory, and has been conducted from the perspectives of teachers, students, and the environment and atmosphere [1–4]. For example, Chih-Hui Chiang et al. explored the factors of teachers, students and technology on the basis of live and recorded contexts to build a model of satisfaction and confirmed that online teacher support services can significantly affect online learning satisfaction in different contexts [1, 2]. Wen Jing and Xu Xiaoqing also found that learners' learning attitudes, learning behaviors, content interaction and teacher-student interaction in online learning are very important to online learning satisfaction [3, 4]; Yin Meng and Liang Lulu studied students' continuous learning behaviors in online courses from both system and user perspectives, and illustrated the importance of learning atmosphere, course quality, teaching quality and users' self-control to students' continuous online learning [5]. Although a large number of studies have demonstrated that online learning platforms, online learning environments, teacher-student interaction and personal perceptions are the main influencing factors of online learning satisfaction, the influence of online course quality and students' learning expectations has been neglected. Therefore, analyzing the satisfaction of online learning only from the factors such as online learning effect does not fully explain the influencing factors of online learning satisfaction of college students, and it is more important to analyze the satisfaction of online learning in relation to the expectation of college students on online learning.

In the study of user satisfaction, expectation confirmation theory has been proven to be one of the main theories for analyzing user expectations, satisfaction and persistent behaviour. Therefore, this paper uses the expectation confirmation theory as a framework to analyse the impact of students' expectation confirmation on the perceived quality of online courses, as well as its role in the realization of value and satisfaction of online learning by university students. The results of this study will provide theoretical support for the design of online learning platforms, courses and teaching activities, in order to improve students' satisfaction with online learning, reduce the dropout rate and improve the effectiveness of online learning.

2 Theoretical Basis and Literature Review

The lack of satisfaction with online learning has a direct impact on the sustainability of online learning and is the main reason why students drop out of online learning. Improving online learning satisfaction is the key point to improve the effectiveness of online learning. Combining previous research and the research scenario of online learning, I believe that the satisfaction of students' online learning comes not only from the comparison between the expectation before online learning and the actual experience after learning, but also from the students' perception of the quality of online courses and the value of online course learning. Therefore, with reference to the research on user behavior of information systems, we introduce the expectation confirmation theory into the study of online learning of college students [6] integrate the factors related to the quality perception of college students' online courses, and study its influence on the satisfaction of college students' online learning.

2.1 Expectation Confirmation Theory and Its Study

Expectation Confirmation Theory (ECT) is a classic theory for studying user behaviour, and is mainly used to analyze the satisfaction of information system users, their continuous behaviour and the factors influencing them [6, 7]. The expectation confirmation theory suggests that users expect the system to meet their needs before using the system, and the higher the degree of expectation confirmation, the higher the satisfaction of users [6, 8] In user behaviour research, expectation confirmation theory generally integrates different theories and influencing factors depending on the research scenario to study user behaviour. This suggests that expectation confirmation theory can be used as a research framework to integrate other theories for the study of user satisfaction and behaviour in different research contexts, and that expectation confirmation has different degrees of influence on perceived usefulness, perceived quality, perceived value, as well as satisfaction and continued use behaviour. The learning of online courses is the process of acquiring knowledge through online learning platforms, which is also part of user behaviour. Therefore, expectation confirmation theory is also applicable to the study of online learning satisfaction, and can be used to construct a research model and conduct empirical research from the perspective of perceived quality.

2.2 A Study of Online Learning Satisfaction and Perceived Quality

Satisfaction is the psychological state that arises when comparing the user's expectations before receiving a product or service with the perceived effects of using it, and is a cognitive differential evaluation of prior expectations and performance perceptions.

Satisfaction with online course learning is also derived from the comparison of expectations before and after the course, and the platform of the online course, the content of the online learning, the atmosphere of the online learning and the effectiveness of the online learning are also important factors that affect the perceived quality and value of online course learning of university students. Perceived quality refers to the user's subjective evaluation and judgement that the product or service they use meets their needs during or after use; perceived value refers to the user's overall subjective perception and judgement of the benefits of using the product or service compared to the cost of using the product or service.

As we can see above, the research model based on expectation confirmation theory has been applied to the study of user satisfaction and its influencing factors by many scholars, but there is less research on the online learning scenario of university students, especially the research that combines expectation confirmation with perceived value and perceived quality to analyze the learning satisfaction behavior. Therefore, based on the expectation confirmation theory, this paper subdivides perceived quality into platform quality, course quality and learning quality, and integrates perceived value to build a research model to investigate the influence of expectation confirmation on perceived quality of online learning, and the influence of different types of perceived quality on students' perceived value and satisfaction of online learning.

3 Model Construction and Research Hypothesis

3.1 Model Construction

Based on previous research, this paper divides perceived quality into three dimensions: platform quality, course quality and learning quality, and concludes that perceived quality affects perceived value and learning satisfaction, while perceived value also affects learning satisfaction. The research model shown in Fig. 1 is used to analyse the effects of expectation confirmation, and perceived quality on perceived value and learning satisfaction.

3.2 The Influential Role of Online Learning Expectation Confirmation

Learning expectation confirmation refers to the user's perceived satisfaction of learning outcomes and results before learning an online course. In the context of online learning research, the perceived quality in this paper includes three dimensions: platform quality, course quality and learning quality. Perceived quality, perceived value and customer satisfaction have been shown to be influenced by customer expectations in studies based on the Consumer Satisfaction Index (ACSI). When users' expectations of online learning are confirmed to a high degree, they subjectively perceive the overall quality of online learning to be higher, i.e. learning expectations have a positive effect on perceived quality.

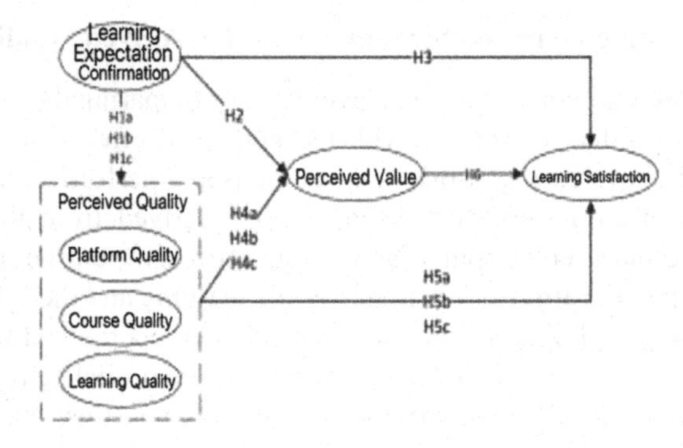

Fig. 1. Research model of factors influencing satisfaction with online course learning

Platform quality includes indicators such as the number of courses in the online learning platform, the ease of use of the learning platform and the clarity of the interface design [6]. The quality of the platform is a key factor in the user experience when using an online course platform, and many users refuse to use an online learning platform because of the quality of the platform. The higher the overall expectation confirmation, the higher the perception of the quality of the online learning platform. Therefore, the following hypothesis is:

H1a: Learning expectations confirm the positive influence on perceived platform quality.

Course quality refers to the richness of the content of the online course, the clarity of the objectives of the online course, and the attractiveness of the online course content. Li et al. show that expectation confirmation has a significant positive effect on perceived usefulness, which generally measures the user's perception of the overall quality of the information system, i.e. the higher the level of overall expectation confirmation of online learning, the more it affects the perceived quality and satisfaction of students. Online courses break the constraints of time and space, which helps to increase user engagement and satisfaction to a certain extent, and they also make it easier for students to access learning materials and content and to understand the objectives of the course. The higher the overall expectations of students in the learning process, the higher the students' perception of the quality of the online course. Therefore, the following hypothesis is:

H1b: Learning expectations confirm the positive influence on perceived course quality.

Learning quality refers to the subjective perception of students' active thinking, participation, knowledge acquisition and learning gains when participating in online courses. The perception of learning quality is closely related to online teaching resources, students' learning initiative and teacher-student interaction, and is the key to measuring the success of online teaching. The higher the quality of learning, the more students can obtain the knowledge they want and satisfy their needs for knowledge through online courses. The confirmation of university students' expectation of online learning includes the confirmation of the convenience of knowledge acquisition, the amount of knowledge acquisition, and the quality of knowledge acquisition. Therefore, the higher the degree of confirmation of students' expectations of online learning, the higher the quality of online learning is perceived by students. Therefore, the following hypothesis is:

H1c: Learning expectations confirm the positive influence on perceived learning quality.

Perceived value refers to users' overall perceptions of the knowledge and value gained from using online learning compared to the cost of time and money spent. The relationship between social networks and perceived value was investigated by Yin and Li, who confirmed that expectation confirmation can influence users' different perceptions of value, i.e. the higher the level of expectation confirmation, the stronger the user's perception of value. When users' expectation confirmation of online learning is high, they subjectively believe that the effectiveness they gain from using online learning is worth the effort, i.e., learning expectation confirmation positively influences perceived value. Therefore, the following hypothesis is:

H2: Learning expectation confirmation has a positive effect on perceived value.

In expectation confirmation theory, expectation confirmation has a direct effect on user satisfaction. A number of studies based on expectation confirmation theory have confirmed the positive and significant effect of expectation confirmation on satisfaction. In the study context of online learning, the higher the degree of expectation confirmation of online learning and the higher the perceived enjoyment and satisfaction after using online learning, the higher the satisfaction of online learning, i.e. expectation confirmation of online learning can enhance the satisfaction of online learning of university students. Therefore, the following hypothesis is:

H3: Confirmation of learning expectations has a positive effect on learning satisfaction.

3.3 Impact of Online Course Satisfaction and Perceived Quality Role

User perceived quality influences perceived value, and satisfaction is influenced by both perceived value and perceived quality. In the context of online learning, the benefits of online learning for students are mainly derived from the overall perception of online learning, including the quality of the online platform, the quality of the online course and the quality of online learning. If students' perceptions of all three are higher, then their perceived benefits will be higher, and their perceived value will be higher for the same cost. Thus, perceived platform quality, perceived course quality and perceived learning quality all affect the value of student learning. Therefore, the following hypothesis is:

H4a: Perceived platform quality positively influences perceived value;

H4b: Perceived course quality positively influences perceived value;

H4c: Perceived learning quality positively influences perceived value.

Previous research has demonstrated the impact of perceived usefulness, perceived ease of use, perceived quality and perceived value on user satisfaction. In the study of online learning, the higher the perceived overall quality of online learning, the higher the user's needs are met, the higher the knowledge gained and the higher the learning performance, the happier the user is, and the higher the overall satisfaction. The overall quality perception of online courses consists of three dimensions: platform quality perception, course quality perception and learning quality perception, with platform quality perception reflecting the convenience and ease of access to knowledge; course quality perception reflecting the richness and effectiveness of online course content; and online learning quality reflecting students' online learning performance. High platform quality, course quality and learning quality bring students a good experience of online learning, i.e. the perceived quality of all three dimensions positively affects students' satisfaction with online learning. Therefore, the following hypothesis is:

H5a: Perceived platform quality positively influences learning satisfaction;

H5b: Perceived course quality positively influences learning satisfaction;

H5c: Perceived quality of learning positively influences learning satisfaction.

Perceived value comes from the user's overall perception of gain and loss. The higher the user's perception of value, the higher the user's benefit and the higher the user's satisfaction. In the context of online course learning, perceived value comes from the perceived cost of time spent on online learning compared to the benefits, the higher the knowledge gained and the higher the performance of the learning, the greater the pleasure of learning online and the higher the satisfaction of the students. Therefore, the following hypothesis is:

H6: Perceived value significantly and positively influences satisfaction with learning.

4 Research Methodology and Empirical Analysis

4.1 Questionnaire Design and Variable Measurements

In this paper, data were collected by means of a questionnaire, processed and statistically analyzed using SPSS, and path analysis and hypothesis testing were carried out using SmartPLS. In order to obtain more valid data, the questionnaire was designed in three parts: firstly, the basic information of the sample such as gender, age and grade; secondly, the measurement of latent variables such as perceived quality, learning expectation and perceived value, which require the respondents to answer according to their actual situation of using the online learning platform; and finally, the influence of each latent variable on the satisfaction of using the online learning platform is measured, and the respondents are required to answer according to their own learning satisfaction.

The research model includes six latent variables, of which platform quality, course quality and learning quality are the three latent variables of perceived quality. In order to ensure the validity of the measures, three questions were designed for each measure, and a questionnaire was developed using a 5-point Likert scale. After the questionnaire was designed, a pre-study was conducted, and the questionnaire was revised based on the results of the pre-study to finalize the questionnaire.

4.2 Data Collection and Statistical Analysis

4.3 Reliability and Validity Tests

4.3.1 Reliability Test

The reliability test reflects the stability and reliability of the measured scale, and the internal consistency is mainly determined by the combined reliability (CR). The overall Cronbach's α value of the sample data was 0.959, which was greater than 0.8, indicating that the sample data had very good reliability and could be used for subsequent data analysis. The results are shown in Table 2, which shows that the alpha and CR values of the latent variables are all greater than 0.8, the CR values are all greater than 0.7, the standard loadings of each measure are all above 0.7, and the average extracted variance (AVE) values are all greater than 0.5 and the confidence level of the sample data is considered to meet the requirements of the data analysis.

4.3.2 Validity Test

The correlation coefficients between the variables and the square root of the AVE were calculated. Table 2 shows that the AVE values for all latent variables were >0.5, indicating good convergent validity of the sample. The results are shown in Table 3, where the values on the diagonal line are the square roots of the AVEs of the latent variables, which are greater than the correlation coefficients between the latent variables, and therefore the discriminant validity of the sample is considered to be satisfactory.

Table 1. Descriptive statistics of the sample (n = 330)

Options	Range of options	Frequency	Percentage (%)	Options	Range of options	Frequency	Percentage (%)
Gender	male	94	28.48		Year 1	9	2.73
		236	71.52		Year 2	106	32.12
	female	2	0.61	Grade	Year 3	176	53.33
		179	54.24		Year 4	39	11.82
Age	<15	147	44.55		Love Course	30	9.09
	16—20	1	0.30		Tencent Classroom	98	29.70
	21—25	1	0.30			35	10.61
	26—30		4.55	Online courses used	Schoolroom Online		
	>30						
School Type	Undergraduate	34	10.31	Platform	Netease Cloud Classroom	132	40.00
		289	87.58		Mucuo	153	46.36
	Senior & High School	7	2.12		Others	101	30.61
	Others						

Table 2. Reliability and validity analysis of the latent variables

Latent variables	Measurements	Average	Standard deviation	Standard load	α	CR	AVE
Platform quality	PTQ1	3.68	0.974	0.805	0.818	0.892	0.734
	PYQ2	3.69	0.900	0.901			
	PTQ3	3.7	0.835	0.861			
Course quality	KCQ1	3.76	0.883	0.837	0.821	0.893	0.736
	KCQ2	3.57	0.876	0.885			
	KCQ3	3.33	0.893	0.851			
Learning quality	XXQ1	3.31	0.841	0.843	0.841	0.904	0.759
	XXQ2	3.35	0.921	0.879			
	XXQ3	3.62	0.835	0.891			
Learning Expectation	PEC1	3.49	0.855	0.927	0.935	0.958	0.884
	PEC2	3.42	0.879	0.953			
	PEC3	3.59	0.828	0.941			
Perceived value	PV1	3.34	0.826	0.878	0.875	0.923	0.800
	PV2	3.35	0.804	0.892			
	PV3	3.37	0.823	0.912			
Satisfaction	XXS1	3.50	0.800	0.934	0.938	0.956	0.878
	XXS2	3.51	0.819	0.950			
	XXS3	3.51	0.837	0.928			

Table 3. Discriminant validity analysis

Latent variables	Platform quality	Course quality	Learning quality	Learning Expectation	Perceived value	Satisfaction
Platform quality	0.857					
Course quality	0.738	0.858				
Learning quality	0.635	0.747	0.871			
Learning Expectation	0.499	0.610	0.679	0.940		
Perceived value	0.617	0.739	0.768	0.727	0.894	
Satisfaction	0.610	0.734	0.751	0.765	0.807	0.937

4.4 Hypothesis Testing

This paper uses SmartPLS to measure the correlation coefficients between the latent variables and the significance levels of the paths, and the results are shown in Fig. 2 and Table 4.

5 Findings, Implications and Prospects

5.1 Research Findings

As can be seen from Fig. 2 and Table 4, hypotheses 4a and 5a were not supported, while all other hypotheses were supported. The results of the study confirm that learning expectation confirmation, course quality, quality of learning and perceived value have a positive effect on learning satisfaction, and that the effect of each latent variable.

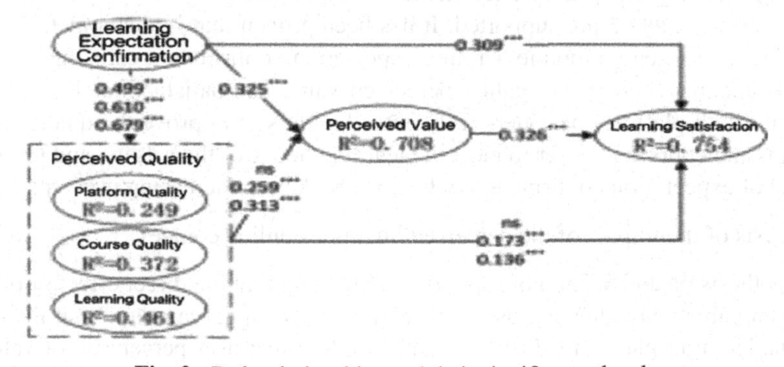

Fig. 2. Path relationships and their significance levels

The analysis is as follows:

Table 4. Summary of study results

Research hypothesis	Path coefficient	T-value	Results	Research hypothesis	Path coefficient	T-value	Results
H1a:Learning Expectation→Platform quality	0. 499***	10.3	Support	H4a:Platform quality→Perceived value	0.065	1.4	No support
H1b:Learning Expectation→Course quality	0. 610***	15.1	Support	H4b:Course quality→Perceived value	0. 259***	4.5	Support
H1c:Learning Expectation→Learning quality	0. 679***	20.3	Support	H4c:Learning quality→Perceived value	0. 313***	5.2	Support
H2:Learning quality→Perceived value	0. 313***	5.2	Support	H5a:Platform quality→Satisfaction	0.040	0.9	No support
H3:Learning Expectation→Satisfaction	0. 309***	6.2	Support	H5b:Course quality→Satisfaction	0. 173***	2.9	Support
H6:Perceived value→Satisfaction	0. 326***	4.7	Support	H5c:Learning quality→Satisfaction	0. 136**	2.0	Support

1. Analysis of the impact of the confirmation of online learning expectations

Hypotheses 1a, 1b and 1c are all supported. For university users, the higher the level of expectation confirmation when learning online through an online learning platform, the stronger the overall experience will be; the better the perception of online course learning, the higher the overall quality of online course learning will be. For online learning platform builders, the key to gaining students' recognition of online learning is to raise their expectations of online learning. The confirmation of students' expectations of online learning comes from two sources: the students' pre-study expectations, and the students' online learning satisfaction of their expectations. There is no way to intervene in students' pre-study expectations, but it is possible to improve the confirmation of students' expectations through optimising the learning platform, enriching the curriculum, enhancing learning supervision and interacting with students.

Hypotheses 2 and 3 are supported. It has been proven that in the context of online course learning research, online learning expectation confirmation can simultaneously improve students' perceived quality, perceived value and satisfaction. It is therefore crucial for both platform providers and course builders to improve the quality of their platforms and courses in order to meet the learning needs of their users, and to increase the level of expectation confirmation, which is also key to increasing user satisfaction.

2. Analysis of the impact of the perceived quality of online courses

Hypothesis 4a and 5a are not supported, indicating that the direct effect of platform quality on perceived value and user satisfaction is not significant, and that the quality of online learning platforms does not significantly affect user perception of value and satisfaction. The main reason for this may be that existing online learning platforms are relatively mature and stable, and that most online learning platforms are highly homogeneous and less differentiated, so that students' experiences when using online learning platforms are not different. However, this does not mean that the quality of the online learning platform is not important, the online learning platform is the foundation, and the technological innovation of the online platform is the key to the innovative development of online learning. With the development of online teaching and intelligent teaching, online learning platforms are also facing the demand for innovation and development. Therefore, the development of online learning should also consider how to innovate the online learning platform, so that it can be more suitable for the online learning of university students, and enhance its competitiveness through the differentiation of platform functions and services.

Hypothesis 4b and 4c are supported by the fact that perceived course quality and perceived learning quality are important factors influencing the perceived value of learning, and that users measure their perceived value by the quality of the course and the quality of learning. With less differentiation in the quality of the platform, users focus more on the quality of the course and the quality of learning, which are the main factors determining their perceived value. Therefore, platform designers should pay more attention to the improvement of course quality, establish a richer and more complete course system, strengthen the interaction, supervision and management of the course learning process, and improve the quality of users' learning through various methods and channels in order to more effectively enhance the perceived value of users and give them a better experience.

Hypothesis 5b and 5c are supported, indicating that users' perceived course quality and learning quality significantly and positively influence users' satisfaction with their learning. Hypothesis 6 is supported, suggesting that the value of online learning can significantly increase the satisfaction of online learning for students. For platform designers to improve user satisfaction, they should focus on building the quality of the courses, such as designing a more complete course system, adding richer course content, making the courses on the platform more extensive, improving the quality of the course content, and inviting more celebrities to teach on the platform. The quality of user learning significantly affects satisfaction, so platform designers should focus on the quality of user learning, such as actively understanding user needs and adding courses that are of more interest to users, planning course time rationally, allowing students to study with high attention span, providing after-class assignments and discussion functions, supervising users' learning, and actively helping users to solve problems.

5.2 Significance of the Study

5.2.1 Theoretical Implications

This paper combines the expectation confirmation theory with perceived quality based on the expectation confirmation theory and the special characteristics of online course learning, and applies it to the study of online learning satisfaction as well as widening the scope of application of expectation confirmation theory. The results of this study confirm that user perceived course quality, perceived learning quality, perceived value and confirmation of learning expectations positively influence user learning satisfaction, with perceived value and confirmation of learning expectations being among the most important influencing factors, and expand the research on factors influencing online learning satisfaction, illustrating the importance of course quality and student learning quality in online courses.

5.2.2 Practical Implications

The main factors influencing user satisfaction are the quality of the course and the quality of learning. This is why online courses should be designed with a view to enhancing the content of the course, for example, by designing online courses with concise and useful content, clear titles and appropriate course lengths. Although the quality of the platform does not have a significant impact on perceived quality and learning satisfaction, the platform is the foundation of online learning, so it is important for designers to keep up with the development trend and to promote innovation in online courses through technological innovation. The confirmation of learning expectations is also an important factor influencing users' satisfaction with online learning, so platform providers should be realistic in their initial promotion and strive to improve the quality of online learning to meet students' learning needs.

5.3 Research Prospects

Based on the expectation confirmation theory, this paper analyses the factors influencing the learning satisfaction of university students in online courses and constructs a research model on the influence of perceived quality on learning satisfaction, and finds the key factors affecting users' learning satisfaction in online courses through empirical research. The study found that the perceived quality of the course and the perceived quality of learning had a significant positive impact on perceived value and learning satisfaction, but the perceived quality of the platform did not have a significant impact on perceived value and learning satisfaction; the perceived expectation confirmation and perceived value had a significant positive impact on learning satisfaction.

There are also shortcomings in the study: firstly, university students are the main group of people using online courses, and this study focuses on university students, but the users of online learning are not only students, but also working professionals and teachers. Therefore, in future research, the scope of the survey can be expanded, for example, to include working professionals and teachers. Therefore, in future research, the scope of the survey can be expanded, such as specialized research on working people and older learners. Secondly, future research could further analyse the impact of personal characteristics such as gender, age and preferences, as well as factors such as the type of subject and the teaching style of the teacher on user satisfaction. Thirdly, user satisfaction is also moderated by moderating factors, such as payment for the course, the purpose of the course, and the type of course, which all moderate the impact of user expectations on satisfaction. Therefore, future studies may include moderators to further expand the study of online learning satisfaction.

Acknowledgement. Project supported by Sanya.

Aviation and Tourism College The ideological and political special project number: SATC2023SZ-04.

References

1. Zhihui, J., Chengling, Z., Hongxia, L., et al.: Factors influencing online learners' satisfaction: a comparison of live and recorded situations. Open Educ. Res. **23**(4), 76–85 (2017)
2. Zhihui, J., Chengling, Z.: Learner satisfaction: the ultimate destination of teacher support services in online learning. Modern Distance Educ. **6**, 51–59 (2018)
3. Jing, W.: Study on university students' learning satisfaction and its influencing factors. China High. Educ. Rev. **4**(1), 134–144 (2013)
4. Xu, X., Zhao, W., Liu, H.: Factors influencing university students' satisfaction with online learning. China Distance Educ. (5), 43–50+79–80 (2017)
5. Meng, Y., Lulu, L.: The study of factors influencing continuous learning in online courses from the perspective of platforms and users. J. Xinyang Normal College (Philosophical Soc. Sci. Ed.) **41**(6), 80–87 (2021)
6. Xin, L., Qi, L., Meng, Y.: A study on the persistent use intention of group purchasing APP: an ECM-based integration approach. J. Dalian Polytechnic Univ. (Soc. Sci. Ed.) **40**(4), 56–65 (2019)
7. Zou, X., Xie, J.: A study on the factors influencing the satisfaction of mobile news users: a survey based on students in five universities in Shanghai. Journalism Univ. (5), 77–85+149–150 (2017)
8. Meng, Y., Qi, L.: A study on the continuous use intention of mobile APPs integrating ECT and IS success theory: an example of health APPs. J. Dalian Polytech. Univ. (Soc. Sci. Ed.) **38**(1), 81–87 (2017)
9. Zhihao, M., Jinping, G., Xiang, Z.: The persistent use behavior and subjective well-being of webcast users based on expectation recognition models and quasi-social relationships. J. Commun. Rev. **73**(2), 29–46 (2020)
10. Sun, J., Pei, L., Liu, H.: A model for continuous use of video websites based on expectation confirmation model. Library Intell. Knowl. (5), 82–88+ 45 (2013)
11. Jiaqi, L., Wan, K., Chun, L.: A study on the factors influencing bicycle sharing users' intention to continue using bicycles based on TAM-ECM model. Soft Sci. **33**(7), 116–121 (2019)
12. Zhao, X., Wang, S.: The factors influencing the persistent willingness of WeChat applet users. Modern Intell. **39**(6), 70–80+90 (2019)
13. Liu, R., Chai, J.: A study of the factors influencing the persistent use behavior of SNS users. Soft Sci. **27**(4), 132–135+ 140 (2013)
14. Zhenyu, L., Chaohui, C.: A comprehensive model of the factors affecting mobile bank persistence: based on the perspective of ECM and TAM. Modern Manag. Sci. **9**, 63–65 (2014)

Analysing the Factors Influencing the High Dropout Rate of MOOCs Based on NVivo Qualitative

Kaicheng Shi and Mengqin Sun(✉)

Guangdong University of Science and Technology, Dongguan, China
sunmengqin@gdust.edu.cn

Abstract. The massive open online course (MOOC) is a new course model that has emerged in the field of open education in recent years. After the New Crown epidemic in 2020, the total number of MOOC courses and the number of learners in Chinese universities are also increasing, but along with this is the high dropout rate of MOOC courses. The author tracked a total of 152 students enrolled in classes 15 to 19 at Y University and used NVivo qualitative software to code and analyse texts related to the reasons for dropping out of MOOC courses for 152 students to study the factors influencing the high dropout rate of MOOC courses. Based on the analysis results, the dropout factors are specifically described in terms of learners, MOOC courses, and MOOC learning platforms.

Keywords: MOOC · High dropout rate · NVivo · Influence factor

1 Research Questions

1.1 A Subsection Sample

MOOCs, also known as MOOCs, are large-scale open courses released on the Internet by individuals or organizations with the spirit of sharing and collaboration and are willing to enhance the dissemination of knowledge. MOOCs are a new model of free and open online courses in the field of education in recent years.

MOOCs provide rich teaching resources (mostly in the form of multimedia) and interactive forums and learning communities based on the concept of student-centered and teacher-led teaching, organize students with similar mass, objectives, interests and prior knowledge, complex types, world distribution and different habits in the network environment, stimulate their interest in learning, bring into play their subjective initiative, make individual learning social and lifelong learning, and influence their lives, thinking and behavior. And influence their way of life, thinking, behavior and worldview [1]. According to data from the Ministry of Education, the number of learners of MOOC

This work is supported Promotion Plan for Key Discipline of Computer Science and Technology under no.GKY-2020COXK-2, and the Characteristic Innovation Project of Guangdong Universities under no.2022WTSCX133.

J. Gan et al. (Eds.): CSEI 2023, CCIS 1899, pp. 346–354, 2024.
https://doi.org/10.1007/978-981-99-9499-1_30

courses online in China has reached 800 million, but only more than 300 million learners have obtained MOOC credits. Despite the booming development of MOOCs and the continuous increase in the number of users, MOOCs suffer from high dropout rates and low completion rates [2]. With the increase in the number of MOOC learners, these problems have seriously restricted the sustainable development of MOOCs and have become a real problem that needs to be solved. High dropout rates have a negative impact on both MOOC platforms and the students themselves and are detrimental to the continued growth of MOOCs globally. From the platform's perspective, dropping out increases the average cost per student, as the cost of enrolling new learners is much greater than the cost of retaining potential dropouts. From the student's perspective, dropping out is a waste of time and energy investment.

To this end, the author tracked and analysed the reasons for dropout among 152 college students' MOOC learning and explored the influencing factors that lead to the dropout behavior of MOOC learners.

2 Research Design

This study mainly uses NVivo software to help the researcher analyse the information related to the reasons for dropping out of MOOC courses by creating projects, importing information, creating nodes, coding nodes and analysing information [3], extracting information related to the factors influencing the high dropout rate of MOOC courses, and then helping the researcher think and obtain useful conclusions.

In this study, "dropout" refers to the behavior of a learner who enrolls in a course through a MOOC platform, enters the course, participates in the teaching and learning activities, and then drops out or fails to complete the follow-up tasks of the course due to some factors. In this study, the MOOC study reports of 152 students from the class of 2015 to 2019 at Y University were collected, including course completion, dropout status, and analysis of their dropout reasons. A total of 152 relevant profiles were harvested throughout the period and analysed using NVivo10 software. First, the data were formatted and imported into NVivo10 software; second, the data were coded, and qualitative analysis was conducted to identify the nodes at each level; third, NVivo10 software was used to analyse the position of the nodes at the first level in the factors affecting the dropout rate of MOOC courses; fourth, NVivo10 software was used to explore the relationship between the nodes at each level.

3 Research Analysis and Results

Through the study and analysis of 152 learning reports, it was found that the completion rate of Chinese MOOC courses chosen by learners independently was 18.5%, and the completion rate of English courses was only 0.03%.

The author introduced "reference points" in the research analysis, which indicates the number of codes under a certain node; the more codes there are, the greater the proportion of reasons for dropping out of the MOOC; after coding, read carefully, merge or reorganize the node names and similar contents; finally, study the logic between tree nodes and adjust some subnodes appropriately [4]. Nodes' positions. The software analysis yielded a coding reference number of 167 points for learners, which accounted for 51% of the coding reference number of the first-level nodes, indicating that learners believed that they attributed most of the dropout reasons of the MOOC course to themselves. The coding reference number for the MOOC courses was 107, which accounted for 33% of the coding reference number of the first-level nodes. The number of coding references for the MOOC platform was 54, which accounted for 16%. Based on the above analysis, learners, MOOC courses, and MOOC platforms are identified as the core factors as the first-level nodes. The coding reference points of the first-level nodes and their subordinate second-level nodes in NVivo are summarized in Table 1.

Table 1. Number of subnode reference points and example statistics.

Level 1 Node	Level 2 Node	Number of code references
Learner	Learning motivation deficits	41
	Learning style differences	15
	Differences in ability levels	23
	Limited time and effort available	34
	Lack of self-management skills	38
	Loneliness of learning	15
MOOC Courses	Instructional design	40
	Course quality	49
	Evaluation methods	18
MOOC Platform	Inadequate learning support services	31
	Inadequate monitoring system	13
	Low recognition of certificates	10

3.1 Learners

The learner is the emitter of the MOOC, and any of the factors that affect the learner's learning may make the learner drop out. There are many learners' own factors that lead to the occurrence of MOOC dropout behavior, both intellectual and nonintellectual factors; intellectual factors are mostly reflected in knowledge level, cognitive characteristics, and cognitive structural variables, while nonintellectual factors mainly involve time, motivation, and learning styles.

First, learners' motivation to learn is lacking. The analysis of the results of the motivation to participate in MOOC courses shows that most learners have clear learning goals and a strong need for self-actualization, and they are mostly based on interest, knowledge pursuit and personal improvement when choosing courses, which shows that learners have a strong willingness to learn. In the analysis of the reasons for learners dropping out in the middle of the course, most of the learners attributed the dropout to their own problems, and according to the coding reference number, it can be seen that the lack of learning motivation is the most important reason. In the prestudy course, the vast majority of learners are motivated by their interest in learning. However, during the learning process, learners' interest may decrease due to time conflicts, their own willpower, learning partners, etc. The lack of learning interest may, to some extent, lead to a decrease in learners' motivation to learn independently and thus drop out.

Second, there are differences in learners' learning styles. Learning styles are the ways in which learners process information during the learning process [5] and are a combination of learning strategies and learning dispositions that are consistent and characterized by the learner's personality. For the same course, different learners have different learning styles, i.e., learners adopt different learning strategies and learning tendencies, and when the teaching style of the MOOC course does not match the learning style of the learners, it will easily lead to learners dropping out.

Third, there are differences in ability levels. For the same MOOC course, the level of learners varies, and this difference not only includes the lack of preliminary basic knowledge and skills but also the difference in the level of ability to receive knowledge. In the learning process, some learners find the course content simple and boring and give up learning; some find the course content difficult and effortless to learn and drop out. When learning English MOOCs, 152 learners could not finish the course due to their poor English level foundation.

Fourth, there was a lack of self-management ability. Unlike traditional school education, MOOCs emphasize the self-organization of learning behavior and process - learners are highly autonomous, choosing their own courses and self managing their progress. In MOOC learning, learners' self-management ability is reflected to a certain extent in the planning of time and personal willpower. Many learners reported that they dropped out of the course because they did not plan their MOOC learning reasonably well and missed the submission time and study time. Additionally, throughout the study, there were no mandatory requirements for learners to complete or drop the MOOC course of their own choice. Only the learners themselves manage and monitor themselves from the beginning to the end of the course. The lack of self-control and impatience of individual learners can lead to dropout.

Fifth, in MOOC learning, most learners have their own studies or careers, and their investment of time and energy is limited, so when there is a conflict between MOOC learning and real-life tasks, learners tend to give up MOOC learning [6].

Sixth, the loneliness of learning. In the MOOC environment, learners learn online. A lack of opportunities to communicate with other learners in a timely manner will lead to loneliness. This sense of learning loneliness will affect learning to a certain extent, resulting in dropout.

3.2 MOOC Courses

First, most MOOC courses are still designed as a replica of traditional teaching, and the core concept is still centered on the course rather than the students. The teaching format is single, and teachers and students are separated in a learning environment, which leads to the gradual loss of learners' interest and motivation, and the difficulties in teacher-student interaction and student–student interaction have undermined learners' confidence in learning.

Second, the large capacity, high difficulty, and uneven teaching quality of MOOC courses are the factors that cause students to drop out. Some MOOC courses have long cycles and many assignments, which can cause learners to burn out and not want to continue learning. The courses are difficult, and learners are unable to keep up with the course progress, which is mainly reflected in the more skill-based courses. In some courses, course quality factors such as boring lectures by teachers, untimely answers to questions, and lectures that are detached from the subject matter are also causes for students to drop out.

Finally, the evaluation methods of MOOCs are imperfect, and the reliability of the evaluation results is low. MOOC learning platforms have introduced the mechanism of mutual evaluation of students' assignments, and peer evaluation has to a certain extent reduced the pressure of labor volume due to the teacher-student ratio, but it has also raised questions about the authority of the evaluation from industry members and learners themselves. The author found that the effect of mutual evaluation is not obvious, and the phenomenon of unreasonable mutual evaluation scores often occurs. This evaluation method makes students have the possibility of cheating, so the reliability is low, which may eventually cause learners to lose confidence in the credibility of the curriculum and drop out of school.

3.3 MOOC Platform

Learning Support Services are not Up to Standard. With the development of "Internet +", various technologies are becoming more convenient and intelligent. The teachers of MOOC courses make up for the lack of emotions in online education through live streaming, WeChat groups or QQ groups and answer the questions raised by students. In the process of learning a MOOC course, everyone's learning ability and acceptance level are different, and each course participant encounters different problems. When a learner's knowledge is weak, the learner may not be aware of the problem and needs targeted instruction and training from the educator, but the instructor cannot take into account every course participant. Without targeted learning support, the participants of MOOC courses need to figure it out by themselves and even put more time and effort into it, which increases the chance of MOOC learners dropping out.

Low Recognition of Certificates. Most MOOC courses are only elective courses for learners, which are not recognized by most schools and cannot replace school courses and credits, so the recognition of both universities and society is low, which reduces the confidence of learners in MOOC courses to a certain extent. The learning of MOOCs is not recognized, and learners naturally do not pay attention to MOOCs, which is one of the reasons for dropping out of MOOCs.

Online Learning Cannot be Regulated. Also the supervision system is not perfect. The access threshold of MOOC courses is low, and there are basically no requirements for learners. In the whole course, the platform cannot effectively supervise the learners, students learn without psychological pressure, and there is no shame in failing the course.

Students with poor self-management ability can drop out at any time. At the same time, it is also easy for learners to cheat in MOOC courses, and in assignments and exams, learners can use the Internet and other means to search for answers to complete their studies and obtain certificates. Due to the lack of regulatory measures, the platform cannot monitor these phenomena.

4 Research Analysis and Results

4.1 MOOC Learners

MOOC learners are different from traditional classroom learners in that they usually have a clearer learning purpose and should carefully consider their knowledge and skills needs as well as their a priori knowledge and abilities before learning and choose the courses they truly need and can master. Second, the motivation of MOOC learners is weakened by various influences during the learning period, and motivation is the driving force for learners to persist in learning, which determines the learners' consciousness, motivation, inclination and selectivity to participate in learning activities. Therefore, strengthening learners' intrinsic and extrinsic motivation to learn is important to help reduce dropout rates. We can improve learners' motivation by improving the credit certification system of MOOCs, such as expanding the scope of MOOCtual recognition of credits, cooperating with universities and launching degree programs and other related measures. It also focuses on MOOC-based blended teaching so that learners can better complete the course with the guidance and assistance of the instructor and avoid the isolation they may encounter when studying alone.

At the same time, to improve their own participation in MOOC courses, learners should understand their own learning characteristics, have a correct understanding of their own learning style, establish motivation based on active knowledge acquisition [7], set clear goals, choose a suitable MOOC course learning style for themselves, put themselves into course learning with an active mindset, monitor their learning process reasonably, complete course learning, actively think and ask questions when encountering problems, help other learners solve problems, and create knowledge while learning knowledge.

4.2 MOOC Teachers

Effective interaction is a more important form of expression in the process of internalizing knowledge and improving ability. In the existing forums and instant social networking software, student–student interaction accounts for a large proportion of the interaction, while teacher-student interaction accounts for a small proportion. Therefore, teachers should be more involved in the interaction and provide professional guidance to learners in a more proactive manner. On the teachers' side, real-time interaction between teachers and students and students can be enhanced through relevant measures. For example, the MOOC platform can establish a QQ group or WeChat group to support the course so that teachers and other learners can receive and respond to the questions posted by learners in the group to improve the active participation of learners; teachers and learners can also organize regular online and offline communication activities to discuss learning perceptions, enhance mutual understanding, improve teaching effectiveness and increase the completion rate of MOOC courses.

On the other hand, embedded activities should be reasonably included in the lecture videos, which is a teacher-student interactive learning mode and a useful supplement to the course evaluation, inserting interactive activities such as preclass mapping, in-class questions and follow-up exercises to simulate the learning atmosphere of a real classroom, where learners can see their own answers, those of other learning partners and the teacher, respectively, which is conducive to reducing learners' loneliness in online online learning and enhancing learners' reliance and trust in the course.

4.3 MOOC Courses

Quality lecture content remains the core of MOOC sustainable development and an effective external thrust for learners to continue their MOOC learning. Some teachers do not pay attention to the MOOC's instructional design and only design and develop the MOOC as a resource, ignoring the pedagogical characteristics and instructional design principles of the MOOC. To improve the quality of MOOC teaching content, this study argues that MOOCs have the basic elements of a curriculum and conform to the general curriculum model. It is necessary to carry out systematic instructional design for MOOCs, which should analyse learning needs, learners and learning content, clarify learning objectives, develop learning outcome measurement and evaluation criteria and teaching strategies, etc. It is important to note that MOOCs are different from the general teaching process and problems faced in traditional classrooms. It is necessary to study the teaching methods, teaching strategies, and teaching organization forms suitable for MOOCs based on learner characteristic analysis combined with relevant curriculum design principles. Improving learner characteristics analysis Learner characteristics analysis is the prerequisite and foundation for selecting and organizing teaching content and designing teaching strategies. In 1989, Heinich et al. pointed out that even some rough analysis of learners' general characteristics is useful for the selection of teaching methods and media [8]. MOOC learners are different from traditional classroom learners in that they have clear learning purposes. They have rich practical experience, strong self-learning ability and focus on teaching efficiency, but they have limited free time, poor self-control ability and uneven foundation. Teachers should understand the learners' original knowledge base and cognitive ability and then conduct a learning needs analysis to clarify the gap between the learners' current level and the desired level to prepare for determining the teaching objectives and selecting the teaching contents; on the course description page, learners should be clearly informed of the teaching objectives, prerequisites, syllabus, course length, course load, content type and other course information, or they can make a 1 to The course description page should clearly inform learners of the course objectives, prerequisites, syllabus, course length, course load, content type and other course information.

MOOCs are different from the general teaching process and problems faced by traditional classrooms. It should combine course design principles such as humanistic learning theory, mastery learning theory, and meaningful learning theory to study teaching methods, teaching strategies, and teaching organization forms that are suitable for

MOOCs. Arrange a reasonable teaching cycle according to the results of learner characteristic analysis so that learners can persist in learning all the contents of the MOOC course.

4.4 MOOC Platform

The results of the study show that MOOC platforms lack the necessary supervision and management for MOOC learners. Some measures can be taken to further improve the supervisory mechanism of MOOC platforms, such as predicting potential dropout points of learners through learning analytics to help teachers keep track of each student's dropout in a given time period. Then, combining the analysis of the difficulty level of the course helps teachers and the platform make more targeted adjustments to the MOOC course organization structure to improve the course quality, make timely interventions, and impose a series of supervisory measures on learners who do not attend the course properly to motivate them to complete the MOOC course and achieve the purpose of reducing MOOC dropouts. Attempts can also be made to charge learners of quality MOOCs a fee, which is returned if the course is completed; if not, the fee can be used both for MOOC platform construction and to reward MOOC completers. The MOOC platform can encourage learners to actively participate in discussions and complete the course through points, scholarships and digital badges. For example, points can be exchanged for paper certificates, fee-based courses, etc., and scholarships can be directly cashed in. At the same time, the MOOC platform can cooperate with recruitment websites to recommend relevant jobs for learners who have completed MOOC learning; it can also cooperate with universities to launch degree courses, and learners can obtain degree or academic certificates issued by universities after completing all courses and successfully passing tests.

5 Conclusion

With the development of MOOCs, an increasing number of users are registering to participate in learning; meanwhile, the phenomenon of a high dropout rate of the course is also attracting attention, the reasons for which can be roughly attributed to learners, MOOC courses and MOOC platforms. In this paper, we analysed 152 MOOC learners' dropout and revealed the influencing factors of MOOC dropout. We concluded that the influencing factors of MOOC learners' dropout behavior are mainly learners' own factors, course factors, and MOOC teaching support platform factors, among which learners' own factors are the first factor, course factors are the second factor, and MOOC teaching support platform factors are the second factor. Among them, learners' own factor is the first factor, course factor is the second factor, and MOOC teaching support platform factor is the last factor. The MOOC course is the main body composed of educators, learners and the MOOC platform, and educators should carefully design the MOOC course to provide the best content for learners. The MOOC platform should also provide good learning support services and find a solution to the high dropout rate of MOOCs.

References

1. Sun, Y., Cheng, Y., Zhu, L.: Research on the construction of university teaching mode based on MOOC. J. Distance Educ. **33**(03), 65–71 (2015)
2. Jing, Z.: Analysis of causes of bridge collapse accident based on NVivo. China University of Geosciences, Beijing (2015)
3. Jiang, L., Han, X., Cheng, J.: Analysis and research on MOOCs learner characteristics and learning effects. China Audio Vis. Educ. (11), 54–59, 65(2013)
4. YongSheng, X.: Attention allocation of local governments in the construction of "double first-class" —NVivo software analysis based on 30 provincial policy texts. Educ. Dev. Res. **37**(21), 31–38(2017)
5. Zoghi, M., et al.: Learning style preferences of Australian health science students. J. Allied Health **39**(2), 95–103(2010)
6. Sisi, L., Ling, Q.: Analysis and reflection on the high dropout rate of MOOC. China Educ. Technol. Equipment (22), 132–133 (2015)
7. Lin, J., Xibin, H., Jiangang, C.: Study on the characteristics of learners and learning effect analysis of MOOCs. China's Electrochem. Educ. (11), 54–59(2013)
8. Heinich, R., Molenda, M., Russell, J.D.: Instructional Media and the New Technologies of Instruction, 3nd edn. Macmillan Publishing Company, New York (1989)

Application and Research of Process Assessment in Computer Course Teaching

Rongqi Liu, Shifen Zhong(✉), and Honghong Chen

Xihua University, Pidu District, Chendu, China
zshifen@qq.com

Abstract. In recent years, online education has developed rapidly. This paper introduces a method for improving the assessment process of curricula by utilizing the main modules of several software platforms, such as Superstar Xuexitong and Tencent Classroom. These modules include live broadcasting, sign-in, question banks, course copying, group and teaching resources, virtual classroom performance, among others. By applying these modules in teaching practice, better performance has been shown for learning computer courses. By improving online teaching evaluation, the level and effectiveness of classroom teaching can be improved, better meeting the learning needs of students.Through multiple semesters of online teaching and blended online and offline teaching practices, some conclusions have been drawn. Teaching practices can fully stimulate students' interest in learning by using mobile communication technology. Mobile communication technology and online education have shifted the role of teachers in the classroom from the central role in traditional teaching to other roles.

Keywords: Xuexitong · Educational platform · Mobile communication · Process assessing · Teaching method

1 Introduction

The rapid popularization of mobile communication has greatly promoted the application of mobile apps in various fields. Compared with 4G, 5G makes life more convenient and faster. 5G is characterized by low latency and high speed, which makes apps faster and more accurate. Apps also play a greater role in education [1, 2].

With the implementation of the national strategy of "mass entrepreneurship and innovation," and the emergence of new generations of information technology such as big data, artificial intelligence, and virtual reality under the background of "Internet plus," computer applications have penetrated into all fields of social and economic development. The progress and innovation of science and technology in various disciplines and industries increasingly depend on the advancement of computer information technology [3].

Under the traditional computer education model, teachers often play the role of leaders in classroom teaching. They explain knowledge to students most of the time

J. Gan et al. (Eds.): CSEI 2023, CCIS 1899, pp. 355–361, 2024.
https://doi.org/10.1007/978-981-99-9499-1_31

while students passively take notes and learn. This approach hinders the development of students' autonomous learning and practical abilities to a great extent [4].

The rapid development of online education has led to the emergence of various mobile internet-based software platforms, such as Superstar Xuexitong, Chinese University MOOC, Rain-Classroom, and Tencent Classroom. These platforms continuously challenge traditional educational ideas, models, and methods. The coronavirus pandemic in early 2020 accelerated their growth. Online sign-in, live broadcasting, recording, replaying, question banks, and resource sharing have all been fully integrated into teaching practices, greatly promoting the revolution of traditional teaching [5].

2 The Significant of Course Assessing

Compared with foreign curriculum assessing methods, the final examination has been paid more attention in China, which typically accounts for over 70% of the total grade, and relatively neglects the process assessment of the curriculum. However, since the final exam has a certain degree of randomness, it may not accurately reflect the ability of students. Some students resort to excessive practice of exam questions before the final exam, which may result in high scores but low ability. Conversely, foreign education emphasizes flexible and diverse process assessment methods, with the final grade accounting for only a relatively small portion, approximately 30–40%.

There are several methods of assessing student progress, including quizzes, homework, attendance, classroom questions, experiment reports, and voting. However, these methods can make calculating grades more complicated. As a result, many teachers choose to either simplify the process or abandon it altogether [6].

Online education platforms, such as Superstar Xuexitong, use internet technology and mobile communication to simplify the complexity of the teachers' recording and assessment process, thereby greatly improving the quality of process teaching. Due to the improved process assessment and result recording method, students must now pay more attention to their usual studies because even if the final score is higher, the total grade may not be better. Xuexitong stores the process assessment results in the cloud database, allowing teachers to specify and adjust various assessment weights anytime and export the process assessment results. Additionally, students can check their grades anytime to avoid a lower grade at the end of the class. The platform also allows students to submit personal assignments and initiate personal discussions, which teachers can address in a timely and effective manner in order to solve student questions and supervise their studying status.

3 Process Assessing Modules of Online Education Platform

At present, there are approximately ten widely used online educational platforms. Of those, the author prefers two: Superstar Xuexitong and Tencent Classroom.

Superstar Xuexitong is a platform for course learning, knowledge dissemination, and management sharing based on microservice architecture. It has three versions: a mobile app version, a computer version, and a web version. Superstar Xuexitong takes advantage of the vast resources, such as books, periodicals, newspapers, videos, and original content, accumulated by Superstar for more than 20 years. It integrates knowledge management, course learning, special creation, and office applications to provide users with a one-stop learning and working environment.

Tencent Classroom is an online educational platform that offers both a computer version and a mobile app. It assists in monitoring student learning and provides a variety of courses that can be accessed from computers and mobile devices. Tencent Classroom also curates a large number of high-quality curriculum resources from educational institutions and teachers. Its main features include online live broadcasting, recording, and replaying.

Some traditional online educational platforms, such as Superstar Xuexitong, offer the convenience of recording students' regular grades. By specifying the weights of the relevant processes, teachers can easily calculate students' grades simultaneously on the platform. This feature is useful for motivating students to study hard. Every assessment result is uploaded to the cloud database for statistical analysis. These weights include homework, classroom interaction, attendance, course audio and video, chapter tests, exams, live broadcasting, and knowledge points, etc.

The main functional modules provided by the online education platforms for process assessment are shown in Fig. 1 (see Fig. 1).

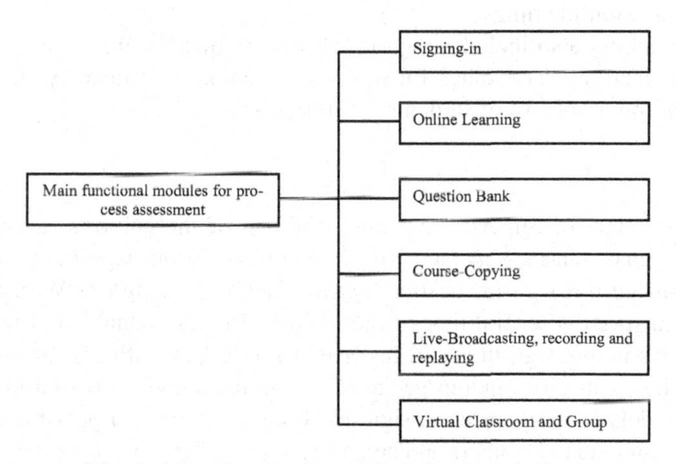

Fig. 1. Main functional modules of online platform.

The main functional modules for process assessment include:

- Sign-in: determines whether students are present in the classroom;
- Online Learning: provides various learning materials such as PPT, audio, video, and live broadcasting;
- Question Bank: facilitates communication, testing, and assessment through a computer database;
- Course-copying: provides a quick way to create a new online course and reduces the workload for teachers;
- Live-broadcasting, recording, and replaying: provides a convenient tool for students to learn;

- Virtual Classroom and group: a learning environment constructed by multimedia communication technology on the computer network, which allows teachers and students in different locations to carry out most teaching activities.

4 Application of Online Education Platform to Improve Process Assessment

During the spring semester of 2021, the author used two online education platforms, Superstar Xuexitong and Tencent Classroom, to teach courses on the Principle of Computer Composition and the Principle and Application of Database. In contrast, the spring semester of 2020 was entirely online. During the semesters of 2022 and 2023, the author used a mix method of online and offline learning. Based on current trends, the combination of online and offline teaching is expected to become more widespread in the future.

Offline teaching is essentially the same as traditional teaching, as it allows for easy communication between students and teachers. However, there is no doubt that in-person learning is more conducive to emotional communication.

Online teaching presents key and challenging examples, along with instructional content, on a platform in the form of videos or notes. Students can replay and review these materials multiple times.

Online teaching also includes sign-in, classroom questioning, after-school homework, online learning, and other functions. The points provided by these modules constitute an important part of students' overall grade.

4.1 Sign-in

The sign-in module of Superstar Xuexitong is one of the author's favorites. Unlike traditional manual sign-in, Superstar Xuexitong offers various sign-in methods such as normal sign-in, gesture sign-in, location sign-in, and QR-code sign-in. With gesture sign-in, the sign-in speed is several times faster than traditional manual sign-in. Even with network delays in 4G, sign-in is still faster in milliseconds with 5G. By using gesture sign-in, teachers can give random gestures, prompting students to sign in on the spot and avoiding delays or advances in sign-in. However, there is a possibility that some students may pretend to be others and help them sign in. To solve this problem, teachers can specify a sign-in time limit of one minute. After the time limit, teachers can review the feedback of the sign-in. With location sign-in, teachers can check if some students are not in the classroom. However, technical issues and students not activating GPS on their mobile devices may cause occasional errors. If some students cannot use the sign-in function (e.g., due to no internet access), teachers can assist them with manual sign-in. Sign-in results are directly stored in the database and can be exported as usual grades at the end of the course.

4.2 Question Bank

The Question Bank of Superstar Xuexitong currently supports various question types, including single-choice questions, multiple-choice questions, true/false, fill-in-the-blank, calculation, programming, and short-answer questions. Some questions, such as multiple-choice questions, single-choice questions, and true/false, can be automatically graded by the computer. However, fill-in-the-blank and other types of questions require manual review. Questions stored on the cloud database can be downloaded to client computers as Word or Excel documents, while questions stored on local computers can be uploaded to the cloud database.

The questions can be re-edited and organized into assignments or tests. Teachers can require students to complete them within a specific time frame. After completion, the computer can automatically assess the student's score based on the answers in the question bank and perform statistical analysis. This analysis can help teachers focus on the topics that most students find difficult. To prevent rote memorization, the answers can be arranged randomly. Students can check the corresponding references and analysis after completing the test. The final result is then uploaded directly to the cloud database. Another advantage of the question bank is that the questions can be used an unlimited number of times.

4.3 Course-Copying

The course-copying module of Superstar Xuexitong is an innovative tool that greatly simplifies teachers' workload and improves their efficiency. The platform offers numerous learning resources, including high-quality courses such as the Principle of Computer Composition. This course includes course PPTs, learning videos, a question bank, assignments, computer-practice questions, computer reports, and test papers. In the new semester, teachers can use course-copying to duplicate all materials from the course. All activities in the course only need to be restarted when necessary, and the deadline can be reset. Joining the course is easy for students too. After the teacher creates a new course, they can share the course number with the students, who can join the course using their real student ID and name. Teachers can also bulk-import the student list into the course and display the course's QR code for students to join. These measures significantly simplify the work of teachers.

4.4 Group

The Superstar Xuexitong group module enables teachers to assign specific students to designated groups. Teachers can use homework, activity library, voting/questionnaire, brainstorming, Q&A/discussion, and testing to provide classroom activities. Since most of these activities involve subjective questions and answers, the teacher can appoint a team leader or have group members evaluate each other after providing reference answers. This greatly reduces the teacher's workload.

4.5 Virtual Classroom Performance

By using the Virtual Classroom Performance module, this platform provides various ways to enhance the classroom experience, such as raising hands, answering questions, group evaluation, and selecting students. These methods can effectively improve student participation and stimulate classroom engagement. Teachers can also save classroom notes as message records or files in the resource library.

4.6 Other Modules

Due to limitations of cloud servers, live broadcasting on certain platforms, such as Superstar Xuexitong, may be relatively weak. To enhance live broadcasting capabilities, one can consider using Tencent Classroom. Tencent Classroom allows for the creation of multiple courses and enables students to ask questions during class. One of its most important functions is the replay feature, which allows students to review past lessons repeatedly. This is an incomparable function compared to traditional teaching methods.

Another function of Superstar Xuexitong is resource database management. This function is similar to the QQ share-folder function. Teachers can upload reference materials, courseware, videos, and other resource files to the database and specify knowledge points. The difference is that browsing knowledge points in the database can be converted into corresponding grades for students.

Figure 2 (see Fig. 2) displays the typical grades of students. It is evident that the fourth student, who rarely attends classes, has a lower grade compared to the others. Notably, some weights are excluded from the grade calculation. Only the following factors are considered: course videos, access times, sign-ins, and classroom interaction. Nevertheless, the teacher can reset all weights as necessary.

Serial No	Student Name	Student Number	Homework -40%	Signing-in -30%	Classroom -30%	Usual grade
1	Li jiayu	312020030663X	23.6	27.69	16	67.29
2	Ren zhezhen	312020030663X	32.66	28.27	8	68.93
3	Luo xianyan	312020030662X	32.05	29.42	27	88.47
4	Gao guochao	312020030662X	28.35	28.85	2	59.2
5	Peng daipen	312020030662X	34.49	29.42	30	93.91
6	He xinhong	312020030662X	33.83	30	30	93.83

Fig. 2. The typical grades of students in Superstar Xuexitong.

With the development of technology, it is now possible to share resources, highlight students' dominant position, and innovate network teaching methods. In addition, by improving network teaching evaluations, we can enhance the classroom teaching level and effectiveness, and better meet the learning needs of students. Through the use of network teaching models, computer education can take advantage of its strengths, allowing students to learn computer knowledge and skills faster and more thoroughly [4].

5 Conclusion

Teaching practices can fully stimulate students' interest in learning by using mobile communication technology. One simple and effective way to do this is by using Superstar Xuexitong. Superstar Xuexitong, available in both PC web and app versions, played a key role in the teaching process by serving as the basic unit of instruction and completing all relevant applications.

The created course has become the fundamental unit of teaching that encompasses all relevant applications. This teaching process includes course creation, uploading teaching materials, course instant-messaging, voting, assignments, resource database sharing, announcements, real-time results, and attendance tracking.

When creating the course for the first time, it may be necessary to create relevant question banks and activities, which can take some time to input and organize, even with the help of other teachers. However, this provides a solid foundation for future teaching. In future teaching practices, the author plans to utilize mobile internet technology more effectively, expand the application of Superstar Xuexitong, and improve the interactivity and quality of teaching.

An education expert once stated, "If we prohibit students from using mobile phones in school today, they will lose tomorrow." While some teachers believe that allowing students to use mobile phones in class may negatively impact teaching quality. Everything has the opposite.With the rational use of advanced technology, we can certainly mobilize students' enthusiasm for learning.

Undoubtedly, the pandemic has accelerated the development of online education, prompting a re-evaluation of traditional teaching methods. Mobile communication technology and online education are expected to transform the role of teachers in the classroom from a central role in traditional teaching to other responsibilities such as organization, coordination, Q&A, and inspection, utilizing existing resources. With the arrival of the 5G era, smartphones are expected to become more integrated into the campus and classroom, and online education will play an increasingly active role in educational activities [7].

Fund Project. Teaching reform project xjjg2021115 and xjjg2021060 of Xihua University; JG2021-929 of Sichuan Provincial Education and Teaching Reform Research Project

References

1. Yang, J., Shi, G., Zhang, R., Wang, Y., Huang, R.: 5G + Smart education: educational reform based on intelligent technology. China Educ. Technol. **2021**(04), 1–7 (2021)
2. Zhong, S., Liu, R., Wei, D.: Design and development of wireless voting teaching system based on intelligent mobile terminal. Softw. Guide **17**(02), 120–123 (2018)
3. Wang, C.: An analysis of research hotspots and frontier trends in university computer education. J. Open Learn. **26**(3), 9 (2021)
4. Zhang, Y.: Research on computer education reform based on network teaching mode. Comput. Knowl. Technol. **017**(015), 166–167 (2021)
5. Ren, Y., Li, T., Zuo, W.: Construction of the teaching system of "data structure" course based on superstar learning and mobile teaching. Educ. Modern. **7**(07), 68–70 (2020)
6. Yang, Q., Fu, Z.: Analysis on the reform of undergraduate course score evaluation in universities. Teacher **2022**(02), 84–86 (2022)
7. Sun, S.: The application of smartphones in physics teaching: taking QQ software teaching application as an example. Dig. Educ. **2016**(3), 4 (2016)

Research on the Experimental Teaching System of Internet of Things Engineering Under the New Infrastructure Perspective

Xiaoyan Zhao[1,2], Junna Zhang[1,2], and Peiyan Yuan[1](✉)

[1] Henan Normal University, Xinxiang, China
peiyan@htu.cn
[2] Engineering Lab. of Intelligence Business and Internet of Things, Xinxiang, Henan, China

Abstract. It is one of the key directions of the new infrastructure to establish an experimental teaching platform for synergy between science and education, thus promoting the construction of intelligent laboratories. As a new engineering major supporting the development of national strategic emerging industries, the experimental teaching of Internet of Things (IoT) engineering is crucial in the process of talent training. However, the existing experimental teaching system is constrained by many factors including funding, location, faculty strength, and network conditions, which make it difficult to implement large-scale and creative IoT experiments, especially process-integrated experiments. This paper focuses on how to build an experimental teaching process and experimental teaching system that meets the needs of the IoT industry and talent training under the new infrastructure perspective. By analysing the IoT curriculum structure and talent demand, the deficiencies of the existing experimental teaching platform are discussed in combination with the school's talent training positioning and the current IoT industry chain situation. Simultaneously, the technical system structure of IoT is set as the main theme to sort out the knowledge points of IoT experimental teaching, and then a virtual simulation platform of IoT experimental teaching is proposed. The practical application on National Cyberspace proves that the proposed experimental platform can meet the needs of basic experiments, engineering practical training, innovation, scientific research assistance, and industrial applications.

Keywords: Internet of Things Engineering · Experimental Teaching · Virtual Simulation · Talent Demand · Project-Based Practice

1 Introduction

New infrastructure refers to the information network-led digital industrial system which involves 5G/6G, big data center, artificial intelligence, and industrial internet etc. [1]. In July 2021, the Ministry of Education and six other departments issued the "Guidance on Promoting the Construction of New Infrastructure for Education to Build a High-Quality Education Support System". It states clearly that the new educational infrastructure is

J. Gan et al. (Eds.): CSEI 2023, CCIS 1899, pp. 362–372, 2024.
https://doi.org/10.1007/978-981-99-9499-1_32

one of the national infrastructures, a traction force for educational transformation in the information era, and a strategic initiative to accelerate the modernization of education and to build an educational power [2]. In 2022, the highlights of the work of the Ministry of Education further emphasizes the need to promote new educational infrastructure, enrich the supply of digital educational resources and services, and enhance the ability of higher education to serve innovation and development [3].

Smart campus is one of the six key directions of the new infrastructure of education. It is clearly stated in the guiding opinions that institutions are supported to deploy discipline-specific classrooms and teaching laboratories to promote the construction of intelligent laboratories, build collaborative platforms for scientific research and provide services such as experimental environments with virtuality and experimental data sharing for scientific research [4]. As a new engineering major set up by the Ministry of Education, the Internet of Things (IoT) engineering major is characterized by strong integration, extensive knowledge, and close connection with engineering applications in emerging industries [5]. This puts forward higher requirements on the quality of talent training. By building a combined virtual and real experimental teaching platform and forming a collaborative teaching mode that integrates physical space and cyberspace, it can provide technical empowerment for the training of IoT professionals and promote the digital transformation and upgrading of IoT professional experimental teaching in the environment of "Internet+ education" [6, 7]. However, in order to meet the needs of the IoT industry and the requirements of talent training, it is a challenging problem that how to combine the characteristics of the profession and build an experimental teaching process and experimental teaching system in the construction of IoT laboratories under the new infrastructure perspective.

IoT is a comprehensive interdisciplinary field that integrates electronic information, computer and communication. It mainly includes electronic technology, sensor technology, wired and wireless communication technology, network technology, software technology, etc. Its knowledge system has the characteristics of complexity, applicability and practicality. Therefore, the training of talents in IoT requires not only solid professional theoretical knowledge, but also rich development experience and strong practical ability, that is to say, the experimental teaching plays a crucial role in the training process. Nevertheless, the existing experimental teaching system is constrained by factors such as funding, venue, faculty strength and network conditions. Thereupon, it is difficult to intuitively present large-scale, personalized and process-oriented comprehensive experiments, which would, in turn, inevitably hinder students to understand and master the theories related to IoT in their studies. Consequently, the students may not have a more macroscopic cognition of the actual IoT project development.

Aiming at this problem, this paper takes Henan Normal University's IoT Engineering major as a case to study the curriculum system. Combined with the positioning of talent training of the school and the current situation of IoT industry chain, the experimental teaching knowledge points of IoT are sorted out through the line of the technical system structure. At the same time, in view of the problems and deficiencies of the existing experimental teaching, a kind of experimental teaching system combining real and virtual for the training of professional talents is proposed.

2 Curriculum Structure of the Internet of Things

At present, the standard academic system of IoT engineering program is 4 years in national higher education. Students are generally required to complete 170 credits within 3–6 years of study. The credit courses can be divided into compulsory public courses, general courses, professional courses and practical teaching courses according to their categories. Take the curriculum of Henan Normal University of Internet of Things Engineering as an example, there are 37 credits of practical teaching, accounting for 22% of the total credits, including 21 credits of professional experiments, 6 credits of practical training, 4 credits of second classroom (such as innovative practice, discipline competition, etc.), 6 credits of thesis. The structure of all courses and the proportion of credits are shown in Fig. 1.

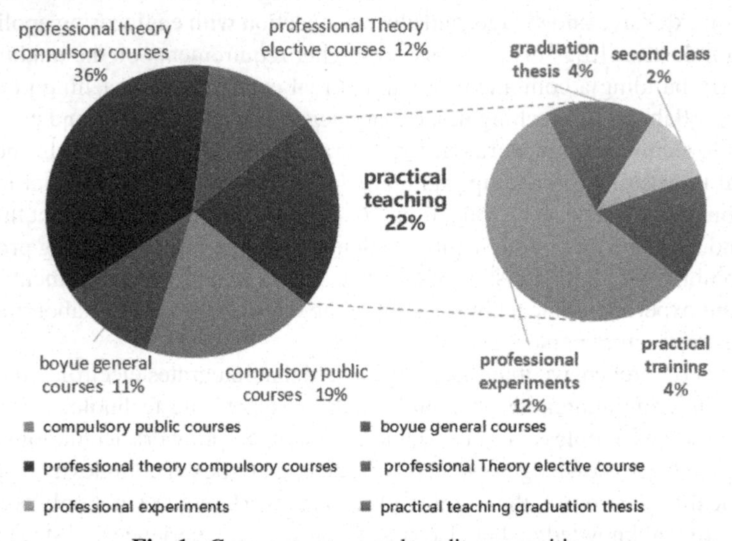

Fig. 1. Course structure and credit composition

From the curriculum, it is easy to see that the IoT profession requires strong engineering consciousness and practical innovation ability, so the practical teaching of IoT plays a much more important role in the talent training process than other disciplines. The professional experiments revolve around the main courses such as IoT communication technology, wireless sensor network, RFID principle and application, embedded system and design, IoT engineering practical training, operating system, computer network, etc. Other practical courses are based on professional experiment-related content for further study and expansion. On the whole, the experimental teaching of IoT engineering should be market demand-oriented, target the basic technology of information disciplines, coordinate the cultivation of applied, compound and innovative talents. After teaching basic theoretical knowledge, it needs a platform for hands-on practice to translate the theoretical knowledge into the practical operation. By providing students with a realistic simulated IoT environment, it can make students master the principles, technologies and applications of various IoT devices, components and systems.

3 IoT Professional Talents Demand

The program of talent training and teaching plan of IoT should be developed around the needs of society and enterprises [8, 9]. Moreover, the construction of curriculum system and the design of experimental teaching should be done according to the talent demand, i.e., the professional orientation should be set reasonably. Cooperating with an IoT company in Wuhan, the authors analyse and research the job demands related to IoT majors by conducting research on many websites such as Zhaopin, China Youth Network and many IoT enterprises in China. According to the IoT industry chain, the positions in the recruitment of IoT professional talents are classified into five major categories, which include the basic discipline quality category, IoT junior engineer, IoT product development category, IoT software development category, and IoT senior engineer. The percentage distribution is shown in Fig. 2.

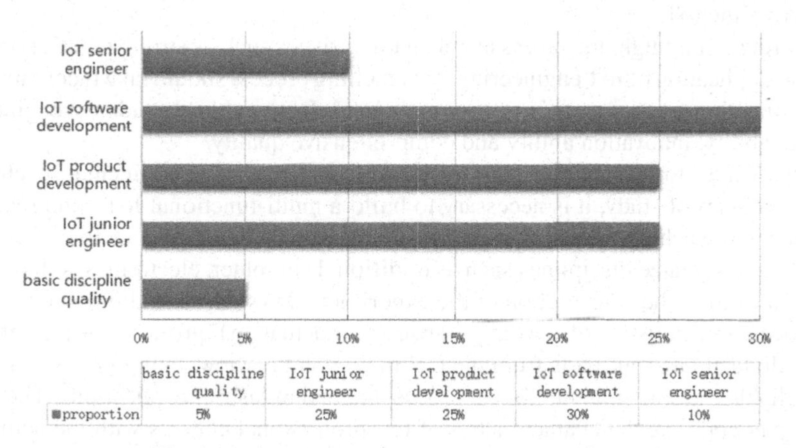

	basic discipline quality	IoT junior engineer	IoT product development	IoT software development	IoT senior engineer
■proportion	5%	25%	25%	30%	10%

Fig. 2. IoT professional talent demand distribution

As illustrated in Fig. 2, the basic discipline quality category mainly accounted for 5 percent, which includes junior jobs such as technical marketing and sales, technical copywriting, bidding and assistant. IoT junior engineer mainly includes IoT industry project implementation and operation and maintenance, system integration and testing, pre-sales and post-sales technical support and other IoT junior professional-type jobs. IoT product development mainly includes IoT project supervisor, embedded system development, one-chip computer development, intelligent gateway and other product development, sensor and embedded hardware designer and other professional design and development work. IoT software development and testing mainly includes UI design, Android application development, Web HTML5 front-end application development and software testing for IoT or mobile internet, industrial internet and other industry directions. IoT senior engineer is mainly responsible for IoT major project system architecture design, development and implementation and other professional work. Senior engineer usually chooses professionals with certain work experience and technical personnel with core skills of IoT hardware or software. It is need to master the finishing system architecture, or familiar with IoT project background design and platform development and other processes.

4 Deficiencies of the Existing Experimental Teaching System

The purpose of experimental teaching is to master the basic theoretical knowledge and key technology of IoT. It is also required to be familiar with IoT system and component application, as well as the structure and composition of IoT project [10, 11]. At the same time, combined with the enterprise talent demand, the students should strengthen the practical ability, pioneering thinking, system concept, management skills and innovation consciousness. Through hands-on ability exercise, students can adapt the needs of different jobs, and be capable of basic and design work such as core components and project development, technology application, system construction and maintenance, and upgrade of the IoT.

In order to highlight the professional characteristics such as strong practice, innovation and application of IoT engineering, the teaching process should take theory teaching and engineering practice teaching as two main lines. It can cultivate students' engineering practice ability, innovation ability and comprehensive quality.

Meanwhile, for giving full play to the practical role of experimental teaching in various courses of study, it is necessary to build a multi-functional IoT comprehensive experimental teaching system that covers all the knowledge points of IoT technology and integrates related disciplines such as traditional computer, electronics, software and communication. The construction of the experimental system should fully consider the relevance characteristics of existing courses and actual IoT projects. In fact, the IoT can be divided into four parts from the technical point of view: comprehensive perception, reliable transmission, intelligent processing and industrial applications. Therefore, in order to correlate the characteristics of the professional courses with the actual IoT projects, this paper divides the IoT engineering knowledge points into four levels based on the technical perspective: perceptual layer, transport layer, business layer and application layer. The experimental teaching knowledge points and professional courses covered by each level are shown in Fig. 3.

However, there is still no special open and shared virtual simulation experiment platform of IoT in domestic universities now. On the other hand, the existing IoT experimental teaching basically adopts hardware test box [10]. Constrained by funding, site and network conditions, existing experimental teaching often faces the following problems:

1) **Unable to do** visually present. Since the working process of devices and wireless networks is abstract and usually more focus on the technical knowledge points such as protocol stack development and interface development, the existing experiments, especially the hardware experiments, cannot visually present the interaction between knowledge points and the linkage with the overall IoT project.
2) **Unable to do** large-scale projects. Due to the complex architecture of IoT comprehensive experiment system, the large number of nodes, the high value and easy destruction of multiple types of test equipment, existing laboratory basically can't do large-scale IoT project in university.

3) **Unable to do** creative project realization. Because of the complex application scenarios of the IoT, existing hardware and software environment cannot fully cover all knowledge points. Therefore, existing experimental platform is difficult to build scenarios, diversified, creative wireless sensor network experiments, as well as it cannot do well in the accurate implementation of creative ideas for projects.
4) **Unable to do** procedural comprehensive experiments. Due to the rapid upgrading of IoT devices, limited hardware experimental equipment is difficult to support multiple users. As a result, students cannot do comprehensive experiments, let alone participate in the entire project progress the installation, debugging, testing, maintenance and other processes of the entire project.

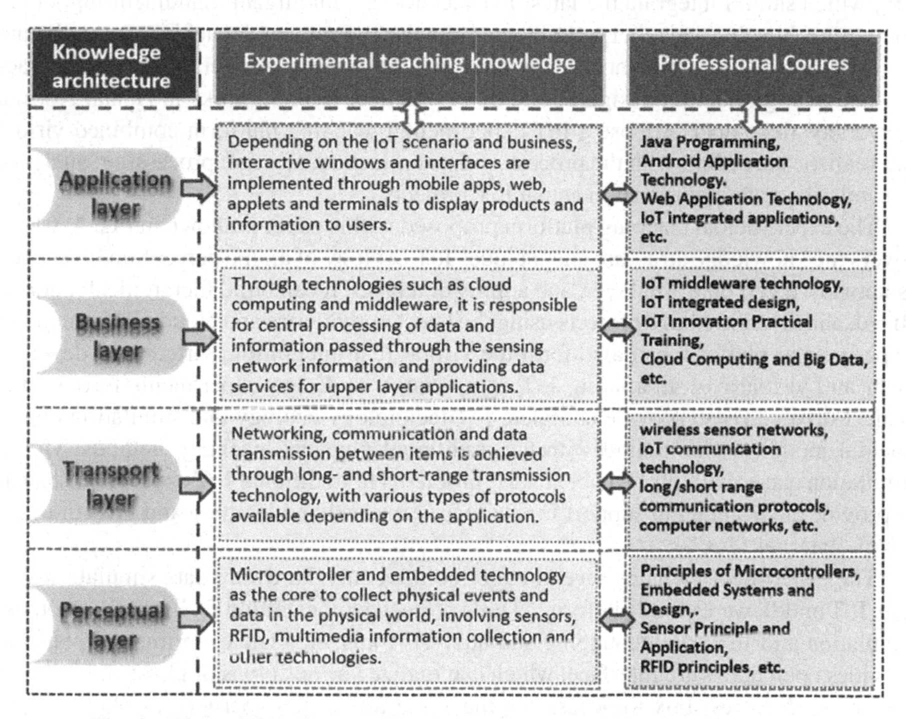

Fig. 3. Hierarchical diagram of IoT experimental teaching knowledge point

The above factors lead to the general feeling that it is difficult to understand and master the related theories and knowledge of IoT projects. This also causes that students is relatively weak in comprehensive ability and advanced thinking ability to solve complex problems, and they need to go through a long period of pre-employment training in enterprises after graduation in order to be competent for the relevant work.

5 Construction and Application of Virtual-Real Combination of IoT Experimental Teaching Platform

Under the background of the new infrastructure, education is constantly changing towards digitization, networking and intelligence. The IoT engineering major should take full advantage of the historical opportunity of the development of new infrastructure of education on the basis of grasping the demand of social talents. Combining the advantages and discipline characteristics of universities, experimental teaching should mainly focus on the development of IoT engineering profession. In order to cultivate students' innovation consciousness, engineering consciousness, practical ability and project development ability, it is necessary to establish the experimental teaching system, which should integrate the latest IoT technology, intelligent manufacturing, cloud computing, big data and other technologies into the experimental teaching. By analyzing the core curriculum experiment, comprehensive curriculum design, professional practice and post-graduation design of and other practical teaching links in Henan Normal University, this paper propose a IoT experimental teaching platform combined virtual and realistic according with the process of data collection, storage, processing, analysis, transmission and application in actual IoT projects.

The experimental teaching platform proposed in this paper is shown in Fig. 4, which covers the knowledge structure and includes IoT ecology of all the perception layer such as network layer, platform layer, and application layer. It can build hierarchical, personalized, and diversified IoT projects using the latest middleware and cloud platform ideas. Experimental platform can also form the virtual-real integration, virtual-real development and virtual-real alternating IoT comprehensive design experiments through the project-driven. These provide complete IoT technology ecology and simulation experimental modules. Combining with the traditional physical teaching methods, virtual simulation can solve four "Unable to do" problems in traditional IoT experiments, so as to provide environmental support for students' personalized learning and growth in the era of "Internet Plus".

The experiment includes several major components: hardware data simulation system, IoT middleware cloud platform, 2D/3D project demonstration, IoT security protocol simulation and IoT data debugging and analysis tools, etc. The experimental platform provides open hardware interface, which can realize various types of physical hardware devices such as test box to access. At the same time, the experimental platform can simulate and generate various intelligent virtual hardware objects through the hardware data virtual simulation system. It can perform parameter configuration and set hardware object meta-attributes, data and execution state settings, etc. Meanwhile, it can provide virtual hardware data source for conventional hardware devices and some high-cost, high-consumption, high-risk and easy lossy sensors.

The IoT middleware cloud platform is the main support platform and data cloud center of the system. It is also the connector between the virtual world and the physical world. The cloud platform realizes the access of IoT sensor data (including data generated by physical hardware and data simulation system) through various intelligent gateway interfaces. Using middleware support technology of data interconnection and big data, it can analyze the process of the massive IoT data such as classification storage, retrieval, mining, real-time analysis and decision making. Meanwhile, the middleware cloud platform provides API secondary development interfaces such as Android library and Web JavaScript library to customize industry application services based on Android or JSP framework according to project requirements.

IoT data debugging and analysis module provides ZXBee data analysis and testing tools under Android and Windows platforms. It supports data access with LabView simulation software and can quickly design IoT configuration project prototype. The realization of data package analysis, network topology, data source query and other functions can facilitate the maintenance and testing of the program.

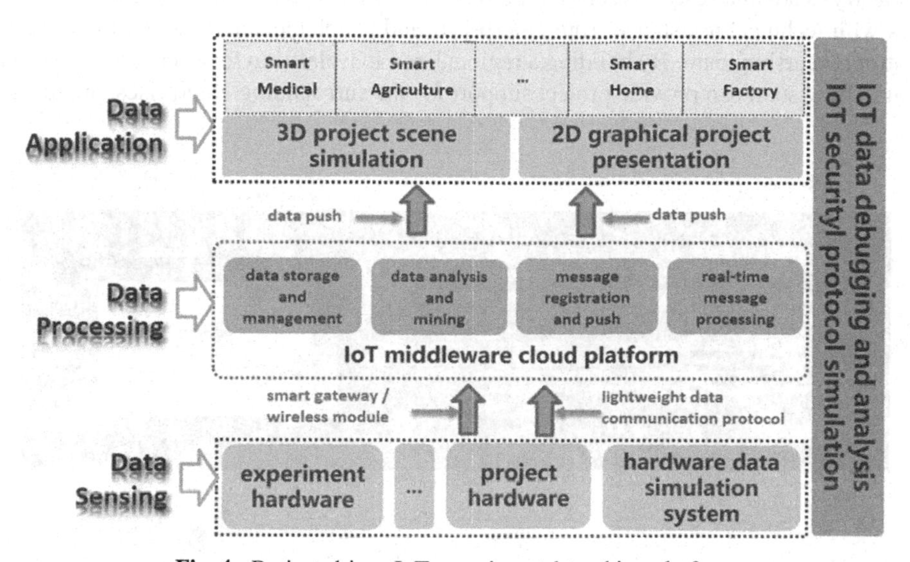

Fig. 4. Project-driven IoT experimental teaching platform

Considering the enterprise talent demand, the experimental platform teaching is associated with the basic, practical training, innovation, application, scientific research and other multi-dimensional applications. It follows the idea of thick foundation, high quality, strong ability, good innovation f to create a large-scale, intelligent, personalized, high-quality internship practice environment for the IoT engineering-related professional. Our proposed experimental teaching platform can meet the following kinds of needs:

Basic experiments, which meets the basic experimental learning of IoT professional knowledge points. Basic experiments cover the teaching experiments of perception layer, network layer, gateway layer, platform layer, application layer, which perform mainly through test boxes, development boards and other conventional test equipment.

Engineering practical training, which meets the comprehensive practical training exercises from IoT professional knowledge point to knowledge area. Each practical training experiment basically covers all the knowledge points of IoT and can make students master the complete process of IoT system. It can be achieved mainly through the practical training table, practical training stations, practical training kits and a variety of IoT application scenarios of the project training table and other equipment.

Innovation and creators, which meets the training of the IoT professional innovation ability and the needs of the cross-cutting knowledge content for different disciplines. Combined with a variety of practical application needs of the industry and the in-depth mastery of the core technology, the platform can innovate and break through the application difficulties vertically. Meanwhile, innovative experimental equipment can provide more open design-based functions and the engineering products who is closer to the actual application.

Research support, which meets the construction of the IoT profession and form an industry-academia research center. The research center can be led by a team of teachers with technical assistance from enterprises and supplemented by a team of student entrepreneurship team. By building a regionalized IoT platform to access cloud and big data, the system can provide project support for the surrounding enterprises and units.

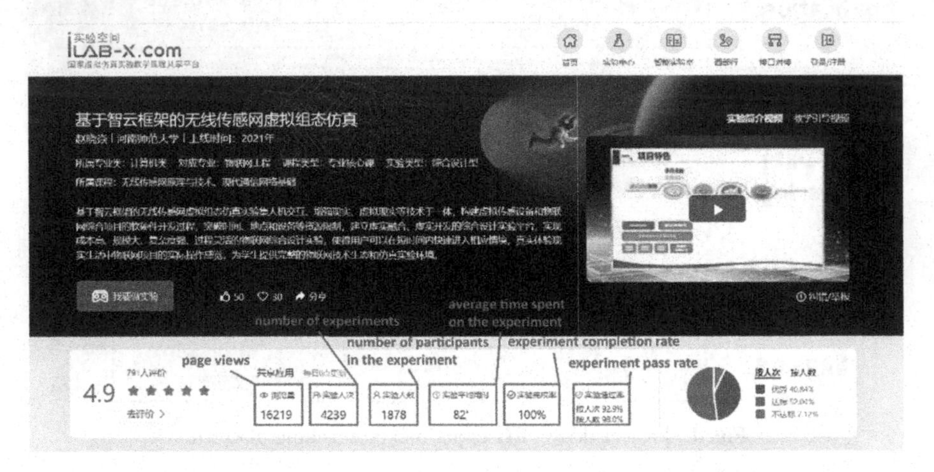

Fig. 5. The actual operation effect of the proposed platform

Industry application, which provides better recognize and experience in IoT scenarios through actual engineering cases and sample models, such as smart home experience hall, smart agriculture sandbox, smart traffic sandbox, smart medical workstation, and so on. At the same time, the platform can be combined with local development characteristics and introduce more localized engineering application scenarios.

Some functions of the proposed platform have been tested in experimental teaching course sharing platform, i.e., the national virtual simulation platform of China (www.ilab-x.com). The results prove that the proposed system has continuously promoted the construction of national and provincial first-class undergraduate programs in Henan Normal University such as the major of computer science and technology and the major of IoT Engineering. Meanwhile, it supports one provincial first-class course and cultivates two provincial virtual simulation experimental projects. At present, the number of people involved in the experiments on the national platform has exceeded 16,000, and the institutions using our proposed platform include universities in Shanghai, Beijing and Kunming and so on. The actual operation effect of the platform is shown in Fig. 5. Overall, the proposed platform can meet the teaching and research needs for key courses such as introduction to IoT, IoT application system design, Middleware technology of IoT and wireless sensor network technology.

6 Conclusion

Under the background of the new infrastructure of education, IoT majors needs to deepen the reform of the experimental teaching under the macro development mode of "new infrastructure-education". It is necessary for professional construction to cultivate high-quality talents with strong engineering consciousness, application ability and practical innovation ability. Combining the curriculum structure of the IoT and the positioning of the school's personnel training, the experimental teaching knowledge points and the shortcomings of the existing experimental teaching platform are analyzed in this paper. And then, an experimental teaching platform for the major of IoT is proposed to realize the experimental environment combined with the virtual and the real. The proposed experimental platform provides a complete IoT technology ecology and test module. It can model and recognize the project prototype in the early stage of the IoT course, and complete the virtual simulation of the project module in the middle and late stage of the IoT course through the reasonable integration the existing teaching experiment platform and hardware equipment. Meanwhile, the proposed platform provides the complete IoT technology ecology and the simulation test environment, which can effectively improve the quality of students' graduation and employment.

Acknowledgements. This work was supported in part by Higher Education Teaching Reform research and practice project in Henan Province 2019SJGLX067, 2021SJGLX110, in part by the New Infrastructure & University Informatization Project XJJ202205009, in part by the Teaching Reform Research Foundation of Henan Normal University 20190035.

References

1. Siqi, Z., Zhaoyong, M., Jie, Y., Baowei, S.: S&T Think-tank development in colleges and universities based on interdisciplinary personnel orientation training for new infrastructure construction: experience of northwestern polytechnical university. Sci. Technol. Manag. Res. **41**(02), 101–106 (2021)
2. Zhiting, Z., Qiuxuan, X., Yonghe, W.: Building new infrastructure for educational informatization: standards and implementation. Dist. Educ. China (10), 1–11 (2021)
3. Ministry of Education of the People's Republic of China: Key Points of the Ministry of Education's Work in 2022. http://www.moe.gov.cn/jyb_sjzl/moe_164/202202/t20220208_597666.html
4. Zhiting, Z., Hao, Z., Lijun, X., Huina, W., Yonghe, W.: Demand analysis and action suggestion of new infrastructure for digital transformation in education. Open Educ. Res. **28**(02), 22–23 (2022)
5. Wang, Y., Zhang, H., Huang, J., et al.: Discussion on the experimental teaching system for internet of things in the background of new engineering. Softw. Eng. (2018)
6. Weiwei, X.: Analysis on employment quality of loT majored graduates in secondary vocational schools in Zhejiang province. Computer Era (01), 80–83 (2020)

7. Xiuxiu, L., Chunwei, K.: Exploration of practical teaching system for IoT engineering major under the mode of engineering and technology talent cultivation. Internet Things Technol. **12**(01), 126–127+130(2022)
8. Naiguo, W., Xiangwei, Z.: Demand for IoT application technology professionals and job analysis for vocational college students. Chin. Vocat. Tech. Educ. (31), 76–79 (2014)
9. Xie, Z., Zhang, H., Yang, S., et al.: Construction of new type of innovative and practical teaching system for Internet of things. Exp. Technol. Manag. (2018)
10. Ye, L.U., Tao, L.I., Gong, X.L., et al.: Research on the construction of experiment curriculum system and practice teaching for Internet of Things. Lab. Sci. (2019)
11. Sarac, M., Adamovic, S., Saracevic, M.: Interactive and collaborative experimental platforms for teaching introductory internet of things concepts. Int. J. Eng. Educ. (4), 37 (2021)

The Internal Drive Force Analysis of Learning for Engineering Students

Xiaoyu Du[1(✉)], Guanying Zhou[2], Zhijie Han[3], Ying Du[1], and Baojun Qiao[1]

[1] College of Computer and Information Engineering, Henan University, Kaifeng 475004, China
dxy@henu.edu.cn

[2] Henan Engineering Laboratory of Spatial Information Processing, Henan University, Kaifeng 475004, China

[3] College of Software, Henan University, Kaifeng 475004, China

Abstract. Emerging Engineering Education is oriented to cultivate the ability to solve complex engineering problems, which required engineering students to have higher learning initiative and self-discipline. This paper explores the formation mechanism of college students' learning drive from teachers, counselors, learning environment and learning motivation, then we propose methods and suggestions for cultivating learning drive for these aspects.

Keywords: Emerging engineering · Internal drive · Self-learning · Engineering Education

1 Introduction

In order to comprehensively deepen the reform and innovation of higher engineering education in the new period, the Ministry of Education of China started the construction of "Emerging Engineering" in 2017, through the evolution of "Fudan Consensus", "Tianda Action" and "Beijing Guide", it points out the direction for the training of new engineering talents [1]. Compared with traditional engineering, the practical teaching link in emerging engineering education plays a pivotal role, which is an important guarantee and basic to adapt to the development of "engineering knowledge", "engineering skills" and "engineering attitude" under the new business form [2]. The emerging engineering education contains more practical education, which puts forward higher requirements for students' independent learning ability. The drive of learning can be divided into two categories: internal drive and external drive. External drive refers to the learning motivation generated by the external influence of parents, teachers or schools, including the parents' expectations, the strict discipline of teachers, and the school's academic requirements, etc. Internal drive is internal driving force, which refers to the spontaneous learning due to interest and learning habits. Internal driving force is affected by many aspects, which is the key factor for students to learn actively and spontaneously. Students with strong internal drive

J. Gan et al. (Eds.): CSEI 2023, CCIS 1899, pp. 373–380, 2024.
https://doi.org/10.1007/978-981-99-9499-1_33

have efficient learning efficiency. This paper takes the emerging engineering education as the research background, analyzes the influencing factors of the learning drive of engineering college students, establishes a new engineering education concept, and improves the students' ability to solve the complex engineering problems.

2 The Main Factors Affecting the Internal Drive of Students

Learning power is derived from the "learning organization" proposed by Professor Jay Forrester in 1965. Learning power is a huge energy for behavioral, cognitive and emotional development through learning. R. D. Crick points out the energy that promotes the interaction between learning willingness and learning outcomes is learning power, which has a direct impact on the effectiveness of learning [3].College students' learning power model is a comprehensive model integrating cognition, behavior and emotion, which shows the mutual relationship between learning driving force, learning strategy force, learning action force, knowledge force, cognitive ability, technical ability and emotional force [4], and an important factor affecting the learning power is the driving force of learning. The drive of learning can transform students' passive learning into active learning, and produce clear learning willingness and learning goals in the students' brain.

The factors affecting students' drive include the following aspects:

2.1 Clear Learning Goals

Psychological research shows that human's behavior has purposeful, and the purpose comes from certain motivation, motivation arises from need. The need to induce motivation, which governs behavior and points to predetermined goals, is a general pattern of human behavior [5,6]. College students, especially when they first enter college, tend to lose themselves in college life, which has a lot to do with high school education. At present, China's high school education is similar to nanny-style education, with a clear goal (that is, to successfully pass the college entrance examination and then receive higher education). Schools and teachers take this as the ultimate goal to manage and train students in an all-round way.

Many teachers express or imply that students in class that their efforts and sweat will be rewarded in the college entrance examination, and they can relax after the college entrance examination.This makes many students lose the goal of struggle after entering the university, without the direction of struggle, thus forming a negative, slack attitude towards learning.

Life is a long-distance running, each stage of education is a component part of this long-distance running, it can be set local goals, but can't take them as the ultimate goal, which will affect the long-term life planning. It has been found that students in the university with clear goals than no target students have strong motivation and learning passion, a valuable goal will become the power of their learning drive, a college student with a firm goal will constantly drive themselves towards goal and struggle, and achieve their goal and ambition. The learning objectives of college students are affected by multi-directional factors. Learning objectives directly affect the persistence and stability of internal drive, and are also one of the important factors affecting students' development. Learning goals are both excitation and motivation. Achieving certain learning goals can make students have a sense of achievement and satisfaction. Figure 1 shows several main factors related to learning goals.

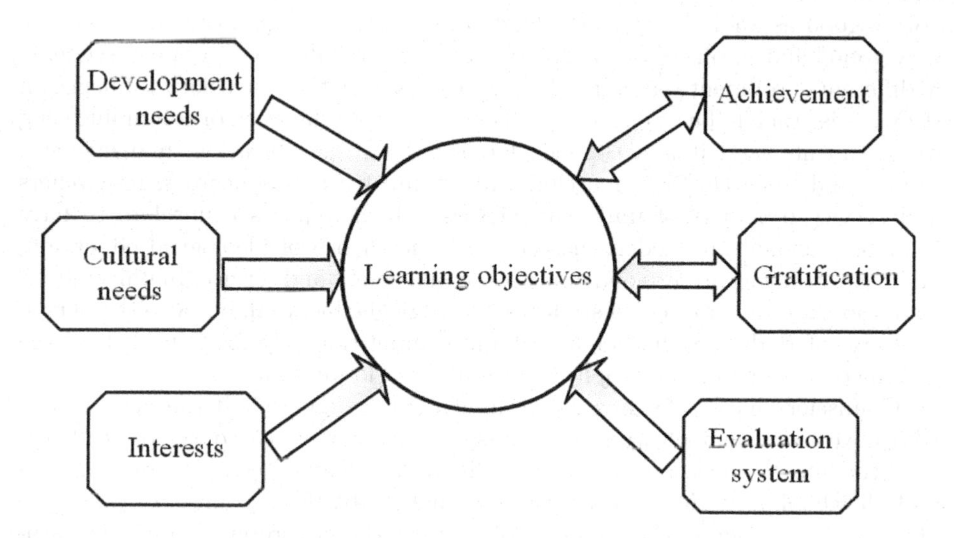

Fig. 1. Main factors related to learning objectives.

2.2 Working Attitude of the Teachers

Teaching is a two-way input and output process. Teachers and students influence each other and achieve each other. Good teachers not only give vivid lectures and responsible work, but also mobilize students' enthusiasm for learning.Similarly, active learning classes will reverse affect teachers 'teaching, and a serious classroom and positive feedback will have a good impact on teachers' teaching motivation.

As the designer and organizer of learning development, teachers are the leader of the whole course. The depth of understanding of the subject, the attitude of teaching, the preparation before class and the organization of the classroom all directly affect the learning effect of students. A serious and responsible teacher attaches importance to the cultivation of students' ability to contact, integrate and transfer, will deeply analyze the learning methods of professional skills, and integrate the current new technologies and new ideas into his own classroom.

This teacher will not only be strict with himself, but also strictly manage the classroom and after-class learning. Teachers' serious working attitude will motivate students' learning. Students will treat the courses seriously in a subtle way, and learn according to the rhythm and requirements of teachers, so as to improve the drive of learning.

2.3 The Guiding Role of the Counselors

In universities, a strange phenomenon is been found that with the same teachers and learning environment the teachers always say that "one class of students is not as good as another student", "one class of students quality and ability are very good" and so on topics. There are not any big differences between students in different enrollment years. In college study and life, the counselor's influence on students is crucial. The work of a counselor is simply the work of communicating with students, and it is a complex labor integrating education, management, service and research [7]. Counselors are administrators, educators, researchers and service providers of university classes, which requires counselors to have solid professional knowledge, master the basic theory of ideological education, and have strong awareness and ability of management and service. In universities, counselors are the pioneers of students 'ideological education, but also the person in charge of student evaluation award and competition organization, and are the guidance of students' philosophy, values and world outlook.

Counselors have a leading role that cannot be ignored. If the class cadres who have more contact with the counselors are sophisticated active students, the students in the class are more inclined to participate in school activities and off-school activities to ignore professional study. If the counselors pay more attention to academic performance, often visit the classroom and diligent students, the overall learning atmosphere is strong, and the students' learning drive is stimulated.

2.4 Learning Atmosphere of the Small Group

It is often been seen about such news: all the members in a dormitory were admitted to graduate students of 985 or 211 universities ,3 students in a 4 members dormitory obtained the maintenance qualification, and most of the students in a laboratory got the offer of top 500 enterprises. This phenomenon shows that the learning drive of science and engineering students is easily affected by the external environment.

Humans are social animals, most people change their behavior in the face of group pressure, so that they can quickly integrate into the group. The willpower of College students has not experienced the social training and beating, and it is more likely to produce conformity behavior. When an individual is in a positive environment, the individual will have a strong willingness to learn, this learning willingness and herd behavior will be transformed into the drive of learning, stimulate students' psychological needs recognized in the group, overcome their own ego and inertia, and let students study actively.

2.5 Learning Significance and Learning Benefits

In an era of data explosion, students have a variety of channels to receive information, affected by the bad social atmosphere, some college students will be eager for quick success and instant benefits, high vision and low action. A considerable number of students in ordinary colleges and universities cannot deeply realize the long-term significance and value of learning, and lack the incentive of short-term learning income, which is tend to produce the psychology of self-abandonment.

The emerging engineering education pays more attention to the cultivation of innovation and creative ability. The problem-oriented training mode can make students have a firm learning motivation of and have certain expectations for the effect of learning [8]. Stimulating the interest of students in learning and having a certain curiosity can keep students' long-term and effective internal drive. In the learning and research process of complex engineering problems in the emerging engineering, the complex problems are decomposed into small problems related to the curriculum. Students can directly realize the learning significance, record and affirm the phased achievements made by students, and improve the contribution value and participation of each student in the learning process in this way. This short-term learning income can further stimulate the growth of students' internal drive. Through the analysis of internal driving force, the main participating roles of various factors can be summarized, as shown in Table 1.

Table 1. The main participating role of the internal drive influencing factors.

Factors affecting internal drive	Participation role
Learning objectives	Students
Working attitude of Teachers	Teachers
Guiding role of Counselors	Counselors, College decision makers
Learning atmosphere of group	Classmates, Friends
Learning significance and benefits	Social environment, School

3 Establishment of Effective Learning Drive Training Mechanism

3.1 Set up Firm Learning Goal

Sun Tzu's Art of War said: "Reality always comes worse than you've expected". One of the responsibilities of universities is to guide students to have the right values, help students set a valuable and lofty goal and keep approaching to this goal. The emerging engineering education makes the learning goal more clear. In the whole university life, it is necessary to constantly strengthen the ideological education of students, strengthen students' belief in realizing their ideals, turn this goal into a steady stream of drive, and promote students to make continuous efforts to achieve the goal.

3.2 Establish Highly Efficient and Strict Teaching Norms

No matter what kind of teaching method, teachers are the controller and leader of the classroom and the core and soul of the whole team. If the performance of teachers in class is too casual and lazy, students will not pay attention to the subject and no longer focus on study. If teachers have strict teaching plans, fast and efficient teaching programs, coupled with strict classroom management, students will be more focused on learning in class. At the same time, if the teachers seriously correct homework, students will be relatively correct attitude; if the teachers do not often correct homework or seriously correct homework, students will be more perfunctory. In the emerging engineering education, a strict and serious and responsible teacher will affect students' study of the subject in all aspects, so as to improve students' self-discipline ability and stimulate potential internal drive.

3.3 Give Full Play to the Leading Role of College Counselors

The influence of teachers on students is usually limited to a certain subject, and the influence of counselors on students can continue throughout college life. In our research, we found that in classes with postgraduate entrance examination dormitories or postgraduate guarantee dormitories, counselors usually release more information about postgraduate examinations; And the classes that have achieved more competition results or successful entrepreneurship, the counselors focus on often publishing information about new technologies and successful people. Therefore, counselors need to help students make clarify their learning goals and significance when they enter school, set excellent and hard-working students as models and examples, and timely release information of learning and competitions, so as to create a positive learning environment.

3.4 Clarify the Significance and Value of Learning and Establish Short-Term Effective Incentives

Everyone has a potential need to be recognized by others. Successful experience in learning can satisfy their sense of achievement, which is the source of everyone's hard work. From the beginning of enrollment, it is necessary to encourage students with the learning experience of advanced alumni and excellent personal deeds in the industry to make them clear the significance and value of learning.

In addition, it is also necessary to sort out, revise and improve the training plan, determine the role and status of each course in the whole discipline system under the background of the emerging engineering, take the ability to help students solve complex engineering problems as the guidance, and carefully record the tasks completed, opinions put forward, phased progress and activities of each fellow student in the whole teaching and research process, Timely affirm the contribution value and participation of each member in the learning process. This approval will stimulate students' learning motivation and stimulate the growth of internal drive, so as to achieve the effect of efficient and active learning, the radar analysis diagram of influencing factors of internal drive as shown in Fig. 2.

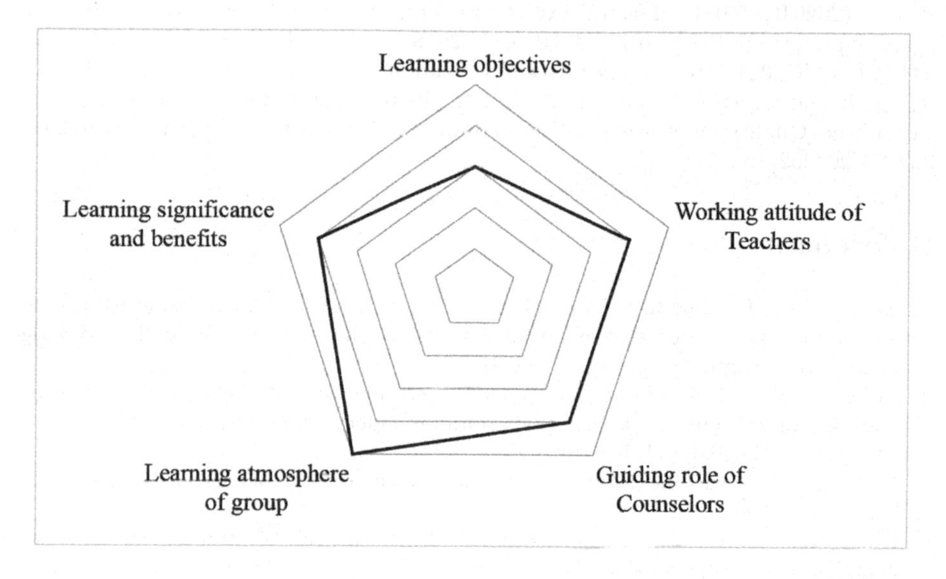

Fig. 2. Radar diagram of core influencing factors.

4 Conclusion

The concept of emerging engineering puts forward new requirements for higher education, and brings new challenges to the ability cultivation of students majoring in engineering. The internal driving force of learning is the comprehensive embodiment of students 'sense of responsibility, self-improvement and initiative. The cultivation of internal driving force can stimulate learning enthusiasm, improve students' self-discipline ability and autonomous learning ability,and correct learning attitude. This paper explores the formation mechanism of college students' learning drive from teachers, counselors, learning environment and learning motivation, and puts forward the methods and suggestions to cultivate the learning drive. Firstly, set valuable goals and ideals to make students understand the role and significance of learning and correct the attitude towards learning. Secondly, establish serious teaching norms to make students realize the pressure and urgency of learning. Thirdly, develop serious and responsible counselors to create a positive learning environment. Finally, by decomposing learning tasks and establishing short-term incentive strategies, students can obtain a sense of achievement, so as to further improve their learning initiative, realize their own life value and realize a virtuous circle.

Acknowledgements. This research was supported by Henan Province Higher Education Teaching Reform Research and Practice Project (2021SJGLX080, 2019SJGLX044);Henan Province Teacher Education Curriculum Reform Research Project (2022-JSJYYB-025); Henan Province New Engineering Research and Practice Project (2020JGLX011); Henan University undergraduate teaching reform research and practice project (HDXJJG2018-04, HDXJJG2019-10, HDXJJG2020-13, HDXJJG2021-047, HDXJJG2021-116); Henan University Graduate education and Teaching Reform Research and Practice Project(YJSJG2022 XJ056); Postgraduate Cultivating Innovation and Quality Improvement Action Plan of Henan University(SYLAL2022018, SYLKC2022022).

References

1. Kun, L., Yu. D.: The first batch of new engineering research and practice project guidelines reached degree evaluation and future development research and judgment[J].Res. High. Educ. Eng., 2021(01), 31–38
2. Hong, M., Wei. Z.: Exploration of practical teaching reform of chemical engineering undergraduate course under the background of emerging engineering[J].High. Educ. Chem. Eng., 2020,37(04):97–102
3. CRICK R D. Learning Power in Practice: a guide for teachers[M].London: Paul Chapman, 2006
4. Fang, W.: A study on the learning ability model of chinese college students[D].Xiamen University, 2019
5. Shumei, S., Jun, W.: Stimulation needs, Stimulate motivation, Enhance the internal drive of learning[J].Vocat. Tech. Educ. Forum, 2004(12):53
6. QingHua, G.: Goal leads, stimulate students to learn the drive[J].Curriculum guidance(Teaching Research) 2020(17):57
7. Yuting, Q.: Research on the Value perspective and path of aesthetic education of college counselor in the new era[J].Policy Scientific Consult, 2021(07), 241–242
8. Cheng, P., Xiaohong, Z.: Exploration and practice of problem-oriented innovation ability cultivation under the background of emerging engineering[J].2020,28(30):139–140

Practical Teaching Exploration and Reform of Signal and Information Processing Courses

Jinyan Hu(✉), Shaojing Song, Yumei Gong, and Haihua Yu

Shanghai Polytechnic University, Shanghai 201209, China
jyhu@sspu.edu.cn

Abstract. In order to develop the students' practical ability, this paper explores and realizes the optimization of practice and applications based on the signal and information processing course system. The constructed course system consists of courses categorized as fundamental theory, theoretical applications and technical practice. A progressive mode of practical teaching is designed and carried out by a dual professional teacher team. At the same time, an effective path to improving students' practical ability is built from basic experiments, to Project Based Learning (PBL) task, and then to extracurricular extensions. Speech signal processing is taken as an example course to show the details of basic experiments design and PBL task arrangement. The practice of adaptive filtering in speech signal is used to demonstrate how to transform signal and information processing algorithms from software simulation to real-time implementation. The statistical results indicate that students' practical ability has been greatly improved through the progressive practice mode in our constructed course system.

Keywords: Application-oriented · Signal and information processing · Progressive practice mode · Project Based Learning

1 Introduction

The demand for application-oriented talents is increasing rapidly with the development of social economy. The main goal of an application-oriented university is to cultivate the talents needed by the industry. So that the undergraduates can improve their independent learning ability, problem-solving ability, communication and teamwork ability concerned by enterprises while acquiring professional and technical ability before graduation. The problems that colleges and universities generally face in the practical teaching of signal and information courses are as follows. First, how to stimulate students' interest and transform their thirst for knowledge into knowledge and ability in the teaching of highly theoretical courses. Second, how to improve students' practical ability and treasure both practice and theory through limited class hours [1, 2]. With many years of teaching experience on signal and information processing, this paper designs and implements the optimization of theoretical and practical teaching content based on the course system architecture, and takes the advantages of dual professional teachers' team to form a progressive practice mode.

J. Gan et al. (Eds.): CSEI 2023, CCIS 1899, pp. 381–389, 2024.
https://doi.org/10.1007/978-981-99-9499-1_34

2 Course System Construction

According to the goal of cultivation and characteristics of the courses, the related courses are integrated to form a signal and information processing course system [3, 4]. As shown in Fig. 1, the course system is divided into three modules including fundamental theory, theoretical applications and technical practice. The fundamental theory module is composed of two specialized elementary courses, signal and system and digital signal processing, which lays a theoretical foundation for signal processing. The theoretical applications module is composed of two specialized courses, speech signal processing and digital image processing. It is respectively oriented to the principle, method and application of one-dimensional digital signal represented by speech and two-dimensional digital signal processing represented by image. The technical practice module is composed of Principle and application of Digital Signal Processor (DSP) and DSP engineering practice courses, which applies professional technology to engineering practice. From the perspective of time line, the courses start from fundamental theory, pass through theoretical applications, and end up with technical practice. From the perspective of application-oriented goal, the fundamental theory module provides the foundation for theoretical applications module, and technical practice module services the realization of theoretical applications.

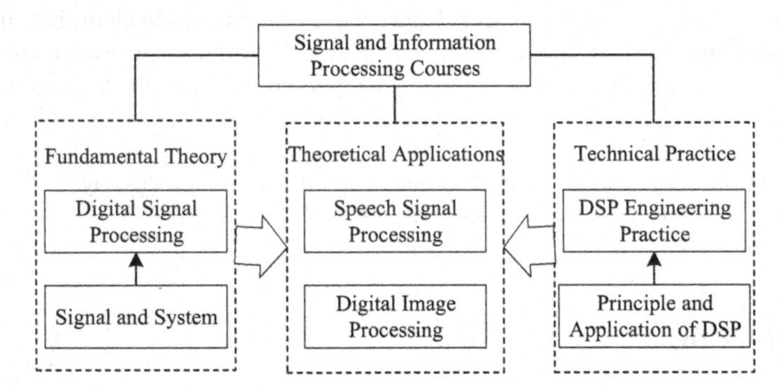

Fig. 1. Course System Architecture

The cultivation of application-oriented talents brings forward higher requirements for the teachers' team. Among the teachers of all the courses in the course system, dual professional teachers with both practical experience and theoretical background account for 90%, and among the teachers of theoretical applications and technical practice module courses, dual professional teachers account for 100%. In teaching and scientific innovation projects, dual professional teachers can combine their industry background and working experience in relevant fields to guide students in practicing innovation and establishing engineering consciousness.

3 Progressive Practice Mode

In the situation of limited class hours, a progressive practice mode is designed to break through the limitations of time and space. The three-level progressive ladder goes from basic experiments, PBL task [5], to extracurricular extensions. Among them, the basic experiments stage uses the experiment class hours of the course itself, the PBL stage uses the after-school time during the course, and the extracurricular extensions stage extends the practice to the college students' innovation projects. The progressive mode creates a learning path of not only improving the students' practical ability but also transforming interest into knowledge and practical ability.

3.1 Basic Experiments and PBL Task

Basic experiments are designed in the courses of fundamental theory, theoretical applications and technical practice. The PBL task is only available in the stages of theoretical applications and technical practice.

Taking the course of speech signal processing [6] as an example, according to the teaching content and class hour arrangement, the basic experiments are mainly verification experiments, as shown in Table 1. The students are required to master the basic short-time analysis and feature extraction of speech signal through experiment 1 and 2, and understand two kinds of applications in speech enhancement and coding through experiment 3 and 4.

Table 1. Basic Experiments of Speech Signal Processing.

No	Experiments	Content	Class hours
1	Speech Signal Analysis	Framing and windowing Time-domain analysis Frequency-domain analysis	2
2	Speech Feature Extraction	End-point detection Pitch extraction Formant extraction	2
3	Speech Enhancement	Sub-spectrum method Weiner filtering method Adaptive filtering method	2
4	Speech Coding	PCM coding ADPCM coding	2

The experiments start with the sampling of speech signals. The students are required to complete the sampling of mono speech signals with 8kHz sampling rate and 16-bit resolution before class, and save them as WAV files. Since there are no restrictions on the acquisition method and the content of speech, some use mobile phone recording to cooperate with the Format Factory Conversion software, some use Audition or GoldWave or other software to record, and some use programing to realize recording, and etc. The content of speech includes speaking, poetry reading, singing and so on. Through the seemingly simple speech signal sampling, the students are prompted to think about why to adopt 8kHz sampling rate instead of lower or 44.1kHz for speech signal, what is the effect of sampling resolution lower than 16 bits, what is the difference between mono and stereo, what is the difference between WAV and MP3 files, and so on. For each basic experiment, the corresponding knowledge point is expanded in depth or breadth through questions and thinking.

The topic directions and specific requirements of the PBL task are introduced during the first class, and the project submission time is before the end of the course. Alternative topics include but not limited to speech recognition, speech enhancement, speech emotion recognition, speech coding, speaker recognition, speech synthesis, speech information hiding and speech blind separation. The projects are implemented in groups, with three people in a group and free combination. The groups are required to deliver the project design and implementation, final project report, and presentation of the selected topic. The students use the time after class to complete the PBL task with team members, and teachers provide after class guidance for the topic selections. Figure 2 shows the statistical results of students' PBL topic selections in recent years. Among them, the most groups choose speech recognition, followed by emotion recognition, speaker recognition, and speech enhancement, from which we can clearly see the students' interest tendency. In terms of task completion, the completion rate of final project report is 100% and the completion rate of project design and implementation is 72%. The programming languages involved include C++, Java, python, and etc. The reasons for 28% not completing the design and implementation mainly include the weakness of prerequisite courses, insufficient time after class and unreasonable time arrangement.

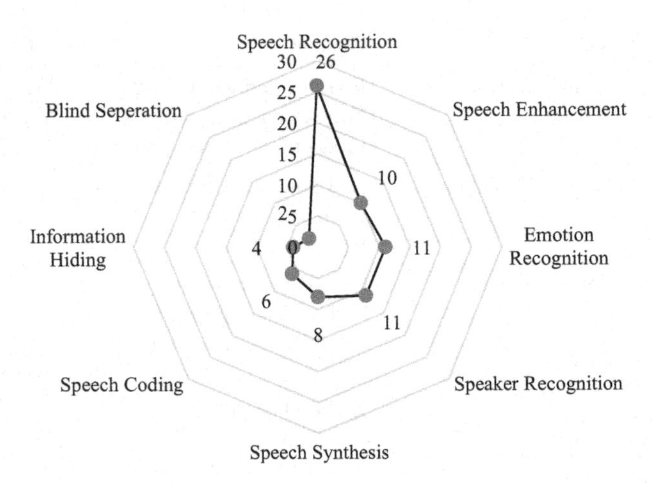

Fig. 2. Statistics of PBL topic selections

In the process of PBL task, the completion of each topic requires learning new knowledge and even mastering new programming language. Various tasks to be completed and problems to be solved during the project execution require reasonable task assignments and close cooperation within the group. Thus not only train students' autonomous learning ability and problem-solving ability, but also improve students' communication ability and teamwork ability.

The assessment methods of PBL task are as follows, final project report accounts for 40%, design and implementation accounts for 40%, and presentation accounts for 20%. The overall assessment methods of the course are as follows, final examination accounts for 50%, basic experiments accounts for 15%, PBL task accounts for 20%, and class performance accounts for 15%.

3.2 Simulation and Real-Time Implementation

The speech and image signal processing algorithms learnt from the theoretical application module can be realized on the DSP hardware platform to turn simulation into real-time implementation. It will help to improve students' engineering application ability. The subjects of comprehensive design project in DSP engineering practice course can be either speech or image processing applications. The hardware platform is TMS320VC5509A DSP development board, and the software development environment is Code Composer Studio (CCS) IDE [7]. The implementation process of the key signal processing algorithm in a comprehensive design project includes progressive steps of algorithm principle design, simulation and verification, algorithm implementation, and performance optimization. For speech signal processing applications, audio CODEC is required in the hardware system to realize the input of analog audio signal and the conversion from analog to digital signal, the conversion from digital to analog signal and the output of analog audio signal. Next, the application of adaptive filtering in speech signal processing based on DSP is taken as an example.

Adaptive filtering is an effective method to deal with nonstationary signals. Without knowing the statistical characteristics of the input signal and noise in advance, the filter can track the statistical characteristics of the estimated signal and adjust its own parameters to achieve the optimal filtering effect under certain criteria [8]. The general form of adaptive filtering is shown in Fig. 3, where it contains the input signal $x(n)$, the output signal $y(n)$, the desired signal $d(n)$, and the error signal $e(n)$.

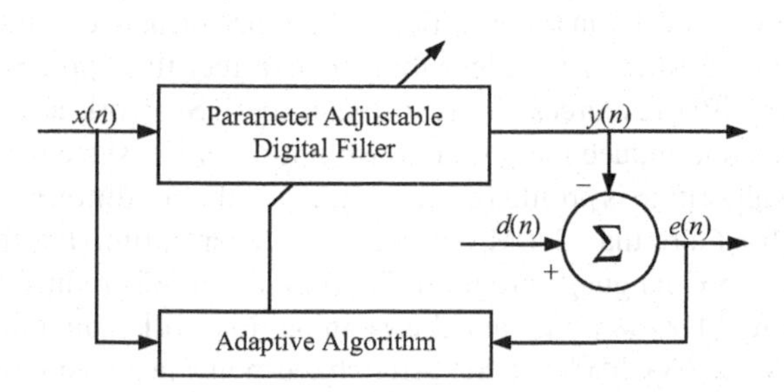

Fig. 3. Adaptive Filtering Theory

The parameter adjustable digital filter is selected as the transverse FIR filter structure, and the weight coefficient vector of m-order FIR filter is expressed as $W(n) = [w_0(n),$

$w_1(n),\ldots, w_{M-1}(n)$]. Then the output of the filter is:

$$y(n) = X(n)W^T(n) \quad (1)$$

where $X(n) = [x(n), x(n-1),\ldots, x(n-M+1)]$, representing the input signal vector. The error signal $e(n)$ is the difference between the filter output signal and the desired signal.

$$e(n) = d(n) - y(n) \quad (2)$$

The most commonly used Least Mean Square (LMS) algorithm is selected as the adaptive algorithm, that is, the least mean square of $e(n)$ is taken as the criterion. The weight coefficient recurrence formula of the algorithm is:

$$W(n+1) = W(n) + 2\mu e(n)X(n) \quad (3)$$

where the range of iteration step μ is $0 < \mu < 1/\lambda_{max}$, and λ_{max} is the maximum eigenvalue of autocorrelation matrix $X(n)$. Each update of the weight coefficient is related to the input signal $x(n)$ and the desired signal $d(n)$ of the filter. In the application of noise elimination of speech signal, taking the reference noise signal related to the actual noise signal as $x(n)$ and the noisy speech signal as $d(n)$, the output signal $y(n)$ of the filter is the best estimation of the actual noise signal, and the error signal $e(n)$ is the speech signal after de-noising.

The above LMS adaptive filtering implementation process first initializes the weight coefficient vector, and then updates the filter output $y(n)$, error signal $e(n)$ and weight coefficient vectors $w(n)$ for each speech signal sampling point with $n = 1,2,\ldots$ According to Eqs. (1)–(3), and $e(n)$ is treated as de-noised speech signals.

After algorithm verification of adaptive filtering in speech signal processing, C language programming is used to port the algorithm to the target DSP platform, carry out system integration and test, and complete the implementation of the algorithm. Figure 4 shows the test results of speech signal adaptive filtering after algorithm implementation. The length of the test signal is 8000 sampling points. The signal-to-noise ratio of the noisy speech signal with Gaussian white noise is 1dB, and the order of FIR filter is 32. The signal-to-noise ratio of the speech signal after de-noising is about 15dB improved.

In the practical engineering application of speech signal processing, performance optimization is very important, and its results will directly affect the performance and cost of products. One of the main objectives of the performance optimization stage is to reduce the running time of the algorithm, realize real-time processing and reduce the occupation of CPU resources, so as to make the DSP work at a main frequency as low as possible, and reduce the power consumption of the system. The ported LMS adaptive filtering algorithm is profiled corresponding to the condition of the above speech test, and it runs for more than 380M clock cycles. After optimizing the floating-point division operation in C language program, the running time is reduced by half, but for speech signal with 8kHz sampling rate, this running time still cannot meet the real-time processing of TMS320VC5509A DSP. After fixed-point processing of floating-point operations in C language program, the running time is reduced to about 10M clock cycles, which can realize real-time processing. Further, by calling the assembly level optimized function in C55x function library, the running time of the algorithm is reduced to 552K clock cycles, which fully meets the real-time requirement and significantly improves the performance.

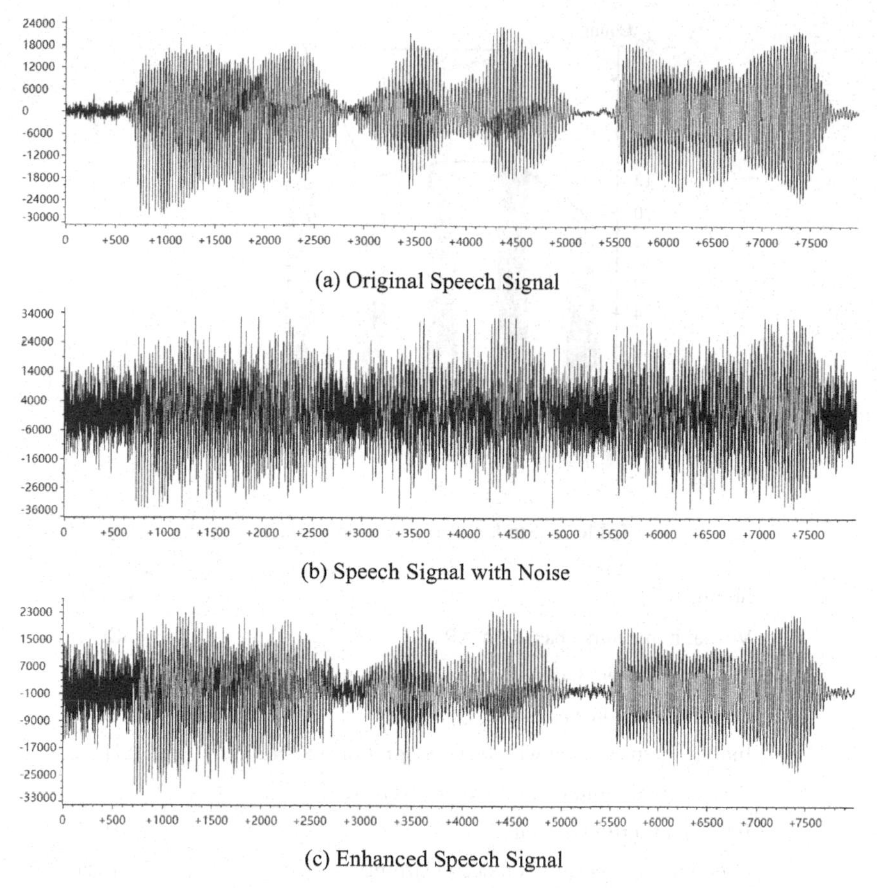

(a) Original Speech Signal

(b) Speech Signal with Noise

(c) Enhanced Speech Signal

Fig. 4. Test Results of Speech Signal Adaptive Filtering

3.3 Extracurricular Practice and Innovation

Based on the interests and abilities cultivated in the courses of speech signal processing and image signal processing, students are encouraged to apply for and complete the innovation and entrepreneurship projects in relevant fields every year. Through these projects, students' comprehensive practice and innovation ability are further improved. The innovation projects can also be converted into credits.

In the past five years, students majoring in Electronics and Information Engineering of Shanghai Polytechnic University (SSPU) have won a total of up to 40 university level innovation projects and 28 municipal (SH) innovation projects, as shown in Fig. 5. It can be seen that both university and Municipal level innovation projects are increasing steadily year by year. And 6 of the municipal innovation projects was rated as national (China) innovation projects. Table 2 lists some of the students' innovation projects related to signal processing applications, including 3 projects each for university level, municipal level and national level.

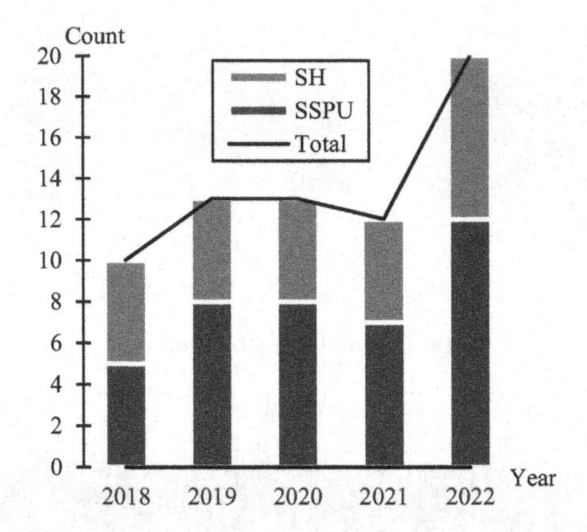

Fig. 5. Statistics of University Students' Innovation Projects

Table 2. Students' Innovation Projects.

No	Subjects	Level
1	Virtual home nurse based on AR	SSPU
2	Tracking Camera based on image recognition	SSPU
3	Personalized voice assistant	SSPU
4	Intelligent interaction with face recognition and NLP	SH
5	Road sign recognition of driverless vehicle	SH
6	Intelligent sorting dustbin	SH
7	Food recognition based on deep learning	China
8	Emotion analysis based on feature fusion	China
9	Driver fatigue monitoring based on machine vision	China

4 Conclusion

Starting from the framework of signal and information processing course system, this paper makes an overall design of the courses' practical teaching, breaks through the boundary of time and space, and constructs a progressive practice mode. In the basic experiments stage, students can obtain a certain depth and breadth of expansion while mastering the knowledge points. In the PBL task stage, students' enthusiasm is stimulated and their abilities of autonomous learning, problem-solving, communication and teamwork are improved. In the extracurricular extension stage, students' engineering practice ability is further improved by combining the signal processing application practice with specific hardware platforms. Some students enhance their comprehensive practice and innovation ability through the university students' innovation and entrepreneurship projects. At each stage, there is a dual professional teacher team with rich practical experience to provide students with professional and efficient guidance and guarantee.

In the next step, continuous improvement will be made in the integration of curriculum politics and the simultaneous optimization of technical practice courses in the course system.

Acknowledgement. This project is supported by 2021–2022 Shanghai University English Teaching Model Course project for foreign students (A30YD210803) and Curriculum Construction project of Shanghai Polytechnic University (A01GY22E021–01).

References

1. Qinghua, H.: Artificial intelligence affects speech signal processing teaching. J. EEE **3**(42), 49–51+64 (2020)
2. Qingyun, W., Ruiyu, L., Li, Z., Yueqin, F., Yongqiang, B.: Research on teaching and experimental methods of speech signal processing under the real-time environment. Res. Explor. Lab. **9**(38), 186–189+220 (2019)
3. Yanfen, W., Xiaoguang, Z., Gang, W., Limei, C.: Construction and reform practice on curriculum group of signal processing for electronic information specialty. Exp. Technol. Manag. **4**(32), 11–14+18 (2015)
4. Min, L., Jun, L.: Reform and practice of signal processing course group experimental practice teaching. Educ. Teach. Forum **23**, 156–158 (2020)
5. Kun, Q., Fang, F.: PBL teaching and practice for DSP technology and course project. J. Electr. Electron. Educ. **1**(37), 68–70 (2015)
6. Lawrence, R., Schafer, R.: Digital speech processing. Froehlich/Kent Encycl. Telecommun. **6**, 237–258 (2011)
7. Hui, L., Shuai, L., Han, T., Hongdang, Z.: Research on heuristic teaching method of "DSP principle and application" course. Exp. Technol. Manag. **5**(38), 167–170+174 (2021)
8. Chunli, Z., Xin, L.: Speech endpoint detection method based on LMS noise reduction and improved dual–threshold. J. Syst. Simul. **9**(29), 1950–1960+1967 (2017)

A Multi-working Mode Switching Technique on ARM Teaching Model Machine

Fujia Zhang, Danfeng Sun(✉), and Yuejun Yu

School of Computer, Hangzhou Dianzi University, Hangzhou, China
{hziee_zfj,yuejun_yu}@hdu.edu.cn, sun_danfeng@foxmail.com

Abstract. The switching of 9 working modes of ARM CPU is one of the difficulties in designing ARM teaching model computer. Based on the independent research and development of ARMv7 architecture teaching model machine, this paper proposes a multi-work mode switching method leveraging the program state register heap structure and coercion conversion strategy. This method simulates the multi-mode switching technology in an ARM chip, provides the hardware foundation for the system-level interrupt design experiment of ARM model machine, and adds a new computer component design method to the traditional Principles of Computer Composition. Supporting by the remote self-learning innovative experiment with the small private online course (RSIE-SPOC) teaching method and self-made remote FPGA experimental platform, student satisfaction is over 90%, which lays the foundation for future systemic ability training of ARM architecture across multiple courses.

Keywords: ARM teaching model machine · Program status register heap · Forced conversion strategy

1 Introduction

For decades, there has been a long-term deviation in the training of domestic computer professionals in the training of emphasis on software rather than hardware, and emphasis on applications rather than foundation", resulting in a lack of high-end computer infrastructure design and underlying software development talents in the industry. Basic research talent training has become a valuable strategy for many countries [1–4].

For computer majors, the root of basic research personnel training lies in the cultivation of system ability. Wang et al. [5] introduced the connotation and needs of the system ability training. In view of the current situation of our higher education and the problems existing in the system ability training, they elaborated the thoughts of the national education reference commission on the system ability training and curriculum setting.

In the research on system capacity training, many universities from the "double world-class project" and "Project 985" of China have played a leading role. Bao et al. [6, 7] developed the teaching program of CPU design and tape-out for undergraduates and organized the "one chip for a lifetime" program for computer majors. In July 2021, Yuan et al. [8] held a computer system ability training 2.0 tutorial class seminar.

J. Gan et al. (Eds.): CSEI 2023, CCIS 1899, pp. 390–400, 2024.
https://doi.org/10.1007/978-981-99-9499-1_35

In the systematic teaching reform, the Principles of Computer Composition is an indispensable core course. In the research on the structure of the new-generation teaching model machine of the traditional Principles of Computer Composition course after MIPS, ARM has become the two main directions of the research of the new-generation teaching model machine together with RISC-V because of its market share in the embedded field such as mobile phone is up to 90% [9–15]. Compared with the advantage of open source of the RISC-V architecture, ARM is difficult to reform because it is not open source, and the number of developers is small. However, the industry has a huge demand for high-end talents who are familiar with the underlying development of ARM, which has prompted the reform of ARM courses to be carried out. The significance of developing the ARM teaching model machine and implementing teaching is not only to allow students to have a deeper understanding of the underlying hardware structure of ARM but also to enable students to learn more high-end computer underlying design methods through diverse examples to meet industry needs and promote National strategies can be better implemented.

Chen Wei translated the textbook "Computer Composition and Design (Hardware/Software Interface) (ARM Edition)" written by Turing Award Winner David A. Patterson et al. [16]. However, Legv8 (ARMv8 simplified version) teaching model machine structure introduced in this textbook has many similarities with MIPS. It is simple in structure and lacks high-level and complex ARM system-level underlying design such as multi-working mode switching and interrupts priority preemption based on it.

Nine working modes are important features of ARMv7 and above architecture chips. These modes are the basis for ARM CPUs to realize system functions such as interrupts, and also the basis for developing multi-course linkage system capability based on ARM architecture. In this paper, a hardware mechanism design method is proposed to realize multiple working modes switching through ARM program status register heap structure design and forced conversion strategy. The method simulates the implementation of multi-working mode switching technology in ARM chips on the underlying hardware of the system and provides a hardware basis for multi-working mode switching of ARM interrupt mechanism. This is a new approach to designing computer components for the traditional Principles of Computer Composition course.

2 Program Status Register Heap and 9 Operating Modes in ARMv7 Architecture

The program status register stack in the ARMv7 architecture CPU contains one current program status register CPSR and seven SPSR registers. The low 5 bits M[4:0] of the current program status register CPSR represents the current processor operating mode. 7 sub-mode backup program status registers SPSR correspond to 7 operating modes such as fiq, irq, and svc, while there is no corresponding SPSR register for User and Sys modes.

3 Operating Mode Switching Based on Program Status Register Heap Structure

Figure 1 shows the program status register heap structure. The backup program status registers SPSR_fiq, SPSR_irq, SPSR_svc, SPSR_mon, SPSR_abt, SPSR_hyp, and SPSR_und are selected according to the operating mode specified by the lower 5 bits M[4:0] in the CPSR.

The backup program status register SPSR writes data from the current program status register CPSR or from the module external data SPSR_New. The selection signal is W_SPSR_s and the write control signal is Write_SPSR. Normally, the control signal Chang_M = 0 of the multiway selector determines which backup program status register to write data to by the lower 5 bits M[4:0] of the CPSR register. The write operation is performed at the clk skip edge.

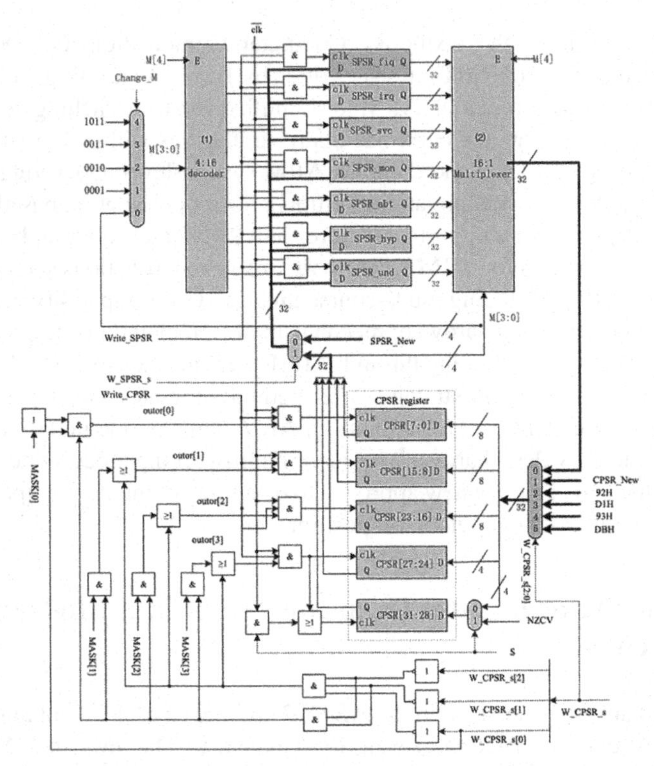

Fig. 1. Multi-working mode switching mechanism based on program status register heap structure

The data written to the current program status register CPSR is either from one of the sub-mode SPSR registers or from data external to the module. The module external data is either the switch input value CPSR_New or the four values 92H, D1H, 93H, and DBH specified by the forced transition policy. The select signal is W_CPSR_s and the write control signal is Write_CPSR, which performs the write CPSR operation at the clk down-jump edge. Marked number of (1) and (2) in Fig. 1, are the decoder and multiplexer, respectively, and their enable terminal E is active high. The highest bit M [4] of the operating mode is connected to the enable terminal E of (1) and (2). (1) and (2) is enabled when M [4] = 1.

The CPSR registers can be written byte by byte, while each sub-mode SPSR register must be written by 32-bit word as a whole. In Fig. 1, the control signal for writing to the CPSR byte by byte is MASK[3:0], and each bit of MASK controls writing one byte to the CPSR. When the data written to the CPSR comes from one of the sub-mode SPSR registers, MASK[3:0] = 1111, which also modifies 4 bytes of the CPSR register. The highest byte of the CPSR register is handled in two segments: CPSR[31:28] holds the four flag bits NZCV of the ALU output, while CPSR[27:24] is handled similarly to the lower three bytes of the CPSR register. When the lowest byte of CPSR, CPSR_C, is modified, the system operating mode is switched.

The control circuits of the 4:16 decoder (1) and the 16:1 multiplexer (2) in Fig. 1 correspond to the operating modes as shown in Table 1. They both have a selection signal of M[3:0] and an enable signal of M [4] = 1, thus ensuring that the operating mode is coded legally.

Table 1. Correspondence table of operating modes of decoder (1) and multiplexer (2)

Operating mode control selection data	Output corresponding register
M[3:0] = 0001	SPSR_fiq
M[3:0] = 0010	SPSR_irq
M[3:0] = 0011	SPSR_svc
M[3:0] = 0110	SPSR_mon
M[3:0] = 0111	SPSR_abt
M[3:0] = 1010	SPSR_hyp
M[3:0] = 1011	SPSR_und

4 Application of Forced Transition Strategy in the Interruption Process

ARM's interrupt handling is based on multi-working mode switching; when the ARM CPU responds to an interrupt, it first switches to svc mode and then to the corresponding target working mode to handle the interrupt. Before switching to the new working mode, the CPU needs to save the breakpoint, and the ARM main stack pointer MSP and user stack pointer PSP have to complete the correspondence with the SP pointer in the old working mode. It is difficult to complete the above operation according to the conventional working mode switching mechanism. In order to simplify the complexity of working mode switching, the ARM teaching model machine adopts a forced switching strategy to achieve the special requirements of interrupt control.

When interrupt response, according to the bit meaning of CPSR register, interrupt hidden instruction forces a new value to the lowest byte of CPSR, CPSR_C. This new value is fixed, as shown in Table 2. For example, the new value corresponding to irq interrupt is 92H, which means off irq interrupt (=1) and on fiq (=0), and does not allow nesting of interrupts of the same level. Fiq interrupt has a higher priority than irq interrupt, which can interrupt the irq interrupt process and go to respond to fiq interrupt when irq interrupt processing is not finished, and then continue to finish the interrupted irq interrupt after fiq interrupt processing is finished The interrupt can be preempted. To handle irq interrupts, you need to switch to irq working mode, so the working mode bit is set to 10010, so CPSR_C should be assigned to 92H.

Table 2. The interrupt setting value specified under the coercion policy

Interrupt Type	CPSR minimum byte new value	Meaning
fiq interruption	D1H	Off irq interrupt, off fiq interrupt, instruction system is ARM instruction set, working mode is set to fiq (10001)
irq interruption	92H	Off irq interrupt, on fiq interrupt, instruction system is ARM instruction set, working mode is set to irq (10010)
SVC exception	93H	Off irq interrupt, on fiq interrupt, instruction system is ARM instruction set, working mode is set to svc (10011)
Undefined instruction exception	DBH	Off irq interrupt, off fiq interrupt, instruction system is ARM instruction set, working mode is set to und (11011)

The multiplexer before the 4:16 decoder (1) in the program status register heap is used to force the value of CPSR into some sub-mode SPSR in the original operating mode before the CPSR is updated. The control signal of the multiplexer is Chang_M. When Chang_M = 1, the input of decoder (1) is 0001, forcing it to fiq mode; when Chang_M = 2, the input of decoder (1) is 0010, forcing it to irq mode; when Chang_M = 3, the input of decoder (1) is 0011, forcing it to svc mode; when Chang_M = 4, the input of decoder (1) is 0011, forcing it to svc mode; when Chang_M = 4, the input of decoder (1) is 0010, forcing it to irq mode. 4, the input of decoder (1) is 1011, forcing it to und mode.

The W_CPSR_s selector has 4 sources, which correspond to the 4 constants in Table 2. From the W_CPSR_s selector to the or gate output before the D flip-flop clock end of the CPSR, the outputs of the 4 or gates are named outer[3:0], respectively. The

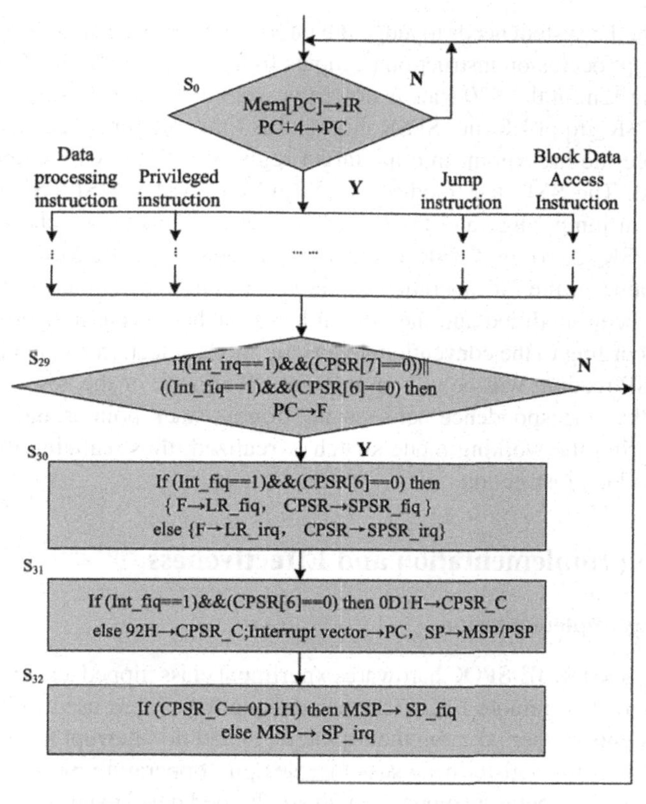

Fig. 2. fiq and irq interrupt control flow chart.

relationship between the selection control signal W_CPSR_s, the byte selection signal MASK, and the outer are shown in the logical expressions (1) to (4).

$$outer[0] = W_{CPSR_{s[0]}} \times MA\overline{S}K[0] \times W_{CP\overline{S}R_{s[1]}} \times W_{CP\overline{S}R_{s[2]}} \quad (1)$$

$$outer[1] = W_{CP\overline{S}R_{s[0]}} \times W_{CP\overline{S}R_{s[1]}} \times W_{CP\overline{S}R_{s[2]}} + W_{CP\overline{S}R_{s[1]}} \times W_{CP\overline{S}R_{s[2]}} \times MASK[1] \quad (2)$$

$$outer[2] = W_{CP\overline{S}R_{s[0]}} \times W_{CP\overline{S}R_{s[1]}} \times W_{CP\overline{S}R_{s[2]}} + W_{CP\overline{S}R_{s[1]}} \times W_{CP\overline{S}R_{s[2]}} \times MASK[2] \quad (3)$$

$$outer[3] = W\_CP\overline{S}R\_s[0] \times W\_CP\overline{S}R\_s[1] \times W\_CP\overline{S}R\_s[2] + W\_CP\overline{S}R\_s[1] \times W\_CP\overline{S}R\_s[2] \times MASK[3] \quad (4)$$

The above program status register heap structure and nine operating mode conversion mechanisms, as well as the forced assignment conversion strategy, can be used with the hardware structures such as MSP/PSP stack pointers and interrupt control circuits on the ARM model machine, to implement the irq interrupt, and fiq to irq interrupt preemption. Fiq and irq interrupt control flowchart is shown in Fig. 2. In the interrupt system where fiq and irq coexist, the system needs to judge the interrupt priority and handle it accordingly, and the interrupt occlusion instruction occupies four clk cycles. In Fig. 2, the operating mode of the system in the S30 state is not fiq or irq, but it needs to save the breakpoint to LR_irq, SPSR_irq or LR_fiq, SPSR_fiq. At this time, the forced conversion strategy is used to store the breakpoint into the target register with the CPSR operating mode bit unchanged. The S31 state modifies CPSR_C and writes MSP/PSP both occur at the clock down-jump edge, and the system's operating mode switch is the result of modifying CPSR_C, so the CPSR_C has not changed when the MSP/PSP is written, and the SP value in the old operating mode is written. When entering the S32 state, CPSR_C has been modified and the system has switched to the new operating mode. Therefore, according to the conventional working mode selection mechanism, the value of MSP or PSP readout will be written into the SP register of the new working mode. In this way, the correspondence between the double stack pointer and the sub-mode SP pointer during the working mode switch is realized, thus realizing the function of interrupting hidden instruction.

5 Teaching Implementation and Effectiveness

5.1 Teaching Implementation

The self-developed RSIE-SPOC hardware experiment class flipped teaching method and self-made interactive remote FPGA experiment platform were used to implement the teaching. Students further program the irq interrupt and fiq interrupt mechanisms based on the program status register heap structure design, 9 operating modes switching and forced conversion of operating modes, which are divided into 3 experiments. In addition, there are two optional exception-handling experiments.

Figure 3 shows the simulation waveform of a group of students' fiq-to-irq interrupts preemption experimental works. As seen from the 32-bit coding of CPSR in the figure, the working mode of the system changes during interrupt preemption, indicating that the experimental design can correctly implement forced working mode switching to support interrupt preemption.

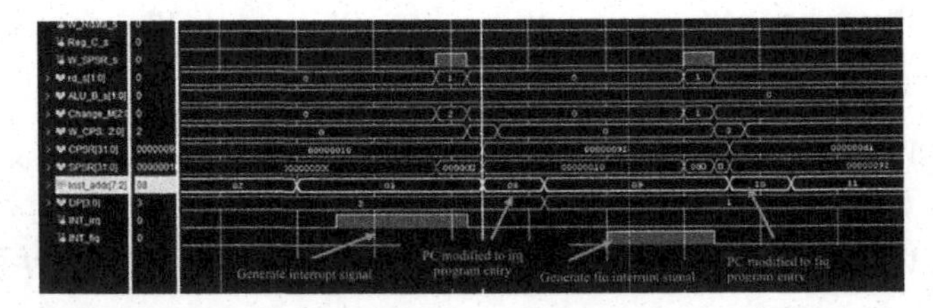

Fig. 3. Student work

The following code is a Verilog HDL program fragment written by a student to write to the CPSR byte by byte in the program status register heap design experiment. This code implements the modification of the lowest byte of the CPSR controlled by the MASK[0] bits, which contains the operating mode bits M[4:0], and CPSR_in[7:0], which contains the new value obtained by the forced conversion strategy, thus achieving the goal of switching the operating mode of the system.

Verilog HDL program fragment

```
always @(posedge rst or negedge clk)
begin
  if (rst == 1) CPSR <= 32'h00000013;
  else
  begin
   if (Write_CPSR && (MASK[0] || (~W_CPSR_s)))
    CPSR[7:0] <= CPSR_in[7:0];
   if (Write_CPSR && (MASK[1] || (~W_CPSR_s)))
    CPSR[15:8] <= CPSR_in[15:8];
   if (Write_CPSR && (MASK[2] || (~W_CPSR_s)))
    CPSR[23:16] <= CPSR_in[23:16];
   if (Write_CPSR && (MASK[3] || (~W_CPSR_s)))
    CPSR[27:24] <= CPSR_in[27:24];
   if (S) CPSR[31:28] <= NZCV;
   else
    if (Write_CPSR && (MASK[3] || (~W_CPSR_s)))
     CPSR[31:28] <= CPSR_in[31:28];
  end
end
```

5.2 Teaching Effect Analysis

Starting from 2021, the program status register heap design experiment, irq interrupt experiment and fiq interrupt experiment, and exception handling experiment are officially put into teaching use. The course implementation survey shows that students' overall satisfaction with the course is over 90%, 90.5% of students believe that the component design experiments (including the program-state register heap design experiment) promote a deeper understanding of the ARM CPU architecture, and 76.2% of students believe that the course has increased their interest in learning computer hardware systems. As shown in Fig. 4.

Figure 4 shows the results of the following survey among students. The component design projects in the lab class are barrel shifter design experiment, multi-function LU design and connection with barrel shifter experiment, general register heap design experiment, program status register heap design experiment, memory design experiment, ARM assembler simulator experiment, and fetch finger today datapath design experiment.

A. Promote a deeper understanding of ARM CPU structure;
B. more than learning MIPS and RISC-V to promote a better connection to the successor class "embedded system design" (the course uses ARM development board teaching);
C. Improve the ability of Verilog HDL programming;
D. Promote understanding of the concept of components forming the whole machine;

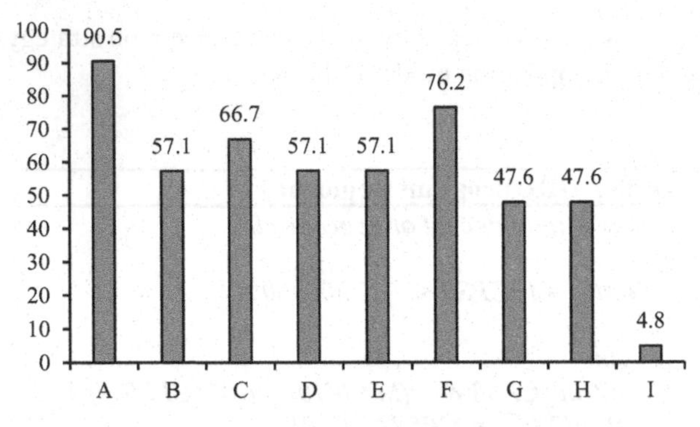

Fig. 4. Student Satisfaction Survey 1

E. promote the learning of hardware debugging methods, improve self-learning ability, and promote the development of complex engineering skills;
F. Improved interest in learning computer hardware systems;
G. Cultivate the ability to analyze and design the components of computer hardware systems, with significant results;
H. The learning of component design experiments promotes the professional knowledge and ability of students;
I. It is useless to learn or not to learn, it is useless to cultivate the system ability and personal ability to improve.

The program status registers heap design experiment obtained a good teaching effect, facilitating the smooth development of the interrupt/exception handling experiment. 21 students in the 2021 teaching class completed 100% of the two system-level interrupt design experiments, irq, and fiq, with an average score of 87.6. The teaching program was generally accepted by the students. 81% of the students considered the interrupt experiments worth learning, as shown in Fig. 5.

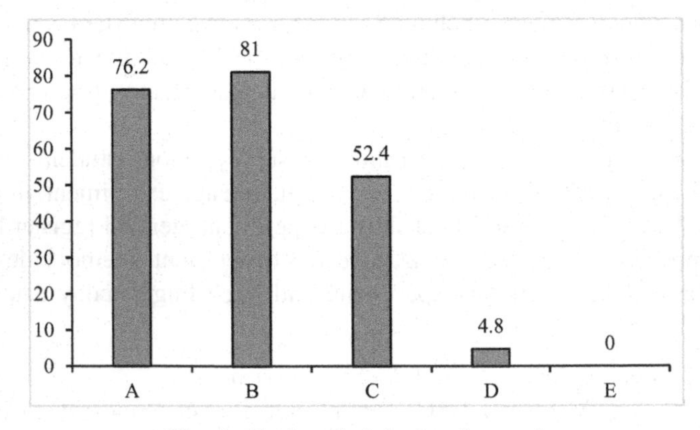

Fig. 5. Student Satisfaction Survey 2

Figure 5 shows the results of the following survey among students. There are 2 ARM interrupt experimental top items and 2 ARM exception experimental items in the lab class, Do you think?

A. It is especially useful to connect with the following classes "Operating System" and "Embedded System Design", etc.;
B. Presented the concept of interrupt priority, covering a variety of ways of ARM interrupts/exceptions, worn learning;
C. despite the lack of in-class hours, after the end of this course, there is interest in continuing to complete these experiments;
D. Insufficient in-class hours, after this course, do not intend to continue to complete these experiments;
E. These experiments have no effect on the course connection and enhance the system's capability. So it is better not to do it.

6 Conclusion

ARM's program status register heap structure is the hardware basis for implementing the 9 operating modes switching, and the forced conversion strategy improves the support of interrupt mechanism for operating mode switching, and its design method is the research result of the high-end model computer architecture design carried out by local universities. The teaching implementation results show that the method can be used to implement irq and fiq interrupt mechanisms on ARM model machines, and the teaching effect is good, which promotes students' deep understanding of ARM CPU architecture, and better mastering of irq, fiq and other computer underlying software/hardware design techniques. For the articulation of Linux operating system, embedded system principles and other courses, and a step to carry out the ARM architecture-based system capability training to lay the foundation.

Acknowledgements. This work was supported by the research project Construction and Educational Reform of an Internationalized System Teaching Platform based on Advanced CPU Architecture (No. jg20220222) funded by the Zhejiang Provincial Department of Education, China. We would like to express our sincere gratitude for their support.

References

1. Yonghe, Z.: Attaching importance to the cultivation of top talents in basic education to solve the problem of "stuck neck" in China', Sci. Soc. **10**(4), 22–24 (2020)
2. Wenhua, R.: Research on the problem of "stuck neck" of key core technology under the perspective of Qian Xuesen's view of technology science'. Sci. Manage. Res. **9**(3), 33–38 (2021)
3. yuliang, Y.: What is "stuck" about "stuck neck"? The problem of "stuck neck" ruminates', Sci. Soc. **10**(4), 1–4 (2020)
4. Dening, C.: Breakthrough "neck" key technology challenges and potential analysis. National Governance Weekly, pp. 29–34 (2020)

5. Zhiying, W., Xingshe, Z., Chunfeng, Y., et al. :Research on system competence cultivation and system curriculum setting for computer science students, Comput. Educ. **9**, 1–6 (2013)
6. Gailun, Z.: Pao Yungang brings down the threshold of chip design. Grand Garden Sci. **10**, 78–79 (2020)
7. Tong, W.: Yungang Bao: Under him, college students can also make chips. Fortune World. **9**, 27–28 (2021)
8. Chunfeng, Y., Jie, T., Feng, S.: Nanjing Computer System Tutorial Course [Z/OL]. https://live.eyunbo.cn/live/68109?uin=1729&refererId=33544167. Accessed 02 March 2022
9. Guangnan, N.: Embracing the new trend of open source chips. Inform. Secur. Commun. Privacy **2**, 10–13 (2019)
10. McGrew, T., Schonauer, E, Jamieson, P.: Framework and tools for undergraduates designing RISC-V processors on an FPGA in computer architecture education. In: 2019 International Conference on Computational Science and Computational Intelligence (CSCI). IEEE, pp. 778–781 (2019)
11. Burnett, D.C., Kilberg, B., Zoll, R., et al.: Tapeout class: taking students from schematic to silicon in one semester. In: 2018 IEEE International Symposium on Circuits and Systems (ISCAS), pp.1–5 IEEE (2018)
12. Lei, K., Xing, L., Hui, L., et al. : 'Design of RISC-V based teaching model machine', pp. 102–106 (2021)
13. Jun, Z., Dongsheng, X., Qilin, Z., et al. : 'Exploration of computer system capability development mechanism based on RISC-V architecture', pp. 72–76 (2020)
14. Moreno, J., Puertas, S., Orts, F., et al.: On stimulating an ARM processor for teaching computer structure. In: 12th annual International Conference of Education, Research and Innovation (ICERI 2019). Seville, Spain: IATED, pp. 3103–3108 (2019)
15. Chunfeng, Y., Zihao, Y.: 'Computer Composition and Design (based on RISC-V architecture)', (Higher Education Press 2020)
16. Patterson, D.A., Hennessy, J.L.: 'Computer composition and design hardware/software interface', (China Machine Press, 2018)

The Construction of Collaborative Education Practical Teaching System Based on Emerging Engineering Oriented Towards the Integration of Production-Education

Qin Qin[1](✉), Tinglong Tang[1], Peng Wang[2], and Guoqiang Gong[1]

[1] College of Computer and Information Technology, China Three Gorges University, Yichang, China
q_qin2000@163.com

[2] Changjiang River Communication Administrations, Yichang, China

Abstract. Emerging engineering construction is a critical strategic decision and deployment for higher engineering education in order to respond to the emergence of new economies and industries. This paper examines in depth the teaching issues that must be addressed in the training of emerging engineering talents, such as the mismatch between the training goal of specialty and the training mode of practical ability, the lack of levels and gradients in the practical teaching system of engineering education, and the lack of engineering teachers' practical ability. Using our university's communication engineering major as an example, from the development of the OBE concept of "3 + 1" talent training mode, to build a multi-level and open system of specialized basic courses and specialized course engineering practice courses, university-enterprise professional co-construction and curriculum co-construction, the development of industry, university, and research institute embodies the student-centered, cultivating "double-qualified" students.

Keywords: Emerging Engineering · Production and Education Integration · Collaborative Education · Practical Teaching

1 Introduction

The OBE concept of professional certification of engineering education in China (student-centered, output-oriented, and continuous improvement) [1] requires that students cultivated by colleges and universities meet the needs of industry, have engineering theory literacy, and basic engineering application ability, emphasize the combination of theory and practice, and advocate for extensive industry participation in the cultivation of engineering talents, so that the integration of production and education can cultivate engineering talents [2].

The application of production and education integration, as well as "integration" and "cooperation," are the cornerstones of growing engineering talent training [3]. To adapt to engineering certification standards under the emerging engineering background, a "3

J. Gan et al. (Eds.): CSEI 2023, CCIS 1899, pp. 401–412, 2024.
https://doi.org/10.1007/978-981-99-9499-1_36

+ 1" talent training system based on the OBE concept and a practical teaching system of university-enterprise collaborative education based on the training objectives and social needs of communication engineering professionals are required. According to the actual situation of students in our college, the university-enterprise joint professional committee, which is made up of senior professors, enterprise experts, professional leaders, and key teachers, has been clear about the professional talent training goal, from the curriculum system, teaching content, teaching means, teaching method, experiment and practice teaching, and many other aspects of the communication engineering talent training scheme. This paper raises the level of enterprise involvement in academe administration by summarizing the knowledge gained over the years as this major was developed at our institution.

Personnel training programs are currently being developed based on the Ministry of Education's ICT Production-Education Integration Innovation Base, Hubei key laboratory of intelligent vision based monitoring of hydroelectric engineering, Hubei engineering technology research center for farmland environment monitoring, and Hubei province engineering technology research center for construction. Cooperate with the Changjiang Yichang Communications Administration, China Mobile, Huawei, Wuhan Lab Tech, Wuhan Easy Start, Shenzhen IUV, and other enterprises to establish practical training and practice bases, promote the integration of production, learning, teaching, and research, and investigate the operation mode of an open practice platform combining in-class and out-of-class activities. We have extensively encouraged university-enterprise collaborative education, enhanced students' ability to tackle complex engineering problems, and gradually raised graduates' recognition and satisfaction with their major.

2 The Main Teaching Problems to be Solved in Order to Improve Students' Engineering Practice Ability

The development of students' engineering practical skills is cross-border. The university's single-subject teaching style has inherent flaws in the development of students' engineering practical competence. Integration of industry and academia, as well as university-enterprise collaboration, is required circumstances for the development of engineering and technical abilities [4]. The following four major teaching challenges must be handled in the practice system teaching reform through multi-party study and communication.

2.1 The Practical Ability Training Style does not Satisfy the Objectives of Professional Training

The goal of the Communication Engineering major is to develop application-oriented professionals who can master the fundamental theory, professional knowledge, and engineering skills of fields related to communication and information, find, research, and find solutions to complex engineering problems in this field, and engage in engineering design, equipment manufacturing, network operation, and technical management in the field of communication engineering and related fields. Engineering training, cognitive practice, production practice, curriculum design, and graduation projects make up the majority of the focused practical teaching in China, which also includes experimental teaching (supporting experiments of theoretical courses and independent experimental courses). The objective of practical teaching is still to validate theoretical understanding and master experimental training techniques, but there are no strict requirements for responsibility, expression ability, innovation ability, or cooperative spirit. In addition, without practical process management and supervision, practical teaching evaluation devolves into a meaningless exercise, and the effectiveness of practical ability training is still far from being established.

2.2 Lack of Levels and Gradients in the Teaching Method for Engineering Education

It is a phenomenon that knowledge learning is prioritized over skill development in China's undergraduate engineering teaching system. The primary features are that the emphasis on teaching the subject's fundamentals outweighs the students' inadequate practice in engineering. Teaching strategies and practical activities lack hierarchy from the perspective of the practical teaching system. A survey and interview with teachers, businesses, and senior students regarding practical teaching were conducted in 2014 by the communication engineering department. The results, which confirmed that experimental teaching was insufficiently thorough and innovative, lacking a gradient and level between cognitive practice, production practice, and graduation practice. Students lacked possibilities for practical training since businesses had their own interests but were also reluctant to accept students for internships. Lack of levels and gradients in the practice teaching method for engineering education.

2.3 Engineering Education Practical Instruction must be Student-Centered

Teaching first, learning second—the idea that teachers are significant while students are not—is a common result of the traditional teacher-centered educational philosophy and methods. Students are typically in a state of passive acquiescence, with little time or opportunity for constructive thought or active expression, and little initiative in their academic work. Students lack problem-finding, problem-solving, innovative concept and consciousness, communication and expression skills, and teamwork abilities.

2.4 Teachers' Engineering Practice Abilities must be Developed

Engineering teachers usually lack engineering practice experience, and their engineering quality and practical expertise are insufficient to be qualified for the critical mission of engineering talent training. Teachers with a strong engineering background and a high academic level are especially scarce. In terms of energy intake, most teachers invest in teaching insufficiently, particularly in practical instruction.

Furthermore, because there is no direct relationship between universities and industries in China, recruiting university engineering lecturers from enterprise engineers with practical expertise is challenging. The absence of engineering experience among engineering teachers has a significant impact on the quality of undergraduate engineering practical teaching. As a result, universities must adopt policies to encourage instructors to take sabbaticals to work in industry, to engage with industrial engineers on research and teaching projects, and to use engineering experience as a recruiting and promotion criterion.

3 The Method of Improved Student Engineering Practice

In the process of teaching research, we primarily use the following strategies to answer the aforementioned teaching challenges.

3.1 Create the "3 + 1" Talent Training Mode of the OBE Idea

In the talent training of communication engineering major, students' output is orientation, combining with the national strategic demand of electronic communications industry and regional industry of the Changjiang Economic Belt and economic demand, optimizing the talent training scheme and curriculum system, practice system, surrounding the Three Gorges Region "hydropower project" and "shipping communication," seizing the Changjiang Economic Belt opportunity.

We decide the professional training of talent positioning and the objective to achieve through collaboration with enterprises, with the support of industry firms familiar with the market and understanding. With this purpose in mind, the "3 + 1" talent training mode and "platform + module" training scheme are proposed, as shown in Fig. 1. That is, students will finish all theoretical courses in the first three years, and in the final year, they will complete practical skill training integrated with engineering practice, such as internship, practical training, and graduation project. The basic idea is to consolidate the professional foundation, universities and enterprises jointly develop professional training, enterprise technical training courses into the direction of communication engineering specialty teaching and engineering practice, enterprise engineers participate in teaching and the process is based on "project-driven" reverse design communication engineering talent training. We will open professional training modules and set up matching professional module courses and practical courses in collaboration with cooperative firms, based on the growth interests of students and the application needs of enterprises. After graduation, students can easily adapt to the working environment of their employer, resulting in a smooth relationship between university and enterprise.

3.2 Create a Multi-level and Open Engineering Practice Course System Comprised of Professional Basic and Professional Courses

Building a professional platform aimed at consolidating the professional foundation, establishing a distinctive major focusing on wireless communication and image information processing, and establishing a practical teaching base inside and outside the university integrating ICT industry, teaching, and research. Professional courses and professional practice courses are integrated into "Estimated budget for communications engineering" "Communication engineering practice" "Project comprehensive practice" and other industry enterprise training courses based on the development of technology

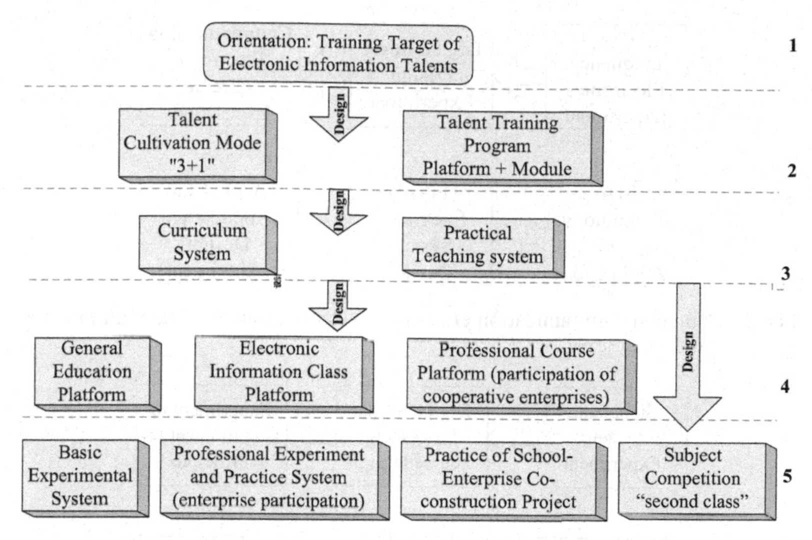

Fig. 1. Mode of communication engineering talent training

and market demand, and the teaching plan and practice content of professional modules are dynamically implemented in collaboration with cooperative enterprises. Furthermore, the related course teaching content is changed in accordance with the needs of the communication engineering professional knowledge system and with reference to feedback on teaching information, and new technology is organically incorporated into the teaching.

We should extend professional caliber, enhance content integration, and create a multi-level, adaptable, and progressive practice teaching system while building a practice training system. Aiming at the existing problem of practice teaching and the future development trend of practice teaching reform of the basic idea for "add levels, update content, open experiment, fit engineering," grasp the basic framework of practice teaching accurately from the macro. The experimental teaching process is divided into three stages: "discipline basis, specialty basis, and specialty direction," resulting in an organized, progressive, and solid practical teaching process. The experimental teaching content is based on three levels: "basic, comprehensive, and innovative," and a multi-level and open practical ability training system are built.

According to its nature, the experimental system of professional basic courses can be divided into three categories, namely, experimental practice courses of communication and electronic system design, experimental practice courses of information processing and transmission, and experimental practice courses of computer, as shown in Figs. 2, 3, and 4.

Since the sophomore year, the practice project's comprehensiveness, design skill, and originality have gradually risen with the increase of knowledge obtained, and it has gradually approached the engineering reality of the communication industry. From the second semester of junior year through the first semester of senior year, the engineering training projects are primarily drawn from the engineering practice of the communication industry. By gradually establishing and forming characteristics of communication

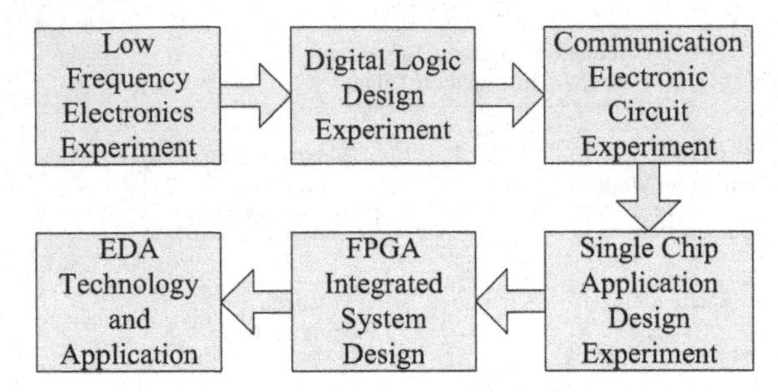

Fig. 2. Course in communication electronic system design experimental practice

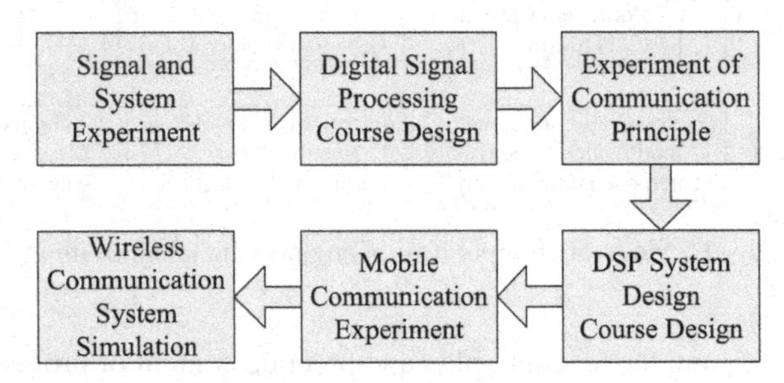

Fig. 3. Experiment with information processing and transmission

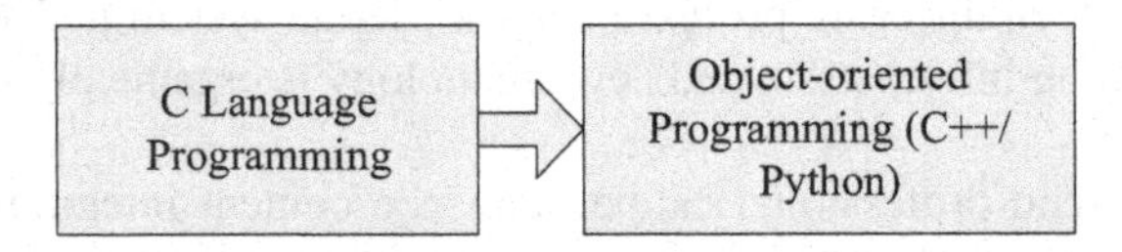

Fig. 4. Course in computer experimental practice

engineering specialty in our university through multi-level and open practice ability training system, graduates can adapt to a wide range of applied positions in the job market and future development, have relatively stable industry tendency, and lay a good foundation for their future development.

3.3 Joint Professional Construction Between Universities and Businesses to Strengthen Professional Construction and Engineering Practice Curriculum Building

We consistently strengthen the strength of university-enterprise joint professional construction and curriculum building in the teaching process in order to grow talents with innovative and practical capacity to tackle complicated engineering challenges.

Enhance University-Business Collaboration in Experimental Practice Courses of Communication Engineering Specialization

Communication engineering is a national first-class construction specialty and a pilot specialty of "comprehensive specialty reform" for undergraduates in Hubei Province, in the course teaching reform, combining with the characteristics of courses and focusing on the current practical problems in the field of industry engineering, using case teaching method, the principle and method through case, so that the students have a comprehensive understanding and mastery of communication engineering. In accordance with university-enterprise cooperation, the combination of virtual and real, and the most recent needs of industrial and technological development to promote the guiding ideology of university talent training reform [5], using production-education integration base to carry out mixed online and offline courses, such as wireless communication system simulation, soft switching technology practice, optical SDH technology practice, the communication engineering practice, project comprehensive practice, virtual simulation course construction, allows our university's professional course and engineering practice teaching to keep up with the development of modern communication technology and link up with market application.

At the moment, a virtual simulation course of 5G communication protocol based on software radio platform has been built, and an emergency communication virtual simulation course based on Changjiang shipping communication is being scripted and refined. By the end of 2021, communication engineering specialty and university-enterprise cooperation units will collaborate to compile professional practice textbooks that can be used not only for communication engineering students' course teaching, but also for technical personnel training in university-enterprise cooperation units.

To improve graduates' and the communication industry's demand fit, improve students' ability to solve practical problems, guide students to apply professional theory knowledge to solve practical problems, develop good working quality and professional ethics, and meet professional needs in advance, the major of communication engineering selects outstanding students to carry out post-practice and graduation projects in the practice base every year. At the moment, the training base has more than ten senior communication engineers and fifteen intermediate communication engineers to provide technical guidance to students. Six senior engineers have been invited to participate in undergraduate and postgraduate graduation defenses in recent years, and six part-time master supervisors and teachers have been hired. It provides students with a comprehensive and professional practice platform by re-creating real work scenes and providing a professional environment.

Conduct Professional Construction Discussions and Exchange Discipline with Industry Firms

Over the last four years, the communication engineering major has had over 30 discussions with university-enterprise cooperation units such as Changjiang Yichang Communication Administration, the Ministry of Education's ICT Industry-education Integration Innovation Base, and Huawei Company on personnel training, scientific and technological cooperation, and the construction of a practical training base, jointly building university-level and provincial-level graduate work. The cooperation units' high-quality information software and hardware resources provide critical support and complement for the teaching of communication engineering major, particularly for the practical links. The win-win concept of production-education integration offers a novel approach to the design and development of communication engineering majors. Cooperation project research has been carried out in the areas of " Bearer network structure adjustment and route optimization ", "Information technology assurance of water traffic safety supervision in administrative areas ", "Research and application of remote power control in CCTV system ", "Application of Beidou System in Changjiang River shipping ", "Regional wireless broadband network and ship big data analysis ", "Research and application of unmanned aerial vehicle audibility ", "Research and application of unmanned aerial vehicle audibility ", "Research and application of an autonomous unmanned aerial vehicle cruise system on water in a 5G scenario."

Actively Pursue Teaching Reform and Research in Specialized Basic and Specialist Courses
Professional teachers have worked on the Ministry of Education's "Construction of Practical Innovation System for Electronic Information Against the Background of Emerging Engineering," "Reform of Practical Teaching System for Electronic Information Against the Background of Emerging Engineering," "Construction of Comprehensive Innovation Platform for Electronic Information Based on Software Radio," and other projects in recent years. The entrusted project "Exploration and Practice of Talents Training Mode of Electronic Information Subject Facing Major Enrollment" and the university level key teaching and research project "Research on Teaching Reform of Information Processing Course Group Facing Major Enrollment" have made a number of achievements in related teaching research and reform. Simultaneously, the development of good courses, online courses, and online open courses in professional foundation core courses has been strengthened. "Digital Signal Processing" and "Communication Principle Experiment" were rated as first-class university-level online courses in 2021.

3.4 The Student-Centered Idea is Reflected in the Co-development of Production, Learning, and Research

Engineering education practice teaching should be based on the CDIO engineering education framework [6], with activity as the center, to create a self-experience for students, independent learning, free creation of the environment, allowing students to carry out project-based learning, learning by doing. This model not only expands the scope of engineering practice teaching, but also the environment of engineering practice teaching put forward the request, a competency-based practical teaching evaluation method is designed to help students gain the competence to apply engineering science and technology knowledge to solve practical engineering problems at various levels through project practice activities.

University-Enterprise Collaboration, Through Internal and External Connections, Produces a Professional Skill Training Mode that Transcends Classroom Teaching Venues and Complies with the Law of Vocational Skill Training
The college experiment center, the ICT production-education integration extracurricular practice base, and the university-enterprise joint practice and training base are the three through-training locations. The experimental center is primarily responsible for conducting in-class basic experiments, specialized basic experiments, and specialized experiments that can meet the fundamental experimental needs of basic, verification, and curriculum design. The university has spent millions of yuan in recent years to construct

the Software Radio Innovation Joint Laboratory, Wireless Communication Laboratory, Modern Communication Technology Laboratory, Electronic System Design Laboratory, Communication Engineering Comprehensive Laboratory, and other professional laboratories.

The Software Radio Innovation Joint Laboratory, Wireless Communication Laboratory, and Electronic System Design Laboratory primarily engage in extracurricular innovative and comprehensive practical training, which serves as an important foundation for cultivating a new generation of communication technology talents with practical ability. As an open laboratory, students can enter at any moment to carry out practical and innovative activities, applying the operation mode of macro direction by teachers and student self-management.

Communication engineering has established a robust collaboration mechanism with businesses and institutions, particularly in the practice of collaborative training. We work closely with Changjiang Yichang Communication Administration, Wuhan Lab Tech, Wuhan Easy Start, Nanjing Runzhong, Wuhan Xinhexin, and 710 Research Institute to improve students' practical and innovative abilities (Fig. 5).

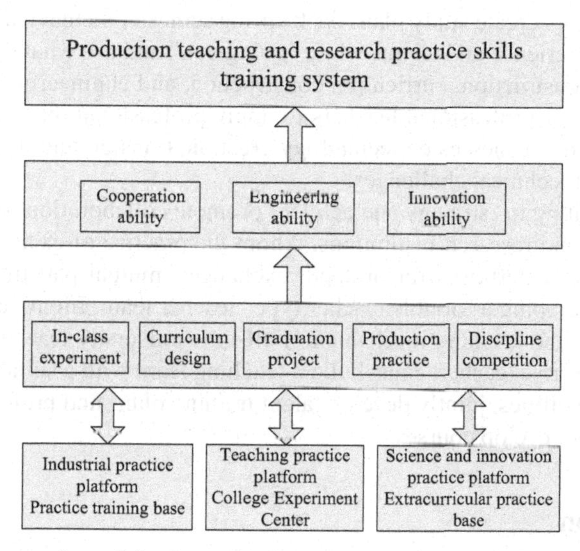

Fig. 5. System for training in production, education, and research practice skills

Through the Adoption of an Undergraduate Tutorial System, University Students' Topic Competitions, and Other Measures, Students' Practical Skill will be Further Developed

The undergraduate tutorial system is a significant method that the college has implemented in recent years to increase students' overall quality, particularly their practical abilities. When undergraduates choose to join the supervisor's team, it not only helps to form the supervisor team's echelon, but it also helps undergraduate students advance the subject, carry out scientific research projects as soon as possible, and form a good sense of teamwork. Students, on the other side, organized teams to compete in several discipline tournaments, led by teachers with extensive experience in competition organizing. In 2021, the university held nine consecutive "FPGA Design Application Competitions," and in the previous five years, students won more than 50 national prizes and more than 20 provincial and ministerial awards in significant contests, achieving remarkable competition outcomes.

3.5 Borrow Wisdom in Order to Introduce Wisdom, and Develop a "Double Teacher Type" Teacher Team

Adopt the "going out and inviting in" strategy, carry out the "project of improving teachers' professional ability," adhere to the combination of backbone teachers entering enterprises and the improvement of all teachers, the combination of off-the-job training and in-service learning, improve teachers' engineering practical ability; university and college actively encourage teachers to take part-time jobs in enterprises, and it is also required that teachers who are promoted to senior professional positions have at least six months of experience working part-time in corresponding firms. Simultaneously, professional instructors create study plans each spring semester so that teachers can enrich their practical experience and talents while "going out," and use what they have learned to professional construction, curriculum construction, and engineering training. It provides a platform for professional teachers to apply professional theoretical knowledge to collaborate with businesses on technology creation, transfer, and innovation, as well as to solve actual technical challenges.

Adopt a "inviting in" strategy and actively promote collaboration between universities, businesses, and research institutions. Adopt the practice of exchanging personnel with the signatory enterprises for in-depth exchanges, mutual part-time labor, and an emphasis on developing a "double teacher type" teacher team. Improve the off-campus specialists' part-time teaching mechanism. Full-time university teachers and part-time cooperative enterprise teachers must build a teaching team with a suitable structure and complementary abilities, jointly develop talent training plans and professional teaching plans, and jointly develop courses.

4 Conclusion

During the seven years of communication engineering teaching practice from 2015 to 2021, the university utilized, refined, and perfected the practice system of university-enterprise joint education, yielding positive outcomes. Except for 2020–2021, the employment rate of communication engineers has been consistent at more than 95% from 2015 to 2019, and employment quality has continuously improved. Every year, a large number of students are admitted to Xi'an Electronic Technology University, China University of Electronic Science and Technology, Xi'an Jiaotong University, Huazhong University of Science and Technology, Beijing University of Posts and Telecommunications, and other industry-renowned and national double-first-class universities. Table 1 shows the employment rate and postgraduate entrance rate for communication engineering.

Table 1. From 2015 through 2021, the employment rate and postgraduate admittance rate for communication engineering majors

Year	Employment rate	Postgraduate admittance rate
2015	98.50%	22.39%
2016	96.77%	27.42%
2017	96.23%	30.77%
2018	95.45%	20.45%
2019	95.08%	28.81%
2020	84.29%	32.86%
2021	91.53%	26.98%

According to a third-party thorough evaluation of the class of 2016, graduates have a 74% job-related degree, students are 86% satisfied with teaching, and alumni are 95% satisfied with their major. To evaluate five years tracking 2010 graduate, working with professional relevance is 72%, professional core courses satisfaction is 87%, from the above statistics, showed that, when compared to this professional and other professional graduate training quality is good, professional employment rate remains high, professional talent training plan and the industry is highly fit, overall employment quality is high, and overall income is in a leading position among all majors in the university.

In the future, the communication engineering major should continue to improve in practice training, continue to implement the undergraduate tutorial system, increase the scale of students' participation in discipline competitions, and deep cooperation with enterprises and institutions in practical aspects, focusing on social needs, and constantly improve the talent training model to better fit the industry's development.

Acknowledgment. This initiative is supported by the Ministry of Education's first batch of Collaborative Education Program funds in 2021 (Item Number 202101345025).

References

1. Shi, X.: Design and execution of course teaching based on the concept of outcome-based education. Res. Higher Educ. Eng. Wuhan. **5**, 154–160 (2018)
2. Shi, X., Xu, Y.: The development of a talent cultivation system based on engineering education accreditation and production-education integration. Res. Higher Educ. Eng. Wuhan. **2**, 33–39,56 (2019)
3. Sun, L.: An investigation into the integration of production and teaching for a talent cultivation path based on emerging engineering. Jiangsu Higher Educ. Nanjing **1**, 74–77 (2021)
4. Xia, J., Zhao, J.: On the reform and development of engineering education in local universities and colleges based on the establishment of emerging engineering education. Res. Higher Educ. Eng. Wuhan. **3**, 15–19,65 (2017)

5. State Council General Office: Several Opinions on Deepening the Integration of Production and Education, GCFA 2017, No. 95 (2017)
6. Gu, P.: The concept, framework and implementation approaches of emerging engineering education (3E) and the new paradigm. Res. Higher Educ. Eng. Wuhan. **6**, 1–13 (2017)

Rethinking Engineering Education on the Teaching and Research Practice of Computer Architecture

Qingzhen Xu[1] and Mingzhi Mao[2](✉)

[1] South China Normal University, Guangzhou 510631, GD, China
[2] Sun Yat-Sen University, Zhuhai 519082, GD, China
mcsmmz@mail.sysu.edu.cn

Abstract. This paper mainly aims at various problems existing in the teaching quality evaluation of the core course computer architecture in engineering education, analyses the influence of factors such as different campuses, different classes, different types of students, the number of students in each course selection and whether to adopt the ideological and political pilot teaching of the course on the teaching quality evaluation, and proposes that the integration of ideological and political elements in the teaching of computer architecture can effectively improve the enthusiasm of students in learning Enhance students' sense of the times and attractiveness towards the great technological rejuvenation of the motherland, and cultivate their innovative thinking of confident development. Finally, we provide application scenarios for data-driven open source vulnerability mining technology. These research results can provide reference and inspiration for research and practice in the field of information and innovation security.

Keywords: Computer Architecture · Engineering Education · Teaching Quality Evaluation · Confident Development

1 Introduction

On December 9, 2016, it was emphasized at the National Conference on Ideological and Political Work in Higher Education Institutions. Integrating ideological and political work throughout the entire process of education and teaching will create a new situation for the development of higher education in China. During the conference, the Chinese Dream was forcefully invoked to promote the youth dream, illuminating the lamp of ideals and the path forward for students, inspiring them to consciously integrate their personal ideal pursuit into the cause of the country and nation, and bravely become pioneers and pioneers who are at the forefront of the times [1].

A new requirement has been put forward for university teachers, especially for our computer major to use new media and technologies to activate teaching work, promote the high integration of ideological and political education with computer course information technology, and further improve the evaluation of computer course teaching quality.

J. Gan et al. (Eds.): CSEI 2023, CCIS 1899, pp. 413–423, 2024.
https://doi.org/10.1007/978-981-99-9499-1_37

2 Curriculum Ideological and Political Education is the Foundation of Teaching Quality Evaluation

China's higher education shoulders the major task of cultivating socialist builders and successors with comprehensive development in morality, intelligence, physical fitness, aesthetics, and labor, and must adhere to the correct political direction. The foundation of establishing a university lies in cultivating morality and cultivating talents. Only universities that cultivate first-class talents can become world-class universities [1].

Enhancing the Four Confidences and cultivating qualified builders of socialism with Chinese characteristics is the basic responsibility of university teachers. A group of experts and scholars have emerged in China to study how to combine ideological and political education with professional teaching in this discipline. Professor Jiang has studied improving the teaching position of the curriculum and comprehensively realizing the tasks undertaken by the curriculum in the talent cultivation system. Actively implement the basic goal of cultivating talents for the Party and the country, and comprehensively build an ecological environment for talent growth. Targeting the achievement of goals, implementing scientific evaluation, and efficiently cultivating high-quality and high-level socialist builders and successors [2].

Professor Mao studied the ideological and political education of IT project management courses in the context of new engineering. The background of the new engineering discipline and the significance of integrating ideological and political education in courses are analyzed. The common problems in ideological and political education in professional courses are analyzed, and the entire process of carrying out ideological and political education is elaborated based on theoretical practice. Corresponding solutions are proposed for specific problems [3, 4].

Wu Yan, an expert from the Ministry of Education, proposed the construction of China's "golden curriculum", which requires great efforts to build five types of "golden curriculum", including offline "golden curriculum", online "golden curriculum", online and offline hybrid "golden curriculum", virtual simulation "golden curriculum", and social practice "golden curriculum" [5, 6]. Strive for every teacher to devote themselves to teaching and educating, do their job well, and their dreams will come true. Building an educational powerhouse will become a reality.

The ideological and political aspects of the construction of the computer architecture curriculum should consider the integration from the dimensions of humanistic value, social responsibility, public welfare, cultural self-confidence, and socialism with Chinese characteristics, so as to avoid the computer majors only learning technology without paying attention to ideological and political integration, and actively guide the computer majors to learn the important role of technology in Serve the People.

Due to the lack of integration of ideological and political education, there have been cases where talented programmers were forced to death by their wives, and high computer students conspired to build gambling websites after graduation, participating in fraud, hacker attacks, and other behaviors, and lost themselves in the face of interests. These are all tragedies caused by the lack of ideological and political education. The integration of ideological and political education in computer courses has a long way to go. In order to better illustrate the importance of ideological and political education in the evaluation of computer course teaching quality, we tracked the results of 16 years of teaching quality evaluation and conducted multidimensional analysis.

3 Big Data Analysis of Teaching Quality Evaluation

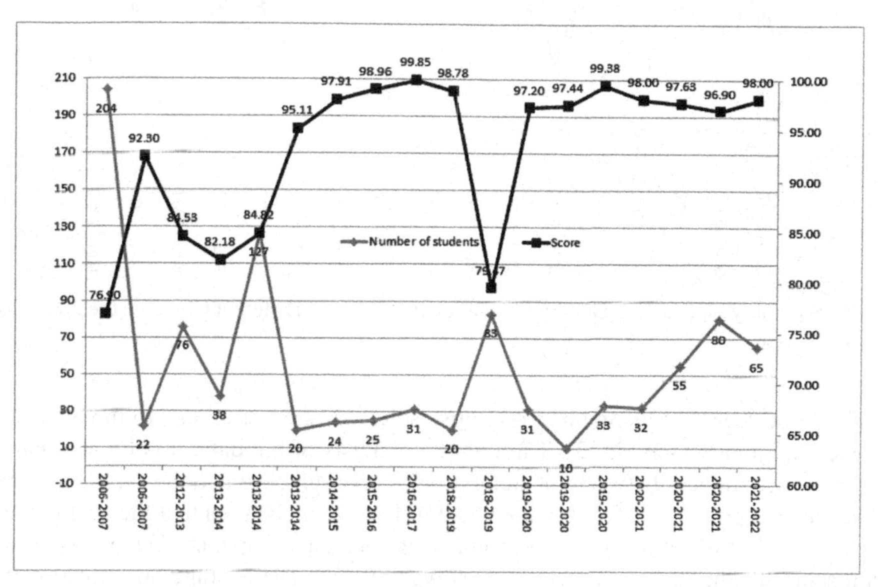

Fig. 1. Overview of Teaching Quality Evaluation in the Main Campus of the 2006–2022 Academic Year.

The number of students (see Fig. 1) is written below, and the evaluation score value is written above. From the curve trend graph (see Fig. 1), it can be seen that the number of students is negatively correlated with the evaluation of teaching quality. Through big data analysis, it is found that there is a negative correlation between the numbers of course selection personnel in the main campus in the past 10 years and the evaluation score, with a correlation coefficient of -0.71862. It can be seen that the evaluation of teaching quality is directly related to the number of course choices. The average evaluation score is 93.0749 points, of which the average evaluation score from 2006 to 2016 was 89.088, and the average evaluation score from 2016 to 2021 was 96.2648. Since the integration of ideological and political education into computer courses in 2016, the overall teaching quality evaluation score has increased by 7.1768 points. After the integration of ideological and political education, the overall teaching quality evaluation has improved significantly. Out of the 18 teaching evaluations, 13 scored > 90, with an excellent rate of 72.2%. From excellent big data analysis, it was found that the average score of excellent students was 97.497, and among the 13 excellent students, the average number of students was 34.462. It can be concluded that a small class of 34 students has the best evaluation of teaching quality.

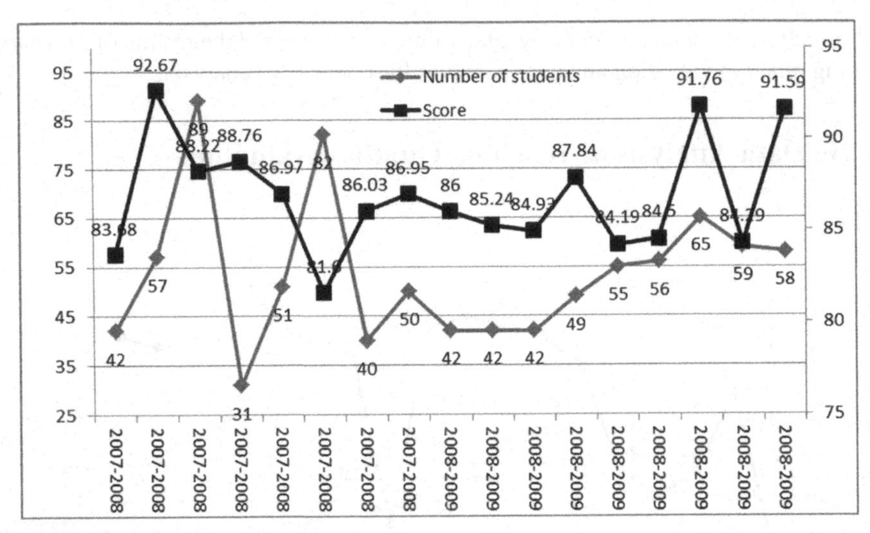

Fig. 2. Summary of Teaching Quality Evaluation by Campus (Different Cities) in the 2007–2009 Academic Year.

It can be seen that the number of course selectors are not related to the evaluation of teaching quality (see Fig. 2). Through the analysis of big data, it is known that the correlation coefficient between the number of course selectors and the evaluation score in the sub campuses from 2007 to 2009 is 0.03157. It can be seen that the evaluation of teaching quality is not related to the number of course participants. The average evaluation score for the three years 2007–2009 was 86.777. The average number of course selectors is 53.53. From the analysis of big data between course hours and evaluation scores, it is found that the correlation coefficient between the two is 0.35564. Out of the 13 evaluations of teaching quality in each campus, 3 scores exceeded 90, with an excellent rate of only 23.08%. The three students with the highest teaching evaluation scores selected courses were 57, 58, and 65, respectively, with the highest teaching quality evaluation in the class of 57 students. On the contrary, the evaluation score of a class with over 80 students significantly decreased. The evaluation score of the class with 82 students is only 81.6, while the evaluation score of the teaching quality of the class with the lowest number of 42 students is 83.68 lower; It can be seen from the analysis results of Big data that it is not good to have too many or too few students selecting courses in different campuses. Slightly above 10% of the average is the best teaching class.

4 Specific Measures for Improving Teaching Quality Evaluation

From the above big data analysis, it can be seen that the new era teaching method based on the construction of computer architecture of ideological and political education should guide students to integrate curriculum ideological and political education from these five aspects: first, humanistic value dimension, second, social responsibility dimension, third, public welfare and mutual benefit dimension, four cultural confidence dimensions, five dimensions of socialism with Chinese characteristics. The improvement of teaching quality of computer architecture based on ideological and political curriculum is the most urgent need of university teachers in the new era.

4.1 The Cultivation of Ideological and Political Thinking Literacy for Teaching Teachers

Starting from the fundamental principles of human beings and relying on their subjective initiative, we aim to cultivate students' humanistic values and achieve common progress in the humanistic values of teachers and students. Guide students to adopt a multi-dimensional thinking mode to enhance their sense of social responsibility. As students majoring in computer science, they should have a sense of information digitization, artificial intelligence thinking, technological innovation, and social responsibility for information. We are in the information age of the information explosion, where computer students have a comprehensive ability and quality to assess the sensitivity and value of big data information. Present contemporary public welfare concepts from the perspective of public welfare and mutual benefit, and make contributions to society through the use of computer technology learned. For example, blockchain, federated learning, itinerary cards, Suikang codes, etc. are all real cases that belong to the dimension of public welfare and mutual benefit. The success of COVID-19 epidemic resistance is enough to reflect the advantages of Chinese cultural self-confidence. Everyone consciously wears masks to block the spread of the virus, and Chinese medicine has no sequelae in treating COVID-19. Behind the success of every success, Chinese cultural self-confidence is displayed. The great rejuvenation of the Chinese nation and the success of the fight against COVID-19 reflect the advantages of the socialist dimension with Chinese characteristics. Our goal in cultivating college students is to cultivate their ability and quality to think about problems from five dimensions.

Professional course teachers should carefully experience and delve deeply into how to better integrate ideological and political elements into the teaching of professional courses, integrate them, inject new vitality into teaching, and cultivate more innovative, technical, and patriotic professional talents.

4.2 Teaching According to One's Aptitude and Improving Teaching Content

The existing computer science textbooks are uneven, with varying degrees of difficulty. Some textbooks are difficult, some are easy, and some are well compiled. During the teaching process, there are too many errors, and the cases in the book cannot be debugged successfully. The book lacks the above five dimensions to integrate ideological and political education with professional textbooks. It is recommended to form a teaching team, absorb the advantages of each textbook, and create teaching PPTs around five dimensions, as well as revise the teaching syllabus and objectives. To truly form a computer course teaching quality evaluation system based on ideological and political education, teaching students according to their aptitude for different courses, and emphasizing the integration of industry and education, and the cultivation model of applying what is learned.

4.3 Evaluation System Based on Ideological and Political Education

According to the characteristics of computer architecture, closed book examination is adopted. In order to better evaluate the learning effectiveness of students and the teaching effectiveness of teachers, it is recommended to incorporate ideological and political elements into the exam questions. Multiple choice questions can be used to specifically examine the names, events, and other famous deeds of high-tech talents who have made contributions to China and are related to their majors. Innovative thinking questions can also be used to test students' professional qualities such as artificial intelligence and big data, and to actively participate in multi-dimensional theoretical and practical tests such as social responsibility and public welfare.

Example 1: Please design an IoT application system for a Mars probe and name it (reference note: China's first Mars exploration mission, Tianwen 1, was successful on May 15, 2021). This type of ideological and political integration question not only tests the ability of professional knowledge, but also conveys to students the superiority of cultural confidence, technological confidence, and the dimension of socialism with Chinese characteristics, enhancing their ability to develop confidence.

Example 2: database design according to the application needs of social prevention and treatment of COVID-19? Consider the specific design of red codes, yellow codes, green codes, and time and space accompanying them. This type of ideological and political integration question not only tests the ability to use professional knowledge to solve practical problems, but also conveys the thinking mode of students in the dimensions of humanistic value, social responsibility, and public welfare.

5 Models and Experimental Data Analysis of Computer Technology Application

5.1 Long and Short Term Memory Model LSTM

LSTM (Long Short Term Memory) is a commonly used Recurrent Neural Network (RNN) model that can better solve problems such as gradient vanishing and exploding when processing sequence data. LSTM was proposed by Hochreiter and Schmidhuber in 1997, with the basic idea of adding gate mechanisms to traditional RNN models to control the flow of information.

The LSTM model includes three gates: forget gate, input gate, and output gate. These gates can control the inflow and outflow of information, as well as whether historical information is retained. Specifically, the forgetting gate determines which historical information should be forgotten at the current time step; the input gate determines which new information should be added at the current time step; the output gate determines which information should be output at the current time step.

In LSTM, each unit has a state vector and an output vector. The state vector is responsible for memorizing historical information, while the output vector is responsible for outputting information in the current state. LSTM controls the update of state vectors and the calculation of output vectors through three gates, thereby better capturing long-term dependencies in sequence data.

Construction of LSTM model:

```
model = Sequential()
model.add(LSTM(128, input_shape = input_shape))
model.add(Dense(128))
model.add(Activation("relu"))
model.add(Dropout(0.5))
model.add(Dense(classes))
model.add(Activation("softmax"))
model.summary()
return model
```

After the construction is completed, the train method is used to train the two models, and the word vector output from the Word2vec model is used as input to obtain a neural network model that can determine whether the code segment contains XSS attacks. For the trained model, input validation and testing sets separately to test the relevant performance of the model.

After completing the preliminary data preprocessing, different CNN model structures and LSTM model structures were constructed, followed by training and testing to find the most suitable model.

5.2 Improvement Process of CNN Model

Firstly, I briefly set up a CNN model with two convolutional layers and two pooling layers (Table 1).

Table 1. CNN Model 1.

Layer Name	Convolutional Kernel Size	Convolutional Kernel Number	Pooled Kernel Size	Neuron Number
Convolutional layer 1	3 * 3	8	—	—
Pooling layer 1	—	—	2 * 2	—
Convolutional layer 2	5 * 5	16	—	—
Pooling layer 2	—	—	2 * 2	—
Fully connected layer	—	—	—	128

After training and testing CNN Model 1, a series of evaluation indicators such as accuracy, accuracy, and recall were found to be low, resulting in severe under fitting. This indicates that the network structure of Model 1 is too simple, and the model cannot obtain and learn key features of the data, unable to complete classification tasks. Therefore, it is necessary to deepen the model structure. After referring to the materials, I improved and set up CNN model 2 (Table 2).

Table 2. CNN Model 2.

Layer Name	Convolutional Kernel Size	Convolutional Kernel Number	Pooled Kernel Size	Neuron Number
Convolutional layer 1	3 * 3	8	—	—
Pooling layer 1	—	—	2 * 2	—
Convolutional layer 2	4 * 4	16	—	—
Pooling layer 2	—	—	2 * 2	—
Convolutional layer 3	5 * 5	32	—	—
Pooling layer 3	—	—	2 * 2	—
Fully connected layer	—	—	—	128

After re inputting the data into CNN Model 2 for training, the test results showed significant improvement compared to CNN Model 1, but there was still a phenomenon of under fitting, and the model's performance on the training and validation sets was still not excellent enough. So I reset CNN model 3 (Table 3).

Table 3. CNN Model 3.

Layer Name	Convolutional Kernel Size	Convolutional Kernel Number	Pooled Kernel Size	Neuron Number
Convolutional layer 1	3 * 3	16	—	—
Pooling layer 1	—	—	2 * 2	—
Convolutional layer 2	4 * 4	32	—	—
Pooling layer 2	—	—	2 * 2	—
Convolutional layer 3	5 * 5	64	—	—
Pooling layer 3	—	—	2 * 2	—
Fully connected layer	—	—	—	128

In CNN Model 3, I did not increase the number of layers in the network, but instead increased the number of convolutional kernels for each convolutional layer. The comparison of the results obtained from the final test set is as follows (Table 4).

Table 4. CNN Model Performance.

Method	Model 1	Model 2	Model 3
Precision	46.4	76.2	92.3
Accuracy	72.7	81.4	89.5
Recall	53.8	78.5	90.2
F1 value	61.8	79.9	89.85

On the basis of CNN model 3, increase the number of network layers or adjusts the relevant parameters, and the final results are reduced, even over fitting occurs. The CNN model is mainly applied to image detection in the field of deep learning, such as face recognition, and is not strong in text data processing. So next, I used the LSTM model of short-term memory network in the recurrent neural network RNN model, which is better at processing text data.

5.3 Improvement Process of LSTM Network Model

One major advantage of the LSTM model is its ability to effectively handle long-term dependencies when processing sequence data. However, the LSTM model also has the problem of vanishing gradients, which can make it difficult for the model to learn long-term dependencies during training.

The reason for the disappearance of gradients is that during the back propagation process of the LSTM model, the gradients are continuously reduced through multiple multiplication operations, resulting in the gradients of earlier time steps approaching zero. This makes it difficult for the model to update the parameters of these time steps, resulting in the model being unable to learn long-term dependencies.

To solve the problem of gradient vanishing, the LSTM model introduces a gating mechanism, which can control the flow of information through some gating units, thereby reducing the problem of gradient vanishing. Specifically, the forget gate in the LSTM model can control which information needs to be forgotten, while the input gate can control which information needs to be input. These gating units enable the LSTM model to better capture long-term dependencies in sequence data, thereby avoiding the problem of gradient vanishing.

In addition, some techniques can also be used to alleviate the problem of gradient disappearance, such as ReLU and other nonlinear activation function, batch normalization, residual connection and other methods. These techniques can make the gradient of the model more stable, thereby avoiding the problem of gradient disappearance. Therefore, the LSTM model structure and related parameters I have set are as follows. The performance of LSTM model 1 is significantly lower than that of LSTM model 2 and the obvious reason is the insufficient number of neurons. However, the performance of LSTM model 3 also lags behind that of LSTM model 2. After multiple model results and parameter adjustments, it is still not as good as LSTM model 2. This indicates that using a layer of LSTM model is more suitable for this project.

5.4 Experimental Data Analysis

In this experiment, the relevant training parameters of the model were set as follows:

- Take 300 epochs for training rounds.
- In the selection of epochs for training rounds, it is important to consider both the effectiveness of the training and the cost of time and space. After considering the effectiveness of the project and the performance of computer hardware, the optimal performance was achieved when the epoch of the training round was set to 300.
- Training batch size is taken as 100.

It can be seen that when batch size is set to 100, the performance of the training and validation sets tends to be consistent (see Fig. 3 and Fig. 4).

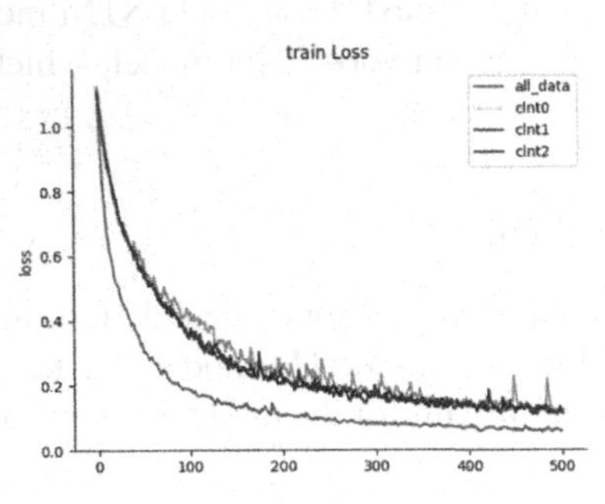

Fig. 3. Train Loss.

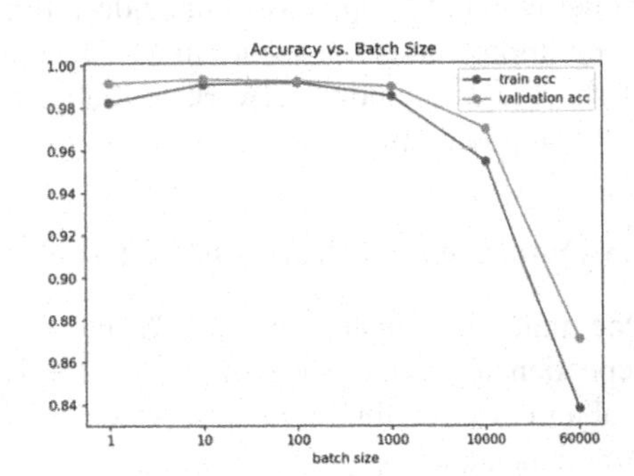

Fig. 4. Accuracy vs. Batch Size.

6 Conclusion

Cultivating computer professionals who are based on multi-dimensional thinking of ideological and political issues is the fundamental aspect of university computer education, and improving the evaluation of computer course teaching quality is the teaching goal. It is the responsibility and obligation of every teacher to integrate the ideological and political elements of the new era into the computer architecture as an important content around the cultivation of students' ability [3, 4, 7]. Through the integration of ideological and political education and computer teaching, students can build a sense of national pride of confident development, and urge each student to think about problems with the five dimensions in the text while learning computer architecture, and we provide practical cases of course application. So as to truly apply their professional knowledge to reality, and achieve the goal of integration of industry and education.

Through the research in this article, several methods are proposed to improve the evaluation of teaching quality:

- Integrating ideological and political elements into the teaching of computer architecture can effectively improve the evaluation of teaching quality.
- Adopting small class teaching, it is recommended to have around 30 students in each class.

- Cultivate students to think from a five dimensional perspective.

Apply what you have learned. Integrate the professional knowledge learned from the dimensions of humanistic value, social responsibility, public welfare, cultural confidence, and socialism with Chinese characteristics into industry and education.

Acknowledgements. Thank you to the corresponding author Mingzhi Mao. This work was supported in part by the postgraduate demonstration course of Guangdong Province Department of Education Programmed Trading (2023SFKC_022), the 2023 computer architecture First Class Course Project of South China Normal University, the 2023 Project of Computer Education Research Association of Chinese Universities (CERACU2023R02).

References

1. Jinping, X.: At the National Conference on Ideological and Political Work in Higher Education Institutions, it was emphasized that ideological and political work should be integrated throughout the entire process of education and teaching, creating a new situation for the development of higher education in China. People's Daily, 09 Dec 2016
2. Zongli, J.: Improve the teaching position of the course. Chin. Univ. Teach. **43**(1–2), 99–110 (2021)
3. Mingzhi, M.: Looking at the curriculum reform of computer majors from the design and implementation of computer problem solving curriculum. Comput. Educ. **12**(1), 24–26 (2014)
4. Mingzhi, M., Zhao, L.: Exploration of ideological and political education in IT project management course under the background of new engineering. Comput. Educ. **20**(4), 21–23 (2022)
5. Yan, W.: Deepen the construction of the "Four New" and take the path of independent talent cultivation'. Chongqing High. Educ. Res. **38**(5), 3–13 (2022)
6. Yan, W.: Building China's "golden course." Chin. Univ. Teach. **40**(12), 4–9 (2018)
7. Xiang, Q., Yutong, L.: A new exploration of integrating computer science education knowledge and competency models. Comput. Educ. **21**(4), 9–14 (2023)

The Practice of Computer Basic Course Teaching for the Training of New Engineering Talents

Yinnan Zhang[1(✉)] and Xiuhua Wang[2]

[1] Zhejiang University of Science and Technology, Hangzhou, China
zyn96@163.com
[2] Shanghai Pudong Foreign Affairs Services School, Shanghai, China

Abstract. With the rapid development of emerging information technology, the cultivation of compound application-oriented talents is indispensable for the cultivation of talents in colleges. Computer application ability and computational thinking have become the basic abilities possessed by high-level talents in various disciplines. The education of computer in universities is one of the imperative pathways to cultivate college students' information literacy. Therefore, by means of the investigations based on the needs of the enterprises, the status quo of teaching, as well as the status of students, the main issues existing in general computer education during the development of new engineering are analyzed. According to the characteristics of application-oriented universities, combined with the requirements of talent training and the current situation of students, the usage of smart technology and the model of hierarchical teaching are proposed. Thereafter, it is further unraveled that formulating the curriculum system for general computer education, updating teaching contents, reforming teaching methods, highlighting capacity building, and cultivating cross-composite application-oriented talents with innovative ability are of vital importance.

Keywords: New Engineering · Computer Basic Course · Talent Training · Teaching Reform

1 Introduction

In 2017, "New Engineering Concept" was carried out by the Ministry of Education to probe a new education model to assist the natural development. According to the trend of a new round of scientific and technological revolution and industrial transformation, the construction of new engineering disciplines is a significant section of higher education in the new era, and it emphasizes the practicality, intersection and comprehensiveness of disciplines.

Concerning the problem how to develop university computer basic education with the concept of general education in application-oriented universities, it is required to constantly explore the reform of computer basic education curriculum system, contents and strategies of teaching for new engineering, continuously promote computational thinking ability of students, and effectively improve the teaching quality of computer courses.

J. Gan et al. (Eds.): CSEI 2023, CCIS 1899, pp. 424–435, 2024.
https://doi.org/10.1007/978-981-99-9499-1_38

2 The Demands of Talent Training

Nowadays, the supply of high-end technical talents still falls short of demand as the requirements of talents by enterprises are still strong. However, it is becoming increasingly difficult for many applicants to search for suitable jobs, manifesting the existence of gap between graduates from colleges and the actual demands of companies.

2.1 Research of Relevant Companies

We visited a part of large and medium-sized enterprises in Zhejiang province on the spot. For the purpose of data pertinence, we issued a questionnaire to the "hidden champion" (cultivation) enterprises in 2018, and made a statistical analysis of the survey [1]. Thereafter, the statistical table concerning the "main difficulties existing in related enterprises" option is shown in Table 1.

Table 1. Main difficulties of the enterprises

Serial number	Options	Votes	Percentage of votes
1	Lacking funding	31	40.8
2	Insufficient talents	55	72.4
3	Not enough attention by leaders	5	6.6
4	Unclear roadmap	12	15.8
5	Others	12	15.8

Seen from the statistics of the questionnaire, it can be found that the main difficulty for enterprises in promoting intelligent manufacturing is the lack of talents, with a percentage of 72.4%. Large-scale enterprises are attractive for talents to some extent, whereas small and medium-sized enterprises are more difficult when it comes to bring in and retain talents. For the brevity, how to attract and retain talents in enterprises has become one of the vital issues restricting enterprises in the developments of intelligent manufacturing.

2.2 Demands of Enterprises for Talent Training

The Requirements of Enterprises for Graduates have Changed in Terms of Levels and Abilities

Enterprise Side: Enterprises have a particularly urgent need for compound talents with a knowledge of design, debugging, programming, engineering implementation, and innovative spirit.

Academic Level: The demand for degree graduates is increasing.

Ability Requirements: Communicative competence, cross-cultural ability, writing and management capacities, etc.

Sparked by this inspiration, it is required to cultivate emerging talents who adapt to industrial revolution and novel economic development with new ideas and new models for higher education. During the education of students, more attention should be payed to practical innovation capacity and thinking ability, thus meeting the demand for high-end compound talents in the fast developing information period.

Application-oriented colleges should meet the demands of China's development agenda, economic and social developments, as well as the overall development of human beings. They should closely integrate development planning of school with economic and practical developments, industrial chain layout, and digital transformation, thus cultivating inter-disciplinary talents for regional economic and social development together with the local industries [2].

Problems in Higher Education

The rapid development of the Internet of Things, big data, artificial intelligence, network security and other emerging economic fields has experienced insufficient talent supply. There also exists a serious talent gap in the digital transformation of traditional industries.

Actually, there are three major problems in talent training in applied colleges: firstly, the integrating degree between talent training and industrial development should be promoted; secondly, the problem of a multi-coordinated talent training system should be solved; furthermore, engineering practice and innovation capabilities of students should be strengthened.

2.3 Emerging Requirements for New Engineering Talent Training

In order to adapt to the changes in the demand for talent training in universities in the new round of scientific and technological revolution as well as industrial transformation, the Ministry of Education has successively launched "new engineering", "new agricultural science", "new medical science" and "new liberal arts" since 2017.

In the "four new" construction, the new generation of information technology is undoubtedly an important section of the curriculum construction and reconstruction of various disciplines. Through the integration and innovative development of the new generation of information technology and traditional courses, the computer application skills of students can be enhanced and thinking ability of students can be empowered.

The propose of new engineering has strengthened the necessity of opening computer general courses, which is of vital importance for cultivating students with profound computational thinking and computer problem-solving ability.

3 Development of Information Technology

3.1 Development of Information Technology

Three waves of information technology popularization have been experienced in our country: the first time was in the 1980s, and the content of popularization was mainly high-level computer languages, especially the BASIC language; the second time was in the 1990s, which mainly popularized office software; the third time is the first decade of the 21st century, and the popular content is mainly the application of the Internet. Nowadays, my country is experiencing the fourth wave, which is characterized by the vigorous popularization of a new generation of information technology represented by artificial intelligence.

Concerning the information literacy of talents, new requirements in terms of living ability, learning ability and work ability have been put forward for the future society. Cultivating innovative talents which meet the current urgent needs of enterprises for innovative talents in information technology application brings new challenges to the training of talents in colleges and universities, and drives the changes in the concepts, connotations, methods, contents and evaluation of traditional teaching model.

3.2 Development of Computer General Education

Since the 21st century, American state universities have introduced a series of strategies to reform general education, and they have pointed out the most important goals of universities: thinking training and knowledge education, that is, increasing the strength of the mind and the reserve of knowledge. The general education curriculum structures of American universities are relatively complete, and the course selection model is more flexible than that of many Chinese universities. In addition, American universities offer students numerous general education courses, a wide range of subject coverage, and a rich gradient of difficulty.

In recent years, the reformation of basic computer courses and general computer courses in colleges and universities has been in full swing. The goal of the reformation is to meet the requirements of the new era, concentrating on the improvement of computer application level and computational thinking ability of students for the adaption to the new era, as well as the professional integration of qualified personnel in this period.

In 2018, Zhejiang University proposed that the university computer basic teaching has a hierarchical "broad, specialized, integrated" curriculum system, and formed a continuous support for four-year professional training [3]. Meanwhile, in June 2018, Shandong University pointed out that the "1 + N" curriculum system for general computer education in the intelligent era [4], and carried out the construction of a series of new technology courses in general computer education based on industry-university cooperation. Harbin Institute of Technology proposed the "Π-type" plan for the new engineering discipline to implement the construction of new engineering disciplines and the training of innovative talents in 2018 [5]. In addition, a "New Engineering F Plan" was claimed in 2019 by researchers from South China University, mentioning a curriculum system that deeply integrates "general knowledge + majors + innovation and entrepreneurship" should be built and "three innovation-oriented" engineering leaders must be fostered [6]. Furthermore, Xiao Zhaohui [7] unraveled that it is necessary to comprehensively reconstruct the general education courses of information technology under the background of new engineering. Wu Chunyan [8] proposed the relationship between general education courses and professional training courses in the curriculum system under the background of large-scale enrollment, and the two systems should integrate and promote each other. Studies concerning the general education courses of information technology remain countless. Liu Yu and his co-workers [9] manifested the design and empirical research on the teaching of innovative thinking and innovative techniques based on the concept of OBE and intersubjectivity education, and signified suggestions on the teaching of general education in colleges under the background of emerging technologies.

4 Analysis and Thinking of Computer Basic Education

Nowadays, basic computer education in the background of general education meets challenges from many aspects. How to realize complete computer education in limited teaching courses and achieve the goal of general education is a major problem for schools and teachers. Many universities have conducted this research, and we have conducted research and analysis on application-oriented universities as shown below.

4.1 Research on Computer Education

We have conducted investigations on conditions of students and computer teaching conditions, from middle schools to universities, and analyzed the conditions of students from two aspects: realistic basis and demand basis.

The Actual Situation of Information Technology Teaching in Middle Schools: The Ministry of Education promulgated the "General High School Information Technology Curriculum Standard (2017 Edition)", which requires students to master the basic knowledge and skills of information technology, enhance information awareness and computational thinking ability, improve digital learning and innovation ability, establish a correct outlook on the world, life and values. The course covers programming, algorithms, computational thinking, software and hardware design applications and many other modules. Attributed to the gradual popularization of information technology courses in high school and the improvement of computer application level, many college freshmen already have good computer operation abilities.

The Actual Situation of College Freshmen Mastering Information Technology: We have conducted a polling survey on the computer knowledge mastery of freshmen in the 2020 and 2021 classes in our school. The total number of students in my class is 955, involving 16 classes. The number of valid voters was 677, and the turnout rate was 70.9%. Each person can choose 2 items, and the total number of voting options is 1301. Herein, a summary of the survey data is shown in Table 2.

It can be seen from the table:

In Senior High School, Which affected by subjective factors such as individual characteristics of teachers (such as gender, educational background, teaching age, professional knowledge level, attitude, etc.), or affected by objective factors such as educational policies, curriculum conditions and geographic, there are huge differences in the level of computer teaching between regions and schools, resulting in large differences in the individual computer application ability of freshmen.

The Demand for Degree Graduates is Increasing. It is not ideal for most freshmen to master computer knowledge, and the number of people who use computers for learning is not very large.

Table 2. Summary of voting surveys on computer knowledge mastery.

Serial number	Options	Votes	Percentage of votes
1	I have studied office software such as Word, and I can use common office software	213	16.4
2	I have learn I have learned a little computer basics, but have forgotten it now	296	22.8
3	I have never learned computer knowledge, and there is little computer contact before	158	12.1
4	I have learned VB language, and I can write simple programs	246	18.9
5	I have learned Python language, and I can write simple programs	51	3.9
6	In the past, computers are commonly applied to surf the Internet, chat and play games, etc.	313	24.1
7	I have learned programming languages, such as VB, C, Java and Python, and I can write applications	24	1.8

4.2 New Demands for Computer Basic Education

From the Background of the Era
Society has entered the digital age in an all-round way, and will enter the age of intelligence. In-depth interdisciplinarity and integration, computing has become an essential core element of interdisciplinary integration. Sparked by this inspiration, new requirements for the knowledge structure, ability structure and quality structure of talents have been put forward.

The Development of the Industry Shows a Need for Numerous High-Level Scientific and Technological Innovation Talents, Multidisciplinary Interdisciplinary Talents and High-Quality Professional and Technical Talents. The content of computer teaching in the general sense can not meet the new demand. Therefore, after analyzing the computer courses offered by non-computer disciplines in domestic and foreign universities, it can be seen that the combination of computing science and various disciplines is becoming closer, and computing science has emerged as an important means and tool for scientific research and problem solving in various disciplines. For the brevity, the status of various disciplines is constantly strengthening.

Judging from the Basic Information Literacy of Contemporary College Students, Computers have been Basically Universalized. However, students own different levels of computer knowledge, uneven application ability, and lack of practical ability.

Novel Computer Knowledge is Strongly Needed for Students. Up to now, the application of information technology such as office software, program design, and IT project development is still not ideal in the specific affairs of students participating in competitions, projects, graduation projects, etc., and the ability of using ICT (Information and Communications Technology) to solve professional problems is insufficient.

In view of the reality of basic computer education, the complex object of teaching, knowledge points and different needs, it is necessary to teach students according to their aptitude. Computer basic education, and proficiency of students' computer application ability, has an important impact on students' follow-up course study, employment, and career development.

4.3 Problems in Computer Basic Education

Problems in the Environment: Limited by multifarious factors like class hours, teachers, conditions, there still exist problems in the connection between production, education and researches. Therefore it is impossible to establish a systematic curriculum system and a practice system, thus better strengthening the cultivation of information integration and innovation ability of students.

Curriculum Construction, Lack of Professional Characteristics: Computer general courses have a wide range of courses, and different majors have different emphasis on computer technology requirements. Each major has a strong personality. During the rapid development period of the Internet nowadays, how to construct the teaching contents and choose the teaching methods according to the characteristics of the major should be considered.

Teaching Content is Lagging Behind, and the Support of Innovation Ability is Not Enough: The lack of cross-integrated teaching content and courses makes computer basic teaching less attractive to students, and students can not learn how to apply computers to solve problems in professional development [10].

Does Not Consider the Level and Differences of Students: At present, the national college entrance examination model is not completely unified, and the curriculum settings at the senior high school level are also different. Since the influence of various factors such as economy, region and education level, computer application abilities of students vary greatly, especially in hands-on ability. If the differences of students are not considered, while the teaching content and progress are arranged in a unified manner, these must cause teaching difficulties.

5 Exploration and Practice of Computer Basic Teaching

According to the characteristics of application-oriented colleges, along with the demands for talent training and the current situation of students, our computer basic teaching department, as the organization unit of computer basic courses, has carried out exploration and practice on computer basic education.

In-depth discussion of the setting of basic computer courses, the update of teaching content and the revolution of teaching methods, especially the in-depth integration of new computing technology and related professional and discipline knowledge, will improve the application of new computer technology in various majors from two levels of depth and breadth.

5.1 Course Objectives

Course Orientation: Meeting the educational concepts of the four new talents in higher education for the new era, with the adaption to the emerging demands for talent training such as new majors, new technologies, and new means, will promote information literacy, strengthen computational thinking, and deepen integration.

Training Objectives: Significantly improve information literacy of college students, strengthen computational thinking of college students, and cultivate their capacity to deal with disciplinary problems. Furthermore, based on the three-level teaching objectives of knowledge, ability and thinking, the engineering practice and innovation capabilities of students can be strengthened.

In order to meet the requirements of each major for basic computer teaching, the differences in basic computer ability of college freshmen and the problems in general computer teaching should be considered, the issue concerning how to design a scientific, practical and forward-looking computer basic education curriculum system and teaching content must be discussed. This will promote the computational thinking and information technology capabilities of students in various majors.

5.2 Reform Thinking

A novel overall reform strategy is proposed for the new system of computer basic education, new teaching content and teaching material resource construction in universities. Combined with intelligent technology, the reform of empowering computer teaching focuses on three-dimensional sections: classified and layered differentiated curriculum system, teaching contents of fresh knowledge and novel technologies, and process-based ability assessment.

Teaching practice can be carried out by adopting the collaborative teaching mode of "classified teaching and graded teaching", thus cultivating the ability of students to solve problems with equipped computer knowledge and technology in the professional fields and providing technical supports for the development of ample disciplines.

5.3 Teaching Mode

Explore the multi-dimensional empowering education and teaching modes under new normal, and carry out a hybrid teaching method that combines online self-study, offline case teaching and practical teaching together.

According to the Characteristics and Teaching Objectives of this Course, a Reasonable Teaching Design is Carried Out. Multifarious teaching methods such as heuristic teaching, case-based teaching, and seminar-based teaching are utilized to mobilize enthusiasm of students for learning and improve the quality of course teaching.

To Solve the Contradiction Between the Limited Class Hours and the Increasing Teaching Content, And to consider the level and differences of students, an online and offline hybrid teaching mode is adopted.

Build a Diversified Practical Experimental Teaching System. In the open experimental platform and system, we must focus on guiding and cultivating students' autonomous learning ability, thinking ability and hands-on ability.

Focus on Innovative Education. Establish an innovation base, and carry out extracurricular science and technology project training combined with the curriculum under the guidance of the instructor.

The Evaluation Method of "Online Grades + Experimental Grades + Classroom Performance + Examination Results" is Utilized, And factors including usual online learning, classroom practice, and final assessment are comprehensively considered, besides, summative evaluation and process evaluation are combined together.

5.4 Curriculum System

Reasonably design courses suitable for the needs of various majors, and explore a flexible curriculum system to support classified and hierarchical computer basic education.

For the Training Plan of Innovative Talents, There is a demand to discuss the deep integration of new computing technology, related professional and subject knowledge, adjust the teaching content and teaching form of "Computer Application" and other courses, and formulate new teaching syllabus and teaching plan.

To Implement Classified and Hierarchical Teaching, The selection of teaching materials and teaching content should be more targeted, and the content of teaching modules for students should be designed according to various levels of students.

For Students with Better Learning Level, We should guide them to participate in science and technology competitions of college students, extracurricular science and technology innovation and practical activities.

New Student Seminars and School-Wide General Electives can be Offered as Expansions to Stimulate Interests and Motivations of Students in Learning, And help students adapt to university studies as soon as possible.

The computer basic course consists of two parts: basic module and extended composite module. Basic modules are compulsory or limited electives, and extended modules are electives. It mainly can be divided into three categories: Computer application and freshmen seminars; Program design courses; Public elective courses and open experiments.

5.5 Teaching Content

Teaching content should grasp the appropriate depth and breadth, focusing on intelligent technology and reflecting the times and frontiers, and there should be an inherent logical relationship between each section; in addition, the cross-integration of IT (Information Technology) and other disciplines should be highlighted, and the cultivation of computational thinking ability should be strengthened.

Theoretical teaching: Emphasizes the understanding, knowledge and experience of knowledge and technology. Practical teaching: Emphasize the unity of theory and practice, and apply the equipped knowledge. Effectively use the program design PTA (Program design experiment auxiliary teaching platform), and make full use of evaluation mechanisms including process evaluation, formative evaluation, and achievement evaluation to heighten the influence of teaching.

According to Graduation Requirements and Social Demands, The personalized content of general education courses in information technology should be optimized, and the construction of curriculum connotation must be strengthened. Taking knowledge teaching and skill training into account, the capacities of computational thinking, problem analysis and solving through computers should be fostered.

Strengthen the Teaching and Investigation of Computer Basic Courses, Accomplish the sharing and co-construction of teaching resources, and constantly develop three-dimensional teaching resources for the training of new engineering talents.

Introduce Typical Cases for Majors, Understand the application of the new generation of information technology in the industry, expand horizons of students, and empower the practical application of their respective majors.

With the Advancement of Curriculum Revolution, Teaching materials must also be adjusted accordingly, and new forms of teaching materials must be compiled to adapt to the new era and new teaching demands, thus achieving two major teaching goals including knowledge explanation and information technology ability training.

5.6 Innovative Education

Talent is the source of innovation, so colleges and universities should focalize attention in the cultivation of innovative talents. Actually, the innovation ability can be cultivated by means of practice. Following that, innovation practice bases can be utilized to guide students to participate in college students' scientific and technological competitions, extracurricular scientific and technological innovation and practical activities under the directions of characteristics based on various disciplines and majors. Furthermore, the effectiveness of innovative talent training can be improved through innovative projects and competition activities, thus giving full play to the guiding role of competition in educating people.

6 Implementation Effect

Continue to track the development trend of information technology, re-plan the course objectives, sort out the course content, build up a teaching content system, revise the syllabus, and finally make the course teaching and content more suitable for practical needs. Actual practice of teaching shows that the teaching based on "Internet+" can effectively improve the quality and efficiency of teaching and learning. The diversified teaching mode cultivates students' abilities of computational thinking, problem solving and autonomous learning, and further improves the overall teaching effect.

Multifarious awards have been received concerning the training of students. Since the freshman year, students could feel that they have learned something and have made the course content more practical. On the basis of classroom and extracurricular learning, many students have participated in extracurricular science and technology innovation and practice projects for college students (such as national innovation projects), college students' ACM programming competition, and college student computer design competition, and excellent results have been received in above competitions. Furthermore, the Outstanding Award of the Text Subject Group in the Course Ideological and Political Students of Zhejiang Province has been won under the instruction.

7 Conclusion

Through the study of basic computer courses, students can strengthen information awareness, improve computational thinking, promote digital innovation and development capabilities, establish correct information society values and sense of responsibility, and lay the foundation for their career development, lifelong learning and society service. Along with the rapid development of new information technologies, we must keep pace with the times, continue to study, and continuously improve teaching to empower students.

The Training of Applied Talents Shows the Demand to Improve the Integrating Degree Between Talent Training and Industry, And it is necessary to build a teaching model for basic computer education. Carry out teaching revolution and improve the curriculum system from the aspects of teaching objectives, course structure, teaching contents, teaching methods, course implementation, classroom teaching, experimental teaching and assessment methods, further building a closed-loop learning oriented to application scenarios.

Using Intelligent Education Technology, And it can provide a guidance for "Internet + education" and "intelligence + education" students to transform their learning methods. Besides, the usage of big data analysis methods can recommend personalized learning resources for learners, customize learning strategies, and contribute to cultivating interdisciplinary and innovative talents.

Establish an Effective Evaluation Mechanism and System, Support individualized study guidance, and improve the efficiency of knowledge acquisition.

Offer Courses Such as Information Technology Application Development, Carry out innovative project training, mobilize the enthusiasm of students to participate in scientific research, guide students to participate in various competitions, and improve students' application capacity.

In brief, the universities must change along with the development of industry, and there exists a demand for general education to cultivate talents according the society needs. As the main power for cultivating high-level application-oriented talents with innovative consciousness and international literacy, application-oriented undergraduate colleges with adaption to social and economic development constantly explore emerging models of engineering and technical personnel training for sustainable competitiveness, and discuss the new training mode of engineering talents driven by demand goal orientation and student learning effect, which shows important practical and practical significance.

Acknowledgment. The paper is support by Computer Basic Education Teaching Research Project in Association of Fundamental Computing Education in Chinese Universities (2022-AFCEC-612), and Curriculum Ideological and Political Teaching Research Project in Zhejiang University of Science and Technology (2022-ksj5).

References

1. Zhang, Y., Luo, C.: Research and analysis on the development of intelligent manufacturing industry in Zhejiang Province. Sci. Technol. Ind. **19**(3), 1–7 (2019)
2. Zhang, Y., Luo, C.: Exploration on the training mode of intelligent manufacturing talents under new engineering education. China Mod. Educ. Equip. (5),98–100 (2019)
3. He, Q., Wang, H.: University computer basic course system and course construction oriented to new engineering. China Univ. Teach. (1),39–43 (2019)
4. Hao, X.W., Zhang, L., Tang, D.K., et al.: Relying on industry-university cooperation, the construction of new technology series courses in computer general education.Comput. Educ. (01), 124–128 (2021)
5. Xu, X.F., Shen, Y., Zhong, S.S.: Exploration and thoughts on the construction of new engineering courses and the innovation practice of educational models in Chinese universities.Comput. Educ. (02), 99–103 (2021)
6. Gao, S.: Implement emerging engineering education F-plan and cultivate engineerleaders. Res. High. Educ. Eng. (04), 19–25 (2019)
7. Xiao, Z.H.: Teaching reform of general education course of new engineering information technology. J. Fujian Comput. **36**(07), 143–145 (2020)
8. Wu, C.Y.: Research on the relationship between general education courses and professional training courses in the curriculum system under the background of general enrollment. Sci. Technol. Innov. (22),70–71 (2020)
9. Liu, Y., Xie, Y., Cui, D.Z.: Teaching practice and thinking of general education courses in colleges and universities under the intelligent learning environment. Softw. Guide **19**(11), 221–226 (2020)
10. Zhu, D.H., Wu, Y.B.: Reform and exploration of computer public basic courses based on emerging engineering education. High. Educ. Chem. Eng. **36**(5), 41–45 (2019)

Exploration of OBE-Based Competence Development Model for Undergraduate Computer Science Students

Juan Luo(✉), Ying Qiao, Degui Xiao, and Huan Zhao

College of Computer Science and Electronic Engineering, Hunan University, Changsha, China
juanluo@hnu.edu.cn

Abstract. The inconsistency and lack of synchronization between computer professional competence education and talents' market demand are the bottleneck problems of undergraduate education. In this paper, we establish a "student-centered" output teaching model based on OBE concept, and construct a computer core competence model based on KSD. We propose a personalized teaching system based on the knowledge graph of teaching contents and students' learning trajectories. It continuously improves and optimizes the training plan according to students' learning outcomes, and improves and adjusts the course contents, which achieves the cultivation of undergraduate students' ability to solve complex engineering problems.

Keywords: KSD · Knowledge graph · OBE · Personalized teaching system

1 Introduction

Human society is rapidly entering a new era of digital society with the integration of information, physics and society. Digital technology gathers energy for innovation drive in the new era. Breakthroughs in digital infrastructure and core technologies require computer talents with the ability to solve complex engineering problems for the new digital era with the characteristic of artificial intelligence, cloud computing, big data and the Internet of Things. The development of such competence is also a cornerstone of talent development from all walks of life in the digital era.

The Organization of Economic Cooperation and Development (OECD) launched a project entitled 'Education 2030: Education and Skills for the Future' in 2015. The project works with participating countries to find answers to two far-reaching questions: the one is what knowledge, skills, attitudes and values will today's students need to thrive and shape their world in 2030? And the other is how can teaching and learning systems effectively develop these knowledge, skills, attitudes and values?

The core of professional computer skills are software design, hardware design and algorithm design in the context of the new engineering discipline [1], which are also the basis of computer system design ability and an important indicator for employers to select outstanding graduates. At present, many employers reflect that they cannot recruit

J. Gan et al. (Eds.): CSEI 2023, CCIS 1899, pp. 436–442, 2024.
https://doi.org/10.1007/978-981-99-9499-1_39

"good students", and the main factor is that the basic skills of graduates cannot meet the requirements. The cultivation of good core computer skills is a process that requires progressive training and continuous cultivation.

Engineering education is an important part of higher education [2]. The accreditation of engineering education majors is an internationally accepted quality assurance system for engineering education, and an important basis for realizing international mutual recognition of engineering education and international mutual recognition of engineers' qualifications. The core of engineering education professional accreditation confirm that engineering graduates meet the established quality standard requirements recognized by the industry [3], which is a kind of qualification evaluation oriented to the cultivation objectives and graduation exit requirements.

OBE (Outcome Based Education) education concept [4, 5] is an advanced education concept of building a curriculum system that is result-oriented and student-oriented, and adopts a reverse thinking approach, which is also called Outcome Oriented Education, Competence Oriented Education, Goal Oriented Education or Demand Oriented Education. OBE is an important concept of engineering education and a core element of cultivating talents based on professional accreditation in engineering education [6, 7]. "How to make students meet the graduation requirements?" is the core question of undergraduate professional education. Based on the understanding in the graduation requirements that "students should be able to develop, select and use modern tools, design and develop solutions for complex engineering problems, and demonstrate a sense of innovation", "the ability to solve complex engineering problems "is the core competence that computer science students should have upon graduation [8]. How to highlight professional characteristics, and effectively strengthen and continuously improve the cultivation of students' ability to solve complex engineering problems is an important issue that needs long-term in-depth exploration and solution.

The undergraduate stage is the most critical stage in the formation of students' worldview, outlook on life and values. Undergraduate education is the most important foundation for improving the comprehensive quality of talents. This paper establishes a scientific talent training system and builds a computer core competence model based on Knowledge-Skills-Dispositions (KSD), which achieves the goal of talent training and solves the bottleneck problem of inconsistency and lack of synchronization between the competence quality education of computer majors and the market demand of talent.

2 OBE-Based Competence Modelling and Visualization

2.1 KSD Based Computer Core Competence Model

OBE is the concept of "Outcomes-Based Education". Unlike the traditional education "teaching-centered" input-based approach, OBE emphasizes "student-centered" output-based teaching, focusing more on student learning outcomes rather than teacher teaching, which achieves a change in the traditional educational paradigm. OBE focuses on students' learning outcomes and the cultivation of higher-order competence to achieve systematic and progressive development of thinking and ability that solve complex engineering problems. Therefore, for learning objective for core competence in solving complex engineering problem for undergraduate computer science students, we construct a model of core computer competence, which is shown in Fig. 1. The model relationship can be illustrated as follows.

Competence = [knowledge + skills + character] in the Task i.e. C = (K + S + D) in T,

where the "Task" consists of four aspects: Role, Goal, Objectives and Constraints. The Task is skilled in building knowledge, skills and the structure to concretize of 'Dispositions'.

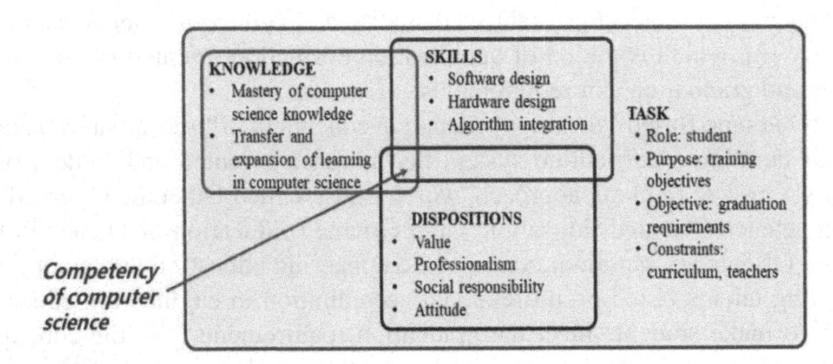

Fig. 1. Computer core competence model

The computer core competence is the professional knowledge of computing + (software, hardware and algorithm) skills + (values, professionalism, social responsibility, etc.) attitude of dispositions in solving complex engineering problems. we enhance students' ability to solve complex engineering problems from three aspects. The first is to cultivate two core ideas for undergraduate students of computational thinking and engineering thinking. The second is to consolidate three basic skills of programming, hardware and algorithms. The third is to face four social factors of society, environment, ethics and economy.

2.2 Building Measurable Computer Core Competence

The new industrial revolution requires a "new type of engineering education", but the core of the "new engineering" is not a "new profession". Complex engineering issues are not only emphasized in the accreditation of engineering education, but are also important in the context of the new engineering discipline, where education must provide support for graduates to adapt to change. The essence of engineering education is to cultivate students' ability, and the teaching reform should be guided by international mainstream concepts and standards, and students' ability should be regarded as the core standard to measure the quality of teaching.

The ability of students to solve complex engineering problems is the most central competence goal of engineering education and the vocation of engineers, as depicted in Fig. 2. Complex engineering problems include six dimensions: problems that require deep knowledge to solve (depth), problems that have no obvious solution (difficulty), problems that require to apply the fundamental professional principles and the latest research findings to solve (breadth), problems that require consideration of multiple constraints in the real world (engineering), multiple constraints, and social impact. Complex engineering problems are embedded in the professional curriculum, particularly in the core and design courses.

The OBE teaching concept is the core of engineering professional accreditation, however the cultivation of the ability to solve complex engineering problems requires the construction of a computer core competence cultivation system, continuous improvement and optimization of the cultivation plan, and improvement and adjustment of the curriculum content. The KSD core competence model is mapped to process-based grading guidelines as criteria for assessing student competence. Each criterion is explicitly listed as a level of achievement, with the aim of correctly reflecting student learning outcomes based on student performance. Clearly measurable competence objectives help to develop students' engineering practice and optimize the content and organization of teaching based on knowledge graph.

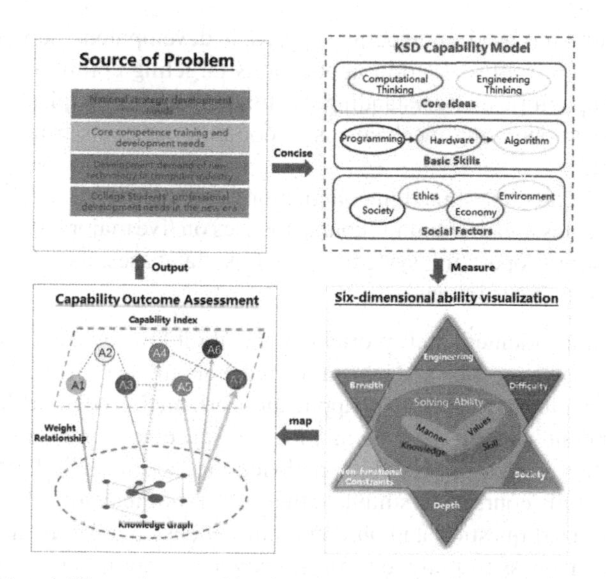

Fig. 2. Measurable, visible and assessable closed-loop capability to solve complex engineering problem

3 A Personalized Teaching System Based on Content Knowledge Graph and Student Learning Trajectories

The establishment of a scientific talent training system can achieve accurate and personalized evaluation of students' learning outcomes in terms of their ability to meet the standards, as shown in Fig. 3. With the rich teaching resources and environment, we build a personalized teaching model based on the knowledge map of teaching contents and students' learning trajectories, construct a knowledge map of course contents based on the computer core competency model with students' learning outcomes, determine the course structure, design teaching planning (teaching resources, teaching activities, and teaching evaluation), implement diverse teaching strategies (case-based, inquiry-based, project-based, and immersion-based), and continuously optimize and improve the course through progressive training pathways and refined teaching evaluation.

Knowledge graph mines, organizes, and effectively manages knowledge from large-scale data to improve the quality of teaching [9, 10].We have established a knowledge graph for each course in the process of developing the ability to solve complex problems, forming a path of "step-by-step introduction to thinking, programming for algorithm design, engineering methods based on complex problems, designing a capstone topics in conjunction with professional directions".

- A step-by-step introduction to thinking: it uses case-based classroom teaching and progressive development of programming skills based on "mimic-rewrite-write".
- Competence enhancement for algorithm design: the seminar and heuristic teach by online and offline flipped classes; the comprehensive problems designed by teamwork, emphasizing the entire training from design, implementation, testing to documentation.
- Complex problem-based engineering approach development: larger-scale simulation cases drawn from real-world applications targeting complex systems analysis and design capabilities, understanding the fundamental principles, logical relationships, and basic operating mechanisms of computer systems from a programmer's perspective.
- The capstone topic is designed in conjunction with the professional orientation: the "Integrated Professional Training" course focuses on five major systems: chip design, computer systems, operating systems, networks, databases, and the development of large software systems in teams.

Insist on output-oriented, ability-oriented, the ability to solve complex engineering problems, progressive practice and innovation teaching mode is driven by case development, student-oriented, "do" oriented, application-oriented, so that the learning process can be "independent" in terms of content, time and space, to stimulate students' interest in learning, so that students can fully experience the "aftertaste" of the integration of knowledge and skills courses, to stimulate their sense of innovation, integrated teacher guidance, centralized question and answer, comprehensive assessment and evaluation of teaching effectiveness from three aspects: knowledge, ability and quality.

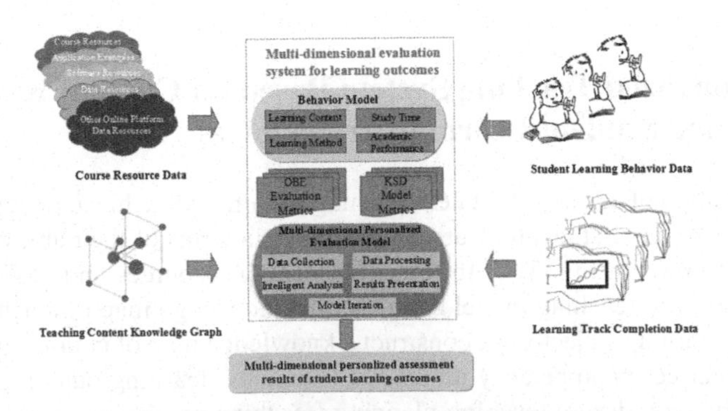

Fig. 3. Student learning outcomes assessment

4 Summary

The OBE teaching concept is the core of engineering professional accreditation. Based on the OBE concept, a " student-centered" output-based teaching mode has been established, and a model of computer core competence has been constructed. To develop the ability to solve complex engineering problems, we need to build a computer core competence training system, continuously improve and optimize the training plan, and improve and adjust the curriculum content. The KSD core competence model has been mapped to process-based grading criteria, which are used to assess students' competence. Each criterion is explicitly listed as a level of achievement and is intended to be based on student performance and to correctly reflect student learning outcomes. Clearly measurable competence targets help to develop students' engineering practice and optimize the content and organization of teaching based on knowledge graph.

There is still a long-term process to guide students' independent learning and assess the effectiveness of the output of teaching outcomes in the undergraduate computer science students' ability to solve complex engineering problems. For example, it is difficult to quantitatively evaluate the feedback of students' interaction in various aspects of teaching in the short term, but the impact of numerous details on students is subtle and needs to continuously promote students' professional learning and career development.

Acknowledgements. This work was supported in part by the National Natural Science Foundation of China under Grant 61972140.

References

1. Ulrich, R., Karen, W., Curfman, M.L., De, S.H.: Research and education in computational science and engineering. SIAM Rev. **60**(3), 707–754 (2018)
2. Huang-Saad, A.Y., Morton, C.S., Libarkin, J.C.: Entrepreneurship assessment in higher education: a research review for engineering education researchers. J. Eng. Educ. **107**(2), 263–290 (2018)
3. Wang, J., Dong, M., Lou, X., Yan, B.: Reform of diversified talents training mode against the background of engineering education accreditation. In: Proceedings of International Conference on 2019 Advanced Education and Social Science Research (2019)
4. Kaliannan, M., Chandran, S.D.: Empowering students through outcome-based education (OBE). Res. Educ. **87**(1), 50–63 (2012)
5. Macayan, J.V.: Implementing outcome-based education (OBE) framework: implications for assessment of students' performance. Educ. Meas. Eval. Rev. **8**(1), 1–10 (2017)
6. Schussler, D.L.: Defining dispositions: wading through murky waters. Teach. Educ. Q. **41**(4), 251–268 (2006)
7. Alison, C., et al.: Designing computer science competency statements: a process and curriculum model for the 21st century. In: Proceedings of International Conference on Working Group Reports on Innovation and Technology in Computer Science Education, pp. 211–246 (2020)

8. Jonassen, D., Strobel, J., Lee, C.B.: Everyday problem solving in engineering: Lessons for engineering educators. J. Eng. Educ. **95**(2), 139–151 (2016)
9. Chen, X., Jia, S., Xiang, Y.: A review: knowledge reasoning over knowledge graph. Expert Syst. Appl. **141**, 112948 (2020)
10. Pujara, J., Miao, H., Getoor, L., Cohen, W.: Knowledge graph identification. In: Alani, H., et al. (eds.) ISWC 2013. LNCS, vol. 8218, pp. 542–557. Springer, Heidelberg (2013). https://doi.org/10.1007/978-3-642-41335-3_34

Author Index

J. Gan et al. (Eds.): CSEI 2023, CCIS 1899, pp. 443–445, 2024.
https://doi.org/10.1007/978-981-99-9499-1

Printed in the United States
by Baker & Taylor Publisher Services

Printed in the United States
by Baker & Taylor Publisher Services